THE
New World
Reader

Thinking and Writing
About the Global Community

Second Edition

Gilbert H. Muller
The City University of New York
LaGuardia College

Houghton Mifflin Company
Boston   New York

For Sadie
Global Girl

Executive Publisher: Patricia A. Coryell
Editor-in-Chief: Carrie Brandon
Senior Sponsoring Editor: Lisa Kimball
Senior Marketing Manager: Tom Ziolkowski
Marketing Assistant: Bettina Chiu
Senior Development Editor: Meg Botteon
Editorial Associate: Sarah Truax
Senior Project Editor: Bob Greiner
Editorial Assistants: Cassandra Gargas and Emily Meyer
Senior Art and Design Coordinator: Jill Haber
Cover Design Manager: Anthony F. Saizon
Senior Photo Editor: Jennifer Meyer Dare
Composition Buyer: Chuck Dutton
New Title Project Manager: Susan Brooks-Peltier

Cover art: Photograph © Jose Cendon/AP Wide World Photos

Printed in the U.S.A.

Library of Congress Catalog Number: 2006935048

Instructor's edition:
ISBN-10: 0-618-83291-2
ISBN-13: 978-0-618-83291-0

For orders, use student text ISBNs:
ISBN-10: 0-618-79653-3
ISBN-13: 978-0-618-79653-3

4 5 6 7 8 9-EB-10 09 08 07

Brief Contents

Contents

2 | New American Mosaic: Are We Becoming a Universal Nation?   29

3 | America and the World: How Do Others Perceive Us?   67

4 | Speaking in Tongues: Does Language Unify or Divide Us?   117

8 | The Clash of Civilizations: Is Conflict Avoidable?   315

Rhetorical Contents

Illustration

Comparison and Contrast

Definition

Classification

Process Analysis

Causal Analysis

Argument and Persuasion

Culture or Conflict?: Images of Globalization

Is Beauty Universal?
Global Body Images

Preface

*We live in a world of transformations, affecting almost
every aspect of what we do. For better or worse, we are
being propelled into a global order that no one fully understands, but which is making its effects felt upon all of us.*

—Anthony Giddens

The New World Reader presents provocative essays about contemporary
global issues and challenges. The book provides students with the resources
needed to think and write in ways that foster varieties of global understanding and citizenship. In a time marked by terrorist attacks and ongoing interventions in Iraq and elsewhere, students have been challenged to reconsider
and reflect upon the relationship between America and its place in the
world. Salman Rushdie observes that the West has met the "rest," and the
writers in this text deal with this reality as well as those global forces that
increasingly shape our lives. These writers from a variety of backgrounds
and perspectives reveal that globalization is *the* big story, the most pressing
issue of our times.

Students using *The New World Reader* will find interconnected chapters
and selections dealing with such strategic global questions as the changing
demographics of the United States, the impact of September 11 on individuals as well as entire populations, the nature of globalization, the clash
of cultures and civilizations, the changing roles of women and men in the
global arena, the ways in which first-world nations can successfully address
global poverty and disease, and the state of the global environment. Challenged by such well-known contemporary thinkers and writers as Richard
Rodriguez, Amy Tan, Francis Fukuyama, Bharati Mukherjee, Kofi Annan,
and Edward Said, today's students will be encouraged to come to grips with
a world that, in Anthony Giddens's words, is now subject to complex and
often mystifying transformations.

This book demonstrates that critical thinking about our new global century begins when students consider unfamiliar perspectives and arguments,
when they are open to new global ideas and perceptions. Put differently, this
text combines and encourages intercultural and transnational inquiry. As
such, the design of the anthology encourages students to ask not only who
they are in this society but also who they are in the world. Many of the
diversity themes that teachers of college writing find especially productive
and stimulating—gender and sexuality, race and ethnicity, class and cultural
orientation—lend themselves to these issues of local and global perception.
The selections in the text present a tapestry of diversity in both a local
and a global light, moving from personalized encounters with cultures to

analytical and argumentative treatment of topics. Students are provided the opportunity to move across cultures and continents, interrogating and assessing authors' insights into our evolving transnational society.

The writers in *The New World Reader* present keen emotional and intellectual insights into our new global era. Most of the essays are relatively brief and provocative and serve as models for the types of personal, analytical, and argumentative papers that college composition teachers ask their students to write. Many of the essays were written after September 11, 2001, and most since 1990. Drawn from a wide variety of authorial backgrounds and sources, and offering diverse angles of opinion and perspectives, the readings in this text lend themselves to thoughtful responses, class debate, small-group discussion, and online research. Some of the longer essays—for example, Jamaica Kincaid on the nature of colonialism and Kwame Anthony Appiah on the challenge to local cultures from globalizing influences—orient students to those forms of academic discourse that they will encounter in the humanities and social sciences. With introductions to chapters and writers, previewing questions, a three-part apparatus following each essay, two four-color photo essays, three appendices offering guidelines on conducting research in the global era and defining rhetorical and global terms, and extensive web resources, *The New World Reader* can serve as the core text in composition courses.

Features

Lively Selections in Chapters That Challenge Our Understanding of Ourselves and Others

The New World Reader presents seventy-four essays in eleven interrelated chapters. The first chapter introduces students to the challenges of thinking, reading, and writing about their place in the new global era. Ten subsequent chapters, each consisting of essays that move from personal and op-ed pieces to more complex selections, focus on key aspects of our increasingly globalized culture, presenting ideas and themes that radiate through the text.

- **Chapter 1. Thinking, Reading, and Writing About the New Global Era.** This concise introductory chapter offers guidelines for students as they think, read, and write about key issues in post–September 11 America and the world. Clear thinking about the "new world order" involves a knowledge of both what has gone before and what lies ahead, as well as mastery of the analytical and cognitive skills at the heart of the reading and writing processes. Three brief essays permit students to practice their critical thinking, reading, and writing skills: Nicholas D. Kristof on how young Americans are increasingly likely to socialize and date across racial lines, Susan Bordo on "The Globalization of Eating Disorders," and Lorraine Ali on how neither jihadists nor most Americans accurately see or portray Muslim women.

- **Chapter 2. New American Mosaic: Are We Becoming a Universal Nation?** Presenting compelling insights into the new American demographics, writers N. Scott Momaday, Moisés Naím, and others stress the ways both native and "fourth wave" patterns of acculturation are changing the face of the American nation while fostering a greater appreciation of other cultures. The chapter introduces students to the idea that globalization is not only "out there" but also "here."

- **NEW Chapter 3. America and the World: How Do Others Perceive Us?** Suggested by teachers who used the first edition of *The New World Reader,* this chapter explores the implications (and reverberations) of America's increasingly interventionist position on the global stage. Fouad Ajami, Alkman Granitsas, and Anne Applebaum are among the multinational writers exploring global attitudes towards the idea of America.

- **Chapter 4. Speaking in Tongues: Does Language Unify or Divide?** Presenting essays by Amy Tan, Ilan Stavans, and other well-known writers, this chapter explores the varied ways in which language forms identity and cultural relationships in our increasingly polyglot world.

- **Chapter 5. Global Relationships: Are Sex and Gender Roles Changing?** Across the globe, the perception of gender and the larger struggle for human rights vary in the amount of change they are undergoing. Ellen Goodman argues for justice for women, while Richard Rodriguez offers a revealing appreciation of his sexual orientation and changing family values. Mohja Kahf offers a challenging new perspective on how contemporary Muslim women see themselves and their faith. The last essay, by Barbara Ehrenreich and Annette Fuentes, "Life on the Global Assembly Line," is a contemporary classic, detailing the exploitation of women in factories overseas.

- **Chapter 6. The Challenge of Globalization: What Are the Consequences?** The debate over globalization, whether framed in economic, political, environmental, or cultural terms, serves increasingly to define our lives in the twenty-first century. Essays by Thomas L. Friedman, Kwame Anthony Appiah, Anthony Giddens, and others argue the benefits and dangers of globalization.

- **Chapter 7. Culture Wars: Whose Culture Is It, Anyway?** This chapter examines the impact of popular American culture on the nation and on the world. From American-style shopping malls in developing nations to the broadcast of American sitcoms in Islamic nations, the new American landscape has had a global impact. Among writers offering critical appraisals of the contemporary culture wars are Henry Louis Gates Jr., Mario Vargas Llosa, and Jamaica Kincaid.

- **Chapter 8. The Clash of Civilizations: Is Conflict Avoidable?** Building on the issues raised in the first seven chapters, this unit offers a critical examination of the clash-of-civilizations debate. Essays by such prominent global analysts as Amartya Sen and Samuel P. Huntington alert students to the fact that today's global conflicts do not spring spontaneously from September 11 but rather have deep historical and political antecedents.

- **Chapter 9. The Age of Terror: What Is the Just Response?** In the second edition of *The New World Reader,* this chapter has been revised to take at once a broader and deeper view of the causes and consequences of international terror. Bill Powell explores the social and cultural frustrations that impel some young men towards jihadist movements, while Greg Campbell traces the terrible impact of first-world greed on the diamond miners of Sierra Leone and the connections between "blood diamonds" and the global marketplace for weapons.

- **NEW Chapter 10. Global Aid: Can We Reduce Disease and Poverty?** Suggested by reviewers and inspired by recent hopeful developments in the global struggle for economic justice, this chapter describes the many ways in which people worldwide are working to raise the living standards of their fellow citizens. Frontline reporting by Alison Katz in Africa and Anuradha Mittal in India, among other perspectives, describes the monumental undertakings of often ordinary citizens and workers.

- **Chapter 11. The Fate of the Earth: Can We Preserve the Global Environment?** From global warming to weapons of mass destruction, the Earth's ecology faces major challenges. Essays by Rachel Carson, Annie Dillard, Jared Diamond, Bill McKibben, and others offer insights into how we might save the environment—and the world—for future generations.

Three Distinctive Appendices

- **Appendix A. Conducting Research in the New Global Era.** This unit provides students with cutting-edge, practical information on the kinds of research skills they are expected to acquire during their college careers. The appendix stresses the new world of information technology that increasingly guides research and offers extensive guidelines on locating and evaluating print and online sources.

- **Appendix B. Glossary of Rhetorical Terms.** Concise definitions of dozens of key rhetorical terms provide a handy reference for students.

- **Appendix C. Glossary of Globalization Terms.** This appendix makes the vocabulary of globalization, drawn from political science, history, economics, and other disciplines, accessible to students.

A Second Table of Contents by Rhetorical Mode

This rhetorical table of contents adds flexibility for teachers who prefer to organize their syllabus around such traditional forms as narration and description, comparison and contrast, process and causal analysis, and argumentation and persuasion.

Consistent Editorial Apparatus with a Sequenced Approach to Exercises

The New World Reader provides brief introductions to all chapters, highlighting the central issues raised by the writers in each section. All readings contain substantial author headnotes followed by a prereading question. Following each essay, three carefully sequenced sets totaling ten questions provide students with the opportunity to respond to the form and content of the text in ways that promote reading, writing, discussion, group work, and Internet exploration.

- **Before Reading.** One question asks students to think about their current understanding or interpretation of an event or a condition.
- **Thinking About the Essay.** Five questions build on the student's ability to comprehend how the writer's ideas develop through essential rhetorical and stylistic techniques.
- **Responding in Writing.** Three writing activities reflect and expand the questions in the first section, offering opportunities for students to write personal, analytical, and argumentative responses to the text.
- **Networking.** Two questions encourage small-group and Internet work. One question promotes collaborative learning. The other question provides practice in the use of Internet and library sources to conduct deeper exploration and research into issues raised by the author.

Exciting Visual Materials

Students today need to read and analyze visual as well as written texts. *The New World Reader* integrates photographs, art work, cartoons, graphs, and maps into the chapters. The second edition includes the popular four-color essay devoted to examining the question of "Culture or Conflict?" as well as a **new** four-color essay on standards of global beauty. These illustrations add a visual dimension to aid students' comprehension of the issues raised by written texts. All visual materials offer questions for informed response and analysis.

Interactive Website

Houghton Mifflin offers dynamic student and instructor websites for this book. The websites include prompts for chapters and essays, answers to questions, additional questions and activities, sample student essays, interactive guidelines for grammar and writing, links to other sites, visual and music portfolios, and additional resources for students and teachers. The instructor's website includes the Instructor's Resource Manual and sample syllabi.

 *Online Study Center*   college.hmco.com/PIC/mullerNWR2e

Instructor's Resource Manual

The Instructor's Resource Manual for *The New World Reader* provides new as well as experienced teachers with suggested reading sequences, additional assignments, resources (both print and online) for further information and research, and possible responses for all activities in the student text. In addition, the IRM discusses classroom management issues unique to the teaching and discussion of challenging, controversial material in the composition classroom.

Acknowledgments

This book is the result of very special relationships—and considerable serendipity—among friends, collaborators, reviewers, and supporters. I was first alerted to the possibility of developing a global reader by my good friend and former colleague John Chaffee, an acclaimed author and specialist in critical thinking and philosophy. To John I offer my gratitude for his faith in an old friend.

Serving as matchmaker, John introduced me to Suzanne Phelps Weir, formerly the executive editor of English at Houghton Mifflin, and she and I began a conversation and collaboration that proceeded rapidly to a proposal, sample chapters, reviews, and a manuscript that was revised and polished by numerous professional hands. Suzanne is any author's dream executive editor; she likes and nourishes writers, and I wish to express my appreciation for her kindness and commitment to this project.

I learned long ago that any college text is only as good as the editorial staff developing it, and here there are several special people who saved me much grief, improved the book, and prevented me from sounding at times like a turgid academician. First and foremost, I thank my development editor, Meg Botteon, whose light touch can be detected in virtually every section of *The New World Reader*. Meg has been more than a development editor. In fact, she has been a partner and collaborator, and I'm deeply grateful for her keen intellect, common sense, and good and gracious humor.

Supporting Meg have been other members of the Houghton Mifflin family who have taken more than ordinary interest in this project. To Bob Greiner, the senior project editor, I express thanks for his expertise and his promise to buy me a Mexican meal in Boston if I hit all targets in the production schedule. To the crack copyeditor, Susan Moore, I express my pleasure and sheer amazement at her knowledge and ability to improve a text right down to the smallest detail. John McHugh, assistant editor, and Cassandra Gargas and Emily Meyer, editorial assistants, helped to keep the project on time and on track.

Derrick Gentry has assisted me in research for the second edition and has revised the online instructor's resource manual.

I would like to thank my friend and agent, John Wright, who negotiated the contract for this book. Finally, I express love and gratitude to my wife, Laleh Mostafavi-Muller, a specialist in international relations and the Middle East, who offered support and advice as the design for this book evolved.

Several reviewers wrote detailed appraisals of the manuscript, recommendations for changes and improvements, praise and cautionary advice, and their collective wisdom informs this book. Thanks go to the following reviewers for the second edition:

> Anne Meade Stockdell-Giesler, Ph.D., University of Tampa
> Gail Samis, Salisbury University English Department
> Dr. Nancy Nanney, Chair, Humanities Division,
>   West Virginia University at Parkersburg
> Debra L. Cumberland, Winona State University

We continue to be grateful for the insights of reviewers whose suggestions helped in the development of the first edition of *The New World Reader:*

> Cathryn Amdahl, Harrisburg Area Community College
> Sandra L. Clark, University of Wyoming
> John Dailey, New Jersey City University
> Stephen F. Evans, University of Kansas
> Eileen Ferretti, Kingsborough Community College
> Len Gougeon, University of Scranton
> Tim Gustafson, University of Minnesota
> Jeff Henderson, Kalamazoo Valley Community College
> Pearlie Peters, Rider University
> Avantika Rohatgi, Butler University
> Renee Schlueter, Kirkwood Community College

Henry Schwarz, Georgetown University
Micheline M. Soong, Hawaii Pacific University
Mark Wiley, California State University, Long Beach
Rosemary Winslow, Catholic University
Randall J. VanderMey, Westmont College
William Vaughn, Central Missouri State University
Julie Yen, California State University, Sacramento

Gilbert Muller

Thinking, Reading, and Writing About the New Global Era

G lobal forces are shaping today's nations and societies as never before. Evolving trends—among them the spread of worldwide communications networks, the "clash of civilizations," **terrorism** in many regions and most continents, environmental challenges, and transnational population shifts—suggest that the last century, the "American century," as *Time* magazine's Henry Luce called it, is over and we have entered a new era. In a world where much seems increasingly interconnected, it is no longer sufficient to think locally. Instead we need to reflect critically on new global realities, assessing the ways in which other peoples, belief systems, traditions, and cultures impact our lives. As the twenty-first century begins, our well-being and arguably our very survival will depend on our ability to harness the forces unleashed by the dynamics of the new global era.

Regardless of what we choose to call this emerging era—the post-9/11 world, the new world order, the post–cold war period, the age of **globalization,** the information age, the age of terror—we exist today in a global landscape characterized by rapid transformations. To comprehend these transformations, we should not confuse, as the historian Francis Fukuyama reminds us, our national needs with our universal ones. We must also consider what writer and *New York Times* syndicated columnist Thomas Friedman terms the "super-story." For Friedman (who asserts in his most recent book that the world is "flat"), the super-story involves all the trends of globalization including world trade, the formation of transnational economic and political alignments, the spread of **information technology,** even new dating and marriage patterns, that affect national and transnational behavior. Writers like

Online Study Center This icon will direct you to web links, audio and visual content, and additional resources on the website: college.hmco.com/pic/mullerNWR2e

An Azad University student uses an Internet café in Tehran, Iran. Access to the Internet is still highly restricted in some countries and by some cultures.

Thinking About the Image

1. Closely examine all of the details of this photograph. (For example, what is on the table next to this woman's elbow?). In what ways does this photograph reinforce standard images in the American media of Muslim women? In what ways is the photograph surprising?
2. Do you agree that access to the Internet provides a kind of empowerment? Why or why not?
3. In her essay "When Afghanistan Was at Peace," Margaret Atwood notes of her book *The Handmaid's Tale* (partly inspired by her travels in Afghanistan) that "there is freedom to and freedom from. But how much of the first should you have to give up in order to assure the second?" How might the woman in this photograph respond?
4. The English-language version of the website for Azad University, where this woman is a student, is http://www.azad.ac.ir/main/INDEX_Eng.htm. Visit this website and compare it to that of your own college. What are the similarities between your schools and how they present themselves? How are they different?

Fukuyama and Friedman, who contribute essays to this book, offer insights into global challenges and the arguments surrounding them.

One of those challenges, of course, and a subject of continuing debate, is worldwide terrorism. The collapse of the World Trade towers and the bombing of the Pentagon on September 11, 2001, as well as subsequent terrorist attacks in Europe, the Middle East, Southeast Asia, and elsewhere, confirm all too graphically the impact of global events on our lives. The 9/11 cataclysm differed from the collapse of the Berlin Wall or the implosion of the Soviet Union: it was an instant in time etched in the minds of an entire generation. And at that moment, we were connected to one another in the United States and to people around the world. No longer isolated by two oceans and seemingly immune to the world's turmoil, we suddenly had to reexamine and re-argue our complex fate.

In order to comprehend our complex fate and prepare for life in the twenty-first century, we will explore in this book some of the key ways we perceive and interact with our new world. In our flattened world, as Thomas Friedman terms it, where everything seems close and immediate—where cell phones, cable, and the Internet connect us instantaneously to a polyglot universe of people and events—we will try to establish parameters for what it means to exist in this global era. Family, community, state, and nation no longer suffice in the construction of our new identity, for today we are citizens of the world. As such, we have to find ways to manage change, negotiate transnational borders, understand diverse viewpoints, and defuse major conflicts if we are to survive and prosper in the new global era.

Critical Thinking

Are you ready for the brave new world of the twenty-first century, the new global era? Do you know enough about *globalization*—the interplay of cultures, societies, economies, and political systems—that is changing your world? Assuredly you will study this new era in various courses, prepare for careers in it, sit next to people from around the world in your classes, and perhaps even marry into it. The three thousand people from around the world who died in the World Trade Center disaster were working, collaborating, and living in this new world. Among the dead were civilians and citizens from sixty-two countries, including 250 Indians, 200 Pakistanis, 200 Britons, and 23 Japanese. Sadly, there were other individuals—call them terrorists—who felt threatened by the new international order represented by the 9/11 victims.

Your success in college hinges in part on your ability to make choices based on knowledge, experience, and careful reflection about the new world order. You will have to think critically about the global contexts that influence you and your nation. *Critical thinking* is clear thinking: it is a type of mental practice in which you respond to issues logically and, for the purposes of this course, deal with texts and the meanings they generate among class members. Often you will have to *rethink* your opinions, beliefs, and attitudes, and this too is a hallmark of critical thinking—the willingness to discard weak ideas or biased opinions for more mature or simply more logical intellectual opinions. For example, how do you define a *terrorist*? Why would Americans define a terrorist as anyone who takes the lives of innocent civilians, while others around the world view such individuals not as terrorists but as freedom fighters or defenders of the faith? Such questions do not admit easy or facile responses. They require deep and complex thought, for we live in a complex world.

To work effectively with the readings in this text, which deal with varieties of global experience, you need to develop a repertoire of critical thinking skills. In all likelihood, you have come to college possessing many of these skills. But it is important to refine, strengthen, and expand these skills to achieve a degree of authority over any given body of knowledge. How then do you think critically—in other words study and interpret—any given text? How do you look closely at the ideas of writers and evaluate them? How do you respond critically in writing? Having a repertoire of critical thinking skills creates the foundation for being a critical reader and writer.

Every writer in this textbook had a project much like the projects that you will develop: to articulate clearly and convincingly a key idea or nucleus of related ideas about an aspect of human experience—whether in the United States or elsewhere. They developed their ideas by using the repertoire of critical thinking skills—which for our purposes we can associate with key rhetorical strategies. **Rhetoric** is the art of writing or speaking, often to convince an audience about a particular issue. **Rhetorical strategies** are the key patterns that writers employ in this effort to clarify ideas and opinions. We divide these patterns into three major groups: *narration* and *description; exposition* (consisting of definition, comparison and contrast, illustration, process analysis, causal analysis, and classification); and *argument* and *persuasion*. These are not just the classic patterns of rhetoric but also powerful ways of thinking about and understanding our world.

Research demonstrates that different people think most effectively in different ways, or **cognitive styles.** You might like to argue—hopefully not in the style of *Crossfire* or *Hardball*—where viewpoints often are reduced simplistically to positions on the political "right" or "left"—but rather with reasonableness and respect. Or you might be great at telling a story to make a point. Or perhaps you have a talent for analyzing global events. All writing reflects one or more of those cognitive styles that we see reflected in narration and description, exposition, and argumentation. You can gain control over your reading and writing practices by selecting from among these major rhetorical strategies or thinking styles.

Narration and Description

Narration can be briefly described as telling a story, and **description** as the use of vivid **sensory detail**—sight, sound, smell, taste, touch—to convey either a specific or an overall impression. Although narration and description are not always treated in studies of reasoning, the truth of the matter is that it is foolish not to consider these strategies as aspects of the thinking process. The study of narration and description reveals that this type of thinking can produce authority in college writing.

Some composition theorists actually believe that narration and description, relying as they do on the creation of a personal **voice**—your personal voice—is the gateway to successful student writing. For example, Where were you during a recent national or global crisis? How did you feel? What was your response? How did you get through the day and the aftermath? If you were answering these questions in an essay, you would need to employ a special kind of thinking and reflection, one in which you get in touch with your feelings and find vivid ways to express and make sense of them. It would be useless to say that you are not engaged in reasoning because you would employ narration and description—perhaps even insert **visual texts** downloaded from the Web—to arrive at your personal form of truth about the event. In all likelihood, you would also state or imply a **thesis** (a main idea) and even other generalizations about the event that go beyond pure narration or description; in fact, the vast majority of essays, while they might reflect one or two dominant rhetorical patterns or styles of organizational thought, tend to reveal mixed patterns or approaches to the writing process.

Consider the way the famous novelist, poet, and essayist John A. Williams begins a piece entitled "September 11, 2001":

> I saw the second plane.
> My wife, Lori, had deserted the radio in the kitchen of our house in Teaneck, New Jersey, having heard something about an explosion in one of the World Trade Center buildings and was now standing before the TV set in the sitting room where I joined her.
> The plane circled slowly past the north tower, then, dipping a wing, turned to ram into the south tower three-quarters of the way from its top. The jet disintegrated in a raging bright-orange inferno that billowed out and up against a sun-streaked blue sky, merging with the whirling orange-brown clouds boiling out of the north tower. At that instant I knew I wouldn't be driving Lori into Manhattan for her dental appointment..
>
> —From *September 11, 2001: American Writers Respond*

Here Williams employs narrative and descriptive skills we see at the outset of his essay to set the stage for personal reflections on the role of the United States in the world. Of course, we would expect a novelist to call up his unique storytelling skills to convey his ideas. He uses narration and description to create a sense of immediacy within the text.

Exposition

Exposition is a relatively broad term that defines a type of writing in which you explain or convey information about a subject. Expository writing is the form of writing that in all likelihood you will be required to produce in college courses. In an expository essay, you set forth facts and ideas—in other words, detailed explanations—to support a thesis, or main idea. As a form of critical thinking, expository writing provides a way of clarifying many of the cultural, political, and economic forces that mold global events today.

To produce effective expository essays, you need to develop skill and fluency in the use of several key rhetorical strategies, among them *definition, comparison* and *contrast, illustration, causal analysis, process analysis,* and *classification.* The use of any one or several of the patterns will dictate your approach to a given topic or problem, and the effective application of these strategies will help to create an authoritative voice, for the readers of your expository essay will see that you are using these rhetorical patterns to think consistently about a body of information and present it coherently. Once again, you employ specific reasoning abilities to make sense of your world.

When you consider the international events that increasingly shape both local and personal life—indeed, that are shaping your identity—it is clear that you must think critically about the best way to approach these events. The way you are able to reason about events, the perspectives you may develop on a particular problem, will inform your understanding of the subject and your ability to convey this understanding in writing.

Think about a term that already has been introduced and that you will encounter in numerous essays in this collection—*globalization.* This is one of the many terms that you will have to look at closely as you come to an understanding of the global forces shaping lives, identities, **cultures,** and civilizations in the twenty-first century. How might you unravel the significance of this word, gain authority over it, explore its relevance to various texts that you will read, and ultimately express your understanding of it in writing?

To start, *definition* of a complex term like *globalization* might be in order. (Definitions for many of the key terms relating to globalization appear in Appendix C.) As a way of thinking about a subject, **definition** is a statement about what a word or phrase means. It is always useful to be able to state this meaning in one or two sentences, as we have already done earlier in this chapter—"the interplay of cultures, societies, economies, and political systems" in the world today. But entire books have been and are being written about globalization, for it is a complex and controversial subject. We call these longer explanations **extended definitions,** which typically rely on other rhetorical strategies to expand the field of understanding. Finally, you might very well have a highly personal understanding of a term like *globalization.* Perhaps you have witnessed or read about workers in overseas factories producing Nikes for a few cents a day and consequently have mixed feelings about the Nikes you are wearing today. In this instance, *globalization* has a special meaning for you, and we term this special meaning a **stipulative definition** because it is colored highly by your experience. Remember, as with all discussions of rhetorical strategies, you are developing and polishing critical thinking skills. With definition, you are taking abstract ideas and making them comprehensible and concrete.

A second way to approach *globalization* would be through comparative thinking. **Comparison** and **contrast** is a cognitive process wherein you consider the similarities and differences of things. Imagine that your instructor asks you to write an essay entitled "Two Ways of Looking at Globalization." The title itself suggests that you have to employ a comparative method to explain and analyze this phenomenon. You would need a thesis to unify this comparative approach, and three or four key points of comparison and/or contrast to support it. The purpose of comparison and contrast is usually to state a preference for one thing over the other or to judge which one is superior. For example, if you maintain that globalization is about inclusion, while those opposing globalization define it as a new form of colonialism or exploitation, you are evaluating and judging two positions.

Any approach to a subject requires a thoughtful and accurate use of **illustration**—that is, the use of examples to support an idea. Illustration, which we also call **exemplification**, enables you to make abstract ideas concrete. Normally several examples or one key extended example serves to illustrate your main and minor ideas about a subject. If, for example, you want to demonstrate that globalization is a trend that will foster understanding among nations and peoples, you would have to provide facts, statistics, examples, details drawn from personal experience, testimonials, and expert opinions to support your position. Illustration is the bedrock of virtually all ways of thinking, reading, and writing about a topic. Whether telling a story, explaining a topic, or arguing a point (which we deal with in the next section), illustration provides the evidence required to produce a powerful text. Illustration teaches the value of using the information of others—typically the texts of others—in order to build a structure for your own paper.

Causal and *process analysis* are two other forms of intellectual practice that can shape your critical approaches to topics. **Causal analysis,** sometimes called **cause-and-effect analysis,** answers the basic human question *Why?* It deals with a chain of happenings and the predictable consequences of these happenings. Like all the forms of thinking presented in this introductory section, causal analysis parallels our everyday thinking patterns. When we ask why terrorists attacked some city or tourist destination, why so many people in the **Third World** oppose globalization, or why the Internet can foster international cooperation, we are looking for causes or conditions and examining consequences and results (or effects). **Process analysis,** on the other hand, answers the question *How?* It takes things apart in order to understand how they operate or function. Many varieties of process analysis deal with "how-to" subjects involving steps in a correct sequence—for example, how to prepare fajitas. But process analysis is also central to the treatment of broad global trends. How did globalization come about? How do we combat terrorism? How do we prevent global warming? Process analysis can help explain the subtle and complex nature of relationships existing within a chain of events.

The last major form of exposition is **classification,** in which information is divided into categories or groups for the purpose of clarifying relationships among them. Some experts would term classification a "higher-order" reasoning skill. In actuality, classification again resembles a great deal of everyday thinking: we classify friends, teachers, types of music, types of cuisine, and so forth. (One writer in this textbook, Octavio Paz, who won the Nobel Prize for Literature, writes an essay classifying types of national foods.) Classification is a way of taking a large body of information and breaking it down (dividing it) into categories for better understanding. It relies on analytical ability—critical thinking that explores parts within a whole. For example, if you were to write an essay entitled "Approaches to Globalization," you could establish three categories—political, economic, and cultural—to divide your subject into coherent parts. The secret to using classification effectively is to avoid the temptation to have your categories overlap excessively. (Did you notice that classification was used to organize this section on exposition?)

Writers skilled in exposition are smart and credible. They write with authority because they can think clearly in a variety of modes. With exposition you make critical thinking choices, selecting those rhetorical strategies that provide the best degree of understanding for your readers, your audience.

Argument and Persuasion

Argument is a special type of reasoning. It appears in texts—written, spoken, or visual—that express a debatable point of view. Stated more rigorously, argument is a process of reasoning in which the truth of some main proposition (or claim) is shown to be true (that is, based on the truth of other minor propositions or premises). Closely allied to argument is **persuasion,** in which you invite an audience through rational, emotional, and ethical appeals to adopt your viewpoint or embark on a course of action. Aristotle in his *Rhetoric* spoke of the appeals as *logos, ethos,* and *pathos*—reason, beliefs, and emotion working together to guide an audience to a proper understanding or judgment of an issue. Argument—the rational component in persuasion—enables you to think responsibly about global issues and present your viewpoints about them in convincing fashion.

The dividing line between various forms of exposition and argumentation is a fine one. Where does a *thesis* leave off and a *claim* (the main argumentative point) begin? Some experts would say that "everything's an argument," and in the arena of global affairs this seems to be true. Issues of religion, race, class, gender, and culture are woven into the very fabric of both our local and global lives, and all of these issues trigger vigorous positions and responses. And the international environment is such that conflict and change seemingly provoke argumentative viewpoints and positions.

The distinctive feature of argumentative thinking is that you give reasons in support of a **claim** or **major proposition.** The claim is what you are trying to prove in an argument. The **reasons,** also called **minor propositions,** offer proof for the major claim. And you support each minor proposition with **evidence**—those various types of illustration mentioned in the previous section as well as logical explanations or abstract thinking used to buttress your basic reasons. If you don't "have the facts"—let's say about global inequality, the Kyoto Protocol on Climate Change, or the worldwide reach of McDonald's—you will not be able to stake a claim and defend it vigorously.

The British philosopher Steven Toulmin emphasizes that underpinning any argument or claim is a **warrant,** which he defines as an assumption, belief, or principle that is taken for granted. The warrant validates the link between the claim and the support. It might be stated or unstated. Many practices of nations, beliefs of citizens, and policies of political groups rest on such warrants. For example, if you assume that the United States is now the world's only **superpower**—a warrant—you can use this principle to claim that the United States should use its power to intervene in rogue states. Or if you believe that people have the right to free themselves from oppression—a warrant at the heart of the Declaration of Independence—you might use this warrant to claim that oppressed citizens have the right to start revolutions to break their chains.

Consider the warrants concerning the war on terrorism embedded in the following paragraph, written by Harold Hongju Koh, a former assistant secretary of state in the Clinton administration and a professor of international law at Yale University:

> Our enemies in this war are out to destroy our society precisely because it is open, tolerant, pluralistic and democratic. In its place, they seek to promote one that is closed, vengeful, repressive and absolutist. To secure genuine victory, we must make sure that they fail, not just in their assault on our safety but also in their challenge to our most fundamental values.
>
> —"Preserving American Values"

Here the writer predicates his claim about the need to achieve victory over our "enemies" on an entire catalog of "fundamental values" that in essence are warrants—that is, principles and beliefs. Also notice the way in which he employs the comparative method to structure his argument in this brief but revealing paragraph.

By their explosive or contentious nature, many global subjects and international issues call for argumentative responses. Your topic might be global warming, the Patriot Act, immigration along the United States–Mexico border, Bush or bin Laden, or the possibility of peace between Israel and the Palestinians. In such instances, your opinions and beliefs will require you to recognize that other people, nations, and cultures might approach the argument from entirely different perspectives. (For instance, you could assert that bin Laden is a terrorist, but millions of people around the world would strongly disagree, viewing him as a freedom fighter and defender of the faith.) Thus one unique challenge when developing arguments on international topics requires you to cross cultural boundaries, understand the attitudes and assumptions held by people outside your country, and contend with diverting opinions in a global context.

Stated differently, arguments on global topics require you to recognize competing global perspectives. In all likelihood, your argumentative paper will be grounded in a Western tradition based in part on rationalism, Judeo-Christian values, and various systems of freedom and individual rights. (It will be based as well on classic Greek and Roman principles of argument.) But warrants inherent in the Western tradition do not necessarily make your claim universal. Consider that newspapers around the world use almost two dozen euphemisms for *terrorist,* including *attacker, bomber, commando, criminal, extremist, fighter, guerrilla, hostage-taker, insurgent, militant, radical, rebel,* and *separatist.* (On the website www.newssafety.com, Reuters' Nidal al-Mughrabi offers advice on this matter to fellow reporters in Gaza: "Never use the word terrorist or terrorism describing Palestinian gunmen and militants; people consider them heroes of the conflict.") How you define and interpret a word can determine the method and purpose of an argument.

Not everyone experiences the world or argues global issues from your system of opinions and beliefs. Fortunately, the Internet and the World Wide Web, various translation engines that open international newspaper sites to research, broadcast and visual clips, and even international discussion groups offer you ways to interact globally with other writers, their text, and their arguments. By searching globally for non-U.S. viewpoints and contending with them, you will be able to write distinctive argumentative papers that go beyond mainstream propositions.

Before launching arguments over "homeland security," the pros and cons of globalization, the Arab-Israeli conflict, the rise of interracial and intercultural dating, or any other global or transnational subject, you once again have an obligation to think clearly and critically about these matters. Argumentation provides a logical way to present a viewpoint, deal fairly with opposing viewpoints, and hopefully arrive at a consensus. The psychologist Carl Rogers offers a new way of looking at argumentation when he suggests that both the communicator presenting an argument and the audience are participants in a dialogue—much like psychotherapy—in which they try to arrive at knowledge, understanding, and truth. At its best, argument results in intelligent discourse, a meeting of the minds, and even a strengthening of civic values.

Thinking About an Essay

Love and Race

NICHOLAS D. KRISTOF

> Nicholas D. Kristof is a reporter and columnist for the
> *New York Times*. He was born in Chicago, Illinois, in
> 1959 and received a B.A. degree from Harvard Univer-
> sity (1981) and a law degree from Oxford University
> (1983). He also has a diploma in Arabic language from
> the American University in Cairo. He writes: "Since my
> student days, when I began to travel with a backpack
> around Africa and Asia, I have had a fascination with
> foreign lands, cultures, and languages." Kristof and his
> wife, Sheryl WuDunn, who is also a *New York Times*
> reporter, won the Pulitzer Prize for their coverage of the
> Tiananmen Square massacre in 1989. Based in Asia for
> many years, Kristof and WuDunn have used their expe-
> riences there to write *China Awakes* (1994), *The Japan-
> ese Economy at the Millennium* (1999), and *Thunder
> from the East: Portrait of a Rising Asia* (2000). In the
> following op-ed essay that appeared in the *New York
> Times* on December 6, 2002, Kristof turns his attention
> from foreign lands to the changing cultural scene in the
> United States.

In a world brimming with bad news, here's one of the happiest trends.   1
Instead of preying on people of different races, young Americans are
falling in love with them.

Whites and blacks can be found strolling together as couples even at the   2
University of Mississippi, once the symbol of racial confrontation.

"I will say that they are always given a second glance," acknowledges   3
C. J. Rhodes, a black student at Ole Miss. He adds that there are still mis-
givings about interracial dating, particularly among black women and a
formidable number of "white Southerners who view this race-mixing as
abnormal, frozen by fear to see Sara Beth bring home a brotha."

Mixed-race marriages in the U.S. now number 1.5 million and are   4
roughly doubling each decade. About 40 percent of Asian-Americans and
6 percent of blacks have married whites in recent years.

Still more striking, one survey found that 40 percent of Americans had   5
dated someone of another race.

In a country where racial divisions remain deep, all this love is an enor-   6
mously hopeful sign of progress in bridging barriers. Scientists who study

the human genome say that race is mostly a bogus distinction reflecting very little genetic difference, perhaps one-hundredth of 1 percent of our DNA.

Skin color differences are recent, arising over only the last 100,000   7 years or so, a twinkling of an evolutionary eye. That's too short a period for substantial genetic differences to emerge, and so there is perhaps 10 times more genetic difference within a race than there is between races. Thus we should welcome any trend that makes a superficial issue like color less central to how we categorize each other.

The rise in interracial marriage reflects a revolution in attitudes. As re-   8 cently as 1958 a white mother in Monroe, N.C., called the police after her little girl kissed a black playmate on the cheek; the boy, Hanover Thompson, 9, was then sentenced to 14 years in prison for attempted rape. (His appeals failed, but he was released later after an outcry.)

In 1963, 59 percent of Americans believed that marriage between blacks   9 and whites should be illegal. At one time or another 42 states banned intermarriage, although the Supreme Court finally invalidated these laws in 1967.

Typically, the miscegenation laws voided any interracial marriages,   10 making the children illegitimate, and some states included penalties such as enslavement, life imprisonment and whippings. My wife is Chinese-American, and our relationship would once have been felonious.

At every juncture from the 19th century on, the segregationists warned   11 that granting rights to blacks would mean the start of a slippery slope, ending up with black men marrying white women. The racists were prophetic.

"They were absolutely right," notes Randall Kennedy, the Harvard   12 Law School professor and author of a dazzling new book, "Interracial Intimacies," to be published next month. "I do think [interracial marriage] is a good thing. It's a welcome sign of thoroughgoing desegregation. We talk about desegregation in the public sphere; here's desegregation in the most intimate sphere."

These days, interracial romance can be seen on the big screen, on TV   13 shows and in the lives of some prominent Americans. Former Defense Secretary William Cohen has a black wife, as does Peter Norton, the software guru. The Supreme Court justice Clarence Thomas has a white wife.

I find the surge in intermarriage to be one of the most positive fronts in   14 American race relations today, building bridges and empathy. But it's still in its infancy.

I was excited to track down interracial couples at Ole Miss, thinking   15 they would be perfect to make my point about this hopeful trend: But none were willing to talk about the issue on the record.

"Even if people wanted to marry [interracially], I think they'd keep it   16 kind of quiet," explained a minister on campus.

For centuries, racists warned that racial equality would lead to the 17
"mongrelization" of America. Perhaps they were right in a sense, for we're
increasingly going to see a blurring of racial distinctions. But these distinctions acquired enormous social resonance without ever having much basis
in biology.

Questions for Critical Thinking

1. What is *your* opinion of interracial love? What assumptions and attitudes
   do you bring to the subject? How open are you to an essay entitled "Love
   and Race"? Why would such a topic invite—almost demand—careful critical thinking? What assumptions do you think Kristof makes about his
   readers?

2. Why does Kristof refer to the University of Mississippi (Ole Miss) at the beginning and end of his essay (paragraphs 3 and 15)? Answer this question
   in groups of three or four class members, pooling your knowledge of civil
   rights history (and perhaps conducting some fast research on someone's
   laptop) to broaden your understanding of Kristof's purpose.

3. Where does Kristof use narration and description to organize part of the
   essay? What is the effect?

4. Kristof employs numerous expository strategies in this essay. Locate and
   identify them, explaining what they contribute to the substance and the organization of the essay.

5. Does Kristof construct an argument in this essay or is he simply reporting
   a cultural development? How do you know?

Reading Critically

Most of the essays in this book were written within the last ten years, but the
ideas in them run through the history of cultures and civilizations. Consequently we have to "read" the contemporary ideas contained in these selections through lenses that scan centuries and continents. We have to read
critically—analyzing, interpreting, and reassessing new and old ideas in the
light of our own experience. When, for example, Jamaica Kincaid, in her
essay "On Seeing England for the First Time" (see p. 304), tells us about her
experience growing up in Antigua, it behooves us to know something about
the legacy of the English **imperialism** before understanding its relevance to us
today. Is the United States the new imperial power? Are we facing the same
conflicts and contradictions that imperial powers through the ages have
confronted? To read critically is to be able to think critically about ideas in
texts, that have deep roots in world history.

As you read the selections in this book, you will discover that careful, critical reading about global issues can complement the talent you already have as a member of the generation that has grown up during the **information age.** Some say that college students have so much trouble with written texts because their culture privileges new forms of technology—call it visual or computer literacy—over older forms of print like the essays you find in this collection. But just as you probably think critically about information acquired through electronic and visual media, you can readily acquire an ability to read written texts critically and to respond to them in discussion and writing. One of the paradoxes of our era is that although we are spending more and more time in front of our computers, we also are buying more books and magazines.

Our most respected thinkers still use the written word to convey their ideas about the issues of our day. They might post these texts on the Web in various forms ranging from online magazines to blogs, but the reality is that these texts appear before us as products of the print universe. Only print can fully convey the intricacy of ideas writers have about our contemporary lives. Speech cannot rival the power of the printed word, as our propensity for tuning out the "talking heads" on television demonstrates. Moreover, with speech we rarely have the opportunity to go back and evaluate what has been said; with written texts, we can assess the presentation of ideas. As a reader, therefore, you have an obligation to deal seriously with the ideas presented by the writers (many of them famous) in this book, and to respond critically and coherently to them. You need to learn strategies that will permit you to read texts in this manner.

There are various ways in which readers can respond to any given text. You, a reader, bring varieties of personal experience—and indeed your personality—to a written text. Your social and cultural background also affects your response to texts. In short, there are several ways to respond critically to both written and visual communication.

You bring numerous personal experiences to the reading of any given text. After all, you have attitudes and opinions, likes and dislikes—a unique range of experience. You construct meaning through these personal experiences, which are rooted in your cultural background and community. If, for example, you read an essay on Islam (there are several in this book) and are Muslim yourself, you probably have personal experience of the text that might or might not be shared by other members of the class.

Along with personal experience, you also *think* about a text in special ways. Cognitive psychologists assert that when you were very young, you probably could not always distinguish fantasy from reality (which is why young children respond so powerfully to fairy tales and cartoons). When you were older—say in junior high school—you were able to seek one true meaning in a text. Then, as in your high school years, you developed an ability to consider multiple meanings and interpretations. The critical intelligence that you bring to a college environment is one that must reason, hypothesize, argue, classify, define, and predict as you contend with any given text that deals with complex global issues.

Of course, the text itself is also important: you cannot center all of its meaning on your personal experience. In fact, some teachers will tell you to eliminate personal experience, moralizing, and impressionistic opinion from your writing and focus on the intrinsic meaning of the text. Thus you become a hunter of the "truth" of a text, which reveals itself in the language, style, and structure of the work. Fortunately, there are rhetorical strategies and **conventions** that govern texts (many introduced in this book) that will help you to discover these formal truths.

The college classroom—especially the English classroom—is the place where you wrestle with the truths of a text. In this environment, you are not an isolated reader but part of a community of readers. This community or society of readers reflects the diverse features of gender, race, and ethnicity, class, education, religion, politics, region, and nation. As a member of this group, you want to share insights with others for the purpose of understanding or consensus (if there is an argument framing the text and discussion). You do not surrender your personal impressions of a text as much as you become a member of what the critic Stanley Fish calls the "interpretive community." In this book, every essay contains an exercise designed to strengthen your reading and writing skills within smaller interpretative or collaborative communities.

Finally, the act of reading critically leads you into the deepest regions of culture and the forces that reveal and inform our experience of the world. Cultural theorists contend that deeply held worldviews and ideologies—for instance, **capitalism** and **socialism**, or Islam and Christianity—are the bedrock of any social configuration. Various institutions, power structures, cultural conventions, gender roles, and "fields of discourse" like medicine and law dictate the ways we respond to a text. As you read the essays in the next chapter, "New American Mosaic," from a cultural perspective, you will have to assess the way your viewpoint on **immigration** has been formed by these deep structures of culture. Through such analysis, you can avoid biased, nationalistic, and religiously intolerant ways of thinking about a text, engaging instead in critical thought and sound, and reflective argument.

When reading argumentative essays in a global context, you should consider these critical questions:

- What is the purpose of the text? What claim or main idea does the writer want to develop?
- What is the writer's background? Was the writer born in the United States or overseas?
- Who is the writer's audience? Does the writer demonstrate an awareness that U.S. and non-U.S. readers might respond differently to the content and method of the text?
- Does the writer consider the values, assumptions, and experiences of readers from other cultures?

- Does the writer treat opposing viewpoints or perspectives, especially if they come from non-U.S. sources, accurately and fairly?
- What reasons or minor propositions support the writer's claim?
- How accurate and representative is the writer's supporting evidence? Does the writer rely solely on evidence from U.S. sources, or does credible evidence from reliable global sources also appear?
- Is the shape of the writer's argument logically convincing?

Steps to Reading Critically

With a basic understanding of how ways of reading influence your approach to a text, you can now follow steps that will enable you to read critically. You should treat any "system" for critical reading flexibly, but with the conviction that it is important to extract and evaluate the meanings that we professional writers want to convey to their audience. Here are guidelines for effective critical reading.

1. *Start with the conviction that critical reading, like critical thinking, requires active reading.* It is not like passively watching television. Instead, critical reading involves intellectual engagement with the text. Consequently, read with a pen or pencil in hand, underlining or circling key words, phrases, and sentences, asking questions in the margins, making observations—a process called **annotation**. These annotations will serve as guidelines for a second reading and additional responses in writing.

2. *Pause from time to time to reflect on what you are reading.* What is the writer's main idea? What are his or her basic methods (recall the rhetorical strategies) for developing ideas? What tone, or voice, does the writer convey, and why? What is the writer's **purpose**? Is it to argue an issue, explain, analyze, or what? What varieties of illustration or evidence does the writer provide?

3. *Employ your critical thinking skills to interrogate the text.* Use some of the reader response theories to explore its deepest meanings. For example, test the text against your personal experience or against certain cultural preconceptions. Think critically about the writer's argument, if there is one, and whether it withstands the test of logic and the conventions of argumentation.

4. *Consider the implied **audience** for the text.* How does the writer address you as part of this audience? Do you actually feel that you are part of this primary audience, a secondary reader, or largely forgotten or excluded? If you feel excluded, what features of the essay have caused you to be removed from this community of readers? How might you make yourself a part of this "universe of discourse" nevertheless?

5. *Write a **précis**, or **summary** of the essay.* These "shorthand" techniques will help you to focus your thoughts and prepare for class discussions and subsequent writing assignments.

These five steps for critical reading should suggest that critical reading, much like critical thinking and critical writing, involves re-reading. If you follow these guidelines, you will be able to enter the classroom community of readers with knowledge and authority and be prepared for productive class discussion.

Reading Visual Texts

You have to read **visual texts**—advertisements, tables and graphs, cartoons, artwork, photographs and illustrations—with the same care you bring to the critical reading of written texts. Indeed, "visuals" seem like the new mother of our information age, for we are bombarded with images that invite, sometimes demand, our response. Whether dealing with spam on our computers, contending with that ubiquitous beer commercial on television, responding to a photograph of the latest disaster in a newspaper account, or trying to decipher what a graph on the federal deficit *really* means, we know that visual texts are constructions designed to influence us in carefully contrived ways.

We must, therefore, attempt to be critical readers of visual texts so that the powerful images of our culture and civilization do not seduce or overwhelm us without proper evaluation. Visual texts, after all, tend to be instruments of persuasion. A symbol like the American eagle, the Islamic crescent, or the red star of China can trigger powerful personal and collective responses. Similarly, political advertisements and commercials often manipulate visual texts to persuade voters to act for a candidate or against (as with negative ads) an opposing candidate. To bring this discussion to the local level, log on to your campus website. What forms of visual text do you encounter that enhance the written text? Look especially for images that suggest that your campus is culturally and globally diverse.

To read visual texts with the same critical authority you bring to scrutinizing written texts, you should consider the following questions:

- In what culture or context did the image originate? Who is the author? What is the source?
- What implicit messages are conveyed by the images and symbols?
- How is the visual designed or organized, and what is the effect of this arrangement?
- What is the purpose of the visual? What does the visual want the viewer to believe?
- What evidence is provided, and how can it be verified?
- What is the relationship of the visual to the printed text?

Visual images complement and at times overwhelm print or even make printed text unnecessary. Whether appearing on T-shirts, in ads in the glossiest fashion magazines, or marching across a computer screen, visual images usher us into a world of meaning. And we need to apply the same critical perspective to this visual universe that we do to its print counterpart.

Reading an Essay Critically

The Globalization of Eating Disorders

SUSAN BORDO

Susan Bordo (b. 1947) was born in Newark, New Jersey. She attended Carleton University (B.A., 1972) and the State University of New York at Stony Brook (Ph.D., 1982). A well-known feminist scholar, Bordo is the Singletary Chair in the Humanities and a professor of English and Women's Studies at the University of Kentucky. In this selection, written as a preface to the tenth anniversary edition of her Pulitzer Prize–nominated book *Unbearable Weight: Feminism, Western Culture, and the Body* (2003), Bordo offers an overview of a new kind of epidemic, fueled by Western media images, that is affecting cultures around the world.

The young girl stands in front of the mirror. Never fat to begin with, she's been on a no-fat diet for a couple of weeks and has reached her goal weight: 115 lb., at 5′4″—exactly what she should weigh, according to her doctor's chart. But in her eyes she still looks dumpy. She can't shake her mind free of the "Lady Marmelade" video from Moulin Rouge. Christina Aguilera, Pink, L'il Kim, and Mya, each one perfect in her own way: every curve smooth and sleek, lean-sexy, nothing to spare. Self-hatred and shame start to burn in the girl, and envy tears at her stomach, enough to make her sick. She'll never look like them, no matter how much weight she loses. Look at that stomach of hers, see how it sticks out? Those thighs—they actually jiggle. Her butt is monstrous. She's fat, gross, a dough girl.

As you read the imaginary scenario above, whom did you picture standing in front of the mirror? If your images of girls with eating and body image problems have been shaped by *People* magazine and Lifetime movies, she's probably white, North American, and economically secure. A child whose parents have never had to worry about putting food on the family table. A girl with money to spare for fashion magazines and trendy clothing, probably college-bound. If you're familiar with the classic psychological literature on eating disorders, you may also have read that she's an

extreme "perfectionist" with a hyper-demanding mother, and that she suffers from "body-image distortion syndrome" and other severe perceptual
and cognitive problems that "normal" girls don't share. You probably
don't picture her as black, Asian, or Latina.

Read the description again, but this time imagine twenty-something   3
Tenisha Williamson standing in front of the mirror. Tenisha is black, suffers from anorexia, and fells like a traitor to her race. "From an African-
American standpoint," she writes, "we as a people are encouraged to
embrace our big, voluptuous bodies. This makes me feel terrible because I
don't want a big, voluptuous body! I don't ever want to be fat—ever, and
I don't ever want to gain weight. I would rather die from starvation than
gain a single pound."[1] Tenisha is no longer an anomaly. Eating and body
image problems are now not only crossing racial and class lines, but gender lines. They have also become a global phenomenon.

Fiji is a striking example. Because of their remote location, the Fiji is-   4
lands did not have access to television until 1995, when a single station was
introduced. It broadcasts programs from the United States, Great Britain,
and Australia. Until that time, Fiji had no reported cases of eating disorders, and a study conducted by anthropologist Anne Becker showed that
most Fijian girls and women, no matter how large, were comfortable with
their bodies. In 1998, just three years after the station began broadcasting,
11 percent of girls reported vomiting to control weight, and 62 percent of
the girls surveyed reported dieting during the previous months.[2]

Becker was surprised by the change; she had thought that Fijian cultural   5
traditions, which celebrate eating and favor voluptuous bodies, would
"withstand" the influence of media images. Becker hadn't yet understood
that we live in an empire of images, and that there are no protective
borders.

In Central Africa, for example, traditional cultures still celebrate volup-   6
tuous women. In some regions, brides are sent to fattening farms, to be
plumped and massaged into shape for their wedding night. In a country
plagued by AIDS, the skinny body has meant—as it used to among Italian,
Jewish, and black Americans—poverty, sickness, death. "An African girl
must have hips," says dress designer Frank Osodi. "We have hips. We have
bums. We like flesh in Africa." For years, Nigeria sent its local version of
beautiful to the Miss World competition. The contestants did very poorly.
Then a savvy entrepreneur went against local ideals and entered Agbani

1. From the Colours of Ana website (http://coloursofana.com//ss8.asp). [This and subsequent notes in the selection are the author's.]
2. Reported in Nancy Snyderma, *The Girl in the Mirror* (New York: Hyperion, 2002), p. 84.

Darego, a light-skinned, hyper-skinny beauty. (He got his inspiration from M-Net, the South African network seen across Africa on satellite television, which broadcasts mostly American movies and television shows.) Agbani Darego won the Miss World Pageant, the first Black African to do so. Now, Nigerian teenagers fast and exercise, trying to become "lepa"—a popular slang phrase for the thin "it" girls that are all the rage. Said one: "People have realized that slim is beautiful."[3]

How can mere images be so powerful? For one thing, they are never   7 "just pictures," as the fashion magazines continually maintain (disingenuously) in their own defense. They speak to young people not just about how to be beautiful but also about how to become what the dominant culture admires, values, rewards. They tell them how to be cool, "get it together," overcome their shame. To girls who have been abused they may offer a fantasy of control and invulnerability, immunity from pain and hurt. For racial and ethnic groups whose bodies have been deemed "foreign," earthy, and primitive, and considered unattractive by Anglo-Saxon norms, they may cast the lure of being accepted as "normal" by the dominant culture.

In today's world, it is through images—much more than parents, teach-   8 ers, or clergy—that we are taught how to be. And it is images, too, that teach us how to see, that educate our vision in what's a defect and what is normal, that give us the models against which our own bodies and the bodies of others are measured. Perceptual pedagogy: "How to Interpret Your Body 101." It's become a global requirement.

I was intrigued, for example, when my articles on eating disorders began   9 to be translated, over the past few years, into Japanese and Chinese. Among the members of audiences at my talks, Asian women had been among the most insistent that eating and body image weren't problems for their people, and indeed, my initial research showed that eating disorders were virtually unknown in Asia. But when, this year, a Korean translation of *Unbearable Weight* was published, I felt I needed to revisit the situation. I discovered multiple reports on dramatic increases in eating disorders in China, South Korea, and Japan. "As many Asian countries become Westernized and infused with the Western aesthetic of a tall, thin, lean body, a virtual tsunami of eating disorders has swamped Asian countries," writes Eunice Park in *Asian Week* magazine. Older people can still remember when it was very different. In China, for example, where revolutionary ideals once condemned any focus on appearance and there have been several disastrous

3. Norimitsu Onishi, "Globalization of Beauty Makes Slimness Trendy," *The New York Times,* Oct. 3, 2002.

famines, "little fatty" was a term of endearment for children. Now, with fast food on every corner, childhood obesity is on the rise, and the cultural meaning of fat and thin has changed. "When I was young," says Li Xiaojing, who manages a fitness center in Beijing, "people admired and were even jealous of fat people since they thought they had a better life. . . . But now, most of us see a fat person and think 'He looks awful.'"[4]

Clearly, body insecurity can be exported, imported, and marketed— 10 just like any other profitable commodity. In this respect, what's happened with men and boys is illustrative. Ten years ago men tended, if anything, to see themselves as better looking than they (perhaps) actually were. And then (as I chronicle in detail in my book *The Male Body*) the menswear manufacturers, the diet industries, and the plastic surgeons "discovered" the male body. And now, young guys are looking in their mirrors, finding themselves soft and ill defined, no matter how muscular they are. Now they are developing the eating and body image disorders that we once thought only girls had. Now they are abusing steroids, measuring their own muscularity against the oiled and perfected images of professional athletes, body-builders, and *Men's Health* models. Now the industries in body-enhancement—cosmetic surgeons, manufacturers of anti-aging creams, spas and salons—are making huge bucks off men, too.

What is to be done? I have no easy answers. But I do know that we need 11 to acknowledge, finally and decisively, that we are dealing here with a cultural problem. If eating disorders were biochemical, as some claim, how can we account for their gradual "spread" across race, gender, and nationality? And with mass media culture increasingly providing the dominant "public education" in our children's lives—and those of children around the globe—how can we blame families? Families matter, of course, and so do racial and ethnic traditions. But families exist in cultural time and space—and so do racial groups. In the empire of images, no one lives in a bubble of self-generated "dysfunction" or permanent immunity. The sooner we recognize that—and start paying attention to the culture around us and what it is teaching our children—the sooner we can begin developing some strategies for change.

Reading and Responding to an Essay

1. After reading Bordo's essay, reread and annotate it. Underline or circle key words, phrases, and sentences. Ask questions and make observations in

---

4. Reported in Elizabeth Rosenthal, "Beijing Journal: China's Chic Waistline: Convex to Concave," *The New York Times*, Dec. 9, 1999.

the margins. Next to the title, write a phrase or sentence explaining what you think the title means.

2. In class groups of three or four, discuss your personal responses to this essay. Share with group members your experience of the text and why you respond to it the way you do. Would you say that your ideal image of physical beauty is based on personal or shared values? Do you know people whose ideas of beauty contrast with your own? Do you think of this difference as a matter of opinion, cultural difference, or simply personal taste?

3. Bordo claims, "In today's world, it is through images—much more than parents, teachers, or clergy—that we are taught to be." How essential is this premise to the writer's claim? What kinds of evidence does she use to support the claim?

4. Examine the language, style, and structure of the essay. Do you find the writer's style to be engaging or accessible? Why or why not? Why does she repeat words and phrases (termed *anaphora* in rhetoric)? Where does she employ description, illustration, comparison, and the basis of case studies followed by general diagnosis—basically a problem-solution method of essay development?

5. Explain the ways in which you could interpret this essay from psychological, cultural, and social perspectives.

Writing in Response to Reading

The distinguished writers in this book, many of them recipients of major awards like the Nobel and Pulitzer Prizes, are professionals. When dealing typically with local and world events—especially with the relationship of a liberal and open society like the United States to the world community—they employ a broad range of stylistic and rhetorical skills to construct meaning. They write for numerous reasons or purposes, although an argumentative edge appears in many of the essays. All engage in strategic thinking and rethinking as they tackle the promises and prospects of our new global era.

It is useful at the outset of a course in college writing to think like a professional writer or at least a professional writer in the making. With each essay you write, imagine that you are trying to produce "publishable prose." Indeed, you will have the opportunity to write letters to the editor, post papers on the Web, pool and present research findings with other classmates, and engage in many tasks that assume the character of the professional writer who composes for a specific audience and for a specific purpose. At the least, by treating yourself as a writer capable of producing publishable prose, you will impress your instructor with your seriousness and aspirations.

Many of the issues and momentous events treated by the writers in this book demand no less than a "professional" response based on your ability to deal critically in writing with the strategic questions the essays raise. Indeed, critical thinking and writing about our common global condition is one measure of a pluralistic and tolerant society. By thinking and rethinking, writing and rewriting about your world, you contribute to the creation of open democratic discourse.

How, then, do you write about the new global era and its many challenges, or about any other topic for that matter? Globalizations has changed the way people think about themselves and their relation to the world. Even ideas have become global; communication of these ideas now can span the world in milliseconds. As a writer in this brave new world of globalization, you need to apply in writing that repertoire of critical thinking skills mentioned at the outset of this chapter to make sense of contemporary life on this planet.

To start, you must have a basic understanding of the world of global interrelationships that characterizes life in the twenty-first century. The noted historian Paul Kennedy, who has an essay in this book, defines globalization as "the ever-growing integration of economies and societies because of new communications, newer trade and investment patterns, the transmissions of cultural images and messages, and the erosion of local and traditional ways of life in the face of powerful economic forces from abroad." Kennedy, as we might expect from a historian, is quick to note that this new world of globalization did not spring immediately from the ashes of 9/11 but can be detected in different guises in the rise and fall of great civilizations. For example, what the British Empire once termed "progress," we now call globalization. Today, the United States is the Great Power, its financial, cultural, military, and hi-tech capacities unrivaled by other nations. Whether or not its Great Power status—its overarching control of the forces of globalization—will create new forms of "progress" for peoples and nations around the world is the central debate underlying the chapters in this book.

Writers like Paul Kennedy are "professional" in the sense that they know their subject. They are informed. But their informed essays do not result from some divinely inspired moment of creativity. When professional writers sit down to tackle an issue of importance, they know that beyond the knowledge they bring to the subject, they will have to consider various perspectives on the subject and even experiment with various methods of composition. Everyone composes differently, but it is fair to say that a good essay is the result of planning, writing, and revision, and such as essay reflects some of the key thinking strategies outlined in the first part of this chapter. There is a common consensus among professionals, including teachers of writing, that a **composing process**, consisting of *prewriting, drafting,* and *revision,* is the best way to approach the creation of a successful essay.

Prewriting

Prewriting is that preliminary stage in the composing process in which you map out mentally and in writing your overall approach to the subject.

Prewriting in the context of this book begins when you read critically and respond to an essay. Perhaps you annotate the essay, summarize it mentally, or take notes on paper or the computer. Or maybe you take notes during class discussion. Next, you size up the nature of the writing project appearing in the exercises at the end of the essay or provided by the instructor. At this early stage, it is clear that already you are thinking, responding, and writing critically about the project at hand.

Composing processes are unique to each writer, but there are certain areas of the prewriting process that are necessary for you to consider:

- *Who is your audience?* A college writing assignment means that your primary audience will be your professor, who knows the "print code" and anticipates well-organized and grammatically correct prose. But there are secondary audiences to consider as well, and you might have to adjust your level of discourse to them. If you are working collaboratively, you have members of the group to satisfy. If you exchange papers with another class member for evaluation, this also creates a new audience. Or perhaps you will need to create an electronic portfolio of your best work as a graduation requirement; here the people who assess the quality of the portfolio become judges of your work.
- *What is your purpose?* Is your purpose to tell a story, describe, inform, argue, evaluate, or combine any number of these basic goals? Knowing your purpose in advance of actually drafting the essay will permit you to control the scope, method, and tone of the composition.
- *What is your thesis or claim?* Every paper requires a controlling idea or assertion. Think about and write down, either in shorthand or as a complete sentence, the main idea or claim that you plan to center your paper on.
- *How will you design your essay?* Planning or outlining your paper in advance of actually writing it can facilitate the writing process. Complete outlines, sketch outlines, sequenced notes, visual diagrams: all serve as aids once the actual drafting begins.
- *How can you generate preliminary content?* Notes can be valuable. **Brainstorming,** in which you write without stop for a certain amount of time, can also activate the creative process. Joining online discussion groups or working collaboratively in the classroom also can result in raw content and ideas for development.

Prewriting provides both content and a plan of operation before moving to the next stage in the composing process.

Drafting

Once you have attended to the preliminary, or prewriting, stage in the composing process, you can move to the second stage, which is the actual **drafting** of the paper. Applying an Aristotelian formula, be certain to have a beginning, middle, and end. Your introduction, ideally one opening paragraph, should center the topic, be sufficiently compelling to engage your reader, and contain a thesis or claim. The body of the essay should offer a series of paragraphs supporting your main idea or central assertion. The conclusion should wrap things up in an emphatic or convincing way.

Here is a checklist for drafting an essay:

- Does your title illuminate the topic and capture the reader's interest?
- Does your opening paragraph "hook" the reader? Does it establish and limit the topic? Does it contain a thesis or claim?
- Do all body paragraphs support the thesis? Is there a main idea (called a **topic sentence**) controlling each paragraph? Are all paragraphs well developed? Do they contain sufficient examples or evidence?
- Does the body hold together? Is there a logical sequence to the paragraphs? In other words, is the body of the essay **unified** and **coherent,** with **transitions** flowing from sentence to sentence and paragraph to paragraph?
- Have you selected the best critical thinking strategies to develop the paper and meet the expectations set out in your introduction?
- Is your conclusion strong and effective?

Think of drafting as the creation of a well-constructed plot. This plot does not begin, develop, and end haphazardly, but rather in a carefully considered sequence. Your draft should reveal those strategies and elements of the composing process that produce an interesting and logically constructed plot.

Revision

There are professional writers who rarely if ever revise their work, and there are others who spend forever getting every word and sentence just right. Yet most professional writers do some amount of **revision**, either on their own initiative or in response to other experts, normally editors and reviewers. As the American poet Archibald MacLeish observed, the composing process consists of the "endless discipline of writing and rewriting and rewriting."

Think of the essay that in all likelihood you have put up on your computer screen not as a polished or final product but as a rough draft. Use the grammar and spell checker features of your software program to clean up this draft, remembering that this software is not infallible and sometimes is even misleading. Then revise your essay, creating a second draft, with the following questions serving as guidelines:

- Is the essay long enough to satisfy the demands of the assignment?
- Is the topic suitable for the assignment?
- Is there a clear thesis or claim?
- Is the purpose or intention of the essay clear?

- Is the essay organized sensibly? Are the best rhetorical patterns used to facilitate reader interest and comprehension?
- Are all sentences grammatically correct and sufficiently varied in structure?
- Is there sufficient evidence, and is all information derived from other sources properly attributed?
- Does the manuscript conform to acceptable guidelines for submitting written work?

Successful writing blends form and content to communicate effectively with an audience. The guidelines offered in this section tap your ability to think and write critically about the global issues raised in this book. To be a global citizen, you must become aware of others, make sense of the world, and evaluate varieties of experience. To be a global writer, you have to translate your understanding of these global relationships into well-ordered and perceptive prose.

Writing in Response to an Essay

Not Ignorant, Not Helpless

LORRAINE ALI

Lorraine Ali writes about music and popular culture. Currently a staff writer for *Newsweek*, Ali was formerly a senior critic for *Rolling Stone* and has also written for *The New York Times*, *The Village Voice*, and *Harper's Bazaar*. She was voted Music Journalist of the Year in 1997 and won a 2002 Excellence in Journalism Award from the National Arab Journalist Association. In this selection, which appeared in the December 12, 2005, issue of *Newsweek*, Ali considers how the image of the oppressed woman of Islamic culture—a stereotype born of Western moral indignation—can become as oppressive as the oppression that is denounced.

If I'd never known a Muslim woman, I'd probably pity any female 1 born into Islam. In America we've come to see these women as timid creatures, covered from head to toe, who scurry rather than walk. They have no voices, no rights and no place outside the home. But I grew up around secular Muslims (my father was an Iraqi Shiite) in Los Angeles, stayed with ultrareligious relatives in Baghdad and met dozens more Muslim women on travels through the Middle East. I've watched them argue politics with men at the dinner table in Baghdad, slap husbands on the back of the head for telling off-color jokes in Egypt and, at a recent Arab

Women's Media Conference in Amman, fiercely debate their notions of democracy from under hijabs and J. Lo-inspired hairdos. The West's exposure to Muslim women is largely based on Islam's most extreme cases of oppression: Taliban-dominated Afghanistan, Wahhabi-ruled Saudi Arabia, and postrevolutionary Iran. Under those regimes, women were and are ordered to cover. Many Afghan women are forbidden to attend school, and no Saudi woman is allowed to drive. Yet despite the spread of ultraconservative versions of Islam over the past few decades, these societies are not the norm in the Muslim world. In Egypt, female cops patrol the streets. In Jordan, women account for the majority of students in medical school. And in Syria, courtrooms are filled with female lawyers. "Women are out working, in every profession, and even expect equal pay," says Leila Ahmed, Harvard Divinity School professor and author of "Women and Gender in Islam." "Though the atmosphere in Muslim countries is becoming more restrictive, no matter how conservative things get they can't put the genie back in the bottle."

Still, Muslim women are feeling like pawns in a political game: jihadists   2
portray them as ignorant lambs who need to be protected from outside forces, while the United States considers them helpless victims of a backward society to be saved through military intervention. "Our empowerment is being exploited by men," says Palestinian Muslim Rima Barakat. "It's a policy of hiding behind the skirts of women. It's dishonorable no matter who's doing it." Scholars such as Khaled Abou El Fadl, an expert on Islamic law and author of "The Great Theft: Wrestling Islam From the Extremists," says this is an age-old problem. "Historically the West has used the women's issue as a spear against Islam," he says. "It was raised in the time of the Crusades, used consistently in colonialism and is being used now. Muslim women have grown very, very sensitive about how they're depicted on either side."

Surely the late feminist Doria Shafik felt the scorn of men—Arab and   3
British—while fighting for the right to vote in 1940s Egypt. Yet Shafik persevered and cast her first ballot in Cairo in 1956. "I render thanks unto God to have been born in the land of mysteries," she later wrote. "To have grown up in the shadow of the palms, to have lived within the arms of the desert, guardian of secrets . . . to have seen the brilliance of the solar disk and to have drunk as a child from the Nile sacred river." Millions of Muslim Arab women still love the societies they're born into, regardless of jihadist manipulation or American intervention. If reform is to come, they will surely be the ones who push it forward.

Responding in Writing

1. As a prewriting strategy, brainstorm about this article for five minutes. Try to capture your impressions of the essay as you respond to the elements in it.

2. In class groups of three or four, list aspects of life in the United States that are (or may be) viewed as "backward" from another culture's point of view (the existence of capital punishment in the United States, for example). Write a brief essay in which you seek to qualify or overturn one of these national stereotypes.

3. Write an analysis of this essay. What evidence in the essay suggests that Ali had a specific audience in mind? Describe her intended audience as it may be inferred from the text. Do you feel included in this group of targeted readers? Why or why not? What is her thesis or claim? How does she develop the introduction, body, and conclusion? What is the nature of her evidence? What ideas about America and world culture does she want the audience to gain from a critical reading of the text?

4. "Professional" writing is partly the result of an author's mastery of the subject. A writer's *ethos* may consist of a wide range of tonal qualities: moral authority, sincerity, good humor, humility, seriousness of purpose. Consider your response to the voice you hear in this essay. Do you feel that Ali's personal disclosure in the opening paragraph contributes to her moral authority? Write a personal disclosure of your own that you feel would establish your authority to speak on a certain subject relating to religion, gender, or American or world culture.

5. Go online and find out more about the roles of Muslim women in a specific country. Write a report on your findings and summarize it in an oral presentation to the class.

New American Mosaic: Are We Becoming a Universal Nation?

M artin Luther King Jr. believed in the need for what he termed a "world house," a commitment to a society of inclusion. "We are all caught up in an inescapable web of mutuality, tied in a single garment of destiny," he declared. Indeed, long before the September 11, 2001, terrorist attacks reminded us of the interconnected forces of our world, we were discovering how the United States (and Canada as well) was starting to reflect the rest of the planet. Accelerating this transformation has been the arrival of tens of millions of immigrants to the United States in the last quarter of the twentieth century. Instead of repeating earlier immigration patterns in which peoples arrived from Europe, these new immigrants travel here from all parts of the globe: Asia, Africa, the Caribbean, Central and South America. Today, new immigrants are changing the traditional notion of what it means to be "American." Arguably, because of the strikingly diverse nature of its citizenry, America is in the process of becoming a universal nation.

The writers in this chapter reflect in their own ethnic and racial origins the broad mosaic—some prefer to call it a kaleidoscope—that characterizes life in the United States today. Consider the historical magnitude of this national transformation. True, North America once belonged to native tribes—as N. Scott Momaday reminds us in one selection in this chapter. And the legacy of slavery, which began in 1621 when a Dutch man-of-war ship brought the first Africans to the Jamestown colony, served to diversify the nation. But from colonial times to 1965, the United States drew its population largely from Europe. First came the English, Scots-Irish, Germans, and French. The second great wave that began in the 1870s and continued up to World War I brought tens of millions of immigrants from southern and eastern

Online Study Center This icon will direct you to weblinks, audio and visual content, and additional resources on the website college.hmco.com/pic/mullerNWR2e

29

Thinking About the Image

1. Are the people portrayed in this cartoon stereotypes? How can you tell? Do you find the stereotypes offensive, or do they help the cartoon make sense? Can you think of any comedians or hip-hop artists who use stereotypes in a way that points out an uncomfortable truth?
2. This cartoon uses irony to make its point. What specifically is ironic about this cartoon?
3. Read the essay in this collection, "The Way to Rainy Mountain" by N. Scott Momaday. What might Momaday think about this cartoon?
4. What political situation or issue is Steve Kelley, the cartoonist, responding to in this cartoon? What is his opinion? Does he make his point effectively?

Europe. For centuries, immigrants from non-European parts of the world were systematically excluded, with restrictive quotas preserving certain assumptions about the racial and ethnic character of the nation. For example, in her haunting memoir *China Men,* the acclaimed writer Maxine

Hong Kingston devotes an entire chapter to listing the dozens of immigration statutes designed to exclude people from China from America's shores.

The Immigration Act of 1965 abolished all such quotas and opened the United States—for the first time in the nation's history—to the world's population. Now everyone presumably had a fair opportunity to achieve the American Dream, whatever this ambiguous term might mean. And arrive they did—from Vietnam, India, Nigeria, Cuba, the Philippines, Iran, China—all seeking a place in the new global nation. Of course, this contemporary collision and intersection of peoples, races, and cultures is not only an American phenomenon; many countries in Europe are dealing with similar patterns. But nowhere is this new global reality more apparent than in the United States. In certain states—California, for example—and in many major American cities, "minorities" are becoming majorities. According to the most recent census data, by 2056 the "average" American will be as likely to trace his or her origins to the Hispanic world, Asia, or the Pacific islands as to Europe. These demographic changes are often reflected on college campuses, with students from scores of national backgrounds speaking dozens of languages sharing classes together.

The story of American civilization is still unfinished, but the authors in this chapter suggest certain directions it will take. They write about conflicts and challenges posed by the new American dream, which is ostensibly open to, if not necessarily desired by, all the peoples of the world. They wrestle with America's complex fate. They ask collectively: How can America continue to be a beacon for peoples from around the planet seeking work, safety, security, freedom, the right to freely practice and preserve their own customs and beliefs? They ask: Can America be—should it be—the model for a universal nation?

All Things Asian Are Becoming Us

ANDREW LAM

Andrew Lam is known as both a prolific journalist and a widely anthologized short story writer. Many listeners also know his voice, as a regular commentator on National Public Radio's *All Things Considered*. Lam's awards include the Society of Professional Journalists' Outstanding Young Journalist Award (1993), The Media Alliance Meritorious award (1994), The World Affairs Council's Excellence in International Journalism Award (1992), the Rockefeller Fellowship at UCLA (1992), and the Asian American Journalists Association National Award (1993; 1995). He co-founded New California Media, an association of 400 ethnic media organizations in California. Lam was born in Vietnam and came to the United States in 1975 when he was eleven years old. His story was featured in the PBS documentary *My Journey Home,* in which a film crew followed him back to his home in Vietnam. In the following selection, Lam reflects on how elements of traditional and popular Asian culture have, within his lifetime, radically altered the cultural identity of Americans and the way they experience the world.

Before Reading

What products of Asian culture attract you the most? When you experience another culture as an imported commodity, do you feel that (in some sense) you become *part* of that culture? Do you have proprietary feelings toward certain aspects of your native culture? Explain your response.

Rudyard Kipling's famous line "East is East and West is West, and never 1
the twain shall meet" no longer applies. Today, East and West are commingled, and in this country, the East is on the rise.

Take movies. American audiences are growing more familiar with 2
movies from China, Japan and South Korea. Quentin Tarantino is planning a kung fu movie entirely in Mandarin, and Zhang Yimou's stylized martial arts films like "Hero" and "House of Flying Daggers" are popular across the country. Hollywood is remaking Japanese blockbusters like "The Ring" and "Shall We Dance?"

What many Asian Americans once considered proprietary culture— 3
kung fu, acupuncture, ginseng, incense, Confucian dramas, beef noodle soup and so on—has spilled irrevocably into the mainstream.

Three decades ago, who would have thought that sushi would become 4
an indelible part of American cuisine? Or that Vietnamese fish sauce would be found on Aisle 3 of Safeway? Or that acupuncture would be accepted by some HMOs? That feng shui would become a household word? Or that Asian writers, especially Indian, would play a large and important role in the pantheon of American letters?

American pundits tend to look at the world through a very old prism— 5
they associate globalization as synonymous with Americanization: i.e., how the United States influences the world. What many tend to overlook, in the age of porous borders, is how much the world has changed the United States.

Evidence of the Easternization of America is piling up.   6

Japanese animation is a good example. There are more than 20 anime 7
shows on cable channels, ranging from "Sailor Moon" to "Pokemon" to the latest teenage craze, "Kagemusha," a series about a half-human, half-demon warrior on a quest. "Spirited Away" beat out Disney movies to win the Oscar for best animation in 2003.

Sales of Japanese comic books, DVDs and videocassettes reached $500 8
million in the United States last year.

Mandarin-language films like "Crouching Tiger, Hidden Dragon," by 9
Ang Lee, and "Hero," by Zhang Yimou, were top draws across the United
States. Asian Americans have been featured as stars as in "Harold and Ku-
mar Go to White Castle" and "Better Luck Tomorrow."

Asian stars in Hollywood include Ang Lee, Joan Chen, Justin Lin, John 10
Woo, Jackie Chan, Jet Li, Chow Yun Fat, Michelle Yeow.

Sandip Roy, host of a San Francisco radio show called "Up Front" and 11
a film critic, points to the "Bollywoodization" of the United States.

"Deepak Chopra has long been managing the spiritual fortunes of Hol- 12
lywood's golden people," he says. "Britney Spears' new album has a
Bhangra remix of one of her singles. Images from old Indian matchbooks
and posters now retail as birthday cards. The vinyl seat covers of Indian
rickshaws are turning into tote bags for Manhattan's chic. And yoga is now
the new aerobics."

That this country is falling under Asia's spell shouldn't be surprising. If 13
the world is experiencing globalization, the union between East and West,
where a new hybrid culture is thriving, is just part of that process.

Suddenly, Beijing, Bombay, Bangkok and Tokyo are much closer to the 14
United States than we thought. And in as much as we feel reassured in seeing the Thai teenager in Bangkok wearing his baseball cap backward under the golden arches of McDonald's, Americans have learned to savor the
taste of lemongrass in our soup and that tangy burnt chili on our fried fish.

Writer Richard Rodriguez once observed that "Each new wave of im- 15
migrants brings changes as radical as Christopher Columbus did to the
Indians."

Eastern religions represent one of those changes. In Los Angeles, there 16
are more than 300 Buddhist temples. Buddhism, writes Diana Eck, professor of comparative religions at Harvard University, "challenges many
Americans at the very core of their thinking about religion—at least, those
of us for whom religion has something to do with one we call God."

One cannot accept that acupuncture works on one's arthritis without 17
considering the essence that lies behind such an art, the flow of the chi—
the energy that flows through all things—and its manipulation with
needles.

One must eventually contemplate what ancient Taoist priests saw, the 18
invisible flow of energy, which involves a radically different way of experiencing the world.

One cannot diligently practice meditation without considering one's 19
psychological transformation and the possibility of enlightenment, of spiritual revelation, waiting at the edge of one's breath.

A century ago, Carl Jung, a great interpreter of the psychic differences 20 between East and West, described the Westerner as basically extroverted, driven by desire to conquer, and the Easterner as a classic introvert, driven by desire to escape suffering. The introvert tends to dismiss the "I," Jung wrote, because in the East, it is identified with selfishness and libidinous delusions. To reach spiritual maturity, the I must be dissolved.

All that has been turned on its head. Many a Westerner, tired of mate- 21 rialism, turns slowly inward in search of spiritual uplift, while introversion and ego-dissolving are no longer consuming Asian quests.

On my wall, I keep two pictures to remind me of the extraordinary 22 ways East and West have changed.

One is from a *Time* magazine issue on Buddhism in the United States. 23 On it, a group of American Buddhists sits serenely in lotus position on a wooden veranda in Malibu contemplating the Pacific Ocean. The other is of the Vietnamese American astronaut Eugene Trinh, who flew on a NASA space shuttle.

Tu Weiming, the Confucian scholar at Harvard, said this is a new "era 24 where various traditions exist side by side for the first time for the picking."

American artists and writers have often looked to the East. What is new 25 in the age of globalization is that Asia is the active agent in the interaction, projecting its vision westward with confidence.

Thinking About the Essay

1. Why do you think Lam chose not to title his essay, "We Are Becoming All Things Asian"?

2. How does Lam develop the meaning of the term *globalization*? What alternate terms (or plays on the term *globalization*) appear in the course of the essay?

3. What is new, according to Lam, about the influence of Asian culture in both the transformation of American culture and the current process of globalization?

4. Why does Lam devote so much attention to Buddhism as an example of a "cultural import" affecting the United States?

5. Does the final paragraph follow logically from preceding paragraphs, or is it simply a restatement of earlier ideas? Does Lam conflate "American" with "Western"? Justify your response.

Responding in Writing

6. Reread the statement by Richard Rodriguez quoted in paragraph 15. List three or four examples of radical changes brought about by past waves of immigration.

7. Do you agree with Lam's statements in paragraphs 17–19 that one must adopt, or at least entertain, the ideologies and values underlying a cultural practice like acupuncture or meditation? Write a brief essay in which you attack or defend this assumption.

8. According to Lam, theories about fundamental differences between Eastern and Western sensibilities (Carl Jung's, for example) have been "turned on [their] head" (paragraph 21). Lam offers a brief illustration, but no other evidence. Write a brief essay in which you present evidence in support of Lam's claim.

Networking

9. List the names of Asian films that you and your classmates have seen. Is there variety among the films on this list, or do they tend to belong to a narrow range of genres or to a single genre (such as the martial arts epic)?

10. Choose one recent Asian film that was also released and marketed in the United States. Visit the United States and Asian online promotional sites that advertise the film to these two different audiences. Is the film promoted in different ways? If you cannot find a version with translated text, then compare the images that appear on each site.

The Way to Rainy Mountain

N. Scott Momaday

Navarre Scott Momaday, born in Oklahoma in 1934, is a Native American—a member of the Kiowa tribe; consequently, he says that he is "vitally interested in American Indian history, art, and culture." After receiving his doctorate from Stanford University, where he studied under the famous poet and critic Ivor Winters, Momaday embarked on his own distinguished career as poet, novelist, critic, autobiographer, and, for many years, professor of English at the University of Arizona. He won the Pulitzer Prize for his novel *House Made of Dawn* (1968). Additional works include *The Way to Rainy Mountain* (1969), *The Names* (1976), *The Ancient Child* (1989), and *In the Presence of the Sun* (1991). In an interview, Momaday stated, "When I was growing up on the reservations of the Southwest, I saw people who were deeply involved in their traditional life, in the memories of their blood. They had, as far as I can see, a certain strength and beauty that I find missing in the modern world at large. I like to celebrate that involvement in my writing." The following essay from

> *The Way to Rainy Mountain* captures the sacredness that Momaday finds in his Native American heritage and the land of his ancestors.

Before Reading

What do you know about Native American history and culture? Where does this knowledge come from? In what ways are Native Americans in the news today? What do you anticipate about the essay that follows from Momaday's title?

A single knoll rises out of the plain in Oklahoma, north and west of the Wichita Range. For my people, the Kiowas, it is an old landmark, and they gave it the name Rainy Mountain. The hardest weather in the world is there. Winter brings blizzards, hot tornadic winds arise in the spring, and in summer the prairie is an anvil's edge. The grass turns brittle and brown, and it cracks beneath your feet. There are green belts along the rivers and creeks, linear groves of hickory and pecan, willow and witch hazel. At a distance in July or August the steaming foliage seems almost to writhe in fire. Great green and yellow grasshoppers are everywhere in the tall grass, popping up like corn to sting the flesh, and tortoises crawl about on the red earth, going nowhere in the plenty of time. Loneliness is an aspect of the land. All things in the plain are isolate; there is no confusion of objects in the eye, but *one* hill or *one* tree or *one* man. To look upon that landscape in the early morning, with the sun at your back, is to lose the sense of proportion. Your imagination comes to life, and this, you think, is where Creation was begun. 1

I returned to Rainy Mountain in July. My grandmother had died in the spring, and I wanted to be at her grave. She had lived to be very old and at last infirm. Her only living daughter was with her when she died, and I was told that in death her face was that of a child. 2

I like to think of her as a child. When she was born, the Kiowas were living the last great moment of their history. For more than a hundred years they had controlled the open range from the Smoky Hill River to the Red, from the headwaters of the Canadian to the fork of the Arkansas and Cimarron. In alliance with the Comanches, they had ruled the whole of the southern Plains. War was their sacred business, and they were among the finest horsemen the world has ever known. But warfare for the Kiowas was preeminently a matter of disposition rather than of survival, and they never understood the grim, unrelenting advance of the U.S. Cavalry. When at last, divided and ill-provisioned, they were driven onto the Staked Plains in the cold rains of autumn, they fell into panic. In Palo Duro Canyon they abandoned their crucial stores to pillage and had nothing then but their lives. In order to save themselves, they surrendered to the soldiers at Fort Sill and were imprisoned in the old stone corral that now stands as a mili- 3 tary museum. My grandmother was spared the humiliation of those high gray walls by eight or ten years, but she must have known from birth the affliction of defeat, the dark brooding of old warriors.

Her name was Aho, and she belonged to the last culture to evolve in   4
North America. Her forebears came down from the high country in western Montana nearly three centuries ago. They were a mountain people, a mysterious tribe of hunters whose language has never been positively classified in any major group. In the late seventeenth century they began a long migration to the south and east. It was a journey toward the dawn, and it led to a golden age. Along the way the Kiowas were befriended by the Crows, who gave them the culture and religion of the Plains. They acquired horses, and their ancient nomadic spirit was suddenly free of the ground. They acquired Tai-me, the sacred Sun Dance doll, from that moment the object and symbol of their worship, and so shared in the divinity of the sun. Not least, they acquired the sense of destiny, therefore courage and pride. When they entered upon the southern Plains they had been transformed. No longer were they slaves to the simple necessity of survival; they were a lordly and dangerous society of fighters and thieves, hunters and priests of the sun. According to their origin myth, they entered the world through a hollow log. From one point of view, their migration was the fruit of an old prophecy, for indeed they emerged from a sunless world.

Although my grandmother lived out her long life in the shadow of   5
Rainy Mountain, the immense landscape of the continental interior lay like memory in her blood. She could tell of the Crows, whom she had never seen, and of the Black Hills, where she had never been. I wanted to see in reality what she had seen more perfectly in the mind's eye, and traveled fifteen hundred miles to begin my pilgrimage.

Yellowstone, it seemed to me, was the top of the world, a region of deep   6
lakes and dark timber, canyons and waterfalls. But, beautiful as it is, one might have the sense of confinement there. The skyline in all directions is close at hand, the high wall of the woods and deep cleavages of shade. There is a perfect freedom in the mountains, but it belongs to the eagle and the elk, the badger and the bear. The Kiowas reckoned their stature by the distance they could see, and they were bent and blind in the wilderness.

Descending eastward, the highland meadows are a stairway to the   7
plain. In July the inland slope of the Rockies is luxuriant with flax and buckwheat, stonecrop and larkspur. The earth unfolds and the limit of the land recedes. Clusters of trees, and animals grazing far in the distance, cause the vision to reach away and wonder to build upon the mind. The sun follows a longer course in the day, and the sky is immense beyond all comparison. The great billowing clouds that sail upon it are shadows that move upon the grain like water, dividing light. Farther down, in the land

of the Crows and Blackfeet, the plain is yellow. Sweet clover takes hold of the hills and bends upon itself to cover and seal the soil. There the Kiowas paused on their way; they had come to the place where they must change their lives. The sun is at home on the plains. Precisely there does it have the certain character of a god. When the Kiowas came to the land of the Crows, they could see the dark lees of the hills at dawn across the Bighorn River, the profusion of light on the grain shelves, the oldest deity ranging after the solstices. Not yet would they veer southward to the caldron of the land that lay below; they must wean their blood from the northern winter and hold the mountains a while longer in their view. They bore Tai-me in procession to the east.

A dark mist lay over the Black Hills, and the land was like iron. At the top of a ridge I caught sight of Devil's Tower upthrust against the gray sky as if in the birth of time the core of the earth had broken through its crust and the motion of the world was begun. There are things in nature that engender an awful quiet in the heart of man; Devil's Tower is one of them. Two centuries ago, because they could not do otherwise, the Kiowas made a legend at the base of the rock. My grandmother said: 8

> Eight children were there at play, seven sisters and their brother. Suddenly the boy was struck dumb; he trembled and began to run upon his hands and feet. His fingers became claws, and his body was covered with fur. Directly there was a bear where the boy had been. The sisters were terrified; they ran, and the bear after them. They came to the stump of a great tree, and the tree spoke to them. It bade them climb upon it, and as they did so it began to rise into the air. The bear came to kill them, but they were just beyond its reach. It reared against the tree and scored the bark all around with its claws. The seven sisters were borne into the sky, and they became the stars of the Big Dipper.

From that moment, and so long as the legend lives, the Kiowas have kinsmen in the night sky. Whatever they were in the mountains, they could be no more. However tenuous their well-being, however much they had suffered and would suffer again, they had found a way out of the wilderness. 9

My grandmother had a reverence for the sun, a holy regard that now is all but gone out of mankind. There was a wariness in her, and an ancient awe. She was a Christian in her later years, but she had come a long way about, and she never forgot her birthright. As a child she had been to the Sun Dances; she had taken part in those annual rites, and by them she had learned the restoration of her people in the presence of Tai-me. She was about seven when the last Kiowa Sun Dance was held in 1887 on the Washita River above Rainy Mountain Creek. The buffalo were gone. In order to consummate the ancient sacrifice—to impale the head of a buffalo bull upon the medicine tree—a delegation of old men journeyed into Texas, 10 there to beg and barter for an animal from the Goodnight herd. She was ten when the Kiowas came together for the last time as a living Sun Dance culture. They could find no buffalo; they had to hang an old hide from the sacred tree. Before the dance could begin, a company of soldiers rode out from Fort Sill under orders to disperse the tribe. Forbidden without cause the essential act of their faith, having seen the wild herds slaughtered and left to rot upon the ground, the Kiowas backed away forever from the medicine tree. That was July 20, 1890, at the great bend of the Washita. My grandmother was there. Without bitterness, and for as long as she lived, she bore a vision of deicide.

Now that I can have her only in memory, I see my grandmother in the 11 several postures that were peculiar to her: standing at the wood stove on a winter morning and turning meat in a great iron skillet; sitting at the south window, bent above her beadwork, and afterwards, when her vision failed, looking down for a long time into the fold of her hands; going out upon a cane, very slowly as she did when the weight of age came upon her; praying. I remember her most often at prayer. She made long, rambling prayers out of suffering and hope, having seen many things. I was never sure that I had the right to hear, so exclusive were they of all mere custom and company. The last time I saw her she prayed standing by the side of her bed at night, naked to the waist, the light of a kerosene lamp moving upon her dark skin. Her long, black hair, always drawn and braided in the day, lay upon her shoulders and against her breasts like a shawl. I do not speak Kiowa, and I never understood her prayers, but there was something inherently sad in the sound, some merest hesitation upon the syllables of sorrow. She began in a high and descending pitch, exhausting her breath to silence; then again and again— and always the same intensity of effort, of something that is, and is not, like urgency in the human voice. Transported so in the dancing light among the shadows of her room, she seemed beyond the reach of time. But that was illusion; I think I knew then that I should not see her again.

Houses are like sentinels in the plain, old keepers of the weather watch. 12 There, in a very little while, wood takes on the appearance of great age. All colors wear soon away in the wind and rain, and then the wood is burned gray and the grain appears and the nails turn red with rust. The window-panes are black and opaque; you imagine there is nothing within, and indeed there are many ghosts, bones given up to the land. They stand here and there against the sky, and you approach them for a longer time than you expect. They belong in the distance; it is their domain.

Once there was a lot of sound in my grandmother's house, a lot of com- 13 ing and going, feasting and talk. The summers there were full of excitement and reunion. The Kiowas are a summer people; they abide the cold and keep to themselves, but when the season turns and the land becomes warm and vital they cannot hold still; an old love of going returns upon them. The aged visitors who came to my grandmother's house when I was a child were made of lean and leather, and they bore themselves upright. They wore great black hats and bright ample shirts that shook in the wind. They rubbed fat upon their hair and wound their braids with strips of colored cloth. Some of them painted their faces and carried the scars of old and cherished enmities. They were an old council of warlords, come to remind and be reminded of who they were. Their wives and daughters served them well. The women might indulge themselves; gossip was at once the mark and compensation of their servitude. They made loud and elaborate talk among themselves, full of jest and gesture, fright and false alarm. They went abroad in fringed and flowered shawls, bright beadwork and German silver. They were at home in the kitchen, and they prepared meals that were banquets.

There were frequent prayer meetings, and great nocturnal feasts. When   14
I was a child I played with my cousins outside, where the lamplight fell upon the ground and the singing of the old people rose up around us and carried away into the darkness. There were a lot of good things to eat, a lot of laughter and surprise. And afterwards, when the quiet returned, I lay down with my grandmother and could hear the frogs away by the river and feel the motion of the air.

Now there is funeral silence in the rooms, the endless wake of some fi-   15
nal word. The walls have closed in upon my grandmother's house. When I returned to it in mourning, I saw for the first time in my life how small it was. It was late at night, and there was a white moon, nearly full. I sat for a long time on the stone steps by the kitchen door. From there I could see out across the land; I could see the long row of trees by the creek, the low light upon the rolling plains, and the stars of the Big Dipper. Once I looked at the moon and caught sight of a strange thing. A cricket had perched upon the handrail, only a few inches away from me. My line of vision was such that the creature filled the moon like a fossil. It had gone there, I thought, to live and die, for there, of all places, was its small definition made whole and eternal. A warm wind rose up and purled like the longing within me.

The next morning I awoke at dawn and went out on the dirt road to   16
Rainy Mountain. It was already hot, and the grasshoppers began to fill the air. Still, it was early in the morning, and the birds sang out of the shadows. The long yellow grass on the mountain shone in the bright light, and a scissortail hied above the land. There, where it ought to be, at the end of a long and legendary way, was my grandmother's grave. Here and there on the dark stones were ancestral names. Looking back once, I saw the mountain and came away.

Thinking About the Essay

1. What aspects of the Native American worldview does Momaday present in this essay? What are the myths and legends? How are they related? What is the relationship of the first paragraph to the central meanings of this essay?

2. In your own words, state the thesis that emerges from Momaday's narrative. Does the thesis emerge from the title? Why or why not? How does the title reflect the writer's purpose?

3. The language in this essay reflects Momaday's reputation as a major poet. Locate instances of "poetic" language in the selection—**imagery, metaphors, symbols,** and other types of **figurative language** and sensory detail. How does this poetic use of language serve to capture Momaday's subject and thesis?

4. Explain the narrative and descriptive patterns that serve to structure and unify the essay. What cinematic elements can you detect?

5. Momaday is quite successful at creating a specific mood or atmosphere in this essay. How would you describe it? How do the land, the Kiowas, and Momaday's grandmother serve as focal points in the creation of this atmosphere? Explain the mood we, as readers, are left with in the concluding paragraph.

Responding in Writing

6. Write a narrative and descriptive essay in which you capture a specific place that you associate with a particular person. Be certain to state your thesis or, if you wish, have it grow from the narrative. Also try to create a specific mood in your essay.

7. Write an analysis of Momaday's essay, focusing on how the writer presents the worldview of the Kiowas.

8. Where is the rest of the United States—other peoples (especially whites) and other communities—in this essay? Is Momaday making any implicit comments about these other peoples, whether it is their relationship to myths, to heritage, to family, or to the land? Answer these questions in a **reflective essay.**

Networking

9. In groups of three or four, discuss what you have learned about Native American culture from Momaday's essay. Identify and list at least three key discoveries. Share your list in discussion with the rest of the class.

10. Go online and find out more about Momaday and about Kiowa culture. Download the most compelling material and share it in class discussion.

America: The Multinational Society

ISHMAEL REED* | Ishmael Reed was born in 1938 in Chattanooga, Tennessee, and is a well-known novelist, poet, and essayist who lives in Oakland and teaches at the University of California at Berkeley. An activist who advocates the rights of people of color, and notably African Americans, he has been at the forefront of major literary and political movements for decades. Reed's extensive literary production includes such works of fiction as *Mumbo Jumbo* (1972) and *Japanese by Spring* (1993), volumes of verse such as *Secretary to the Spirits* (1975), and several collections of essays, among them *Airing Dirty Laundry* (1993). Reed also has been an editor, playwright, songwriter, television producer, and publisher. In the following essay, which first appeared in *Writin' Is Fightin'* (1988) and has become a contemporary classic, Reed argues for a new definition of American culture.

Before Reading

Do you think that the United States is becoming a universal nation, composed of peoples and cultural styles from around the world? Why or why not?

> At the annual Lower East Side Jewish Festival yesterday, a Chinese woman ate a pizza slice in front of Ty Thuan Duc's Vietnamese grocery store. Beside her a Spanish-speaking family patronized a cart with two signs: "Italian Ices" and "Kosher by Rabbi Alper." And after the pastrami ran out, everybody ate knishes.
>
> —*The New York Times*, June 23, 1983

On the day before Memorial Day, 1983, a poet called me to describe a   1
city he had just visited. He said that one section included mosques, built by the Islamic people who dwelled there. Attending his reading, he said, were large numbers of Hispanic people, forty thousand of whom lived in the same city. He was not talking about a fabled city located in some mysterious region of the world. The city he'd visited was Detroit.

A few months before, as I was leaving Houston, Texas, I heard it an-   2
nounced on the radio that Texas's largest minority was Mexican American,
and though a foundation recently issued a report critical of bilingual education, the taped voice used to guide the passengers on the air trams connecting terminals in Dallas Airport is in both Spanish and English. If the
trend continues, a day will come when it will be difficult to travel through
some sections of the country without hearing commands in both English
and Spanish; after all, for some western states, Spanish was the first written language and the Spanish style lives on in the western way of life.

Shortly after my Texas trip, I sat in an auditorium located on the cam-   3
pus of the University of Wisconsin at Milwaukee as a Yale professor—
whose original work on the influence of African cultures upon those of the
Americas has led to his ostracism from some monocultural intellectual
circles—walked up and down the aisle, like an old-time southern evangel-
ist, dancing and drumming the top of the lectern, illustrating his points before some serious Afro-American intellectuals and artists who cheered and
applauded his performance and his mastery of information. The professor
was "white." After his lecture, he joined a group of Milwaukeeans in a
conversation. All of the participants spoke Yoruba, though only the professor had ever traveled to Africa.

One of the artists told me that his paintings, which included African   4
and Afro-American mythological symbols and imagery, were hanging in
the local McDonald's restaurant. The next day I went to McDonald's and
snapped pictures of smiling youngsters eating hamburgers below paintings
that could grace the walls of any of the country's leading museums. The
manager of the local McDonald's said, "I don't know what you boys are
doing, but I like it," as he commissioned the local painters to exhibit in his
restaurant.

Such blurring of cultural styles occurs in everyday life in the United   5
States to a greater extent than anyone can imagine and is probably more
prevalent than the sensational conflict between people of different backgrounds that is played up and often encouraged by the media. The result is
what the Yale professor, Robert Thompson, referred to as a cultural bouillabaisse, yet members of the nation's present educational and cultural Elect
still cling to the notion that the United States belongs to some vaguely defined entity they refer to as "Western civilization," by which they mean,
presumably, a civilization created by the people of Europe, as if Europe
can be viewed in monolithic terms. Is Beethoven's Ninth Symphony,
which includes Turkish marches, a part of Western civilization, or the late
nineteenth- and twentieth-century French paintings, whose creators were

influenced by Japanese art? And what of the cubists, through whom the influence of African art changed modern painting, or the surrealists, who were so impressed with the art of the Pacific Northwest Indians that, in their map of North America, Alaska dwarfs the lower forty-eight in size?

Are the Russians, who are often criticized for their adoption of "West-   6
ern" ways by Tsarist dissidents in exile, members of Western civilization? And what of the millions of Europeans who have black African and Asian ancestry, black Africans having occupied several countries for hundreds of years? Are these "Europeans" members of Western civilization, or the Hungarians, who originated across the Urals in a place called Greater Hungary, or the Irish, who came from the Iberian Peninsula?

Even the notion that North America is part of Western civilization be-   7
cause our "system of government" is derived from Europe is being challenged by Native American historians who say that the founding fathers, Benjamin Franklin especially, were actually influenced by the system of government that had been adopted by the Iroquois hundreds of years prior to the arrival of large numbers of Europeans.

Western civilization, then, becomes another confusing category like   8
Third World, or Judeo-Christian culture, as man attempts to impose his small-screen view of political and cultural reality upon a complex world. Our most publicized novelist recently said that Western civilization was the greatest achievement of mankind, an attitude that flourishes on the street level as scribbles in public restrooms: "White Power," "Niggers and Spics Suck," or "Hitler was a prophet," the latter being the most telling, for wasn't Adolph Hitler the archetypal monoculturalist who, in his pigheaded arrogance, believed that one way and one blood was so pure that it had to be protected from alien strains at all costs? Where did such an attitude, which has caused so much misery and depression in our national life, which has tainted even our noblest achievements, begin? An attitude that caused the incarceration of Japanese-American citizens during World War II, the persecution of Chicanos and Chinese Americans, the near-extermination of the Indians, and the murder and lynchings of thousands of Afro-Americans.

Virtuous, hardworking, pious, even though they occasionally would   9
wander off after some fancy clothes, or rendezvous in the woods with the town prostitute, the Puritans are idealized in our schoolbooks as "a hardy band" of no-nonsense patriarchs whose discipline razed the forest and brought order to the New World (a term that annoys Native American historians). Industrious, responsible, it was their "Yankee ingenuity" and practicality that created the work ethic. They were simple folk who produced a number of good poets, and they set the tone for the American writing style,

of lean and spare lines, long before Hemingway. They worshiped in churches whose colors blended in with the New England snow, churches with simple structures and ornate lecterns.

The Puritans were a daring lot, but they had a mean streak. They hated 10 the theater and banned Christmas. They punished people in a cruel and inhuman manner. They killed children who disobeyed their parents. When they came in contact with those whom they considered heathens or aliens, they behaved in such a bizarre and irrational manner that this chapter in the American history comes down to us as a late-movie horror film. They exterminated the Indians, who taught them how to survive in a world unknown to them, and their encounter with the calypso culture of Barbados resulted in what the tourist guide in Salem's Witches' House refers to as the Witchcraft Hysteria.

The Puritan legacy of hard work and meticulous accounting led to the 11 establishment of a great industrial society; it is no wonder that the American industrial revolution began in Lowell, Massachusetts, but there was the other side, the strange and paranoid attitudes toward those different from the Elect.

The cultural attitudes of that early Elect continue to be voiced in every- 12 day life in the United States: the president of a distinguished university, writing a letter to the *Times,* belittling the study of African civilizations; the television network that promoted its show on the Vatican art with the boast that this art represented "the finest achievements of the human spirit." A modern up-tempo state of complex rhythms that depends upon contacts with an international community can no longer behave as if it dwelled in a "Zion Wilderness" surrounded by beasts and pagans.

When I heard a schoolteacher warn the other night about the invasion 13 of the American educational system by foreign curriculums, I wanted to yell at the television set, "Lady, they're already here." It has already begun because the world is here. The world has been arriving at these shores for at least ten thousand years from Europe, Africa, and Asia. In the late nineteenth and early twentieth centuries, large numbers of Europeans arrived, adding their cultures to those of the European, African, and Asian settlers who were already here, and recently millions have been entering the country from South America and the Caribbean, making Yale Professor Bob Thompson's bouillabaisse richer and thicker.

One of our most visionary politicians said that he envisioned a time 14 when the United States could become the brain of the world, by which he meant the repository of all of the latest advanced information systems. I thought of that remark when an enterprising poet friend of mine called to say that he had just sold a poem to a computer magazine and that the editors were delighted to get it because they didn't carry fiction or poetry. Is that the kind of world we desire? A humdrum homogeneous world of all brains but no heart, no fiction, no poetry; a world of robots with human attendants bereft of imagination, of culture? Or does North America deserve a more exciting destiny? To become a place where the cultures of the world crisscross. This is possible because the United States is unique in the world: The world is here.

Thinking About the Essay

1. How does the author's introductory paragraph set the stage for the development of his main claim or argument? Explain his argument in your own words. Does Reed develop his argument through **induction** or **deduction?** How do you know?

2. Reed begins in a personal mode of discourse, frequently using an "I" **point of view.** He then shifts to a more objective analytical and argumentative style before returning to the first-person point of view at the end of the essay. What is his purpose here? Do you find this strategy to be effective or confusing, and why?

3. What types of details and examples does the author employ? Why does Reed use so many examples in a relatively brief essay?

4. Identify and analyze the various rhetorical strategies—especially definition and comparison and contrast—that appear in this essay.

5. Why does Reed develop a series of questions in his closing paragraph?

Responding in Writing

6. Demonstrate in a personal essay the ways in which you come into contact with various races, ethnicities, and cultures on a daily basis. Be certain that you establish a clear thesis and develop several examples.

7. Write an argumentative essay in which you state your position on Reed's key assertion that the idea of Western or European civilization is wrong-headed.

8. In an analytical essay, explain some of the ways in which America's perception of itself as a **monoculturalist** or **Eurocentric** nation has caused problems in its relationship with the rest of the world.

Networking

9. In small groups, discuss your response to Reed's key assertion that "the United States is unique in the world: The world is here."

10. Select a partner and search the Internet together for information on American Puritanism. Present a brief oral report on your findings, explaining how the Puritan legacy continues to operate—as Reed suggests—in American society.

Two Americas?

JOSEPH CONTRERAS

A native Californian, Joseph Contreras joined the staff of *Newsweek* in 1980 as a correspondent in the magazine's Los Angeles bureau. His reporting on global issues is truly global in scope: Contreras has served as *Newsweek* bureau chief in Miami, Mexico City, Buenos Aires, Johannesburg, and Jerusalem. He was appointed *Newsweek*'s Latin America Regional Editor in 2002. Contreras, who is known for his expertise on Latin American issues, established his early reputation with a series of articles on the Colombian drug wars of the 1980s and the revolution in Peru. As Jerusalem bureau chief, Contreras reported on the political rise of Benjamin Netanyahu in the 1990s and the deterioration of the Middle East peace process in the years following Israel's 1996 election. As Miami bureau chief, he covered the Elian Gonzalez custody battle and the controversy over the 2000 presidential election. In the following selection from the March 22, 2004, issue of *Newsweek International*, Contreras seeks to redefine what some critics have characterized as a "clash of cultures" in the United States.

Before Reading

How would you define a "clash of cultures"? What sort of conflict would prompt you to employ this dramatic-sounding phrase?

In his provocative 1996 book "The Clash of Civilizations," Samuel P. Huntington argued that culture would replace ideology as the principal cause of conflict in the 21st century. The Harvard professor foresaw a collision of "Western arrogance, Islamic intolerance and [Chinese] assertiveness" that would dominate global politics in the post-cold-war era. In his new book, "Who Are We? The Challenges to America's National Identity," the conservative Cassandra looks at American society through that same cultural prism and discerns an internal clash of civilizations: the new war is between the country's white majority and its burgeoning Hispanic population.

"The most serious challenge to America's traditional identity comes   2
from the immense and continuing immigration from Latin America, especially from Mexico," writes Huntington in an excerpt from the forthcom-
ing book published in Foreign Policy magazine. "As their numbers
increase, Mexican Americans feel increasingly comfortable with their own
culture and often contemptuous of American culture." Never one to shrink
from controversy, the 76-year-old academic asks pointedly: "Will the
United States remain a country with a single national language and a core
Anglo-Protestant culture? By ignoring this question, Americans acquiesce
to their eventual transformation into two peoples with two cultures (Anglo and Hispanic) and two languages (English and Spanish).

The backlash has not been long in coming—from both sides of the Rio   3
Grande. The Mexican author Carlos Fuentes labeled Huntington a
"racist" in the influential Mexico City newspaper Reforma last week and
deplored the professor's "stigmatizing of the Spanish language as a practically subversive factor of division." The self-described conservative U.S.
columnist David Brooks took issue with Huntington's Kulturkampf scenario in *The New York Times*. "The mentality that binds us is not well described by the words 'Anglo' or 'Protestant,' wrote Brooks. "There are no
significant differences between Mexican-American lifestyles and other
American lifestyles."

At a time when white U.S. politicians are tripping over each other in hot   4
pursuit of the Latino voter, Huntington's Hispanophobia has reopened
some unresolved questions about identity and integration. Are Hispanics
rejecting the powerful forces of American cultural assimilation, which
swallowed up the successive waves of European immigrants who preceded
them? Are their swelling ranks and enduring loyalty to Latin American culture and the Spanish language carving out Hispanic-dominated enclaves
like Miami where, as Huntington puts it, native Anglos and African-
Americans become "outside minorities that [can] often be ignored"? Or are
Hispanics simply redefining the meaning of mainstream in an ever more diverse, multicultural United States of America?

Statistics amply document the rise of the Hispanic American. Native   5
and foreign-born U.S. residents of Latin American ancestry overtook
blacks as the largest American minority three years ago and are fast approaching the 40 million mark. Between 8 million and 10 million of these
Hispanics are thought to be illegal immigrants, and nearly 70 percent are
Mexicans. If current birthrates and rising levels of immigration continue,
Hispanics could attain majority status in California by 2018, and may account for fully one quarter of all Americans by the middle of this century.

It is the roughly 22 million Mexicans in America who most trouble   6
Huntington. He contrasts the success story of Miami's Cuban-Americans—

who transformed that city into the economic capital of Latin America—with the Mexican immigrants of the American Southwest, the overwhelming percentage of whom are described as "poor, unskilled and poorly educated." The children of this Mexican underclass, concludes Huntington, "are likely to face similar conditions."

Mexican-Americans and other Hispanics are not quite the insular tail 7 of American society that Huntington contends. They are moving up the socioeconomic ladder—albeit more slowly than the white ethnic groups who preceded them. Historically speaking, it's important to remember that this wave of immigration is still relatively young. In the case of Mexican immigration, it soared after 1965: 2.2 million Mexicans legally moved to the United States in the 1990s, up sharply from the 640,000 who lawfully immigrated to El Norte in the 1970s, and these figures don't encompass the possibly larger numbers who entered the country illegally.

More Latinos are going to college—the rate has risen from 16 percent 8 in 1980 to 22 percent in 2000—and they're making more money: their median household income rose by 4.3 percent between 1988 and 1999. The Washington-based Pew Hispanic Center reports that teenage and young-adult Latinos work and earn more than anyone else in their age group, whites included. Admittedly, one reason is that many do not go to college, and the center found high unemployment rates among second-generation Hispanic youths. But beyond the age of 25, second-generation Latinos with college degrees earn more on average than white workers with comparable educational backgrounds.

Rocky Chavez spent many childhood summers picking grapes in Cali- 9 fornia's San Joaquin Valley alongside his Mexican-American aunts and uncles. The Los Angeles native recalls telling his U.S.-born father, one of 18 children, how much he disliked the backbreaking menial labor. "Then get an education," his father responded. Rocky did, earning a college degree. Today the 52-year-old retired Marine colonel speaks little Spanish; he is the principal of a new charter high school in the town of Oceanside, California, and wants to run for mayor as a Republican. "When my father moved us to Torrance he pulled us away from the Latino community," says Chavez, the proud father of three college-educated children. "I assimilated, and I tell my kids, 'You know, we went from a migrant family to a family with a son who just graduated from the best medical school in the nation'."

Hispanics have become accepted in one important respect—as con- 10 sumers. Their—enormous buying power has opened the eyes of big business, especially in an era when Latino celebrities like J. Lo and Ricky Martin vie for top billing with Britney Spears and Brad Pitt. Anna Brockway, the brand-marketing director at jeans maker Levi Strauss, says she doesn't think in terms of Hispanic culture versus mainstream U.S. culture anymore. An English-language ad for Levi's that aired during the January 2002 Super Bowl featured a young Latino model strutting along the grimy streets of Mexico City. Some of Brockman's colleagues asked her why the company picked a "Hispanic ad" for the broadcast. "Hispanic culture is American culture at this point," she explained.

That's especially true among young people. Latinos account for the   11 highest percentage of youths under the age of 18 in seven of the 10 largest U.S. cities. Their numbers will continue to swell for the foreseeable future: the Latino teen population is projected to grow by 36 percent over the next 16 years, while their white peers will decline by 3 percent, according to California-based Hispanic marketing expert Isabel Valdes.

There is disagreement about the degree to which these youngsters and   12 their parents are learning and speaking English. A recent study by the U.S. Association of Hispanic Advertising Agencies (AHAA) found that 68 percent of Latinos between the ages of 18 and 34 are either bilingual or identify Spanish as their language of choice. But other research has turned up very different results pointing in the direction of assimilation. A nationwide 2002 survey by the Pew Hispanic Center and the Kaiser Family Foundation found that among adult Latinos whose parents were immigrants, only 7 percent relied on Spanish as their primary language. Nearly half had no Spanish skills at all, and the rest were bilingual. The corresponding figures were even lower for the U.S.-born children of those second-generation Hispanic adults: less than a quarter were bilingual, and the number of those Latinos who spoke only Spanish was not statistically significant. "The transition from Spanish to English is virtually complete in one generation," says Pew Hispanic Center director Roberto Suro. "Hispanics are undergoing a powerful process of change no less than anyone else who has come to these shores."

Lest he be accused of being a xenophobic bigot, Huntington concedes   13 that biculturalism is not in itself a bad thing. But he is troubled by the concept of bilingual education and by the idea that Americans may need to learn Spanish to communicate with their fellow citizens. In fact, the United States already is a profoundly bilingual society throughout the Southwest and Texas, in most of California, and in cities from Chicago and New York to Miami. The days when one country meant one language, one culture and apparently one Protestant faith are long gone—if they ever existed in the first place. Millions of Hispanics are assimilating, but they are also putting their own distinctive stamp on what assimilation will signify for future generations. And that is not the result of some apocalyptic showdown between two antithetical civilizations.

Thinking About the Essay

1. How does Contreras characterize Huntington? What are some cues in the essay (phrases, epithets, etc.) that indicate the author's attitude toward Huntington and his views?

2. Highlight two or three allusions and explain their function in the essay. (Or explain why you consider them to be gratuitous and unjustified.)

3. Where does Contreras offer an illustration? What is the purpose of this digression and how effectively does it serve this larger purpose?

4. Why does Contreras shift attention from projected future statistics (paragraph 5) to Huntington's preoccupation with the 22 million Mexicans in America today? How does Contreras use this theme of past versus future to structure his critique of Huntington?

5. Contreras returns to consider Huntington's position in the final paragraph of the essay. Do you feel the author is fair in his oblique characterization of Huntington as a "xenophobic bigot"?

Responding in Writing

6. Highlight places in the essay where the author regards Huntington ironically. Replace these ironic gestures with phrases, epithets, adjectives, allusions of your own. What is the tonal effect of each of these revisions?

7. Contreras emphasizes the analogies between Mexican assimilation and the experience of earlier generations of immigrants to the United States. In a brief essay, consider those points where the analogy fails.

8. Is the "acceptance" of an ethnic group as a consumer demographic a positive sign of *cultural* assimilation? Can commodification be a form of assimilation? Answer these questions in an argumentative essay.

Networking

9. Does bilingualism subvert the idea of cultural assimilation? Form two groups and debate the merits and flaws of the idea of establishing English as an official language of the United States.

10. Go online and read at least three different reviews, published in three different journals, of the book by Samuel P. Huntington referred to in the article. (A review by Louis Menand, for example, appeared in the May 17, 2004, issue of *The New Yorker*: http://www.newyorker.com/critics/books/?040517crbo_books). How do the reviews reflect the political orientations of the author and of the periodical in which the review was published? How much attention does each reviewer give to the issue of Mexican-American immigration as it is treated in the book?

American Dreamer

BHARATI MUKHERJEE

Bharati Mukherjee was born in Calcutta, India, in 1940. She attended the universities of Calcutta and Baroda, where she received a master's degree in English and ancient English culture. In 1961 she came to the United States to attend the Writer's Workshop at the University of Iowa, receiving a Ph.D. degree in English and comparative literature. Mukherjee became an American citizen in 1988; she is married to the writer Clark Blaise, with whom she has published two books, *Days and Nights in Calcutta* and *The Sorrow of the Terror.* Mukherjee's books of fiction include *The Middleman and Other Stories,* which won the 1988 National Book Critics Circle Award for fiction; *Jasmine* (1989); *The Holder of the World* (1993); and *The Tree Bride* (2004). She is currently professor of English at the University of California at Berkeley. In the following essay, which was published in 1993 in *Mother Jones,* Mukherjee displays both narrative power and keen analytical strength in rejecting any hyphenated status as an American.

Before Reading

Mukherjee, writing in 1993, hyphenates such words as African-American and Asian-American. As a matter of style, why don't we use hyphenated race compounds today? Why do these terms even exist?

The United States exists as a sovereign nation. "America," in contrast, exists as a myth of democracy and equal opportunity to live by, or as an ideal goal to reach. 1

I am a naturalized U.S. citizen, which means that, unlike native-born citizens, I had to prove to the U.S. government that I merited citizenship. What I didn't have to disclose was that I desired "America," which to me is the stage for the drama of self-transformation. 2

I was born in Calcutta and first came to the United States—to Iowa City, to be precise—on a summer evening in 1961. I flew into a small airport surrounded by cornfields and pastures, ready to carry out the two commands my father had written out for me the night before I left Calcutta: Spend two years studying creative writing at the Iowa Writers' Workshop, then come back home and marry the bridegroom he selected for me from our caste and class. 3

In traditional Hindu families like ours, men provided and women were 4
provided for. My father was a patriarch and I a pliant daughter. The neighborhood I'd grown up in was homogeneously Hindu, Bengali-speaking,
and middle-class. I didn't expect myself to ever disobey or disappoint my
father by setting my own goals and taking charge of my future.

When I landed in Iowa 35 years ago, I found myself in a society in 5
which almost everyone was Christian, white, and moderately well-off. In
the women's dormitory I lived in my first year, apart from six international
graduate students (all of us were from Asia and considered "exotic"), the
only non-Christian was Jewish, and the only nonwhite an African-
American from Georgia. I didn't anticipate then, that over the next 35
years, the Iowa population would become so diverse that it would have
6,931 children from non-English-speaking homes registered as students in
its schools, nor that Iowans would be in the grip of a cultural crisis in which
resentment against immigrants, particularly refugees from Vietnam, Sudan, and Bosnia, as well as unskilled Spanish-speaking workers, would become politicized enough to cause the Immigration and Naturalization
Service to open an "enforcement" office in Cedar Rapids in October for
the tracking and deporting of undocumented aliens.

In Calcutta in the '50s, I heard no talk of "identity crisis"—communal 6
or individual. The concept itself—of a person not knowing who he or she
is—was unimaginable in our hierarchical, classification-obsessed society.
One's identity was fixed, derived from religion, caste, patrimony, and
mother tongue. A Hindu Indian's last name announced his or her forefathers' caste and place of origin. A Mukherjee could *only* be a Brahmin
from Bengal. Hindu tradition forbade intercaste, interlanguage, interethnic
marriages. Bengali tradition even discouraged emigration: To remove one-
self from Bengal was to dilute true culture.

Until the age of 8, I lived in a house crowded with 40 or 50 relatives. My 7
identity was viscerally connected with ancestral soil and genealogy. I was
who I was because I was Dr. Sudhir Lal Mukherjee's daughter, because I was
a Hindu Brahmin, because I was Bengali-speaking, and because my *desh*—
the Bengali word for homeland—was an East Bengal village called Faridpur.

The University of Iowa classroom was my first experience of coeducation. 8
And after not too long, I fell in love with a fellow student named Clark
Blaise, an American of Canadian origin, and impulsively married him dur-
ing a lunch break in a lawyer's office above a coffee shop.

That act cut me off forever from the rules and ways of upper-middle- 9
class life in Bengal, and hurled me into a New World life of scary improvi-
sations and heady explorations. Until my lunch-break wedding, I had seen

myself as an Indian foreign student who intended to return to India to live. The five-minute ceremony in the lawyer's office suddenly changed me into a transient with conflicting loyalties to two very different cultures.

The first 10 years into marriage, years spent mostly in my husband's na- 10 tive Canada, I thought of myself as an expatriate Bengali permanently stranded in North America because of destiny or desire. My first novel, *The Tiger's Daughter,* embodies the loneliness I felt but could not acknowledge, even to myself, as I negotiated the no man's land between the country of my past and the continent of my present. Shaped by memory, textured with nostalgia for a class and culture I had abandoned, this novel quite naturally became an expression of the expatriate consciousness.

It took me a decade of painful introspection to put nostalgia in per- 11 spective and to make the transition from expatriate to immigrant. After a 14-year stay in Canada, I forced my husband and our two sons to relocate to the United States. But the transition from foreign student to U.S. citizen, from detached onlooker to committed immigrant, has not been easy.

The years in Canada were particularly harsh. Canada is a country that 12 officially, and proudly, resists cultural fusion. For all its rhetoric about a cultural "mosaic," Canada refuses to renovate its national self-image to include its changing complexion. It is a New World country with Old World concepts of a fixed, exclusivist national identity. Canadian official rhetoric designated me as one of the "visible minority" who, even though I spoke the Canadian languages of English and French, was straining "the absorptive capacity" of Canada. Canadians of color were routinely treated as "not real" Canadians. One example: In 1985 a terrorist bomb, planted in an Air-India jet on Canadian soil, blew up after leaving Montreal, killing 329 passengers, most of whom were Canadians of Indian origin. The prime minister of Canada at the time, Brian Mulroney, phoned the prime minister of India to offer Canada's condolences for India's loss.

Those years of race-related harassments in Canada politicized me and 13 deepened my love of the ideals embedded in the American Bill of Rights. I don't forget that the architects of the Constitution and the Bill of Rights were white males and slaveholders. But through their declaration, they provided us with the enthusiasm for human rights, and the initial framework from which other empowerments could be conceived and enfranchised communities expanded.

I am a naturalized U.S. citizen and I take my American citizenship very 14 seriously. I am not an economic refugee, nor am I a seeker of political asylum. I am a voluntary immigrant. I became a citizen by choice, not by simple accident of birth.

Yet these days, questions such as who is an American and what is Amer- 15
ican culture are being posed with belligerence, and being answered with violence. Scapegoating of immigrants has once again become the politicians'
easy remedy for all that ails the nation. Hate speeches fill auditoriums for
demagogues willing to profit from stirring up racial animosity. An April
Gallup poll indicated that half of Americans would like to bar almost all
legal immigration for the next five years.

The United States, like every sovereign nation, has a right to formulate 16
its immigration policies. But in this decade of continual, large-scale diasporas, it is imperative that we come to some agreement about who "we"
are, and what our goals are for the nation, now that our community includes people of many races, ethnicities, languages, and religions.

The debate about American culture and American identity has to date 17
been monopolized largely by Eurocentrists and ethnocentrists whose rhetoric has been flamboyantly divisive, pitting a phantom "us" against a demonized "them."

All countries view themselves by their ideals. Indians idealize the cultural 18
continuum, the inherent value system of India, and are properly incensed
when foreigners see nothing but poverty, intolerance, strife, and injustice.
Americans see themselves as the embodiments of liberty, openness, and individualism, even as the world judges them for drugs, crime, violence, big-
otry, militarism, and homelessness. I was in Singapore in 1994 when the
American teenager Michael Fay was sentenced to caning for having spray-
painted some cars. While I saw Fay's actions as those of an individual, and
his sentence as too harsh, the overwhelming local sentiment was that van-
dalism was an "American" crime, and that flogging Fay would deter Singapore youths from becoming "Americanized."

Conversely, in 1994, in Tavares, Florida, the Lake County School Board 19
announced its policy (since overturned) requiring middle school teachers to
instruct their students that American culture, by which the board meant
European-American culture, is inherently "superior to other foreign or historic cultures." The policy's misguided implication was that culture in
the United States has not been affected by the American Indian, African-
American, Latin-American, and Asian-American segments of the population. The sinister implication was that our national identity is so fragile
that it can absorb diverse and immigrant cultures only by recontextualiz-
ing them as deficient.

Our nation is unique in human history in that the founding idea of 20
"America" was in opposition to the tenet that a nation is a collection of
like-looking, like-speaking, like-worshipping people. The primary criterion

for nationhood in Europe is homogeneity of culture, race, and religion—which has contributed to blood-soaked balkanization in the former Yugoslavia and the former Soviet Union.

America's pioneering European ancestors gave up the easy homogeneity of their native countries for a new version of Utopia. Now, in the 1990s, we have the exciting chance to follow that tradition and assist in the making of a new American culture that differs from both the enforced assimilation of a "melting pot" and the Canadian model of a multicultural "mosaic."   21

The multicultural mosaic implies a contiguity of fixed, self-sufficient, utterly distinct cultures. Multiculturalism, as it has been practiced in the United States in the past 10 years, implies the existence of a central culture, ringed by peripheral cultures. The fallout of official multiculturalism is the establishment of one culture as the norm and the rest as aberrations. At the same time, the multiculturalist emphasis on race- and ethnicity-based group identity leads to a lack of respect for individual differences within each group, and to vilification of those individuals who place the good of the nation above the interests of their particular racial or ethnic communities.   22

We must be alert to the dangers of an "us" vs. "them" mentality. In California, this mentality is manifesting itself as increased violence between minority, ethnic communities. The attack on Korean-American merchants in South Central Los Angeles in the wake of the Rodney King beating trial is only one recent example of the tragic side effects of this mentality. On the national level, the politicization of ethnic identities has encouraged the scapegoating of legal immigrants, who are blamed for economic and social problems brought about by flawed domestic and foreign policies.   23

We need to discourage the retention of cultural memory if the aim of that retention is cultural balkanization. We must think of American culture and nationhood as a constantly reforming, transmogrifying "we."   24

In this age of diasporas, one's biological identity may not be one's only identity. Erosions and accretions come with the act of emigration. The experience of cutting myself off from a biological homeland and settling in an adopted homeland that is not always welcoming to its dark-complexioned citizens has tested me as a person, and made me the writer I am today.   25

I choose to describe myself on my own terms as an American, rather than as an Asian-American. Why is it that hyphenation is imposed only on non-white Americans? Rejecting hyphenation is my refusal to categorize the cultural landscape into a center and its peripheries; it is to demand that the   26

American nation deliver the promises of its dream and its Constitution to all its citizens equally.

My rejection of hyphenation has been misrepresented as race treachery 27 by some India-born academics on U.S. campuses who have appointed themselves guardians of the "purity" of ethnic cultures. Many of them, though they reside permanently in the United States and participate in its economy, consistently denounce American ideals and institutions. They direct their rage at me because, by becoming a U.S. citizen and exercising my voting rights, I have invested in the present and not the past; because I have committed myself to help shape the future of my adopted homeland; and because I celebrate racial and cultural mongrelization.

What excites me is that as a nation we have not only the chance to re- 28 tain those values we treasure from our original cultures but also the chance to acknowledge that the outer forms of those values are likely to change. Among Indian immigrants, I see a great deal of guilt about the inability to hang on to what they commonly term "pure culture." Parents express rage or despair at their U.S.-born children's forgetting of, or indifference to, some aspects of Indian culture. Of those parents I would ask: What is it we have lost if our children are acculturating into the culture in which we are living? Is it so terrible that our children are discovering or are inventing homelands for themselves?

Some first-generation Indo-Americans, embittered by racism and by 29 unofficial "glass ceilings," construct a phantom identity, more-Indian-than-Indians-in-India, as a defense against marginalization. I ask: Why don't you get actively involved in fighting discrimination? Make your voice heard. Choose the forum most appropriate for you. If you are a citizen, let your vote count. Reinvest your energy and resources into revitalizing your city's disadvantaged residents and neighborhoods. Know your constitutional rights, and when they are violated, use the agencies of redress the Constitution makes available to you. Expect change, and when it comes, deal with it!

As a writer, my literary agenda begins by acknowledging that America 30 has transformed me. It does not end until I show that I (along with the hundreds of thousands of immigrants like me) am minute by minute transforming America. The transformation is a two-way process: It affects both the individual and the national-cultural identity.

Others who write stories of migration often talk of arrival at a new 31 place as a loss, the loss of communal memory and the erosion of an original culture. I want to talk of arrival as a gain.

Thinking About the Essay

1. What is the significance of the title? How is Mukherjee a dreamer? Why does the idea of America inspire dreams? What impact does the American Dream have on one's identity? For example, Mukherjee says in paragraph 6 that she had a clear sense of identity when she was in India. How has this sense of identity changed now that she is an American?

2. What is Mukherjee's purpose in writing this essay? Does she want to tell a story, analyze an issue, argue a position? Remember that this article appeared in *Mother Jones,* a progressive or left-of-center magazine. What does her primary audience tell you about her intentions?

3. Why does Mukherjee divide her essay into four parts? What are the relationships among these sections? Why has she used this pattern of organization? Where does she employ comparison and contrast and definition to achieve coherence among these parts?

4. Mukherjee refers to Eurocentrics and ethnocentrics. What do these terms mean to you? Discuss your understanding of these terms with other members of the class.

Responding in Writing

5. Write a summary of Mukherjee's essay, capturing as many of her major ideas as possible in no more than 300 words.

6. Write your own essay titled "American Dreamer," referring specifically to the dreams that immigrants—perhaps even you or members of your family—have had about coming to this country.

7. Mukherjee asserts, "We must be alert to the dangers of an 'us' vs. 'them' mentality (paragraph 23)." Write an argumentative essay responding to this statement, referring to other assertions by Mukherjee to amplify your own position.

Networking

8. In small groups, develop a summary of Mukherjee's essay. Next, compose a list of outstanding questions you still might have about her essay. For example, has she overlooked or diminished the importance of a specific topic, or has she personalized the subject too much? Finally, collaborate on a letter to the author in which you lay out your concerns.

9. Download from a search engine all the information that you can find about Bharati Mukherjee. Then compose a brief analytical profile of the author in which you highlight her career and the impact that living in several cultures has had on her work. Use "American Dreamer" as a foundation for this presentation, and be certain to provide citations for your web research. (For information on citing online sources, see Appendix A: Conducting Research in the New Global Era.)

The Cult of Ethnicity

ARTHUR M. SCHLESINGER JR.

Arthur Meine Schlesinger Jr. was born in Columbus, Ohio, in 1917. Graduating from Harvard University in 1938, he embarked on a multifaceted career as historian, popular writer, university professor, political activist, and advisor to presidents. Among other positions he has held, he served as President Kennedy's special assistant for Latin American affairs. Schlesinger published dozens of books, most notably *The Age of Jackson,* which received the 1946 Pulitzer Prize for history, and *A Thousand Days,* which won the Pulitzer for biography in 1966. Although he never received an advanced degree, Schlesinger was awarded numerous honorary doctorates and for years was distinguished professor at the Graduate Center of the City University of New York. In the essay that follows, which was published in *Time* Magazine in 1991, Schlesinger offers a critique of multiculturalism and an endorsement of those values and attitudes that frame our commonality.

Before Reading

Do you support various ethnic studies programs and departments on your campus? Would you major in such a discipline? Why or why not?

The history of the world has been in great part the history of the mixing of peoples. Modern communication and transport accelerate mass migrations from one continent to another. Ethnic and racial diversity is more than ever a salient fact of the age.

But what happens when people of different origins, speaking different languages and professing different religions, inhabit the same locality and live under the same political sovereignty? Ethnic and racial conflict—far more than ideological conflict—is the explosive problem of our times.

On every side today ethnicity is breaking up nations. The Soviet Union, India, Yugoslavia, Ethiopia, are all in crisis. Ethnic tensions disturb and divide Sri Lanka, Burma, Indonesia, Iraq, Cyprus, Nigeria, Angola, Lebanon, Guyana, Trinidad—you name it. Even nations as stable and civilized as Britain and France, Belgium and Spain, face growing ethnic troubles. Is there any large multiethnic state that can be made to work?

The answer to that question has been, until recently, the United States. "No other nation," Margaret Thatcher has said, "has so successfully

combined people of different races and nations within a single culture."
How have Americans succeeded in pulling off this almost unprecedented
trick?

We have always been a multiethnic country. Hector St. John de Creve-   5
coeur, who came from France in the 18th century, marveled at the astonishing diversity of the settlers—"a mixture of English, Scotch, Irish,
French, Dutch, Germans and Swedes . . . this promiscuous breed." He pro-
pounded a famous question: "What then is the American, this new man?"
And he gave a famous answer: "Here individuals of all nations are melted
into a new race of men." *E pluribus unum.*

The U.S. escaped the divisiveness of a multiethnic society by a brilliant   6
solution: the creation of a brand-new national identity. The point of America was not to preserve old cultures but to forge a new, American culture.
"By an intermixture with our people," President George Washington told
Vice President John Adams, immigrants will "get assimilated to our customs, measures and laws: in a word, soon become one people." This was
the ideal that a century later Israel Zangwill crystallized in the title of his
popular 1908 play *The Melting Pot.* And no institution was more potent
in molding Crevecoeur's "promiscuous breed" into Washington's "one
people" than the American public school.

The new American nationality was inescapably English in language,   7
ideas and institutions. The pot did not melt everybody, not even all the
white immigrants; deeply bred racism put black Americans, yellow Americans, red Americans and brown Americans well outside the pale. Still, the
infusion of other stocks, even of nonwhite stocks, and the experience of the
New World reconfigured the British legacy and made the U.S., as we all
know, a very different country from Britain.

In the 20th century, new immigration laws altered the composition of   8
the American people, and a cult of ethnicity erupted both among non-
Anglo whites and among nonwhite minorities. This had many healthy consequences. The American culture at last began to give shamefully overdue
recognition to the achievements of groups subordinated and spurned during the high noon of Anglo dominance, and it began to acknowledge the
great swirling world beyond Europe. Americans acquired a more complex
and invigorating sense of their world—and of themselves.

But, pressed too far, the cult of ethnicity has unhealthy consequences.   9
It gives rise, for example, to the conception of the U.S. as a nation composed not of individuals making their own choices but of inviolable ethnic

and racial groups. It rejects the historic American goals of assimilation and integration.

And, in an excess of zeal, well-intentioned people seek to transform our   10 system of education from a means of creating "one people" into a means of promoting, celebrating and perpetuating separate ethnic origins and identities. The balance is shifting from *unum* to *pluribus*.

That is the issue that lies behind the hullabaloo over "multiculturalism"   11 and "political correctness," the attack on the "Eurocentric" curriculum and the rise of the notion that history and literature should be taught not as disciplines but as therapies whose function is to raise minority self-esteem. Group separatism crystallizes the differences, magnifies tensions, intensifies hostilities. Europe—the unique source of the liberating ideas of democracy, civil liberties and human rights—is portrayed as the root of all evil, and non-European cultures, their own many crimes deleted, are presented as the means of redemption.

I don't want to sound apocalyptic about these developments. Education   12 is always in ferment, and a good thing too. The situation in our universities, I am confident, will soon right itself. But the impact of separatist pressures on our public schools is more troubling. If a Kleagle of the Ku Klux Klan wanted to use the schools to disable and handicap black Americans, he could hardly come up with anything more effective than the "Afrocentric" curriculum. And if separatist tendencies go unchecked, the result can only be the fragmentation, resegregation and tribalization of American life.

I remain optimistic. My impression is that the historic forces driving to-   13 ward "one people" have not lost their power. The eruption of ethnicity is, I believe, a rather superficial enthusiasm stirred by romantic ideologues on the one hand and by unscrupulous con men on the other: self-appointed spokesmen whose claim to represent their minority groups is carelessly accepted by the media. Most American-born members of minority groups, white or nonwhite, see themselves primarily as Americans rather than primarily as members of one or another ethnic group. A notable indicator today is the rate of intermarriage across ethnic lines, across religious lines, even (increasingly) across racial lines. "We Americans," said Theodore Roosevelt, "are children of the crucible."

The growing diversity of the American population makes the quest for   14 unifying ideals and a common culture all the more urgent. In a world savagely rent by ethnic and racial antagonisms, the U.S. must continue as an example of how a highly differentiated society holds itself together.

Thinking About the Essay

1. Why does the writer employ the word *cult* in the title? What connotations does this word have? How does it affect the tone of the essay?

2. Consider the first two paragraphs of this essay, which constitute the writer's introduction. What thesis or claim does the writer advance? Why does he present his main idea in two brief paragraphs instead of one?

3. Summarize Schlesinger's argument. How does he state the problem and then proceed to offer a solution?

4. Note the many references to historical figures that the writer presents. Why has he employed this technique?

5. Examine paragraph 11, which consists of two very long sentences and one shorter one. How does the writer achieve coherence? Why does he place certain words within quotation marks? What assumptions does he make about his audience in presenting relatively complex sentence structures?

Responding in Writing

6. Schlesinger writes, "The balance is shifting from *unum* to *pluribus*" (paragraph 10). Write an essay in which you agree or disagree with this statement, offering your own reasons and support for the position you take.

7. Write an essay with the title "The Cult of_____." You might want to select sports, celebrity, thinness, or any other subject that appeals to you.

8. Do you think that our commonality as Americans and citizens of the world outweighs our uniqueness? How can the two be reconciled? Write an essay that explores this issue.

Networking

9. In small groups talk about whether Schlesinger's portrait of America rings true, whether it describes you and your classmates as college students. What would you add to the writer's remarks? What, if anything, do you consider misleading or exaggerated? On the basis of your collective views, write notes for a letter to Schlesinger about his essay.

10. Using any search engine, download information on multiculturalism. Use the material you have assembled to write an essay in which you offer your own extended definition of this term. Be certain to cite at least three sources that you have discovered. (For information on citing online sources, see Appendix A.)

Arabs in Foreign Lands

MOISÉS NAÍM | Moisés Naím is currently editor and publisher of *Foreign Policy* magazine. He received a Ph.D. from the Massachusetts Institute of Technology and returned to his native Venezuela to serve as professor and dean at Instituto de Estudios Superiores de Administración, in Caracas. As Venezuela's minister of trade and industry in the 1990s, Naím helped to engineer major economic reforms. He was also the director of the projects on economic reforms and on Latin America at the Carnegie Endowment for International Peace and worked for the World Bank as executive director and senior advisor to the president. Naím is the author or editor of eight books and numerous essays dealing with a wide range of subjects: the political economy of international trade and investment, multilateral organizations, economic reforms, globalization. In this selection, which was posted on *foreignpolicy.com* in 2005, Naím attempts to explain the socioeconomic success of Arabs who have immigrated to the United States.

Before Reading

To what extent do you consider your own work ethic to be a *cultural* value or a reaction to a cultural value? Do you feel individually responsible for (or protective of) a culture's being perceived as "progressive" or "backward"? Why or why not?

People of Arab descent living in the United States are doing far better than the average American. That is the surprising conclusion drawn from data collected by the U.S. Census Bureau in 2000 and released last March. The census found that U.S. residents who report having Arab ancestors are better educated and wealthier than average Americans. 1

Whereas 24 percent of Americans hold college degrees, 41 percent of Arab Americans are college graduates. The median income for an Arab family living in the United States is $52,300—4.6 percent higher than other American families—and more than half of all Arab Americans own their home. Forty-two percent of people of Arab descent in the United States work as managers or professionals, while the same is true for only 34 percent of the general U.S. population. For many, this success has come on quickly: Although about 50 percent of Arab Americans were born in the United States, nearly half of those born abroad did not arrive until the 1990s. 2

That immigrants do better than their compatriots back home is of   3
course no surprise. What is far less common is for immigrants to perform
that much better than the average population of their adopted home. This
fact should prompt important debates that transcend how Arab immigrants are faring in the United States.

Consider, for example, the popular notion that cultural factors loom   4
large behind the Middle East's appalling poverty. Cultural explanations for
why some succeed when others fail have a long history. In 1904, German
sociologist Max Weber famously argued that the "Protestant ethic" was
more compatible with capitalism than religions such as Confucianism and
Taoism. Of course, the Asian economic miracle forced a revision of these
assumptions. The same thing happened to "Asian values," the idea that
cultural factors explained the region's phenomenal rates of economic
growth. The Asian financial crisis of the late 1990s gave that cultural theory an even shorter shelf life.

The Middle East's poor economic and social performance today has   5
also prompted explanations of some malignancy in the prevailing culture.
The respected Harvard University historian David S. Landes wrote in his
1998 book, *The Wealth and Poverty of Nations,* that the ill that plagues
these countries "lies with the culture, which (1) does not generate an informed and capable work force; (2) continues to mistrust or reject new
techniques and ideas that come from the enemy West (Christendom) and
(3) does not respect such knowledge as members do manage to achieve."

Such views are common, given the inexcusably poor performance of   6
Arab nations. In the last two decades, no region besides sub-Saharan Africa
has seen income per person grow as slowly as in the Middle East. At the
current rate, it will take the average Arab 140 years to double his or her income. Asians, Europeans, and North Americans are expected to double
their incomes in the next 10 years. The total economic output—including
oil—of all Arab countries is less than that of Spain, the Middle East's unemployment rates are the highest in the developing world, and its literacy
rates rank near the bottom.

But if cultural impediments are behind the Arab world's disappointing   7
performance, what explains Arab Americans' incredible success? The answer, of course, is opportunities and institutions. Arabs in the United States
have access to ample opportunities to prosper and can rely on powerful institutions to protect their civil, political, and economic rights to do so. Indeed, the census data show that Arab ancestry mixed with markets and
meritocracy creates a potent fuel for success.

Of course, many will explain the success of Arab Americans by point-   8
ing out that people who emigrate tend to be younger, more motivated, am-

bitious, and entrepreneurial. The Arab immigrants who are doing so well in the United States, according to this view, would have made it anywhere.

Sadly, that isn't true, either. Otherwise, how does one explain why Arab immigrants in Europe are worse off than those in the United States? Why are leaders of Arab communities in France warning that social and racial tensions are in danger of creating a "social and political atom bomb"? Sure, France may be an extreme case, but the situation of Arabs in the rest of Europe is hardly better. In general, Muslims living in Europe—of which Arabs constitute a significant proportion—are poorer, less educated, and in worse health than the rest of the population. In the Netherlands, the unemployment rate for ethnic Moroccans is 22 percent, roughly four times the rate for the country as a whole. In Britain, the Muslim population has the highest unemployment rate of all religious groups. The failure of Arabs in Europe is particularly worrisome given that 10 of the states or entities along Europe's eastern and southern borders are home to nearly 250 million Muslims—most of them Arabs—with a birthrate more than double that of Europeans.

This census data should prompt soul-searching in many quarters. Cultural determinists may want to revise their theories of Arab backwardness. Arab leaders should be ashamed when they see their emigrants prospering in the United States while their own people are miserable. And Europe should wake up to the possibility that it may have less of an "Arab problem" than a "European problem." Then again, maybe the cultural determinists have an explanation for why Europeans are so predisposed against Arab success.

Thinking About the Essay

1. How is the essay structured around reactions of "surprise" and "disappointment"? Why is Naím "sad" (paragraph 9) to acknowledge the failure of one explanation he has considered?

2. What are *necessary* conditions, as opposed to *sufficient* conditions? Identify examples of *necessary but not sufficient* conditions in Naím's causal analysis.

3. Naím devotes much of the essay to the systematic exposure and elimination of flawed explanations. In paragraph 7, Naím offers some answers of his own. Do you accept these assertions as self-evident, or do you find them just as problematic as the explanations rejected earlier in the essay? Explain your response.

4. This essay is about the limitations of theories, but the author is also interested in what makes certain theories attractive and therefore popular. Where in the essay does Naím inquire into the psychological motives of those who subscribe to theories?

5. In his concluding paragraph, Naím introduces the term "cultural determinist" to categorize a range of theories regarded with suspicion earlier in the essay. Naím concludes the essay, however, by invoking cultural determinism as a possible explanation. What is the purpose of ending the essay in this way?

Responding in Writing

6. Consider American exceptionalism—a point of view Naím entertains in this essay—as one example of a culturally deterministic theory. List some events in the history of the United States that you believe would undermine the explanatory value of this theory. Present this evidence in an argumentative essay.

7. Write a "sequel" to Naím's essay in which you extend his causal analysis to consider religion as a cultural factor.

8. In a brief essay, employ a comparison/contrast strategy to attack one current example of what you see as a deterministic, reductive, or essentialist view of a culture.

Networking

9. In small groups, construct profiles of assimilated cultures within the United States based on popular stereotypes about a culturally specific work ethic, and so forth. List cultural attributes that have been linked (in the popular mind) with that culture's success as an immigrant population. Does a coherent vision of "success" emerge from these lists? As a class, list and discuss some other indicators of "success" (artistic achievement, for example) that Naím fails to consider in his essay.

10. Naím cites a famous cultural explanation proposed by sociologist Max Weber (paragraph 4) and notes that the Asian economic miracle in the period following the Second World War "forced a revision" of Weber's assumptions. Conduct online research to discover the initial reception of Weber's theory and its earliest critics. Why were these ideas thought to be in need of revision even at the time of their publication in 1904? Write a brief report on your findings.

Culture or Conflict?
Images of Globalization

This portfolio of images from around the world presents a visual paradox: Is global culture a happy consumer wonderland where the fries are always crisp and the music always loud? Or has globalization simply packaged and marketed a bland, simplified version of the basics of culture, such as food and fashion, to an increasingly busy and distracted global population?

For millennia, trade between nation-states has introduced and shared aspects of culture, but the electronic telecommunication that is available now between countries has enabled instant blending of customs and has caused regional cultures and languages to fight to keep their own traditions vibrant. French-speaking Quebecois agitate for independence from the rest of English-speaking Canada. The ecotourism movement struggles to maintain the integrity of fragile cultures and environments even as it imports Western tourists with their cash, cameras, and expectations for plumbing. The slow-food movement, which originated in Italy, calls on communities to nurture biodiversity and sustainable agriculture through renewed appreciation of their culinary heritage.

As you examine the following images, be especially attentive to the irony that lies in the details. *Irony* is a quality of being unexpected, incongruous, or out of place, juxtapositions that make something as seemingly common as a bottle of soda seem suddenly, entirely strange. That strangeness leads to a realization that there's more to the image than meets the eye; the nomad's tent topped by a satellite dish or the camel carrying an expensive mountain bicycle can be perceived either as a widening of opportunities and experiences or a flattening out of cultural vitality.

Many readings in this book describe the clashing of cultures and civilizations. Can consumer culture, based on these images, foster cooperation rather than clashes? After all, in a 1996 *New York Times* op-ed piece, foreign correspondent Thomas Friedman argued that no two countries that both have a McDonald's have ever fought a war against each other. What do you think?

Coca-Cola in Egypt. An Egyptian girl drinks from a bottle of Coca-Cola in a shop in downtown Cairo, Egypt. After an Internet rumor that the Coca-Cola logo, if looked at upside-down or in a mirror, reads "No Mohammed, No Mecca" in Arabic, a top religious authority in Egypt studied the label and finally declared that "there is no defamation to the religion of Islam from near or far."

Considering the Image

1. Why would Coca-Cola be a target for such a rumor? Can you think of other examples in which consumer goods were boycotted as the symbols of a larger culture, value system, or belief?

2. What, to your eye, is particularly revealing or compelling about this image? What does the photographer want you to see? Does this image support or contradict images that you see in the media about women in the Middle East?

Big Bird in Shanghai.   More than 90 percent of the households in the twelve major cities of the People's Republic of China have television sets. One of the favorite programs, reaching 120 million Chinese viewers, is *Sesame Street.* Here, Big Bird, known as *Zhima Jie,* appears on Shanghai television.

Considering the Image

1. How did the photographer capture a specific mood in this picture? What is the expression on the children's faces? Why does Big Bird loom over them? Do you think that there are universal values that make *Sesame Street* popular not just in China but throughout the world? Justify and explain your response.

2. Do you think the photographer wants to make a statement about "cultural imperialism" or the impact of globalization on national cultures, or simply capture a specific moment and scene? Explain your response. Why might globalization, which involves in part the transnational movement of media across cultures, be a force for democracy in China and elsewhere?

Ecotourists. Tourists photograph a Huli Wigman, a representative of the Huli people of Papua New Guinea. The Huli are an indigenous people whose subsistence-based way of life has changed little for centuries. They have a particular reverence for birds; the Wigmen (certain men in this intricate clan-based society) wear elaborate headdresses woven of human hair and decorated with flowers and feathers to perform ritual dances that suggest the behavior of local birds.

Considering the Image

1. This photograph was used to illustrate a report on the rights and responsibilities of ecotourists and the groups that sponsor and profit from ecotourism. Why would that group, which advocates for the well-being of indigenous peoples and the preservation of endangered environments, consider this photograph a compelling example of the need for rights to be respected and responsibilities to be upheld?

2. Whose perspective do you assume as you look at this photograph: the native person's, the tourists', or the photographer's taking in the entire scene?

Sophisticated Ladies. Nakshatra Reddy is a biochemist who is married to a prosperous businessman in Mumbai (formerly Bombay). Her daughter, Meghana, dressed in a PVC suit of her own design, is a model and former host on a local music channel.

Considering the Image

1. How does the photographer stage or set up this scene? How does the photographer emphasize certain cultural contrasts between mother and daughter, and what is the purpose? Why is it important for viewers to know that mother and daughter represent a wealthy Indian family rather than a middle–class or poor one?

2. The daughter in this family represents a familiar Western type. How would you describe her? What are her sources of imitation? Do you think that the daughter has succumbed to the lure of Western popular culture, or might she be making a statement about her global identity? Explain your response.

Inclusion Movement.   In 2001, immigrants from several countries in Europe rallied in Valencia, Spain, to protest a new Spanish law that threatened to expel tens of thousands of undocumented aliens. The banner in the foreground reads, "We are human beings. We have rights."

Considering the Image

1. From what vantage point did the photographer shoot this image? What is the effect or dominant impression? If you know Spanish, what other inscriptions on placards can you translate? Does the photographer want to make a statement or simply capture a moment in time? How do you know?

2. The essays in Chapter 2 deal with the impact of immigration on the United States. Were you surprised to discover from this photograph that nations in Europe contend today with similar issues? Why would Spain want to expel undocumented aliens? Conduct research with two other class members to find out more about the impact of recent immigration on Spain, France, Italy, Germany, or Great Britain.

Modern Conveniences. The *ger* is the traditional, portable home of the nomadic people of Mongolia. A cone-shaped structure of felt stretched over a timber frame, with an opening in the top or a pipe to vent smoke from the stove, the *ger* is a symbol both of freedom and of hospitality. Many residents of Mongolia's capital, Ulaan Baatar, still live in traditional *gers,* and in keeping with their nomadic routes, any visitor is warmly greeted and offered shelter and food, as well as many modern conveniences. Here, a *ger* is outfitted with a satellite dish.

Considering the Image

1. This photo suggests not so much a clash of cultures as a fusion of ancient ways and modern technology. Why might a nomadic culture, like that of rural Mongolia, value the latest in communications technology?

2. Many writers define the so-called electronic gap or digital divide as one of the great challenges—and opportunities—for the new century. What does this image suggest to you about the digital divide? Granted, we don't know from this photograph if that satellite dish is being used to watch CNN or MTV; should that even matter? Why or why not?

Masai Men in Kenya. Two Masai warriors participate in an initiation rite. One of the men wears an odd amalgamation of African tribal and Western dress while the second warrior dresses in Western clothing.

Considering the Image

1. How does this photograph highlight the impact of Western popular culture on traditional African culture? What details stand out? How is the photograph composed so as to illustrate the blending (or conflict) of cultures?

2. Do you think that the photographer advances a thesis or claim about traditional Masai rituals, the clash of civilizations, or the viability of old cultural practices in an age of globalization? Justify your response.

America and the World: How Do Others Perceive Us?

O ne of the key elements supporting the idea of America is a belief in freedom, democracy, and human rights. This ideal, as we saw in the previous chapter, has been a motivating impulse in all waves of immigration, especially for the flood of peoples from around the world that have found their way to the United States since 1965, transforming the nation into a global village. But does the rest of the world believe that the United States is truly a "city upon a hill" as President Reagan (borrowing a phrase from one of the nation's first immigrants, Governor John Winthrop of Massachusetts Bay Colony) declared? Are we truly a beacon of democratic promise for other nations? Do we promote democracy and human rights everywhere? What ideals and values—especially when projected by American foreign policy—do we actually represent?

Today the conflicts inherent in the "war on terror" and "clash of civilizations"—framed by a suspicion of American-style capitalism, democracy, and imperialism—fuel a widespread belief that the world's reigning superpower acts out of self-interest rather than altruism. For many, the United States is not a bastion of democracy but a destructive element—a Great Satan in the minds of some. That we led the wars of the last century against the totalitarian forces of nazism, fascism, and communism apparently has become a historic footnote. That we provide international aid today to developing nations and victims of natural disasters, that we share information and technology openly, that we promote democracy at great human and material cost: all seem lost in a maelstrom of anti-Americanism. In a world of predators, the United States appears to many as the most insatiable enemy.

The truth, of course, is that the image America projects to the world has always been a function of what others have projected onto it. As the world's superpower, the United States faces today the option of not only

 **Online Study Center** This icon will direct you to weblinks, audio and visual content, and additional resources on the website college.hmco.com/pic/mullerNWR2e

67

Protesters in Canada rally against President Bush and the war in Iraq.

Thinking About the Image

1. What is your response to this image of a generally friendly and support-ive North American neighbor of the United States protesting the Bush administration and the war in Iraq?
2. Identify and analyze the elements in this photograph that contribute to the dominant impression or overall effect. What point of view, if any, does the photographer want to convey?
3. What ironic elements appear in this image? What is the historical allusion?
4. Research Canadian attitudes concerning the situation in Iraq. In light of this information, would you say that the image is representative of Canadian opinion or an isolated instance of protest? Explain.

inspiring ideals of democracy and freedom in the rest of the world, but of trying to remake nations and regions—as in the case of Iraq and the broader Middle East—according to those ideals. The problem is that the very *idea* of America is symbolically saturated with conflicting aspirations and associations. The ideals that America would transmit to the world will inevitably clash with rival ideals that have been projected from afar. If, for example, we are guardians of the free world, then what forces are we guarding the world *against*? How can the United States unilaterally pursue debatable policies and still maintain moral authority on the world stage? What ideals, beyond self-interest, would justify intervention in the affairs of other nations? For instance, the current administration promotes secular democracy in the Middle East; but many in the area view American actions as an amoral attempt to control the region, destroy traditional societies, and guarantee access to oil.

Of course, not everyone hates the United States or is cynical about its role in the world. The Islamic Republic of Iran might denounce America as the Great Satan (and England as the Lesser Satan), but Iranians love Americans in particular and the West in general. Again, the truth lies in the beholder and the ways in which we construct national mythologies for ourselves. Some might engage in a frenzy of anti-Americanism and even want to harm the United States for what they perceive America does to the rest of the world; but many others around the world, especially in moments of crisis, are thankful for American food during famine, tents and medical supplies after earthquakes and tsunamis, the promotion of human rights, and even military intervention (as in Bosnia) to prevent genocide. The global village does admire America's political and economic freedoms, along with its wealth, culture, and technology, even as it might be appalled by certain foreign policy doctrines and behavior on the world stage.

The essays in this chapter deal with America's complex relationship with the rest of the world, and with the psychological factors behind both current anti-American and pro-American attitudes. The invasion of Iraq in 2003, an attempt to transmit ideals to another part of the world, has changed the image of America in ways that we are only beginning to understand. ("As the savagery of the images coming out of Iraq demonstrate all too well," writes Sasha Abramsky in an essay appearing in this chapter, "we live in a world where image is if not everything, at least crucial.") The famous film footage of the cavalry charge up San Juan Hill that made Theodore Roosevelt's reputation during the Spanish-American War was, as we now know, a staged re-enactment filmed after the real charge took place. Today, a hundred years after Roosevelt's charge, it is no easy task to alter the perception of America as an aggressive imperialist power; but it is still possible, after the fact, to examine and learn from the images, actions, and mythologies that are at its source.

Stranger in the Arab-Muslim World

FOUAD AJAMI

Fouad Ajami was born in Lebanon in 1946 and immigrated to the United States in 1964. He was raised as a Shiite Muslim. A political scientist with a doctorate from the University of Washington, Ajami has taught at Princeton University and, since 1980, at Johns Hopkins University, where today he is Majid Khadduri Professor of Islamic studies and director of Middle Eastern studies. He is also a contributing editor to *U.S. News & World Report* and a consultant to *CBS News*. Ajami received a prestigious MacArthur Fellowship in 1982 for his work on Middle Eastern politics and culture. His work includes *The Vanished Imam: Musa al Sadr and the Shia of Lebanon* (1986), *Beirut: City of Regrets* (1988), *The Arab Predicament* (1981, revised edition 1992), and *The Dream Palace of the Arabs* (1998). In the following essay, published in *The Wilson Quarterly* in the spring of 2001, Ajami argues that the chroniclers of Arab-Islamic history must come to terms with the spread of American pop culture and a rising trend of anti-Americanism.

Before Reading

Do you see the United States as a generally positive or benevolent force in world affairs? What, in your view, is the primary cause of anti-American sentiment in the Arab-Islamic world?

That wily, flamboyant Egyptian ruler Anwar al-Sadat contracted an af-   1
fection for things and people American when he dominated his land in the 1970s. In the distant, powerful United States, which had ventured into Egypt, he saw salvation for his country—a way out of the pan-Arab captivity, the wars with Israel, and the drab austerity of a command economy. But Sadat was struck down in October 1981. The following year Sherif Hetata, a distinguished Egyptian man of letters, published a novel called *alShabaka* (*The net*), into which he poured the heartbreak and unease of his political breed (the secular Left) at America's new role in Egypt.

It is not a brilliant novel. The fiction is merely a vehicle for Hetata's rad-   2
ical politics. A net (an American net) is cast over Egypt and drags the old, burdened land into a bewildering new world. The protagonist of the novel,

Khalil Mansour Khalil, is an educated Egyptian who works for the public sector in the pharmaceutical industry and has known the setbacks and the accomplishments of the Nasser years. The Six-Day War shattered the peace and promise of his world in 1967, but vindication came six years later, in October 1973, when Egyptian armor crossed the Suez Canal. "We lived through a period of great enthusiasm, but it did not last." American diplomacy changed things, "weaned" Egypt away from its old commitments.

Khalil feels the new world's temptations when Ruth Harrison, a mysterious American woman with some command of Arabic, enters his life. Glamorous and alluring, Harrison offers him a contract with an American multinational, and Khalil's drab world and marriage to Amina Tewfic, a woman with "roots deep in the ground," are set against the dazzle of Harrison's world: "Amina always faced me with the facts, laid bare the contradictions in my life; perhaps that is why I kept running away from her. But Ruth was different. She exercised an attraction I found difficult to resist. Was it just the fascination of the unknown, of visiting another world where everything is there for the asking?" 3

Khalil throws over his life and is doomed. Harrison is a spy come to this new American sphere of influence to decimate the Egyptian Left. Predictably, the affair ends in disaster. Harrison is murdered, and Khalil, insisting on his innocence, is put to death. American spies and tricksters and the Egyptians who fall under their sway dismantle the old world and erect in its place a world of betrayal. Egypt wades beyond its depth and barters time-honored truths for glitter, grief, and ruin, the chroniclers of Arab-Islamic history since the mid-1970s must come to terms with two especially puzzling developments: the spread of American pop culture through vast stretches of the Arab world, and the concomitant spread of a furious anti-Americanism. Thus, even as Egypt was incorporated into the American imperium, a relentless anti-Americanism animated Egyptian Islamists and secularists alike. It flowed freely through Egyptian letters and cinema and seemed to be the daily staple of the official and semiofficial organs of the regime. A similar situation now prevails throughout the Arabian Peninsula and the Persian Gulf, where an addiction to things American co-exists with an obligatory hostility to the power whose shadow lies across the landscape. 4

Historians who take note of these developments will not explain them adequately if they believe that the anti-Americanism at play in the Muslim world merely reflects the anti-Americanism now visible in France or Russia or India, or among a certain segment of the Latin American intelligentsia. America's primacy in the world since the defeat of communism has whipped up a powerful strain of resentment. Envy was the predictable response of many societies to the astonishing American economic performance in the 5

1990s—the unprecedented bull run, the "New Economy," the wild valuations in American equities, the triumphant claims that America had discovered a new economic world, free of the market's discipline and of the business cycle itself.

This global resentment inevitably made its way to Arab and Muslim 6 shores. But the Muslim world was a case apart for Pax Americana and sui generis in the kind of anti-Americanism it nurtured. José Bové, the provocateur attacking the spread of McDonald's outlets in France, is not to be compared with Osama bin Laden, the Saudi-born financier suspected of bankrolling a deadly campaign of terror against American embassies and military barracks. The essayists of *Le Monde Diplomatique* may rail against mondialisation American-style (the business schools, the bad food, the unsentimental capitalism of a Wall Street–U.S. Treasury alliance). But a wholly different wind blows through Arab lands, where a young boy drove a Mercedes truck loaded with TNT into an American military compound in Beirut in October 1983; where terrorists targeted a housing complex for the American military in Saudi Arabia in June 1996; where two men in a skiff crippled an American destroyer on a re-fueling stop in Aden, Yemen. Grim, defining episodes of that sort, and many others like them, mark the American presence in Arab-Muslim domains.

In the aftermath of the October 1973 war, the Arab and Iranian heart- 7 land slipped under American sway, and America acquired a kind of Muslim imperium. The development gained momentum from the needs of both the rulers and the social elites who had taken to American ways. The poorer states (read Egypt) needed sustenance; the wealthier states (read the states of the Arabian Peninsula and the Persian Gulf), protection against the covetous poorer states. A monarch in Iran, at once imperious and possessed of a neurotic sense of dependency on American judgment, effectively brought down his own regime. The order he had put together became inseparable in the popular psyche from the American presence in Iran. And they were torched together. The tribune of the revolution, Ayatollah Ruhollah Khomeini, was particularly skilled at turning the foreign power into the demon he needed. Iran alternated between falling for the foreigner's ways and loathing itself for surrendering to the foreigner's seduction. It swung wildly, from the embrace of the foreigner into a faith in the authority of the ancients and the reign of a clerical redeemer.

In the years to come, there would be no respite for America. Khomeini 8 had shown the way. There would be tributaries of his revolution and emulators aplenty. A world had flung wide its own floodgates. It let the foreigner in and lost broad segments of its young to the hip, freewheeling culture of America. By violent reaction the seduction could be covered up, or undone.

A public display of anti-American sentiment in Tehran.

Consider Osama bin Laden's description of America, as reported by a 9
young Sudanese follower of bin Laden who defected and turned witness for
American authorities: "The snake is America, and we have to stop them.
We have to cut off the head of the snake. We cannot let the American army
in our area. We have to do something. We have to fight them."

The American military force that troubles Osama bin Laden, that hov- 10
ers over his Saudi homeland and reaches the ports of his ancestral land in
Yemen, is there because the rulers of those lands acquiesced in its presence,
even sought it. Bin Laden and his followers cannot overturn the ruling order in the Arabian Peninsula and the Persian Gulf—entrenched dynasties
that have mastered the art of governing and struck workable social con-
tracts with the governed. But the rebels cannot concede that harsh truth.
Better to hack at the foreign power. More flattering to the cause to say that

the political orders in the region would fall of their own weight were it not for the armadas of the Americans and the military installations and weapons they have stored in the ports of the Persian Gulf and the Arabian Peninsula. Pax Americana may insist on its innocence, but, inevitably, it is caught in the crossfire between the powers that be and the insurgents who have taken up arms against them and who seek nothing less than the extirpation of America's presence from Muslim lands.

In fact, as Muslim societies become involved in a global economy they 11 can neither master nor ignore, both rulers and insurgents have no choice but to confront the American presence. America has become part of the uneven, painful "modernity" of the Islamic world. Even American embassies have acquired an ambivalent symbolic character: they are targeted by terrorists and besieged by visa seekers—professionals who have given up on failed economies and a restricted way of life; the half-educated and the urban poor, who in earlier times would never have sought opportunity and a new life in a distant land.

Denial is at the heart of the relationship between the Arab and Muslim 12 worlds and America. There can be no written praise of America, no acknowledgment of its tolerance or hospitality, or of the yearnings America has stirred in Karachi and Teheran, Cairo and Beirut, and in the streets of Ramallah. In November 2000, America extended a special gift to Jordan: a free-trade agreement between the two nations. Jordan was only the fourth country to be so favored, after Canada, Mexico, and Israel. The agreement was an investment in peace, a tribute to the late Jordanian ruler, King Hussein, and an admission of America's stake in the reign of his young heir, Abdullah II. But it did not dampen the anti-Americanism among professionals and intellectuals in Jordan.

There, as elsewhere, no intellectual can speak kindly of America. The at- 13 traction has to be hidden, or never fully owned up to. From Afghanistan to the Mediterranean, from Karachi to Cairo, human traffic moves toward America while anti-American demonstrations supply the familiar spectacle of American flags set to the torch. I know of no serious work of commentary in Arab lands in recent years that has spoken of the American political experience or the American cultural landscape with any appreciation. The anti-Americanism is automatic, unexamined, innate. To self-styled "liberals," America is the upholder of reaction; to Islamists, a defiling presence; to pan-Arabists, the backer of a Zionist project to dominate the region.

In the pan-Arab imagination, there would be a measure of Arab unity 14 had America not aborted it. There would be a "balance" of wealth and some harmony between the sparsely populated Arab oil states and the poorer, more populous Arab lands of the Levant had America not driven a wedge between them. There would be wealth for things that matter had those oil states not been tricked into weapons deals and joint military exercises they neither need nor can afford. "I hate America," a young Palestinian boy in the streets of Gaza said late last year to Michael Finkel, an American reporter who had come to cover the "Second Intifada" for the *New York Times Magazine*. But the matter is hardly that simple. Like the larger world to which he belongs, the boy hates America and is drawn to it. His world wants American things without having to partake of American ways. It has beckoned America, and then bloodied America.

America entered Arab lands on particular terms. The lands were, in the   15 main, authoritarian societies, and such middle classes as existed in them were excluded from meaningful political power. Monarchs and rulers of national states claimed the political world, and it was precisely through their good graces that America came on the scene. Pax Americana took to this transaction. It neither knew nor trusted the civil associations, the professional classes, the opposition. America had good reasons to suspect that the ground was not fertile for democratic undertakings. It was satisfied that Egypt's military rulers kept the peace. Why bother engaging those who opposed the regime, even the fragile bourgeois opposition that emerged in the late 1970s? Similarly, the only traffic to be had with Morocco was through its autocratic ruler, Hassan II. The man was harsh and merciless (his son, and successor, Mohammad VI, has all but admitted that), but he kept order, was "our man" in North Africa, and could be relied on to support America's larger purposes.

America extended the same indulgence to Yasir Arafat, the latest, and   16 most dubious, ruler to be incorporated into its designs. In the Palestinian world, the security arrangements and the political arrangements had been struck with Arafat. His American handlers ignored such opposition as had arisen to him. With no real access to the Palestinian world, and precious little knowledge of Arafat's opponents, America seemed to have to choose between the Islamic movement Hamas and Arafat's Palestinian National Authority. An easy call. The Palestinian strongman, in turn, accepted America's patronage but frustrated America's wishes.

The middle classes in the Arab world were mired in the politics of na-   17 tionalism, whereas the rulers always seemed supple and ready to wink at reality. There was precious little economic life outside the state-dominated oil sectors, and little business to be done without recourse to the custodians of the command economies. It was the prudent and, really, inevitable solution to negotiate American presence and American interests with those who, as the Arabic expression has it, have eaten the green and the dry and monopolized the life of the land.

The populations shut out of power fell back on their imaginations and   18
their bitterness. They resented the rulers but could not overthrow them. It
was easier to lash out at American power and question American purposes.
And they have been permitted the political space to do so. They can burn
American flags at will, so long as they remember that the rulers and their
prerogatives are beyond scrutiny. The rulers have been particularly sly in
monitoring the political safety valves in their domains. They know when
to indulge the periodic outbursts at American power. Not a pretty spectacle, but such are the politics in this sphere of American influence.

America's primacy will endure in Arab and Muslim lands, but the for-   19
eign power will have to tread carefully. "England is of Europe, and I am a
friend of the Ingliz, their ally," Ibn Saud, the legendary founder of the Saudi
state, once said of his relationship with the British. "But I will walk with
them only as far as my religion and honor will permit." In Arab and Muslim domains, it is the stranger's fate to walk alone.

Thinking About the Essay

1. Why does Ajami open with mention of the late Anwar al-Sadat? How does
   Ajami regard Sadat and the moderate, pragmatic brand of leadership he
   represented?

2. Ajami begins this essay with a detailed summary of a novel, *The Net,* by
   the Egyptian writer Sherif Hetata. What is his purpose? How does his summary of the novel set the stage for the rest of the essay?

3. How successful do you think Ajami is in presenting the paradox that he
   finds at the heart of Middle Eastern life today? What exactly is this paradox? How convincing is Ajami in supporting his claim?

4. Motifs of necessity and inevitability recur throughout the essay: Ajami
   writes of "obligatory hostility" (paragraph 4), for example, and of "automatic, unexamined, innate" anti-Americanism (paragraph 13). Trace these
   motifs and explain how they develop in the essay.

5. In the opening paragraph, Ajami writes that Sherif Hetata expressed the
   views of the "political breed" to which he belonged. What other "breeds" of
   Arab society does Ajami refer to in the essay? Does this social classification strategy become reductive at any point in the essay? If so, what makes
   it reductive?

Responding in Writing

6. Ajami ranges outside the Middle East to present a global sketch of anti-
   Americanism. What are some examples that he provides? What additional
   examples can you think of? In a brief essay, make your own attempt to explain the virulent anti-Americanism existing in the world today.

7. This article was written and published before the events of September 11, 2001, but Ajami does refer to Osama bin Laden and the rise of anti-Americanism among radical Islamists. Why didn't American policymakers listen to voices like Ajami's, who were warning of these dangers? In a brief essay, describe the role you think should be played by public intellectuals like Fouad Ajami.

8. In paragraph 15, Ajami writes that America "entered Arab lands on particular terms" with "good reasons to suspect that the ground was not fertile for democratic undertakings." In a brief essay, explain how the rationale for anti-American sentiments in Arab countries may have changed since the nation-building invasion of Iraq and the interventionist policy of the Bush administration.

Networking

9. Divide into two groups and construct profiles of an average disadvantaged youth in the Arab/Muslim world who is stereotypically anti-American (group one) and (group two) an average disadvantaged youth living in a large American city. Compare your lists of hypothetical attributes. To what extent can you attribute a scapegoating impulse to the universal factor of limited socioeconomic opportunities?

10. Locate two English-language versions of Middle Eastern newspapers that are available online. You may also consider Arabic newspapers published abroad, notably in London. Scan at least three articles for evidence of anti-American sentiment. Can you classify the source of this sentiment as fundamentalist, secular leftist, or pan-Arabic?

Americans Are Tuning Out the World

ALKMAN GRANITSAS

Alkman Granitsas is an American-born journalist who has reported on global issues in Asia and Europe for more than ten years. He has been a staff writer for the *Asian Wall Street Journal* and has contributed articles to *Business Week*, the *Far Eastern Economic Review*, and numerous other journals. Granitsas is currently based in Athens, where he is writing a book on the Balkans. In the following essay, from the November 24, 2005, issue of the online journal *YaleGlobal*, Granitsas warns against the consequences of a trend toward cultural and political isolationism in the United States.

Before Reading

Do you believe that America is "a shining city on the hill"? Why or why not?

For all the talk about a global village, there are actually two communi-   1
ties in the world today: Americans and everyone else. The average
Frenchman, Brazilian, or Pakistani is becoming more attuned to the American way of life, but Americans themselves are increasingly tuning out the
rest of the globe. At a time when U.S. power, benefiting from globalization,
is unchallenged in the world, a disinterested electorate could be a recipe for
trouble.

Foreigners have long bemoaned the "isolationist" attitude of Americans—   2
safely protected by two oceans and their tabula rasa history. But over the last
several decades, that isolation has deepened. Americans now pay less attention to international affairs, and read less foreign news than at any time in
the last two generations. Relative to the global boom in international travel,
tourism, and business, fewer Americans go overseas or study a foreign language at university. The truth is that Americans are becoming relatively
less—not more—engaged with the world in general.

A few facts. Since the early 1970s, the American public has paid less   3
and less attention to foreign affairs. According to Gallup polls from presidential election years 1948 through 1972, Americans used to rank foreign
affairs as the most important issue facing the nation. Since then, however,
with the single exception of the 2004 elections, the economy has been
ranked first.

Over the same period, the percentage of American university students   4
studying a foreign language has steadily declined. According to a report
funded by the U.S. Department of Education, in 1965, more than 16 percent of all American university students studied a foreign language. Now
only 8.6 percent do.

It has long been known that fewer Americans have passports, and U.S.   5
citizens travel less than their counterparts in other developed economies.
And while a record 21 percent of all Americans now have passports and
are traveling more, the number going overseas in the past 20 years—not
just to neighboring Canada and Mexico—has grown at a slower rate than
the number of overseas visitors to America or the growth in international
tourism in general. And indeed, during the late 1980s and early 1990s, the
number of Americans even applying for a passport declined in several
years.

American media coverage of foreign affairs has also been diminishing.   6
For example, according to a 2004 Columbia University survey, the presence of foreign news stories in American newspapers has been dropping

since the late 1980s. In 1987, overseas news accounted for about 27 percent of front page stories in American newspapers—about the same as a
decade earlier. By 2003, foreign news accounted for just 21 percent of front
page stories, while coverage of domestic affairs more than doubled over the
same period. On television, both the number of American network news
bureaus overseas and the amount of air-time spent on foreign news fell by
half in the 1990s.

Why are Americans progressively tuning out the rest of the world? The   7
reason is twofold. But both confirm the cherished belief of most Americans: that their country is a "shining city on the hill." And the rest of the
world has relatively little to offer.

Consider first, that for the past 45 years, Americans have witnessed a   8
massive immigration boom. Since 1960, more than 20 million immigrants
have come to the United States—the greatest influx of newcomers in the last
hundred years, surpassing even the wave of immigrants that arrived in the
first three decades of the 20th century. Two-thirds of these newcomers—
more than 15 million—have come in just the past 25 years.

That they should come bears out the myth that America is a melting pot   9
of peoples. Indeed, the iconic images of the first Plymouth Rock Pilgrims and
the Ellis Island immigrants of the early 1900s are at the very center of American popular mythology. More recently, news footage of Mexican-Americans
rushing the fences on the southern borders shows that America attracts all
comers. And every single American—from the mid-western blue collar
worker to the pedigreed New England blueblood—knows their forebears
came from someplace else. Chances are they've met or know someone—the
Bangladeshi working at the 7 Eleven, the Chinese scientist on TV, the Somali
cab driver at the airport—who has come even more recently.

With the whole world apparently trying to get to America, the average   10
American can only ask: why look to the rest of the world? After all, why
would everyone try to come here if there was anything worthwhile over
there? It is telling that according to a 2002 National Geographic survey, 30
percent of Americans believed the population of America to be between 1
and 2 billion people. For most Americans, it must seem like everyone is
rushing the fences these days.

The second reason is that for much of the last two decades most (but   11
not all) Americans have seen their economic well-being grow relative to the
rest of the world. Through much of the 1990s, American consumer confidence and real disposable income have risen at their fastest levels since the
relatively golden age of U.S. economic growth of the 1960s. These have
been matched by perceptions of increased wealth from a stock market rally
that, with interruptions, lasted from the early 1980s until three years ago.

Why should that matter? Because since the days of ancient Rome, it is 12
an axiom of political science that economic well-being dulls the appetite of
citizens to participate in civil affairs. It is something that de Tocqueville observed more than a hundred years ago.

"There is, indeed, a most dangerous passage in the history of a demo- 13
cratic people," de Tocqueville observed. "When the taste for physical grat-
ifications among them has grown more rapidly than their education and
their experience of free institutions . . . the discharge of political duties appears to them to be a troublesome impediment which diverts them from
their occupations and business."

Long before 9/11, the Asian tsunami, SARS, the bird flu, and the rela- 14
tively weaker dollar, Americans were already growing less interested in the
rest of the world. Since then, they have found even more reasons to tune
out.

The implications, however, are disturbing. Because of America's pre- 15
eminent position in world affairs—and its role in "globalization," its foreign policy matters more than any other country on earth. But can America
shape a responsible foreign policy with such an uninformed electorate? The
world may be turning into a "global village," but the average American has
moved to the suburbs.

Thinking About the Essay

1. Why, according to Granitsas, are most Americans "tuning out the rest of
   the world"?

2. How does Granitsas connect perceptions about immigration to the United
   States to the isolationist attitude of the average American?

3. Where does the essay shift from factual support of a claim to the causal
   analysis and attribution of psychological motives?

4. Why does Granitsas quote Alexis de Tocqueville at length (paragraph 13)?
   Who was de Tocqueville, and what does quoting him add to the argument
   of the essay?

5. Where in the essay does the author provide answers immediately following
   the question he has posed? Are there rhetorical questions anywhere in the
   essay? Why are these questions left unanswered, and what function do
   they serve in the essay?

Responding in Writing

6. In a brief essay, critique the "axiom" that economic well-being dulls the appetite of citizens to participate in civil affairs. Can you think of exceptions
   to this rule?

7. Write down your response to the popular view that Americans have a "*tab-ula rasa* history." Why would non-Americans view American history in this way?

8. Make a list of the factual indicators Granitsas mentions in the essay as measures of the engagement of the American public. What are the diagnostic limitations of each indicator? Analyze these indicators in an essay.

Networking

9. Do you rank foreign affairs as the most important issue facing the United States? Poll members of your class and, in a class discussion, attempt to explain the majority opinion.

10. Compare the coverage of one foreign affairs issue over the course of a week in two online journals, one published in the United States and one published in a foreign country (the French *Le Monde,* for example, or the British *Guardian*).

An Obsession the World Doesn't Share

ROGER COHEN

Roger Cohen was born in London and attended Oxford University. He joined *The New York Times* in 1990 and was appointed international writer at large after serving as bureau chief in Berlin and as correspondent in Paris and Zagreb. As foreign correspondent for *The Wall Street Journal,* Cohen reported on issues in South America and established the newspaper's office in Rio de Janeiro. From 1979 to 1983, Cohen was based in London, Brussels, and Rome as foreign correspondent for Reuters. Cohen is the author of *Hearts Grown Brutal: Sagas of Sarajevo,* an account of the Balkan wars that he reported on in the early 1990s. In the following essay, published in the March 28, 2005, *New York Times,* Cohen looks at perceptions of the United States' war on terror in other parts of the world.

Before Reading

How important is it that the United States preserve a positive image in the world? Has the Bush administration's war on terror distracted attention from other domestic or foreign policy issues that you feel are more important? Justify your response.

The United States has a strategic problem: Its war on terror, unlike its   1
long fight against Communism, is not universally perceived as the piv-
otal global struggle of the age.

Rather, it is often portrayed abroad as a distraction from more critical   2
issues: It's seen as America's attempt to cultivate fear and impose an aggressive culture on a world still taken with the notion that the Cold War's
end has opened unprecedented possibilities for dialogue and peace.

In Brazil, a country plagued by problems of poverty and development,   3
the policies of Al Qaeda arouse far less interest than those of the International Monetary Fund, which provides struggling countries with vital economic assistance, but usually forces them to undertake painful economic
reforms as well. The violence Brazilians are debating is not that of Islamic
holy warriors but of drug barons and their private militias occupying the
favelas, or slums, of Rio de Janeiro and São Paulo.

In South Africa, the issues of the day are the country's 40 percent job-   4
less rate, crime, and disease, not to mention the poverty that grips the continent as a whole. Many of the 1.3 billion people in the world who live on
less than $1 a day are in Africa. Terrorism isn't the theme of the hour.

Not Like the Cold War

The Cold War and its countless battles around the globe divided Latin   5
America and Africa between countries that sided with the United States or
the Soviet Union. But the war on terror has neither divided nor engaged
these continents in the same way. That, on balance, is a good thing: The
American-Soviet struggle took a huge toll on societies from Argentina to
Angola that still bear the scars.

What is less good, from the American perspective, is that Latin Amer-   6
ica and Africa are more or less united in a critical view of an American
power routinely described as hegemonic, or geared toward dominance over
other countries, and intent on using the Sept. 11, 2001, attacks to impose
what Candido Mendes, a Brazilian political analyst, calls "a civilization of
fear."

Mendes, who has written several books about Brazil's left-leaning Pres-   7
ident, Luiz Inácio Lula da Silva, says: "The exploitation of fear is a highly
developed and refined science, but Brazil is not convinced by this culture
that triumphed in the American election. What concerns us in Latin America is that, in the name of defending its security, the United States will es-
calate the wars it has begun."

The Cold War world adhered to a simple pattern: free societies, led by   8
the U.S., confronting Communism, with its headquarters in the Kremlin,

the walled complex of government buildings in Moscow that became a symbol of Soviet power.

Notwithstanding President Bush's frequent attempts to frame the cur- 9
rent conflict against Islamic terrorism as one of equal importance, it is now clear that most of the world has resisted making it a top priority.

In Asia, Economic Concerns

In wide swaths of the Southern Hemisphere, including Africa and Latin 10
America, the central preoccupation is economic development and trade.

In Asia, in addition to trying to recover from December's tsunami, the 11
focus is on China's spectacular rise, with India not far behind. The rest of Asia worries about losing business to these burgeoning giants and, especially in the case of China, fears that economic power will translate into military might.

In Europe, the bulk of political energy is still absorbed by the develop- 12
ment of the European Union—the multinational organization established in 1993 that now includes 25 independent states attempting to coordinate their military, economic, and political policies.

Because America's central preoccupation—the war on terror—is not 13
widely shared, it tends to isolate the United States, whose power is now so overwhelming as to invite dissent and outright opposition.

Bush seems aware of the problem he and the U.S. face abroad. While 14
visiting Canada last November, he described his second term as "an important opportunity to reach out to our friends," and thanked those Canadians who waved at him "with all five fingers."

Many Americans might be tempted to reply to a stubborn global com- 15
munity: Your memories are short, and if a bunch of crazed Islamic jihadists get their hands on nuclear weapons, you'll understand why we are fighting this war. They might care to use a quotation often attributed to *1984* author George Orwell: "People sleep peaceably in their beds at night only because rough men stand ready to do violence on their behalf."

But for now, the image of rough Americans ready to do violence is more 16
alienating than comforting.

"Anti-Americanism is generalized and growing," says Luiz Felipe Lam- 17
preia, a former Brazilian foreign minister.

"The whole Iraq situation has brought back memories of the big stick— 18
American power as used in Nicaragua or Chile during the Cold War," he says. "The problem is the perception that Bush uses immense power in an egotistical way."

The resulting animosity was evident during Bush's visit last November to 19
Santiago, Chile, where he encountered angry crowds who were not waving.

This situation has its contradictions: The Bush administration's policies toward Latin America have generally been practical and restrained.

Trade differences with Brazil, once acute over steel, have been quietly 20 patched up, although Brazil continues to push the fight against subsidies to farmers in rich countries, which make it harder for countries like Brazil to compete. Presidents Bush and da Silva get along well, two straight-talking guys who like to brush past details, including the fact that they come from opposing political camps. In theory, this could be a time marked more by harmony than hostility.

Billions to Fight Aids

A similar situation prevails in South Africa. The United States is pouring 21 more money into tackling the AIDS epidemic than any other country, having pledged $2.4 billion to the Global Fund to Fight AIDS, Tuberculosis, and Malaria—the organization central to the UN's fight against AIDS. Bush, who has made this fight a priority of his administration, also launched the $15 billion President's Emergency Fund for AIDS relief in 2003.

Personal relations between Bush and Thabo Mbeki, the President of 22 South Africa, are good. The African Growth and Opportunity Act, strongly supported by Bush, has provided important new trade openings by removing tariffs in several sectors, including automobiles.

Yet President Bush is routinely dismissed in the South African media as 23 the Texas Twit and gets no credit for any of the U.S. policies that are helping the country of Africa as a whole. Jendayi E. Frazer, the American ambassador to South Africa, says that government-to-government relations are excellent, but that the prevailing atmosphere means that "people who support the United States cannot come out and say it."

Here lies part of the price of the war on terror, particularly the war in 24 Iraq, for the United States and Bush: The good done quietly on other fronts gains scant recognition because war against a constant terrorist threat is seen to be the overriding message from the administration.

If Secretary of State Condoleezza Rice is to change this negative im- 25 pression, she may have to concede that the war on terror is not, like the Cold War, a label for an era.

It describes the focus of America—a new principle and project guiding 26 national policy—but it describes no more than that, because other countries have other agendas. What these countries want, above all, is to sense that the Bush administration, in its second term, hears them.

Thinking About the Essay

1. What is the analogy at the center of the essay? In what sense does Cohen endorse the analogy, and in what sense does he reject it?

2. According to Cohen, what are the analogous sources of "terror" in African and Latin American nations? Is it possible to characterize some of these forces as organized *agents* of terror like Al Qaeda?

3. What evidence does Cohen provide to support the claim that Latin America and Africa are "more or less united in a critical view of an American power" (paragraph 6)?

4. Why does the opening paragraph refer to the problem as a *strategic* problem?

5. Where in the essay does Cohen present a particular point of view by assuming a voice that is not his own? How effective is this method of characterization?

Responding in Writing

6. How does a label for an era (like "the cold war" or the "war on terror") reflect and/or define the era to which it is meant to apply? Choose one past era that is often referred to as "The Age of. . . ." In a brief essay, defend or critique the adequacy of this label. Do you think it reflects the general interests and concerns of people who lived at the time?

7. Write a presidential speech addressed to a contemporary Latin American audience in which you attempt to persuade your listeners of the central importance of the global war on terror.

8. In a brief essay, respond to the quotation attributed to George Orwell (paragraph 15). Do you agree with this statement? Why or why not?

Networking

9. In groups of four or five, agree on one national issue (foreign or domestic) that you feel is more important or in more urgent need of attention than the war on terror. Sketch an argument for this position and present it to the class.

10. Go online and locate the texts of two speeches given by President George W. Bush since September 11, 2001—an early speech and a more recent one, both addressed (like a State of the Union or Inaugural speech) to a wider global audience. How is the war on terror addressed differently on each occasion?

Fashionable Anti-Americanism

DOMINIC HILTON

A self-described satirist, Dominic Hilton is a commissioning editor and regular columnist for openDemocracy.net, which is where the following selection first appeared in January of 2005. In the column, Hilton explores some of the causes of anti-American sentiment at home and abroad and argues that "most of the time, it's not America's fault the world so condemns it."

Before Reading

Do you associate certain attitudes toward the United States with specific regions or with "types" of Americans? What would be your definition of "anti-American" criticism?

The United States of America is on a *hiding to nothing*.   1

In the conspiratorial alleys of the "Arab Street," Uncle Sam is flogged   2
like a habitual adulterer. In the bars and cafés of Europe, Yankee Doodle is lashed like a mutinous sailor. Even in the privacy of his own backyard, Brother Jonathan is grilled like a jumbo dog.

Ritual condemnation of the USA has been *la tendance du jour* since the   3
Mayflower hauled anchor at Plymouth in 1620. But mankind has advanced some over the past four centuries: nowadays, taking pot-shots at the United States is a booming multi-billion dollar industry, and one my bank manager is keen I invest in.

Regrettably, however, I can't indulge in the unceasing chorus of Yank-   4
bashing. My financial balance suffers for it, but I'm what's known in intellectual circles as an "Americaphile." I told this to an American pal who'd taken shore leave on a recent trip past Europe. "Oh, so you're the one," he grinned.

His story is important. A pleasant chap—polite, open-minded, affable   5
and adorably moral—he'd nevertheless found it hard to ignore the clear anti-American sentiment swilling around the old continent like the contents of an open sewer. In Paris, he explained, waiters had served him swiftly and attentively—a sure sign they'd identified him as an American pig and been keen to see the back of him.

I listened to his sad tale, then told him to quit worrying. While undeni-   6
ably profuse these days, I said, anti-Americanism is not as alarming as many Americans are making out. Much of it is not serious. In fact, I

qualified, most America-thumping is pathetically hypocritical, embarrassingly imbecilic, perilously ruinous and, worst of all, as derisorily fashionable as those ludicrous woolly boots everyone's presently sporting. "But the world hates me and my nation!" he cried in response. "Fahgedaboudit," I shrugged, in a hopeless attempt at a New York accent that nobody was buying.

Still, despite the best efforts of myself, most of Washington, and the en- 7
tire populace of the Midwestern states, the fact remains it's difficult for Americans not to notice how they're the subject of global derision. Most of us would find that kind of thing hard to handle. We'd start to worry about ourselves and feel painfully conscious of our shortcomings. We'd look in the mirror, analysing, criticising, assessing and judging. We might consider therapy, confessional. We'd be reborn and either guest on *Oprah* or volunteer on Karl Rove's staff.

Since 9/11, America has been aware of and concerned about the 8
amount of anti-Americanism inside and outside its borders. Some of this has been caricatured, some of it earnestly analysed. Interest goes right to the top. "Why do they hate us?" President George W Bush asked Congress two weeks after 9/11. His administration splashes out $68 million per an num on "Al-hurra," an Arabic satellite station which aims to tell "the truth about the values of the policies of the United States" to Middle Eastern couch potatoes. It was Bush who hired the legendary Madison Avenue advertising guru Charlotte Beers to market his nation to the Muslim world. She quit after eighteen months.

Some of this is understandable. It's also understandable that "Why do 9
they hate us?" has limits. In a recent *Newsweek* article, Fareed Zakaria expressed concern that with his lofty second inaugural address, Bush had ripened the opportunity for America's critics to charge his nation with hypocrisy for the cavernous gap between its high ideals and its not-so-pure actions. But when Bush declared "America's vital interests and our deepest beliefs are now one," he was also telling the world how (with some noteworthy exceptions) the charge of American hypocrisy might lose legitimacy. The speech combined time-honoured American idealism with a smidgen of "put up or shut up." Two birds with one stone. "Will you give us a break?" the president was saying. "We're doing our best here. Cut us some slack, why don't you?"

Quite right. It would be futile for America to respond in a soul-searching 10
manner to the trash talk of its detractors. Why? Because most of the time, it's not America's fault the world so condemns it. It's not that America does everything right. America is imperfect, thank God. Its commitment to (and achievement of) imperfection is arguably its greatest feat. For this, we should

love it. Criticism remains entirely valid. If America makes a bonehead move—something it does as well as most of us—we should jeer and blow raspberries. Though this is not what we do. The industry of anti-American sentiment is just that—an industry. It should not be mistaken for legitimate and considered concern. "I hate America" is the world's default position. Knocking America is a form of displacement. It helps non-Americans avoid focusing on their own big problems. In fact, strip it of its lacy hosiery and the world's relationship with America is disgustingly Freudian.

Threats and Fads

First, let's distinguish between different types of anti-Americanism. 11 Thomas Friedman put it well in a recent column: "for Europeans, anti-Americanism is a hobby. For too many in the Muslim world it has become a career." In other words, anti-Americanism that breeds terrorism and tyranny is a big, big problem. But anti-Americanism that falls into the category of "indulgent fad" is generally immaterial. Except this is not quite true, is it? Friedman missed something. For more and more Europeans, and more and more Americans, anti-Americanism is an ever more profitable career path. It is very material.

So let's rework this: anti-Americanism that breeds terrorism and 12 tyranny is a major problem for us all and one the United States of America must fully address; anti-Americanism that doesn't result in suicide missions is not America's problem, it's the problem of its moron perpetrators—though it benefits nobody good. Non-Americans that find comfort in blaming America for all the world's ills—poverty, war, environmental destruction, the death of high culture, their own pitiful inadequacies—suffer for such fatuous bunkum. Their own houses rot as they drone on at dinner parties and terrorist camps about American "crimes against humanity." The rhetoric of Osama bin Laden is curiously similar to that of Harold Pinter (though notably less profane). Pinter, I hazard a guess, is less dangerous.

They are all morons, but the difference is that America can and should 13 ignore the dinner guests. They pose no threat. Especially not an intellectual one. The philosophy of "damn you if you do, damn you if you don't" is not worthy of serious contemplation. Insularly isolationist or intensely imperial, America is castigated for both, often by the same people. This is what's technically known as a no-win situation. "The illogicality at base consists in reproaching the United States for some shortcoming, and then for its opposite," writes Jean-Francois Revel in his aptly-titled *Anti-Americanism*. "Here is a convincing sign that we are in the presence, not of rational analysis, but of obsession."

Many of those who say America does not live up to its own ideals and 14
rhetoric would surely be the first to protest if it did. If America invades and
"liberates" Iraq, they say, it should also invade and liberate North Korea,
Burma, China, Zimbabwe, etcetera. I'd love to see their reaction if America took up the challenge. Yes, America talks a good game—but this should
be celebrated, and, yes, held to account. As it stands, though, whether the
"indispensable nation," the "universal country," the "last, best hope," the
"shining city upon a hill," the "global policeman," the "lone superduper-
power," the "empire in denial" or Jefferson's "empire of liberty," the US
plays the traditional lead role of the world's whipping-boy. We might suppose this is inevitable. *C'est le prix du pouvoir* (as Jacques Chirac might
put it).

American Booty

America does not want to be charged with hypocrisy by hypocrites. By def- 15
inition, however, it always will be. In all its guises, anti-Americanism is an
infatuation and an excuse. Anti-Americanism is "the dog ate my homework" of international relations.

"Power is fascinating. . . . But being fascinating is also power," says 16
Timothy Garton Ash in his new book *Free World*. Fair point. But fascination quickly spills into fixation.

> "At least part of the Western left—or rather the Western far left—is
> now so anti-American, or so anti-Bush, that it actually prefers authori-
> tarian or totalitarian leaders to *any* government that would be friendly
> to the United States,"

writes Anne Applebaum in *The Washington Post*.

> "Many of the same people who would refuse to condemn a dictator
> who is anti-American cannot bring themselves to admire democrats
> who admire, or at least don't hate, the United States."

Applebaum is on to something. This goes beyond Saddam apologia. It's 17
getting into the realm of anti-democracy. To some, democratic movements
are only legitimate if also anti-American. Ukrainians in Independence
Square were pro-American, not pro-Castro. Must've been a CIA plot.

In a recent sweeping commentary for *Commentary* magazine entitled 18
"Americanism—and Its Enemies," David Gelernter suggested "Americanism" is a religion and that

> "anti-Americanism is closely associated with anti-Christianism *and* anti-
> Semitism. . . . America has *remained* an object of hatred within nations
> that have themselves gone over to American-style democracy; has been
> hated by people who had nothing whatsoever to fear from American
> power."

Actually, it's worse than that. America has *remained* an object of hatred   19
from those who directly gain from American generosity. Some of America's
most sour critics preach their gospels in America's palatial universities. A
highly desirable standard of living is endowed on those who make their living attacking America's highly desirable standard of living. Ditto its liberty.

"Since the end of the cold war, anti-Americanism has overtaken soccer   20
as the world's most popular sport," Tom Friedman writes in *Longitudes
and Attitudes*.

> "And there is this general assumption in intellectual circles that America
> is to be blamed first for whatever happens, and a given that American
> intellectuals will play along and accept this role as the world's punching
> bag. And when you refuse to do this in mixed company, it's as if you
> unleashed a huge fart at a cocktail party—people look at you funny and
> just start to back away."

American Cool

But it's not just the left-leaning intellectual class that's guilty of rank   21
hypocrisy in its attitude towards Uncle Sam. It'd be comforting to think so,
but you don't have to wear elbow pads on your corduroy jacket to participate in this orgy of anti-American infantilism. The kids are at it too.

As 2004 faded into history, the *Financial Times* ran a feature under the   22
headline "Tarnished image: is the world falling out of love with U.S.
brands?"

> "Poll after poll has shown that allegations of human rights abuses and
> the failure to find weapons of mass destruction in Iraq have tarnished
> the international reputation of the U.S.,"

the article reckoned, worrying aloud about a "subtle tarnishing of brands
in the minds of millions of ordinary consumers." Joseph Nye, of Harvard
and "soft power" fame, offered his wisdom:

> "U.S. brands have benefited from a sense that it is fashionable, chic and
> modern to be American. The other side of that coin is when U.S. poli-
> cies become unpopular, there is a cost."

A net incline in Abu Ghraib scandals = A net decline in Pepsi sales? Im-   23
possible to measure, even with the advent of Mecca Cola. Besides, "It is
more a subject of debate between intellectuals than something that is ham-
pering the development of these brands with consumers," says Maurice
Levy, chief executive of the marketing group Publicis. But subheads like
"Cool would come from Tokyo rather than LA" are not entirely bullshit.
Cool is important. The most popular is never the coolest. America has become like a manufactured pop band. Kids go for thrash metal.

Though hang on, where did thrash metal originate? America's diversity, 24
its sheer vastness, makes life hard for its opponents. The land of Disney is
the land of *Easy Rider*. The home of televangelists is the home of hip-hop.
America *is* "cool"—even in its failings. The bad trip that was the Vietnam
war was replayed in a succession of überhip purple haze movies like *Apoc-
alypse Now!, The Deerhunter, Rambo, Platoon, Full Metal Jacket, Born on
the Fourth of July*, and TV shows like *Tour of Duty* with its Rolling Stones
soundtrack.

My generation grew up with these movies, the Sheen-Duvall-Hopper- 25
Brando-DeNiro-Walken-Stallone-Sheen-Defoe-Berenger-Cruise out-of-control
American soldier with a bandanna, an ironic peace tattoo on their helmet—
wild-eyed boys in the fug of drugs. We pretended these were *negative* images
of an out-of-control America. Nonsense. To my generation, these movies
were an updated confirmation of American cool. How cool to burn villages,
to collect skulls, to play Russian roulette, to rape and pillage your way across
the jungle to the psychedelic strains of Jim Morrison, then return home and
be messed-up about what you done out in 'Nam—or what, ahem, you were
made to do. These movies were so very, very *American*.

In essence, what we are witnessing is a pseudo-rejection of the USA. All 26
this "I hate America as much as you hate America!" baloney is a cultural
phenomenon, little to do with any meaningful or cultivated sense of "politics." Across Europe, gigantic music stores stuffed to the gunwales with
American pop, rock and urban do a sideline in hipster books. Virtually without exception these dazzling paperback digests are rabidly anti-American
(*Why Do We Hate America?*), anti-Bush/anti-American (*The Bush-Haters'
Handbook*), anti-globalisation/anti-American (*American Dream/Global
Nightmare*), anti-American culture/anti-American (*Fat Land: How Ameri-
cans Became the Fattest People in the World*).

For the most part adorned with colourful depictions of the universally 27
attractive symbols of Americana, the covers tell a story of their own: as
beacon or pariah, America sells. Here lies the reading choice of today's
youth, of societies most cool, and these cash-in volumes are horribly high
in the sales charts. It's not just the dreadlocked, nose-ringed student-
acolytes who pack the theatres to hear the nasal drone of the world's Noam
Chomskys, it's the kids who lap up American culture, obese and spotty
from a diet of McDonald's and Coca-Cola, baggily clad in Nike, Gap and
Levi's, plugged into their iPods digitally replete with Eminem or 50 Cent.
These are the kids whose street cred relies on their miserable detestation of
the shallow, candied, military behemoth that is the USA.

Unlike back in '68, "I hate America" is now "organised." Not or- 28
ganised in the leftist sense, I mean organised in the Ben and Jerry's sense.

Attractively-packaged, nice tasting, creamy, chocolaty, cookie-dough anti-Americanism that clogs the arteries and numbs the brain.

Fashion trumps sophistication. America's insignia are ubiquitous— 29 from Ralph Lauren jumpers to Primal Scream album covers to the end of a flaming match in the Arab Street, looking modish even when being burned. I've seen kids on TV in Osama bin Laden t-shirts and New York Yankees' baseball caps (Hello? You don't see the irony?). I've watched young British men in the nondescript north-of-London town of Luton clad in "New York" sweatshirts holding up banners of the extremist Islamic group al-Muhajiroun.

Our rebels are American. So are our anti-Americans. Michael Moore is 30 one of America's biggest exports. America makes anti-Americanism profitable for America. What a country!

Ideals and Piggybacks

Now, even I admit there's something a little fishy at times about America's 31 claim to moral exceptionality. When Gelenter writes about Americans being "positive that their nation is superior to all others—*morally* superior, closer to God," I can only think of Hegel's conviction that 1830s Prussia was the perfect and ultimate achievement of mankind, and how this applesauce led to Marxism.

Nevertheless, there's something too easy about knocking the believer. 32 America is going to say and think big things about itself. Look at its history, and then understand that the United States is a nation, and acts as such—in its own interests and with a powerful identity. In his response to Bush's second inaugural, the American commentator David Brooks identified "this weird intermingling of high ideals with gross materialism" which so defines his country. In the spirit of Washington and Kennedy, the president waxed lyrical on mankind's highest ideals. Later that evening, "drunken, loud and privileged twentysomethings" carried each other piggyback down K Street.

"The people who detest America take a look at this odd conjunction and 33 assume the materialistic America is the real America; the ideals are a sham," Brooks wrote. "The real America, they insist, is the money-grubbing, resource-wasting, TV-drenched, unreflective bimbo of the earth. The high-toned language, the anti-Americans say, is just a cover for the quest for oil, or the desire for riches, dominion and war. But of course they've got it exactly backward. It's the ideals that are real."

The ideals *are* real. Not because they are America's, but because they 34 are ideals and they are the right ideals. Those who don't revel in extremism, dictatorship and political stagnation have to decide whose camp they want to be in. Does Europe really feel more allied to communist China than conservative America? The European Union and China share "a convergence of views about the United States, its foreign policy and its global behaviour," says David Shambaugh of George Washington University. This should send a shudder down the spine of democrats. Who truly wants to believe the late Susan Sontag and her assertion that America is "a doomed country . . . founded on a genocide"? Get over yourself. I'm sticking with my stateside compadre John Hulsman, who believes

> "there is little doubt we have all benefited from the 'naïve' optimism that has enabled America to do amazing things not just for itself, but also for all mankind."

Into the Mirror

Anti-Americanism, when not perpetrated by *true* haters, is often a stale 35 mockery of America, born of our own fascination. This is our (the world's) problem, not America's. Jean-Francois Revel suggests that we "project our faults onto America so as to absolve ourselves." As he says of his native France, and Barry Rubin and Judith Colp Rubin say of the last four hundred years, some of this "Hating America" is born of fear, some of plain old weakness, some of outright jealousy. The left, in particular, is green with envy. 20th-century Communism only served to augment belief in the American Dream. "The success of America was thus a devastating blow to the Left," writes Michael Ledeen. "It wasn't supposed to happen. And American success was particularly galling because it came at the expense of Europe itself, and of the embodiment of the Left's most utopian dream: the Soviet Union."

But some leftists are getting tired of it. The narrative of left-wing anti- 36 Americanism "has ceased to be critical, but become predestinarian," says John Lloyd. Such stasis serves nobody except the tyrants, the terrorists, and the unoriginal, knee-jerk loudmouths who cash in on the fashionability of the flaming Spangled Banner (categorised by Barry Rubin as "self-interest").

Even Americans are caught up in this silly love-hate relationship. "How 37 can you have patience for people who claim they love America but clearly can't stand Americans?," Annette Bening's flag-burning power-woman asks the eponymous Michael Douglas in Aaron Sorkin and Rob Reiner's eco-friendly, anti-gun liberal dream *The American President*. Same question, the other way round, from rightwing firebrand Ann Coulter: a recent explosion was hilariously titled "Liberals love America like O.J. loved Nicole."

This is all a little daft. After the fascistic and communistic horrors of 38 the 20th century, we are bloody lucky to live in a world led by the United States in which the central geopolitical questions are "Should we spread liberty and democracy? And if so, how far?" We should ride our luck a little, before we run it out. "[America's] interaction with the rest of the world must be a conversation, not a monologue," says the new U.S. secretary of state, Condoleezza Rice. That goes both ways. In Asia, "consumers are increasingly indifferent to U.S. brands and are paying great attention to Asian trends and products," reports the *Financial Times*. The rest of the world should swallow a spoonful of this medicine. When President Bush declares how, "In a world moving towards liberty, we are determined to show the meaning and promise of liberty," we should let him get on with it, and try dusting off our own promises.

America is not the panacea, nor is it the devil. Our problems are gen-   39
erally *our* problems. The world would do well to be a little more like America, a tad more insular, self-involved.

Non-Americans love to quote John Kennedy's famous call, "And so, my   40
fellow Americans, ask not what your country can do for you; ask what you can do for your country." Why? It is the second part of Kennedy's couplet we should heed and let roll off our tongues: "My fellow citizens of the world, ask not what America will do for you, but what together we can do for the freedom of man." This still stands. And freedom, like charity, discipline and intelligence, begins at home.

Thinking About the Essay

1. What is your reaction to the abrasive irony of the opening paragraph? Does the paragraph establish a tone that remains consistent throughout the essay? Are you offended by the author's poking fun at Islamic laws and customs? Why or why not?

2. Highlight instances of caricature, hyperbole, and synechdoche (using a part or individual for a whole or class) in the essay. How do these strategies function to establish tone? Look up some definitions of *satire*. Does this essay qualify as satire, or is it best described by another term? Explain your response.

3. What function do the quotations serve in this essay? Does Hilton quote other writers in order to critique their ideas, as corroboration for his own views, or as a way of challenging and complicating the argument of the essay?

4. In the final paragraphs of the essay, Hilton seems to defend the current Bush administration's interventionist policies at the same time he argues for an isolationist attitude. How do these two aspects of the argument complement or contradict each other?

5. Paraphrase the psychological explanation for anti-American feelings Hilton offers in the final section of the essay. Where does this appear as a theme earlier in the essay?

Responding in Writing

6. In a brief essay, explain what it means for an attitude to become a commodity. Are there any popular attitudes that you would characterize in terms of a self-sustaining "industry"? What makes them so?

7. Use Hilton's statement in the fifth section of the essay (his response to David Brooks) to compose an argumentative essay: "The ideals *are* real. Not because they are America's, but because they are ideals and they are the right ideals." What do you consider to be genuinely American ideals? Why are they "right"? Do you feel comfortable speaking of them as universal ideals?

8. In a comparative essay, analyze what you see as important differences between anti-American attitudes and anti-Bush attitudes. Are there any analogies to be made with the anti-globalization/anti-American distinction?

Networking

9. In groups of three or four, discuss one example of an anti-American attitude mentioned in the essay and explain to the class why it should or should not be considered a species of anti-Americanism.

10. This article was published in an online journal and generated a considerable amount of online discussion. Find a blog or discussion group in which the article is referenced and post a response of your own.

America's New Empire for Liberty

PAUL JOHNSON | Paul Johnson, a British historian and author, is also known as a conservative spokesperson and a widely read journalist who appears frequently in *The New York Times, The Wall Street Journal, The Spectator,* and *The Daily Telegraph.* In the early 1980s, he served as speechwriter and adviser to British Prime Minister Margaret Thatcher. Johnson was educated at Magdalen College, Oxford, and first came to prominence in the 1950s as a writer for the *New Statesman* (which he would later edit). Johnson is currently a distinguished visiting fellow at the Hoover Institution. In the following selection, published in *The Hoover Digest* of July 16, 2003, Johnson defines and defends his concept of "defensive imperialism" and envisions a future role for the United States as an imperial power.

Before Reading

Can you think of any terms ("final solution," for example) so loaded with meaning that they resist any possible attempt at redefinition?

For America, September 11 was a new Great Awakening. It realized, for the first time, that it was itself a globalized entity. It no longer had frontiers. Its boundaries were the world, for from whatever part of the world harbored its enemies, it could be attacked and, if such enemies possessed weapons of mass destruction, mortally attacked. For this reason America was obliged to construct a new strategic doctrine, replacing totally that of National Security Council Paper 68 of 1949, which laid down the doctrine of containment. In a globalized world the United States now has to anticipate its enemies, search out and destroy their bases, and disarm states likely to aid them. I call this "defensive imperialism." It is a novel kind but embraces elements of all the old. NSC-68 of 1949, significantly, specifically repudiates imperialism. Its replacement will necessarily embrace it in its new form. There are compelling reasons why the United States is uniquely endowed to exercise this kind of global authority. 1

First, America has the language of the twenty-first century. English is already the premier world language in many respects, and this century will see its rapid extension and consolidation. As first the Greeks, then the Romans, discovered, possession of a common language is the first vital and energizing step toward embracing common norms of law, behavior, and culture. A more secure world will be legislated for, policed, and adjudicated in English. Second, America has, and will continue to acquire, the pioneering technology of the twenty-first century, its lead being widened by its success in providing a clear climate of freedom in which inventors and entrepreneurs of all kinds can operate. 2

In the nineteenth century, the great age of the formal empires, the imperialist thrust was backed by the Industrial Revolution, producing manufactured goods much cheaper and in far greater quantity than ever before. In 1800 it was Asia that produced the majority (57 percent) of world manufactured output, the West only 29 percent; by 1900 the West was producing 86 percent, Asia only 10 percent. Today, America's production of world wealth, both absolutely and relatively, is accelerating. In the last quarter of the twentieth century, it added $5 trillion to its annual GDP. By 2050 the U.S. share of global output will constitute more than a quarter of the world total and will be as much as three times as big, for instance, as that of the European Union. 3

Traditionally, successful imperialism has reflected high birthrates and the ability to export large surplus populations. The climax of European 4 imperialism in the nineteenth century coincided with the European population explosion. America has never exported people overseas. On the contrary, its growing power and wealth have reflected its ability to attract and absorb immigrants. That continues. America now accepts more immigrants than the rest of the world put together. The amazing ability of groups such as the Cubans, the Hong Kong Chinese, the Vietnamese, and other new arrivals to grow roots and create wealth is a key part of America's continuing success story. But America also has a high birthrate. Its population is now coming up to the 300 million mark. By 2050 it will be more than 400 million. By contrast, Europe's population will shrink and the percentage of working age will fall rapidly. The ability of America to sustain a global role is demonstrated by the demographic figures, especially those on the working population. By 2050, the Japanese working population will have shrunk by 38 percent; that of Russia, Ukraine, and Belarus, by 46 percent; and the 15 EU nations, by various totals—8 percent in France, 41 percent in Italy, 35 percent in Spain, 21 percent in Germany. In the EU countries as a whole—both members and candidate members— only Great Britain and Ireland will have increased their working population by 2050. All the rest (except Luxembourg) will decline by an average of 19 percent in existing members, 38 percent in the rest.

Meanwhile America's working population will have increased by more 5 than 54 million (31 percent), an increase greater than the present working population of Germany. This does not take into account either working hours or productivity, both of which hugely increase the productive power of America over Europe.

Population forecasts are notoriously unreliable, and some predictions 6 of what is likely to happen in Europe (and Japan) in this century are so alarming as to be discounted. But clearly there is a marked and growing contrast between old Europe and young America. And the combination of accelerating technology and an expanding workforce will be irresistible in terms of economic and military power. America is able to shoulder its burdens with courage and determination. But it is not alone. Britain, with much smaller resources but with long and varied experience, has a resolve equal to America's to do its fair share. When I was a boy in the 1930s, a quarter of the world on the map was colored red—that is, part of the British Empire and Commonwealth of Nations. It was a liberal empire and a democratic commonwealth, and its aim, as with America in the Philippines, was to prepare its components for self-government. There have been some outstanding successes: Canada, Newfoundland, New Zealand, Australia, Singapore, Hong Kong, and, most of all, India; with a billion inhabitants it has become the world's largest democracy. There have been tragic failures too, notably in Africa. But we have learned from the failures too. The knowledge we gained is at America's disposal, particularly in the training of military and civilian administrators who must take on the kind of work now being done in Iraq and Afghanistan. One idea I would like to see explored—with all deliberate speed—is the creation of an Anglo-American staff college for training men and women, both from the armed forces and from government, in the skills to rescue failed or fragile nations and to take former tyrannies and dictatorships into the magic circle of justice and democracy. We have a vast project ahead of us, and we need to be educated for it.

In this project, what part is there for continental Europe? The answer   7
is as large a one as the Europeans wish to play, are capable of playing, and are anxious to play in good faith. But I am bound to say recent events have not shown Europeans in a good light. It will be some time before the expanded European Union shows whether it is viable, economically and politically, and whether it can generate the resources and display the will to make a worthwhile contribution in military or any other terms. My guess is that the United States of Europe, a ramshackle structure already, is heading for disaster: economic bankruptcy and political implosion. Looking at it from Britain's viewpoint, we should keep well clear of the mess. In emotional and cerebral terms, the English Channel is wider than the Atlantic, and I would prefer to see the expansion of the North Atlantic free trade area rather than that of a bureaucratic, antidemocratic, and illiberal Europe.

The Bush administration is only beginning to grasp the implications of   8
the course on which it has embarked. It still, albeit with growing difficulty, speaks the language of anti-imperialism. But that is the jargon of the twentieth century or at least its second half. Who says it will be the prevailing discourse of the twenty-first? As it happens, imperialism became a derogatory term in America only during the Civil War, when the South accused the North of behaving like a European empire. It then became politically correct to speak only of "American exceptionalism." Internationally *imperialism* became a dirty word early in the twentieth century, and it was the Communists who were chiefly responsible for turning it into a hate word. And it is worth recalling too that up to 1860 empire was not a term of abuse in the United States. George Washington himself spoke of "the rising American Empire." Thomas Jefferson, aware of the dilemma, claimed that America was "an empire for liberty." That is what America is becoming again, in fact if not in name. America's search for security against terrorism and rogue states goes hand in hand with liberating their oppressed

peoples. From the Evil Empire to an Empire for Liberty is a giant step, a contrast as great as the appalling images of the wasted twentieth century and the brightening dawn of the twenty-first. But America has the musculature and the will to take giant steps, as it has shown in the past.

Another factor has received too little attention. It may be that humanity is on the eve of an entirely new age of exploration and settlement—in space. In 1450 no one in old Europe imagined that the discovery and colonization of the New World was just over the historical horizon. Yet the technology of oceanic ships and navigation was already in place and within 50 years in use, and an entire new hemisphere was brought into our grasp. No forethought had been given to who might own it. Today imperialism is a technical possibility and may become a reality much sooner than we think. And when it happens it will develop as with the age of Columbus, with dramatic speed, the adventurous moving much faster than the international lawyers and statesmen. We ought to be thinking about it now. One thing is certain. The United States will be in the forefront of this new imperialism. Indeed it has already taken the first steps by imposing a unilateral ban on rival weapons systems in space. The role of first space imperialist is likely to be imposed on America simply by its wealth, power, and technology.   9

———

One thing is clear: America is unlikely to cease to be an empire in the fundamental sense. It will not share its sovereignty with anyone. It will continue to promote international efforts of proven worth, such as the General Agreement on Tariffs and Trade, and to support military alliances such as NATO where appropriate. But it will not allow the United Nations or any other organization to infringe on its natural right to defend itself as it sees fit. The new globalization of security will proceed with the United Nations if possible, without it if necessary. The empire for liberty is the dynamic of change.   10

Thinking About the Essay

1. What is the significance of Johnson's allusion, in the opening paragraph, to a new "Great Awakening"? Where do you find related metaphors in the essay?

2. According to Johnson, what distinguishes America as a unique imperialist power?

3. How does Johnson employ illustration in this essay? Are the illustrations essential to his argument? Do they seem arbitrarily chosen? Why or why not?

4. Why does Johnson switch abruptly to a digression on the exploration and settlement of space (paragraph 9)? Does this paragraph fit logically within the larger argument of the essay?

5. How would you describe the tone of the final paragraph? Why does Johnson wait until the end of the essay to address the future role of the United Nations?

Responding in Writing

6. Johnson coins the term "defensive imperialism" in his opening paragraph. Write a two- or three-sentence definition that might serve as a dictionary entry.

7. In paragraph 6, Johnson notes that some imperialist exploits of the past have resulted in "tragic failures." In an essay, speculate on some unintended consequences that may arise (or have arisen) from imperialist projects of the kind Johnson envisions.

8. The essay by Roger Cohen included in this chapter discusses the cold war as a period of imperialist expansion. In an essay of your own, consider how the example of cold war *geopolitical* imperialism changes the connotations of a term that Johnson seems to associate more with the example of the British Commonwealth. What is the difference between imperialism and colonialism?

Networking

9. In groups of three or four, write down a cluster of connotations you associate with the term *imperialism*. Share your findings with the class.

10. Go online and look up the text of National Security Council Paper 68 of 1949. What "twentieth-century" concept of imperialism is contained in the language of its repudiation?

In Search of Pro-Americanism

ANNE APPLEBAUM

Anne Applebaum is a columnist and member of the editorial board of *The Washington Post*. In 1988, she became the Warsaw correspondent for *The Economist* and wrote about the collapse of communism across Central and Eastern Europe. Applebaum moved to London in 1992, where she wrote a weekly column on British politics and foreign affairs for *The Daily Telegraph* and reported on the 1997 British election campaign as political editor for the *Evening Standard*. During this period, she also wrote the "Foreigners" column in *Slate* magazine. Applebaum's most recent book, *Gulag: A History*, won the 2004 Pulitzer Prize for Nonfiction and has been translated into more than two dozen languages. In the following selection, which appeared in the July/August, 2005 issue of *Foreign Policy* magazine, Applebaum seeks to understand the psychology of pro-American sentiment in its various manifestations throughout the world.

Before Reading

Did you personally witness any spontaneous gestures of pro-American sympathy by foreigners immediately following September 11, 2001? Do you think those gestures stemmed from innate pro-American feelings, or did they arise only on that occasion?

I was in London on the afternoon of Sept. 11, 2001, a day when strangers 1 in shops, hearing my American accent, offered their cell phones in case I wanted to call home. That evening, parties were cancelled. The next day, political events were called off. An American friend who lives in London received a condolence card from his neighbors, whom he'd never met—and he was not alone. Overwhelmingly, the first British reaction to the terrorist attacks on Washington and New York was deeply sympathetic, and profoundly pro-American.

But so were the reactions of many others, across Europe and around the 2 world. Several days after September 11, I left London and returned to Poland, where I was then living. That evening I attended a concert in a provincial city. In the foyer of the symphony hall, someone had put up a large American flag and surrounded it with candles. At the start of the concert, the conductor announced that there would be a change: Instead of the planned program, the orchestra would play only Mozart's *Requiem*, in honor of the 9/11 victims. These decisions were completely spontaneous and utterly apolitical: No one had reason to think that there would be even a single American in the audience. Within a few days, of course, a second reaction had set in. In London, a television studio audience attacked the former American ambassador on the air, accusing the United States of provoking international hatred and therefore bearing responsibility for the attacks. *The New Statesman*, an influential British left-wing magazine, ran a cover story, saying more or less the same thing. "American bond traders, you may say, are as innocent and undeserving of terror as Vietnamese or Iraqi peasants," the editors wrote. "Well, yes and no. . . . If America seems a greedy and overweening power, that is partly because its people have willed it. They preferred George Bush to both Al Gore and Ralph Nader." Elsewhere in Europe, then French Prime Minister Lionel Jospin had already urged the United States to be "reasonable in its response," and German Chancellor Gerhard Schröder took it upon himself to remind the United States that "we are not at war."

Since then, that initial trickle of post-9/11 anti-Americanism has grown   3
to a flood. A Pew Research Center poll released in March 2004, showed that 62 percent of French, 59 percent of Germans, and 34 percent of Britons had a "very" or "somewhat" unfavorable opinion of the United States. In January 2005, a poll published by the BBC showed that 54 percent of French, 64 percent of Germans, and 50 percent of Britons consider the United States a "negative influence" in the world. These numbers and others like them have spawned a mini-industry. Front-page news stories, television documentaries, and entire books have been devoted to the phenomenon of anti-Americanism, and there is no sign that interest is flagging. Earlier this year, *Newsweek International* once again put the subject on its cover, under the headline "America Leads . . . But Is Anyone Following?"

Given all of the attention that has been lavished upon anti-Americanism   4
in the past four years, however, it is surprising how little analysis has been applied to that first, spontaneous pro-American reaction to 9/11, and to pro-Americanism in general. After all, the population of some countries continues to show approval of the United States, of the American president, and of U.S. foreign policy, even now. Even the most damning evidence, such as the BBC poll quoted above, also reveals that some percentage of the population of even the most anti-American countries in Europe and Latin America remains pro-American. Some 38 percent of the French, 27 percent of Germans, 40 percent of Chinese, and 42 percent of Brazilians remain convinced that the United States exerts a "positive influence on the world." Who are they?

America's Best Behavior

Anecdotally, it isn't hard to come up with examples of famous pro-Americans, even on the generally anti-American continents of Europe and Latin America. There are political reformers such as Vaclav Havel, who has spoken of how the U.S. Declaration of Independence inspired his own country's founding fathers. There are economic reformers such as José Piñera, the man who created the Chilean pension system, who admire American economic liberty. There are thinkers, such as the Iraqi intellectual Kanan Makiya, who openly identify the United States with the spread of political freedom. At a recent event in his honor in Washington, Makiya publicly thanked the Americans who had helped his country defeat Saddam Hussein. (He received applause, which was made notably warmer by the palpable sense of relief: At least someone over there likes us.) All of these are people with very clear, liberal, democratic philosophies, people who either identify part of their ideology as somehow "American," or who are grateful for American support at some point in their countries' history.

There are also countries that contain not only individuals but whole groups of people with similar ideological or nostalgic attachments to the United States. I am thinking here of British Thatcherites—from whom Prime Minister Tony Blair is in some sense descended—and of former associates of the Polish Solidarity movement. Although Lady Thatcher (who was herself stridently pro-American) is no longer in office, her political heirs, and those who associate her with positive economic and political changes in Britain, are still likely to think well of the United States. Their influence is reflected in the fact that the British, on the whole, are more likely to think positively of the United States than other Europeans. Polish anticommunists, who still remember the support that President Ronald Reagan gave their movement in the 1980s, have the same impact in their country, which remains more pro-American than even the rest of Central Europe.

In some countries, even larger chunks of the population have such associations. In the Philippines, for example, the BBC poll shows that 88 percent of the population has a "mainly positive" view of the United States, an unusually high number anywhere. In India, that number is 54 percent, and in South Africa, it's 56 percent, particularly high numbers for the developing world. In the case of the first two countries, geopolitics could be part of the explanation: India and the Philippines are both fighting Islamist terrorist insurgencies, and they see the United States as an ally in their struggles. (Perhaps for this reason, both of these countries are also among the few who perceived the reelection of U.S. President George W. Bush as "mainly positive" for the world as well.) But it is also true that all three of these countries have experienced, in the last 20 years, political or economic change that has made them richer, freer, or both. And in all three cases, it's clear that people would have reasons to associate new prosperity and new freedom with the actions of the United States.

These associations are not just vague, general sentiments either. New 8 polling data from the international polling firm GlobeScan and the Program on International Policy Attitudes at the University of Maryland break down pro- and anti-American sentiments by age, income, and gender. Looking closely at notably pro-American countries, it emerges that this pro-Americanism can sometimes be extraordinarily concrete. It turns out, for example, that in Poland, which is generally pro-American, people between the ages of 30 and 44 years old are even more likely to support America than their compatriots. In that age group, 58.5 percent say they feel the United States has a "mainly positive" influence in the world. But perhaps that is not surprising: This is the group whose lives would have been most directly affected by the experience of the Solidarity movement and martial law—events that occurred when they were in their teens and 20s—and they would have the clearest memories of American support for the Polish underground movement.

Younger Poles, by contrast, show significantly less support: In the 9 15–29-year-old group, only 45.3 percent say they feel the United States has a "mainly positive" influence in the world—a drop of more than 13 percent. But perhaps that is not surprising either. This generation has only narrow memories of communism, and no recollection of Reagan's support for Solidarity. The United States, to them, is best known as a country for which it is difficult to get visas—and younger Poles have a very high refusal rate. Now that Poland is a member of the European Union, by contrast, they have greater opportunities to travel and study in Europe, where they no longer need visas at all. In their growing skepticism of the United States, young Poles may also be starting to follow the more general European pattern.

Looking at age patterns in other generally anti-American countries can 10 be equally revealing. In Canada, Britain, Italy, and Australia, for example, all countries with generally high or very high anti-American sentiments, people older than 60 have relatively much more positive feelings about the United States than their children and grandchildren. When people older than 60 are surveyed, 63.5 percent of Britons, 59.6 percent of Italians, 50.2 percent of Australians, and 46.8 percent of Canadians feel that the United States is a "mainly positive" influence on the world. For those between the ages of 15 and 29, the numbers are far lower: 31.9 percent (Britain), 37.4 percent (Italy), 27 percent (Australia), and 19.9 percent (Canada). Again, that isn't surprising: All of these countries had positive experiences of American cooperation during or after the Second World War. The British of that generation have direct memories, or share their parents' memories, of Winston Churchill's meetings with Franklin Roosevelt; the Canadians and Australians fought alongside American G.I.s; and many Italians remember that those same G.I.s evicted the Nazis from their country, too.

These differences in age groups are significant, not only in themselves, 11 but because they carry a basic but easily forgotten lesson for American foreign policymakers: At least some of the time, U.S. foreign policy has a direct impact on foreigners' perceptions of the United States. That may sound like a rather obvious principle, but in recent years it has frequently been questioned. Because anti-Americanism is so often described as if it were mere fashion, or some sort of unavoidable, contagious virus, some commentators have made it seem as if the phenomenon bore no relationship whatsoever to the United States' actions abroad. But America's behavior overseas, whether support for anticommunist movements or visa policy, does matter. Here, looking at the problem from the opposite perspective is proof: People feel more positive about the United States when their personal experience leads them to feel more positive.

An Inspiration—to Some

Direct political experience is not, however, the only factor that shapes for- 12 eigners' perceptions of the United States. Around the world, there are millions of people who associate the United States not merely with a concrete political ideal, or even a particular economic theory, but with more general notions of upward mobility, of economic progress, and of a classless society (not all of which exist in the United States anymore, but that's another matter). Advertising executives understand very well the phenomenon of ordinary women who read magazines filled with photographs of clothes they could not possibly afford. They call such women "aspirational." Looking around the world, there are classes of people who are "aspirational" as well. And these aspirational classes, filled with people who are upwardly mobile or would like to be, tend to be pro-American as well.

Looking again at some relatively anti-American countries is instruc- 13 tional. In Britain, for example, it is absolutely clear that the greatest support for the United States comes from people in the lowest income brackets, and those with the least amount of formal education. In Britain, 57.6 percent of those whose income is very low believe the United States has a mainly positive influence. Only 37.1 percent of those whose income is very high, by contrast, believe the same. Asking the same question, but breaking down the answers by education, the same pattern holds in South

Korea, where 69.2 percent of those with a low education think the United States is a positive influence, and only 45.8 percent of those with a high education agree. That trend repeats itself in many developed countries: those on their way up are pro-American, and those who have arrived are much less so.

In developing countries, by contrast, the pattern is sometimes reversed. 14 It turns out, for example, that Indians are much more likely to be pro-American if they are not only younger but wealthier and better educated. And that too makes sense: Younger Indians have had the experience of working with American companies and American investors, whereas their parents did not. Only in recent decades have Indians been full members of the international economy, and only in recent years was India fully open to foreign investment. The poor in India are still untouched by globalization, but the middle and upper-middle classes—those who see for themselves a role in the English speaking, America-dominated international economy— are aspirational, and therefore pro-American. In fact, some 69 percent of Indians with very high incomes think the United States is a mainly positive influence; 43.2 percent of those with average incomes feel that way; and only 29.6 percent of those with very low incomes are likely to think of American influence as positive.

Taking a slightly different tack, it is possible to identify countries in 15 which the country as a whole could be described as aspirational, rather than one particular class. Here it is worth looking at Spain, Portugal, and Italy. Again, none of these countries can be described as overwhelmingly pro-American as can, for example, the Philippines. Spain in particular has registered very high opposition to the American war in Iraq and even overturned a government on those grounds. But these countries are slightly different from others in Europe, not only because, unlike France and Germany, they follow the Canadian and British pattern—the less educated and the least wealthy are relatively pro-American—but also because all three have, at some point in the past several years, elected notably pro-American leaders. Former Prime Ministers José María Aznar in Spain and Pedro Santana Lopes in Portugal as well as current Prime Minister Silvio Berlusconi in Italy made close relations with the United States a central part of their foreign policies, and all three sent troops to fight in Iraq.

True, their support for the United States following 9/11 is more directly 16 explained by European politics: Like Britain and Denmark, the three southern European countries dislike the increasing Franco–German dominance of Europe, and see the American presence in Europe as an important counterweight. But it is also the case that Italy, Spain, and Portugal are Europe's nouveau riche: All have grown wealthier in the past generation, and all still have large numbers of "upwardly mobile" citizens. That too might help explain their politicians' fondness for the United States, a country that is, by older European standards, a true arriviste. This same phenomenon might also account for the persistence of a surprising degree of popular pro-Americanism in such places as Vietnam, Indonesia, Brazil, and, again, the Philippines: They're getting richer—like Americans—but aren't yet so rich as to feel directly competitive.

Portrait of a Pro-American Man

There is, finally, one other factor that is associated almost everywhere in 17 the world with pro-Americanism: In Europe, Asia, and South America, men are far more likely than women to have positive feelings about the United States. In some cases, the numbers are quite striking. Asking men and women how they feel about the United States produces an 11 percent gender gap in India, a 17 percent gender gap in Poland, and even a 6 percent gap in the Philippines. This pattern probably requires more psychological analysis than I can muster, but it's possible to guess at some explanations. Perhaps the United States is associated with armies and invasions, which historically appeal more to men. Perhaps it is because the United States is also associated with muscular foreign policy, and fewer women around the world are involved in, or interested in, foreign policy at all. Perhaps it's because men are more attracted to the idea of power, entrepreneurship, or capitalism. Or it may just be that the United States appeals to men in greater numbers for the same intuitive reasons that President George W. Bush appeals to men in greater numbers, whatever those are.

Although not as surprising as some of the other numbers, this gender 18 gap does help us come up with a clearer picture of who the typical pro-American might be. We all know the stereotypes of the anti-Americans: The angry Arab radical, demonstrating in the mythical Arab street; or the left-wing newspaper editor, fulminating at Berlin dinner parties; or the French farmer, railing against McDonald's. Now, perhaps, we should add new stereotypes: The British small businessman, son of a coal miner, who once admired Thatcher and has been to Florida on holiday. Or the Polish anticommunist intellectual, who argued about Reagan with his Parisian friends in the 1980s, and disagrees with them about the Iraqi war now. Or the Indian stockbroker, the South Korean investment banker, and the Philippine manufacturer, all of whom have excellent relations with their American clients, all of whom support a U.S. military presence in their parts of the world, and all of whom probably harbor a fondness for President Bush that they wouldn't confess to their wives. These stock figures should be as firmly a part of the columnists' and commentators' repertoire as their opponents have become.

They also matter, or should matter, to the United States. These people, 19 and their equivalents in other countries, are America's natural constituents. They may not be a majority, either in the world or in their own countries. But neither are they insignificant. After all, pro-Americans will vote for pro-American politicians, who sometimes win, even in Europe. They can exert pressure on their governments to support U.S. foreign policy. They will also purchase American products, make deals with American companies, vacation in the United States, and watch American movies.

They are worth cultivating, in other words, because their numbers can 20 rise or fall, depending on U.S. policies. Their opinions will change, according to how American ambassadors conduct business in their countries, according to how often the U.S. secretary of state visits their cities, and according to how their media report on American affairs. Before the United States brushes away Europe as hopelessly anti-American, Americans should therefore remember that not all Europeans dislike them. Before Americans brush off the opinion of "foreigners" as unworthy of cultivation either, they should remember that whole chunks of the world have a natural affinity for them and, if they are diligent, always will.

Thinking About the Essay

1. How does the author make her transition from the personal narrative of the opening paragraphs to more general questions?

2. Where does the author's claim appear in the essay? Why is there a delay in its appearance?

3. According to Applebaum, why is the relatively pro-American attitude in Great Britain an exception among European states?

4. How does Applebaum borrow her definition of "aspirational" and adapt it for her own purposes (an example of a stipulative definition)?

5. How, finally, does Applebaum reconcile what seem to be two contradictory accounts: that pro-American feelings are the lasting imprint of a personal experience and that these feelings also result from changing experience of America's changing foreign policy?

Responding in Writing

6. In this essay, Applebaum is vigilantly self-conscious about her methods of inquiry and announces her frequent shifts from one level of analysis to another (personal, anecdotal, intuitive, demographic, etc.). In a brief essay,

follow a similar pattern of inquiry in your own attempt to explain the demographic behavior of a sociological "type."

7. Do you believe in the concept of a collective national (or generational) consciousness? In a persuasive essay, argue for or against the validity of the concept.

8. Following the examples Applebaum gives in the final section of her essay, write a profile of your own political sympathies and attempt to explain them in terms of your age, gender, ethnicity, and socioeconomic background.

Networking

9. Record your earliest impressions of a foreign country and share them with the class. Do people in your class who belong to the same age group share these memories?

10. Go online and locate three or four blogs posted by foreign-bom individuals who express what appear to be pro-American sentiments. Based on what you see posted, attempt to construct a profile of one type of individual with pro-American feelings.

Waking Up from the American Dream

SASHA ABRAMSKY

Sasha Abramsky is a freelance journalist and author who writes on politics and culture. He was born in England and studied politics, philosophy, and economics at Balliol College, Oxford, and moved to New York in 1993 to study journalism at Columbia University. His first book, *Hard Time Blues: How Politics Built a Prison Nation* (2002), examines the American prison system. Abramsky is currently a Senior Fellow at the New York City-based Demos Foundation. In the following essay, published in the July 23, 2004, issue of *The Chronicle of Higher Education*, Abramsky asks why foreign sympathy for America, inspired by faith in the American Dream, has dissipated at the turn of the new century.

Before Reading

Do you feel that the recent crisis of confidence in the United States among other nations also reflects a global loss of confidence in the ideal of the American Dream?

Last year I visited London and stumbled upon an essay in a Sunday paper written by Margaret Drabble, one of Britain's pre-eminent ladies of letters. "My anti-Americanism has become almost uncontrollable," she wrote. "It has possessed me, like a disease. It rises up in my throat like acid reflux, that fashionable American sickness. I now loathe the United States and what it has done to Iraq and the rest of the helpless world." 1

The essay continued in the same rather bilious vein for about a thousand words, and as I read it, two things struck me: The first was how appalled I was by Drabble's crassly oversimplistic analysis of what America was all about, of who its people were, and of what its culture valued; the second was a sense somewhat akin to fear as I thought through the implications of the venom attached to the words of this gentle scribe of the English bourgeoisie. After all, if someone whose country and class have so clearly benefited economically from the protections provided by American military and political ties reacts so passionately to the omnipresence of the United States, what must an angry, impoverished young man in a failing third world state feel? 2

I grew up in London in the 1970s and 1980s, in a country that was struggling to craft a postcolonial identity for itself, a country that was, in many ways, still reeling from the collapse of power it suffered in the post–World War II years. Not surprisingly, there was a strong anti-American flavor to much of the politics, the humor, the cultural chitchat of the period; after all, America had dramatically usurped Britannia on the world stage, and who among us doesn't harbor some resentments at being shunted onto the sidelines by a new superstar? 3

Today, however, when I talk with friends and relatives in London, when I visit Europe, the anti-Americanism is more than just sardonic asides, rueful Monty Python-style jibes, and haughty intimations of superiority. Today something much more visceral is in the air. I go to my old home and I get the distinct impression that, as Drabble put it, people really *loathe* America somewhere deep, deep in their gut. 4

A Pew Research Center Global Attitudes Project survey recently found that even in Britain, America's staunchest ally, more than 6 out of 10 people polled believed the United States paid little or no attention to that country's interests. About 80 percent of French and German respondents stated that, because of the war in Iraq, they had less confidence in the trustworthiness of America. In the Muslim countries surveyed, large majorities believed the war on terror to be about establishing U.S. world domination. 5

Indeed, in many countries—in the Arab world and in regions, such as Western Europe, closely tied into American economic and military structures—popular opinion about both America the country and Americans as 6

individuals has taken a serious hit. Just weeks ago, 27 of America's top retired diplomats and military commanders warned in a public statement,
"Never in the 2¼ centuries of our history has the United States been so isolated among the nations, so broadly feared and distrusted."

If true, that suggests that, while to all appearances America's allies con- 7
tinue to craft policies in line with the wishes of Washington, underneath the
surface a new dynamic may well be emerging, one not too dissimilar to the
Soviet Union's relations with its reluctant satellite states in Eastern Europe
during the cold war. America's friends may be quiescent in public, deeply
reluctant to toe the line in private. Drabble mentioned the Iraq war as her
primary *casus belli* with the United States. The statement from the biparti-
san group calling itself Diplomats and Military Commanders for Change
focused on the Bush administration's recent foreign policy. But to me it
seems that something else is also going on.

In many ways, the Iraq war is merely a pretext for a deeper discontent 8
with how America has seemed to fashion a new global society, a new economic, military, and political order in the decade and a half since the end
of the cold war. America may only be riding the crest of a wave of modernization that, in all likelihood, would have emerged without its guiding
hand. But add to the mix a discontent with the vast wealth and power that
America has amassed in the past century and a deep sense of unease with
the ways in which a secular, market-driven world divvies up wealth and influence among people and nations, and you have all the ingredients for a
nasty backlash against America.

I'm not talking merely about the anti-globalism of dispossessed Third 9
World peasants, the fears of the loss of cultural sovereignty experienced by
societies older and more traditional than the United States, the anger at a
perceived American arrogance that we've recently been reading so much
about. I'm talking about something that is rooted deeper in the psyches of
other nations. I guess I mean a feeling of being marginalized by history; of
being peripheral to the human saga; of being footnotes for tomorrow's historians rather than main characters. In short, a growing anxiety brought
on by having another country and culture dictating one's place in the society of nations.

In the years since I stood on my rooftop in Brooklyn watching the 10
World Trade Center towers burn so apocalyptically, I have spent at least a
part of every day wrestling with a host of existential questions. I can't help
it—almost obsessively I churn thoughts over and over in my head, trying
to understand the psychological contours of this cruel new world. The
questions largely boil down to the following: Where has the world's faith
in America gone? Where is the American Dream headed?

What is happening to that intangible force that helped shape our mod- 11 ern world, that invisible symbiotic relationship between the good will of foreigners and the successful functioning of the American "way of life," that willingness by strangers to let us serve as the repository for their dreams, their hopes, their visions of a better future? In the same way that the scale of our national debt is made possible only because other countries are willing to buy treasury bonds and, in effect, lend us their savings, so it seems to me the American Dream has been largely facilitated by the willingness of other peoples to lend us their expectations for the future. Without that willingness, the Dream is a bubble primed to burst. It hasn't burst yet—witness the huge numbers who still migrate to America in search of the good life—but I worry that it is leaking seriously.

Few countries and cultures have risen to global prominence as quickly 12 as America did in the years after the Civil War. Perhaps the last time there was such an extraordinary accumulation of geopolitical, military, and economic influence in so few decades was 800 years ago, with the rise of the Mongol khanates. Fewer still have so definitively laid claim to an era, while that era was still unfolding, as we did—and as the world acknowledged— during the 20th century, "the American Century."

While the old powers of Europe tore themselves apart during World 13 War I, the United States entered the war late and fought the fight on other people's home terrain. While whole societies were destroyed during World War II, America's political and economic system flourished, its cities thrived, and its entertainment industries soared. In other words, as America rose to global pre-eminence during the bloody first half of the 20th century, it projected outward an aura of invulnerability, a vision of "normalcy" redolent with consumer temptations and glamorous cultural spectacles. In an exhibit at the museum on Ellis Island a few years back, I remember seeing a copy of a letter written by a young Polish migrant in New York to his family back home. Urging them to join him, he wrote that the ordinary person on the streets of America lived a life far more comfortable than aristocrats in Poland could possibly dream of.

In a way America, during the American Century, thus served as a safety 14 valve, allowing the world's poor to dream of a better place somewhere else; to visualize a place neither bound by the constraints of old nor held hostage to the messianic visions of revolutionary Marxist or Fascist movements so powerful in so many other parts of the globe.

Throughout the cold war, even as America spent unprecedented 15 amounts on military hardware, enough was left over to nurture the mass-consumption culture, to build up an infrastructure of vast proportions. And despite the war in Vietnam, despite the dirty wars that ravaged Latin

America in the 1980s, despite America's nefarious role in promoting coups and dictatorships in a slew of countries-cum-cold-war-pawns around the globe, somehow much of the world preserved a rosy-hued vision of America that could have been culled straight from the marketing rooms of Madison Avenue.

Now something is changing. Having dealt with history largely on its 16 own terms, largely with the ability to deflect the worst of the chaos to arenas outside our borders (as imperial Britain did in the century following the defeat of Napoleon in 1815, through to the disastrous events leading up to World War I in 1914), America has attracted a concentrated fury and vengeful ire of disastrous proportions. The willingness to forgive, embodied in so much of the world's embrace of the American Dream, is being replaced by a rather vicious craving to see America—which, under the Bush administration, has increasingly defined its greatness by way of military triumphs—humbled. Moreover, no great power has served as a magnet for such a maelstrom of hate in an era as saturated with media images, as susceptible to instantaneous opinion-shaping coverage of events occurring anywhere in the world.

I guess the question that gnaws at my consciousness could be rephrased 17 as: How does one give an encore to a bravura performance? It's either an anticlimax or, worse, a dismal failure—with the audience heading out the doors halfway through, talking not of the brilliance of the earlier music, but of the tawdriness of the last few bars. If the 20th century was the American Century, its best hopes largely embodied by something akin to the American Dream, what kind of follow-up can the 21st century bring?

In the immediate aftermath of September 11, an outpouring of genuine, 18 if temporary, solidarity from countries and peoples across the globe swathed America in an aura of magnificent victimhood. We, the most powerful country on earth, had been blindsided by a ruthless, ingenious, and barbaric enemy, two of our greatest cities violated. We demanded the world's tears, and, overwhelmingly, we received them. They were, we felt, no less than our due, no more than our merit. In the days after the trade center collapsed, even the Parisian daily *Le Monde*, not known for its pro-Yankee sentimentality, informed its readers, in an echo of John F. Kennedy's famous "Ich bin ein Berliner" speech, that "we are all Americans now."

Perhaps inevitably, however, that sympathy has now largely dissipated. 19 Powerful countries under attack fight back—ruthlessly, brutally, with all the economic, political, diplomatic, and military resources at their disposal. They always have; like as not, they always will. In so doing, perhaps they cannot but step on the sensibilities of smaller, less powerful dare I say it, less *imperial* nations and peoples. And as Britain, the country in which I grew up, discovered so painfully during the early years of World War II, sometimes the mighty end up standing largely alone, bulwarks against history's periodic tidal waves. In that fight, even if they emerge successful, they ultimately emerge also tarnished and somewhat humbled, their power and drive and confidence at least partly evaporated on the battlefield.

In the post-September 11 world, even leaving aside Iraq and all the distortions, half-truths, and lies used to justify the invasion, even leaving aside the cataclysmic impact of the Abu Ghraib prison photographs, I believe America would have attracted significant wrath simply in doing what had to be done in routing out the Taliban in Afghanistan, in reorienting its foreign policy to try and tackle international terror networks and breeding grounds. That is why I come back time and again in my mind to the tactical brilliance of Al Qaeda's September 11 attacks: If America hadn't responded, a green light would have been turned on, one that signaled that the country was too decadent to defend its vital interests. Yet in responding, the response itself was almost guaranteed to spotlight an empire bullying allies and enemies alike into cooperation and subordination and, thus, to focus an inchoate rage against the world's lone standing superpower. Damned if we did, damned if we didn't. 20

Which brings me back to the American Dream. In the past even as our power grew, much of the world saw us, rightly or wrongly, as a moral beacon, as a country somehow largely outside the bloody, gory, oft-tyrannical history that carved its swath across so much of the world during the American Century. Indeed, in many ways, even as cultural elites in once-glorious Old World nations sneered at upstart, crass, consumerist America, the masses in those nations idealized America as some sort of Promised Land, as a place of freedoms and economic possibilities simply unheard of in many parts of the globe. In many ways, the American Dream of the last 100-some years has been more something dreamed by foreigners from afar, especially those who experienced fascism or Stalinism, than lived as a universal reality on the ground in the United States. 21

Things look simpler from a distance than they do on the ground. In the past foreigners might have idealized America as a place whose streets were paved if not with gold, at least with alloys seeded with rare and precious metals, even while those who lived here knew it was a gigantic, complicated, multifaceted, continental country with a vast patchwork of cultures and creeds coexisting side by messy side. Today, I fear, foreigners slumber with dreamy American smiles on their sleeping faces no more; that intangible faith in the pastel-colored hue and soft contours of the Dream risks 22 being shattered, replaced instead by an equally simplistic dislike of all things and peoples American.

Paradoxically these days it is the political elites—the leaders and policy 23 analysts and defense experts—who try to hold in place alliances built up in the post–World War II years as the *pax Americana* spread its wings, while the populaces shy away from an America perceived to be dominated by corporations, military musclemen, and empire-builders-in-the-name-of-democracy; increasingly they sympathize with the unnuanced critiques of the Margaret Drabbles of the world. The Pew survey, for example, found that sizable majorities in countries such as Jordan, Morocco, Turkey, Germany, and France believed the war on terror to be largely about the United States wanting to control Middle Eastern oil supplies.

In other words, the *perception*—never universally held, but held by 24 enough people to help shape our global image—is changing. Once our image abroad was of an exceptional country accruing all the power of empire without the psychology of empire; now it is being replaced by something more historically normal—that of a great power determined to preserve and expand its might, for its own selfish interests and not much else. An exhibit in New York's Whitney Museum last year, titled "The American Effect," presented the works of 50 artists from around the world who portrayed an America intent on world dominance through military adventurism and gross consumption habits. In the run-up to the war in Iraq, Mikhail Gorbachev lambasted an America he now viewed as operating in a manner "far from real world leadership." Nelson Mandela talked of the United States as a country that "has committed unspeakable atrocities in the world."

Maybe the American Dream always was little more than marketing 25 hype (the author Jeffrey Decker writes in *Made in America* that the term itself was conjured up in 1931 by a populist historian named James Truslow Adams, perhaps as an antidote to the harsh realities of Depression-era America). But as the savagery of the images coming out of Iraq demonstrate all too well, we live in a world where image is if not everything, at least crucial. Perhaps I'm wrong and the American Dream will continue to sweeten the sleep of those living overseas for another century. I certainly hope, very much, that I'm wrong—for a world denuded of the Dream, however far from complex reality that Dream might have been, would be impoverished indeed. But I worry that that encore I mentioned earlier won't be nearly as breathtaking or as splendid as the original performance that shaped the first American century.

Thinking About the Essay

1. Why does Abramsky wait until paragraph 3 to inform the reader that he grew up in London? What effect does this strategic withholding of information have upon you as a reader?

2. List some of the illustrations that Abramsky invokes as "barometers" of public sentiment.

3. According to Abramsky, why is it important for the future of America that foreigners continue to idealize the country and believe in some concept of an American Dream?

4. How does Abramsky characterize American power as being the result of a symbiotic relationship or exchange with the rest of the world?

5. The concluding sentence picks up an extended metaphor (or conceit) that was introduced earlier in the essay. How effective is this metaphor as a structuring device?

Responding in Writing

6. Do you feel that the Iraq war is merely a pretext for a deeper discontent with America? In a brief essay, speculate on the nature of the discontent underlying one critique of the Iraq war that you have heard expressed.

7. Reread the no-win scenario outlined in paragraph 20. Do you agree with Abramksy's statement that America "would have attracted significant wrath simply in doing what had to be done"? Defend your opinion in an argumentative essay.

8. Have you ever felt "marginalized by history," as a result of your place of birth, time of birth, or other factors beyond your control? Write an essay explaining some of the factors that would contribute to that feeling.

Networking

9. In groups of three or four, list some key features of the American Dream, and share these lists with the class. Is there a concept of the American Dream common to everyone in the class?

10. Go online and view (or read about) some of the works that were on display in "The American Effect" exhibit at New York's Whitney Museum. Do you detect a "party line" in the way these artists view America? Are there perceptions of America that Abramsky might consider "nuanced"?

Speaking in Tongues: Does Language Unify or Divide Us?

The multicultural voices in the previous chapters reflect some of the numerous ethnic and racial diversities of the American mosaic. Along with this mosaic comes a variety of languages. Of course, you have been taught to speak and write the same language—that standard variety of English that places you in the college classroom today. Knowing the standard English "code" provides you with a powerful tool, offering pragmatic and liberating ways to gain control over your world. However, other languages might compete for your attention, especially if there are other languages that you speak at home or in your community. Powerful constituencies—politicians and advertisers among them—exploit this fact; for example, some decidedly Anglo politicians try to speak Spanish to Latino crowds (often to the amusement of native Spanish speakers). Other constituencies, threatened by our multilingual world, try to enact "English-only" laws in various states. Language can unify or divide a community or country, but basically it quite simply is a mark of your identity. To know a language or languages permits you to navigate your community, culture, and even global society.

Imagine, for example, what it would be like if you were illiterate. You wouldn't be here in college. You might not be able to read a menu or fill out a job application. You might not be interested in voting because you cannot read the names of the candidates. Illiteracy in reality is common around the world—and far more common in the United States than you might think.

We have vivid reminders of both the cost of illiteracy and also the power of literacy in film and literature. In the film *Driving Miss Daisy*, the character played by Morgan Freeman goes through most of his life

*Online Study Center*   This icon will direct you to weblinks, audio and visual content, and additional resources on the website college.hmco.com/pic/mullerNWR2e

117

The neighborhood of Elmhurst, Queens, in New York City, is one of the most ethnically and linguistically diverse places in the world. At Elmhurst's Newtown High School alone, students come from more than 100 countries and at least 39 languages are spoken. In this photograph, local schoolchildren take part in the neighborhood's annual International Day Festival on May 27, 1999.

Thinking About the Image

1. Recall a class photograph from your childhood. Was your school as diverse as this group of schoolchildren, or not? What are the advantages of being exposed to so many nationalities and languages at such a young age? What are the disadvantages?
2. News photographers often shoot many images of the same event, sometimes even multiple rolls of film, and then decide with their editors which unique image best captures the spirit of the event. Why do you think this photo was selected?
3. Are there parades for various ethnic or social groups in your community? How are those events covered in the local news media?
4. Would this parade have achieved its purpose, or appealed to its audience, as effectively if the marchers were adults instead of children? Why or why not? Would the message (or purpose) have been different? In what way?

pretending to read the daily newspaper. When Daisy (played by Jessica Tandy) teaches him to read, his world—and his comprehension of it—expands. Or consider one of the memorable sequences in *The Autobiography of Malcolm X*. Malcolm teaches himself to read and write when he is in prison. He starts at the beginning of the dictionary and works his way to the end. Going into prison as Richard Little, he comes out as Malcolm X, his identity reconstructed not only by the acquisition of a new system of belief—Islam—but also by a newly acquired literacy. In his writing and in his recovered life, Malcolm X harnessed the power of language to transform himself and his understanding of the world.

Think of language, then, as a radical weapon. Language permits you to share experiences and emotions, process information, analyze situations and events, defend a position, advocate a cause, make decisions. Language contributes to the growth of the self. Language is the bedrock of our academic, social, and professional lives. Language is a liberating force.

The idea that language is the key to our identity and our perception of the world is not new. Early Greek and Roman philosophers believed that you could not be a good thinker or writer unless you were a good person. Assuming that you are a good person, you possess a repertoire of mental skills that you can bring to bear on various situations and dimensions of your life. You can draw inferences, interpret conditions, understand causal relationships, develop arguments, make intelligent choices, and so forth. But have you ever found yourself in a situation where you know what you mean but not how to say it? Or think of how difficult it must be for people acquiring a second language; they know what they mean in their primary language but cannot express it in their new one. The essays in this chapter deal with precisely this situation.

The writers in this chapter illuminate the power and paradox of language. They link language, culture, and identity. They use language with skill and feeling. They work with the problems and contradictions of language, seeking answers to the question, Who am I, and where do my words—my languages—fit into the American as well as the world mosaic?

Mother Tongue

AMY TAN | Amy Tan was born in San Francisco, California, in 1952, only two and a half years after her parents emigrated from China to the United States. She was educated at San Jose State University and the University of California at Berkeley and then worked as a reporter and technical writer. Tan is best known as a novelist whose fiction focuses on the conflict in culture between

Chinese parents and their Americanized children. Her first novel, *The Joy Luck Club* (1989), was highly popular and adapted by Hollywood as a feature film. Tan's other novels are *The Kitchen God's Wife* (1991), *The Hundred Secret Senses* (1995), and *The Bonesetter's Daughter* (2001). Tan's complicated relationship with her mother, Daisy, who died of Alzheimer's disease in 1999 at the age of eighty-three, is central to much of her fiction. In this essay, published in 1990 in *The Threepenny Reviews*, Tan, who has a master's degree in linguistics, invokes her mother in exploring the "Englishes" that immigrants employ as they navigate American culture.

Before Reading

How many "Englishes" do you speak, and what types of English do you speak in various situations? Is the English you speak in the classroom the same as you speak in your home or dormitory?

I am not a scholar of English or literature. I cannot give you much more 1 than personal opinions on the English language and its variations in this country or others.

I am a writer. And by that definition, I am someone who has always 2 loved language. I am fascinated by language in daily life. I spend a great deal of my time thinking about the power of language—the way it can evoke an emotion, a visual image, a complex idea, or a simple truth. Language is the tool of my trade. And I use them all—all the Englishes I grew up with.

Recently, I was made keenly aware of the different Englishes I do use. I 3 was giving a talk to a large group of people, the same talk I had already given to half a dozen other groups. The nature of the talk was about my writing, my life, and my book, *The Joy Luck Club*. The talk was going along well enough, until I remembered one major difference that made the whole talk sound wrong. My mother was in the room. And it was perhaps the first time she had heard me give a lengthy speech, using the kind of English I have never used with her. I was saying things like, "The intersection of memory upon imagination" and "There is an aspect of my fiction that relates to thus-and-thus"—a speech filled with carefully wrought grammatical phrases, burdened, it suddenly seemed to me, with nominalized forms, past perfect tenses, conditional phrases, all the forms of standard English that I had learned in school and through books, the forms of English I did not use at home with my mother.

Just last week, I was walking down the street with my mother, and I   4
again found myself conscious of the English I was using, the English I do
use with her. We were talking about the price of new and used furniture
and I heard myself saying this: "Not waste money that way." My husband
was with us as well, and he didn't notice any switch in my English. And
then I realized why. It's because over the twenty years we've been together
I've often used that same kind of English with him, and sometimes he even
uses it with me. It has become our language of intimacy, a different sort of
English that relates to family talk, the language I grew up with.

So you'll have some idea of what this family talk I heard sounds like,   5
I'll quote what my mother said during a recent conversation which I videotaped and then transcribed. During this conversation, my mother was talking about a political gangster in Shanghai who had the same last name as
her family's, Du, and how the gangster in his early years wanted to be
adopted by her family, which was rich by comparison. Later, the gangster
became more powerful, far richer than my mother's family, and one day
showed up at my mother's wedding to pay his respects. Here's what she
said in part:

"Du Yusong having business like fruit stand. Like off the street kind.   6
He is Du like Du Zong—but not Tsung-ming Island people. The local people call putong, the river east side, he belong to that side local people. That
man want to ask Du Zong father take him in like become own family. Du
Zong father wasn't look down on him, but didn't take seriously, until that
man big like become a mafia. Now important person, very hard to inviting
him. Chinese way, came only to show respect, don't stay for dinner. Respect
for making big celebration, he shows up. Mean gives lots of respect. Chinese custom. Chinese social life that way. If too important won't have to
stay too long. He come to my wedding. I didn't see, I heard it. I gone to
boy's side, they have YMCA dinner. Chinese age I was nineteen."

You should know that my mother's expressive command of English be-   7
lies how much she actually understands. She reads the *Forbes* report, lis-
tens to *Wall Street Week*, converses daily with her stockbroker, reads all of
Shirley MacLaine's books with ease—all kinds of things I can't begin to understand. Yet some of my friends tell me they understand 50 percent of
what my mother says. Some say they understand 80 to 90 percent. Some
say they understand none of it, as if she were speaking pure Chinese. But
to me, my mother's English is perfectly clear, perfectly natural. It's my
mother tongue. Her language, as I hear it, is vivid, direct, full of observation and imagery. That was the language that helped shape the way I saw
things, expressed things, made sense of the world.

Lately, I've been giving more thought to the kind of English my mother   8
speaks. Like others, I have described it to people as "broken" or "frac-
tured" English. But I wince when I say that. It has always bothered me that
I can think of no way to describe it other than "broken," as if it were dam-
aged and needed to be fixed, as if it lacked a certain wholeness and soundness. I've heard other terms used, "limited English," for example. But they
seem just as bad, as if everything is limited, including people's perceptions
of the limited English speaker.

I know this for a fact, because when I was growing up, my mother's   9
"limited" English limited *my* perception of her. I was ashamed of her English. I believed that her English reflected the quality of what she had to say.
That is, because she expressed them imperfectly her thoughts were imperfect. And I had plenty of empirical evidence to support me: the fact that
people in department stores, at banks, and at restaurants did not take her
seriously, did not give her good service, pretended not to understand her,
or even acted as if they did not hear her.

My mother has long realized the limitations of her English as well.   10
When I was fifteen, she used to have me call people on the phone to pretend I was she. In this guise, I was forced to ask for information or even to
complain and yell at people who had been rude to her. One time it was a
call to her stockbroker in New York. She had cashed out her small portfolio and it just so happened we were going to go to New York the next week,
our very first trip outside California. I had to get on the phone and say in
an adolescent voice that was not very convincing, "This is Mrs. Tan."

And my mother was standing in the back whispering loudly, "Why he   11
don't send me check, already two weeks late. So mad he lie to me, losing
me money."

And then I said in perfect English, "Yes, I'm getting rather concerned.   12
You had agreed to send the check two weeks ago, but it hasn't arrived."

Then she began to talk more loudly. "What he want, I come to New   13
York tell him front of his boss, you cheating me?" And I was trying to calm
her down, make her be quiet, while telling the stockbroker, "I can't tolerate any more excuses. If I don't receive the check immediately, I am going
to have to speak to your manager when I'm in New York next week." And
sure enough, the following week there we were in front of this astonished
stockbroker, and I was sitting there red-faced and quiet, and my mother,
the real Mrs. Tan, was shouting at his boss in her impeccable broken
English.

We used a similar routine just five days ago, for a situation that was far   14
less humorous. My mother had gone to the hospital for an appointment, to
find out about a benign brain tumor a CAT scan had revealed a month ago.

She said she had spoken very good English, her best English, no mistakes. Still, she said, the hospital did not apologize when they said they had lost the CAT scan and she had come for nothing. She said they did not seem to have any sympathy when she told them she was anxious to know the exact diagnosis, since her husband and son had both died of brain tumors. She said they would not give her any more information until the next time and she would have to make another appointment for that. So she said she would not leave until the doctor called her daughter. She wouldn't budge. And when the doctor finally called her daughter, me, who spoke in perfect English—lo and behold—we had assurances the CAT scan would be found, promises that a conference call on Monday would be held, and apologies for any suffering my mother had gone through for a most regrettable mistake.

I think my mother's English almost had an effect on limiting my possi- 15
bilities in life as well. Sociologists and linguists probably will tell you that a person's developing language skills are more influenced by peers. But I do think that the language spoken in the family, especially in immigrant families which are more insular, plays a large role in shaping the language of the child. And I believe that it affected my results on achievement tests, IQ tests, and the SAT. While my English skills were never judged as poor, compared to math, English could not be considered my strong suit. In grade school I did moderately well, getting perhaps B's, sometimes B-pluses, in English and scoring perhaps in the sixtieth or seventieth percentile on achievement tests. But those scores were not good enough to override the opinion that my true abilities lay in math and science, because in those areas I achieved A's and scored in the ninetieth percentile or higher.

This was understandable. Math is precise; there is only one correct an- 16
swer. Whereas, for me at least, the answers on English tests were always a judgment call, a matter of opinion and personal experience. Those tests were constructed around items like fill-in-the-blank sentence completion, such as, "Even though Tom was _____, Mary thought he was _____." And the correct answer always seemed to be the most bland combinations of thoughts, for example, "Even though Tom was shy, Mary thought he was charming," with the grammatical structure "even though" limiting the correct answer to some sort of semantic opposites, so you wouldn't get answers like, "Even though Tom was foolish, Mary thought he was ridiculous." Well, according to my mother, there were very few limitations as to what Tom could have been and what Mary might have thought of him. So I never did well on tests like that.

The same was true with word analogies, pairs of words in which you 17
were supposed to find some sort of logical, semantic relationship—for example, "*Sunset* is to *nightfall* as _____ is to _____." And here you

would be presented with a list of four possible pairs, one of which showed the same kind of relationship: *red* is to *stoplight, bus* is to *arrival, chills* is to *fever, yawn* is to *boring*. Well, I could never think that way. I knew what the tests were asking, but I could not block out of my mind the images already created by the first pair, "*sunset* is to *nightfall*"—and I would see a burst of colors against a darkening sky, the moon rising, the lowering of a curtain of stars. And all the other pairs of words—red, bus, stoplight, boring—just threw up a mass of confusing images, making it impossible for me to sort out something as logical as saying: "A sunset precedes nightfall" is the same as "a chill precedes a fever." The only way I would have gotten that answer right would have been to imagine an associative situation, for example, my being disobedient and staying out past sunset, catching a chill at night, which turns into feverish pneumonia as punishment, which indeed did happen to me.

I have been thinking about all this lately, about my mother's English, about 18 achievement tests. Because lately I've been asked, as a writer, why there are not more Asian Americans represented in American literature. Why are there few Asian Americans enrolled in creative writing programs? Why do so many Chinese students go into engineering? Well, these are broad sociological questions I can't begin to answer. But I have noticed in surveys—in fact, just last week—that Asian students, as a whole, always do significantly better on math achievement tests than in English. And this makes me think that there are other Asian-American students whose English spoken in the home might also be described as "broken" or "limited." And perhaps they also have teachers who are steering them away from writing and into math and science, which is what happened to me.

Fortunately, I happen to be rebellious in nature and enjoy the challenge 19 of disproving assumptions made about me. I became an English major my first year in college, after being enrolled as pre-med. I started writing nonfiction as a freelancer the week after I was told by my former boss that writing was my worst skill and I should hone my talents toward account management.

But it wasn't until 1985 that I finally began to write fiction. And at first 20 I wrote using what I thought to be wittily crafted sentences, sentences that would finally prove I had mastery over the English language. Here's an example from the first draft of a story that later made its way into *The Joy Luck Club*, but without this line: "That was my mental quandary in its nascent state." A terrible line, which I can barely pronounce.

Fortunately, for reasons I won't get into today, I later decided I should 21 envision a reader for the stories I would write. And the reader I decided upon was my mother, because these were stories about mothers. So with this reader in mind—and in fact she did read my early drafts—I began to write stories using all the Englishes I grew up with: the English I spoke to my mother, which for lack of a better term might be described as "simple"; the English she used with me, which for lack of a better term might be described as "broken"; my translation of her Chinese, which could certainly be described as "watered down"; and what I imagined to be her translation of her Chinese if she could speak in perfect English, her internal language, and for that I sought to preserve the essence, but neither an English nor a Chinese structure. I wanted to capture what language ability tests can never reveal: her intent, her passion, her imagery, the rhythms of her speech and the nature of her thoughts.

Apart from what any critic had to say about my writing, I knew I had 22 succeeded where it counted when my mother finished reading my book and gave me her verdict: "So easy to read."

Thinking About the Essay

1. Explain the multiple meanings of Tan's title and how they illuminate the essay. What are the four ways Tan says language can work?

2. What is Tan's thesis, and where does it appear? How do we know her point of view about other "Englishes"? Does she state it directly or indirectly, and where?

3. How do narration and description interact in this essay? How does Tan describe her mother? What is the importance of dialogue?

4. What is Tan's viewpoint about language? Does she state that language should always be "simple"? Why or why not? To the extent that Tan's mother is an intended audience for her essay, is her language simple? Explain your answer by specific reference to her words and sentences. Finally, why does Tan's mother find her daughter's writing easy to understand?

5. How and where does Tan use humor in this essay? Where does Tan employ amusing anecdotes? What is her purpose in presenting these anecdotes, and how do they influence the essay's overall tone?

Responding in Writing

6. Tan suggests that the way we use language reflects the way we see the world. Write an essay based on this observation. Feel free to present an analytical paper or a narrative and descriptive essay, or to blend these patterns as does Tan.

7. Should all Americans speak and write the same language? Answer this question in an argumentative essay.

8. Tan writes about the "shame" she once experienced because of her mother's speech (paragraph 9). Write an essay about the dangers of linking personality or behavior to language. Can this linkage be used to promote racist, sexist, or other discriminatory ideas?

Networking

9. With two other class members, draw up a list of all the "Englishes" you have encountered. For example, how do your parents speak? What about relatives? Friends? Classmates? Personalities on television? Share your list with the class.

10. Conduct Internet or library research on the role of stereotyping by language in American radio and/or film. You might want to look into the popularity of the Charlie Chan series or Amos and Andy, or focus on a particular film that stereotypes a group. Present your information in an analytical and evaluative essay.

Mute in an English-Only World

CHANG-RAE LEE | Chang-rae Lee was born in 1965 in Seoul, South Korea. He and his family emigrated to the United States in 1968. Lee attended public schools in New Rochelle, New York; graduated from Yale University (B.A., 1987); and received an M.F.A. degree from the University of Oregon (1993). His first novel, *Native Speaker* (1995), won several prizes, including the Ernest Hemingway Foundation/PEN Award for First Fiction. He has also written *A Gesture Life* (1999) and *Aloft* (2004), and he has published fiction and nonfiction in many magazines, including *The New Yorker* and *Time*. Lee has taught in the creative writing programs at the University of Oregon and Hunter College; today he is part of the Humanities Council and creative writing program at Princeton University. In the following essay, which appeared on the op-ed page of *The New York Times* in 1996, Lee remembers his mother's efforts to learn English, using literary memoir to comment on recent laws passed by certain towns in New Jersey requiring English on all commercial signs.

Before Reading

Should all commercial signs have English written on them, in addition to any other language? What about menus in ethnic restaurants?

When I read of the troubles in Palisades Park, N.J., over the prolifer-   1
ation of Korean-language signs along its main commercial strip, I
unexpectedly sympathized with the frustrations, resentments and fears of
the longtime residents. They clearly felt alienated and even unwelcome in
a vital part of their community. The town, like seven others in New Jersey,
has passed laws requiring that half of any commercial sign in a foreign language be in English.

Now I certainly would never tolerate any exclusionary ideas about who   2
could rightfully settle and belong in the town. But having been raised in a
Korean immigrant family, I saw every day the exacting price and power of
language, especially with my mother, who was an outsider in an English-
only world.

In the first years we lived in America, my mother could speak only the   3
most basic English, and she often encountered great difficulty whenever she
went out.

We lived in New Rochelle, N.Y., in the early 70's, and most of the local   4
businesses were run by the descendants of immigrants who, generations
ago, had come to the suburbs from New York City. Proudly dotting Main
Street and North Avenue were Italian pastry and cheese shops, Jewish tai-
lors and cleaners and Polish and German butchers and bakers. If my
mother's marketing couldn't wait until the weekend, when my father had
free time, she would often hold off until I came home from school to buy
the groceries.

Though I was only 6 or 7 years old, she insisted that I go out shopping   5
with her and my younger sister. I mostly loathed the task, partly because it
meant I couldn't spend the afternoon playing catch with my friends but
also because I knew our errands would inevitably lead to an awkward
scene, and that I would have to speak up to help my mother.

I was just learning the language myself, but I was a quick study, as chil-   6
dren are with new tongues. I had spent kindergarten in almost complete silence, hearing only the high nasality of my teacher and comprehending little
but the cranky wails and cries of my classmates. But soon, seemingly mere
months later, I had already become a terrible ham and mimic, and I would
crack up my father with impressions of teachers, his friends and even himself. My mother scolded me for aping his speech, and the one time I attempted to make light of hers I rated a roundhouse smack on my bottom.

For her, the English language was not very funny. It usually meant trou-   7
ble and a good dose of shame, and sometimes real hurt. Although she had
a good reading knowledge of the language from university classes in South
Korea, she had never practiced actual conversation. So in America, she
used English flashcards and phrase books and watched television with us

kids. And she faithfully carried a pocket workbook illustrated with stick-figure people and compound sentences to be filled in.

But none of it seemed to do her much good. Staying mostly at home to care for us, she didn't have many chances to try out sundry words and phrases. When she did, say, at the window of the post office, her readied speech would stall, freeze, sometimes altogether collapse. 8

One day was unusually harrowing. We ventured downtown in the new Ford Country Squire my father had bought her, an enormous station wagon that seemed as long—and deft—as an ocean liner. We were shopping for a special meal for guests visiting that weekend, and my mother had heard that a particular butcher carried fresh oxtails—which she needed for a traditional soup. 9

We'd never been inside the shop, but my mother would pause before its window, which was always lined with whole hams, crown roasts and ropes of plump handmade sausages. She greatly esteemed the bounty with her eyes, and my sister and I did also, but despite our desirous cries she'd turn us away and instead buy the packaged links at the Finast supermarket, where she felt comfortable looking them over and could easily spot the price. And, of course, not have to talk. 10

But that day she was resolved. The butcher store was crowded, and as we stepped inside the door jingled a welcome. No one seemed to notice. We waited for some time, and people who entered after us were now being served. Finally, an old woman nudged my mother and waved a little ticket, which we hadn't taken. We patiently waited again, until one of the beefy men behind the glass display hollered our number. 11

My mother pulled us forward and began searching the cases, but the oxtails were nowhere to be found. The man, his big arms crossed, sharply said, "Come on, lady, whaddya want?" This unnerved her, and she somehow blurted the Korean word for oxtail, soggori. 12

The butcher looked as if my mother had put something sour in his mouth, and he glanced back at the lighted board and called the next number. 13

Before I knew it, she had rushed us outside and back in the wagon, which she had double-parked because of the crowd. She was furious, almost vibrating with fear and grief, and I could see she was about to cry. 14

She wanted to go back inside, but now the driver of the car we were blocking wanted to pull out. She was shooing us away. My mother, who had just earned her driver's license, started furiously working the pedals. But in her haste she must have flooded the engine, for it wouldn't turn over. The driver started honking and then another car began honking as well, and soon it seemed the entire street was shrieking at us. 15

In the following years, my mother grew steadily more comfortable with 16
English. In Korean, she could be fiery, stern, deeply funny and ironic; in
English, just slightly less so. If she was never quite fluent, she gained
enough confidence to make herself clearly known to anyone, and particularly to me.

Five years ago, she died of cancer, and some months after we buried her 17
I found myself in the driveway of my father's house, washing her sedan. I
liked taking care of her things; it made me feel close to her. While I was
cleaning out the glove compartment, I found her pocket English workbook, the one with the silly illustrations. I hadn't seen it in nearly 20 years.
The yellowed pages were brittle and dog-eared. She had fashioned a plain-
paper wrapping for it, and I wondered whether she meant to protect the
book or hide it.

I don't doubt that she would have appreciated doing the family shopping 18
on the new Broad Avenue of Palisades Park. But I like to think, too, that she
would have understood those who now complain about the Korean-only
signs.

I wonder what these same people would have done if they had seen my 19
mother studying her English workbook—or lost in a store. Would they
have nodded gently at her? Would they have lent a kind word?

Thinking About the Essay

1. What is the author's purpose? Is he trying to paint a picture of his mother,
   describe an aspect of the immigrant experience, convey a thesis, argue a
   point, or what? Explain your response.

2. What is unusual about Lee's introduction? How does his position on the issue raised defy your expectations?

3. Lee offers stories within stories. How are they ordered? Which tale receives greatest development, and why?

4. Lee uses **colloquial language** in this essay. Identify some examples. What
   is the effect?

5. What is the dominant impression that you have of Lee's mother? How does
   he bring her to life?

Responding in Writing

6. Construct a profile of the writer. What do we learn about Lee? What are his
   values? What is his attitude toward English? How does this son of immigrant parents establish himself as an authority? How does he surprise us
   with his perspective on language?

7. In a personal essay, tell of a time when you were embarrassed either by the language of someone close to you or by your own use of language in a social or business situation.

8. Both Amy Tan and Chang-rae Lee focus on their mothers' handling of their second language—English. Write a comparative essay in which you explain the similarities and differences in the authors' approaches to their subject.

Networking

9. With two other class members, discuss the emotional appeal of Lee's essay. Look especially at his conclusion. Share your responses with the class.

10. Write an e-mail to your instructor, suggesting two additional questions you would ask about Lee's essay if you were teaching it.

If You Can't Master English, Try Globish

MARY BLUME

Mary Blume moved to Paris in 1960 and was soon hired as a writer for the *New York Herald Tribune*. She has covered the Paris beat for the *Herald Tribune* for more than four decades, and the collection *A French Affair* (1999) gathers together a wide range of pieces that Blume wrote in Paris between 1960 and 1998. In the following essay, which originally appeared in the April 22, 2005, *International Herald Tribune*, Blume profiles the inventor of Globish and describes the properties and uses of this new "universal language."

Before Reading

Do you use a hybrid language to communicate with friends or family? Do you feel any limitations in what you can express in this language?

It happens all the time: during an airport delay the man to the left, a Korean perhaps, starts talking to the man opposite, who might be Colombian, and soon they are chatting away in what seems to be English. But the native English speaker sitting between them cannot understand a word.

They don't know it, but the Korean and the Colombian are speaking Globish, the latest addition to the 6,800 languages that are said to be spoken across the world. Not that its inventor, Jean-Paul Nerrière, considers it a proper language.

"It is not a language, it is a tool," he says. "A language is the vehicle 3 of a culture. Globish doesn't want to be that at all. It is a means of communication."

Nerrière doesn't see Globish in the same light as utopian efforts such as 4 Kosmos, Volapuk, Novial or staunch Esperanto. Nor should it be confused with barbaric Algol (for Algorithmic language). It is a sort of English lite: a means of simplifying the language and giving it rules so it can be understood by all.

"The language spoken worldwide, by 88 percent of mankind, is not ex- 5 actly English," Nerrière says. "I don't think people who think this gives them an edge are right because it's not useful if they cannot be understood by English speakers." His primer, Parlez Globish, is an attempt to codify worldspeak and since its publication by Eyrolles in Paris last year, he says, his Web site www.jpn-globish.com has had almost 36,000 hits.

A retired IBM marketing executive, Nerrière speaks excellent English 6 but switches to Globish if he is not getting through. "I look at their faces. Lack of understanding is very easy to decipher."

The main principles of Globish are a vocabulary of only 1,500 words 7 in English (the OED lists 615,000), gestures and repetition. Grammar will be dealt with in the next volume, "Découvrez le Globish," due next month.

The Web site also includes song lyrics because Nerrière reckons this is 8 an excellent way to learn words, even if they are not on the Globish 1,500. "Strangers in the Night" is one choice, but what is the student to do when Sinatra goes "scoobie-doobie-do"?

"Doesn't matter," Nerrière replies buoyantly. "I saw 'A Chorus Line' 9 three or four times on Broadway and I know all the songs by heart. I never understood the line 'If Troy Donahue can be a movie star you can be a movie star,' but I managed to reproduce it well enough in a way it could be understood."

The point, he says, is to reach the threshold of understanding. But nei- 10 ther threshold nor understanding is on the 1,500-word list. "In Globish it would be the target, the goal, the objective. I use three words to reach the point where you would be understood everywhere."

The list goes from "able" to "zero." Niece and nephew, for example, 11 are not included, "but you can replace them with the children of my brother," Nerrière says. He feels he erred in putting in both beauty and beautiful and in including "much" and "many" but not "lot."

"Much is for ideas, many is for things you can count. A lot works for 12 both cases, the others require a little more understanding."

The seeds for Globish came about in the 1980s when Nerrière was 13 working for IBM in Paris with colleagues of about 40 nationalities. At a meeting where they were to be addressed by two Americans whose flight had been delayed, they started exchanging shoptalk in what Nerrière calls "une certaine forme d'anglais perverti." Then the Americans arrived and beyond their opening phrases, "Call me Jim," "Call me Bill," no one understood a word. And Jim and Bill, needless to say, did not understand perverted English.

One might say that, except for Jim and Bill of course, everyone was   14 speaking Globish though they didn't know it. "They all, like me, spoke low-quality English, not really Globish. One might have a vocabulary of 2,000 words, another of 1,200 and not the same words. One of the things of interest in Globish is that with 1,500 words you can express everything. People all over the world will speak with the same limited vocabulary."

With many corporations imposing English as the lingua franca wher-   15 ever their base, Nerrière sees a great future for Globish, which he has trademarked. Learning it by computer and practicing it by free-access telephone will make things even easier. And there is a new law in France that gives employees the right to 20 hours per year of instruction in a given subject.

"The idea is to increase their employability by teaching them skills un-   16 related to their present employment. For me, the odds of someone asking for a course in macramé are very small and the odds of asking for a course in Maltese are also small. Why not Globish? If it could be of use in this small grocery shop where I work maybe it will help me in the big hotel where I hope to be."

There is an other advantage, he argues. "At 20 hours a year you need   17 24 years to learn English with no result whatsoever since it would be spread too thin for the learner to remember what had been said two weeks earlier. With Globish you not only have free telephone access via the Internet but you could get cheap lessons in places like India where people speak good English and wages are low."

Nerrière reckons that with 182 hours plus learning "Strangers in the   18 Night," the student should be able to communicate in Globish. It is not a pretty language—full of redundancies and lumpy constructions—but Nerrière repeats that it is nothing but a tool when proper English is not understood. "It is not the language of Hamlet, Faulkner or Virginia Woolf," he explains.

But the worst thing for the French about this international language is   19 that it isn't French. Nerrière argues rather subtly that if people learned Globish, the French language would remain unsullied because franglais would die out.

"It would end this crazy French terror about English and francophonie. 20
The French say you are killing the French language and I say, no, we are
saving it from being killed by English."

There is one possible hiccup in this scheme. The fluent Globish speaker 21
will not be understood by native English speakers. No problem: Nerrière
already is preparing a Globish version in English in addition to the Italian
and Spanish editions, which will be out shortly. So he is not only protecting French from invasion but he is getting Americans to become, so to
speak, bilingual.

"Absolutely!" Nerrière says triumphantly. "This is the way to get 22
Americans to learn another language."

Thinking About the Essay

1. How effectively does the opening paragraph anticipate the description of
   the event that actually inspired the invention of Globish?

2. How does the author alternate between direct quotation and paraphrase to
   give the effect of an interview exchange as it might have sounded while in
   progress? How successful is the simulation?

3. What is the purpose of the self-reflexive gesture in paragraph 6?

4. What is the author's tone with regard to her subject? Point to evidence in
   the text.

5. Why does the French response to Globish receive special attention in the
   essay?

Responding in Writing

6. Is there a fundamental difference between language considered as a "vehicle of a culture" and language as "a means of communication"? Defend or
   attack the distinction in a brief essay.

7. The inventor of Globish is quoted as saying (paragraph 14) that "with
   1,500 words you can express everything." In a brief essay, consider one
   form of expression that you feel cannot be translated into a more limited,
   pragmatic vocabulary. What aspects of this use of language explain its resistance to paraphrase?

8. How do you respond to the sentiment expressed by Nerrière in the quotation that ends the essay? Do you think Globish constitutes, or would encourage, the learning of another language? Defend your position in a brief
   essay.

Networking

9. In groups of three or four, come up with one complex, tonally nuanced sentence that draws from the full repertoire of "standard," OED English. Exchange sentences with other groups and attempt, as a group, to translate the sentence you are given into Globish.

10. Go online and visit the Globish website (www.jpn-globish.com). List three words that you are surprised are not listed in the 1,500-word Globish dictionary.

Lingua Franchise

CHARLES FORAN | Charles Foran is from Toronto and holds degrees from the University of Toronto and University College, Dublin. He has taught at universities in China, Hong Kong, and Canada. Foran is the author of seven books, including four novels, and writes regularly for Canadian journals. He has also produced radio documentaries for the Canadian Broadcasting Company's *Ideas* program on subjects ranging from Hong Kong Cinema to contemporary Indian writing. In the following piece, which first appeared in *The Walrus Magazine* in November of 2004, Foran looks at how English has been adopted and adapted in the global marketplace.

Before Reading

What elements of a slang dialect make an appearance in your casual speech? How many people do you know who practice this dialect?

In a restaurant in Singapore's Little India district I chatted recently with a   1
man doling out bowls of fish-head curry. He called me a *"mat saleh,"*
Malay for 'white foreigner.' He also dubbed a woman who walked past us
an "S.P.G."—a 'Sarong Party Girl.' According to him, upper-crust Singaporians who put on posh accents were "chiak kantang." "Chiak" is Hokkien
for 'eating,' "kantang" a mangling of the Malay for 'potatoes.' 'Eating potatoes': affecting Western mannerisms.

Singapore has four official languages: Mandarin, English, Malay, and   2
Tamil. At street level, however, there is no mother tongue. Except for
among older Chinese, who still speak the Hokkien dialect, the city-state's
lingua franca is actually Singlish, a much-loved, much-frowned-upon
hodge-podge of languages and slang. When the man in the restaurant asked
if I could pay with a smaller bill, he expressed it this way: "Got, lah?" I rec-

ognized that bit of cobbling. In Hong Kong, where I was then living, Cantonese speakers sprinkle their English with similar punctuation. 'Lah' often denotes a question, like 'eh' for Canadians. 'Wah' infers astonishment. Once, when I was walking through that city's nightclub district with a Chinese friend, we nearly knocked into a Canto-pop star, a young man of smouldering Elvis looks. "Wah, now can die!" my friend said, only half-jokingly.

If English is the region's compromise tongue, default neutral terrain for doing deals and making friends, loan words and hybrid street dialects serve to advance its utility. It is the same across most of Asia. In the Philippines, Tagalog speakers refer to a look-alike as a "Xerox" and an out-dated fad as a "chapter." "Golets," they say, meaning 'Let's go.' Anything first-rate in Bombay gets called "cheese," from 'chiz,' the Hindi word for 'object.' In Japan, students on a Friday night announce "Let's beer!" and salarymen quit smoking because of a "dokuto-sutoppu" a 'doctor-stop,' or orders from their physician. The majority of these word constructions would be no more comprehensible to a North American than the latest slang out of England or Australia. They belong to the places that formed them.

All this activity marks an interesting point from which to examine the latest evidence surrounding the explosion of English, which now boasts 1.9 billion competent speakers worldwide. In the view of Montreal writer Mark Abley, author of *Spoken Here: Travels Among Threatened Languages*, "no other language has ever enjoyed the political, economic, cultural, and military power that now accompanies English." English, he says, acts like a "brand name" and serves as a "repository of global ambition." Describing a quiz given to young Malaysians that contained references to American culture, Abley reports: "The obvious theme is the United States. But the subtler theme, I think, is power."

"Language annihilation," he writes, may just be one battle in the "wider war"—"the fight to sustain diversity on a planet where globalizing, assimilating, and eradicating occur on a massive scale." Mark Abley is far from alone in linking the spread of English with fears of a bland consumerist empire—i.e. with a certain vision of American might. Geoffrey Hull, an Australian linguist quoted in *Spoken Here*, advises the banning of unsubtitled English programming on TV in East Timor. "English," Hull warns, "is a killer language."

Such unease isn't hard to understand. Of the 6,000 living languages, some ninety percent are at risk of vanishing before the end of this century. These are tongues spoken by fewer than 100,000 people, and rarely as the only means of communication. For some linguists, the death of each marks the disappearance of a world view. Without a language to call one's own, original stories stop being told and unique conversations with God diminish. English triumphs just one set of stories and one conversation.

But is the link between the "tidal wave" of English, as Abley describes 7
it, and the threat to variety so direct? History isn't without precedents for this kind of upheaval. With a few centuries of the empire in Ancient Greece, for instance, languages spoken by Trojans, Sumerians, Lydians, Etruscans and Sycthians, to name a few, had been rendered extinct. Each of those societies contributed to the first great renaissance in western civilization. Classical Greek itself went on to serve as a foundation for a few other languages, including this one.

Cries of English the cultural barbarian aren't new, either. In the 19th 8
century, France's *civilisatrice* and Germany's *kultur* programs granted the colonial aggressions of those nations a patina of benevolence. England's ambitions, in contrast, were given no similar benefit of the doubt, being equated from the start with an unbridled lust for power. Over the past fifty years, as the U.S. has come to supplant Cruel Britannia as the primary 'exporter' of the tongue, it has come to bear most of the criticisms. When a Muslim group recently denounced the Arabic version of the *Idol* TV series because it "facilitates the culture of globalization led by America," it didn't matter that the program had originated in England. In certain minds, English can only ever be the language of McDonald's and Nike, Madonna and Cruise.

By this reasoning, English couldn't form a natural part of Singaporian 9
street life or Filipino cross-language talk. It couldn't be the rightful possession of the millions of Indians who now call it their mother tongue. But the truth is, English isn't just exploding across the universe; it is being exploded on contact with other societies and languages. No single political power or region, it could be argued, can fairly claim it as its exclusive spokesperson.

In Asia, at least, English certainly feels this protean. The Hong Kong 10
author Nury Vittachi has been charting the emergence of a pan-Southeast-Asian argot. He calls the argot 'Englasian,' the wonky dialect of international business types and youthful hipsters. Vittachi even penned a short play in Englasian called *Don't Stupid Lah, Brudder*. The setting is a bar in a Jakarta hotel and the characters are a Malaysian investor, an Indian accountant, and an Australian entrepreneur. The Malay says things like "No nid-lah, sit-sit, don't shy." The Auzzie counters with "Don't do yer lolly, mate. Let's have a squiz." Of the three, the Indian is the most readily intelligible. She speaks of how she might be able to "facilitate my cousin-brother, a revered Sydneysider."

Spend any time in the region and two things become obvious. First, 11
English still makes only a minor noise, and only in the major cities. Its consumer blandishments pale against home-grown magazines, movies, and

pop singers. No major Asian language, be it Mandarin, Malay, Japanese, or any of the fourteen principal Indian tongues, is at risk of vanishing. Interestingly, those languages are themselves killing off their own sub-dialects and non-standard variants. The world is everywhere too connected for the health of the linguistically vulnerable.

The second observation relates to the playfulness of inventions like 12 Singlish. If Asians are threatened by the growing presence of English, they are expressing their fear in the strangest manner—by inviting the danger into their homes. Linguists praise a language for its capacity to acquire and assimilate expressions from elsewhere. Such openness is taken as a sign of confidence and growth. The principal languages of nearly half of humanity are, by this measure, prospering. English isn't storming these cultures to wage war on them. The locals, at least, aren't under that impression. They view the language mostly as a tool, one they can manipulate, and even make their own.

Thinking About the Essay

1. What is the pun in the title? Is this, in your opinion, an appropriate title for the essay?

2. What is the effect of the rapid translations of phrases and terms given in the first two paragraphs? How important is the narrator's identity or point of view?

3. According to the author, how do languages work at the "street level," in contrast to the "official" level? In what sense do loan words and hybrid street dialects "advance [the] utility" of English (paragraph 3)?

4. What is the author's attitude toward the critic Mark Abley and his conclusion that English is a "killer language" (paragraph 5)?

5. What does Foran mean when he writes (in paragraph 11) that the "world is everywhere too connected for the health of the linguistically vulnerable"?

Responding in Writing

6. Is it true that the death of a language "marks the disappearance of a world view" (paragraph 6)? In a brief essay, consider the relationship between language and thought. How can language *give birth* to a worldview?

7. Do you agree with Foran's claim that "no single political power or region . . . can fairly claim [English] as its exclusive spokesperson" (paragraph 9)? Respond to this statement in an argumentative essay.

8. Compare Foran's critique of those who view language as an instrument of commercial exploitation with Kwame Anthony Appiah's argument in "Toward a New Cosmopolitanism" (Chapter 6). Where do these authors' positions overlap?

Networking

9. As a class, make a list of words or phrases that have been recently acquired and assimilated in American English. Is it accurate to say of any of these new acquisitions that they also introduce a new set of *concepts*?

10. Go online and perform a Google search of one of the terms or phrases Foran heard in the Singapore restaurant (paragraphs 1–2). How does this language appear in print, online, in contrast to the spoken context Foran describes?

Spanglish: The Making of a New American Language

ILAN STAVANS

Ilan Stavans was born in Mexico in 1961 to an Eastern European Jewish family and moved to New York City in the mid-1980s to attend Columbia University. Stavans is the editor of *The Oxford Book of Latin American Essays, The Oxford Book of Jewish Stories,* and the author of numerous works on Hispanic literature and culture. In genres ranging from literary criticism to the memoir, he has explored issues of language and identity in books including *Imagining Columbus: The Literary Voyage* (2001); *The Hispanic Condition: The Power of a People* (1995); and with Chicano artist Lalo Alcaraz, *LatinoUSA: A Cartoon History* (2000). A collection of his short stories, *The One-Handed Pianist and Other Stories*, appeared in 1996. Stavans, the recipient of a Guggenheim Fellowship and the Latino Literature Prize, is currently the Lewis-Sebring Professor in Latin-American and Latino Culture at Amherst College. In the following selection, which appears in *Spanglish: The Making of a New American Language* (2003), Stavans combines personal and analytical writing to explore a popular form of discourse.

Before Reading

What is your response to being required to speak or write a certain kind of English in the classroom and, perhaps, in the workplace? Why do these requirements, which may create tensions between people of different backgrounds, exist?

¿Cómo empezó everything? How did I stumble upon it? Walking the   1
streets of El Barrio in New York City, at least initially. Wandering

around, as the Mexican expression puts it, con la oreja al vuelo, with ears wide open. Later on, of course, my appreciation for Spanglish evolved dramatically as I traveled around los Unaited Esteits. But at the beginning was New York. It always is, isn't it?

I had arrived in Manhattan in the mid-eighties. My first one-room   2 apartment, which I shared with three roommates, was on Broadway and 122nd Street. The area was bustling with color: immigrants from the Americas, especially from the Dominican Republic, Mexico, El Salvador, and Colombia, intermingling with students from Columbia University, Barnard and Teacher's College, and with future ministers and rabbis from Union Theological Seminary and The Jewish Theological Seminary. The ethnic juxtaposition was exhilarating indeed. But sight wasn't everything. Sound was equally important. Color and noise went together, as I quickly learned.

I was enthralled by the clashing voices I encountered on a regular walk   3 in the Upper West Side: English, Spanish, Yiddish, Hebrew . . . Those voices often changed as one oscillated to different areas of the city: Arabic, French, Polish, Russian, Swahili and scores of other tongues were added to the mix. What kind of symphony was I immersed in? Was this the sound of the entire universe or only of my neighborhood?

There was a newspaper stand on the corner of 110th and Broadway,   4 next to a bagel bakery and a Korean grocery store. I regularly made my shopping in those blocks, so I regularly stopped to browse. Newspapers and magazines in English predominated in it, and Chinese and Israeli periodicals were also for sale. But the owner displayed the Spanish-language items with emphasis: *El Diario/La Prensa, Noticias del Mundo, Diario de las Américas, Cosmopolitan, Imagen* . . . As a Mexican native, I often bought one of them in the morning, "just to keep up with what's up," as I would tell my friends. But to keep up with these publications was also to invite your tongue for a bumpy ride. The grammar and syntax used in them was never fully "normal," e.g., it replicated, often unconsciously, English-language patterns. It was obvious that its authors and editors were americanos with a loose connection to la lengua de Borges. "Están contaminaos . . . ," a teacher of mine in the Department of Spanish at Columbia would tell me. "Pobrecitos . . . They've lost all sense of verbal propriety."

Or had they?   5

My favorite section to read in *El Diario/La Prensa,* already then the   6 fastest-growing daily in New York, where I eventually was hired to be a columnist, was the hilarious classified section. "Conviértase en inversor del Citibank," claimed an ad. Another one would state: "Para casos de divorcio y child support, llame a su advocate personal al (888) 745-1515." And:

"¡¡¡ Alerta!!! Carpinteros y window professionals. Deben tener 10 años de experiencia y traer tools." Or, "Estación de TV local está buscando un editor de lineal creativo. Debe tener conocimiento del 'Grass Valley Group VPE Series 151'. En The Bronx. Venga en persona: (718) 601-0962." One morning I came across one that announced pompously: "Hoy más que nunca, tiempo is money." And I stumbled upon another that read: "Apartments are selling like pan caliente and apartments de verdad."

Today I use the term *hilarious* in a reverent fashion. Over the years my admiration for Spanglish has grown exponentially, even though I'm perfectly conscious of its social and economic consequences. Only 14 percent of Latino students in the country graduate from college. The majority complain that the cultural obstacles along the way are innumerable: the closely knit family dynamic, the need to help support their family, the refusal to move out from home in order to go to school . . . And language, naturally: for many of them proficiency in the English language is too high a barrier to overcome. English is the door to the American Dream. Not until one masters el inglés are the fruits of that dream attainable.

Spanglish is often described as the trap, la trampa Hispanics fall into on the road to assimilation—el obstáculo en el cainino. Alas, the growing lower class uses it, thus procrastinating the possibility of un futuro mejor, a better future. Still, I've learned to admire Spanglish over time. Yes, it is the tongue of the uneducated. Yet, it's a hodgepodge . . . But its creativity astonished me. In many ways, I see in it the beauties and achievements of jazz, a musical style that sprung up among African-Americans as a result of improvisation and lack of education. Eventually, though, it became a major force in America, a state of mind breaching out of the ghetto into the middle class and beyond. Will Spanglish follow a similar route?

Back then, as my early immigrant days unfolded, it was easier to denigrate it. Asked by a reporter in 1985 for his opinion on el espanglés, one of the other ways used to refer to the linguistic juxtaposition of south and north—some other categories are casteyanqui, inglañol, argot sajón, español bastardo, papiamento gringo, and caló pachuco—Octavio Paz, the Mexican author of *The Labyrinth of Solitude* (1950) and a recipient of the Nobel Prize for Literature, is said to have responded with a paradox: "ni es bueno ni es malo, sino abominable"—it is neither good nor bad but abominable. This wasn't an exceptional view: Paz was one of scores of intellectuals with a distaste for the bastard jargon, which, in his eyes, didn't have gravitas. Una lengua bastarda: illegitimate, even wrongful.

The common perception was that Spanglish was sheer verbal chaos— el habla de los bárbaros. As I browsed through the pages of Spanish-language periodicals, as I watched TV and listened to radio stations en español, this approach increasingly made me uncomfortable. There was something, un yo no sé qué, that was simply exquisite . . . Of course, it took me no time to recognize that standard English was the lingua franca of the middle and upper classes, but its domain was in question in the lower strata of the population. In that segment, I wasn't able to recognize the English I expected to hear: monolithic, homogenous, single-minded. Instead, I constantly awakened to a polyphonic reality.

Depending on the individual age, ethnicity, and educational back- 11 ground, a vast number of dispossessed nuyorquinos spoke a myriad of tongues, a sum of parts impossible to define. Indeed, the metropolis seemed to me a veritable Tower of Babel. And among Hispanics—the rubric *Latino* was only then emerging—this hullabaloo, this mishmash was all the more intense.

Mishmash is a Hebrew term that means fusion. In and of itself, the 12 word Spanglish is that mixture: a collage, part Spanish, part English. I'm an etymological freak, always on the lookout for a lexicographic definition. I've sought for the inclusion and explanation of the word *Spanglish* in dictionaries.

Doctor Samuel Johnson, an idol of mine, once said that "dictionaries 13 are like watches: the worst is better than none, and the best cannot be expected to go quite true." Perhaps that is the reason why so many ignore so common a verbal phenomenon: the best lexicon is never good enough, or the worst will build a fence around it not to let undignified terms erupt on its pages. For shouldn't a lexicon, seeking to categorize the rowdy and infinite Spanglish exchanges, "to go as true as it might," in Johnson's mindset, begin by giving the meaning of the word?

Again, think of el jazz. In the seventies, Herbie Hancock offered a bril- 14 liant analogy: "It is something very hard to define," he said, "but very easy to recognize." Spanglish, I'm convinced, fits the same bill: it's not that it is impossible to define, but that people simply refuse to do it. And yet, nobody has the slightest doubt that it has arrived, que ya llegó . . . It is also a common vehicle of communication in places like Miami, Los Angeles, San Antonio, Houston, Albuquerque, Phoenix, Denver, and Tallahassee, as well as in countless rural areas, wherever the 35.3 million documented Latinos—this is the official number issued by the 2000 U.S. Census Bureau, which in 2003 jumped to 38.8 million, de facto making Hispanics the largest minority north of the Rio Grande—find themselves.

And, atención, Spanglish isn't only a phenomenon that takes place en los 15 Unaited Esteits: in some shape or form, with English as a merciless global force, it is spoken—and broken: no es solamente hablado sino quebrado— all across the Hispanic world, from Buenos Aires to Bogotá, from Barcelona to Santo Domingo.

Beware: Se habla el espanglés everywhere these days!   16

To contradict Paz—and perhaps to correct him—let me attempt my   17
own definition of Spanglish, once as succinct and encompassing as possible: "Spanglish, n. The verbal encounter between Anglo and Hispano
civilizations."

As is always the case with these types of dictionary "explications," it   18
already makes me unhappy. For one thing, I was tempted to write *clash* instead of *encounter,* and *language* instead of *civilization.* But then again, by
doing so I would have reduced Spanglish to a purely linguistic phenomenon, which it isn't. Para nada . . .

At any rate, one thing is to get exposed to Spanish in the streets of New   19
York, another altogether different is to use it effortlessly. As an immigrant,
my road to full participation in American life was—as it has been and continues to be for any immigrant, regardless the origin—through English. I
had come with primitive skills in Shakespeare's tongue, so during almost
my entire first decade this side of the Rio Grande, my sole objective was to
master it de la mejor manera posible, to the best of my capacity. Spanish
was the language of the past for me, English the language of my future. It
was only when I was already comfortable in both Spanish and English (as
comfortable as one is ever likely to be) that I suddenly detected the possibilities of Spanglish.

This sequence of events, no doubt, has enlarged my overall apprecia-   20
tion of it. I date my full-grown descubrimiento in the early nineties. By then
I had already left Manhattan and was living in a small New England town,
where I taught at a small liberal arts college. My responsibilities included
courses on colonial and present-day Latin America, and, on occasion, also
on Hispanic culture in Anglolandia. The latter courses were invariably
more challenging for me to teach. Students didn't register for them with the
mere hope of learning about a specific period in history. Instead, their objective was psychological; they were eager to turn the classroom into a lab-
oratory of identity.

They wanted to ask out loud: Quiénes somos? What makes us unique?   21
And why are we here? Are we members of a single minority—the Latinos—
or are we instead peoples of different ethnic, class, religious, and national
backgrounds? In the isolated milieu of Amherst, Massachusetts, the language my Latino students used was recognizable to me. But I didn't pay
much notice until Lisa Martinez showed up. (The name is fictitious and so
are some of her circumstances.) Or better, until she was a punto de
desvanecerse, about to disappear.

Originally from Istlos (e.g., East Los Angeles), Lisa, a junior, had taken   22
a number of classes with me: on popular culture—comic strips, TV soaps,

thrillers, music . . .—on autobiography, and on Argentine letters. We had established a solid relationship. Her odyssey was remarkable: Lisa had grown up in the inner city; she had been an active gang member and had seen a number of relatives and friends shot or imprisoned—vapuleados por el sistema; and she was initiated into Catholic life by an activist priest. Her tenure in Amherst, Massachusetts, was, hence, a radical change of scene for Lisa.

During her freshman year, Lisa felt disoriented, nostalgic for la casa, 23 anxious to finish and return home. She also expressed her ambivalence at being an affirmative action student, enticed to the place by a full fellowship, but often looked at suspiciously by her Anglo counterparts because of her skin color, su pigmentación mestiza and her ethnic idiosyncrasy. Still, in her third year of college she appeared to have found inner and outer balance.

However, in recent times, whenever we stumbled across one another in 24 the hallway, Lisa looked at peace with herself. It was somewhat surprising, therefore, that one frigid February, Lisa came to my office to say adiós.

"Ya me voy, profe . . . ," she announced. 25

I wasn't completely sure I understood her statement, so I asked Lisa 26 where she was going. She answered that she was going back to her hood, to Califas, where people "no son tan fregados. They are más calientes, with a little bit of dignidad." Lisa was tired of the WASPy culture of the small liberal arts college she was invited to attend with an ethnic scholarship.

"Aqui no soy más que un prieto, profe. They want me pa'las quotas, so 27 the place might say 'Chicanos are also part of our diverse student population.' Pero pa'qué, profe? I don't feel bien. I'm just a strange animal brought in a cage to be displayed pa'que los gringos no sientan culpa."

I begged her to be patient. 28

She was almost finished with her education, I said. Estaba casi de sal- 29 ida . . . One and a half more years—is that too much? But she wouldn't listen. Our entire tête-à-tête took approximately five minutes.

I never succeeded in changing Lisa's mind, nunca la convencí, and to 30 this day I regret it. Somehow, seeing her walk toward the podium during Commencement to get her Bachelor's diploma would have been a better conclusion to the New England chapter of her journey.

In retrospect, Lisa's goodbye, su partida, was quite painful. Me rompió 31 el corazón. I felt genuine affection for her. But the scene that took place between us in my office was more than about dropping out from college—at least for me. For, as I recall the occasion, the moment I opened my mouth, I realized every one of the words I uttered felt artificial, anomalous. I had wanted to tell Lisa that the separation from home is painful for everyone, that for some, like her, the separation isn't only emotional but also geographical and cultural. I told her it was important to keep in mind that H*O*M*E—and I pronounced the word patiently, comfortably, sweetly—acquires a different value, it becomes symbolic, the moment one leaves it behind. Or doesn't it? Even if she went back, her status as her mother's daughter would be different. And . . .

Pero no habia vuelta de hoja.   32

To my consternation, though, I couldn't express myself. The more I   33
tried to articulate my words, first in Spanish, then in English, the more dissatisfied I became. Any why? Because I was overwhelmed with envy. To announce her sudden farewell, Lisa wasn't using the traditional college language a pupil is expected to articulate in the professor's designated space. Instead, judging by her vocabulary and syntax, she had already departed New England for Los Angeles: she was inhabiting the language of her turf, su propia habla, not the language of the alien environment where she found herself at present.

And what was expected of me: to ask her, in that troublesome situation,   34
to switch to a more proper lengua?

That, no doubt, would have been counterproductive. What I desper-   35
ately needed was for her to feel cómoda.

But what actually happened to me is that, instead of wanting her to   36
"talk like me," my secret desire was the other way around: I wanted to use her own lingo.

Yes, en Spanglish—Lisa and I began to communicate in the jargon I had   37
frequently heard, and had been enthralled by, en las calles de Nuyol.

Was I happy with my switch?   38

To my chagrin, I was . . . And what did I do? Nothing, absolutamente   39
nada. I just let myself be taken by the verbal cadence of the conversation. Where is it written that faculty should elevate itself intellectually far beyond the reach of the students? Where does it say that professors cannot talk slang too? No sooner did I switch to Spanglish, though, that I realized that, as a teacher, I had crossed a dangerous line—una línea peligrosa.

My immediate, mechanical reaction was in tune with the milieu I came   40
from as a middle-class Jew from Mexico whose choice it was to emigrate to El Norte: What on earth es ésto? I asked myself. Why was I mimicking Lisa? Wasn't my role as an intellectual and teacher to protect the purity and sanctity of el español and el inglés, rather than endorse this verbal promiscuity?

If I, and others like me, endorse this chaos of words, where is this syn-   41
tactical amalgam leading us if not to hell? These were not easy questions. My tongue was moving in one direction and my heart in another. The more I rationalized what I was doing, the more guilt I felt. But I also realized that, through my standard English and Spanish, I lived in a verbal stratosphere

remote from the universe I purported to invoke—and teach—in the classroom, for pupils just like my dear Lisa Martinez. Besides, in Spanglish I felt freer, más libre. I didn't sense it as an imported, unnatural self. On the contrary, using it made me blissful.

Me sentí feliz!   42

Over the years, I've returned to that fated encounter hundreds of times.   43
A door closed for Lisa Martinez that day but another one opened for me, a door se abrió and I walked through only to be radically transformed by the path I followed. That door has led me to more difficult questions.

Thinking About the Essay

1. What is Stavans's thesis?

2. What connections does Stavans draw between racism and language? How does he develop this connection? Point to specific passages to support your answer.

3. Stavans combines narrative and exposition in this essay. What stories does he tell? How does he order them within the essay? What comparative elements does he develop?

4. Part of our interest in this essay—and in Stavans—is his personal voice, the way in which he struggles to find a language to capture his identity. How does he go about doing this? What self-image does he create? Justify your answer by reference to the text.

5. Stavans develops extended definitions of Spanglish. What are some of the rhetorical techniques he uses to flesh out this extended definition? What is the primary audience for his definition? How do you know?

Responding in Writing

6. Stavans speaks of his discovery of Spanglish. Have you undergone a similar connection of your language to your identity? Write a personal essay on this topic.

7. In his conversations with his student Lisa, Stavans comes to realize that it is "important to keep in mind that H*O*M*E—and I pronounce the word patiently, comfortably, sweetly—acquires a different value, it becomes symbolic, the moment one leaves it behind" (paragraph 31). Write an essay responding to his observation, focusing on the role of language in creating a sense of "home."

8. Write an essay on Stavans's contention that "English is the door to the American Dream" (paragraph 7). Do you agree or disagree with his statement? Be surc to support your argument with examples and illustrations.

Networking

9. With another class member, look into popular websites for Latino/Latina/ Hispanic culture in urban North America. To what extent do these websites use "Spanglish"?

10. Search the Internet for information on the Mexican Jewish community. Prepare notes for a five-minute lecture on the subject.

Multilingual America

WILLIAM H. FREY

> William H. Frey is a senior fellow of demographic studies at the Milken Institute in Santa Barbara, California. He is also on the faculty of the Population Studies Center at the University of Michigan. In the following essay, which appeared in the July/August 2002 issue of *American Demographics,* Frey analyzes the rise in American households where the inhabitants speak a language other than English. The writer offers data drawn from the 2000 United States Census to trace recent population shifts, the rise of ethnic communities in urban and nonurban areas, and the impact on the American "melting pot" of people who speak a language other than English at home.

Before Reading

How can English be taught to new immigrants who stay in their own ethnic communities and prefer to speak their own language at home? If you were involved in policymaking, what programs would you design for these individuals?

America's identity as a melting pot now extends beyond multiple races 1 and cultures to also include numerous languages. Ours is an increasingly multilingual nation, due to a new wave of immigration.

The number of individuals who speak a language other than English at 2 home is on the rise. This population is also on the move: No longer restricted to traditional port-of-entry cities, such as New York and Los Angeles, foreign-language speakers are now sprouting up in certain Southeastern and Western states.

For the first time, thanks to Census 2000 long-form data, we are able to 3 identify these new locations where residents who speak a foreign language are making their presence felt. Although relatively small, this population is beginning to constitute a critical mass in many communities—reason alone for businesses seeking new markets to take note.

Nationally, Americans age 5 and older who speak a language other   4
than English at home grew 47 percent in the past decade. According to
Census 2000, this group now accounts for slightly less than 1 in 5 Americans (17.9 percent). About three-fifths of this group speak Spanish at home
(59.9 percent), another fifth speaks another Indo-European language (21.3
percent) and almost 15 percent speak an Asian language.

Overall, foreign-language speakers grew by about 15 million during the   5
1990s, with new Spanish speakers contributing about 11 million people
and new Asian speakers almost 2.5 million. Continued immigration from
Latin America and Asia has increased the number of people who speak languages native to those regions.

Foreign-Language Havens

These foreign-language speakers are concentrated in 10 states, each where   6
20 percent or more of the residents speak a language other than English at
home. Led by California (40 percent), this group includes several other
Western states as well as New York, New Jersey, Florida and Rhode Island.
The concentration is even more evident when one looks at individual metropolitan areas. (See Table 4.1.)

In six metros, including Miami and Laredo, Texas, those who speak   7
only English at home are in the minority. In five Mexican border towns in
this category, Spanish accounts for more than 96 percent of non-English
languages spoken.

Other areas where more than one-third of the population speaks a lan-   8
guage other than English at home include Los Angeles, San Antonio, San
Francisco, New York and San Diego.

By far, the two largest metros that house the most foreign-language-   9
speakers are Los Angeles and New York, with more than 7 million and 6
million foreign-language speakers, respectively. Together, these two gate-
ways increased their foreign-language-speaking populations by 3.5 million
between 1990 and 2000, accounting for 24 percent of the country's total
gain. (See Figure 4.1.)

Eight metropolitan areas with the largest populations that speak a for-   10
eign language accounted for almost half (46 percent) of the nation's total
gain. Others include Phoenix, Atlanta, Las Vegas, Seattle and Denver—cities
that became secondary magnets for new immigrant groups during the 1990s.

Multilingual Expansion

Although many immigrant gateway metros still hold the lion's share of in-   11
habitants who speak a foreign language, the 1990s was a decade of extensive redistribution of foreign-born residents and hence, of foreign-language

TABLE 4.1   Spanish and Asian Language Magnets

There is some overlap between the lists of communities forming new, fast-growing enclaves of speakers of Spanish and Asian languages. The areas below all have at least 5,000 Spanish-speaking or Asian-speaking residents.

Persons speaking Spanish at home: Metro areas with greatest growth, 1990–2000	% Increase 1990–2000
Fayetteville-Springdale-Rogers, AR MSA*	609%
Elkhart-Goshen, IN MSA	403%
Raleigh-Durham–Chapel Hill, NC MSA	381%
Charlotte-Gastonia–Rock Hill, NC-SC MSA	376%
Greensboro-Winston-Salem–High Point, NC MSA	367%
Green Bay, WI MSA	354%
Hickory-Morganton-Lenoir, NC MSA	338%
Atlanta, GA MSA	314%
Fort Smith, AR-OK MSA	310%
Sioux City, IA-NE MSA	306%
Persons speaking Asian language at home: Metro areas with greatest growth, 1990–2000	
Hickory-Morganton-Lenoir, NC MSA	467%
Las Vegas, NV-AZ MSA	220%
Charlotte-Gastonia–Rock Hill, NC-SC MSA	182%
Lincoln, NE MSA	172%
Greenville-Spartanburg-Anderson, SC MSA	170%
Atlanta, GA MSA	157%
Greensboro-Winston-Salem–High Point, NC MSA	156%
Austin-San Marcos, TX MSA	156%
Raleigh-Durham–Chapel Hill, NC MSA	128%
Grand Rapids-Muskegon-Holland, MI MSA	127%

Source: William H. Frey analysis, 1990 and 2000 U.S. Census.
*MSA = Metropolitan Statistical Area as defined by the Office of Management and Budget.

speakers. Areas that had little prior familiarity with Spanish-speaking residents or those who speak an Asian language gained exposure to cultural as well as linguistic differences in their communities.

States that now have the fastest growing non-English-speaking popula- 12 tions are not typically those with the highest percentages of such people. (See Figure 4.2.) Most are Southeastern and Western states that began to attract new immigrants, often in response to an increased demand for services due to an influx of migrants from other states.

FIGURE 4.1   Native Tongues

Ten states have the largest shares of foreign-language speakers (more than one in five speaks a foreign language at home). These include several Western states, New York, New Jersey, Florida, and Rhode Island.

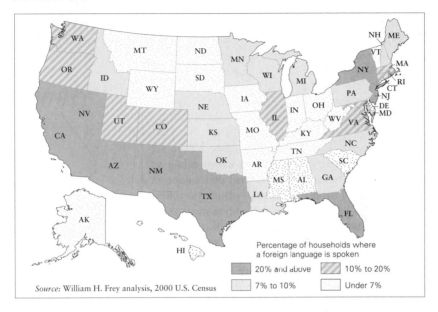

Source: William H. Frey analysis, 2000 U.S. Census

In the Southeast, this includes Georgia, North Carolina, Arkansas, Tennessee and Virginia; in the West, Arizona, Nevada, Utah, Oregon, Washington, Idaho and Colorado. Several interior states with small foreign-born populations, such as Nebraska, are also attracting new non-English-speaking residents to take a variety of service jobs.

Similar geographic patterns are evident in metropolitan areas with the fastest growth of foreign-language speakers. For example, Fayetteville, Ark., increased its non-English-speaking population by a whopping 368 percent during the 1990s. Six of the seven fastest-growing areas (Las Vegas being the exception) are in the South, including the North Carolina metros of Hickory, Raleigh-Durham–Chapel Hill, Charlotte and Greensboro.

Although in many of these enclaves foreign-language speakers account for only a small percentage of the area's total population, this is not the case for all. Las Vegas, for example, increased its share of residents who speak a foreign language to 24 percent, from 13 percent, between 1990 and 2000. Similar increases can be seen for Orlando and Naples, Fla.; Phoenix and Dallas. Significant gains also occurred in small Iowa cities, such as Sioux City, Waterloo and Des Moines.

FIGURE 4.2   Foreign-Language Growth, 1990–2000

The states with the fastest-growing non-English-speaking populations are not typically those with the highest percentages of foreign-language speakers. Such states include Georgia and North Carolina as well as Nebraska and Washington.

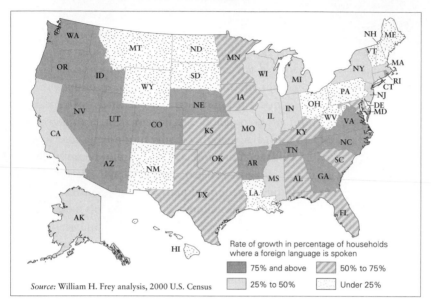

Rate of growth in percentage of households where a foreign language is spoken

- 75% and above
- 50% to 75%
- 25% to 50%
- Under 25%

Source: William H. Frey analysis, 2000 U.S. Census

Spanish and Asian Language Magnets

While Spanish dominates the foreign languages spoken at home on the na-   16
tional level, this is not true for all parts of the United States. For example,
fewer than half the foreign-language speakers in San Francisco and New
York City speak Spanish. In the former, nearly as many speak Asian languages; in the latter, a large number of residents continue to speak other
European languages at home.

Spanish represents more than half the foreign languages spoken at   17
home in only nine states. These are located mostly on the Mexican border
and in the West. Metro areas with the largest Spanish-speaking shares of
their populations reflect the same geographic pattern.

In contrast, metropolitan areas that house large shares of Asian popu-   18
lations are fewer and farther between. Honolulu tops the group, with Asian
languages spoken by almost 9 out of 10 people who speak a non-English
language at home, followed by San Francisco, Los Angeles, San Diego and
Stockton, Calif.

TABLE 4.2   Metros with Highest Shares of Foreign-Language Speakers, 2000
Six metros, including Laredo and Miami, have populations where the minority speak only English at home. In five Mexican border towns in this category, Spanish is the non-English language spoken in more than 96 percent of homes.

Name	Percent speaking non-English language at home	Spanish	Asian language	European language	Other
Laredo, TX MSA	91.9%	99.4%	0.3%	0.3%	0.0%
McAllen-Edinburg-Mission, TX MSA	83.1%	99.0%	0.5%	0.4%	0.0%
Brownsville-Harlingen–San Benito, TX MSA	79.0%	99.1%	0.4%	0.4%	0.1%
El Paso, TX MSA	73.3%	97.1%	1.0%	1.6%	0.3%
Las Cruces, NM MSA	54.4%	96.7%	0.7%	1.9%	0.7%
Miami–Fort Lauderdale, FL CMSA	51.5%	80.0%	1.9%	16.7%	1.4%
Salinas, CA MSA	47.3%	83.5%	9.1%	6.5%	0.9%
Los Angeles–Riverside–Orange County, CA CMSA	46.8%	70.7%	18.2%	9.1%	1.9%
Yuma, AZ MSA	45.5%	95.6%	1.5%	1.9%	0.9%
Merced, CA MSA	45.2%	77.7%	11.6%	10.4%	0.4%

Source: William H. Frey analysis, 2000 U.S. Census.

Considerable overlap exists between communities forming new, fast- 19 growing enclaves for Spanish speakers and those who speak an Asian language. (See Tables 4.2 and 4.3.) Of the 15 metro areas with the fastest-growing Spanish-speaking populations, six are on the list of fast-growing, Asian-language-speaking areas. These include Atlanta and Las Vegas, as well as North Carolina metros Raleigh-Durham, Charlotte, Greensboro and Hickory.

These areas are attracting new residents as a result of local universities 20 or the labor market pulls associated with general population growth and the fast-growing economies of the "New Sun Belt."

TABLE 4.3   Metros with Largest Number of Foreign-Language Speakers, 2000
The two largest metros with foreign-language speakers are Los Angeles and New York. Together they increased their foreign-language-speaking population by 3.5 million during the 1990s—about 24 percent of the nation's total gain.

Largest number of foreign-language speakers, 2000	*Number of people*
Los Angeles–Riverside–Orange County, CA CMSA	7,080.474
New York–Northern New Jersey–Long Island, NY-NJ-CT-PA CMSA	6,614.354
San Francisco–Oakland–San Jose, CA CMSA	2,368.377
Chicago-Gary-Kenosha, IL-IN-WI CMSA	2,116.043
Miami–Fort Lauderdale, FL CMSA	1,869.966
Houston-Galveston-Brazoria, TX CMSA	1,372.010
Dallas–Fort Worth, TX CMSA	1,163.502
Washington-Baltimore, DC-MD-VA-WV CMSA	1,158.677
Boston-Worcester-Lawrence, MA-NH-ME-CT CMSA	1,042.727

Source: William H. Frey analysis, 1990 and 2000 U.S. Census.

English Proficiency

One issue raised when people who speak a foreign language become new   21
residents of a community is how well they can conduct their lives in English. While it's no surprise that immigrants who have lived in the U.S. for a long time become fluent in English, Census 2000 reveals that this may not be the case with new arrivals.

The Census Bureau asked people who speak a language other than English at home this question: How well does this person speak English? (The   22
choices were: very well, well, not well or not at all.) Between 1990 and 2000, there was a larger increase of Spanish speakers who could not speak English very well than of those who could. However, for Asian language speakers, there was a larger increase between 1990 and 2000 of those who could speak English very well.

To a great extent, Spanish speakers arriving in non-gateway areas are   23
less likely to speak English very well. Among the metros with the lowest percentages of Spanish speakers speaking English very well are Greensboro, Raleigh-Durham, Charlotte and Hickory in North Carolina; Atlanta and other newer destinations for Spanish-speaking residents.

Among areas where Spanish speakers have high levels of English profi-   24
ciency are university towns like Gainesville, Fla., and Lubbock, Texas, as

well as locales with long-standing Spanish-speaking residents, such as Albuquerque, N.M.

The same pattern occurs among residents who speak an Asian language, 25 with lower levels of proficiency where such settlers are relatively new (e.g., Lincoln, Neb.; Grand Rapids, Mich.; Minneapolis–St. Paul, Minn.; Greensboro, N.C. and Atlanta). High levels of proficiency tend to be in university communities such as Gainesville, Fla.; Raleigh-Durham and Chapel Hill, N.C.; Champagne-Urbana, Ill. and Colorado Springs, Colo.

These patterns of English proficiency mirror the national picture. States 26 with the lowest levels of English proficiency tend to be those that had the fastest growth of foreign-language residents during the 1990s. Nebraska, Nevada, Oregon, North Carolina and Georgia are part of this group of states, which also includes some longer-term havens for foreign-born and foreign-language-speaking residents. For example, less than half (49 percent) of California's foreign-born residents speak English very well.

The new census data provides insights into this fast growing group of 27 Americans who speak a language other than English at home. It also highlights the fact that if the U.S. is to continue to live up to its reputation as a melting pot, this influx of foreign-language speakers will require special efforts on the parts of schools, local organizations and grassroots groups to enable these new residents to become fully integrated members of their communities.

Thinking About the Essay

1. How would you describe the writer's audience for this essay? What assumptions does he make about this audience? How does he mold his style to the expectations of the audience?

2. Explain the significance of the writer's title. What approach does he take to his subject? In other words, what is his purpose? How does his purpose govern his thesis?

3. Where is the thesis stated? How does the conclusion reinforce the thesis or color it with a mildly argumentative edge?

4. Frey employs a considerable amount of data in this essay. How relevant are these data? What aspects of the data do you find interesting? What aspects, if any, do you find weak or irrelevant?

5. The author divides his essay into sections. Summarize each section. How does each section flow from the previous unit? Is the author able to achieve unity and coherence? Justify your response.

6. There are several visual illustrations in this essay. What types are they? How do you "read" them in terms of their significance? What do they contribute to the article?

Responding in Writing

7. Use the data provided by Frey to write your own essay entitled "Our Shrinking Language Tapestry." Make your essay more argumentative than Frey's. Take a stand on the demographics Frey provides, and back up your claim with at least three good reasons or minor propositions.

8. If you belong to a family in which members normally speak a language other than English, tell about their attitude toward the use of English. Or imagine that you are part of such a household. What would your perception of your native language and this second language—English—be?

9. In the last paragraphs, Frey implies that it is important to learn English to become "fully integrated" into one's community. In an argumentative essay, agree or disagree with his statement.

Networking

10. In groups of four, obtain a copy of the 2000 United States Census, and focus on the data about immigration patterns and language use that this document provides. Then construct a group report of approximately 1,000 words highlighting and interpreting this data.

11. Go to one or more search engines and type in "English only" or "English Only Movement." Try other combinations if necessary. Download relevant information, and then participate in a class discussion of this controversy.

Reading the History of the World

ISABEL ALLENDE
Isabel Allende, the daughter of a Chilean diplomat, was born in 1942 in Lima, Peru. Isabel moved from Peru to Chile, where she was living and working at the time her uncle, Salvador Allende, the president of Chile, was assassinated during an army coup, assisted by the CIA, in 1973. "In that moment," she says, "I realized that everything was possible—that violence was a dimension that was always around you." The Allende family did not think that the new regime would last, and Isabel Allende continued to work as a noted journalist. However, when it became too dangerous to remain in Chile, the family went into exile in Venezuela. Allende's first novel, *The House of the Spirits* (1985), established her as a significant writer in the tradition of "magic realism" associated with the Nobel Prize winner Gabriel García Márquez. Other novels include *Of Love and Shadows* (1987), *Eva Luna* (1988), *Daughter of*

Fortune (1999), and *Zorro* (2005). Allende has also written an autobiography, *Paula* (1995), and stories for children. Allende has spoken of the "wind of exile" that makes it necessary to recover memories of one's native land. In this essay, which appears in a collection of essays on reading by well-known writers, *Speaking of Reading* (1995), she invokes the act of reading as one way to salvage these memories.

Before Reading

Allende declares that only through reading can we fully become aware of "injustice and misery and violence." Would you agree or disagree, and why?

Reading is like looking through several windows which open to an infinite landscape. I abandon myself to the pleasure of the journey. How could I know about other people, how could I know about the history of the world, how could my mind expand and grow if I could not read? I began to read when I was very small; I learned to read and write practically when I was a baby. For me, life without reading would be like being in prison, it would be as if my spirit were in a straitjacket; life would be a very dark and narrow place.

I was brought up in a house full of books. It was a big, strange, somber house, the house of my grandparents. My uncle, who lived in the house, had a lot of books—he collected them like holy relics. His room held a ton of books. Few newspapers were allowed in that house because my grandfather was a very patriarchal, conservative man who thought that newspapers, as well as the radio, were full of vulgar ideas (at that time we didn't have TV), so the only contact I had with the world, really, was through my uncle's books. No one censored or guided my reading; I read anything I wanted.

I began reading Shakespeare when I was nine, not because of the language or the beauty, but because of the plot and the great characters. I have always been interested in adventure, plot, strong characters, history, animals. As a child, I read children's books, most of the Russian literature, many French authors, and later, Latin American writers. I think I belong to the first generation of writers in Latin America who were brought up reading Latin American literature; earlier generations read European and North American literature. Our books were very badly distributed.

Books allow me to see my feelings put into words. After I read the feminist authors from North America, I could finally find words for the anger that I had all my life. I was brought up in a male chauvinist society and I had accumulated much anger, yet I couldn't express it. I could only be angry and do crazy things, but I couldn't put my anger into words and use it in a rational, articulate way. After I read those books, things became clearer to me, I could talk about that anger and express it in a more positive way.

The same thing happened with politics. I was aware of injustice and misery and political violence, but I couldn't express my feelings until I read about those issues and realized that other people had been dealing with them for centuries, and had already invented the words to express what I was feeling.

I have often been separated from my mother, whom I love very much. She now lives in Chile and we write a letter to each other every day. We talk about what we've read or what we are writing. I do it the first thing every morning of my life, even when I'm traveling. It's as if I were writing a journal. It's like having a long conversation with her; we are connected with a strong bond. This same bond also connects me with my daughter, who is living in Spain, because when I write the letter to my mother, I make a copy that goes to my daughter, and they do the same. This is becoming a very strange network of letters.

My mother is a much better reader than I. My reading is very fast, hectic, disorganized, and impatient. If I'm not caught in the first pages I abandon the book. My mother, however, is very patient and goes very slowly. She is the only person who reads my manuscripts, helping me to edit, revise, and correct them. She has a strong sense of poetry and such good taste. She's very well informed, very cultivated, very sensitive, and loves reading.

I have tried to give my children the love of books. My daughter is a good reader. She's a psychologist and has to read a lot of professional books, but she loves novels, short stories, poetry. My son, however, doesn't read any fiction. He's a scientific person with a mathematical mentality. I've tried to imagine how his mind and heart work, without nourishment from books, but I can't. He's a great boy, but how can he do it? I don't know.

My uncle, Salvador Allende, who was President of Chile before he was assassinated during the military coup, hardly affected my life. I liked him and loved him, but only as I do other relatives. He was the best man at my wedding. I was never involved in politics, and never participated in his government. (I became interested in politics only after the coup.) He was not a very strong reader of fiction, actually. He was always reading reports, essays, books about politics, sociology, economy, etc. He was a very well-informed person and he read very fast, his eyes practically skimming across the page to get the necessary information, but when he wanted to relax, he would rather watch a movie than read.

During the three years of Allende's government, any Chilean could buy 10 books of "Quimantu," the state publishing house, for very little money, the equivalent of two newspapers. In this way he hoped to promote culture. His goal was that every single Chilean could read and write and be able to buy as many books as he or she wanted by the end of his term.

My own experience of life, my biography, my feelings, my self as a per- 11 son, affect my reading. The writer puts out half of the book, but then I read the book in my own unique manner. This is why reading is so interesting; we as readers don't have passive roles, but very active ones. We must integrate into the text our own experiences of life and our own feelings. While reading a book, we are constantly applying our own knowledge.

Our backgrounds determine our strengths and interests as readers. 12 Many themes that are extremely popular in North America are impossible for me to read because they aren't part of my culture—I just don't care about them. For example, I can't relate to those books by daughters who write against their mothers. But if I read a book by Toni Morrison or Louise Erdrich that deals with being a woman and part of an ethnic minority, I can relate to its content. Also, I like Latin American authors very much, especially Jorge Amado, García Márquez, Mario Vargas Llosa, Juan Rulfo, Jorge Luis Borges, and many others. There are a few Latin American women writers that I enjoy as well, but they have been badly distributed and poorly reviewed. Latin American literature has been an exclusively male club, to say the least.

I have met many people, including well-informed, educated people, 13 who actually take pride in the fact that they haven't read anything by a woman. Recently, I received a clipping from a newspaper in Chile. It was a public letter to me from a Chilean entertainer apologizing that he had never before read any of my books because I am a woman. He wrote that he never read literature written by women. After he made a special effort to read my books, he felt he must apologize to me and say that I could actually write.

I will always be interested in programs of illiteracy because it is such a 14 common problem in my continent: 50 percent of the population of Latin America cannot read or write, and of those who can, only a few can afford books or have the habit of reading. To me, not reading is like having the spirit imprisoned.

Thinking About the Essay

1. List the images, metaphors, and **similes** that Allende presents in her introductory paragraph. What is her purpose? What is the effect?

2. State Allende's thesis. Is it stated or implied? Explain.

3. What strategies does Allende employ to blend personal experience and analysis? What, specifically, is she analyzing, and how does she develop her topics?

4. Allende devotes two paragraphs to her uncle, Salvador Allende (paragraphs 9 and 10). Why? How do these paragraphs influence the tone of the entire essay?

5. What causal connections does Allende establish between the acts of reading and writing and the state of society in Latin America?

Responding in Writing

6. Write an essay in which you describe your reading habits as a child and as an adult. Did you live in a house filled with books? Did you enjoy reading? What were your favorite books? Who were the readers and nonreaders in your family? Answer these questions in a personal essay.

7. Allende refers to the fact that half of the population in Latin America is illiterate. Write an analytical essay that examines the impact of illiteracy on a society or nation.

8. Imagine a reading plan for your children, and write about it. Will you leave reading development exclusively to teachers? How will you regulate your child's reading and television viewing habits? Do you agree with Allende that reading can open children to "an infinite landscape" (paragraph 1)?

Networking

9. Discuss in small groups the nature of your reading habits during various stages in your life. Report to the class on your discoveries.

10. Find out more about Salvador Allende and the Allende family. Search the Internet or conduct an advanced search with the assistance of a college librarian. Try to find specific information on Allende's literacy crusade.

Global Relationships: Are Sex and Gender Roles Changing?

5

CHAPTER

As we move into the twenty-first century, the roles of men and women in the United States and around the world are in flux. In the United States, there are increasing numbers of American women in many professional fields—medicine, law, education, politics, corporate life. And, with more men staying home and caring for their children, either by preference or necessity, there is greater equality in domestic responsibilities. At the same time, a woman's right to choose or even obtain social services is under attack. And it was only in the summer of 2003 that the United States Supreme Court struck down a Texas law that had made sex between consenting adult males in the privacy of their homes a crime. This national opposition in certain quarters to equality of rights in human relations is reflected in reactionary global attitudes and practices. Issues of race, sexual orientation, and ethnicity complicate the roles of women and men on a global scale.

American women do seem to have advantages over many of their global counterparts, for when we consider the situation of women globally, the issue of equal rights and human rights becomes acute. From increasing AIDS rates among global women, to their exploitation as cheap labor or sex workers, to female infanticide, to the continuing resistance of men in traditional societies to any thought of gender equality, the lives of women in many parts of the world are perilous. Gendered value systems in traditional societies change glacially, and often under only the most extreme conditions. For example, before the massacre of more than 800,000 Tutsi by their Hutu neighbors in Rwanda in 1993, women could not work or appear alone in the market; with the killing of so many of the men, Rwandan women suddenly had to assume responsibility for tasks they formerly had been

 **Online Study Center** This icon will direct you to weblinks, and audio and visual content, and additional resources on the website college.hmco.com/pic/mullerNWR2e

Hindu women take part in a speed-dating event at a London nightclub. Daters meet for a few minutes before moving on to the next date. Traditionally, relationships and marriages in this community were arranged by the families of the potential bride and groom.

Thinking About the Image

1. You probably know how awkward it can be to meet someone new. How do you think this photographer captured such an intimate, difficult moment between these two people?
2. What key characteristics do you see that distinguish groups of people or ethnicities in this photograph?
3. This photograph originally accompanied "Arranged Marriages Get a Little Reshuffling" by Lizette Alvarez (p. 161) How accurately does the photograph illustrate the article? Newspaper editors have a limited amount of space to fill each day—why do you think this newspaper's editors wanted to include a photograph with this story?
4. If you could take a snapshot of dating culture in your own social group, what would you need to include in order to best capture its essence? Describe the image using very specific language.

excluded from. Women are the ones who are displaced disproportionately by wars, ethnic conflicts, famine, and environmental crises.

In this new global era, the destinies of women and men around the world are intertwined. Global forces have brought them together. The role of democracy in promoting human rights, the challenge to spread wealth from North to South and West to East, the need to prevent wars, even the degradation of the environment—have notable implications for men and women. Some argue that global forces—which we will detect in some essays in this chapter and study in detail in the next chapter—are notably hostile to women. Others argue that to the extent that nations can promote peace and democracy, produce prosperity, improve health and the environment, and reduce racism and ethnocentrism, both women and men will be the beneficiaries.

The essays in this chapter present insights into the roles of men and women around the world. The writers inquire into the impact of economics, politics, race, gender and sexual orientation, and culture on the lives of women and men. They invite us to reconsider the meaning of human rights, self-determination, and equality from a gendered perspective. In the twenty-first century, new ideas have emerged about the roles and rights of women and men. The essays that follow reveal some of the challenges that must be overcome before the concept of equal rights and opportunities for women and men can be realized.

Arranged Marriages Get a Little Reshuffling

LIZETTE ALVAREZ

> In the following article, which appeared in *The New York Times* in 2003, Lizette Alvarez, a journalist for the newspaper, examines the changing attitudes and rituals concerning the traditional practice of arranged marriages. Writing from London, she focuses on "young, hip, South Asians." These young people do not reject traditions governing relations between the sexes. Instead, they "reshuffle" these conventions so that they may work successfully for them in the twenty-first century.

Before Reading

What is your attitude toward arranged marriage? In many Western nations, divorce rates approach 50 percent. Why not try arranged marriage if choosing your own mate is so frustrating and perilous?

They are young, hip, South Asians in their 20's who glide seamlessly be-   1
tween two cultures, carefully cherry picking from the West to modernize the East.

They can just as easily listen to Justin Timberlake, the pop star, as Rishi   2
Rich, the Hindu musical dynamo. They eat halal meat but wear jeans and
T-shirts to cafes.

Now these young Indians and Pakistanis are pushing the cultural   3
boundaries created by their parents and grandparents one step further:
they are reshaping the tradition of arranged marriages in Britain.

While couples were once introduced exclusively by relatives and   4
friends, the Aunt Bijis, as Muslims call their matchmakers, are now being
slowly nudged out by a boom in Asian marriage Web sites, chat rooms and
personal advertisements. South Asian speed dating—Hindus one night,
Muslims the next—is the latest phenomenon to hit London, with men and
women meeting each other for just three minutes at restaurants and bars
before moving on to the next potential mate.

Arranged marriages are still the norm within these clannish, tight-knit   5
communities in Britain, but, with the urging of second- and third-generation
children, the nature of the arrangement has evolved, mostly by necessity.

What the young Indians and Pakistanis of Britain have done, in effect,   6
is to modernize practices that had evolved among the urban middle class
in India in recent decades, allowing the prospective bride and groom a little more than one fleeting meeting to make up their minds.

The relaxation that had crept in since the 1960's allowed the couple, af-   7
ter an initial meeting before their extended families, to meet alone several
times, either with family members in another room or at a restaurant, before delivering a verdict. Now, the meetings take place in public venues
without the family encounter first.

"The term we use now is 'assisted' arranged marriage," said Maha   8
Khan, a 23-year-old London Muslim woman. "The whole concept has
changed a lot. Parents have become more open and more liberal in their
concept of marriage and courtship."

Gitangeli Sapra, a trendy, willowy British Sindhu who at 25 jokes that   9
she is on her way to spinsterhood, is an avid speed dater with no qualms
about advertising her love of modern arranged marriages. She even wrote
a column about it for *The Sunday Times.*

"It's not based on love," she said, "which can fizzle out."   10

Ms. Sapra had attended 10 of the more formal arranged meetings—   11
awkward, drawn-out affairs in which the young man, his mother and several other relatives came over to meet the young woman and her family.
She wore her best Indian outfit, a sari or elegant Indian pants and top. She

sat quietly, which is almost impossible to fathom, considering her chattiness. When called upon, she poured tea, and then talked briefly to her potential mate in a side room.

"The matriarchs do the talking," she said over a glass of wine at an Italian restaurant. "You sit there looking cute and like the ideal housewife." 12

"To be honest, it's an easy way to get a rich man, with my mother's blessing," she added, with a laugh. 13

None of them worked out, though, and Ms. Sapra has moved on to speed dating with the blessings of her mother. 14

The very concept raises the hackles of some more old-fashioned parents, but many are coming around, in part out of desperation. If Ms. Sapra finds someone on a speed date, she will quickly bring him home to her mother. 15

The abiding principles behind an arranged marriage still remain strong—lust does not a lasting marriage make and family knows best. But parents and elders, eager to avoid alienating their children, making them miserable or seeing them go unmarried, have shown considerable flexibility. This is especially pronounced among the middle class, whose members tend to have integrated more into British life. 16

"The notion of arrangement has become more fluid," said Yunas Samad, a sociology professor at Bradford University, who has studied marriage in the Muslim community. "What is happening is that the arranged marriage is becoming a bit more open and children are getting a bit more say in this so it becomes a nice compromise. There is the comfort of family support and a choice in what they are doing." 17

"It's a halfway house, not completely traditional and not completely the same as what is happening in British society," he added. 18

To the surprise of parents and elders, this new hybrid between East and West has actually stoked enthusiasm for an age-old tradition that many young people privately viewed as crusty and hopelessly unhip. 19

Now they see it as an important way to preserve religion and identity, not to mention a low-maintenance way of finding a mate. "It's like your parents giving you a black book of girls," said Ronak Mashru, 24, a London comedian whose parents are from India. 20

The young people also recognize that arranged marriages—in which similar education and income levels, religious beliefs and character outweigh the importance of physical attraction—can well outlast love marriages. 21

"The falling-in-love system has failed," said Rehna Azim, a Pakistani family lawyer who founded an Asian magazine, *Memsahib*. 22

South Asian unions are viewed as marriages between families, not in- 23
dividuals. Divorce is anathema, while respect and standing within a community are paramount. A lot of people have much invested in making a
match work.

Similarly, several customs have survived dating: decisions have to be 24
made relatively quickly, often after the second or third meeting, and, Ms.
Sapra said, "once you've said yes, there is no turning back."

Dowries remain common and background still matters, too. 25

"Our mums look at the C.V.'s," said Vani Gupta, 30, a speed dater. 26
"They figure out whether we're compatible on paper—right job, right
background, right caste. It's nice to know your parents have done the work
for you. You feel more secure."

These middle-class women, most of them educated professionals or 27
university students, are looking for more modern men, who accept working wives and help around the house. But a "mechanic won't try for a
lawyer and a lawyer would not look for a mechanic," she said.

Ms. Sapra, for example, is looking for a fellow Sindhu, and a Gujarati 28
Indian typically seeks another Gujarati.

Muslims still keep it mostly within the family and the same region of 29
Pakistan. Cousins still frequently marry cousins, or at least second or third
cousins, and many British Pakistanis still find their brides back in Pakistan.
But now more men are marrying white British women who convert to Islam, and others insist on finding a Muslim bride there who speaks English,
eats fish and chips and watches "East Enders," a popular soap opera.

Parents and elders have had to adapt, in large part because the number 30
of potential partners is much smaller here than in their home countries.
Rather than see an educated daughter go unwed, parents and elders have
accepted these more modern approaches, "Women are not going to be put
back in some kind of bottle," Professor Samad said.

Ms. Azim said, "Parents can say my child had an arranged marriage, 31
and he can say, 'Yeah, it's arranged. But I like her.'"

Thinking About the Essay

1. Writing for *The New York Times*, Alvarez knows her primary audience. What
   assumptions does she make about this audience? What secondary audiences would be interested in her topic, and why?

2. Does this article have a thesis? If so, where is it? If not, why not?

3. How does this essay reflect journalistic practice? Point to aspects of style,
   paragraph organization, article length, and other journalistic features. Is

the tone of the article strictly neutral and objective (one aspect of journalistic method), or does it shade toward commentary or perhaps even contain an implicit argument? Explain.

4. How many people were interviewed for this article? Who are they, and what are their backgrounds? Taken together, how do they embody some of the main points that Alvarez wants to make about courtship practices among some Asians today?

5. What rhetorical practices—for example, definition, comparison and contrast, process and causal analysis—can you locate in this essay? Toward what purpose does the writer use them?

Responding in Writing

6. What is the difference between people who use Internet dating sites to make their own contacts and establish their own relationships, and people from traditional societies who use the Internet to "cherry pick" prospective mates, whom they then present to their parents for appraisal. Which method strikes you as safer or potentially more successful, and why?

7. What is so great about "modern" dating and courtship practices if they often end in frustration and failure? Why not try something old, tried, and tested—like arranged marriage? Imagine that your parents insist on an arranged marriage for you. Write a personal response to this situation. Do not write that you would try to subvert the entire ritual. Instead, explain how you might "manage" this process to make the outcome acceptable.

8. Alvarez, presenting one principle behind the need for arranged marriages, writes that "lust does not a lasting marriage make" (paragraph 16). Do you agree or disagree with this claim? Provide at least three reasons to justify your response.

Networking

9. In class discussion, design a questionnaire about attitudes toward arranged marriage. Aim for at least five questions that can be answered briefly. Then have each class member obtain several responses to the questionnaire from other students. Compile the results, discuss them, and arrive at conclusions.

10. Investigate an Internet dating site. Sign up for it if you feel comfortable, or simply monitor the site for information. Report your findings to the class.

In Africa, AIDS Has a Woman's Face

KOFI A. ANNAN │ Kofi A. Annan was born in the Gold Coast, as Ghana was known under British rule, in 1938. The son of a Fonte nobleman, he graduated in1957 from Mfantsipim, a prestigious boarding school for boys that had been founded by the Methodist Church; Ghana won its independence from Great Britain that same year. After studies at the University of Science and Technology in Kumasi, Annan came to the United States on a Ford Foundation fellowship in 1959, completing his degree in economics at Macalester College in St. Paul, Minnesota. He also has a master's degree in management from the Massachusetts Institute of Technology (1972). Annan has worked for the United Nations in various capacities for four decades and has been secretary general of the United Nations since 1997. In the following essay, which appeared in *The New York Times* in 2003, he writes about one of the many "problems without borders" that he believes we must deal with from an international perspective.

Before Reading

Consider the impact that AIDS has on a developing nation or an entire region. What are the economic consequences of the AIDS epidemic in these countries? What happens to the condition of women in such societies?

A combination of famine and AIDS is threatening the backbone of   1
Africa—the women who keep African societies going and whose work makes up the economic foundation of rural communities. For decades, we have known that the best way for Africa to thrive is to ensure that its women have the freedom, power and knowledge to make decisions affecting their own lives and those of their families and communities. At the United Nations, we have always understood that our work for development depends on building a successful partnership with the African farmer and her husband.

Study after study has shown that there is no effective development strat-   2
egy in which women do not play a central role. When women are fully involved, the benefits can be seen immediately: families are healthier; they are

better fed; their income, savings and reinvestment go up. And, what is true of families is true of communities and, eventually, of whole countries.

But today, millions of African women are threatened by two simulta-   3
neous catastrophes: famine and AIDS. More than 30 million people are now at risk of starvation in southern Africa and the Horn of Africa. All of these predominantly agricultural societies are also battling serious AIDS epidemics. This is no coincidence: AIDS and famine are directly linked.

Because of AIDS, farming skills are being lost, agricultural development   4
efforts are declining, rural livelihoods are disintegrating, productive capacity to work the land is dropping and household earnings are shrinking—all while the cost of caring for the ill is rising exponentially. At the same time, H.I.V. infection and AIDS are spreading dramatically and disproportionately among women. A United Nations report released last month shows that women now make up 50 percent of those infected with H.I.V. worldwide—and in Africa that figure is now 58 percent. Today, AIDS has a woman's face.

AIDS has already caused immense suffering by killing almost 2.5 mil-   5
lion Africans this year alone. It has left 11 million African children orphaned since the epidemic began. Now it is attacking the capacity of these countries to resist famine by eroding those mechanisms that enable populations to fight back—the coping abilities provided by women.

In famines before the AIDS crisis, women proved more resilient than   6
men. Their survival rate was higher, and their coping skills were stronger. Women were the ones who found alternative foods that could sustain their children in times of drought. Because droughts happened once a decade or so, women who had experienced previous droughts were able to pass on survival techniques to younger women. Women are the ones who nurture social networks that can help spread the burden in times of famine.

But today, as AIDS is eroding the health of Africa's women, it is erod-   7
ing the skills, experience and networks that keep their families and communities going. Even before falling ill, a woman will often have to care for a sick husband, thereby reducing the time she can devote to planting, harvesting and marketing crops. When her husband dies, she is often deprived of credit, distribution networks or land rights. When she dies, the household will risk collapsing completely, leaving children to fend for themselves. The older ones, especially girls, will be taken out of school to work in the home or the farm. These girls, deprived of education and opportunities, will be even less able to protect themselves against AIDS.

Because this crisis is different from past famines, we must look beyond   8
relief measures of the past. Merely shipping in food is not enough. Our effort will have to combine food assistance and new approaches to farming
with treatment and prevention of H.I.V. and AIDS. It will require creating
early-warning and analysis systems that monitor both H.I.V. infection rates
and famine indicators. It will require new agricultural techniques, appropriate to a depleted work force. It will require a renewed effort to wipe out
H.I.V.-related stigma and silence.

It will require innovative, large-scale ways to care for orphans, with   9
specific measures that enable children in AIDS-affected communities to
stay in school. Education and prevention are still the most powerful
weapons against the spread of H.I.V. Above all, this new international effort must put women at the center of our strategy to fight AIDS.

Experience suggests that there is reason to hope. The recent United Na-   10
tions report shows that H.I.V. infection rates in Uganda continue to decline. In South Africa, infection rates for women under 20 have started to
decrease. In Zambia, H.I.V. rates show signs of dropping among women in
urban areas and younger women in rural areas. In Ethiopia, infection levels have fallen among young women in the center of Addis Ababa.

We can and must build on those successes and replicate them else-   11
where. For that, we need leadership, partnership and imagination from the
international community and African governments. If we want to save
Africa from two catastrophes, we would do well to focus on saving Africa's
women.

Thinking About the Image

1. Although the map on the facing page did not appear with Kofi Annan's editorial, it was produced by a United Nations group formed to educate people
   about, and actively combat, H.I.V./AIDS. In what ways does this map visu-
   ally represent the trends Annan describes? How does the map make the urgency of his argument more immediate?

2. Is there any information on the map that surprises you?

3. If you were a delegate to the United Nations from an African or Asian nation, what questions or responses would you have for Secretary-General
   Kofi Annan?

4. Use the information in this map to support your answer to any of the "Responding in Writing" questions.

FIGURE 5.1   Regional Estimates of H.I.V./AIDS Infection as of December 2002.

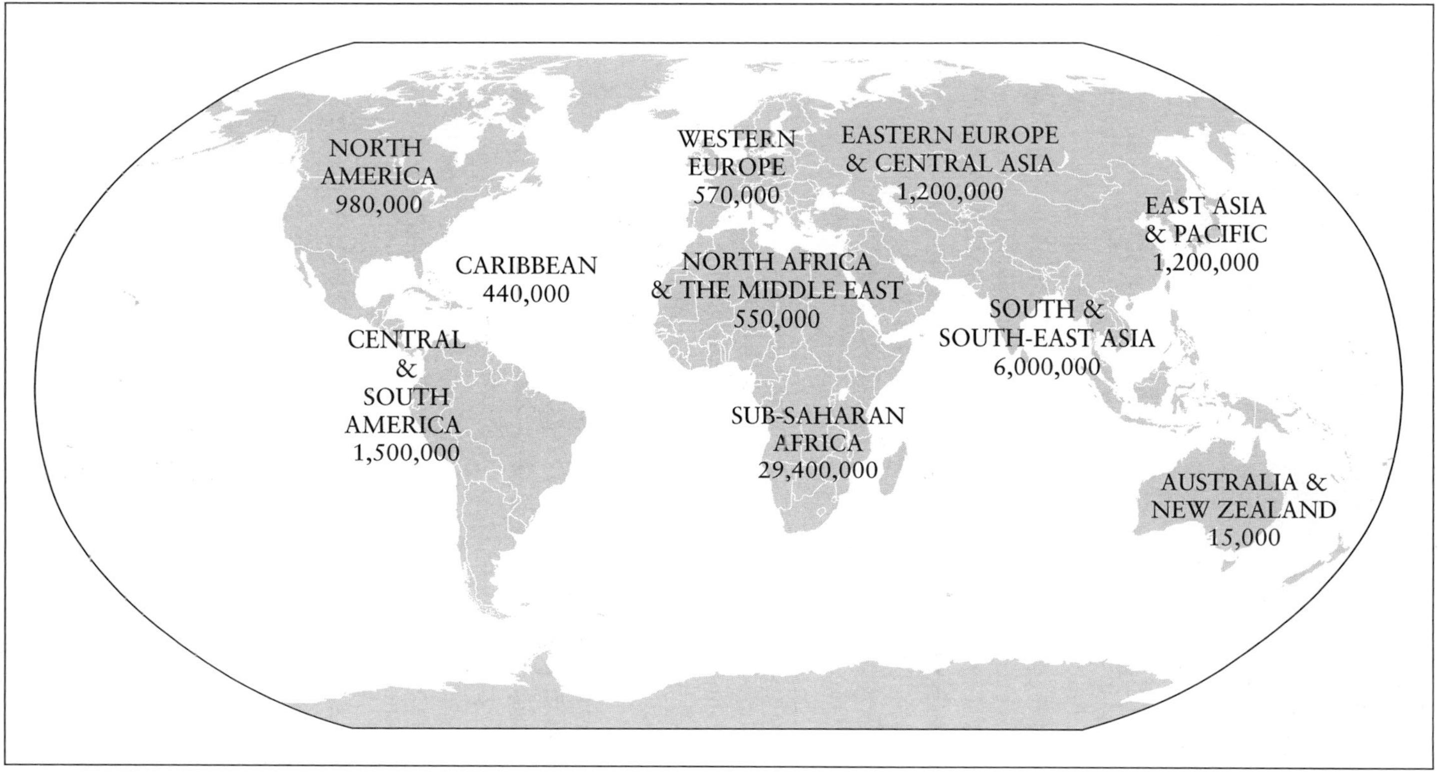

NORTH
AMERICA
980,000

CENTRAL
&
SOUTH
AMERICA
1,500,000

CARIBBEAN
440,000

WESTERN
EUROPE
570,000

EASTERN EUROPE
& CENTRAL ASIA
1,200,000

NORTH AFRICA
& THE MIDDLE EAST
550,000

SUB-SAHARAN
AFRICA
29,400,000

EAST ASIA
& PACIFIC
1,200,000

SOUTH &
SOUTH-EAST ASIA
6,000,000

AUSTRALIA &
NEW ZEALAND
15,000

Source: Estimated number of adults and children living with H.I.V./AIDS during 2002, from "UNAIDS/WHO H.I.V./AIDS Regional Estimates as of the end of 2002" (United Nations/World Health Organization), October 2003.

Thinking About the Essay

1. What is the tone of Annan's introductory paragraph and the entire essay? What is his purpose? Point to specific passages to support your answer.

2. Annan employs causal analysis to develop this essay. Trace the causes and effects that he presents. What are some of the primary causes and effects? What secondary causes and effects does he mention?

3. This essay is rich in the use of examples. What types of illustration does Annan present to support his thesis?

4. Locate other rhetorical strategies—for example, comparison and contrast—that appear as structuring devices in this essay.

5. This essay presents a problem and offers a solution. Explain this strategy, paying careful attention to how the pattern evolves.

Responding in Writing

6. In a brief essay, explain what you have learned about AIDS in Africa from Annan's essay. Do you share his sense of optimism about the ability of the nations involved and the international community to solve the problem? Why or why not?

7. Explain your personal viewpoint on the increase of AIDS among the women of the world—not just in Africa but in Asia, Russia, Europe, and elsewhere.

8. Write an essay on another threat to women—either in a particular country or region, or around the world.

Networking

9. Form working groups of four or five class members, and draw up an action plan to solicit funds on your campus for United Nations AIDS relief efforts in sub-Saharan Africa. Then create a master plan based on the work of other class groups. Decide if you want to present this plan to the campus administration for approval.

10. Search the Internet for information on the United Nations programs to alleviate the AIDS epidemic around the world. Then write a letter to your congressional representative explaining why (or why not) Congress should support these efforts.

The Muslim in the Mirror

MOHJA KAHF | Mohja Kahf is associate professor of comparative litera-
ture at the University of Arkansas. Her book *Western
Representations of the Muslim Woman* (1999) is a
pioneering study of gender and Islam in early Western
literatures. Kahf is also known as a poet and writer of
fiction, and for nonscholarly books such as *Emails
From Scheherazad* (2003). Kahf grew up in a Muslim
family in Indiana, and her mixed feelings toward traditional Muslim culture, as a Muslim American, are a
central theme of her work. Kahf contributes a regular
column on sexuality to the progressive Muslim website
www.MuslimWakeUp.com. In the following essay,
included in the collection *Living Islam Out Loud:
American Muslim Women Speak* (2005), Kahf reflects
on her ambivalent relationship with traditional Islamic
religion and culture.

Before Reading

How is your perception of Islamic culture affected by the popular image of
Islamic-sanctioned misogyny? How do you distinguish between Islamic religious
doctrine and Islamic *culture?* Or between liberal and orthodox religious
doctrine?

"I don't care if I never see another Muslim for as long as I live." That 1
thought became a refrain in my mind somewhere around 1998. Fine,
I amended, except the one I sleep with. He can stay. And my children. Parents. Five brothers, a sister. In-laws, I guess. Several best friends.

Oh, yeah, and the Muslim in the mirror: Myself. 2

But I didn't want to hear another word of Islam-talk for as long as I live. 3
Islam is a way of life this. Islamic identity that. Sunni this, Shi'a that. Dawah
this, shari'a that. Conservative Muslims. Muslim feminists. Liberal Muslims. Nation Muslims. Ahmediya. Wahhabiya. Sufis. Traditionals. Orthodox. Arab-hating Muslims and racist Arab Muslims. Converts and
"reverts." Political Islam. From radical revolutionaries to flag-waving Republican Muslims. Palestine, Kashmir, and the latest Muslim cause *du jour*.
Hijab yes, hijab no, hijab maybe. Sister do, sister don't. When "sister"
means the brother wants me to toe the line, then I ain't your sister, mister.

I was sick of the scene. And of the God that went with the Islam-talk. 4
God and the Prophet. Do it for the sake of God. For the pleasure of God.
For obeying God. All that glib talk of God. All my life I've heard it.

I was fed up with Islam-talk. There are other things in life besides the religion game, you know. Good things. Beautiful things. I discovered that it is entirely possible to ditch the Islam-scene and still seek God. It is possible that all that busy religion work was what was keeping me from spirituality.

Oh, I was still a Muslim. No one was gonna take that away from me. Especially not the anti-Muslim bigots. If there's anyone I was more sick and tired of than Muslims, it's Muslim-bashers. No one is allowed to criticize Islam and Muslims but those who do it from love. Those who do it from hate, step aside. And step aside, those who do it as a way to fame and fortune funded by neo-conservatives who think they can *kaCHING* up genuine "reform" in Islam and manufacture docile little McMuslims for the maintenance of U.S. McHegemony in the world. Neocons can kiss my Islamic ass.

Neither will I swerve away from forthrightly criticizing my beloved faith community because such criticism is seen as aiding and abetting the bigots who are vying to close our charities, to criminalize our beliefs and practices and even our Arabic script, and to isolate us inside a barbed wire of hate. I will not circle my wagons around the mosque, will not yield in fearful worry to the entreaties of the wagon-circlers inside nor to the shouts of the hatemongers outside. I function within this double bind. I strategize around it with every move I make, every piece I write.

Back at that moment when I said "I've had it with Islam-talk," even then I still acknowledged the wisdom and beauty in the tradition. I rejoiced in it. I just didn't want all the other crap that comes with it in many contemporary Islamic worldviews. I was tired of butting my head up against an Islam-brickwall that would not move.

Why I need a migraine every Friday after the *khutba* (that is, when I was in places that allowed me to attend *juma*; my local mosque until recently had little space or welcome for women at *juma*, and now that the new mosque is built women can pray *juma* only on a mezzanine with opaque fiberglass cutting off all visual contact with the main hall). I was tired of feeling isolated in the Islamic conversation. I had years ago left the conservative worldview and hung with the liberal modernist Muslims, who emphasize the flexibility and versatility of Islamic laws and traditions, but that didn't help for long. In the end the liberals were still inside the box, as far as I could tell, unable to think outside the forms into which Islam had rigidified over the centuries. Something more radical was needed. Not to dump all of tradition, but to take the best strands of it and create Islam afresh for a new generation.

Maybe I was crazy. No one else I knew seemed to want to do that, and 10
by myself, I didn't know how. Well, okay, not "no one"; there were a few
scattered individuals here and there who had similar thoughts. But maybe
they were as crazy as I was. The fight took too much high logic for my brain
to handle. Too much sadness for my tired heart. I dropped out. I would
rather have new ground to explore. Culture, art, music, poetry. Not
polemics but beauty. Wherever you turn, there is the Face of God. So let
me come at life a different way for a while.

It was the summer of 2001. I got a phone call. Decided to try a little 11
volunteering. Not for Islam, but for humanity at large. Do some service in
the world. The women's shelter called me, needing a translator for a beaten
woman. Muslim, the religious kind. Scared, the battered woman kind. I
went. Better me than some Muslim who'd try to send her back to him, saying, "Sister mustn't stay with these kaffir kind, in the home is where you
belong." Better me than some non-Muslim trying to help her while believing that her religion was the problem and if she'd only dump it, take that
veil off her head, and follow a Western model, she'd be suddenly liberated.
That would only send a very traditional woman, attached to her religious
symbols, recoiling right back into the arms of the batterer.

I found out that beaten women horrify me. Their abjection, their de- 12
featedness, reminded me of something inside me, something cringing and
afraid and weak. I know that the battered woman has an altered sense of
reality in which he is all-powerful, that she can't help her schizoid dance of
"I want to live—but I'm going to return and live abjectly under his raised
arm. I don't want to die—but I won't take strong steps to protect my life."
But she can. She can help herself. It's the voice inside that won't let her, the
voice of the man-pleasing woman she thinks she has to be.

This particular woman's man-pleasing and self-killing voice implicated 13
Islam. Oh, there was no dancing out of this one with the neat steps of Islamic apologetics, like the stuff I was raised on, the stuff I learned to spout
as a youth: "Islam gave women their rights fourteen hundred years ago."
Nor was the sellout speech of the Muslim woman I used to be, lauded for
her Islamic knowledge, any help: "It's just that Muslim women aren't educated about their rights." Blame Muslim women for not being educated
about their rights? No, not the women alone—blame the *ulema*, the Islamic
activists and preachers, the mosque communities, along with the women
for not educating themselves with a consciousness of their inner liberation
in God, and for instead inculcating in women, day in, day out, that an ethic
of wifely submission to male authority is godly. Blame ourselves for perpetuating and defending a sexist set of assumptions we keep calling Islam.

Blame our Muslim American leaders for running our mosques and organizations like "men's clubs" (in the words of Dr. Ingrid Mattson, vice president of the Islamic Society of North America, in an interview with Asra Nomani). Blame the masses of our community members for passively accepting this Muslim sexism. Blame them for trying to silence women and men who try to change this, by mistrusting their motives, mocking them, and casting doubt on their faith.

And don't even try "It's not Islam, it's just culture." Our sexism is embedded in Islam itself. Because Islam is not just some pie-in-the-sky ideal, but what people practice as Islam and what the scholars preach as Islam. They are reality and we deal with them daily as Islam. If you think such a thing as "pure Islam" existed, even for five minutes in C.E. 623, think again. Islam is always manifested inside a particular culture and in specific, earth-rooted human bodies, and our job now is to birth a new Islam, a new Islamic culture. This Islam-on-the-ground-as-a-lived-reality needs to step up and take credit for the specific ways in which it oppresses women as well as the ways in which it liberated women fourteen hundred years ago. 14

This woman at the shelter sincerely believed that Islam required of her submission to a man who was regularly beating her black-and-blue, burning her with hot iron instruments, strangling her with his hands. When I saw her worldview and how Islam figured in it, I was outraged, horrified, disgusted. She actually believed she deserved the beatings because she had defied orders of her husband. She felt herself deeply, profoundly, to be the one in the wrong, and she felt she'd multiplied the wrong by leaving the house. A disobedient woman deserves chastisement, right? Never mind that she disobeyed him from an instinct for survival that—thank God—had not been totally killed in her by Islam, by her Islam-inculcated, Muslim-community-supported belief in wifely obedience. 15

What kind of a horrible God did she believe in, I asked myself, who would let her be trapped like this, in a death-in-life, without letting her believe in a means of escape? What kind of horrible God did we—Muslims—believe in to allow any number of women to go around with this idea in their heads, that they are supposed to live these lives of abject subordination in order to be good Muslim women? 16

The shelter case may be a pathological example of how Islam manifested in one woman's life. There are kinder, gentler faces of patriarchal Islam. But it took an extreme case to shock me out of my paralysis about participating in the modern Islamic conversation. Because the internalized vision of Islam this woman had is one of the faces of Islam that we have allowed to evolve and exist and thrive. For it is not just this one woman who believes in this hopelessly inegalitarian version of Islam, it is many, and we 17 are all implicated. For our cowardice. For not fighting the ethic of wifely submission in Islamic discourses. For not rescuing the compassionate and pro-woman face of Islam.

Victims of the pre-Islamic Arab custom of female infanticide were tra- 18 ditionally murdered by burial alive. They were rescued by the Qur'an in the seventh century, rescued by a vision of social change that addressed their human rights in a bold, emphatic way never before thought of in that society. We have allowed the bodies of women to become the sacrificial victims again. And we have allowed the feminine body of Islam to be buried alive in the sand, over and over again.

We are implicated for dropping out of the community and its discourses 19 when we are alienated. For giving up on changing Islam. Like I had. For giving up on being part of the conversation, the Islam-talk. Instead of staying and rolling up our sleeves and working for reform, even though it may mean a weekly headache and getting splattered by the mudslingers in personal attacks on our Islamic legitimacy, our moral character, our right to have a say in the Muslim community, and our faith.

Why I need this Islam-talk? Because it was the only talk that would get 20 this battered woman out of her old worldview. She would not leave without Islam. She had to take Islam with her to make a new life, a new way of thinking about life as a woman alone in the world. I had to give her a jolt of Islam-CPR, and I needed it myself, too.

To help the woman back at the shelter, I had to go back into the forest of 21 liberal Islam and seek the Muslim feminists with whom I had lost patience because their work was too slow and piecemeal for me. They worked within existing Islamic paradigms but tried to craft a more woman-affirming manifestation of the laws. I dug out my old dog-eared copies of Dr. Rifaat Hassan and Dr. Amina Wadud to arm the woman with Qur'anic concepts so as to refute the abject woman she thought she had to be with other concepts firmly rooted in Islam. I looked up things on the website of the Muslim Women's League. I called up my ever-helpful and enduring best friend Dr. Asifa Quraishi, an Islamic law expert, to get some answers.

But it was not only liberal Islam that helped me with the woman at the 22 shelter. I sought aid from conservative Islam, too. Look, conservative Muslims do not want wives to get pummeled any more than progressives, okay? The conservative Muslim vision, despite its inegalitarian views of gender, is not ultimately one of a home devoid of safety and dignity for women, after all. I called up the imam of a major Midwestern mosque. As soon as he saw the police report of the beating, he wrote up an Islamic divorce for the woman from the man she thought she couldn't divorce Islamically.

The battered woman did not know that she had the Islamic right to leave   23
her husband unilaterally because of *darrar*, harm that he inflicted on her. I
knew that she did have this right, had spent many years of my life pursuing
these concepts and rights, and could tell her all about them, but she would
not take these Islamic concepts from me and act on them, because she, being a traditional woman, had to hear it from a man. A man with a beard
who looked to her like an Islamic authority. Thank God for the supportive
conservative Muslim men—even the ones who parse the meaning of the
"beat verse" by saying, "Yes, but he can only beat her with a handkerchief,"
which is still too conservative for me. But if the alternative is this traditional
Muslim woman thinking her husband had the right to beat her uncondi-
tionally, I'll take it, and pass it to her happily, as a first step anyway. I called
upon my conservative Muslim family. My father, an Islamic economics
scholar, gave me a review of the woman's rights according to Islamic law
and helped me brush up on empowering Islamic concepts to pass on to her.
The rest of my family—mother, uncles, aunts, brothers—sent money for her
and gave me moral support and encouragement.

And it worked. I could see her latch on to the concepts, which were new   24
to her but whose grounding in Qur'anic values she immediately recognized
with a deep *yaqin*-certainty. I actually watched her gird herself around with
them and fend off the well-meaning mosque community members, the next
time they came at her with "A wife leaving the husband's house to spend
the night outside with strangers is un-Islamic, a disgrace!" Now she could
say, "Tell you what the un-Islamic, disgrace is, it is his beating me nearly
to death, because *darrar* is not allowed in Islam, and shari'a is there to protect five things, and one of them is life, physical well-being. My physical
well-being is as important to God as husbandly authority. And I am not
with strangers, I am in a place where they have provided me with a Muslim woman with Islamic answers. She brought me a Qur'an and a prayer
rug the very first night. So how can this be such a den of iniquity and im-
morality and a compromise to my family's honor?" And if the local Muslim people said to her, "You can't get divorced Islamically unless he grants
it!" she now responded, "Yes I can, I can initiate unilateral divorce through
a judge, or I can get *khul*. How could you think God would not legislate a
way out for me in this deadly situation? That would not be just or merci-
ful, and God is just and Rahman."

Even though I reentered contemporary Muslim discourse by seeking   25
old allies among conservative and liberal Muslims, I could not stay in their
modes of thinking about Islam. More daring Muslim thought had been go-

ing on for years, but my ears had not been equipped to pick it up. Now I had new antennae, and I tuned in. I didn't feel isolated anymore: Everywhere I turned, the faces of freethinking Muslims and alternative Islamic discourses—from other periods of Islamic history as well as in today's world—were becoming visible to me. Even many Muslim figures I had formerly encountered as conservative or liberal were themselves shifting in their orientation. For example, I discovered that Amina Wadud had already moved past the borderlands of liberal Islamic discourse and was moving deeply into what we now seem to be calling the progressive part of the Islamic spectrum. For another example, Sufi discourse, whose deeply traditional, hierarchical side I had known for years, now showed me its other face through members of the Jerrahi order and of the Bawa Muhaiyaddeen Fellowship, a Sufism that still respected tradition but was far more fluid and open in its form.

Finally, with the help of friends and guides on the path, I began to free 26 myself of the false god who lived within, the god whose obsession is obedience. I had been battered by an internalized idea of this god. My prior clumsy attempts to make my way around him by myself gave me that crazy schizoid feeling—that I must be doing something terribly wrong in going outside the house of tradition, disobeying, while a *yaqin*-certainty told me that not to do so violated everything I knew to be sacred.

Grateful for the guidance that had come my way, I began to seek al- 27 Rahman, the Divine whose countenance is compassion, loving kindness, mercy: Rahma. A word which comes from the Arabic root *rahm*: the womb. I began to seek the womanly body of Islamic discourse, to pull her out of the sand in which she has been half-buried and struggling for a long, long time. The distressed woman I was sent to help was myself in another form, an abject form my selfhood has taken sometimes, a cringing woman inside me that I tried to forget. She straightened up, uncringed. I am back. I am back and kicking.

Thinking About the Essay

1. What is the purpose and effect of the author's use, early in the essay, of staccato rhythms and subject-free sentence fragments? Why does she change her prose style in other places in the essay?

2. Where does Kahf shift from use of colloquial language in (American) English to use of Arabic terms associated with the Qur'an and Islamic law? What is the purpose of these transitions between two radically different discourses?

3. Respond to the statement at the end of paragraph 6: "Neocons can kiss my Islamic ass." What effect does this gesture have upon Kahf's authorial *ethos*? How does her voice sound differently to you at the end of the essay?

4. Where does Kahf defend her own approach toward Islam against the possible charge that she is engaging in the Islamic apologetics and special pleading that were rejected earlier in the essay (paragraph 13)? Do you think Kahf defends her approach successfully? Justify your response.

5. Describe Kahf's final concept of tradition. How does this concept of tradition relate to different versions she entertained at other moments in her life (as related in the essay)?

Responding in Writing

6. In a brief essay, reflect on a moment when you have felt trapped in a "double bind," when you feared that your criticism of a position that you disagreed with would appear (even if only to yourself) to lend support to an opposing view with which you also disagreed.

7. Explain, in a brief essay, what you see as the relationship between belief inculcated by religious doctrine and belief as supported by a community.

8. Is it possible, or desirable, to enter into the terms of a given discourse and still remain "outside the house of tradition"? How does one avoid the charges of moral relativism or disingenuousness? In a brief essay, consider this challenge in light of another test case.

Networking

9. Divide into two groups and conduct a mock trial of the abusive husband mentioned in the essay. One group should present a case against the husband based on the tenets of Islamic law mentioned in Kahf's essay; the other group should base their prosecution on secular, liberal humanist beliefs about individual rights.

10. Go online and read at least three of Kahf's columns posted on www. MuslimWakeUp.com. Are you surprised to read her views on other issues, or do these views seem consonant with what you have read in this essay? Why or why not?

Justice for Women

ELLEN GOODMAN

Ellen Goodman was born in 1941 in Newton, Massachusetts, and received a B.A. degree from Harvard University in 1963. She is an award-winning journalist and columnist whose syndicated writing appears regularly in more than 250 newspapers. Goodman won the Pulitzer Prize for Distinguished Commentary in 1980. She also has been a commentator on radio and television. Among her books are *Close to Home* (1979), *At Large* (1981), *Value Judgments* (1993), and with Patricia O'Brien, *I Know Just What You Mean: The Power of Friendship in Women's Lives* (2000). Goodman is an adept practitioner of the personal essay, frequently bringing keen wit and humor to her subjects. However, Goodman employs invective and biting irony in the following essay from *The Boston Globe* (2002), in which she excoriates the Bush administration for its failure to promote women's rights.

Before Reading

Do you think that women have equal standing before courts of law in the United States? Around the world? Explain.

This time the dateline was Multan, Pakistan, although it could have happened in any other place on the globe where women are the designated punching bags of injustice. An 18-year-old girl was "sentenced" to gang rape. Rape was the punishment allotted by a tribal council for her 11-year-old brother's "crime" of walking with an unchaperoned girl from a different tribe. For the sake of honor, four men took turns at sexual revenge, inflicting the "law" on the sister as she cried for help.

What shall we do with this unforgettable horror story? Shall we put it in the folder next to stories of Nigerian women sentenced to be stoned to death for the crime of "adultery," whether sex was forced or consensual? Shall we add it to the studies coming out of the Barcelona AIDS conference reminding us that women's stunning vulnerability to this epidemic in sub-Saharan Africa is not just physiology but culture?

Ever since Afghanistan came upon our radar screen as the homeland of woman-hating, we've paid more mind to the world's women. In one speech after another, President Bush has described the liberation of women as an American value worth fighting for. "A thriving nation," he told West Point graduates, "will respect the rights of women, because no society can prosper while denying opportunity to half its citizens."

In this atmosphere, how is it possible that our country cavalierly un-   4
dermines its own stand on human rights?

Twenty-three years ago [1979] the United States helped write an inter-   5
national women's bill of rights. Since then, 170 countries have ratified the
UN's Convention on the Elimination of All Forms of Discrimination
Against Women.

Words like "discrimination" seem far too mild to describe female gen-   6
ital mutilation or sexual trafficking. But women from Colombia to
Rwanda have used the treaty as a standard to rewrite laws on inheritance
and domestic abuse, to change the patterns of education and employment.
The treaty has been a tool in the long, slow evolution toward women's human rights. But who has not ratified the treaty? Countries like Somalia, Sudan, Iran. And the United States of America.

This year, I thought we would leave such embarrassing companions be-   7
hind. After all, the Bush administration offered a "general approval" for
the treaty early on. The Senate Foreign Relations Committee finally held
hearings in June [2000].

But on the way to ratification, women's rights took a right turn. First,   8
the conservative watchdog John Ashcroft declared that the treaty needed
more "study." Last Monday, Colin Powell made it clear to Joe Biden, the
chair of the Senate Foreign Relations Committee, that the State Department is not cramming to finish this "study." Powell's letter placed the
women's rights treaty behind 17 others waiting for Senate approval.

The administration is clearly trying to balance international women's   9
rights and the domestic political right. And politics may win.

The UN treaty brings out all the ancient enemies and hoary arguments   10
once launched against the Equal Rights Amendment. Conservative op-ed
mills and politicians proclaim that the treaty is simultaneously toothless
and radical. They offer a litany of alarms about the destruction of the family and even the bizarre idea that the treaty would eliminate, maybe even
criminalize, Mother's Day.

This international agreement can't trump national laws. Saudi Arabia,   11
no poster child for women's rights, has signed the treaty. So has Pakistan,
the scene of the rape sentence.

Slowly, though, more citizens hold countries up to their own signatures.   12
This new consciousness about human rights was surely one reason for the
Pakistani government's arrest of the rapist-jurists.

By not joining the international community, America damages its au-   13
thority to call others to account. As human rights advocate Steve Rickard
says, "We powerfully assist the Talibans of the world who want to argue
that the treaty isn't universal because we're not a party to it."

Biden, joining in, says, "The plain fact of the matter is that we should 14
provide a tool for women fighting for their lives in these countries." He
plans to bring up this plain fact next week in executive session of the Foreign Relations Committee and expects it to be voted onto the Senate floor.
"I want people to be counted," he says. But will that count add up to a two-
thirds majority?

Over the past two decades, nearly every president has signed an inter- 15
national human rights treaty. Ronald Reagan signed the genocide treaty.
The first George Bush signed the torture convention. Clinton signed the
race treaty. Will the man who takes pride in freeing Afghan women see
himself as a liberator or a rear guard?

Meanwhile, the stories accumulate. Every time we read about the 16
women of the world, there is an impulse to do something. This treaty is the
least we can do.

Thinking About the Essay

1. This is a topical essay, filled with references to figures in the Bush administration. Do these references limit the importance or lasting significance of
   the article? Why or why not?

2. How would you describe Goodman's tone in this essay? How does the tone
   affect her selection of information and her approach to the political environment she discusses?

3. Explain the effectiveness of Goodman's introduction. What is her purpose?

4. Trace the development of Goodman's argument. What is her claim? What
   reasons and evidence in support of her claim does she present?

5. Goodman's paragraphs are brief, reflecting the demands and expectations
   of opinion writing for the **op-ed** page of newspapers. What benefits do you
   see in her paragraphs, some of which are only one sentence? What is the
   downside to this strategy? How well, do you think, does she operate within
   the conventions of the op-ed piece?

Responding in Writing

6. Write an essay in which you agree or disagree with Goodman's charges
   against the Bush administration.

7. Write a letter to the editor of your college newspaper in which you explain
   how your campus can be more involved in the campaign for equal rights for
   women around the world.

8. Argue for or against the proposition that women need a human rights treaty
   to protect them and to achieve equality.

Networking

9. In groups of four or five class members, research the status of the UN's Convention on the Elimination of All Forms of Discrimination Against Women. Also determine the current administration's position on this document. Share your findings with the class.

10. Do a computer search for information on women's rights in India or Pakistan. Draft a report outlining your findings.

The Veiled Threat

AZAR NAFISI

Azar Nafisi was born in Iran. She completed graduate study in the United States at the University of Oklahoma, where she received a Ph.D. degree in English in 1979. Nafisi was a professor of English at the University of Tehran, the Free Islamic University, and Allameh Tabatabai University. She was fired from all three institutions for criticism of the Islamic regime, including her refusal to wear the veil. Subsequently she held a literature class for a small group of her former female students in her home, a narrative recounted in her book *Reading Lolita in Tehran: A Memoir in Books* (2003). Nafisi left Iran in 1997 and now teaches at Johns Hopkins University. She has published articles in *The New York Times* and *The Washington Post* and has appeared as a radio and television commentator on Iranian affairs. In the following essay, which first appeared in *The New Republic* in 1999 but remains relevant today, Nafisi explains how the Islamic regime in Iran, while attempting to suppress women, has paradoxically invested them with authority and power.

Before Reading

How do you respond to media images from Iran that you see today? Do you infer a different reality beneath the surface appearance?

I would like to begin with a painting. It is Edgar Degas's *Dancers Practic-* 1 *ing at the Barre*, as reproduced in an artbook recently published in the Islamic Republic of Iran. Under the heading "Spatial Organization," the book gives a two-paragraph explanation of Degas's placement of the ballerinas: "The two major forms are crowded into the upper right quadrant of the painting, leaving the rest of the canvas as openspace. . . ."

Edgar Degas, *Dancers Practicing at the Barre*, 1877. The original painting, with its practicing ballerinas.

So far, everything seems normal. But, like most things in Iran today, it 2 is not. Upon closer inspection, there is something disturbingly wrong with the illustration accompanying this description, something that makes both the painting and the serious tone of its discussion absurdly unreal: the ballerinas, you see, have been airbrushed out. Instead, what meet the eye are an empty space, the floor, the blank wall, and the bar. Like so many other images of women in Iran, the ballerinas have been censored.

Of course, the irony is that, by removing the dancers, the censors have 3 succeeded only in making them the focus of our attention. Through their absence, the dancers are rendered glaringly present. In this way, Degas's painting is emblematic of a basic paradox of life in Iran, on the eve of the twentieth anniversary of the 1979 Islamic Revolution. On the one hand, the ruling Islamic regime has succeeded in completely repressing Iranian women. Women are forbidden to go out in public unless they are covered by clothing that conceals everything but their hands and faces. At all

Reproduction of *Dancers Practicing at the Barre,* from an art book published in Iran. The censored version reflects what Nafisi calls a "basic paradox of life in Iran."

government institutions, universities, and airports, there are separate entrances for women, where they are searched for lipstick and other weapons of mass destruction. No infraction is too small to escape notice. At the university where I used to teach, one woman was penalized for "laughter of a giggling kind." And, just recently, a female professor was expelled because her wrist had shown from under her sleeve while she was writing on the blackboard.

Yet, while these measures are meant to render women invisible and powerless, they are paradoxically making women tremendously visible and powerful. By attempting to control and shape every aspect of women's lives—and by staking its legitimacy on the Iranian people's supposed desire for this control—the regime has unwittingly handed women a powerful weapon: every private act or gesture in defiance of official rules is now a strong political statement. Meanwhile, because the regime's extreme regulation of women's lives necessarily intrudes on the private lives of men as well (whose every interaction with women is closely governed), the regime has alienated not just women but many men who initially supported the revolution.

4

This tension between the Islamic ruling elite and Iranian society at large has been vastly underestimated by Western observers of Iran. In part this is because, over the past 20 years, American analysts and academics, as well as the Iranian exile community, have had little or no access to Iran. Thus they have relied unduly on the image presented by Iran's ruling clerics.

At present that image is one of increased openness—as symbolized by the election of the moderate cleric Mohammed Khatami to the presidency back in 1997. Recently, for example, CNN cheerfully informed us that, after 20 years, the Islamic Republic has begun to show Hollywood movies. What CNN failed to mention was that Iranian television's version of, for example, *Mary Poppins* showed less than 45 minutes of the actual film. All portions featuring women dancing or singing were cut out and instead described by an Iranian narrator. In *Popeye*, all scenes involving Olive Oyl, whose person and whose relationship with Popeye are considered lewd, were excised from the cartoon. Meanwhile, even as the regime purports to have softened its hostile stance toward the United States, it has not softened the punishment meted out to Iranians who dare show an interest in American culture. In fact, soon after he was appointed, Khatami's new education minister issued a new directive forbidding students to bring material bearing the Latin alphabet or other "decadent Western symbols" to class.

However, these are just the mildest examples of the many ways in which the new openness that characterizes Khatami's rule has been accompanied by increased repression. The brief spring that followed his victory—during which freedom of speech flourished in public demonstrations and new newspapers—was brought to an end with an abrupt crackdown. The government has since banned most of the new papers and harassed or jailed their editors. (They have since been released.) Many of the progressive clergymen who took advantage of the opening to protest the current legal system were also arrested and, in one case, defrocked. The regime has also taken the opportunity to clamp down on members of Iran's Bahai minority.

Meanwhile, the parliament has passed two of the most reactionary laws on women in the republic's history. The first requires that all medical facilities be segregated by sex. The second effectively bans publication of women's pictures on the cover of magazines as well as any form of writing that "creates conflict between the sexes and is opposed to the Islamic laws."

This past fall, two nationalist opposition leaders, Daryush and Parvaneh Forouhar, were murdered, and three prominent writers disappeared. All three were later found dead. Many Iranians were outraged, and tens of thousands attended the Forouhars' funeral in a tacit protest. The government's initial response gave these Iranians some reason for hope. President

Khatami condemned the killings and set up a committee to investigate them. The committee's first conclusion was that those responsible were members of the Information Ministry. However, within days, the committee was proffering a different story, alleging that, on second thought, the murderers were just part of a rogue group within the ministry and that the killings were not political. The committee also has yet to name the killers—much less bring them to justice. Furious, Iranians have flooded the progressive newspapers with angry calls and letters.

To the extent that the Western media have taken note of such incidents, 10 they have mainly cast them as the symptoms of a struggle between the moderate Khatami and his reactionary fellow clerics. More often than not, the media portray acts of repression as measures taken by the hard-liners against Khatami—as if he, and not the people who were actually murdered or oppressed, was the real victim.

This simplistic portrayal of Khatami versus the hard-liners completely 11 misunderstands the current situation in Iran. Khatami does not represent the opposition in Iran—and he cannot. True, in order to win a popular mandate he had to present an agenda for tearing down some of the fundamental pillars of the Islamic Republic. But in order to even be eligible for election he had to have impeccable political and religious credentials. In other words, he had to be, and clearly is, committed to upholding the very ideology his constituents so vehemently oppose.

Khatami's tenure, then, has revealed the key dilemma facing the Islamic 12 regime. In order to maintain the people's support, the government must reform, but it cannot reform without negating itself. The result has been a kind of chaos, a period marked by the arbitrariness of its events. One day a new freedom is granted; the next day an old freedom is rescinded. Both events are symptoms of the deep struggle under way in Iran today, not just between Khatami and the reactionary clerics, but between the people of Iran and all representatives of the government. And at the center of this struggle is the battle over women's rights.

A second image comes to mind—a woman from the past, Dr. 13 Farokhroo Parsa. Like the ballerinas, her presence is felt through her absence. I try to conjure her in my mind's eye. Parsa had given up her medical practice to become the principal of the girls' school in Tehran I attended as a teenager. Slowly her pudgy, stern face looms before me, just as it did when she used to stand outside the school inspecting the students as we entered the building. Her smile was always accompanied by the shadow of a frown, as if she were afraid that we would take advantage of that smile and betray the vision she had created for her school. That vision, her life's goal, was for us, her girls, to be "truly" educated. Under the Shah,

Parsa rose to become one of the first Iranian women to be elected to the Iranian parliament, and then, in 1968, she became Iran's first female Cabinet minister, in charge of higher education. In that post Parsa tried not only to raise the quality of education but to purge the school textbooks of sexist images of women.

When the Shah was ousted in 1979 by a diverse group of opposition 14 figures that included Muslim clerics, leftists, and nationalists, Parsa was one of the many high functionaries of the previous government whom the revolutionaries summarily tried and executed. At her trial she was charged with "corruption on earth," "warring against God," and "expansion of prostitution." She was allowed no defense attorney and was sentenced by hooded judges.

At the time, the new revolutionary regime took a great deal of pride in 15 its executions, even advertising them and printing pictures of its victims in the newspapers afterward. But Parsa's photograph was never published. Even more exceptional, in that exceptional time, was the manner of her death. Before being killed she was put in a sack. The only logic behind such an act could be the claim that Islam forbade a man to touch the body of a woman, even during her death. There is some debate about the method of her execution. Some say she was beaten, others that she was stoned, still others that she was machine-gunned. Nonetheless, the central image of her murder remains the same: that of a living, breathing woman made shapeless, formless, in order to preserve the "virtue" and "dignity" of her executioners.

I had not thought of Parsa for many years until the news of her exe- 16 cution resurrected her in my memory. Since then, time and again, I have tried to imagine her moment of death. But, while I can see her living face with its smile and frown, I cannot envision her features at the specific moment when that smile and frown forever disappeared in that dark sack. Could she have divined how, not long afterward, her students and her students' students would also be made shapeless and invisible not in death but in life?

For this, on a broader scale, is precisely what the clerics have done to 17 all Iranian women. Almost immediately upon seizing power, Ayatollah Khomeini began taking back women's hard-won rights. He justified his actions by claiming that he was actually restoring women's dignity and rescuing them from the degrading and dangerous ideas that had been imposed on them by Western imperialists and their agents, among which he included the Shah.

In making this claim, the Islamic regime not only robbed Iran's women 18 of their rights; it robbed them of their history. For the true story of women's liberation in Iran is not that of an outside imperialist force imposing alien ideas, or—as even some opponents of the Islamic regime contend—that of a benevolent Shah bestowing rights upon his passive female subjects. No, the advent of women's liberation in Iran was the result of a homegrown struggle on the part of Iranian women themselves for the creation of a modern nation—a fight that reached back more than a century. At every step of the way, scores of women, unassuming, without much sense of the magnitude of their pioneering roles, had created new spaces, the spaces my generation and I had taken for granted. This is not to say that Iranian women—including those of my own generation—never made mistakes, never wavered in their commitment to freedom. But the fact that Iran's women were fallible does not change the fact that so many of them were vital leaders in Iran's long struggle for modernization.

Probably the first of these leaders was a poet who lived in the middle of the last century, a woman named Tahereh who was said to be stunningly beautiful. At the time, Iran was ruled by the despotic and semi-feudal Qajar dynasty, whose reign was supported by fundamentalist Muslim clerics. The alliance between the mullahs and the despotic regime prompted various groups to begin questioning the basic tenets of Islam. One such group were the Babis—a dissident movement of Islamic thinkers who were the precursors to the Bahais—who eventually broke with Islam to create a new religion, and who are the victims of vicious persecution by the Iranian government to this day. Tahereh was one of the Babis' most effective leaders. She was among the first to demand that religion be modernized. She debated her ideas with men and took the unprecedented step of leaving her husband and children in order to tour the country preaching her ideas. Tahereh was also the first woman to unveil publicly. Perhaps not surprisingly, she paid for her views with her life. In 1852, she was secretly taken to a garden and strangled. Her body was thrown into a well. She was 36.

As Iran began to have increasing contact with the West, many sectors of the population—intellectuals, minorities, clerics, and even ordinary people—became increasingly aware of their nation's backwardness as compared to the West. From the mid-nineteenth century these forces continually struggled with Iran's rulers over the degree to which Iran should close the gap by modernizing itself. By 1908, this struggle had come to a head, with the ruling Shah threatening to undermine the constitution that the modernizers had forced his predecessor to agree to accept in 1906. The new Shah soon began bombarding the parliament.

Once again, women were at the forefront. Many of them actually fought in the violent skirmishes that ensued, sometimes disguised as men. They even marched to the parliament, carrying weapons under their veils and, once inside, demanded that the men holed up there hand over the jobs if they could not protect the constitution.

The constitutionalists prevailed, and, although the constitution con- 22 tained no language advancing women's rights, the next 20 years saw significant progress in this area thanks to the determined efforts of countless women. Leafing through the books about the women's movements from this era, one is amazed at their members' courage and daring. So many names and images crowd the pages of these books. I pick one at random: Sediqeh Dowlatabadi, daughter of a learned and religious man from an old and highly respected family, who was the editor of a monthly journal for women. In the 1910s she was beaten and detained for three months for establishing a girls' school in Isfahan. One can only guess the degree of her rage and resentment against her adversaries by her will, in which she proclaimed: "I will never forgive women who visit my grave veiled." It was only appropriate that those who murdered Farokhroo Parsa should also not tolerate Dowlatabadi, even in her death. In August 1980, Islamic vigilantes demolished her tomb and the tombs of her father and brother who, although men of religion, had supported her activities.

It was an American, Morgan Shuster, who best appreciated the efforts 23 of Iranian women during Dowlatabadi's period. "The Persian women since 1907 had become almost at a bound the most progressive, not to say radical, in the world," he wrote in his 1912 book *The Strangling of Persia*. "That this statement upsets the ideas of centuries makes no difference. It is the fact."

As part of their push toward modernization, the women of Iran also 24 supported a general movement in favor of greater cultural pluralism. Writers and poets led heated and exciting debates on the need to change the old modes of artistic and literary expression, with many calling for a "democratization" of the Persian language. New literary and artistic forms were introduced to Iran.

The reactionary elements in the clerical ranks and other supporters of 25 despotism rightly recognized that the ideas in these cultural products represented a threat to their dominance and immediately attacked them as "poisonous vapors" coming from the West to destroy the minds of Iranian youth. To the mullahs the idea of women's rights fell in the same category—and they opposed them in the same breath. Two prominent clerics, Sheikh Fazolah Nuri and Sayyid 'Ali Shushtari—mentors of Ayatollah Khomeini—even issued a fatwa against women's education.

But the charge that Iran's women's rights activists—and the moderniz- 26 ers in general—were agents of the West is patently unjust. To be sure, they were keenly interested in bringing in Western ideas. But this desire stemmed from their acute awareness of Iran's shortcomings and their belief that Iran's road to independence and prosperity lay in understanding and internalizing the best of the Western systems of government and thought. It also meant fighting back when the Western nations began brutally exploiting Iran's wealth and natural resources. And Iranian women were at the forefront of this battle—for instance, organizing a large-scale boycott of foreign textiles in favor of Iranian-manufactured products and frequently demonstrating in support of national independence. In fact, it is safe to say that, more than any other group, women, the same women who were several decades later demonized as the agents of imperialism, symbolized the nationalistic and anti-imperialist mood of those times.

Over the ensuing years, the modernizers gained ground. Whatever else 27 might be said about him, Shah Reza Pahlevi, who came to power in 1925, was a committed modernizer who in 1936 even attempted to mandate that all women cease wearing veils. When this failed due to popular outrage, he worked to encourage unveiling in other ways. His son, Shah Muhammad Reza, who was in power at the time of the 1979 revolution, continued in this tradition—for example, granting women the right to vote in 1963. (Of course, it should be remembered that, contrary to the claims of both the Shahs and the clerics who opposed them, these actions merely ratified the progress that had been achieved by Iranian women themselves. Long before the mandatory unveiling law was imposed and long after that law was annulled, scores of Iranian women chose to throw off their veils of their own volition.)

By 1979, women were active in all areas of life in Iran. The number of 28 girls attending schools was on the rise. The number of female candidates for the universities had risen sevenfold during the first half of the 1970s. Women were encouraged to participate in areas normally closed to them through a quota system that gave preferential treatment to eligible girls. Women were scholars, police officers, judges, pilots, and engineers—active in every field except the clergy. In 1978, 333 of 1,660 candidates for local councils were women. Twenty-two were elected to the parliament; two to the Senate. There were one female Cabinet minister, three sub-Cabinet undersecretaries (including the second-highest ranking officials in the Ministries of Labor and Mines and Industries), one governor, one ambassador, and five mayors.

That Khomeini ousted them by resorting to the clergy's old tactic of ac- 29 cusing them of betraying Iranian culture and tradition was not surprising. What was surprising was that the leftist members of his revolutionary coalition went along. The leftists had traditionally appeared to support women's rights. However, this support never ran very deep. The leftists operated under a totalitarian mindset that was ultimately far more at ease with the rigid rules espoused by the reactionary clerics than with the pluralistic approach favored by the women's movement. Thus, when the Ayatollah began his crackdown, he had the leftists' full support.

Most Iranian women, on the other hand, were not so pliant. Another 30 image surfaces—this one a photograph that appeared in an American magazine, I can't remember which. I found it recently among the scraps I had kept from the early days of the revolution. It was taken on a snowy day in March 1979 and reveals tens of thousands of shouting women massed into one of Tehran's wide avenues. Their expressions are arresting, but that is not what is most striking about this photo. No, what draws my attention is how, in contrast to today's pictures of women in Iran—depressing images of drab figures cloaked in black cloth—this photograph is filled with color! The women are dressed in different shades—vibrant reds, bright blues—almost as if they had purposely tried to make themselves stand out as much as possible. In fact, perhaps this was their objective, because, on that March day, these women had gathered to express their resistance to—and their outrage at—Ayatollah Khomeini's attempt to make them invisible.

Some days prior, the Ayatollah had launched the first phase of his clamp- 31 down on women's rights. First, he had announced the annulment of the Family Protection Law that had, since 1967, helped women work outside the home and given them more rights in their marriages. In its place, the traditional Islamic law, known as Sharia, would apply. In one fell swoop the Ayatollah had set Iran back nearly a century. Under the new system, the age of consent for girls has been changed from 18 to nine. Yet no woman no matter what age can marry for the first time without the consent of her father, and no married woman can leave the country without her husband's written and notarized consent. Adultery is punishable by stoning. On the witness stand it takes the testimony of two women to equal that of one man. If a Muslim man kills a Muslim woman and is then sentenced to death, her family must first pay him compensation for his life. As if all this were not enough, Khomeini also announced the reimposition of the veil—decreeing that no woman could go to work unless she is fully covered.

The March 8 demonstration began as a commemoration of the Inter- 32 national Day of the Woman. But, as hundreds of women poured into the streets of Tehran, its character spontaneously changed into a full-fledged protest march against the new regime's measures. "Freedom is neither Eastern nor Western; it is global," the women shouted. "Down with the reactionaries! Tyranny in any form is condemned!"

The March 8 event led to further protests. On the third day, a huge 33 demonstration took place in front of the Ministry of Justice. Declarations of support from different associations and organizations were read, and an eight-point manifesto was issued. Among other things, it called for gender equality in all areas of public and private life as well as a guarantee of fundamental freedoms for both men and women. It also demanded that "the decision over women's clothing, which is determined by custom and the exigencies of geographical location, should be left to women."

In the face of such widespread protest, the Ayatollah backed down. His   34 son-in-law emerged to say that Khomeini had merely meant to encourage women to dress "respectably" in the workplace. But the Ayatollah's retreat proved only temporary. Even as he was officially relenting on his proclamation on the veil, his vigilantes continued to attack unveiled women in public—often by throwing acid at them. And the Ayatollah soon proceeded to reinstate the veiling laws—this time taking care to move step by step. In the summer of 1980, his regime made the veil mandatory in government offices. Later, it prohibited women from shopping without a veil. As they had before, many women resisted and protested these acts. And, once again, they were attacked and beaten by government goons and denounced by the leftist "progressive" forces. Later, the veil was made mandatory for all women regardless of their religion, creed, or nationality. By the early '80s, and after much violence, the regime had succeeded in making the veil the uniform of all Iranian women.

Yet, even as it enabled the regime to consolidate its control over every   35 aspect of its subjects' lives, this act firmly established the separation between the regime and the Iranian population. In order to implement its new laws, the regime created special vice squads that patrol the cities on the lookout for any citizen guilty of a "moral offense." The guards are allowed to raid not just public places but private homes, in search of alcoholic drinks, "decadent" music or videos, people playing cards, sexually mixed parties or unveiled women. Those arrested go to special courts and jails. The result was that ordinary Iranian citizens—both men and women—immediately began to feel the presence and intervention of the state in their most private daily affairs. These officers were not there to arrest criminals who threatened the lives or safety of the populace; they were there to control the populace, to take people away, and to flog and imprison them. Bazaars and shopping malls were surrounded and raided; young girls and boys were arrested for walking together in the streets, for not wearing the proper clothing. Nail polish and Reebok shoes were treated as lethal weapons. Young girls were subjected to virginity tests. Soon, even people who originally supported the regime began to question it.

The government had claimed that only a handful of "Westernized"   36 women had opposed its laws, but now, 20 years after the revolution, its most outspoken and daring opponents are the very children of revolution, many of whom were the most active members of Islamic students' associations. To cite just one statistic, of the 802 men and women the vice squads detained in Tehran in July 1993, 80 percent were under the age of 20. The suppression of culture in the name of defending against the West's "cultural invasion" and the attempts at coercive "Islamization" have made these youths almost obsessed with the culture they are being deprived of.

The regime has also succeeded in alienating many of the traditionalist 37 women who had initially supported it. Committed religious believers, these women had long felt uncomfortable with the modernization and secularization that had taken place in Iran during the century leading up to the revolution. So, when Ayatollah Khomeini first arrived on the scene, they welcomed him with open arms. So powerful an ally were they that Khomeini, who had vehemently protested when women were granted the right to vote in 1963, decided against repealing it so that he could rely on these women's votes.

After the revolution, these women began to venture into the work- 38 place—which they now deemed sufficiently hospitable to their traditionalist lifestyle. There they encountered those secular women who had not been a part of the Shah's government and who had therefore been allowed to remain in their jobs so that the regime could benefit from their know-how. As time went by, the traditionalist women began to find that they actually had quite a lot in common with their secular counterparts, who they had previously criticized as Westernized. The line between "us" and "them" gradually blurred.

One issue that solidified this bond was the law. For some traditional 39 women, the imposition of the veil was an affront to their religiosity—changing what had been a freely chosen expression of religious faith into a rote act imposed on them by the state. My grandmother was one such woman. An intensely religious woman who never parted with her chador, she was nonetheless outraged at those who had defiled her religion by using violence to impose their interpretation of it on her grandchildren. "This is not Islam!" she would insist.

Meanwhile, other traditional women felt alienated by some of the more 40 draconian aspects of Sharia. The debate around the Islamic laws inevitably led to a critical reappraisal of the basic tenets that had created them. It also led to a discussion of more fundamental issues pertaining to the nature of male-female relations as well as public and private spaces. The regime had changed the laws, claiming that they were unjust, that they were products of alien rule and exploitation. Now that the "alien rulers" were gone, these claims were being tested. Iranian women from all walks of life were discovering that the biggest affront to them was the law itself. It did not protect the most basic rights of women; it violated them. As Zahra Rahnavard, the wife of the last Iranian Prime Minister Mir Hossein Musavi and an ardent Islamist, has lamented to the Iranian press: "The Islamic government has lost the war on the hejab [veil]. . . . The Islamic values have failed to protect women and to win their support."

The incompatibility of these laws with the reality of modern Iran thus   41
became apparent to the more openminded elements that had previously supported the regime. Many of them distanced themselves from the official policies and joined ranks with those on the "other" side. The transformation of the editor and part of the staff of an official women's journal, *Zane Rooz*, is a good example. They left office in the mid-'80s and created a new magazine, *Zanan*, sharply critical of many government policies and practices. They invited secular women to participate in the publication of their journal. Some from the ranks of clergy joined them in criticizing the existing laws on women. Such transformations have frightened the hard-liners into passing even more reactionary laws, further suppressing the progressive elements working for creation of a civil society and, in the process, fueling a vicious cycle.

The consequence has been that the regime has become far more de-   42
pendent on women for its survival than women are on the regime. The regime can make all sorts of deals with the imperialist powers, even with the Great Satan itself, but it cannot allow its women to change the public image imposed on them; since the regime's legitimacy rests so heavily on the notion that its rules represent the will of the Iranian people, the presence of even one unveiled woman in the streets has become more dangerous than the grenades of an underground opposition. And Iranian women appear to have taken notice. Young girls in particular have turned the veil into an instrument of protest. They wear it in attractive and provocative ways. They leave part of their hair showing from under their scarves or allow colorful clothing to show underneath their uniforms. They walk in a defiant manner. And in doing so they have become a constant reminder to the ruling elite that it is fighting a losing battle.

I would like to end with a final image—this one a joyous one that   43
negates the other mutilated half-images of women I have described. It happened in 1997, when the Iranian soccer team defeated Australia in the World Cup qualifying tournament. The government had repeatedly warned against any secular-style celebrations. But, as soon as the game was over, millions of Iranians spilled into the streets, dancing and singing to loud mu-

sic. They called it the "football revolution." The most striking feature of this "revolution" was the presence of thousands of women who broke through police barricades to enter the football stadium, from which they are normally banned. Some even celebrated by taking off their veils. Time and again I replay not the actions but the atmosphere of jubilation and defiance surrounding this event. The Iranian nation, having no political or national symbols or events to celebrate as its own, chose the most nonpolitical of all events, soccer, and turned it into a strong political statement.

As usual, the Western press described these events as a message to the 44 hard-liners from Khatami's supporters. But the main addressees of the football revolution's message were not the hard-liners; they had heard the message many times before and had ignored it. If anyone were to learn any lessons from this event it should have been the more "moderate" faction. It was clear then, and it has become clearer since thanks to subsequent demonstrations, protest meetings, and publications, that the majority of Iranians see the current Islamic regime as the main obstacle to the creation of a civil society.

It is this problem that faces President Khatami today. He has impressed 45 the West by proclaiming himself a man who stands for the rule of law. But the law in the Islamic Republic is what most Iranians today are protesting against. In reaction the hard-liners have become increasingly repressive; the small openings and freedoms enjoyed by the Iranian people at the start of President Khatami's victory have come with arbitrary crackdowns in which ordinary citizens are stoned for adultery; writers and prominent members of the opposition are not only jailed but murdered; Bahais are deprived of their most basic human rights; and the revolutionary guards and morality police treat the Iranian citizens as strictly as ever.

But these actions are taken from a position of weakness, not strength. 46 Unlike in the past, repressive measures have failed to quell the protests. Side by side with the daily struggle that has turned the business of living into a protracted war, there are public debates, protest meetings, and demonstrations, reminders of those sunny-snowy days 20 years ago. And, just as in those days past, women are once again playing a decisive role.

In fact, there is an almost artistic symmetry to the way Iranian women 47 at the end of the twentieth century, as at its beginning, are at the center of the larger struggle for the creation of an open and pluralistic society in Iran. The future twists and turns of this struggle are uncertain, but of one thing I am sure: a time will come when the Degas ballerinas return to their rightful place.

Thinking About the Essay

1. How is the essay structured, like a slide presentation, around four images? How are the images related? By what logic does Nafisi progress from one image to the next? Why is the work of Edgar Degas an appropriate illustration for Nafisi's purposes, in ways that she does not explicitly mention? (You may want to do some research on Degas.)

2. Where in the essay does Nafisi employ process analysis? How do these analyses function as digressions within the essay?

3. How is the second image (introduced in paragraph 13) transformed, over the course of several paragraphs, into a *metaphor*? How is the image of this person made to relate to the censored Degas painting?

4. How did the association with "modern" Western values harm the Iranian women's movement later in the twentieth century? What are some of the ironic parallels Nafisi draws between the association of the women's movement with Western values and the postrevolutionary Iranian government's alignment with anti-Western attitudes?

5. How does Nafisi's hostility toward the current Iranian regime surface in this essay? Does she present a convincing argument, or, as a woman who has experienced difficulty at clerical hands, is she too opinionated or biased? Explain with reference to the text.

Responding in Writing

6. In *Reading Lolita in Tehran*, Nafisi presents a list of novels, including Nabokov's *Lolita* and F. Scott Fitzgerald's *The Great Gatsby*, that she taught to her seven female students. What do you think her motivation was? Why didn't she teach Persian literature? Why did she select, of all novels she might have taught, *Lolita*, which is (at one literal level) about an older man who seduces a teenaged girl?

7. What range of private acts are available today to women in the United States who want to make a strong political statement? In a brief essay, describe how one such act could be considered a gesture in defiance of a cultural norm.

8. How have recent political events in Iran either supported or refuted Nafisi's predictions in this essay? (You may want to consider, for example, the results of the most recent election, or the role that Iran played in the international controversy, in early 2006, over a cartoon that appeared in a European newspaper.)

Networking

9. In groups of three or four, choose one recently published media image in which an absence strongly implies a presence. Describe (or show) the image to the class and explain what (or who) is absent from the photo and why this is a meaningful absence.

10. With two or three other students, go online and find out more about the lives of women in Iran today. Share your findings in class discussion.

Family Values

RICHARD RODRIGUEZ

Richard Rodriguez, born in San Francisco in 1944, has gained national fame for his articles, books, and radio and television broadcasts on issues of race, immigration, multiculturalism, and gender. After receiving degrees from Stanford University and Columbia University, Rodriguez pursued graduate work at the University of California at Berkeley and the Warburg Institute, London. In his autobiography, *Hunger of Memory: The Education of Richard Rodriguez* (1982), he offers a memorable portrait of a young man trying to reconcile his Hispanic heritage and the dominant American culture. Rodriguez's opposition to bilingualism and affirmative action, as well as his advocacy of gay rights (which we see in the following essay), has been controversial, but he brings sharp critical insights to every subject he treats. Rodriguez's most recent book is *Brown: The Last Discovery of America* (2002). In "Family Values," published in the *Los Angeles Times* in 1992, Rodriguez argues that contrary to certain claims, homosexuality actually strengthens rather than weakens family structures.

Before Reading

Many college instructors see homophobia as the most intractable problem to deal with in the classroom—much more than sexism, racism, or any other type of discrimination. Why might this be the case? What is your own attitude toward homosexuality? What is your family's attitude? What is your culture or religion's attitude?

I am sitting alone in my car, in front of my parents' house—a middle-aged 1 man with a boy's secret to tell. What words will I use to tell them? I hate the word *gay,* find its little affirming sparkle more pathetic than assertive.

I am happier with the less polite *queer.* But to my parents I would say *homosexual,* avoiding the Mexican slang *joto* (I had always heard it said in our house with hints of condescension), though *joto* is less mocking than the sissy-boy *maricon.*

The buzz on everyone's lips now: Family values. The other night on TV, the vice president of the United States, his arm around his wife, smiled into the camera and described homosexuality as "mostly a choice." But how would he know? Homosexuality never felt like a choice to me.

A few minutes ago Rush Limbaugh, the radio guy with a voice that reminds me, for some reason, of a butcher's arms, was banging his console and booming a near-reasonable polemic about family values. Limbaugh was not very clear about which values exactly he considers to be family values. A divorced man who lives alone in New York?

My parents live on a gray, treeless street in San Francisco not far from the ocean. Probably more than half of the neighborhood is immigrant. India lives next door to Greece, who lives next door to Russia. I wonder what the Chinese lady next door to my parents makes of the politicians' phrase *family values.*

What immigrants know, what my parents certainly know, is that when you come to this country, you risk losing your children. The assurance of family—continuity, inevitability—is precisely what America encourages its children to overturn. *Become your own man.* We who are native to this country know this too, of course, though we are likely to deny it. Only a society so guilty about its betrayal of family would tolerate the pieties of politicians regarding family values.

On the same summer day that Republicans were swarming in Houston (buzzing about family values), a friend of mine who escaped family values awhile back and who now wears earrings resembling intrauterine devices, was complaining to me over coffee about the Chinese. The Chinese will never take over San Francisco, my friend said, because the Chinese do not want to take over San Francisco. The Chinese do not even see San Francisco! All they care about is their damn families. All they care about is double-parking smack in front of the restaurant on Clement Street and pulling granny out of the car—and damn anyone who happens to be in the car behind them or the next or the next.

Politicians would be horrified by such an American opinion, of course. But then what do politicians, Republicans or Democrats, really know of our family life? Or what are they willing to admit? Even in that area where they could reasonably be expected to have something to say—regarding the relationship of family life to our economic system—the politicians say nothing. Republicans celebrate American economic freedom, but Republicans don't seem to connect that economic freedom to the social breakdown they find appalling. Democrats, on the other hand, if more tolerant of the drift from familial tradition, are suspicious of the very capitalism that creates social freedom.

How you become free in America: Consider the immigrant. He gets a 8 job. Soon he is earning more money than his father ever made (his father's authority is thereby subtly undermined). The immigrant begins living a life his father never knew. The immigrant moves from one job to another, changes houses. His economic choices determine his home address—not the other way around. The immigrant is on his way to becoming his own man.

When I was broke a few years ago and trying to finish a book, I lived 9 with my parents. What a thing to do! A major theme of America is leaving home. We trust the child who forsakes family connections to make it on his own. We call that the making of a man.

Let's talk about this man stuff for a minute. America's ethos is anti- 10 domestic. We may be intrigued by blood that runs through wealth—the Kennedys or the Rockefellers—but they seem European to us. Which is to say, they are movies. They are Corleones. Our real pledge of allegiance: We say in America that nothing about your family—your class, your race, your pedigree—should be as important as what you yourself achieve. We end up in 1992 introducing ourselves by first names.

What authority can Papa have in a country that formed its identity in 11 an act of Oedipal rebellion against a mad British king? Papa is a joke in America, a stock sitcom figure—Archie Bunker or Homer Simpson. But my Mexican father went to work every morning, and he stood in a white smock, making false teeth, oblivious of the shelves of grinning false teeth mocking his devotion.

The nuns in grammar school—my wonderful Irish nuns—used to push 12 Mark Twain on me. I distrusted Huck Finn, he seemed like a gringo kid I would steer clear of in the schoolyard. (He was too confident.) I realize now, of course, that Huck is the closest we have to a national hero. We trust the story of a boy who has no home and is restless for the river. (Huck's Pap is drunk.) Americans are more forgiving of Huck's wildness than of the sweetness of the Chinese boy who walks to school with his mama or grandma. (There is no worse thing in America than to be a mama's boy, nothing better than to be a real boy—all boy—like Huck, who eludes Aunt Sally, and is eager for the world of men.)

There's a bent old woman coming up the street. She glances nervously 13 as she passes my car. What would you tell us, old lady, of family values in America?

America is an immigrant country, we say. Motherhood—parenthood— 14
is less our point than adoption. If I had to assign gender to America, I
would note the consensus of the rest of the world. When America is burned
in effigy, a male is burned. Americans themselves speak of Uncle Sam.

Like the Goddess of Liberty, Uncle Sam has no children of his own. He 15
steals children to make men of them, mocks all reticence, all modesty, all
memory. Uncle Sam is a hectoring Yankee, a skinflint uncle, gaunt, un-
couth, unloved. He is the American Savonarola—hater of moonshine, destroyer of stills, burner of cocaine. Sam has no patience with mamas' boys.

You betray Uncle Sam by favoring private over public life, by seeking 16
to exempt yourself, by cheating on your income taxes, by avoiding jury
duty, by trying to keep your boy on the farm.

Mothers are traditionally the guardians of the family against Amer- 17
ica—though even Mom may side with America against queers and desert-
ers, at least when the Old Man is around. Premature gray hair. Arthritis in
her shoulders. Bowlegged with time, red hands. In their fiercely flowered
housedresses, mothers are always smarter than fathers in America. But in
reality they are betrayed by their children who leave. In a thousand ways.
They end up alone.

We kind of like the daughter who was a tomboy. Remember her? It was 18
always easier to be a tomboy in America than a sissy. Americans admired
Annie Oakley more than they admired Liberace (who, nevertheless, always
remembered his mother). But today we do not admire Annie Oakley when
we see Mom becoming Annie Oakley.

The American household now needs two incomes, everyone says. 19
Meaning: Mom is *forced* to leave home out of economic necessity. But lots
of us know lots of moms who are sick and tired of being mom, or only
mom. It's like the nuns getting fed up, teaching kids for all those years and
having those kids grow up telling stories of how awful Catholic school
was! Not every woman in America wants her life's work to be forgiveness.
Today there are moms who don't want their husbands' names. And the
most disturbing possibility: What happens when Mom doesn't want to be
Mom at all? Refuses pregnancy?

Mom is only becoming an American like the rest of us. Certainly, peo- 20
ple all over the world are going to describe the influence of feminism on
women (all over the world) as their "Americanization." And rightly so.

Nothing of this, of course, will the politician's wife tell you. The politi- 21
cian's wife is careful to follow her husband's sentimental reassurances that
nothing has changed about America except perhaps for the sinister influence of deviants. Like myself.

I contain within myself an anomaly at least as interesting as the Re-   22
publican Party's version of family values. I am a homosexual Catholic, a
communicant in a tradition that rejects even as it upholds me.

I do not count myself among those Christians who proclaim themselves   23
protectors of family values. They regard me as no less an enemy of the family than the "radical feminists." But the joke about families that all homosexuals know is that we are the ones who stick around and make families
possible. Call on us. I can think of 20 or 30 examples. A gay son or daughter is the only one who is "free" (married brothers and sisters are too busy).
And, indeed, because we have admitted the inadmissible about ourselves
(that we are queer)—we are adepts at imagination—we can even imagine
those who refuse to imagine us. We can imagine Mom's loneliness, for example. If Mom needs to be taken to church or to the doctor or ferried between Christmas dinners, depend on the gay son or lesbian daughter.

I won't deny that the so-called gay liberation movement, along with   24
feminism, undermined the heterosexual household, if that's what politicians mean when they say family values. Against churchly reminders that
sex was for procreation, the gay bar as much as the birth-control pill taught
Americans not to fear sexual pleasure. In the past two decades—and, not
coincidentally, parallel to the feminist movement—the gay liberation
movement moved a generation of Americans toward the idea of a childless
adulthood. If the women's movement was ultimately more concerned
about getting out of the house and into the workplace, the gay movement
was in its way more subversive to puritan America because it stressed the
importance of play.

Several months ago, the society editor of the morning paper in San   25
Francisco suggested (on a list of "must haves") that every society dame
must have at least one gay male friend. A ballet companion. A lunch date.
The remark was glib and incorrect enough to beg complaints from homosexual readers, but there was a truth about it as well. Homosexual men
have provided women with an alternate model of masculinity. And the
truth: The Old Man, God bless him, is a bore. Thus are we seen as preserving marriages? Even Republican marriages?

For myself, homosexuality is a deep brotherhood but does not involve   26
domestic life. Which is why, my married sisters will tell you, I can afford
the time to be a writer. And why are so many homosexuals such wonderful teachers and priests and favorite aunts, if not because we are freed from
the house? On the other hand, I know lots of homosexual couples (male
and female) who model their lives on the traditional heterosexual version
of domesticity and marriage. Republican politicians mock the notion of a

homosexual marriage, but ironically such marriages honor the heterosexual marriage by imitating it.

"The only loving couples I know," a friend of mine recently remarked, 27 "are all gay couples."

This woman was not saying that she does not love her children or that 28 she is planning a divorce. But she was saying something about the sadness of American domestic life: the fact that there is so little joy in family intimacy. Which is perhaps why gossip (public intrusion into the private) has become a national industry. All day long, in forlorn houses, the television lights up a freakish parade of husbands and mothers-in-law and children upon the stage of Sally or Oprah or Phil. They tell on each other. The audience ooohhhs. Then a psychiatrist-shaman appears at the end to dispense prescriptions—the importance of family members granting one another more "space."

The question I desperately need to ask you is whether we Americans 29 have ever truly valued the family. We are famous, or our immigrant ancestors were famous, for the willingness to leave home. And it is ironic that a crusade under the banner of family values has been taken up by those who would otherwise pass themselves off as patriots. For they seem not to understand America, nor do I think they love the freedoms America grants. Do they understand why, in a country that prizes individuality and is suspicious of authority, children are disinclined to submit to their parents? You cannot celebrate American values in the public realm without expecting them to touch our private lives. As Barbara Bush remarked recently, family values are also neighborhood values. It may be harmless enough for Barbara Bush to recall a sweeter America—Midland, Texas, in the 1950s. But the question left begging is why we chose to leave Midland, Texas. Americans like to say that we can't go home again. The truth is that we don't want to go home again, don't want to be known, recognized. Don't want to respond in the same old ways. (And you know you will if you go back there.)

Little 10-year-old girls know that there are reasons for getting away 30 from the family. They learn to keep their secrets—under lock and key—addressed to Dear Diary. Growing up queer, you learn to keep secrets as well. In no place are those secrets more firmly held than within the family house. You learn to live in closets. I know a Chinese man who arrived in America about 10 years ago. He got a job and made some money. And during that time he came to confront his homosexuality. And then his family arrived. I do not yet know the end of this story.

The genius of America is that it permits children to leave home, it per- 31 mits us to become different from our parents. But the sadness, the loneliness of America, is clear too.

Listen to the way Americans talk about immigrants. If, on the one 32
hand, there is impatience when today's immigrants do not seem to give up
their family, there is also a fascination with this reluctance. In Los Angeles,
Hispanics are considered people of family. Hispanic women are hired to be
at the center of the American family—to babysit and diaper, to cook and
to clean and to ease the dying. Hispanic attachment to family is seen by
many Americans, I think, as the reason why Hispanics don't get ahead. But
if Asians privately annoy us for being so family oriented, they are also
stereotypically celebrated as the new "whiz kids" in school. Don't Asians
go to college, after all, to honor their parents?

More important still is the technological and economic ascendancy of 33
Asia, particularly Japan, on the American imagination. Americans are
starting to wonder whether perhaps the family values of Asia put the
United States at a disadvantage. The old platitude had it that ours is a vi-
brant, robust society for being a society of individuals. Now we look to
Asia and see team effort paying off.

In this time of national homesickness, of nostalgia, for how we imagine 34
America used to be, there are obvious dangers. We are going to start blaming each other for the loss. Since we are inclined, as Americans, to think of
ourselves individually, we are disinclined to think of ourselves as creating
one another or influencing one another.

But it is not the politician or any political debate about family values 35
that has brought me here on a gray morning to my parents' house. It is
some payment I owe to my youth and to my parents' youth. I imagine us
sitting in the living room, amid my mother's sentimental doilies and the
family photographs, trying to take the measure of the people we have
turned out to be in America.

A San Francisco poet, when he was in the hospital and dying, called a 36
priest to his bedside. The old poet wanted to make his peace with Mother
Church. He wanted baptism. The priest asked why. "Because the Catholic
Church has to accept me," said the poet. "Because I am a sinner."

Isn't willy-nilly inclusiveness the point, the only possible point to be 37
derived from the concept of family? Curiously, both President Bush and
Vice President Quayle got in trouble with their constituents recently for
expressing a real family value. Both men said that they would try to dis-
suade a daughter or granddaughter from having an abortion. But, finally,
they said they would support her decision, continue to love her, never
abandon her.

There are families that do not accept. There are children who are forced 38
to leave home because of abortions or homosexuality. There are family

secrets that Papa never hears. Which is to say there are families that never learn the point of families.

But there she is at the window. My mother has seen me and she waves 39 me in. Her face asks: Why am I sitting outside? (Have they, after all, known my secret for years and kept it, out of embarrassment, not knowing what to say?) Families accept, often by silence. My father opens the door to welcome me in.

Thinking About the Essay

1. Rodriguez's title is exceedingly compelling in light of his essay. Why is this title so powerful? What ironies do the title and the text reveal? Point to specific instances of irony in the essay.

2. Consider the introduction and conclusion of this essay. Why does Rodriguez begin and end on a personal note? What is his purpose? How does personal narrative enhance what is basically an expository essay?

3. How would you describe the writer's style in this essay? What types of sentences does he prefer? What are some of his more arresting phrases and figures of speech? How does he generate an emotional mood and tone that pervades the entire essay? How would you describe this tone?

4. In many ways, this essay involves a definition—and a meditation—on the family and family values. What rhetorical strategies does Rodriguez use to develop his extended definitions? Would you say that his definitions are stipulative (that is, strictly personal and therefore limited in application) or universally true? Explain.

5. Analyze this essay as an argument. What is Rodriguez's claim? What are his key reasons supporting his claim? What types of evidence does he provide in support of these reasons? Finally, how convincing is his argument? Does he convince you? Has your thinking been changed in any way? Explain.

Responding in Writing

6. Rodriguez states that gay men and women frequently are the strongest defenders of traditional values within families (paragraph 23). Write an argumentative essay in which you agree or disagree with this proposition.

7. Write your own definition of "family values." Be certain to create a tone that captures your feelings about this term and about the people and groups who use it to advance a certain agenda.

8. Write an argumentative essay supporting or rejecting the concept of gay marriage. State your claim or major proposition, back it up with at least three key minor propositions, and provide supporting evidence. Throughout the essay, focus on the notion of "family values."

Networking

9. With two other class members, have a serious discussion of the issues raised by Rodriguez in his essay and your personal response to them. Share your opinions and feelings with the rest of the class.

10. Locate a "family values" website. What does this website say about homosexuality? Report your findings to the class.

Life on the Global Assembly Line

Barbara Ehrenreich and Annette Fuentes

Barbara Ehrenreich was born in 1941 in Butte, Montana. She attended Reed College (B.A., 1963) and Rockefeller University (Ph.D. in biology, 1968). A self-described socialist and **feminist**, Ehrenreich uses her scientific training to investigate a broad range of social issues: health care, the plight of the poor, the condition of women around the world. Her scathing critiques of American health care in such books as *The American Health Empire* (with John Ehrenreich, 1970), *Complaints and Disorders: The Sexual Politics of Sickness* (with Deirdre English, 1973), and *For Her Own Good* (with English, 1978) established her as an authority in the field. In her provocative *The Hearts of Men: American Dreams and the Flight from Commitment* (1983), Ehrenreich surveys the decline of male investment in the family from the 1950s to the 1980s. A prolific writer during the 1980s and 1990s, Ehrenreich most recently published the award-winning book *Nickel and Dimed: On (Not) Getting By in America* (2001). She is also a frequent contributor to magazines, including *Nation, Esquire, Radical America, New Republic,* and *The New York Times,* while serving as a contributing editor to *Ms.* and *Mother Jones.* The classic essay that appears here, written for *Ms.* in 1981 with Annette Fuentes, a New York–based journalist and adjunct professor at Columbia University, was among the first articles to expose the plight of working women around the world.

Before Reading

What experiences or expectations do you bring to a new job? What happens if you discover you are being exploited?

Ms.; 1981 January 1
flash forward 2

> Globalization has changed the rules of the game. The nation-state as we 3
> understand it is a state that is bargaining, struggling, being swallowed
> up by the forces of globalization. In 1985, on the eve of the Nairobi
> conference, our message about development was really new, that you
> can't just talk about gender equality without considering equality of
> what. Do you want equal shares of a poisoned pie? It was a message
> that had a galvanizing effect on people, because by Beijing, globaliza-
> tion issues had become part of everyone's vocabulary. No longer was it
> a situation where the North worries about gender equality and the
> South about development.
>
> —Economist Gita Sen, *Ford Foundation Report,* Winter 2000

Every morning, between four and seven, thousands of women head out 4
for the day shift. In Ciudad Juarez, they crowd into *ruteras* (run-down
vans) for the trip from the slum neighborhoods to the industrial parks on
the outskirts of the city. In Penang they squeeze, 60 or more at a time, into
buses for the trip to the low, modern factory buildings of the Bayan Lepas
free trade zone. In Taiwan, they walk from the dormitories—where the
night shift is already asleep in the still-warm beds—through the checkpoints in the high fence surrounding the factory zone.

This is the world's new industrial proletariat: young, female, Third 5
World. Viewed from the "first world," they are still faceless, genderless
"cheap labor," signaling their existence only through a label or tiny imprint
"made in Hong Kong," or Taiwan, Korea, the Dominican Republic, Mexico, the Philippines. But they may be one of the most strategic blocs of
womanpower in the world. Conservatively, there are 2 million Third World
female industrial workers employed now, millions more looking for work,
and their numbers are rising every year.

It doesn't take more than second-grade arithmetic to understand what's 6
happening. In the U.S., an assembly-line worker is likely to earn, depending on her length of employment, between $3.10 and $5 an hour. In many
Third World countries, a woman doing the same work will earn $3 to $5
a day.

And so, almost everything that can be packed up is being moved out to 7
the Third World: garment manufacture, textiles, toys, footwear, pharmaceuticals, wigs, appliance parts, tape decks, computer components, plastic
goods. In some industries, like garment and textile, American jobs are lost
in the process, and the biggest losers are women, often black and Hispanic.
But what's going on is much more than a matter of runaway shops. Economists are talking about a "new international division of labor," in which the
process of production is broken down and the fragments are dispersed to

This three-year-old in India helps her mother and sisters make soccer balls—for 75 cents a day.

different parts of the world, while control over the overall process and technology remains safely at company headquarters in "first world" countries.

The American electronics industry provides a classic example: circuits are printed on silicon wafers and tested in California; then the wafers are shipped to Asia for the labor-intensive process by which they are cut into tiny chips and bonded to circuit boards; final assembly into products such as calculators or military equipment usually takes place in the United States. Garment manufacture too is often broken into geographically separated steps, with the most repetitive, labor-intensive jobs going to the poor countries of the southern hemisphere. 8

So much any economist could tell you. What is less often noted is the gender breakdown of the emerging international division of labor. Eighty to 90 percent of the low-skilled assembly jobs that go to the Third World are performed by women in a remarkable switch from earlier patterns of 9 foreign-dominated industrialization. Until now, "development" under the aegis of foreign corporations has usually meant more jobs for men and—compared to traditional agricultural society—a diminished economic status for women. But multinational corporations and Third World governments alike consider assembly-line work—whether the product is Barbie dolls or missile parts—to be "women's" work.

It's an article of faith with management that only women can do, or will do, the monotonous, painstaking work that American business is export-   10
ing to the Third World. The personnel manager of a light assembly plant in Taiwan told anthropologist Linda Gail Arrigo, "Young male workers are too restless and impatient to do monotonous work with no career value. If displeased, they sabotage the machines and even threaten the foreman. But girls? At most, they cry a little."

A top-level management consultant who specializes in advising Ameri-   11
can companies on where to relocate, gave us this global generalization: "The [factory] girls genuinely enjoy themselves. They're away from their families. They have spending money. Of course it's a regulated experience too—with dormitories to live in—so it's a healthful experience."

What is the real experience of the women in the emerging Third World industrial work force? Rachael Grossman, a researcher with the Southeast   12
Asia Resource Center, found women employees of U.S. multinational firms in Malaysia and the Philippines living four to eight in a room in boarding-houses, or squeezing into tiny extensions built onto squatter huts near the factory. Where companies do provide dormitories, they are not of the "healthful," collegiate variety. The American Friends Service Committee reports that dormitory space is "likely to be crowded—while one shift works, another sleeps, as many as twenty to a room."

Living conditions are only part of the story. The work that multinational corporations export to the Third World is not only the most tedious, but of-   13
ten the most hazardous part of the production process. The countries they go to are, for the most part, those that will guarantee no interference from health and safety inspectors, trade unions, or even freelance reformers.

Consider the electronics industry, which is generally thought to be the safest and cleanest of the exported industries. The factory buildings are low   14
and modern, like those one might find in a suburban American industrial park. Inside, rows of young women, neatly dressed in the company uniform or Tshirt, work quietly at their stations. There is air conditioning (not for the women's comfort, but to protect the delicate semiconductor parts they work with), and high-volume piped-in Bee Gees hits (not so much for entertainment, as to prevent talking).

For many Third World women, electronics is a prestige occupation, at 15 least compared to other kinds of factory work. They are unlikely to know that in the United States the National Institute on Occupational Safety and Health (NIOSH) has placed electronics on its select list of "high health-risk industries using the greatest number of toxic substances." If electronics assembly work is risky here, it is doubly so in countries where there is no equivalent of NIOSH to even issue warnings. In many plants toxic chemicals and solvents sit in open containers, filling the work area with fumes that can literally knock you out. "We have been told of cases where ten to twelve women passed out at once," an AFSC field worker in northern Mexico told us, "and the newspapers report this as 'mass hysteria.'"

Some of the worst conditions have been documented in South Korea, 16 where the garment and textile industries have helped spark that country's "economic miracle." Workers are packed into poorly lit rooms, where summer temperatures rise above 100 degrees. Textile dust, which can cause permanent lung damage, fills the air. Management may require forced overtime of as much as 48 hours at a stretch, and if that seems to go beyond the limits of human endurance, pep pills and amphetamine injections are thoughtfully provided. In her diary (originally published in a magazine now banned by the South Korean government) Min Chong Suk, 30, a sewing-machine operator, wrote of working from 7 A.M. to 11:30 P.M. in a garment factory: "When [the apprentices] shake the waste threads from the clothes, the whole room fills with dust, and it is hard to breathe. Since we've been working in such dusty air, there have been increasing numbers of people getting tuberculosis, bronchitis, and eye diseases. Since we are women, it makes us so sad when we have pale, unhealthy, wrinkled faces like dried-up spinach. It seems to me that no one knows our blood dissolves into the threads and seams, with sighs and sorrow."

In all the exported industries, the most invidious, inescapable health 17 hazard is stress. Lunch breaks may be barely long enough for a woman to stand in line at the canteen or hawkers' stalls. Visits to the bathroom are treated as privileges. Rotating shifts—the day shift one week, the night shift the next—wreak havoc with sleep patterns. Because inaccuracies or failure to meet production quotas can mean substantial pay losses, the pressures are quickly internalized; stomach ailments and nervous problems are not unusual.

As if poor health and the stress of factory life weren't enough to drive 18 women into early retirement, management actually encourages a high turnover in many industries. "As you know, when seniority rises, wages rise," the management consultant to U.S. multinationals told us. He explained that it's cheaper to train a fresh supply of teenagers than to pay experienced women higher wages. "Older" women, aged 23 or 24, are likely to be laid off and not rehired.

The lucky ones find husbands. The unlucky ones find themselves at the 19 margins of society—as bar girls, "hostesses," or prostitutes.

There has been no international protest about the exploitation of Third 20 World women by multinational corporations—no thundering denunciations from the floor of the United Nations' General Assembly, no angry resolutions from the Conference of the Non-Aligned Countries. Sociologist Robert Snow, who has been tracing the multinationals on their way south and east-ward for years, explained why. "The Third World governments want the multinationals to move in. There's cutthroat competition to attract the corporations."

The governments themselves gain little revenue from this kind of in- 21 vestment—especially since most offer tax holidays and freedom from export duties in order to attract the multinationals in the first place. Nor do the people as a whole benefit, according to a highly placed Third World woman within the U.N. "The multinationals like to say they're contributing to development," she told us, "but they come into our countries for one thing—cheap labor. If the labor stops being so cheap, they can move on. So how can you call that development? It depends on the people being poor and staying poor." But there are important groups that do stand to gain when the multinationals set up shop in their countries: local entrepreneurs who subcontract to the multinationals; "technocrats" who become local management; and government officials who specialize in cutting red tape for an "agent's fee" or an outright bribe.

In the competition for multinational investment, local governments ad- 22 vertise their women shamelessly. An investment brochure issued by the Malaysian government informs multinational executives that: "the manual dexterity of the Oriental female is famous the world over. Her hands are small, and she works fast with extreme care. . . . Who, therefore, could be better qualified by nature and inheritance, to contribute to the efficiency of a bench-assembly production line than the Oriental girl?"

Many "host" governments are willing to back up their advertising with 23 whatever brutality it takes to keep "their girls" just as docile as they look in the brochures. Even the most polite and orderly attempts to organize are likely to bring down overkill doses of police repression:

In Guatemala in 1975 women workers in a North American-owned 24 garment factory drew up a list of complaints that included insults by management, piecework wages that turned out to be less than the legal minimum, no overtime pay, and "threats of death." In response, the American boss called the local authorities to report that he was being harassed by

"Communists." When the women reported for work the next day they found the factory surrounded by two fully armed contingents of military police. The "Communist" ringleaders were picked out and fired.

In the Dominican Republic in 1978, workers who attempted to organ- 25 ize at La Romana industrial zone were first fired, then obligingly arrested by the local police. Officials from the AFLCIO have described the zone as a "modern slave-labor camp," where workers who do not meet their production quotas during their regular shift must stay and put in unpaid overtime until they do meet them, and many women workers are routinely strip-searched at the end of the day. During the 1978 organizing attempt, the government sent in national police in full combat gear armed with automatic weapons. Gulf & Western supplements the local law with its own company-sponsored motorcycle club, which specializes in terrorizing suspected union sympathizers.

In Inchon, South Korea, women at the Dong-II Textile Company (which 26 produces fabrics and yarn for export to the United States) had succeeded in gaining leadership in their union in 1972. But in 1978 the government-controlled, male-dominated Federation of Korean Trade Unions sent special "action squads" to destroy the women's union. Armed with steel bars and buckets of human excrement, the goons broke into the union office, smashed the office equipment, and smeared the excrement over the women's bodies and in their hair, ears, eyes, and mouths.

Crudely put (and incidents like this do not inspire verbal delicacy), the 27 relationship between many Third World governments and the multinational corporations is not very different from the relationship between a pimp and his customers. The governments advertise their women, sell them, and keep them in line for the multinational "johns." But there are other parties to the growing international traffic in women—such as the United Nations' Industrial Development Organization (UNIDO), the World Bank, and the United States government itself.

UNIDO has been a major promoter of "free trade zones." These are en- 28 claves within nations that offer multinationals a range of creature comforts, including: freedom from paying taxes and export duties; low-cost water, power, and buildings; exemption from whatever labor laws may apply in the country as a whole; and, in some cases, such security features as barbed-wire, guarded checkpoints, and government-paid police.

Then there is the World Bank, which over the past decade has lent sev- 29 eral billion dollars to finance the roads, airports, power plants, and even the first-class hotels that multinational corporations need in order to set up business in Third World countries.

But the most powerful promoter of exploitative conditions for Third 30
World women workers is the United States government itself. For example,
the notoriously repressive Korean textile industry was developed with the
help of $400 million in aid from the U.S. State Department. Malaysia be-
came a low-wage haven for the electronics industry thanks to technical assistance financed by AID and to U.S. money (funneled through the Asian
Development Bank) to set up free trade zones.

But the most obvious form of United States involvement, according to 31
Lenny Siegel, the director of the Pacific Studies Center, is through "our consistent record of military aid to Third World governments that are capitalist, politically repressive, and are not striving for economic independence."

What does our government have to say for itself? According to AID 32
staffer Emmy Simmons, "we can get hung up in the idea that it's exploitation without really looking at the alternatives for women. These people
have to go somewhere."

Anna, for one, has nowhere to go but the maquiladora. Her family left 33
the farm when she was only six, and the land has long since been bought
up by a large commercial agribusiness company. After her father left to find
work north of the border, money was scarce for years. So when the factory
where she now works opened, Anna felt it was "the best thing that had ever
happened" to her. As a wage-earner, her status rose compared to her brothers with their on-again, off-again jobs. Partly out of her new sense of confidence she agreed to meet with a few other women one day after work to
talk about wages and health conditions. That was the way she became
what management called a "labor agitator" when, six months later, 90 percent of the day shift walked out in the company's first south-of-the-border
strike.

Women like Anna need their jobs desperately. They know the risks of 34
organizing. Beyond that—if they do succeed in organizing—the company
can always move on in search of a still-docile, job-hungry work force. Yet
thousands of women in the Third World's industrial work force have chosen to fight for better wages and working conditions.

One particularly dramatic instance took place in South Korea in 1979. 35
Two hundred young women employees of the YH textile-and-wig factory
staged a peaceful vigil and fast to protest the company's threatened closing
of the plant. On the fifth day of the vigil, more than 1,000 riot police,
armed with clubs and steel shields, broke into the building where the
women were staying and forcibly dragged them out. Twenty-one-year-old
Kim Kyong-suk was killed during the melee. It was her death that touched
off widespread rioting throughout Korea that many thought led to the
overthrow of President Park Chung Hee.

So far, feminism, first-world style, has barely begun to acknowledge the 36 Third World's new industrial womanpower. Jeb Mays and Kathleen Connell, cofounders of the San Francisco-based Women's Network on Global Corporations, are two women who would like to change that: "There's still this idea of the Third World woman as 'the other'—someone exotic and totally unlike us," Mays and Connell told us. "But now we're talking about women who wear the same styles in clothes, listen to the same music, and may even work for the same corporation. That's an irony the multinationals have created. In a way, they're drawing us together as women."

Saralee Hamilton, an AFSC staff organizer says: "The multinational 37 corporations have deliberately targeted women for exploitation. If feminism is going to mean anything to women all over the world, it's going to have to find new ways to resist corporate power internationally." She envisions a global network of grass-roots women capable of sharing experiences, transmitting information, and—eventually—providing direct support for each other's struggles. It's a long way off; few women anywhere have the money for intercontinental plane flights or even long-distance calls, but at least we are beginning to see the way. "We all have the same hard life," wrote Korean garment worker Min Chong Suk. "We are bound together with one string."

Thinking About the Essay

1. Describe the writers' argumentative purpose in this essay. Is it to convince or persuade—or both? Explain.

2. Who is the intended audience for this essay? What is the level of diction? How are the two connected?

3. Examine the writers' use of illustration in this essay. How do they use these illustrations to support a series of generalizations? Ehrenreich and Fuentes cite various studies and authorities. Identify these instances and explain the cumulative effect.

4. Ehrenreich and Fuentes draw on a number of rhetorical strategies to advance their argument. Explain their use of comparison and cause-and-effect analysis.

5. Evaluate the writers' conclusion. Does it effectively reinforce their argument? Why or why not?

Responding in Writing

6. Ehrenreich and Fuentes wrote this article originally for *Ms.* magazine. Why would the essay appeal to the *Ms.* audience? What elements would also appeal to a general audience? Write a brief essay that answers these questions, providing specific examples from the text.

7. Write a personal essay in which you describe a job that you had (or have) in which you were exploited. Provide sufficient illustrations to support your thesis.

8. The writers imply that workforce women around the world are exploited more than men. Write an essay in which you agree or disagree with their claim.

Networking

9. Form small groups, and read the drafts of each other's essays. After general comments about how to improve the first draft, concentrate on ways to provide even greater illustration to support each writer's thesis or claim.

10. With another class member, do a web search for new examples of the global exploitation of working women. Limit your focus to one of the countries mentioned by Ehrenreich and Fuentes. Think about whether the conditions that the two writers exposed more than twenty years ago are better or worse today. Share your conclusions with the rest of the class.

The Challenge of
Globalization: What
Are the Consequences?

Q uick! Where was your cell phone manufactured? Where was the
clothing you are wearing today made—and how much do you
think the workers were paid to produce it? What type of food do
you plan to eat for lunch or dinner: pizza, fried rice, tacos, a Big Mac?
The ordinary features of our daily lives capture the forces of globalization that characterize our new century and our changed world. *New
York Times* columnist Thomas Friedman, who writes persuasively on
the subject—and who has an essay in this chapter—terms globalization
the "super-story," the one all-embracing subject that dominates national
and transnational developments today. As we see from the essays in this
chapter, the concept of globalization already influences many major
trends in economic, social, cultural, and political life in the twenty-first
century.

It could be argued, of course, that globalization is nothing new:
after all, Greece "globalized" much of the known world as far as India.
Then Rome created its global dominion from England to Persia. More
recently, for almost three centuries—from the seventeenth to the
twentieth—England ruled the waves and a majority of the world's
nations. And from the twentieth century to the present, the United
States has assumed the mantle of the world's major globalizing power.
(Some critics claim that globalization might simply be a mask for
"Americanization.") With anti-globalization demonstrations and riots
now commonplace in the United States, Europe, and the Third World,
we have to acknowledge that there *is* something about contemporary

Online Study Center This icon will direct you to web links, audio and visual
content, and additional resources on the website
college.hmco.com/pic/mullerNWR2e

215

A multiethnic group of protesters representing a wide range of causes marches in Richmond, California, to protest globalization.

Thinking About the Image

1. How many different ideas or causes do you see represented in this photograph? What does that suggest about this particular protest? About the anti-globalization movement in general?
2. What is the photographer's perspective on this event? Is anyone looking directly at the lens? Would your response to the photograph—or the story it tells—be different if there was a focus on just one or two people? If the photographer was further away and captured a larger crowd in the frame?
3. What other kinds of images do you associate with street protests? Based on the fact that this one photograph was chosen to represent an entire day of protest, what can you infer about the tone of the protest and the response of the community?
4. Street protest is a kind of rhetoric, in that the demonstrators have a purpose and an audience. How clear is the purpose of these protesters? Who is their audience? Do you think such protests will make any difference to people like the child on p. 207?

globalization that prompts debate and demands critical analysis. Ralph Nader states the case against globalization boldly: "The essence of globalization is a subordination of human rights, of labor rights, consumer rights, environmental rights, democracy rights, to the imperatives of global trade and investment." But is Nader correct? Robert Rubin, the very able secretary of the treasury during the Clinton administration and highly respected throughout the world financial community, objects: "I think a healthy economy is the best environment in which to pursue human rights." The oppositional viewpoints of Nader and Rubin suggest that discussion of globalization often produces diverse opinions, and that consequently we must think carefully and openly about the globalizing trends molding our lives today.

One trend that is clear today, as the twenty-first century begins, is that capitalism has triumphed over all its main rivals: communism, fascism, and socialism. Thus capitalism is the dominant if not the sole model of development for the nations of the world. Where capitalism collides with alternative visions of development—for example, Islamic economics in Iran—the result proves disastrous. The question that many people—especially young people on college and university campuses around the world—ask is whether or not capitalism can meaningfully address the numerous questions of social justice raised by globalization. If, for example, the environmental policy of the United States aids the interests of its energy companies, can this policy benefit others in the developing world? Or does the policy exclude almost everyone in a developing nation? Such questions can be asked about virtually every key issue raised by Ralph Nader and others who are skeptical of globalization as an overpowering economic force around the world.

The writers in this chapter and the next offer a variety of perspectives and critical insights into the nature and effects of globalization trends. Because of developments in information technology, peoples in the most distant parts of the world now are as close to us as someone in the dorm room next door—and perhaps more compelling. We certainly see poverty, famine, the degradation of the environment, and civil wars close up. But is all this suffering the result of predatory multinational corporations and runaway capitalism? After all, both globalization *and* civil society are increasing worldwide, and the connections between the two require subtle critical analysis. The writers in this chapter bring such critical ability to their treatment of the social implications of current globalization trends.

Prologue: The Super-Story

THOMAS L. FRIEDMAN

> A noted author, journalist, and television commentator, and currently an op-ed contributor to *The New York Times,* Thomas L. Friedman writes and speaks knowledgeably about contemporary trends in politics and global development. He was born in Minneapolis, Minnesota, in 1953, and was educated at Brandeis University (B.A., 1975) and St. Anthony's College (M.A., 1978). Friedman covered the Middle East for *The New York Times* for ten years, and for five years he was bureau chief in Beirut, writing about both the Lebanese civil war and the Israel-Palestine conflict. He recorded these experiences in *From Beirut to Jerusalem* (1989), for which he won the National Book Award for nonfiction. A strong proponent of American intervention to solve seemingly intractable problems like the Arab-Israeli conflict, Friedman writes at the end of *From Beirut to Jerusalem,* "Only a real friend tells you the truth about yourself. An American friend has to help jar these people out of their fantasies by constantly holding up before their eyes the mirror of reality." In 2002, Friedman received the Pulitzer Prize for Commentary for his reports on terrorism for *The New York Times.* His other books include *The Lexus and the Olive Tree: Understanding Globalization* (2000), *The World Is Flat* (2005), and a collection of articles and essays, *Longitudes and Attitudes: Exploring the World After September 11* (2002), in which the following selection serves as the book's prologue.

Before Reading

How would you define the word *globalization?* Is it simply a trend in which nations interrelate economically, or are other forces involved? Do you think that globalization is good or bad? Justify your response.

I am a big believer in the idea of the super-story, the notion that we all 1
carry around with us a big lens, a big framework, through which we look
at the world, order events, and decide what is important and what is not.
The events of 9/11 did not happen in a vacuum. They happened in the context of a new international system—a system that cannot explain everything but *can* explain and connect more things in more places on more days
than anything else. That new international system is called globalization.

It came together in the late 1980s and replaced the previous international system, the cold war system, which had reigned since the end of World War II. This new system is the lens, the super-story, through which I viewed the events of 9/11.

I define globalization as the inexorable integration of markets, trans- 2 portation systems, and communication systems to a degree never witnessed before—in a way that is enabling corporations, countries, and individuals to reach around the world farther, faster, deeper, and cheaper than ever before, and in a way that is enabling the world to reach into corporations, countries, and individuals farther, faster, deeper, and cheaper than ever before.

Several important features of this globalization system differ from those 3 of the cold war system in ways that are quite relevant for understanding the events of 9/11. I examined them in detail in my previous book, *The Lexus and the Olive Tree,* and want to simply highlight them here.

The cold war system was characterized by one overarching feature— 4 and that was *division.* That world was a divided-up, chopped-up place, and whether you were a country or a company, your threats and opportunities in the cold war system tended to grow out of who you were divided from. Appropriately, this cold war system was symbolized by a single word— *wall,* the Berlin Wall.

The globalization system is different. It also has one overarching fea- 5 ture—and that is *integration.* The world has become an increasingly inter- woven place, and today, whether you are a company or a country, your threats and opportunities increasingly derive from who you are connected to. This globalization system is also characterized by a single word—*web,* the World Wide Web. So in the broadest sense we have gone from an in- ternational system built around division and walls to a system increasingly built around integration and webs. In the cold war we reached for the hot- line, which was a symbol that we were all divided but at least two people were in charge—the leaders of the United States and the Soviet Union. In the globalization system we reach for the Internet, which is a symbol that we are all connected and nobody is quite in charge.

Everyone in the world is directly or indirectly affected by this new sys- 6 tem, but not everyone benefits from it, not by a long shot, which is why the more it becomes diffused, the more it also produces a backlash by people who feel overwhelmed by it, homogenized by it, or unable to keep pace with its demands.

The other key difference between the cold war system and the global- 7 ization system is how power is structured within them. The cold war sys- tem was built primarily around nation-states. You acted on the world in that system through your state. The cold war was a drama of states confronting states, balancing states, and aligning with states. And, as a system, the cold war was balanced at the center by two superstates, two superpowers: the United States and the Soviet Union.

The globalization system, by contrast, is built around three balances, 8 which overlap and affect one another. The first is the traditional balance of power between nation-states. In the globalization system, the United States is now the sole and dominant superpower and all other nations are subordinate to it to one degree or another. The shifting balance of power between the United States and other states, or simply between other states, still very much matters for the stability of this system. And it can still explain a lot of the news you read on the front page of the paper, whether it is the news of China balancing Russia, Iran balancing Iraq, or India confronting Pakistan.

The second important power balance in the globalization system is be- 9 tween nation-states and global markets. These global markets are made up of millions of investors moving money around the world with the click of a mouse. I call them the Electronic Herd, and this herd gathers in key global financial centers—such as Wall Street, Hong Kong, London, and Frankfurt—which I call the Supermarkets. The attitudes and actions of the Electronic Herd and the Supermarkets can have a huge impact on nation-states today, even to the point of triggering the downfall of governments. Who ousted Suharto in Indonesia in 1998? It wasn't another state, it was the Supermarkets, by withdrawing their support for, and confidence in, the Indonesian economy. You also will not understand the front page of the newspaper today unless you bring the Supermarkets into your analysis. Because the United States can destroy you by dropping bombs, but the Supermarkets can destroy you by downgrading your bonds. In other words, the United States is the dominant player in maintaining the globalization game board, but it is hardly alone in influencing the moves on that game board.

The third balance that you have to pay attention to—the one that is re- 10 ally the newest of all and the most relevant to the events of 9/11—is the balance between individuals and nation-states. Because globalization has brought down many of the walls that limited the movement and reach of people, and because it has simultaneously wired the world into networks, it gives more power to *individuals* to influence both markets and nation-states than at any other time in history. Whether by enabling people to use the Internet to communicate instantly at almost no cost over vast distances, or by enabling them to use the Web to transfer money or obtain weapons designs that normally would have been controlled by states, or by enabling them to go into a hardware store now and buy a five-hundred-dollar global positioning device, connected to a satellite, that can direct a hijacked airplane—globalization can be an incredible force-multiplier for individuals. Individuals can increasingly act on the world stage directly, unmediated by a state.

So you have today not only a superpower, not only Supermarkets, but   11
also what I call "super-empowered individuals." Some of these super-empowered individuals are quite angry, some of them quite wonderful—but all of them are now able to act much more directly and much more powerfully on the world stage.

Osama bin Laden declared war on the United States in the late 1990s.   12
After he organized the bombing of two American embassies in Africa, the U.S. Air Force retaliated with a cruise missile attack on his bases in Afghanistan as though he were another nation-state. Think about that: on one day in 1998, the United States fired 75 cruise missiles at bin Laden. The United States fired 75 cruise missiles, at $1 million apiece, at a person! That was the first battle in history between a superpower and a super-empowered angry man. September 11 was just the second such battle.

Jody Williams won the Nobel Peace Prize in 1997 for helping to build   13
an international coalition to bring about a treaty outlawing land mines. Although nearly 120 governments endorsed the treaty, it was opposed by Russia, China, and the United States. When Jody Williams was asked, "How did you do that? How did you organize one thousand different citizens' groups and nongovernmental organizations on five continents to forge a treaty that was opposed by the major powers?" she had a very brief answer: "E-mail." Jody Williams used e-mail and the networked world to super-empower herself.

Nation-states, and the American superpower in particular, are still   14
hugely important today, but so too now are Supermarkets and super-empowered individuals. You will never understand the globalization system, or the front page of the morning paper—or 9/11—unless you see each as a complex interaction between all three of these actors: states bumping up against states, states bumping up against Supermarkets, and Supermarkets and states bumping up against super-empowered individuals—many of whom, unfortunately, are super-empowered angry men.

Thinking About the Essay

1. Friedman constructs this essay and entitles it a "prologue." What is the purpose of a prologue? What subject matter does the writer provide in his prologue?

2. The writer is not afraid to inject the personal "I" into his analysis—a strategy that many composition teachers will warn you against. Why does Friedman start with his personal voice? Why can he get away with it? What does the personal voice contribute to the effect of the essay?

3. In addition to his personal voice, what other stylistic features make Friedman's essay, despite its complicated subject matter, accessible to ordinary readers? How does he establish a colloquial style?

4. This essay offers a series of definitions, comparisons, and classifications as structuring devices. Locate instances of these three rhetorical strategies and explain how they complement each other.

5. Friedman uses September 11 as a touchstone for his essay. Why does he do this? What is the effect?

Responding in Writing

6. Write a 250-word summary of Friedman's essay, capturing all the important topics that he presents.

7. Take one major point that Friedman makes in this essay and write a paper on it. For example, you might want to discuss why September 11 represents a key transition point in our understanding of globalization. Or you might focus on the concept of the Supermarket or the Electronic Herd.

8. Think about the world today, and write your own "super-story" in which you define and classify its primary features.

Networking

9. Divide into two roughly equal groups, and conduct a debate on whether or not globalization is a good or bad phenomenon. Use Friedman's essay as a reference point. Your instructor should serve as the moderator for this debate.

10. Join the Electronic Herd and develop a list of links to sites that deal with globalization. Contribute your list to the others generated by class members in order to create a superlist for possible future use.

The Global Village Finally Arrives

PICO IYER

Pico Iyer was born in 1957, in Oxford, England, to Indian parents, both of them university professors. Educated at Oxford University and Harvard University, Iyer has been a writer for *Time* magazine since 1982 and a prolific author of travel books, essays, and fiction. His first full-length travel book is the acclaimed *Video Night in Kathmandu: And Other Reports from the Not-so-Far East* (1988). He followed the success of this book with *The Lady and the Monk: Four Seasons in Kyoto* (1991), *Tropical Classical: Essays from Several Directions* (1997), and *The Global Soul: Jet Lag, Shopping Malls, and the Search for Home* (2000), and *Sun after Dark: Flights into the Foreign* (2004), among others. Iyer also has published a novel, *Cuba and the Night* (1995). Iyer calls writing "an intimate letter to a stranger." In this essay, published in *Time* Magazine on December 2, 1993, he invites us to view his world in southern California—and the world in general—in polyglot terms.

Before Reading

Look around you or think about your college—its students, courses, clubs, cultural programs, and so forth. Would you say that your campus reflects what Iyer terms a "diversified world"? Why or why not?

This is the typical day of a relatively typical soul in today's diversified 1 world. I wake up to the sound of my Japanese clock radio, put on a T-shirt sent me by an uncle in Nigeria and walk out into the street, past German cars, to my office. Around me are English-language students from Korea, Switzerland and Argentina—all on this Spanish-named road in this Mediterranean-style town. On TV, I find, the news is in Mandarin; today's baseball game is being broadcast in Korean. For lunch I can walk to a sushi bar, a tandoori palace, a Thai cafe or the newest burrito joint (run by an old Japanese lady). Who am I, I sometimes wonder, the son of Indian parents and a British citizen who spends much of his time in Japan (and is therefore—what else?—an American permanent resident)? And where am I?

I am, as it happens, in Southern California, in a quiet, relatively unin- 2 ternational town, but I could as easily be in Vancouver or Sydney or London or Hong Kong. All the world's a rainbow coalition, more and more; the whole planet, you might say, is going global. When I fly to Toronto, or

Paris, or Singapore, I disembark in a world as hyphenated as the one I left. More and more of the globe looks like America, but an America that is itself looking more and more like the rest of the globe. Los Angeles famously teaches 82 different languages in its schools. In this respect, the city seems only to bear out the old adage that what is in California today is in America tomorrow, and next week around the globe.

In ways that were hardly conceivable even a generation ago, the new 3
world order is a version of the New World writ large: a wide-open frontier of polyglot terms and postnational trends. A common multiculturalism links us all—call it Planet Hollywood, Planet Reebok or the United Colors of Benetton. Taxi and hotel and disco are universal terms now, but so too are karaoke and yoga and pizza. For the gourmet alone, there is tiramisu at the Burger King in Kyoto, echt angel-hair pasta in Saigon and enchiladas on every menu in Nepal.

But deeper than mere goods, it is souls that are mingling. In Brussels, a 4
center of the new "unified Europe," 1 new baby in every 4 is Arab. Whole parts of the Paraguayan capital of Asunción are largely Korean. And when the prostitutes of Melbourne distributed some pro-condom pamphlets, one of the languages they used was Macedonian. Even Japan, which prides itself on its centuries-old socially engineered uniculture, swarms with Iranian illegals, Western executives, Pakistani laborers and Filipina hostesses.

The global village is defined, as we know, by an international youth cul- 5
ture that takes its cues from American pop culture. Kids in Perth and Prague and New Delhi are all tuning in to *Santa Barbara* on TV, and wriggling into 501 jeans, while singing along to Madonna's latest in English. CNN (which has grown 70-fold in 13 years) now reaches more than 140 countries; an American football championship pits London against Barcelona. As fast as the world comes to America, America goes round the world—but it is an America that is itself multi-tongued and many hued, an America of Amy Tan and Janet Jackson and movies with dialogue in Lakota.

For far more than goods and artifacts, the one great influence being 6
broadcast around the world in greater numbers and at greater speed than ever before is people. What were once clear divisions are now tangles of crossed lines: there are 40,000 "Canadians" resident in Hong Kong, many of whose first language is Cantonese. And with people come customs: while new immigrants from Taiwan and Vietnam and India—some of the so-called Asian Calvinists—import all-American values of hard work and family closeness and entrepreneurial energy to America, America is sending its values of upward mobility and individualism and melting-pot hopefulness to Taipei and Saigon and Bombay.

Values, in fact, travel at the speed of fax; by now, almost half the 7
world's Mormons live outside the U.S. A diversity of one culture quickly
becomes a diversity of many: the "typical American" who goes to Japan
today may be a third-generation Japanese American, or the son of a Japanese woman married to a California serviceman, or the offspring of a Salvadoran father and an Italian mother from San Francisco. When he goes
out with a Japanese woman, more than two cultures are brought into play.

None of this, of course, is new: Chinese silks were all the rage in Rome 8
centuries ago, and Alexandria before the time of Christ was a paradigm of
the modern universal city. Not even American eclecticism is new: many a
small town has long known Chinese restaurants, Indian doctors and
Lebanese grocers. But now all these cultures are crossing at the speed of
light. And the rising diversity of the planet is something more than mere
cosmopolitanism: it is a fundamental recoloring of the very complexion of
societies. Cities like Paris, or Hong Kong, have always had a soigné, international air and served as magnets for exiles and émigrés, but now smaller
places are multinational too. Marseilles speaks French with a distinctly
North African twang. Islamic fundamentalism has one of its strongholds in
Bradford, England. It is the sleepy coastal towns of Queensland, Australia,
that print their menus in Japanese.

The dangers this internationalism presents are evident: not for nothing 9
did the Tower of Babel collapse. As national borders fall, tribal alliances, and
new manmade divisions, rise up, and the world learns every day terrible new
meanings of the word Balkanization. And while some places are wired for
international transmission, others (think of Iran or North Korea or Burma)
remain as isolated as ever, widening the gap between the haves and the have-
nots, or what Alvin Toffler has called the "fast" and the "slow" worlds.
Tokyo has more telephones than the whole continent of Africa.

Nonetheless, whether we like it or not, the "transnational" future is 10
upon us: as Kenichi Ohmae, the international economist, suggests with his
talk of a "borderless economy," capitalism's allegiances are to products, not
places. "Capital is now global," Robert Reich, the Secretary of Labor, has
said, pointing out that when an Iowan buys a Pontiac from General Motors,
60% of his money goes to South Korea, Japan, West Germany, Taiwan, Singapore, Britain and Barbados. Culturally we are being reformed daily by the
cadences of world music and world fiction: where the great Canadian writers of an older generation had names like Frye and Davies and Laurence,
now they are called Ondaatje and Mistry and Skvorecky.

As space shrinks, moreover, time accelerates. This hip-hop mishmash is 11
spreading overnight. When my parents were in college, there were all of
seven foreigners living in Tibet, a country the size of Western Europe, and in

its entire history the country had seen fewer than 2,000 Westerners. Now a Danish student in Lhasa is scarcely more surprising than a Tibetan in Copenhagen. Already a city like Miami is beyond the wildest dreams of 1968; how much more so will its face in 2018 defy our predictions of today?

It would be easy, seeing all this, to say that the world is moving toward 12 the Raza Cosmica (Cosmic Race), predicted by the Mexican thinker José Vasconcelos in the '20s—a glorious blend of mongrels and mestizos. It may be more relevant to suppose that more and more of the world may come to resemble Hong Kong, a stateless special economic zone full of expats and exiles linked by the lingua franca of English and the global marketplace. Some urbanists already see the world as a grid of 30 or so highly advanced city-regions, or technopoles, all plugged into the same international circuit.

The world will not become America. Anyone who has been to a base- 13 ball game in Osaka, or a Pizza Hut in Moscow, knows instantly that she is not in Kansas. But America may still, if only symbolically, be a model for the world. E Pluribus Unum, after all, is on the dollar bill. As Federico Mayor Zaragoza, the director-general of UNESCO, has said, "America's main role in the new world order is not as a military superpower, but as a multicultural superpower."

The traditional metaphor for this is that of a mosaic. But Richard Rod- 14 riguez, the Mexican-American essayist who is a psalmist for our new hybrid forms, points out that the interaction is more fluid than that, more human, subject to daily revision. "I am Chinese," he says, "because I live in San Francisco, a Chinese city. I became Irish in America. I became Portuguese in America." And even as he announces this new truth, Portuguese women are becoming American, and Irishmen are becoming Portuguese, and Sydney (or is it Toronto?) is thinking to compare itself with the "Chinese city" we know as San Francisco.

Thinking About the Essay

1. How does Iyer's introductory paragraph set the stage for the rest of the essay? What is the setting? Why does he use a personal voice? What is his reason for writing? Is his thesis stated or implied? Explain.

2. Iyer presents us with an interesting example of an illustrative essay. Draw up a list of all the examples, references, authorities, and allusions that he presents. Why—from start to finish and in every paragraph—does he offer so many illustrations? What is the overall effect?

3. Does the writer have an argument or claim that he develops in this essay, or does he merely want to make a major point? Explain your response.

4. What is the tone of this essay? Put differently, do you think that Iyer embraces his new "transnational" world, likes it, dislikes it, is worried about it, or what? Locate passages that confirm your response.

5. How does Iyer use definitions in constructing his analysis of the global village? Cite examples of his approach.

Responding in Writing

6. Narrate—as Iyer does at the start of his essay—a typical day in your life. Turn this day into an exploration of how you fit into the "Global Village." Provide examples throughout the essay to support your thesis.

7. "The world," writes Iyer, "will not become America" (paragraph 13). Write an essay arguing for or against his view.

8. Write an extended definition of globalization. Refer to Iyer's essay for ideas as you develop this paper.

Networking

9. Iyer's professional address is Time Magazine, 1271 Avenue of the Americas, Rockefeller Center, New York, NY 10021. Discuss his essay with class members, and then write a collective letter telling him of the group's discussion. Ask about his interest in travel and globalization, and pose one or two questions for his response.

10. As a travel writer, Iyer has visited some of the more remote and exotic parts of the planet. What exotic or romantic part of the world interests you? Go online and find information about this place. Plan travel arrangements and a budget. Prepare an outline or itinerary for a two-week trip to your dream destination.

The Noble Feat of Nike

JOHAN NORBERG

Johan Norberg contributed this article to London's *The Spectator* in June 2003. In the essay, he takes issue with those who think that globalization is the invention of "ruthless international capitalists." In arguing his case, Norberg centers his discussion on one symbol of globalization—Nike—suggesting that we simply have to look at our "feet" to understand Nike's "feat" in advancing a benign form of globalization. Norberg is the author of *In Defense of Global Capitalism,* and writer and presenter of the recent documentary *Globalization Is Good.*

Before Reading

Check your sneakers. Where were they made? What do you think the workers earned to manufacture them? Do you think they were exploited? Explain your response.

Nike. It means victory. It also means a type of expensive gym shoe. In 1 the minds of the anti-globalisation movement, it stands for both at once. Nike stands for the victory of a Western footwear company over the poor and dispossessed. Spongy, smelly, hungered after by kids across the world, Nike is the symbol of the unacceptable triumph of global capital.

A Nike is a shoe that simultaneously kicks people out of jobs in the 2 West, and tramples on the poor in the Third World. Sold for 100 times more than the wages of the peons who make them, Nike shoes are hate-objects more potent, in the eyes of the protesters at this week's G8 riots, than McDonald's hamburgers. If you want to be trendy these days, you don't wear Nikes; you boycott them.

So I was interested to hear someone not only praising Nike sweatshops, 3 but also claiming that Nike is an example of a good and responsible business. That someone was the ruling Communist party of Vietnam.

Today Nike has almost four times more workers in Vietnam than in the 4 United States. I travelled to Ho Chi Minh to examine the effects of multi-national corporations on poor countries. Nike being the most notorious multinational villain, and Vietnam being a dictatorship with a documented lack of free speech, the operation is supposed to be a classic of conscience-free capitalist oppression.

In truth the work does look tough, and the conditions grim, if we com- 5 pare Vietnamese factories with what we have back home. But that's not the comparison these workers make. They compare the work at Nike with the way they lived before, or the way their parents or neighbours still work. And the facts are revealing. The average pay at a Nike factory close to Ho Chi Minh is $54 a month, almost three times the minimum wage for a state-owned enterprise.

Ten years ago, when Nike was established in Vietnam, the workers had 6 to walk to the factories, often for many miles. After three years on Nike wages, they could afford bicycles. Another three years later, they could af-ford scooters, so they all take the scooters to work (and if you go there, be-ware; they haven't really decided on which side of the road to drive). Today, the first workers can afford to buy a car.

But when I talk to a young Vietnamese woman, Tsi-Chi, at the factory, 7 it is not the wages she is most happy about. Sure, she makes five times more than she did, she earns more than her husband, and she can now afford to build an extension to her house. But the most important thing, she says, is that she doesn't have to work outdoors on a farm any more. For me, a Swede with only three months of summer, this sounds bizarre. Surely working conditions under the blue sky must be superior to those in a sweatshop? But then I am naively Eurocentric. Farming means 10 to 14 hours a day in the burning sun or the intensive rain, in rice fields with water up to your ankles and insects in your face. Even a Swede would prefer working nine to five in a clean, air-conditioned factory.

Furthermore, the Nike job comes with a regular wage, with free or sub- 8 sidised meals, free medical services and training and education. The most persistent demand Nike hears from the workers is for an expansion of the factories so that their relatives can be offered a job as well.

These facts make Nike sound more like Santa Claus than Scrooge. But 9 corporations such as Nike don't bring these benefits and wages because they are generous. It is not altruism that is at work here; it is globalisation. With their investments in poor countries, multinationals bring new machinery, better technology, new management skills and production ideas, a larger market and the education of their workers. That is exactly what raises productivity. And if you increase productivity—the amount a worker can produce—you can also increase his wage.

Nike is not the accidental good guy. On average, multinationals in the 10 least developed countries pay twice as much as domestic companies in the same line of business. If you get to work for an American multinational in a low-income country, you get eight times the average income. If this is exploitation, then the problem in our world is that the poor countries aren't sufficiently exploited.

The effect on local business is profound: "Before I visit some foreign 11 factory, especially like Nike, we have a question. Why do the foreign factories here work well and produce much more?" That was what Mr. Kiet, the owner of a local shoe factory who visited Nike to learn how he could be just as successful at attracting workers, told me: "And I recognise that productivity does not only come from machinery but also from satisfaction of the worker. So for the future factory we should concentrate on our working conditions."

If I was an antiglobalist, I would stop complaining about Nike's bad 12 wages. If there is a problem, it is that the wages are too high, so that they are almost luring doctors and teachers away from their important jobs.

But—happily—I don't think even that is a realistic threat. With grow- 13 ing productivity it will also be possible to invest in education and healthcare for Vietnam. Since 1990, when the Vietnamese communists began to liberalise the economy, exports of coffee, rice, clothes and footwear have surged, the economy has doubled, and poverty has been halved. Nike and

Coca-Cola triumphed where American bombs failed. They have made Vietnam capitalist.

I asked the young Nike worker Tsi-Chi what her hopes were for her   14 son's future. A generation ago, she would have had to put him to work on the farm from an early age. But Tsi-Chi told me she wants to give him a good education, so that he can become a doctor. That's one of the most impressive developments since Vietnam's economy was opened up. In ten years 2.2 million children have gone from child labour to education. It would be extremely interesting to hear an antiglobalist explain to Tsi-Chi why it is important for Westerners to boycott Nike, so that she loses her job, and has to go back into farming, and has to send her son to work.

The European Left used to listen to the Vietnamese communists when   15 they brought only misery and starvation to their population. Shouldn't they listen to the Vietnamese now, when they have found a way to improve people's lives? The party officials have been convinced by Nike that ruthless multinational capitalists are better than the state at providing workers with high wages and a good and healthy workplace. How long will it take for our own anticapitalists to learn that lesson?

Thinking About the Essay

1. Examine the writer's introduction. Why is it distinctive? How does Norberg "hook" us and also set the terms of his argument? Why is Nike an especially potent symbol around which to organize an essay on globalization?

2. Explain the writer's claim and how he defends it. Identify those instances in which he deals with the opposition. How effective do you think his argument is? Justify your answer.

3. What is the writer's tone in this essay? Why is the tone especially effective in conveying the substance of Norberg's argument?

4. Analyze the writer's style and how it contributes to his argument. Identify specific stylistic elements that you consider especially effective.

5. To a large extent, the writer bases his argument on direct observation. How can you tell that he is open-minded and truthful in the presentation of facts? What is the role of a newspaper or journal in claiming responsibility for the accuracy of this information?

Responding in Writing

6. Select a symbol of globalization and write an essay about it. You may use Nike if you wish, or Coca-Cola, McDonald's, or any other company that has a global reach.

7. Write a rebuttal to Norberg's essay. Try to answer him point by point.

8. Why have clothing manufacturing and other forms of manufacturing fled from the United States and other industrialized nations to less developed parts of the world? Write a causal analysis of this trend, being certain to state a thesis or present a claim that illustrates your viewpoint on the issue.

Networking

9. In groups of four, examine your clothes. List the countries where they were manufactured. Share the list with the class, drawing a global map of the countries where the various items were produced.

10. Check various Internet sites for information on Nike and its role in globalization. On the basis of your findings, determine whether or not this company is sensitive to globalization issues. Participate in a class discussion of this topic.

Fear Not Globalization

Joseph S. Nye Jr.

Joseph Samuel Nye Jr. was born in South Orange, New Jersey, in 1937; his father was a stockbroker and his mother an art gallery owner. He received undergraduate degrees from Princeton University (1958) and Oxford University (1960), and a Ph.D. degree from Harvard University (1964) in political science. Currently he is dean of Harvard's Kennedy School of Government. A prolific writer and well-known authority in international relations, Nye has served in the U.S. Department of State and on the committees of such prominent organizations as the Ford Foundation and the Carnegie Endowment for International Peace. A frequent guest on television programs, including *Nightline* and the *Mc-Neil-Lehrer Report,* Nye also writes frequently for *The New York Times, The Christian Science Monitor, Atlantic Monthly,* and *The New Republic.* His most recent book is *Soft Power: The Means to Success in World Politics* (2004). The title of the following essay, which appeared in *Newsday* on October 8, 2002, captures Nye's essential thesis about the forces of globalization in today's world.

Before Reading

Is globalization a force for good or bad? Will it turn all nations, cultures, and peoples into reflections of each other?

When anti-globalization protesters took to the streets of Washington   1
recently, they blamed globalization for everything from hunger to
the destruction of indigenous cultures. And globalization meant the United
States.

The critics call it Coca-Colonization, and French sheep farmer Jose Bove   2
has become a cult figure since destroying a McDonald's restaurant in 1999.

Contrary to conventional wisdom, however, globalization is neither ho-   3
mogenizing nor Americanizing the cultures of the world.

To understand why not, we have to step back and put the current pe-   4
riod in a larger historical perspective. Although they are related, the long-
term historical trends of globalization and modernization are not the same.
While modernization has produced some common traits, such as large
cities, factories and mass communications, local cultures have by no means
been erased. The appearance of similar institutions in response to similar
problems is not surprising, but it does not lead to homogeneity.

In the first half of the 20th century, for example, there were some sim-   5
ilarities among the industrial societies of Britain, Germany, America and
Japan, but there were even more important differences. When China, India
and Brazil complete their current processes of industrialization and modernization, we should not expect them to be replicas of Japan, Germany or
the United States.

Take the current information revolution. The United States is at the   6
forefront of this great movement of change, so the uniform social and cultural habits produced by television viewing or Internet use, for instance, are
often attributed to Americanization. But correlation is not causation.
Imagine if another country had introduced computers and communications at a rapid rate in a world in which the United States did not exist. Major social and cultural changes still would have followed. Of course, since
the United States does exist and is at the leading edge of the information
revolution, there is a degree of Americanization at present, but it is likely
to diminish over the course of the 21st century as technology spreads and
local cultures modernize in their own ways.

The lesson that Japan has to teach the rest of the world is that even a   7
century and a half of openness to global trends does not necessarily assure
destruction of a country's separate cultural identity. Of course, there are
American influences in contemporary Japan (and Japanese influences such
as Sony and Pokemon in the United States). Thousands of Japanese youths
are co-opting the music, dress and style of urban black America. But some
of the groups they listen to dress up like samurai warriors on stage. One
can applaud or deplore such cultural transfers, but one should not doubt
the persistence of Japan's cultural uniqueness.

The protesters' image of America homogenizing the world also reflects 8
a mistakenly static view of culture. Efforts to portray cultures as unchanging more often reflect reactionary political strategies than descriptions of reality. The Peruvian writer Mario Vargas Llosa put it well when he said that arguments in favor of cultural identity and against globalization "betray a stagnant attitude toward culture that is not borne out by historical fact. Do we know of any cultures that have remained unchanged through time? To find any of them one has to travel to the small, primitive, magico-religious communities made up of people . . . who, due to their primitive condition, become progressively more vulnerable to exploitation and extermination."

Vibrant cultures are constantly changing and borrowing from other 9
cultures. And the borrowing is not always from the United States. For example many more countries turned to Canada than to the United States as a model for constitution-building in the aftermath of the Cold War. Canadian views of how to deal with hate crimes were more congenial to countries such as South Africa and the post-Communist states of Eastern Europe than America's First Amendment practices.

Globalization is also a two-edged sword. In some areas, there has been 10
not only a backlash against American cultural imports, but also an effort to change American culture itself. American policies on capital punishment may have majority support inside the United States, but they are regarded as egregious violations of human rights in much of Europe and have been the focus of transnational human rights campaigns. American attitudes toward climate change or genetic modification of food draw similar criticism. More subtly, the openness of the United States to the world's diasporas both enriches and changes American culture.

Transnational corporations are changing poor countries but not ho- 11
mogenizing them. In the early stages of investment, a multinational company with access to the global resources of finance, technology and markets holds the high cards and often gets the best of the bargain with the poor country. But over time, as the poor country develops a skilled workforce, learns new technologies, and opens its own channels to global finance and markets, it is often able to renegotiate the bargain and capture more of the benefits.

As technical capabilities spread and more and more people hook up to 12
global communications systems, the U.S.' economic and cultural preponderance may diminish. This in turn has mixed implications for American "soft" power, our ability to get others to do what we want by attraction rather than coercion. Less dominance may mean less anxiety about Americanization, fewer complaints about American arrogance and a little less

intensity in the anti-American backlash. We may have less control in the future, but we may find ourselves living in a world somewhat more congenial to our basic values of democracy, free markets and human rights.

Thinking About the Essay

1. What is Nye's purpose in writing this article? How can you tell? What type of audience does Nye have in mind for his essay? Why does he produce such an affirmative tone in dealing with his subject?

2. Which paragraphs constitute Nye's introduction? Where does he place his thesis, and how does he state it?

3. Break down the essay into its main topics. How does Nye develop these topics? What strategies does he employ—for example, causal analysis, comparison and contrast, illustration—and where?

4. Analyze Nye's topic sentences for his paragraphs. How do they serve as clear guides for the development of his paragraphs? How do they serve to unify the essay?

5. How does Nye's concluding paragraph serve as an answer both to the issue raised in his introduction and to other concerns expressed in the body of the essay?

Responding in Writing

6. From your own personal experience of globalization, write an essay in which you agree or disagree with Nye's assertion that there is little to fear from globilization.

7. Try writing a rebuttal to Nye's argument, explaining why there is much to fear about globalization. Deal point by point with Nye's main assertions. Be certain to provide your own evidence in support of your key reasons.

8. Write an essay that responds to the following topic sentence in Nye's essay: "Vibrant cultures are constantly changing and borrowing from other cultures" (paragraph 9). Base your paper on personal experience, your reading, and your knowledge of current events.

Networking

9. With four other classmates, imagine that you have to teach Nye's essay to a class of high school seniors. How would you proceed? Develop a lesson plan that you think would appeal to your audience.

10. With the entire class, arrange a time when you can have an online chat about Nye's essay. As a focal point for your discussion, argue for or against the idea that he does not take the dangers of globalization seriously enough.

Globalisation

ANTHONY GIDDENS

Anthony Giddens, born in 1938, is arguably England's most prominent sociologist and cultural critic. He received his B.A. degree from the University of Hull (1959), an M.A. degree (with distinction) from the London School of Economics (1961), and a Ph.D. degree from the University of Cambridge (1976). Director of the London School of Economics and chairman of Polity Press, Giddens enjoys an international reputation; he has been a distinguished lecturer and professor at universities around the world, including Harvard University, Stanford University, the University of Rome, and the University of Paris. He has published dozens of books on modern social theory, including *The Consequences of Modernity* (1990), *The Third Way: The Renewal of Social Democracy* (1999), and *Runaway World: How Globalization Is Reshaping Our Lives* (2000). With "Globalisation," part of a series he presented for the BBC Reith Lectures in 1999, Giddens offers a succinct definition of globalization as "a complex set of processes."

Before Reading

In this essay, Giddens asks, "Is globalisation a force promoting the general good?" Based on your reading and writing so far, what is your answer?

A friend of mine studies village life in central Africa. A few years ago, 1 she paid her first visit to a remote area where she was to carry out her fieldwork. The evening she got there, she was invited to a local home for an evening's entertainment. She expected to find out about the traditional pastimes of this isolated community. Instead, the evening turned out to be a viewing of *Basic Instinct* on video. The film at that point hadn't even reached the cinemas in London.

Such vignettes reveal something about our world. And what they reveal 2 isn't trivial. It isn't just a matter of people adding modern paraphernalia—videos, TVs, personal computers and so forth—to their traditional ways of life. We live in a world of transformations, affecting almost every aspect of what we do. For better or worse, we are being propelled into a global order that no one fully understands, but which is making its effects felt upon all of us.

Globalisation is the main theme of my lecture tonight, and of the lec-   3
tures as a whole. The term may not be—it isn't—a particularly attractive or
elegant one. But absolutely no-one who wants to understand our prospects
and possibilities at century's end can ignore it. I travel a lot to speak abroad.
I haven't been to a single country recently where globalisation isn't being in-
tensively discussed. In France, the word is *mondialisation*. In Spain and
Latin America, it is *globalización*. The Germans say *Globalisierung*.

The global spread of the term is evidence of the very developments to   4
which it refers. Every business guru talks about it. No political speech is
complete without reference to it. Yet as little as 10 years ago the term was
hardly used, either in the academic literature or in everyday language. It
has come from nowhere to be almost everywhere. Given its sudden popularity, we shouldn't be surprised that the meaning of the notion isn't always
clear, or that an intellectual reaction has set in against it. Globalisation has
something to do with the thesis that we now all live in one world—but in
what ways exactly, and is the idea really valid?

Different thinkers have taken almost completely opposite views about   5
globalisation in debates that have sprung up over the past few years. Some
dispute the whole thing. I'll call them the sceptics. According to the sceptics, all the talk about globalisation is only that—just talk. Whatever its
benefits, its trials and tribulations, the global economy isn't especially different from that which existed at previous periods. The world carries on
much the same as it has done for many years.

Most countries, the sceptics argue, only gain a small amount of their in-   6
come from external trade. Moreover, a good deal of economic exchange is
between regions, rather than being truly world-wide. The countries of the
European Union, for example, mostly trade among themselves. The same
is true of the other main trading blocs, such as those of the Asia Pacific or
North America.

Others, however, take a very different position. I'll label them the rad-   7
icals. The radicals argue that not only is globalisation very real, but that its
consequences can be felt everywhere. The global marketplace, they say, is
much more developed than even two or three decades ago, and is indifferent to national borders. Nations have lost most of the sovereignty they
once had, and politicians have lost most of their capability to influence
events. It isn't surprising that no one respects political leaders any more, or
has much interest in what they have to say. The era of the nation state is
over. Nations, as the Japanese business writer Keniche Ohmae puts it, have
become mere "fictions." Authors like Ohmae see the economic difficulties
of last year and this as demonstrating the reality of globalisation, albeit
seen from its disruptive side.

The sceptics tend to be on the political left, especially the old left. For 8 if all of this is essentially a myth, governments can still intervene in economic life and the welfare state remain intact. The notion of globalisation, according to the sceptics, is an ideology put about by free-marketeers who wish to dismantle welfare systems and cut back on state expenditures. What has happened is at most a reversion to how the world was a century ago. In the late 19th Century there was already an open global economy, with a great deal of trade, including trade in currencies.

Well, who is right in this debate? I think it is the radicals. The level of 9 world trade today is much higher than it ever was before, and involves a much wider range of goods and services. But the biggest difference is in the level of finance and capital flows. Geared as it is to electronic money—money that exists only as digits in computers—the current world economy has no parallels in earlier times. In the new global electronic economy, fund managers, banks, corporations, as well as millions of individual investors, can transfer vast amounts of capital from one side of the world to another at the click of a mouse. As they do so, they can destabilise what might have seemed rock-solid economies—as happened in East Asia.

The volume of world financial transactions is usually measured in U.S. 10 dollars. A million dollars is a lot of money for most people. Measured as a stack of thousand dollar notes, it would be eight inches high. A billion dollars—in other words, a million million—would be over 120 miles high, 20 times higher than Mount Everest.

Yet far more than a trillion dollars is now turned over each day on 11 global currency markets, a massive increase from only 10 years ago, let alone the more distant past. The value of whatever money we may have in our pockets, or our bank accounts, shifts from moment to moment according to fluctuations in such markets. I would have no hesitation, therefore, in saying that globalisation, as we are experiencing it, is in many respects not only new, but revolutionary.

However, I don't believe either the sceptics or the radicals have prop- 12 erly understood either what it is or its implications for us. Both groups see the phenomenon almost solely in economic terms. This is a mistake. Globalisation is political, technological and cultural, as well as economic. It has been influenced above all by developments in systems of communication, dating back only to the late 1960's.

In the mid-19th century, a Massachusetts portrait painter, Samuel 13 Morse, transmitted the first message, "What hath god wrought?," by electric telegraph. In so doing, he initiated a new phase in world history. Never before could a message be sent without someone going somewhere to carry it. Yet the advent of satellite communications marks every bit as dramatic a break with the past. The first communications satellite was launched only just over 30 years ago. Now there are more than 200 such satellites above the earth, each carrying a vast range of information. For the first time ever, instantaneous communication is possible from one side of the world to the other. Other types of electronic communication, more and more integrated with satellite transmission, have also accelerated over the past few years. No dedicated transatlantic or transpacific cables existed at all until the late 1950's. The first held less than 100 voice paths. Those of today carry more than a million.

On the first of February 1999, about 150 years after Morse invented 14
his system of dots and dashes, Morse code finally disappeared from the world stage, discontinued as a means of communication for the sea. In its place has come a system using satellite technology, whereby any ship in distress can be pinpointed immediately. Most countries prepared for the transition some while before. The French, for example, stopped using Morse as a distress code in their local waters two years ago, signing off with a Gallic flourish: "Calling all. This is our last cry before our eternal silence."

Instantaneous electronic communication isn't just a way in which news 15
or information is conveyed more quickly. Its existence alters the very texture of our lives, rich and poor alike. When the image of Nelson Mandela maybe is more familiar to us than the face of our next door neighbour, something has changed in the nature of our everyday experience.

Nelson Mandela is a global celebrity, and celebrity itself is largely a 16
product of new communications technology. The reach of media technologies is growing with each wave of innovation. It took 40 years for radio in the United States to gain an audience of 50 million. The same number were using personal computers only 15 years after the PC was introduced. It needed a mere four years, after it was made available for 50 million Americans to be regularly using the Internet.

It is wrong to think of globalisation as just concerning the big systems, 17
like the world financial order. Globalisation isn't only about what is "out there" remote and far away from the individual. It is an "in here" phenomenon too, influencing intimate and personal aspects of our lives. The debate about family values, for example, that is going on in many countries, might seem far removed from globalising influences. It isn't. Traditional family systems are becoming transformed, or are under strain, in many parts of the world, particularly as women stake claim to greater equality. There has never before been a society, so far as we know from the historical record, in which women have been even approximately equal to men. This is a truly global revolution in everyday life, whose consequences are being felt around the world in spheres from work to politics.

Globalisation thus is a complex set of processes, not a single one. And these operate in a contradictory or oppositional fashion. Most people think of it as simply "pulling away" power or influence from local communities and nations into the global arena. And indeed this is one of its consequences. Nations do lose some of the economic power they once had. However, it also has an opposite effect. Globalisation not only pulls upwards, it pushes downwards, creating new pressures for local autonomy. The American sociologist Daniel Bell expresses this very well when he says that the nation becomes too small to solve the big problems, but also too large to solve the small ones.

Globalisation is the reason for the revival of local cultural identities in different parts of the world. If one asks, for example, why the Scots want more independence in the UK, or why there is a strong separatist movement in Quebec, the answer is not to be found only in their cultural history. Local nationalisms spring up as a response to globalising tendencies, as the hold of older nation-states weakens.

Globalisation also squeezes sideways. It creates new economic and cultural zones within and across nations. Examples are the Hong Kong region, northern Italy, or Silicon Valley in California. The area around Barcelona in northern Spain extends over into France. Catalonia, where Barcelona is located, is closely integrated into the European Union. It is part of Spain, yet also looks outwards.

The changes are being propelled by a range of factors, some structural, others more specific and historical. Economic influences are certainly among the driving forces, especially the global financial system. Yet they aren't like forces of nature. They have been shaped by technology, and cultural diffusion, as well as by the decisions of governments to liberalise and deregulate their national economies.

The collapse of Soviet communism has added further weight to such developments, since no significant group of countries any longer stands outside. That collapse wasn't just something that happened to occur. Globalisation explains both why and how Soviet communism met its end. The Soviet Union and the East European countries were comparable to the West in terms of growth rates until somewhere around the early 1970s. After that point, they fell rapidly behind. Soviet communism, with its emphasis upon state-run enterprise and heavy industry, could not compete in the global electronic economy. The ideological and cultural control upon which communist political authority was based similarly could not survive in an era of global media.

The Soviet and the East European regimes were unable to prevent the reception of western radio and TV broadcasts. Television played a direct role in the 1989 revolutions, which have rightly been called the first "television revolutions." Street protests taking place in one country were watched by the audiences in others, large numbers of whom then took to the streets themselves.

Globalisation, of course, isn't developing in an even-handed way, and 24 is by no means wholly benign in its consequences. To many living outside Europe and North America, it looks uncomfortably like Westernisation—or, perhaps, Americanisation, since the U.S. is now the sole superpower, with a dominant economic, cultural and military position in the global order. Many of the most visible cultural expressions of globalisation are American—Coca-Cola, McDonald's.

Most of giant multinational companies are based in the U.S. too. Those 25 that aren't all come from the rich countries, not the poorer areas of the world. A pessimistic view of globalisation would consider it largely an affair of the industrial North, in which the developing societies of the South play little or no active part. It would see it as destroying local cultures, widening world inequalities and worsening the lot of the impoverished. Globalisation, some argue, creates a world of winners and losers, a few on the fast track to prosperity, the majority condemned to a life of misery and despair.

And indeed the statistics are daunting. The share of the poorest fifth of 26 the world's population in global income has dropped from 2.3% to 1.4% over the past 10 years. The proportion taken by the richest fifth, on the other hand, has risen from 70% to 85%. In Sub-Saharan Africa, 20 countries have lower incomes per head in real terms than they did two decades ago. In many less developed countries, safety and environmental regulations are low or virtually non-existent. Some trans-national companies sell goods there that are controlled or banned in the industrial countries—poor quality medical drugs, destructive pesticides or high tar and nicotine content cigarettes. As one writer put it recently, rather than a global village, this is more like global pillage.

Along with ecological risk, to which it is related, expanding inequality 27 is the most serious problem facing world society. It will not do, however, merely to blame it on the wealthy. It is fundamental to my argument that globalisation today is only partly Westernisation. Of course the western nations, and more generally the industrial countries, still have far more influence over world affairs than do the poorer states. But globalisation is becoming increasingly de-centred—not under the control of any group of nations, and still less of the large corporations. Its effects are felt just as much in the western countries as elsewhere.

This is true of the global financial system, communications and media, 28 and of changes affecting the nature of government itself. Examples of "reverse colonization" are becoming more and more common. Reverse colonisation means that non-western countries influence developments in the west. Examples abound—such as the Latinising of Los Angeles, the emergence of a globally-oriented high-tech sector in India, or the selling of Brazilian TV programmes to Portugal.

Is globalisation a force promoting the general good? The question can't 29 be answered in a simple way, given the complexity of the phenomenon. People who ask it, and who blame globalisation for deepening world inequalities, usually have in mind economic globalisation, and within that, free trade. Now it is surely obvious that free trade is not an unalloyed benefit. This is especially so as concerns the less developed countries. Opening up a country, or regions within it, to free trade can undermine a local subsistence economy. An area that becomes dependent upon a few products sold on world markets is very vulnerable to shifts in prices as well as to technological change.

Trade always needs a framework of institutions, as do other forms of 30 economic development. Markets cannot be created by purely economic means, and how far a given economy should be exposed to the world marketplace must depend upon a range of criteria. Yet to oppose economic globalisation, and to opt for economic protectionism, would be a misplaced tactic for rich and poor nations alike. Protectionism may be a necessary strategy at some times and in some countries. In my view, for example, Malaysia was correct to introduce controls in 1998, to stem the flood of capital from the country. But more permanent forms of protectionism will not help the development of the poor countries, and among the rich would lead to warring trade blocs.

The debates about globalisation I mentioned at the beginning have con- 31 centrated mainly upon its implications for the nation-state. Are nation-states, and hence national political leaders, still powerful, or are they becoming largely irrelevant to the forces shaping the world? Nation-states are indeed still powerful and political leaders have a large role to play in the world. Yet at the same time the nation-state is being reshaped before our eyes. National economic policy can't be as effective as it once was. More importantly, nations have to rethink their identities now the older forms of geopolitics are becoming obsolete. Although this is a contentious point, I would say that, following the dissolving of the cold war, nations no longer have enemies. Who are the enemies of Britain, or France, or Japan? Nations today face risks and dangers rather than enemies, a massive shift in their very nature.

It isn't only of the nation that such comments could be made. Every- 32
where we look, we see institutions that appear the same as they used to be
from the outside, and carry the same names, but inside have become quite
different. We continue to talk of the nation, the family, work, tradition, nature, as if they were all the same as in the past. They are not. The outer shell
remains, but inside all is different—and this is happening not only in the
U.S., Britain, or France, but almost everywhere. They are what I call shell
institutions, and I shall talk about them quite a bit in the lectures to come.
They are institutions that have become inadequate to the tasks they are
called upon to perform.

As the changes I have described in this lecture gather weight, they are 33
creating something that has never existed before, a global cosmopolitan society. We are the first generation to live in this society, whose contours we
can as yet only dimly see. It is shaking up our existing ways of life, no matter where we happen to be. This is not—at least at the moment—a global
order driven by collective human will. Instead, it is emerging in an anar-
chic, haphazard, fashion, carried along by a mixture of economic, technological and cultural imperatives.

It is not settled or secure, but fraught with anxieties, as well as scarred 34
by deep divisions. Many of us feel in the grip of forces over which we have
no control. Can we re-impose our will upon them? I believe we can. The
powerlessness we experience is not a sign of personal failings, but reflects
the incapacities of our institutions. We need to reconstruct those we have,
or create new ones, in ways appropriate to the global age.

We should and we can look to achieve greater control over our run- 35
away world. We shan't be able to do so if we shirk the challenges, or pretend that all can go on as before. For globalisation is not incidental to our
lives today. It is a shift in our very life circumstances. It is the way we
now live.   *Conclusion*

Thinking About the Essay

1. Did you notice how Giddens spells *globalisation*? Why does the English
   spelling differ from the American? Where does Giddens allude to the word
   in other languages? What can you infer from these variant spellings and
   translations?

2. Giddens begins his essay with the personal example of an unnamed friend.
   Why? What other types of illustration does he use in this essay?

3. The writer presents an *extended definition* of globalization. What aspects of globalization does he define and in what sequence? What thesis emerges from this definition? In what place (or places) does his thesis appear?

4. According to Giddens, how did globalization come about? What historical processes, causes and effects does he trace in his presentation?

5. How does Giddens use the comparative method and classification to frame his analysis of globalization? Identify specific paragraphs and passages where these strategies serve his purpose.

Responding in Writing

6. Giddens suggests—most clearly in his conclusion—that today we live in a "runaway world." Do you have the same thoughts or feelings? Is your response a result of the forces of globalization? Write an essay that answers these questions.

7. Giddens wrote this piece as a lecture. Write your own lecture, about ten minutes long, on globalization. Assume that you must define and discuss the word for an educated radio or television audience. Adjust your style to the expectations of this audience.

8. Giddens speaks of "sceptics," "radicals," and a third group he doesn't name but whom we might call "comparative analysts" who are capable of understanding the complexities of globalization. Write a classification essay in which you present at least three types or ways of looking at globalization. Feel free to use one or more of Giddens's categories in your paper.

Networking

9. In small groups, construct an extended definition of globalization. Feel free to use information in Giddens's essay as well as other selections in this chapter. Then distill this definition to a 300-word summary that one member of your group presents to the class.

10. Go online and locate transcripts of the entire series of lectures on globalization given by Giddens on the British Broadcasting System. Review the content and write a brief report on your findings.

Thinking About the Image

1. What is ironic about the narrative in this cartoon?

2. What do the visual images contribute to this man's story?

3. Giddens divides people who think about globalization into "sceptics," "radicals," and what might be called "comparative analysts." How would each group respond to this cartoon?

4. Cartoons are also a kind of rhetoric, in that they have a purpose and an audience. A cartoonist uses visuals as well as language to move or persuade that audience. How effective is Horsey's rhetoric in serving his purpose? Who is his audience, and how effectively does he address them?

Toward a New Cosmopolitanism

KWAME ANTHONY APPIAH

Kwame Anthony Appiah was born in London in 1954 to socially prominent and politically active parents: His father was a barrister and statesman from the African nation of Ghana; his mother came from the English landed gentry. Appiah attended school in Ghana, but he returned to England to study at Cambridge. While an undergraduate, Appiah met the African American scholar Henry Louis Gates Jr., with whom he would later collaborate on a number of books and other projects. After graduating from Cambridge, Appiah moved to the United States and taught at Yale, Cornell, Duke, Harvard, and (most recently) Princeton, where he is the Lawrence Rockefeller Professor in Philosophy. Appiah currently lives in Manhattan and is also known as an editor and writer for *The New Yorker* magazine. His many books include *In My Father's House* (1992), *Color Conscious: The Political Morality of Race* (1996), and his most recent book, *Cosmopolitanism: Ethics in a World of Strangers* (2006), from which the following essay was adapted for publication in the January 1, 2006, issue of *The New York Times Magazine*.

Before Reading

What attitudes do you associate with the term *cosmopolitan*? What attitudes do you associate with the term *provincial*?

1.

I'm seated, with my mother, on a palace veranda, cooled by a breeze from the royal garden. Before us, on a dais, is an empty throne, its arms and legs embossed with polished brass, the back and seat covered in black-and-gold silk. In front of the steps to the dais, there are two columns of people, mostly men, facing one another, seated on carved wooden stools, the cloths they wear wrapped around their chests, leaving their shoulders bare. There is a quiet buzz of conversation. Outside in the garden, peacocks screech. At last, the blowing of a ram's horn announces the arrival of the king of Asante, its tones sounding his honorific, *kotokohene*, "porcupine chief." (Each quill of the porcupine, according to custom, signifies a warrior ready to kill and to die for the kingdom.) Everyone stands until the king has settled on the throne. Then, when we sit, a chorus sings songs in praise of him, which are interspersed with the playing of a flute. It is a Wednesday festival day in Kumasi, the town in Ghana where I grew up.

Unless you're one of a few million Ghanaians, this will probably seem   2
a relatively unfamiliar world, perhaps even an exotic one. You might suppose that this Wednesday festival belongs quaintly to an African past. But before the king arrived, people were taking calls on cellphones, and among those passing the time in quiet conversation were a dozen men in suits, representatives of an insurance company. And the meetings in the office next to the veranda are about contemporary issues: H.I.V./AIDS, the educational needs of 21st-century children, the teaching of science and technology at the local university. When my turn comes to be formally presented, the king asks me about Princeton, where I teach. I ask him when he'll next be in the States. In a few weeks, he says cheerfully. He's got a meeting with the head of the World Bank.

Anywhere you travel in the world—today as always—you can find cer-   3
emonies like these, many of them rooted in centuries-old traditions. But you will also find everywhere—and this is something new—many intimate connections with places far away: Washington, Moscow, Mexico City, Beijing. Across the street from us, when we were growing up, there was a large house occupied by a number of families, among them a vast family of boys; one, about my age, was a good friend. He lives in London. His brother lives in Japan, where his wife is from. They have another brother who has been in Spain for a while and a couple more brothers who, last I heard, were in the United States. Some of them still live in Kumasi, one or two in Accra, Ghana's capital. Eddie, who lives in Japan, speaks his wife's language now. He has to. But he was never very comfortable in English, the language of our government and our schools. When he phones me from time to time, he prefers to speak Asante-Twi.

Over the years, the royal palace buildings in Kumasi have expanded.   4
When I was a child, we used to visit the previous king, my great-uncle by marriage, in a small building that the British had allowed his predecessor to build when he returned from exile in the Seychelles to a restored but diminished Asante kingship. That building is now a museum, dwarfed by the enormous house next door—built by his successor, my uncle by marriage—where the current king lives. Next to it is the suite of offices abutting the veranda where we were sitting, recently finished by the present king, my uncle's successor. The British, my mother's people, conquered Asante at the turn of the 20th century; now, at the turn of the 21st, the palace feels as it must have felt in the 19th century: a center of power. The president of Ghana comes from this world, too. He was born across the street from the palace to a member of the royal Oyoko clan. But he belongs to other

worlds as well: he went to Oxford University; he's a member of one of the Inns of Court in London; he's a Catholic, with a picture of himself greeting the pope in his sitting room.

What are we to make of this? On Kumasi's Wednesday festival day, I've seen visitors from England and the United States wince at what they regard as the intrusion of modernity on timeless, traditional rituals—more evidence, they think, of a pressure in the modern world toward uniformity. They react like the assistant on the film set who's supposed to check that the extras in a sword-and-sandals movie aren't wearing wristwatches. And such purists are not alone. In the past couple of years, Unesco's members have spent a great deal of time trying to hammer out a convention on the "protection and promotion" of cultural diversity. (It was finally approved at the Unesco General Conference in October 2005.) The drafters worried that "the processes of globalization . . . represent a challenge for cultural diversity, namely in view of risks of imbalances between rich and poor countries." The fear is that the values and images of Western mass culture, like some invasive weed, are threatening to choke out the world's native flora.   5

The contradictions in this argument aren't hard to find. This same Unesco document is careful to affirm the importance of the free flow of ideas, the freedom of thought and expression and human rights—values that, we know, will become universal only if we make them so. What's really important, then, cultures or people? In a world where Kumasi and New York—and Cairo and Leeds and Istanbul—are being drawn ever closer together, an ethics of globalization has proved elusive.   6

The right approach, I think, starts by taking individuals—not nations, tribes or "peoples"—as the proper object of moral concern. It doesn't much matter what we call such a creed, but in homage to Diogenes, the fourth-century Greek Cynic and the first philosopher to call himself a "citizen of the world," we could call it cosmopolitan. Cosmopolitans take cultural difference seriously, because they take the choices individual people make seriously. But because cultural difference is not the only thing that concerns them, they suspect that many of globalization's cultural critics are aiming at the wrong targets.   7

Yes, globalization can produce homogeneity. But globalization is also a threat to homogeneity. You can see this as clearly in Kumasi as anywhere. One thing Kumasi isn't—simply because it's a city—is homogeneous. English, German, Chinese, Syrian, Lebanese, Burkinabe, Ivorian, Nigerian, Indian: I can find you families of each description. I can find you Asante people, whose ancestors have lived in this town for centuries, but also Hausa households that have been around for centuries, too. There are   8 people there from every region of the country as well, speaking scores of languages. But if you travel just a little way outside Kumasi—20 miles, say, in the right direction—and if you drive off the main road down one of the many potholed side roads of red laterite, you won't have difficulty finding villages that are fairly monocultural. The people have mostly been to Kumasi and seen the big, polyglot, diverse world of the city. Where they live, though, there is one everyday language (aside from the English in the government schools) and an agrarian way of life based on some old crops, like yams, and some newer ones, like cocoa, which arrived in the late 19th century as a product for export. They may or may not have electricity. (This close to Kumasi, they probably do.) When people talk of the homogeneity produced by globalization, what they are talking about is this: Even here, the villagers will have radios (though the language will be local); you will be able to get a discussion going about Ronaldo, Mike Tyson or Tupac; and you will probably be able to find a bottle of Guinness or Coca-Cola (as well as of Star or Club, Ghana's own fine lagers). But has access to these things made the place more homogeneous or less? And what can you tell about people's souls from the fact that they drink Coca-Cola?

It's true that the enclaves of homogeneity you find these days—in Asante as in Pennsylvania—are less distinctive than they were a century ago, but mostly in good ways. More of them have access to effective medicines. More of them have access to clean drinking water, and more of them have schools. Where, as is still too common, they don't have these things, it's something not to celebrate but to deplore. And whatever loss of difference there has been, they are constantly inventing new forms of difference: new hairstyles, new slang, even, from time to time, new religions. No one could say that the world's villages are becoming anything like the same.   9

So why do people in these places sometimes feel that their identities are threatened? Because the world, their world, is changing, and some of them don't like it. The pull of the global economy—witness those cocoa trees, whose chocolate is eaten all around the world—created some of the life they now live. If chocolate prices were to collapse again, as they did in the early 1990's, Asante farmers might have to find new crops or new forms of livelihood. That prospect is unsettling for some people (just as it is exciting for others). Missionaries came awhile ago, so many of these villagers will be Christian, even if they have also kept some of the rites from earlier days. But new Pentecostal messengers are challenging the churches they know and condemning the old rites as idolatrous. Again, some like it; some don't.   10

Above all, relationships are changing. When my father was young, a man in a village would farm some land that a chief had granted him, and his maternal clan (including his younger brothers) would work it with him.   11

When a new house needed building, he would organize it. He would also make sure his dependents were fed and clothed, the children educated, marriages and funerals arranged and paid for. He could expect to pass the farm and the responsibilities along to the next generation.

Nowadays, everything is different. Cocoa prices have not kept pace 12 with the cost of living. Gas prices have made the transportation of the crop more expensive. And there are new possibilities for the young in the towns, in other parts of the country and in other parts of the world. Once, perhaps, you could have commanded the young ones to stay. Now they have the right to leave—perhaps to seek work at one of the new data-processing centers down south in the nation's capital—and, anyway, you may not make enough to feed and clothe and educate them all. So the time of the successful farming family is passing, and those who were settled in that way of life are as sad to see it go as American family farmers are whose lands are accumulated by giant agribusinesses. We can sympathize with them. But we cannot force their children to stay in the name of protecting their authentic culture, and we cannot afford to subsidize indefinitely thousands of distinct islands of homogeneity that no longer make economic sense.

Nor should we want to. Human variety matters, cosmopolitans think, 13 because people are entitled to options. What John Stuart Mill said more than a century ago in "On Liberty" about diversity within a society serves just as well as an argument for variety across the globe: "If it were only that people have diversities of taste, that is reason enough for not attempting to shape them all after one model. But different persons also require different conditions for their spiritual development; and can no more exist healthily in the same moral, than all the variety of plants can exist in the same physical, atmosphere and climate. The same things which are helps to one person towards the cultivation of his higher nature are hindrances to another. . . . Unless there is a corresponding diversity in their modes of life, they neither obtain their fair share of happiness, nor grow up to the mental, moral, and aesthetic stature of which their nature is capable." If we want to preserve a wide range of human conditions because it allows free people the best chance to make their own lives, we can't enforce diversity by trapping people within differences they long to escape.

2.

Even if you grant that people shouldn't be compelled to sustain the older 14 cultural practices, you might suppose that cosmopolitans should side with those who are busy around the world "preserving culture" and resisting "cultural imperialism." Yet behind these slogans you often find some curious assumptions. Take "preserving culture." It's one thing to help people sustain arts they want to sustain. I am all for festivals of Welsh bards in Llandudno financed by the Welsh arts council. Long live the Ghana National Cultural Center in Kumasi, where you can go and learn traditional Akan dancing and drumming, especially since its classes are spirited and overflowing. Restore the deteriorating film stock of early Hollywood movies; continue the preservation of Old Norse and early Chinese and Ethiopian manuscripts; record, transcribe and analyze the oral narratives of Malay and Masai and Maori. All these are undeniably valuable.

But preserving culture—in the sense of such cultural artifacts—is different from preserving cultures. And the cultural preservationists often pursue the latter, trying to ensure that the Huli of Papua New Guinea (or even Sikhs in Toronto) maintain their "authentic" ways. What makes a cultural expression authentic, though? Are we to stop the importation of baseball caps into Vietnam so that the Zao will continue to wear their colorful red headdresses? Why not ask the Zao? Shouldn't the choice be theirs? 15

"They have no real choice," the cultural preservationists say. "We've dumped cheap Western clothes into their markets, and they can no longer afford the silk they used to wear. If they had what they really wanted, they'd still be dressed traditionally." But this is no longer an argument about authenticity. The claim is that they can't afford to do something that they'd really like to do, something that is expressive of an identity they care about and want to sustain. This is a genuine problem, one that afflicts people in many communities: they're too poor to live the life they want to lead. But if they do get richer, and they still run around in T-shirts, that's their choice. Talk of authenticity now just amounts to telling other people what they ought to value in their own traditions. 16

Not that this is likely to be a problem in the real world. People who can afford it mostly like to put on traditional garb—at least from time to time. I was best man once at a Scottish wedding at which the bridegroom wore a kilt and I wore kente cloth. Andrew Oransay, the islander who piped us up the aisle, whispered in my ear at one point, "Here we all are then, in our tribal gear." In Kumasi, people who can afford them love to put on their kente cloths, especially the most "traditional" ones, woven in colorful silk strips in the town of Bonwire, as they have been for a couple of centuries. (The prices are high in part because demand outside Asante has risen. A fine kente for a man now costs more than the average Ghanaian earns in a year. Is that bad? Not for the people of Bonwire.) 17

Besides, trying to find some primordially authentic culture can be like peeling an onion. The textiles most people think of as traditional West African cloths are known as Java prints; they arrived in the 19th century 18 with the Javanese batiks sold, and often milled, by the Dutch. The traditional garb of Herero women in Namibia derives from the attire of 19th-century German missionaries, though it is still unmistakably Herero, not least because the fabrics used have a distinctly un-Lutheran range of colors. And so with our kente cloth: the silk was always imported, traded by Europeans, produced in Asia. This tradition was once an innovation. Should we reject it for that reason as untraditional? How far back must one go? Should we condemn the young men and women of the University of Science and Technology, a few miles outside Kumasi, who wear European-style gowns for graduation, lined with kente strips (as they do now at Howard and Morehouse, too)? Cultures are made of continuities and changes, and the identity of a society can survive through these changes. Societies without change aren't authentic; they're just dead.

3.

The preservationists often make their case by invoking the evil of "cultural [19] imperialism." Their underlying picture, in broad strokes, is this: There is a world system of capitalism. It has a center and a periphery. At the center—in Europe and the United States—is a set of multinational corporations. Some of these are in the media business. The products they sell around the world promote the creation of desires that can be fulfilled only by the purchase and use of their products. They do this explicitly through advertising, but more insidiously, they also do so through the messages implicit in movies and in television drama. Herbert Schiller, a leading critic of "media-cultural imperialism," claimed that "it is the imagery and cultural perspectives of the ruling sector in the center that shape and structure consciousness throughout the system at large."

That's the theory, anyway. But the evidence doesn't bear it out. Re- [20] searchers have actually gone out into the world and explored the responses to the hit television series "Dallas" in Holland and among Israeli Arabs, Moroccan Jewish immigrants, kibbutzniks and new Russian immigrants to Israel. They have examined the actual content of the television media—whose penetration of everyday life far exceeds that of film—in Australia, Brazil, Canada, India and Mexico. They have looked at how American popular culture was taken up by the artists of Sophiatown, in South Africa. They have discussed "Days of Our Lives" and "The Bold and the Beautiful" with Zulu college students from traditional backgrounds.

And one thing they've found is that how people respond to these cultural [21] imports depends on their existing cultural context. When the media scholar Larry Strelitz spoke to students from KwaZulu-Natal, he found that they were anything but passive vessels. One of them, Sipho—a self-described "very, very

strong Zulu man"—reported that he had drawn lessons from watching the
American soap opera "Days of Our Lives," "especially relationship-wise." It
fortified his view that "if a guy can tell a woman that he loves her, she should
be able to do the same." What's more, after watching the show, Sipho "realized that I should be allowed to speak to my father. He should be my friend
rather than just my father." It seems doubtful that that was the intended message of multinational capitalism's ruling sector.

But Sipho's response also confirmed that cultural consumers are not   22
dupes. They can adapt products to suit their own needs, and they can decide for themselves what they do and do not approve of. Here's Sipho
again:

"In terms of our culture, a girl is expected to enter into relationships   23
when she is about 20. In the Western culture, a girl can be exposed to a relationship as early as 15 or 16. That one we shouldn't adopt in our culture.
Another thing we shouldn't adopt from the Western culture has to do with
the way they treat elderly people. I wouldn't like my family to be sent into
an old-age home."

It wouldn't matter whether the "old-age homes" in American soap op-   24
eras were safe places, full of kindly people. That wouldn't sell the idea to
Sipho. Dutch viewers of "Dallas" saw not the pleasures of conspicuous
consumption among the superrich—the message that theorists of "cultural
imperialism" find in every episode—but a reminder that money and power
don't protect you from tragedy. Israeli Arabs saw a program that confirmed that women abused by their husbands should return to their fathers.
Mexican telenovelas remind Ghanaian women that, where sex is at issue,
men are not to be trusted. If the telenovelas tried to tell them otherwise,
they wouldn't believe it.

Talk of cultural imperialism "structuring the consciousnesses" of   25
those in the periphery treats people like Sipho as blank slates on which
global capitalism's moving finger writes its message, leaving behind another cultural automaton as it moves on. It is deeply condescending. And
it isn't true.

In fact, one way that people sometimes respond to the onslaught of   26
ideas from the West is to turn them against their originators. It's no accident that the West's fiercest adversaries among other societies tend to come
from among the most Westernized of the group. Who in Ghana excoriated
the British colonizers and built the movement for independence? Not the
farmers and the peasants. Not the chiefs. It was the Western-educated
bourgeoisie. And when Kwame Nkrumah—who went to college in Pennsylvania and lived in London—created a nationalist mass movement, at its
core were soldiers who had returned from fighting a war in the British

Army, urban market women who traded Dutch prints, unionists who worked in industries created by colonialism and the so-called veranda boys, who had been to colonial schools, learned English and studied history and geography in textbooks written in England. Who led the resistance to the British Raj? An Indian-born South African lawyer, trained in the British courts, whose name was Gandhi; an Indian named Nehru, who wore Savile Row suits and sent his daughter to an English boarding school; and Muhammad Ali Jinnah, founder of Pakistan, who joined Lincoln's Inn in London and became a barrister at the age of 19. The independence movements of the postwar world that led to the end of Europe's African and Asian empires were driven by the rhetoric that had guided the Allies' own struggle against Germany and Japan: democracy, freedom, equality. This wasn't a conflict between values. It was a conflict of interests couched in terms of the same values.

4.

Sometimes, though, people react to the incursions of the modern world not by appropriating the values espoused by the liberal democracies but by inverting them. One recent result has been a new worldwide fraternity that presents cosmopolitanism with something of a sinister mirror image. Indeed, you could think of its members as counter-cosmopolitans. They believe in human dignity across the nations, and they live their creed. They share these ideals with people in many countries, speaking many languages. As thoroughgoing globalists, they make full use of the World Wide Web. They resist the crass consumerism of modern Western society and deplore its influence in the rest of the world. But they also resist the temptations of the narrow nationalisms of the countries where they were born, along with the humble allegiances of kith and kin. They resist such humdrum loyalties because they get in the way of the one thing that matters: building a community of enlightened men and women across the world. That is one reason they reject traditional religious authorities (though they disapprove, too, of their obscurantism and temporizing). Sometimes they agonize in their discussions about whether they can reverse the world's evils or whether their struggle is hopeless. But mostly they soldier on in their efforts to make the world a better place. 27

These are not the heirs of Diogenes the Cynic. The community these comrades are building is not a polis; it's what they call the *ummah*, the global community of Muslims, and it is open to all who share their faith. They are young, global Muslim fundamentalists. The ummah's new globalists consider that they have returned to the fundamentals of Islam; much of what passes for Islam in the world, much of what has passed as Islam 28 for centuries, they think a sham. As the French scholar Olivier Roy has observed, these religionists—his term for them is "neofundamentalists"— wish to cleanse Islam's pristine and universal message from the contingencies of mere history, of local cultures. For them, Roy notes, "globalization is a good opportunity to dissociate Islam from any given culture and to provide a model that could work beyond any culture." They have taken a set of doctrines that once came with a form of life, in other words, and thrown away that form of life.

Now, the vast majority of these fundamentalists are not going to blow 29 anybody up. So they should not be confused with those other Muslims— the "radical neofundamentalists," Roy calls them—who want to turn jihad, interpreted as literal warfare against the West, into the sixth pillar of Islam. Whether to endorse the use of violence is a political decision, even if it is to be justified in religious terms. Nonetheless, the neofundamentalists present a classic challenge to cosmopolitanism, because they, too, offer a moral and, in its way, inclusive universalism.

Unlike cosmopolitanism, of course, it is universalist without being tol- 30 erant, and such intolerant universalism has often led to murder. It underlay the French Wars of Religion that bloodied the four decades before the Edict of Nantes of 1598, in which Henri IV of France finally granted to the Protestants in his realm the right to practice their faith. In the Thirty Years' War, which ravaged central Europe until 1648 and the Peace of Westphalia, Protestant and Catholic princes from Austria to Sweden struggled with one another, and hundreds of thousands of Germans died in battle. Millions starved or died of disease as roaming armies pillaged the countryside. The period of religious conflict in the British Isles, from the first Bishop's War of 1639 to the end of the English Civil War in 1651, which pitted Protestant armies against the forces of a Catholic king, resulted in the deaths of perhaps 10 percent of the population. All these conflicts involved issues beyond sectarian doctrine, of course. Still, many Enlightenment liberals drew the conclusion that enforcing one vision of universal truth could only lead the world back to the blood baths.

Yet tolerance by itself is not what distinguishes the cosmopolitan from 31 the neofundamentalist. There are plenty of things that the heroes of radical Islam are happy to tolerate. They don't care if you eat kebabs or meatballs or kung pao chicken, as long as the meat is halal; your hijab can be silk or linen or viscose. At the same time, there are plenty of things that cosmopolitans will not tolerate. We will sometimes want to intervene in other places because what is going on there violates our principles so deeply. We, too, can see moral error. And when it is serious enough—genocide is the least-controversial case—we will not stop with conversation. Toleration has its limits.

Nor can you tell us apart by saying that the neofundamentalists believe 32 in universal truth. Cosmopolitans believe in universal truth, too, though we are less certain that we already have all of it. It is not skepticism about the very idea of truth that guides us; it is realism about how hard the truth is to find. One tenet we hold to, however, is that every human being has obligations to every other. Everybody matters: that is our central idea. And again, it sharply limits the scope of our tolerance.

To say what, in principle, distinguishes the cosmopolitan from compet- 33 ing universalisms, we plainly need to go beyond talk of truth and tolerance. One distinctively cosmopolitan commitment is to pluralism. Cosmopolitans think that there are many values worth living by and that you cannot live by all of them. So we hope and expect that different people and different societies will embody different values. Another aspect of cosmopolitanism is what philosophers call fallibilism—the sense that our knowledge is imperfect, provisional, subject to revision in the face of new evidence.

The neofundamentalist conception of a global ummah, by contrast, ad- 34 mits of local variations—but only in matters that don't matter. These counter-cosmopolitans, like many Christian fundamentalists, do think that there is one right way for all human beings to live; that all the differences must be in the details. If what concerns you is global homogeneity, then this utopia, not the world that capitalism is producing, is the one you should worry about. Still, the universalisms in the name of religion are hardly the only ones that invert the cosmopolitan creed. In the name of universal humanity, you can be the kind of Marxist, like Mao or Pol Pot, who wants to eradicate all religion, just as easily as you can be the Grand Inquisitor supervising an auto-da-fé. All of these men want every one on their side, so we can share with them the vision in their mirror. "Indeed, I'm a trustworthy adviser to you," Osama bin Laden said in a 2002 "message to the American people." "I invite you to the happiness of this world and the hereafter and to escape your dry, miserable, materialistic life that is without soul. I invite you to Islam, that calls to follow of the path of Allah alone Who has no partners, the path which calls for justice and forbids oppression and crimes." Join us, the counter-cosmopolitans say, and we will all be sisters and brothers. But each of them plans to trample on our differences—to trample us to death, if necessary—if we will not join them. Their motto might as well be the sardonic German saying *Und willst du nicht mein Bruder sein, So schlag' ich Dir den Schädel ein.* (If you don't want to be my brother, then I'll smash your skull in.)

That liberal pluralists are hostile to certain authoritarian ways of life— 35 that they're intolerant of radical intolerance—is sometimes seen as kind of self-refutation. That's a mistake: you can care about individual freedom and still understand that the contours of that freedom will vary considerably from place to place. But we might as well admit that a concern for individual freedom isn't something that will appeal to every individual. In politics, including cultural politics, there are winners and losers—which is worth remembering when we think about international human rights treaties. When we seek to embody our concern for strangers in human rights law, and when we urge our government to enforce it, we are seeking to change the world of law in every nation on the planet. We have declared slavery a violation of international law. And, in so doing, we have committed ourselves, at a minimum, to the desirability of its eradication everywhere. This is no longer controversial in the capitals of the world. No one defends enslavement. But international treaties define slavery in ways that arguably include debt bondage, and debt bondage is a significant economic institution in parts of South Asia. I hold no brief for debt bondage. Still, we shouldn't be surprised if people whose incomes and style of life depend upon it are angry.

It's the same with the international movements to promote women's 36 equality. We know that many Islamists are deeply disturbed by the way Western men and women behave. We permit women to swim almost naked with strange men, which is our business, but it is hard to keep the news of these acts of immodesty from Muslim women and children or to protect Muslim men from the temptations they inevitably create. As the Internet extends its reach, it will get even harder, and their children, especially their girls, will be tempted to ask for these freedoms, too. Worse, they say, we are now trying to force our conception of how women and men should behave upon them. We speak of women's rights. We make treaties enshrining these rights. And then we want their governments to enforce them.

Like many people in every nation, I support those treaties; I believe that 37 women, like men, should have the vote, should be entitled to work outside their homes, should be protected from the physical abuse of men, including their fathers, brothers and husbands. But I also know that the changes these freedoms would bring will change the balance of power between men and women in everyday life. How do I know this? Because I have lived most of my adult life in the West as it has gone through just such a transition, and I know that the process is not yet complete.

So liberty and diversity may well be at odds, and the tensions between 38 them aren't always easily resolved. But the rhetoric of cultural preservation isn't any help. Again, the contradictions are near to hand. Take another look at that Unesco Convention. It affirms the "principle of equal dignity of and respect for all cultures." (What, all cultures—including those of the K.K.K. and the Taliban?) It also affirms "the importance of culture for social cohesion in general, and in particular its potential for the enhancement of the status and role of women in society." (But doesn't "cohesion" argue for uniformity? And wouldn't enhancing the status and role of women involve changing, rather than preserving, cultures?) In Saudi Arabia, people can watch "Will and Grace" on satellite TV—officially proscribed, but available all the same—knowing that, under Saudi law, Will could be beheaded in a public square. In northern Nigeria, mullahs inveigh against polio vaccination while sentencing adulteresses to death by stoning. In India, thousands of wives are burned to death each year for failing to make their dowry payments. *Vive la différence?* Please.

5.

Living cultures do not, in any case, evolve from purity into contamination; change is more a gradual transformation from one mixture to a new mixture, a process that usually takes place at some distance from rules and rulers, in the conversations that occur across cultural boundaries. Such conversations are not so much about arguments and values as about the exchange of perspectives. I don't say that we can't change minds, but the reasons we offer in our conversation will seldom do much to persuade others who do not share our fundamental evaluative judgments already. When we make judgments, after all, it's rarely because we have applied well-thought-out principles to a set of facts and deduced an answer. Our efforts to justify what we have done—or what we plan to do—are typically made up after the event, rationalizations of what we have decided intuitively to do. And a good deal of what we intuitively take to be right, we take to be right just because it is what we are used to. That does not mean, however, that we cannot become accustomed to doing things differently. 39

Consider the practice of foot-binding in China, which persisted for a thousand years—and was largely eradicated within a generation. The anti-foot-binding campaign, in the 1910's and 1920's, did circulate facts about the disadvantages of bound feet, but those couldn't have come as news to most people. Perhaps more effective was the campaign's emphasis that no other country went in for the practice; in the world at large, then, China was "losing face" because of it. (To China's cultural preservationists, of course, the fact that the practice was peculiar to the region was entirely a mark in its favor.) Natural-foot societies were formed, with members for swearing the practice and further pledging that their sons would not marry women with bound feet. As the movement took hold, scorn was heaped on older women with bound feet, and they were forced to endure the agonies of unbinding. What had been beautiful became ugly; ornamentation became disfigurement. The appeal to reason can explain neither the custom nor its abolition. 40

So, too, with other social trends. Just a couple of generations ago, most 41
people in most of the industrialized world thought that middle-class
women would ideally be housewives and mothers. If they had time on their
hands, they could engage in charitable work or entertain one another; a
few of them might engage in the arts, writing novels, painting, performing
in music, theater and dance. But there was little place for them in the
"learned professions"—as lawyers or doctors, priests or rabbis; and if they
were to be academics, they would teach young women and probably remain unmarried. They were not likely to make their way in politics, except
perhaps at the local level. And they were not made welcome in science.

How much of the shift away from these assumptions is a result of ar- 42
guments? Isn't a significant part of it just the consequence of our getting
used to new ways of doing things? The arguments that kept the old pattern
in place were not—to put it mildly—terribly good. If the *reasons* for the old
sexist way of doing things had been the problem, the women's movement
could have been done in a couple of weeks.

Consider another example: In much of Europe and North America, in 43
places where a generation ago homosexuals were social outcasts and homosexual acts were illegal, lesbian and gay couples are increasingly being
recognized by their families, by society and by the law. This is true despite
the continued opposition of major religious groups and a significant and
persisting undercurrent of social disapproval. Both sides make arguments,
some good, most bad. But if you ask the social scientists what has produced
this change, they will rightly not start with a story about reasons. They will
give you a historical account that concludes with a sort of perspectival
shift. The increasing presence of "openly gay" people in social life and in
the media has changed our habits. And over the last 30 years or so, instead
of thinking about the private activity of gay sex, many Americans and Europeans started thinking about the public category of gay people.

One of the great savants of the postwar era, John von Neumann, liked 44
to say, mischievously, that "in mathematics you don't understand things,
you just get used to them." As in mathematical arguments, so in moral
ones. Now, I don't deny that all the time, at every stage, people were talking, giving one another reasons to do things: accept their children, stop
treating homosexuality as a medical disorder, disagree with their churches,
come out. Still, the short version of the story is basically this: People got
used to lesbians and gay men. I am urging that we should learn about people in other places, take an interest in their civilizations, their arguments,
their errors, their achievements, not because that will bring us to agreement
but because it will help us get used to one another—something we have a
powerful need to do in this globalized era. If that is the aim, then the fact

that we have all these opportunities for disagreement about values need not put us off. Understanding one another may be hard; it can certainly be interesting. But it doesn't require that we come to agreement.

6.

The ideals of purity and preservation have licensed a great deal of mischief 45 in the past century, but they have never had much to do with lived culture. Ours may be an era of mass migration, but the global spread and hybridization of culture—through travel, trade or conquest—is hardly a recent development. Alexander's empire molded both the states and the sculpture of Egypt and North India; the Mongols and then the Mughals shaped great swaths of Asia; the Bantu migrations populated half the African continent. Islamic states stretch from Morocco to Indonesia; Christianity reached Africa, Europe and Asia within a few centuries of the death of Jesus of Nazareth; Buddhism long ago migrated from India into much of East and Southeast Asia. Jews and people whose ancestors came from many parts of China have long lived in vast diasporas. The traders of the Silk Road changed the style of elite dress in Italy; someone buried Chinese pottery in 15th-century Swahili graves. I have heard it said that the bagpipes started out in Egypt and came to Scotland with the Roman infantry. None of this is modern.

Our guide to what is going on here might as well be a former African 46 slave named Publius Terentius Afer, whom we know as Terence. Terence, born in Carthage, was taken to Rome in the early second century B.C., and his plays—witty, elegant works that are, with Plautus's earlier, less-cultivated works, essentially all we have of Roman comedy—were widely admired among the city's literary elite. Terence's own mode of writing—which involved freely incorporating any number of earlier Greek plays into a single Latin one—was known to Roman littérateurs as "contamination."

It's an evocative term. When people speak for an ideal of cultural pu- 47 rity, sustaining the authentic culture of the Asante or the American family farm, I find myself drawn to contamination as the name for a counterideal. Terence had a notably firm grasp on the range of human variety: "So many men, so many opinions" was a line of his. And it's in his comedy "The Self-Tormentor" that you'll find what may be the golden rule of cosmopolitanism—*Homo sum: humani nil a me alienum puto*; "I am human: nothing human is alien to me." The context is illuminating. A busybody farmer named Chremes is told by his neighbor to mind his own affairs; the homo sum credo is Chremes's breezy rejoinder. It isn't meant to be an ordinance from on high; it's just the case for gossip. Then again, gossip—the fascination people have for the small doings of other people—has been a powerful force for conversation among cultures.

The ideal of contamination has few exponents more eloquent than 48
Salman Rushdie, who has insisted that the novel that occasioned his fatwa
"celebrates hybridity, impurity, intermingling, the transformation that
comes of new and unexpected combinations of human beings, cultures,
ideas, politics, movies, songs. It rejoices in mongrelisation and fears the absolutism of the Pure. Mélange, hotch-potch, a bit of this and a bit of that
is how newness enters the world." No doubt there can be an easy and spu-
rious utopianism of "mixture," as there is of "purity" or "authenticity."
And yet the larger human truth is on the side of contamination—that endless process of imitation and revision.

A tenable global ethics has to temper a respect for difference with a re- 49
spect for the freedom of actual human beings to make their own choices.
That's why cosmopolitans don't insist that everyone become cosmopolitan.
They know they don't have all the answers. They're humble enough to
think that they might learn from strangers; not too humble to think that
strangers can't learn from them. Few remember what Chremes says after
his "I am human" line, but it is equally suggestive: "If you're right, I'll do
what you do. If you're wrong, I'll set you straight."

Thinking About the Essay

1. What is the thematic significance of the descriptive details given in the
   opening paragraph? Why, for example, does Appiah include a parenthetical
   aside on the traditional meaning of the porcupine quills?

2. Where does Appiah most directly and explicitly define *cosmopolitanism*? If
   the essay is an extended definition of the term, then what is lost by limiting
   one's attention to a passage containing what appears to be a stipulative
   definition (i.e., a definition in the form of a self-contained statement)?

3. How does Appiah reverse one currently accepted meaning of the term *homogeneous*? What is the polemical effect of repeating the phrase "islands
   [or enclaves] of homogeneity"? What are some other instances of semantic
   reversal in the essay?

4. How does Appiah employ personal reminiscence as illustration throughout
   the essay? Do these passages function as logical support for the author's
   argument? What other purpose(s) do they serve?

5. What is the "cultural imperialism" argument, and what evidence does Appiah offer in section 3 to refute this argument?

Responding in Writing

6. Is there a difference between "preserving culture" and "preserving cultures"? In an argumentative essay, explain why you agree or disagree with

Appiah's distinction. How many definitions of *culture* can you come up with? Do these definitions conflict with each other? Why or why not?

7. Compare Appiah's argument in paragraph 27 to a similar argument made by Dominic Hilton in his essay "Fashionable Anti-Americanism" (included in Chapter 3). Which version of the argument do you find most persuasive? Why? Explain in an argumentative essay.

8. Respond, in a brief essay, to the statement at the end of section 2 of the essay: "Societies without change aren't authentic; they're just dead." Can you think of one cultural practice (or an example of a society) that has atrophied as a result of preservationist zeal?

Networking

9. In groups of three or four, make lists of what everyone in the group agrees are "universal" values. Share your list with the class, and (in a class discussion) list a set of possible or likely conflicts between these values and the value system of one culture that exists in the world today.

10. Go online and look up the text of the UNESCO convention on cultural diversity mentioned in the essay. (It was approved in October, 2005.) What are some other passages in the approved text that are not mentioned by Appiah but which seem to run counter to Appiah's concept of cosmopolitanism?

The Educated Student: Global Citizen or Global Consumer?

BENJAMIN BARBER

Born in New York City in 1939, Benjamin Barber attended school in Switzerland and London before receiving a B.A. degree from Grinnell College in 1960 and a Ph.D. degree from Harvard University in 1966. For years he was Walt Whitman Professor of Political Science and director of the Walt Whitman Center for the Culture and Politics of Democracy at Rutgers University. Currently he holds an endowed professorship at the University of Maryland and is principal of the Democracy Collaborative. A charismatic speaker in great demand at major conferences and a frequent guest on television news programs, Barber is also a prolific writer on a wide range of issues, many of them centering on the need for participatory democracy around the world. His numerous books include *Jihad Versus McWorld* (1995), *A Passion for Democracy* (1998), and *A*

> *Place for Us: Civilizing Society and Domesticating the Marketplace* (1998). He is also a playwright and author, with Patrick Watson, of *The Struggle for Democracy* television series. In the essay that appears next, which appeared in the magazine *Liberal Education* (a publication of the Association of Colleges and Universities) in 2002, Barber raises important questions about the status of civic education in the contemporary global era.

Before Reading

Should today's college students be educated in global affairs? If so, how should such programs be handled by schools and colleges? If not, why not? What connections do you see between education and citizenship?

I want to trace a quick trajectory from July 4, 1776 to Sept. 11, 2001. It 1 takes us from the Declaration of Independence to the declaration of interdependence—not one that is actually yet proclaimed but one that we educators need to begin to proclaim from the pulpits of our classrooms and administrative suites across America.

In 1776 it was all pretty simple for people who cared about both edu- 2 cation and democracy. There was nobody among the extraordinary group of men who founded this nation who did not know that democracy—then an inventive, challenging, experimental new system of government—was dependent for its success not just on constitutions, laws, and institutions, but dependent for its success on the quality of citizens who would constitute the new republic. Because democracy depends on citizenship, the emphasis then was to think about what and how to constitute a competent and virtuous citizen body. That led directly, in almost every one of the founders' minds, to the connection between citizenship and education.

Whether you look at Thomas Jefferson in Virginia or John Adams in 3 Massachusetts, there was widespread agreement that the new republic, for all of the cunning of its inventive and experimental new Constitution, could not succeed unless the citizenry was well educated. That meant that in the period after the Revolution but before the ratification of the Constitution, John Adams argued hard for schools for every young man in Massachusetts (it being the case, of course, that only men could be citizens). And in Virginia, Thomas Jefferson made the same argument for public schooling for every potential citizen in America, founding the first great public university there. Those were arguments that were uncontested.

By the beginning of the nineteenth century this logic was clear in the 4 common school movement and later, in the land grant colleges. It was clear in the founding documents of every religious, private, and public higher education institution in this country. Colleges and universities had to be committed above all to the constituting of citizens. That's what education was about. The other aspects of it—literacy, knowledge, and research—were in themselves important. Equally important as dimensions of education and citizenship was education that would make the Bill of Rights real, education that would make democracy succeed.

It was no accident that in subsequent years, African Americans and 5 then women struggled for a place and a voice in this system, and the key was always seen as education. If women were to be citizens, then women's education would have to become central to suffragism. After the Civil War, African Americans were given technical liberty but remained in many ways in economic servitude. Education again was seen as the key. The struggle over education went on, through *Plessy vs. Ferguson* in 1896—separate, but equal—right down to the 1954 *Brown vs. Board of Education,* which declared separate but equal unconstitutional.

In a way our first 200 years were a clear lesson in the relationship be- 6 tween democracy, citizenship, and education, the triangle on which the freedom of America depended. But sometime after the Civil War with the emergence of great corporations and of an economic system organized around private capital, private labor, and private markets, and with the import from Europe of models of higher education devoted to scientific research, we began to see a gradual change in the character of American education generally and particularly the character of higher education in America's colleges and universities. From the founding of Johns Hopkins at the end of the nineteenth century through today we have witnessed the professionalization, the bureaucratization, the privatization, the commercialization, and the individualization of education. Civics stopped being the envelope in which education was put and became instead a footnote on the letter that went inside and nothing more than that.

With the rise of industry, capitalism, and a market society, it came to 7 pass that young people were exposed more and more to tutors other than teachers in their classrooms or even those who were in their churches, their synagogues—and today, their mosques as well. They were increasingly exposed to the informal education of popular opinion, of advertising, of merchandising, of the entertainment industry. Today it is a world whose messages come at our young people from those ubiquitous screens that define modern society and have little to do with anything that you teach. The large screens of the multiplex promote content determined not just by Hollywood but by multinational corporations that control information, technology, communication, sports, and entertainment. About ten of those corporations control over 60 to 70 percent of what appears on those screens.

Then, too, there are those medium-sized screens, the television sets that peek from every room of our homes. That's where our children receive not the twenty-eight to thirty hours a week of instruction they might receive in primary and secondary school, or the six or nine hours a week of classroom instruction they might get in college, but where they get anywhere from forty to seventy hours a week of ongoing "information," "knowledge," and above all, entertainment. The barriers between these very categories of information and entertainment are themselves largely vanished.   8

Then, there are those little screens, our computer screens, hooked up to the Internet. Just fifteen years ago they were thought to be a potential new electronic frontier for democracy. But today very clearly they are one more mirror of a commercialized, privatized society where everything is for sale. The Internet which our children use is now a steady stream of advertising, mass marketing, a virtual mall, a place where the violence, the values—for better or worse—of these same universal corporations reappear in video games and sales messages. Ninety-five to 97 percent of the hits on the Internet are commercial. Of those, 25 to 30 percent are hits on pornographic sites. Most of our political leaders are deeply proud that they have hooked up American schools to the Internet, and that we are a "wired nation." We have, however, in effect hooked up our schools to what in many ways is a national sewer.   9

In the nineteenth century, Alexis de Tocqueville talked about the "immense tutelary power" of that other source of learning, not education, but public opinion. Now public opinion has come under the control of corporate conglomerates whose primary interest is profit. They are willing to put anything out there that will sell and make a profit.   10

We have watched this commercialization and privatization, a distortion of the education mission and its content, going to the heart of our schools themselves. Most American colleges and universities now are participants—and in some ways beneficiaries—but ultimately victims of the cola wars. Is your college a Pepsi college or a Coke college? Which do you have a contract with? And which monopoly do your kids have to drink the goods of? While you are busy teaching them the importance of critical choices, they can only drink one cola beverage on this campus. Choice ends at the cafeteria door.   11

Go to what used to be the food services cafeteria of your local college or university and in many cases you will now find a food court indistinguishable from the local mall featuring Taco Bell, Starbucks, McDonald's, and Burger King. Yes, they are feeding students, but more importantly, they   12 are creating a venue in the middle of campus for what is not education, but an acquisition-of-brands learning. Brand learning means getting young people on board: any merchandiser will tell you, "If we can get the kids when they are in high school and college to buy into our brand, we've got them for life."

Consequences of De-funding

Part of privatization means the de-funding of public institutions, of culture 13 and education, and the de-funding of universities, and so these institutions make a pact with the devil. A real mischief of the modern world (one that colleges haven't yet encountered) is Channel One, which goes into our nation's junior high schools and high schools—particularly the poor ones, those in the inner-city that can't afford their own technology or their own equipment. It makes this promise: "We're not going to give it to you, but we'll lease you some equipment: television sets, maybe a satellite dish, some modems, maybe even a few computers, if you do one thing. Once a day make sure that every student in this school sits in the classroom and watches a very nice little twelve-minute program. Only three minutes of it will be advertising. Let us feed advertising to your kids during a history or a social studies class, and we will lend you some technology."

Most states—New York state is the only one that has held out—in 14 America have accepted Channel One, which is now in over twelve or thirteen thousand high schools around the nation. Our students sit during class time, possibly a social studies or history class, and watch advertising. I dare say, if somebody said they were going to give you some equipment as long as you watch the message of Christ or the church of Christ for three minutes a day, or said they were going to give you some equipment as long as you listen to the message of the Communist Party or the Democratic party during class for three out of twelve minutes, there would be an outcry and an uproar. Totalitarianism! State propaganda! Theocracy! But because they have been so degradingly de-funded, we have allowed our schools to be left without the resources to resist this deal with the devil.

Tell me why it is in the modern world that when a political party or a 15 state takes over the schools and spews its propaganda into them and takes over every sector of society, we call that political totalitarianism and oppose it as the denial of liberty. And when a church or a religion takes over every sector of society and spews its propaganda forth in its schools, we call it theocratic and totalitarian and go to war against it. But when the market comes in with its brands and advertising and takes over every sector of society and spews its propaganda in our schools, we call it an excellent bargain on the road to liberty. I don't understand that, and I don't think we should put up with it, and I don't think America should put up with it. I know the people who sell it would not sit still for a minute if their own children, sitting in private schools somewhere, were exposed to that commercial advertising. They're not paying $25,000 a year to have their kids watch advertising in the classroom. But, of course, it's not their children's schools that are at risk; it's mostly the schools of children of families who don't have much of a say about these things.

Imagine how far Channel One has come from Jefferson's dream, from   16
John Adams's dream, the dream of the common school. And how low we have sunk as a society where we turn our heads and say, "Well, it's not so bad, it's not really, it's just advertising." Advertisers know how valuable the legitimizing venue of the classroom is and pay double the rates of prime time to advertise on Channel One, not because the audience is so broad but because it is the perfect target audience and because it gets that extraordinary legitimization of the American classroom where what kids believe you "learn" in your classroom has to be true.

Commercialization and privatization go right across the board. You see   17
them in every part of our society. You see cultural institutions increasingly dependent on corporate handouts. Because we will not fund the arts, the arts, too, like education have to make a profit. In our universities and colleges, scientists are now selling patents and making deals that the research they do will benefit not humanity and their students, but the shareholders of corporations, and so their research will otherwise be kept private. Again, most administrators welcome that because they don't have to raise faculty research budgets. The corporate world will take care of that.

These practices change the nature of knowledge and information. They   18
privatize, making research a part of commercial enterprise. That's the kind of bargain we have made with our colleges and universities. We hope that somehow the faculty will remain insulated from it. We hope the students won't notice, but then when they're cynical about politics and about the administration, and cynical about their own education, and when they look to their own education as a passport to a hot job and big money—and nothing else—we wonder what's going on with them.

But of course students see everything; they have noses for hypocrisy.   19
Students see the hypocrisy of a society that talks about the importance of education and knowledge and information while its very educational institutions are selling their own souls for a buck, and they're doing it because the society otherwise won't support them adequately, is unwilling to tax itself, is unwilling to ask itself for sufficient funds to support quality education. That's where we are. That's where we were on September 10.

What We've Learned

On September 11 a dreadful, pathological act occurred, which nonetheless 20 may act in a brutal way as a kind of tutorial for America and for its educators. On that day, it suddenly became apparent to many people who'd forgotten it that America was no longer a land of independence or sovereignty, a land that could "go it alone." America was no longer capable of surviving as a free democracy unless it began to deal in different terms with a world that for 200 years it had largely ignored and in the last fifty or seventy-five years had treated in terms of that sad phrase "collateral damage." Foreign policy was about dealing with the collateral damage of America being America, America being commercialized, America being prosperous, America "doing well" in the economic sense—if necessary, at everybody else's expense.

September 11 was a brutal and perverse lesson in the inevitability of in- 21 terdependence in the modern world—and of the end of independence, where America could simply go it alone. It was the end of the time in which making a buck for individuals would, for those that were doing all right, be enough; somehow the fact that the rest of the world was in trouble and that much of America was in trouble—particularly its children (one out of five in poverty)—was incidental. After thirty years of privatization and commercialization, the growing strength of the ideology that said the era not just of government, but of big government was over; that said, this was to be the era of markets, and markets will solve every problem: education, culture, you name it, the markets can do it.

On September 11 it became clear that there were areas in which the 22 market could do nothing: terrorism, poverty, injustice, war. The tragedy pointed to issues of democracy and equality and culture, and revealed a foreign policy that had been paying no attention. In the early morning of September 12, nobody called Bill Gates at Microsoft or Michael Eisner at Disney and said "Help us, would you? You market guys have good solutions. Help us get the terrorists." Indeed, the heroes of September 11 were public officials, public safety officers: policemen, firemen, administrators, even a mayor who found his soul during that period. Those were the ones we turned to and suddenly understood that they played a public role representing all of us.

Suddenly, Americans recognized that its citizens were the heroes. Not 23 the pop singers, fastball pitchers, and the guys who make all the money in the NBA; not those who've figured out how to make a fast buck by the time they're thirty, the Internet entrepreneurs. In the aftermath of 9/11, it was particularly those public-official-citizens. All citizens because in what they do, they are committed to the welfare of their neighbors, their children, to future generations. That's what citizens are supposed to do: think about the communities to which they belong and pledge themselves to the public good of those communities.

Hence the importance of the civic professions like teaching. In most 24 countries, in fact, teachers and professors are public officials. They are seen, like firemen and policemen, as guardians of the public good, of the res publica, those things of the public that we all care about. On September 11 and the days afterwards, it became clear how important those folks were. As a consequence, a kind of closing of a door occasioned by the fall of the towers became an opening of a window of new opportunities, new possibilities, new citizenship: an opportunity to explore interdependence. Interdependence is another word for citizenship.

Citizenship in the World

The citizen is the person who acknowledges and recognizes his or her in- 25 terdependence in a neighborhood, a town, a state, in a nation—and today, in the world. Anyone with eyes wide open during the last thirty to forty years has known that the world has become interdependent in ineluctable and significant ways. AIDS and the West Nile Virus don't carry passports. They go where they will. The Internet doesn't stop at national boundaries; it's a worldwide phenomenon. Today's telecommunications technologies define communications and entertainment all over the world without re- gard to borders. Global warming recognizes no sovereignty, and nobody can say he or she won't have to suffer the consequences of polluted air. Ecology, technology, and of course economics and markets are global in character, and no nation can pretend that its own destiny is any longer in its own hands in the manner of eighteenth and nineteenth century nations.

In particular, this nation was the special land where independence had 26 been declared, and our two oceans would protect us from the world. We went for several hundred years thinking America was immune to the prob- lems and tumult and prejudices of the wars of the world beyond the oceans. And then 9/11—and suddenly it became clear that no American could ever rest comfortably in bed at night if somewhere, someone else in the world was starving or someone's children were at risk. With 9/11 it became ap- parent that whatever boundaries once protected us and whatever new borders we were trying to build including the missile shield (a new technological "virtual ocean" that would protect us from the world) were irrelevant.

Multilateralism becomes a new mandate of national security, a neces- 27 sity. There are no oceans wide enough, there are no walls high enough to protect America from the rest of our world. What does that say about education? It means that for the first time a lot of people who didn't care about civic education—the education of citizens, the soundness of our own democracy, the ability of our children to understand the world—now suddenly recognize this is key, that education counts. Multicultural education counts because we have to understand the cultures of other worlds. Language education counts because language is a window on other cultures and histories.

Citizenship is now the crucial identity. We need to think about what an   28
adequate civic education means today, and what it means to be a citizen. We need education-based community service programs. We need experiential learning, not just talking about citizenship but exercises in doing it. We need to strongly support the programs around the country that over the '80s and '90s sprang up but have recently been in decline.

But we also need new programs in media literacy. I talked about the   29
way in which a handful of global corporations control the information channels of television, the Internet, and Hollywood. We need young people who are sophisticated in media, who understand how media work, how media affect them, how to resist, how to control, how to become immune to media. Media literacy and media studies from my point of view become a key part of how we create a new civic education. Of course history, the arts, sociology, and anthropology, and all of those fields that make young people aware of the rest of the world in a comparative fashion are more important than ever before.

We are a strange place because we are one of the most multicultural na-   30
tions on Earth with people in our schools from all over the world, and yet we know less than most nations about the world from which those people come. At one and the same time, we are truly multicultural, we represent the globe, and yet we know little about it.

Coming Full Circle

In coming full circle, the trajectory from the Declaration of Independence   31
200 years ago to the declaration of interdependence that was sounded on September 11 opens an opportunity for us as educators to seize the initiative to make civic education central again. The opportunity to free education from the commercializers and privatizers, to take it back for civic education and for our children, and to make the schools of America and the world the engines of democracy and liberty and freedom that they were supposed to be. And that's not just an abstraction. That starts with addressing commercialization directly: confronting Channel One and the food court at your local college, the malling of your cafeterias, and the sellout of corporate research.

There are things that every one of us can do inside our own colleges and   32
universities. If we do, our students will notice. And if we really make our
colleges and universities democratic, civic, independent, autonomous, international, and multilateral again, we will no longer even need civics
classes. Our students will take one look at what we've done in the university and understand the relationship between education and democracy.
That must be our mission. I hope that as individual citizens, teachers, administrators, you will take this mission seriously. I certainly do, and I know
that as before, the future of liberty, the future of democracy in both America and around the world, depends most of all on its educational institutions and on the teachers and administrators who control them. Which
means we really are in a position to determine what our future will be.

Thinking About the Essay

1. This essay reflects Barber's deep historical and political knowledge and his
   passionate concern for the role of education in civic and global life. What
   assumptions does he make about his primary audience—who, we can infer
   from the place of publication—are educators? What "message" does he
   want to convey to his primary audience? What secondary audiences might
   he have in mind, and how does he manage to appeal to them?

2. State Barber's thesis in your own words. Does he ever present a thesis
   statement or does he imply it? Explain.

3. In part, this essay reflects a rhetorical strategy known as process analysis.
   How does Barber take us through a step-by-step historical process? Point
   to specific stages in this process. How does the process come full circle?
   In other words, how does he tie September 11, 2001, to July 4, 1776?

4. Barber divides his essay into five parts. Summarize each part. What logical
   relationships do you see between and among them? How do these sections progress logically from one stage of Barber's argument to the next?

5. What definitions does Barber offer for such key terms as *democracy, education, civic responsibility, globalization,* and *multilateralism*? What is his
   purpose? Why does he introduce such abstract terms? What other broad
   abstractions does he discuss, and where?

Responding in Writing

6. In a personal essay, discuss the quality of your own education. To what extent do you feel your education has provided you with a sense of what it
   takes to create or sustain a democracy or a sense of civic responsibility?
   To what extent have you been encouraged to think of yourself as a citizen

of the world? To what extent have you been affected by the forces of consumerism? Explore these issues—and any others raised by Barber—in your paper.

7. Barber writes that "students see everything; they have noses for hypocrisy" (paragraph 19). Clearly you agree with this notion. But what precisely are you hypocritical about when you think about education, democracy, terrorism, consumerism, and some of the other "big" words that Barber discusses? In fact, do you have a nose for hypocrisy or might you actually be hypocritical? (For example, if you believe in democracy as a necessary civic institution, do you vote in elections?) Write an essay exploring the subject of hypocrisy.

8. Are you a global citizen or a global consumer? Must you be one or the other, or can you be both and still be a good citizen—of your country and of the world? Examine this subject in a reflective essay.

Networking

9. In small groups, look over the syllabi for the various courses that you are taking this term. Which ones explicitly address some of the main issues raised by Barber? Does the English course in which you're presently enrolled reflect these issues? Present your findings to the class.

10. Locate websites for the Walt Whitman Center for the Culture and Politics of Democracy or the Democracy Collaborative. Take notes on these organizations, and then prepare a paper on their missions and programs.

7

CHAPTER

Culture Wars:
Whose Culture Is It, Anyway?

A s we have seen in earlier chapters, the power and influence of the United States radiate outward to the rest of the world in many ways. Nowhere is this more visible than in the impact of various American cultural manifestations—ranging from food, to clothing, to music, to television and film—on other countries. When a French farmer burns down a McDonald's or terrorists destroy a disco in Bali, killing more than two hundred people, we sense the opposition to American cultural hegemony. Conversely, when young Iranians turn on their banned satellite systems to catch the latest *Simpsons* episode, or when street merchants in Kenya sell University of Michigan T-shirts, we detect the flip side of the culture wars—the mesmerizing power of American culture throughout the world. Sometimes it seems that American culture, wittingly or unwittingly, is in a battle for the world's soul.

We also have to acknowledge that the culture wars color American life as well. At home, current debates over immigration, affirmative action, bilingual education, and much more impinge on our daily lives and dominate media presentations. It might be fashionable to say that we all trace our DNA to Africa and that ideally we are all citizens of the world, but the issue of what sort of culture we represent individually or collectively is much more complicated. Tiger Woods might be the icon for the New American, or for the new Universal Person, but his slightest actions and words prompt cultural controversy. American culture cuts many ways; it is powerful, but also strange and contradictory.

The culture wars take us to the borders of contradiction both at home and abroad. It is too facile to say that we are moving "beyond"

 *Online Study Center*   This icon will direct you to web links, audio and visual content, and additional resources on the website college.hmco.com/pic/mullerNWR2e

French farmer José Bové, who leads a radical farmer's union in France protesting the encroachments of American fast-food culture, is shown here after having been released from prison for vandalizing a McDonald's restaurant in France. To celebrate, he dines on local French bread, Roquefort cheese, and wine.

Thinking About the Image

1. If McDonald's is stereotypically American, what is stereotypically French about this image? Why do you think José Bové is emphasizing those stereotypes?
2. Think about other images of protest you have seen in this book. Clearly, José Bové's delicious meal was intended for an audience and had a clear purpose. How effective is the "rhetoric" of his protest here?
3. In 2003, some Americans boycotted French products (such as wine and cheese) in protest over France's refusal to support the United States in its war against Iraq. Why is something so seemingly basic as food such a potent symbol of cultural meaning and pride?

monoculturalism at home or that the rest of the world doesn't have to embrace American culture if it doesn't want to. What is clear is that the very *idea* of American culture, in all its diversity, is so pervasive that it spawns numerous viewpoints and possibilities for resolution. After all, culture is a big subject: it embraces one's ethnic, racial, class, religious, sexual, and national identity. We can't be uncritical about culture. We have to understand how culture both molds and reflects our lives.

The writers in this chapter offer perspectives—all of them provocative and engaging—on national and transnational culture. They deal with the ironies of culture at home and the paradoxes of American cultural influence abroad. Some of the writers engage in self-reflection, others in rigorous analysis. All refuse to view culture in simplistic terms. In reading them, you might discover that whether you grew up in the United States or another country, culture is at the heart of who you are.

Cultural Baggage

BARBARA EHRENREICH

Barbara Ehrenreich was born in 1941 in Butte, Montana. She attended Reed College (B.A., 1963) and Rockefeller University (Ph.D. in biology, 1968). A self-described socialist and feminist, Ehrenreich uses her scientific training to investigate a broad range of social issues: health care, the plight of the poor, the condition of women around the world. Her scathing critiques of American health care in such books as *The American Health Empire* (with John Ehrenreich, 1970), *Complaints and Disorders: The Sexual Politics of Sickness* (with Deirdre English, 1973), and *For Her Own Good* (with English, 1978) established her as an authority in the field. In her provocative *The Hearts of Men: American Dreams and the Flight from Commitment* (1983), Ehrenreich surveys the decline of male investment in the family from the 1950s to the 1980s. A prolific writer during the 1980s and 1990s, Ehrenreich most recently published the award-winning book, *Nickel and Dimed: On (Not) Getting By in America* (2001). She is also a frequent contributor to magazines, including *Nation, Esquire, Radical America, New Republic,* and *The New York Times,* while serving as a contributing editor to *Ms.* and *Mother Jones.* Her fresh insights into the complex contours of American society can be seen in "Cultural Baggage," published in *The New York Times* Magazine in 1992, where Ehrenreich offers a new slant on the idea of "heritage."

Before Reading

What is your ethnic or religious heritage? Do you feel comfortable explaining or defending it? Why or why not?

An acquaintance was telling me about the joys of rediscovering her eth- 1
nic and religious heritage. "I know exactly what my ancestors were doing 2,000 years ago," she said, eyes gleaming with enthusiasm, "and I can do the same things now." Then she leaned forward and inquired politely, "And what is your ethnic background, if I may ask?"

"None," I said, that being the first word in line to get out of my mouth. 2
Well, not "none," I backtracked. Scottish, English, Irish—that was something, I supposed. Too much Irish to qualify as a WASP; too much of the hated English to warrant a "Kiss Me, I'm Irish" button; plus there are a number of dead ends in the family tree due to adoptions, missing records, failing memories and the like. I was blushing by this time. Did "none" mean I was rejecting my heritage out of Anglo-Celtic self-hate? Or was I revealing a hidden ethnic chauvinism in which the Britannically derived serve as a kind of neutral standard compared with the ethnic "others"?

Throughout the 1960s and '70s I watched one group after another— 3
African Americans, Latinos, Native Americans—stand up and proudly reclaim their roots while I just sank back ever deeper into my seat. All this excitement over ethnicity stemmed, I uneasily sensed, from a past in which their ancestors had been trampled upon by my ancestors, or at least by people who looked very much like them. In addition, it had begun to seem almost un-American not to have some sort of hyphen at hand, linking one to more venerable times and locales.

But the truth is, I was raised with none. We'd eaten ethnic foods in my 4
childhood home, but these were all borrowed, like the pasties, or Cornish meat pies, my father had picked up from his fellow miners in Butte, Montana. If my mother had one rule, it was militant ecumenism in all matters of food and experience. "Try new things," she would say, meaning anything from sweet-breads to clams, with an emphasis on the "new."

As a child, I briefly nourished a craving for tradition and roots. I im- 5
mersed myself in the works of Sir Walter Scott. I pretended to believe that the bagpipe was a musical instrument. I was fascinated to learn from a grandmother that we were descended from certain Highland clans and longed for a pleated skirt in one of their distinctive tartans.

But in *Ivanhoe*, it was the dark-eyed "Jewess" Rebecca I identified 6
with, not the flaxen-haired bimbo Rowena. As for clans: Why not call them tribes—those bands of half-clad peasants and warriors whose idea of cuisine was stuffed sheep gut washed down with whisky? And then there was

the sting of Disraeli's remark—which I came across in my early teens—to the effect that his ancestors had been leading orderly, literate lives when my ancestors were still rampaging through the Highlands daubing themselves with blue paint.

Motherhood put the screws on me, ethnicity-wise. I had hoped that by marrying a man of Eastern European Jewish ancestry I would acquire for my descendants the ethnic genes that my own forebears so sadly lacked. At one point I even subjected the children to a seder of my own design, including a little talk about the flight from Egypt and its relevance to modern social issues. But the kids insisted on buttering their matzos and snickering through my talk. "Give me a break, Mom," the older one said. "You don't even believe in God."   7

After the tiny pagans had been put to bed, I sat down to brood over Elijah's wine. What had I been thinking? The kids knew that their Jewish grandparents were secular folks who didn't hold seders themselves. And if ethnicity eluded me, how could I expect it to take root in my children, who are not only Scottish English Irish, but Hungarian Polish Russian to boot?   8

But, then, on the fumes of Manischewitz, a great insight took form in my mind. It was true, as the kids said, that I didn't "believe in God." But this could be taken as something very different from an accusation—a reminder of a genuine heritage. My parents had not believed in God either, nor had my grandparents or any other progenitors going back to the great-great level. They had become disillusioned with Christianity generations ago—just as, on the in-law side, my children's other ancestors had shaken off their Orthodox Judaism. This insight did not exactly furnish me with an "identity," but it was at least something to work with: We are the kind of people, I realized—whatever our distant ancestors' religions—who do not believe, who do not carry on traditions, who do not do things just because someone has done them before.   9

The epiphany went on: I recalled that my mother never introduced a procedure for cooking or cleaning by telling me, "Grandma did it this way." What did Grandma know, living in the days before vacuum cleaners and disposable toilet mops? In my parents' general view, new things were better than old and the very fact that some ritual had been performed in the past was a good reason for abandoning it now. Because what was the past, as our forebears knew it? Nothing but poverty, superstition and grief. "Think for yourself," Dad used to say. "Always ask why."   10

In fact, this may have been the ideal cultural heritage for my particular ethnic strain—bounced as it was from the Highlands of Scotland across the sea, out to the Rockies, down into the mines and finally spewed out into high-tech, suburban America. What better philosophy, for a race of mi-   11 grants, than "think for yourself"? What better maxim, for a people whose whole world was rudely inverted every 30 years or so, than "try new things"?

The more tradition-minded, the newly enthusiastic celebrants of Purim 12 and Kwanzaa and Solstice, may see little point to survival if the survivors carry no cultural freight—religion, for example, or ethnic tradition. To which I would say that skepticism, curiosity and wide-eyed ecumenical tolerance are also worthy elements of the human tradition and are at least as old as such notions as "Serbian" or "Croatian," "Scottish" or "Jewish." I make no claims for my personal line of progenitors except that they remained loyal to the values that may have induced all of our ancestors, long, long ago, to climb down from the trees and make their way into the open plains.

A few weeks ago I cleared my throat and asked the children, now 13 mostly grown and fearsomely smart, whether they felt any stirrings of ethnic or religious identity, which might have been, ahem, insufficiently nourished at home. "None," they said, adding firmly, "and the world would be a better place if nobody else did, either." My chest swelled with pride, as would my mother's, to know that the race of "none" marches on.

Thinking About the Essay

1. Why is Ehrenreich's title perfect for the essay that she writes?

2. What is Ehrenreich's purpose in asking so many questions in this essay? Is the strategy effective? Why or why not?

3. How would you describe the tone of this essay—the writer's attitude or approach to her subject? Locate phrases, sentences, and passages that support your response.

4. Ehrenreich traces a pattern of causality in this essay as she describes not only her own experience of ethnic and religious heritage but that of others as well. Trace this pattern of cause and effect throughout the article. Where do other rhetorical strategies—for example, illustration, comparison, or definition—come into play?

5. Examine paragraphs 10–13. How do they serve as an extended conclusion to the argument Ehrenreich presents?

Responding in Writing

6. Write your own personal essay with the title "Cultural Baggage." Like Ehrenreich, use the personal, or "I," point of view and focus on your own experience of your ethnic and religious heritage. Be certain to have a clear thesis that helps to guide your approach to the subject.

7. As an exercise, argue against Ehrenreich's claim that it is best to have "no cultural freight—religion, for example, or ethnic tradition" (paragraph 12).

8. Write a comparative paper in which you analyze the concepts of cultural pride and cultural baggage. Establish a controlling thesis, and develop at least three major comparative topics for this essay.

Networking

9. Form two equal groups of class members. One group should develop an argument in favor of cultural heritage, the other opposing it. Select one spokesperson from each group and have them debate the issue in front of the class.

10. Ehrenreich says she is a socialist. Go online and locate information on this term, as well as additional information on Ehrenreich herself. Then use this information to write a paper describing how "Cultural Baggage" reflects Ehrenreich's socialist views.

It's a Mall World After All

MAC MARGOLIS

In the following piece, which appeared in the December 5, 2005, *Newsweek International*, columnist Mac Margolis defends a much maligned and distinctively American export to the world by looking at the variety of its manifestations around the world and its almost inadvertent role as a social and political institution.

Before Reading

In what sense do you regard malls as an institution? Do you associate malls with democratic or other values?

When the Los Angeles firm Altoon + Porter Architects set out to design a shopping arcade in Riyadh, Saudi Arabia, a few years ago, it faced a delicate mission: to raise a glitzy pleasure dome full of Western temptations in the maw of fundamentalist Islam. Not that the Saudis were consumer innocents; King Khalid airport in Riyadh fairly hums with wealthy Arabs bound for the lavish shops of Paris and London. But the trick was to lure women buyers—the royalty of retail—who are not allowed to shed their veils in public. "Women can't be expected to buy anything if they can't try it on," says architect Ronald Altoon, managing partner of the firm. So Altoon + Porter came up with an ecumenical solution: the Kingdom Centre, a three-story glass-and-steel Xanadu of retail with an entire floor—Women's Kingdom—devoted exclusively to female customers. "We took the veil off the women and put it on the building," says Altoon.

The modest proposal paid off. In Women's Kingdom, Saudi women can   2
shop, schmooze, dine or even loll about at the spa without upsetting the sheiks or subverting Sharia, the country's strict Islamic laws. Normally the third level of any mall is a dud, but it's become the most profitable floor in the whole arcade. The Kingdom Centre may not be revolutionary; no one is burning veils at the food court. Still, it represents a small but meaningful freedom for Saudi women. And its success points to the irrepressible global appetite for consumer culture, as well as to the growing role that the right to shop plays in fostering democratization and development.

It's been more than two decades since John B. Hightower, the director   3
of New York City's South Street Seaport Museum, a combination cultural center and shopping arcade, brazenly declared that "shopping is the chief cultural activity of the United States." Since then, it has also become one of America's chief exports: shopping malls, once a peculiarly American symbol of convenience and excess, now dot the global landscape from Santiago to St. Petersburg and Manila to Mumbai. In 1999, India boasted only three malls. Now there are 45, and the number is expected to rise to 300 by 2010. The pint-size Arab Emirate of Dubai, sometimes known as the Oz of malls, clocked 88.5 million mall visitors last year; nearly 180 million Brazilians mob shopping arcades every month—almost as many as in the United States. Where elephants and giraffes once gamboled along the Mombasa road leading into Nairobi, the African mall rat is now a far more common sight, with four gleaming new malls to scavenge in at the Kenyan capital and three more in the works. And no one can keep pace with China, where foreign investors are scrambling to get a piece of a real-estate boom driven in part by mall mania. "The same energy and dynamism that the shopping industry brought to North America 30, 40 years ago is now reaching overseas," says Michael Kercheval, head of the International Council of Shopping Centers, an industry trade association and advisory group. "Now it's reached the global masses."

Indeed, the planet appears deep in the grip of the retail version of an   4
arms race. For years, the West Edmonton Mall in Alberta, Canada, with 20,000 parking spaces, an ice-skating rink, a miniature-golf course and four submarines (more than in the Canadian Navy) on display, had reigned as the grandest in the world. Last October it was overtaken by the $1.3 billion Golden Resources Shopping Center in northwest Beijing, with 20,000 employees and nearly twice the floor space of the Pentagon. Developers in Dubai are breaking ground on not one but two malls they claim will be

even bigger, one of which boasts a man-made, five-run ski slope. Yet all these have been eclipsed by the behemoth South China Mall, which opened its doors in the factory city of Dongguan this year. By the end of the decade, China is likely to have at least seven of the world's 10 largest malls—many of them equipped with hotels, on the theory that no one can possibly see everything in a single day.

To those who malign malls as the epitome of all that is wrong with   5 American culture, their spread is like a pestilence upon the land. Dissident scholars churn out one dystopian tract—"One Nation Under Goods," "The Call of the Mall"—after another. Critics despair of whole nations willing to cash in their once vibrant downtowns and street markets for a wasteland of jerry-built nowhere, epic traffic jams and marquees ablaze with fatuous English names (Phoenix High Street, Palm Springs Life Plaza and Bairong World Trade Center Phase II). To some, this is an assault on democracy itself. "Shopping malls are great for dictatorships," says Emil Pocock, a professor of American studies at Eastern Connecticut State University, who takes students on field trips to malls to study consumer society. "What better way to control folks than to put them under a dome and in enclosed doors?" The "malling of America," in the words of author and famous mall-basher William Kowinski, has become the malling of the world.

As it turns out, that may not be such a bad thing. Rather than presage   6 or hasten the decline of the traditional downtown, as many critics fear, the rise of the mall is actually serving as a catalyst for growth, especially in developing nations. In China, the booming retail sector has sucked in a fortune in venture capital and spawned dozens of joint ventures with international investors looking to snap up Chinese urban properties. In late July, the Simon Property Group, a major U.S. developer, teamed up with Morgan Stanley and a government-owned Chinese company to launch up to a dozen major retail centers throughout China over the next few years. Malls are a leading force in driving India's $330 billion retailing industry, which already accounts for a third of national GDP and recently overtook Russia's. Similarly, a burst of consumer spending in the Philippines— thanks to overseas nationals who send between $6 billion and $7 billion back every year—has fueled a real-estate boom, led by megamalls.

Most developing-world malls are integrated in the heart of the inner   7 cities instead of strewn like beached whales along arid superhighways. "In China, 80 percent of shoppers walk to the mall," says Kercheval of the ICSC. In some megacities, including New Delhi, Nairobi and Rio, urban sprawl has flung customers into outlying neighborhoods, many of which spring up around brand-new shopping centers. That means malls are no longer catering just to the elite. "We used to talk exclusively about A-class shoppers," says Kercheval. "Now we are seeing the arrival of B-, C- and D-class customers. The developing-world mall is becoming more democratic."

In many places, malls are welcome havens of safety and security. In Rio, where teenagers (especially young men) are the main victims of street crime, parents breathe easier when they know their kids are at play in the mall, some of which deploy 100 or more private police. "Safety is one of our biggest selling points," says Paulo Malzoni Filho, president of the Brazilian Association of Shopping Centers. "When I enter into one of these malls, it feels like I have landed in a foreign country," says Parag Mehta, a regular at the Inorbit mall in the busy northern Mumbai suburb of Malad.

And as malls break new ground around the world, the one-size-fits-all business model created in North American suburbia is giving way to regionalized versions. Malls may conjure up the specter of a flood of U.S. brands and burgers, but in reality, local palates and preferences often prevail. On a recent evening in Beijing's Golden Resources Shopping Center, Kentucky Fried Chicken and Papa John's were nearly deserted, while the Korean restaurant just around the corner was packed. Chile has long welcomed foreign investors, yet the leading retailers at malls in Santiago are two local chains, Falabella and Almacenes Paris. In San Salvador, capital of El Salvador, the Gallerias shopping arcade houses a Roman Catholic church that holds mass twice a day—an intriguing metaphysical twist on the concept of the anchor store. In many developing countries, malls have attracted banks, art galleries, museums, car-rental agencies and even government services such as passport offices and motor-vehicle departments, becoming de facto villages instead of just shopping centers.

For residents of the developing world, malls increasingly serve as surrogate civic centers, encouraging social values that go beyond conspicuous spending. China is home to some 168 million smokers, but they are not allowed to partake at the smoke-free malls. That's not the only environmental plus; many Chinese malls are equipped with a soft-switching system that stabilizes the electrical current and conserves energy. In the Middle East, arcades such as Riyadh's Kingdom Centre are among the few public spaces where women can gather, gab or just walk about alone in public. "Malls are not just places to shop, they are places to imagine," says Xia Yeliang, a professor at Beijing University's School of Economics. "They bring communities together that might not otherwise encounter one another and create new communities."

For some societies, malls even offer a communal respite from the past. In Warsaw, where World War II demolished most of the historic shopping district—and dreary chockablock communist-era architecture finished the job—one of the most revered public spaces around is the local mall. "For decades Poles dressed up for Sunday mass," says Grzegorz Makowski, a sociologist at Warsaw University and expert on consumer culture. "Now they dress for a visit to the shopping mall."

Still, for some critics, no amount of social or economic development 12 can hide the fact that all modern malls are at heart temples of rampant consumerism. Jan Gehl, a leading Danish champion of urban renaissance and a professor of architecture at the Royal Academy of Fine Arts in Copenhagen, likes to show his students pictures of malls around the world and ask them where each one is located. Many look so indistinguishable that they can't tell. (Only now are some clues beginning to appear.) Even Victor Gruen, the Viennese Jewish emigre who fled Hitler's Europe and created the first indoor-shopping arcade in the Minneapolis suburbs in the 1950s, eventually grew disgusted by the soulless concrete-box-with-parking monstrosities rendered in his name. "I refuse to pay alimony to these bastards of development," he growled during a 1978 speech in London, fleeing back to Europe. By then there was no escape; malls were already marching on the Old World.

Half a century on, some of the resistance to malls speaks more to nos- 13 talgia for an illusory past than a rejection of the present. Ancient Turkey certainly had its bazaar rats. And what is the contemporary shopping center if not a souk with a Cineplex? "Maybe the mall is just a modern and more comfortable version of what has always been," says Stephen Marshall of the Young Foundation, a London think tank. "It's quite possible the ancients would have seen our malls with all that technology as terrific places."

Certainly mall developers seem to have learned from their early ex- 14 cesses. Instead of garish bunkers with blind walls and plastic rain forests, newer malls boast sculpture gardens, murals, belvederes and gentle lighting. Lush creepers, great ferns, cacti and feathery palms tumble down the interior of the Fashion Mall, a boutique arcade, in Rio de Janeiro. The Kingdom Centre in Riyadh won an international design award in 2003. And while "big" may still be beautiful in mallworld, more and more developers are launching arcades built to modest scale, deliberately emulating yesterday's main streets or the Old World piazzas they replaced. This may not be the much-vaunted consumer's arcadia the mallmeisters had always hoped for, but global malls seem oddly to come closer to the bold democratic ideal than the originals ever did. And when it rains, everybody stays dry.

Thinking About the Essay

1. Highlight three passing allusions that occur in the essay (the allusion to Xanadu in the opening paragraph, for example). Is there a chain of association between the series of allusions you see in the essay?

2. What is the "ecumenical solution" devised by the architectural firm Altoon + Porter?

3. Where in the essay does Margolis address critics of malls as a cultural phenomenon? What is his response to these critics?

4. How does Margolis connect the "right to consumer culture" with democratic rights and values? Do you feel he is successful in making this connection? Why or why not?

5. Margolis concludes the piece by asserting that "global malls seem oddly to come closer to the bold democratic ideal than the originals ever did." Where in the essay has Margolis considered those precedents? Do you feel he has offered enough historical evidence to support his conclusion?

Responding in Writing

6. Do you see evidence in your own community that mall developers "have learned from their early excesses"? Write a brief critique of the architectural style and layout of your local mall.

7. Respond to Margolis's observation in paragraph 11 that malls "offer a communal respite from the past." Do you see this as a stereotypically American attitude toward the past? Would you characterize what malls offer as a "respite from the past" or as an "*escape* from the past"?

8. In a brief essay, reflect on the reasons for your own resistance to or enthusiasm for malls. Would you describe your feelings in terms of nostalgia for a past model in the process of being replaced, or in terms of progress? What is the nature of this progress? What is lost or gained in the move to a new model of commerce?

Networking

9. In groups of three or four, list at least three "social values" (i.e., not consumer values) that are promoted or made possible by your local mall.

10. Go online and look up images of at least five different malls located in five different countries. What signs of individual character do you see?

Whose Culture Is It, Anyway?

HENRY LOUIS GATES JR.

Henry Louis Gates Jr. is one of the most respected figures in the field of African American studies. Born in 1950 in Keyser, West Virginia, he received a B.A. degree (summa cum laude) from Harvard University (1973) and M.A. (1974) and Ph.D. degrees (1979) from Clare College, Cambridge University. A recipient of numerous major grants, including the prestigious MacArthur Prize Fellowship, and a professor at Harvard University, Gates in numerous essays and books argues for a greater diversity in arts, literature, and life. In one of his best-known works, *Loose Canons: Notes on the Culture Wars* (1992), Gates states, "The society we have made simply won't survive without the values of tolerance. And cultural tolerance comes to nothing without cultural understanding." Among his many publications are *The Signifying Monkey: Toward a Theory of Afro-American Literary Criticism* (1988), which won both a National Book Award and an American Book Award; *Colored People, A Memoir* (1994); *The Future of the Race* (with Cornel West, 1996); and *Wonders of the African World* (1999). In the following essay, which appeared originally in *The New York Times* on May 4, 1991, Gates analyzes the cultural diversity movement in American colleges and universities.

Before Reading

Gates argues elsewhere that we must reject "ethnic absolutism" of all kinds. What do you think he means by this phrase? Exactly how does a college or university—perhaps your institution—transcend this problem?

I recently asked the dean of a prestigious liberal arts college if his school   1
would ever have, as Berkeley has, a 70 percent non-white enrollment. "Never," he replied. "That would completely alter our identity as a center of the liberal arts."

The assumption that there is a deep connection between the shape of a   2
college's curriculum and the ethnic composition of its students reflects a disquieting trend in education. Political representation has been confused with the "representation" of various ethnic identities in the curriculum.

The cultural right wing, threatened by demographic changes and the   3
ensuing demands for curricular change, has retreated to intellectual pro-

tectionism, arguing for a great and inviolable "Western tradition," which contains the seeds, fruit and flowers of the very best thought or uttered in history. (Typically, Mortimer Adler has ventured that blacks "wrote no good books.") Meanwhile, the cultural left demands changes to accord with population shifts in gender and ethnicity. Both are wrongheaded.

I am just as concerned that so many of my colleagues feel that the ra- 4
tionale for a diverse curriculum depends on the latest Census Bureau report as I am that those opposed see pluralism as forestalling the possibility of a communal "American" identity. To them, the study of our diverse cultures must lead to "tribalism" and "fragmentation."

The cultural diversity movement arose partly because of the fragmen- 5
tation of society by ethnicity, class and gender. To make it the culprit for this fragmentation is to mistake effect for cause. A curriculum that reflects the achievement of the world's great cultures, not merely the West's, is not "politicized"; rather it situates the West as one of a community of civilizations. After all, culture is always a conversation among different voices.

To insist that we "master our own culture" before learning others—as 6
Arthur Schlesinger Jr. has proposed—only defers the vexed question: What gets to count as "our" culture? What has passed as "common culture" has been an Anglo-American regional culture, masking itself as universal. Significantly different cultures sought refuge underground.

Writing in 1903, W. E. B. Du Bois expressed his dream of a high culture 7
that would transcend the color line: "I sit with Shakespeare and he winces not." But the dream was not open to all. "Is this the life you grudge us," he concluded, "O knightly America?" For him, the humanities were a conduit into a republic of letters enabling escape from racism and ethnic chauvinism. Yet no one played a more crucial role than he in excavating the long buried heritage of Africans and African-Americans.

The fact of one's ethnicity, for any American of color, is never neutral: 8
One's public treatment, and public behavior, are shaped in large part by one's perceived ethnic identity, just as by one's gender. To demand that Americans shuck their cultural heritages and homogenize themselves into a "universal" WASP culture is to dream of an America in cultural white face, and that just won't do.

So it's only when we're free to explore the complexities of our hyphen- 9
ated culture that we can discover what a genuinely common American culture might actually look like.

Is multiculturalism un-American? Herman Melville didn't think so. As 10
he wrote: "We are not a narrow tribe, no. . . . We are not a nation, so much as a world." We're all ethnics; the challenge of transcending ethnic chauvinism is one we all face.

We've entrusted our schools with the fashioning and refashioning of a   11
democratic polity. That's why schooling has always been a matter of political judgment. But in a nation that has theorized itself as plural from its in-
ception, schools have a very special task.

Our society won't survive without the values of tolerance, and cultural   12
tolerance comes to nothing without cultural understanding. The challenge
facing America will be the shaping of a truly common public culture, one
responsive to the long-silenced cultures of color. If we relinquish the ideal
of America as a plural nation, we've abandoned the very experiment America represents. And that is too great a price to pay.

Thinking About the Essay

1. Gates poses a question in his title. How does he answer it? Where does he state his thesis?

2. The essay begins with an anecdote. How does it illuminate a key aspect of the problem Gates analyzes?

3. Gates makes several references to other writers—Mortimer Adler, Arthur Schlesinger Jr. (who appears in an earlier chapter), W. E. B. Du Bois, and Herman Melville. Who are these figures, and how do they provide a frame or context for Gates's argument?

4. How does the writer use comparison and contrast and causal analysis to advance his argument?

5. How does the concluding paragraph serve as a fitting end to the writer's argument?

Responding in Writing

6. Write a comparative essay in which you analyze the respective approaches to multiculturalism by Arthur Schlesinger Jr. (see Chapter 2) and Gates.

7. Gates speaks of "our hyphenated culture" (paragraph 9). Write a paper examining this phrase and applying it to your own campus.

8. Are you on "the cultural left" or "the cultural right" (to use Gates's words in paragraph 3), or somewhere in the middle? Write a personal essay responding to this question.

Networking

9. Form four working groups of classmates. Each group should investigate the ethnic composition of your campus, courses and programs designed to foster pluralism and multiculturalism, and the institution's policy on affirmative action. Draft a document in which you present your findings and conclusions concerning the state of the cultural diversity movement on your campus.

10. Search the World Wide Web for sites that promote what Gates terms "'universal' WASP culture" (paragraph 8). What sort of ideology do they promote? Where do they stand in terms of the culture wars? What impact do you think they have on the course of contemporary life in the United States?

Hygiene and Repression

OCTAVIO PAZ

Octavio Paz was born in 1914 near Mexico City, into a family that was influential in the political and cultural life of the nation. Paz published poetry and short stories as a teenager and came to the attention of the famous Chilean poet Pablo Neruda, who encouraged him to attend a congress of leftist writers in Spain. Subsequently, Paz was drawn into the Spanish Civil War, fighting against the Fascist forces of Francisco Franco. Paz moved continuously for decades—Los Angeles, New York, Mexico City, and France—and served in his country's diplomatic corps for twenty years. During this time he published one of his most famous works, *The Labyrinth of Solitude* (1950), a study of Mexican culture and identity. A prolific writer of both poetry and prose, the author of more than four dozen books, Paz was awarded the Nobel Prize for Literature in 1990. He died in April 1998. Paz was a professor of comparative literature at Harvard University from 1973 to 1980, and during this period he wrote the following essay, which appears in *Convergences Essays on Art and Literature* (1997). In this essay, Paz offers a fine comparative investigation of rival cultural cuisines.

Before Reading

How would you describe "American" food? How does it reflect American culture? And how would you describe Spanish or French or Indian cuisine and the ways it captures its respective culture?

Traditional American cooking is a cuisine without mystery: simple, 1 nourishing, scantily seasoned foods. No tricks: a carrot is a homely, honest carrot, a potato is not ashamed of its humble condition, and a steak is a big, bloody hunk of meat. This is a transubstantiation of the democratic virtues of the Founding Fathers: a plain meal, one dish following another like the sensible, unaffected sentences of a virtuous discourse. Like the conversation among those at table, the relation between substances and flavors is direct: sauces that mask tastes, garnishes that entice the eye, condiments that confuse the taste buds are taboo. The separation of one food from another is analogous to the reserve that characterizes the relations between sexes, races, and classes. In our countries food is communion, not only between those together at table but between ingredients; Yankee food, impregnated with Puritanism, is based on exclusions. The maniacal preoccupation with the purity and origin of food products has its counterpart in racism and exclusivism. The American contradiction—a democratic universalism based on ethnic, cultural, religious, and sexual exclusions—is reflected in its cuisine. In this culinary tradition our fondness for dark, passionate stews such as moles, for thick and sumptuous red, green, and yellow sauces, would be scandalous, as would be the choice place at our table of *huitlacoche,* which not only is made from diseased young maize but is black in color. Likewise our love for hot peppers, ranging from parakeet green to ecclesiastical purple, and for ears of Indian corn, their grains varying from golden yellow to midnight blue. Colors as violent as their tastes. Americans adore fresh, delicate colors and flavors. Their cuisine is like watercolor painting or pastels.

American cooking shuns spices as it shuns the devil, but it wallows in   2
slews of cream and butter. Orgies of sugar. Complementary opposites: the almost apostolic simplicity and soberness of lunch, in stark contrast to the suspiciously innocent, pregenital pleasures of ice cream and milkshakes. Two poles: the glass of milk and the glass of whiskey. The first affirms the primacy of home and mother. The virtues of the glass of milk are twofold: it is a wholesome food and it takes us back to childhood. Fourier detested the family repast, the image of the family in civilized society, a tedious daily ceremony presided over by a tyrannical father and a phallic mother. What would he have said of the cult of the glass of milk? As for whiskey and gin, they are drinks for loners and introverts. For Fourier, Gastrosophy was the science of combining not only foods but guests at table: matching the variety of dishes is the variety of persons sharing the meal. Wines, spirits, and liqueurs are the complement of a meal, hence their object is to stimulate the relations and unions consolidated round a table. Unlike wine, pulque, champagne, beer, and vodka, neither whiskey nor gin accompanies meals. Nor are they apéritifs or digestifs. They are drinks that accentuate uncommunicativeness and unsociability. In a gastrosophic age they would not enjoy much of a reputation. The universal favor accorded them reveals the situation of our societies, ever wavering between promiscuous association and solitude.

Ambiguity and ambivalence are resources unknown to American cook-   3
ing. Here, as in so many other things, it is the diametrical opposite of the extremely delicate French cuisine, based on nuances, variations, and modulations—transitions from one substance to another, from one flavor to

another. In a sort of profane Eucharist, even a glass of water is transfigured into an erotic chalice:

> *Ta lèvre contre le cristal*
> *Gorgée à gorgée y compose*
> *Le souvenir pourpre et vital*
> *De la moins éphémère rose.**

It is the contrary as well of Mexican and Hindu cuisine, whose secret is the shock of tastes: cool and piquant, salt and sweet, hot and tart, pungent and delicate. Desire is the active agent, the secret producer of changes, whether it be the transition from one flavor to another or the contrast between several. In gastronomy as in the erotic, it's desire that sets substances, bodies, and sensations in motion; this is the power that rules their conjunction, commingling, and transmutation. A reasonable cuisine, in which each substance is what it is and in which both variations and contrasts are avoided, is a cuisine that has excluded desire.

Pleasure is a notion (a sensation) absent from traditional Yankee cuisine. Not pleasure but health, not correspondence between savors but the satisfaction of a need—these are its two values. One is physical and the other moral; both are associated with the idea of the body as work. Work in turn is a concept at once economic and spiritual: production and redemption. We are condemned to labor, and food restores the body after the pain and punishment of work. It is a real *reparation,* in both the physical and the moral sense. Through work the body pays its debt; by earning its physical sustenance, it also earns its spiritual recompense. Work redeems us and the sign of this redemption is food. An active sign in the spiritual economy of humanity, food restores the health of body and soul. If what we eat gives us physical and spiritual health, the exclusion of spices for moral and hygienic reasons is justified: they are the signs of desire, and they are difficult to digest.

Health is the condition of two activities of the body, work and sports. In the first, the body is an agent that produces and at the same time redeems; in the second, the sign changes: sports are a wasteful expenditure of energy. This is a contradiction in appearance only, since what we have here in reality is a system of communicating vessels. Sports are a physical expenditure that is precisely the contrary of what happens in sexual pleasure, since sports in the end become productive—an expenditure that produces health. Work in turn is an expenditure of energy that produces goods and thereby transforms biological life into social, economic, and moral life. There is, moreover, another connection between work and sports: both

*Your lip against the crystal/Sip by sip forms therein/The vital deep crimson memory/ Of the least ephemeral rose.—Stéphane Mallarmé, "Verre d'eau."

take place within a context of rivalry; both are competition and emulation. The two of them are forms of Fourier's "Cabalist" passion. In this sense, sports possess the rigor and gravity of work, and work possesses the gratuity and levity of sports. The play element of work is one of the few features of American society that might have earned Fourier's praise, though doubtless he would have been horrified at the commercialization of sports. The preeminence of work and sports, activities necessarily excluding sexual pleasure, has the same significance as the exclusion of spices in cuisine. If gastronomy and eroticism are unions and conjunctions of substances and tastes or of bodies and sensations, it is evident that neither has been a central preoccupation of American society—as ideas and social values, I repeat, not as more or less secret realities. In the American tradition the body is not a source of pleasure but of health and work, in the material and the moral sense.

The cult of health manifests itself as an "ethic of hygiene." I use the   6
word ethic because its prescriptions are at once physiological and moral. A despotic ethic: sexuality, work, sports, and even cuisine are its domains. Again, there is a dual concept: hygiene governs both the corporeal and the moral life. Following the precepts of hygiene means obeying not only rules concerning physiology but also ethical principles: temperance, moderation, reserve. The morality of separation gives rise to the rules of hygiene, just as the aesthetics of fusion inspires the combinations of gastronomy and erotics. In India I frequently witnessed the obsession of Americans with hygiene. Their dread of contagion seemed to know no bounds; anything and everything might be laden with germs: food, drink, objects, people, the very air. These preoccupations are the precise counterpart of the ritual preoccupations of Brahmans fearing contact with certain foods and impure things, not to mention people belonging to a caste different from their own. Many will say that the concerns of the American are justified, whereas those of the Brahman are superstitions. Everything depends on the point of view: for the Brahman the bacteria that the American fears are illusory, while the moral stains produced by contact with alien people are real. These stains are stigmas that isolate him: no member of his caste would dare touch him until he had performed long and complicated rites of purification. The fear of social isolation is no less intense than that of illness. The hygienic taboo of the American and the ritual taboo of the Brahman have a common basis: the concern for purity. This basis is religious even though, in the case of hygiene, it is masked by the authority of science.

In the last analysis, the cult of hygiene is merely another expression of   7
the principle underlying attitudes toward sports, work, cuisine, sex, and races. The other name of purity is separation. Although hygiene is a social

morality based explicitly on science, its unconscious root is religious. Nonetheless, the form in which it expresses itself, and the justifications for it, are rational. In American society, unlike in ours, science from the very beginning has occupied a privileged place in the system of beliefs and values. The quarrel between faith and reason never took on the intensity that it assumed among Hispanic peoples. Ever since their birth as a nation, Americans have been modern; for them it is natural to believe in science, whereas for us this belief implies a negation of our past. The prestige of science in American public opinion is such that even political disputes frequently take on the form of scientific polemics, just as in the Soviet Union they assume the guise of quarrels about Marxist orthodoxy. Two recent examples are the racial question and the feminist movement: are intellectual differences between races and sexes genetic in origin or a historico-cultural phenomenon?

The universality of science (or what passes for science) justifies the de-   8
velopment and imposition of collective patterns of normality. Obviating the necessity for direct coercion, the overlapping of science and Puritan morality permits the imposition of rules that condemn peculiarities, exceptions, and deviations in a manner no less categorical and implacable than religious anathemas. Against the excommunications of science, the individual has neither the religious recourse of abjuration nor the legal one of *habeas corpus*. Although they masquerade as hygiene and science, these patterns of normality have the same function in the realm of eroticism as "healthful" cuisine in the sphere of gastronomy: the extirpation or the separation of what is alien, different, ambiguous, impure. One and the same condemnation applies to blacks, Chicanos, sodomites, and spices.

Thinking About the Essay

1. Paz's title is intriguing—as challenging perhaps as the essay. How does the title capture the substance of the essay?

2. Explain Paz's argument. What is his claim? What are his warrants? What support does he present, and how is it organized?

3. The writer composes dense, relatively long paragraphs, filled with figurative language, various allusions (notably to Fourier), difficult words, and complex sentences. Take one paragraph and analyze it as completely as possible. Would you say that Paz is writing for a Harvard audience? What exactly is a Harvard audience?

4. Sexuality is a theme, or motif, that runs through this essay. Trace its development in the essay and explain its contribution to the selection.

5. Paz uses a variety of rhetorical strategies—notably comparison and contrast—to organize his essay. Identify these strategies and explain how they function.

Responding in Writing

6. Select your favorite cuisine, and in an analytical essay explain why you prefer it to all other cuisines.

7. Write an essay comparing any two cuisines. Be certain to link these two cuisines to the nations or cultures they illuminate.

8. Paz makes an implicit criticism of American food in his essay. Write an argumentative essay in which you agree or disagree with his thoughts on the subject.

Networking

9. In small groups, select just one dish—for example, pizza or tacos or hamburger—and discuss ways in which this food reflects its culture. Draw up a list of these cultural attributes, and present it to the class.

10. Go to Google or another search engine and find out more about Octavio Paz. Focus on his thoughts about politics and then, in class discussion, show how his political views are reflected in the tone of "Hygiene and Repression."

Besieged by "Friends"

HEATHER HAVRILESKY

> Heather Havrilesky is TV and entertainment correspondent for *Salon.com*. She attended Duke University before becoming an online journalist. With illustrator Terry Colon, she created the popular weekly cartoon *Filler* for *Suck.com*. Her writing has appeared in *New York* magazine, *Spin*, *The Washington Post*, and National Public Radio's *All Things Considered*. In the following essay, which appeared in *Salon.com* in September 2005, Havrilesky reviews a new documentary that investigates the reaction in the Middle East to Hollywood's depictions of the Arab world.

Before Reading

How do you respond to depictions of Americans and American culture that you see in foreign films and television?

It must be tough living in the Middle East, what with all the dust and the   1
camels and the angry terrorists running around, looking for stuff to blow up. I bet it's hard to get your coffee in the morning, with all those terrorists shouting that the line is too long, or threatening to level the joint be-

cause they specifically said "soy" or "no foam" and the little drummer boy behind the counter didn't hear them right the first time.

Despite the fact that most Arabs on the big screen have several sticks of dynamite packed into their BVDs, most of us aren't stupid enough to think that the Muslim world is filled with Wile E. Coyotes in robes. Still, when kids grow up watching "True Lies," "The Siege" and "Rules of Engagement," in which even a one-legged Yemeni girl totes a machine gun, it's not too hard to see how their perspectives get twisted beyond recognition. In his documentary "Hollywood in the Muslim World" Charles C. Stuart discovers a well of anger and frustration in the Middle East over American depictions of Arabs, anger that some believe stokes the flames of extremism.

As Stuart points out at the start of his film, by the year 2000, Arab television had grown into a half-billion dollar a year industry. With 100 satellite channels, Arab governments can no longer control the content of every broadcast. These days, people in Cairo, Egypt; Beirut, Lebanon; and Qatar are familiar with shows like "Friends," "Sex and the City" and "Will & Grace," as well as countless American movies. Two months before the war with Iraq began, Stuart visited the Middle East and talked with citizens in Egypt, Iraq, Lebanon and Qatar about the influence of Hollywood and American pop culture in the Middle East.

Many of those interviewed resented the pervasive influence of Hollywood, claiming that such "cultural pollution" is a threat to Muslim identity. One filmmaker in Beirut expressed regret at the way kids in Lebanon grow up with so many American influences. "I feel that Lebanon has lost part of its identity by imitating or having all the American things here. This winter I didn't go to any Starbucks café, I don't like Dunkin Donuts . . . But the marketing of all these things is done in such a way that it reaches the children. I mean, who goes to McDonald's here? The children. Because at the same time, you have a McDonald's, a ticket to see a Disney film and you have a gadget. It's a market."

When Stuart interviewed a bunch of kids about their favorite American movies, a 19-year-old man interrupted them, fearing that the filmmaker was exploiting the children. When Stuart asked for the young man's point of view, he angrily railed off a list of Hollywood's stereotypes. "Do you see any camels around here?" he asked.

Others Stuart interviewed saw the influx of American culture as part of a U.S. campaign to stereotype Arabs. "We know that there is a war, a war of propaganda, and a media war against the Arabs and the Muslims," said one network representative.

Whether or not they agreed with the assertion that American stereotypes are intentionally denigrating, many subjects feel certain that Americanization in the Muslim world is pushing some Arabs to embrace more extremist beliefs. Or, as professor Abdullah Schleifer of the American University in Cairo put it, "Radical fundamentalism is a reaction to radical Westernization or modernization."

As paranoid, oversensitive or wildly professorial as such remarks might   8
seem, consider how American stereotypes conveniently mirror our government's foreign policy at any given time. While mid-century movies about World War II seem laughably dated in their depiction of psychotically evil Japanese soldiers, the trauma of Pearl Harbor stoked paranoia and hatred toward Japan in such a way that prejudices were absolutely taken for granted as holding some grain of truth. Meanwhile, in early Hollywood movies like "The Sheik" and "Lawrence of Arabia," Arabs were depicted as exotic, wildly sexual beings. By the early '80s, with the Iran hostage crisis and rising turmoil in the Middle East, Hollywood's depictions of Arabs and Muslims became darker and more foreboding. Today, the trauma of Sept. 11 enables many to cast a blind eye on the way Hollywood perpetuates extreme prejudice against Arabs in America and in the Middle East.

Unfortunately, Stuart doesn't explore such points. As fascinating as it is   9
to meet the writers of the Arab sitcom "Shabab Online," which appears to be a badly blocked "Friends" with perpetually grinning actors, or to visit "The Friends Cafe," a coffee joint in Beirut modeled after "Central Perk," most of Stuart's interviews don't move past surface observations and he seems to touch on a wide range of subjects without delving too deep or pulling the threads together into a cohesive narrative.

Still, at a time when the "patriotic" view often simply means pervasive   10
xenophobia, it's valuable to witness the resentment and anger welling up from those who feel their cultural identity has been taken hostage by Hollywood. And we can hardly blame them—if we were forced to watch reruns of "Shabab Online" on every channel, we'd be angry, too.

Thinking About the Essay

1. What is the purpose of Havrilesky's ironic opening? Does she avoid sounding flippant? How does she control (or fail to control) her use of irony?

2. According to the writer, how have American stereotypes of foreign cultures changed in response to wars and other events in American history?

3. Why do you think the 19-year-old man interrupted the interview of the children (paragraph 5)? Why does Havrilesky mention this incident?

4. What is Havrilesky's major criticism of the documentary? Is the documentary itself the primary focus of the review, or is it more of a stimulus for the reviewer's own meditations on the issue?

5. How effective is Havrilesky's conclusion? In what ways does it relate to the thematic concerns of the opening paragraph?

Responding in Writing

6. In paragraph 8, Havrilesky characterizes theories about the Americanization of the Muslim world as "paranoid, oversensitive, or wildly professorial. . . ." Other authors included in this chapter have characterized reservations about cultural hegemony as "academic" or merely theoretical. Evaluate this stereotype in an essay. Do you think it is a fair characterization? What are the limitations and dangers of appealing to this stereotype?

7. Respond to the views expressed by the Beirut filmmaker and quoted in paragraph 4. Do you believe those who market American products target children, or is there another explanation for the way Middle Eastern youth respond to American culture?

8. Charles C. Stuart conducted his interviews two months before the war with Iraq began in 2003. How do you think those interviewed in the Middle East would respond differently to Stuart's questions if they were asked today? Speculate on their likely responses in a brief essay, and offer some explanation for the change of attitude.

Networking

9. In groups of three or four, make a list of popular stereotypes currently associated with America and Americans that have been transmitted by Hollywood to other parts of the world. Then discuss how these stereotypes have complicated your relations with people from other cultures. Share your stories with the rest of the class.

10. Go online and locate the program schedule for a Middle Eastern television satellite network. How much of the programming is American in origin? What programs (like "Shabab Online") appear to be a repackaging of an American program?

The Culture of Liberty

MARIO VARGAS LLOSA

Mario Vargas Llosa, born in Arequipa, Peru, in 1936, is a major figure in contemporary Latin American and world literature. An acclaimed novelist, playwright, critic, and essayist, Vargas Llosa was a self-imposed exile from his native land for three decades, living in Paris, London, and Barcelona. He received a Ph.D. degree from the University of Madrid in 1959. Returning to Peru, he ran for president in 1990; he had a big lead initially but lost in the end to Alberto Fujimori. In his writing, broadcasting, and frequent lecturing, Vargas Llosa has been a persistent critic of violence, tyranny, and all forms of political oppression. A Marxist in his youth, Vargas Llosa in recent years has been a strong supporter of democracy. "If you are a writer in a country like Peru," he told an interviewer, "you're a privileged person because you know how to read and write, you have an audience, and you are respected. It is a moral obligation of a writer in Latin America to be involved in civic activities." Today Vargas Llosa is a citizen of Spain. Among his many notable novels are *Aunt Julia and the Scriptwriter* (1982), *In Praise of the Stepmother* (1990), and *The Feast of the Goat* (2001). In the essay that follows, which appeared in the journal *Foreign Policy* in 2001, Vargas Llosa examines the relationship between local culture and globalization.

Before Reading

Do you think that it is too simplistic to say that local cultures around the world cannot survive the impact of globalization? Why or why not?

The most effective attacks against globalization are usually not those 1
related to economics. Instead, they are social, ethical, and, above all, cultural. These arguments surfaced amid the tumult of Seattle in 1999 and have resonated more recently in Davos, Bangkok, and Prague. They say this:

The disappearance of national borders and the establishment of a world 2
interconnected by markets will deal a deathblow to regional and national cultures and to the traditions, customs, myths, and mores that determine each country or region's cultural identity. Since most of the world is incapable of resisting the invasion of cultural products from developed countries—or, more to the point, from the superpower, the United States—that inevitably trails the great transnational corporations, North American culture will ultimately impose itself, standardizing the world and annihilating its rich flora of diverse cultures. In this manner, all other peoples, and not just the small and weak ones, will lose their identity, their soul, and will become no more than 21st-century colonies—zombies or caricatures modeled after the cultural norms of a new imperialism that, in addition to ruling over the planet with its capital, military might, and scientific knowledge, will impose on others its language and its ways of thinking, believing, enjoying, and dreaming.

This nightmare or negative utopia of a world that, thanks to globaliza-   3
tion, is losing its linguistic and cultural diversity and is being culturally appropriated by the United States, is not the exclusive domain of left-wing
politicians nostalgic for Marx, Mao, or Che Guevara. This delirium of persecution—spurred by hatred and rancor toward the North American giant—is also apparent in developed countries and nations of high culture
and is shared among political sectors of the left, center, and right.

The most notorious case is that of France, where we see frequent gov-   4
ernment campaigns in defense of a French "cultural identity" supposedly
threatened by globalization. A vast array of intellectuals and politicians is
alarmed by the possibility that the soil that produced Montaigne,
Descartes, Racine, and Baudelaire—and a country that was long the arbiter
of fashion in clothing, thought, art, dining, and in all domains of the
spirit—can be invaded by McDonald's, Pizza Hut, Kentucky Fried
Chicken, rock, rap, Hollywood movies, bluejeans, sneakers, and T-shirts.
This fear has resulted, for instance, in massive French subsidies for the local film industry and demands for quotas requiring theaters to show a certain number of national films and limit the importation of movies from the
United States. This fear is also the reason why municipalities issued severe
directives penalizing with high fines any publicity announcements that littered with Anglicisms the language of Molière. (Although, judging by the
view of a pedestrian on the streets of Paris, the directives were not quite respected.) This is the reason why José Bové, the farmer-cum-crusader
against *la malbouffe* (lousy food), has become no less than a popular hero
in France. And with his recent sentencing to three months in prison, his
popularity has likely increased.

Even though I believe this cultural argument against globalization is un-   5
acceptable, we should recognize that deep within it lies an unquestionable
truth. This century, the world in which we will live will be less picturesque
and imbued with less local color than the one we left behind. The festivals,
attire, customs, ceremonies, rites, and beliefs that in the past gave humanity its folkloric and ethnological variety are progressively disappearing or
confining themselves to minority sectors, while the bulk of society aban-
dons them and adopts others more suited to the reality of our time. All
countries of the earth experience this process, some more quickly than others, but it is not due to globalization. Rather, it is due to modernization, of
which the former is effect, not cause. It is possible to lament, certainly, that
this process occurs, and to feel nostalgia for the eclipse of the past ways of
life that, particularly from our comfortable vantage point of the present, seem
full of amusement, originality, and color. But this process is unavoidable.

Totalitarian regimes in countries like Cuba or North Korea, fearful that any opening will destroy them, close themselves off and issue all types of prohibitions and censures against modernity. But even they are unable to impede modernity's slow infiltration and its gradual undermining of their so-called cultural identity. In theory, perhaps, a country could keep this identity, but only if—like certain remote tribes in Africa or the Amazon—it decides to live in total isolation, cutting off all exchange with other nations and practicing self-sufficiency. A cultural identity preserved in this form would take that society back to prehistoric standards of living.

It is true that modernization makes many forms of traditional life disappear. But at the same time, it opens opportunities and constitutes an important step forward for a society as a whole. That is why, when given the option to choose freely, peoples, sometimes counter to what their leaders or intellectual traditionalists would like, opt for modernization without the slightest ambiguity.   6

The allegations against globalization and in favor of cultural identity reveal a static conception of culture that has no historical basis. Which cultures have ever remained identical and unchanged over time? To find them we must search among the small and primitive magical-religious communities that live in caves, worship thunder and beasts, and, due to their primitivism, are increasingly vulnerable to exploitation and extermination. All other cultures, in particular those that have the right to be called modern and alive, have evolved to the point that they are but a remote reflection of what they were just two or three generations before. This evolution is easily apparent in countries like France, Spain, and England, where the changes over the last half century have been so spectacular and profound that a Marcel Proust, a Federico García Lorca, or a Virginia Woolf would hardly recognize today the societies in which they were born—the societies their works helped so much to renew.   7

The notion of "cultural identity" is dangerous. From a social point of view, it represents merely a doubtful, artificial concept, but from a political perspective it threatens humanity's most precious achievement: freedom. I do not deny that people who speak the same language, were born and live in the same territory, face the same problems, and practice the same religions and customs have common characteristics. But that collective denominator can never fully define each one of them, and it only abolishes or relegates to a disdainful secondary plane the sum of unique attributes and traits that differentiates one member of the group from the others. The concept of identity, when not employed on an exclusively individual scale, is inherently reductionist and dehumanizing, a collectivist and ideological   8 abstraction of all that is original and creative in the human being, of all that has not been imposed by inheritance, geography, or social pressure. Rather, true identity springs from the capacity of human beings to resist these influences and counter them with free acts of their own invention.

The notion of "collective identity" is an ideological fiction and the   9 foundation of nationalism. For many ethnologists and anthropologists, collective identity does not represent the truth even among the most archaic communities. Common practices and customs may be crucial to the defense of a group, but the margin of initiative and creativity among its members to emancipate themselves from the group is invariably large, and individual differences prevail over collective traits when individuals are examined on their own terms, and not as mere peripheral elements of collectivity. Globalization extends radically to all citizens of this planet the possibility to construct their individual cultural identities through voluntary action, according to their preferences and intimate motivations. Now, citizens are not always obligated, as in the past and in many places in the present, to respect an identity that traps them in a concentration camp from which there is no escape—the identity that is imposed on them through the language, nation, church, and customs of the place where they were born. In this sense, globalization must be welcomed because it notably expands the horizons of individual liberty.

One Continent's Two Histories

Perhaps Latin America is the best example of the artifice and absurdity of   10 trying to establish collective identities. What might be Latin America's cultural identity? What would be included in a coherent collection of beliefs, customs, traditions, practices, and mythologies that endows this region with a singular personality, unique and nontransferable? Our history has been forged in intellectual polemics—some ferocious—seeking to answer this question. The most celebrated was the one that, beginning in the early 20th century, pitted Hispanists against indigenists and reverberated across the continent.

For Hispanists like José de la Riva-Agüero, Victor Andrés Belaúnde,   11 and Francisco Garcia Calderón, Latin America was born when, thanks to the Discovery and the Conquest, it joined with the Spanish and Portuguese languages and, adopting Christianity, came to form part of Western civilization. Hispanists did not belittle pre-Hispanic cultures, but considered that these constituted but a layer—and not the primary one—of the social and historical reality that only completed its nature and personality thanks to the vivifying influence of the West.

Indigenists, on the other hand, rejected with moral indignation the al-   12
leged benefits that Europeans brought to Latin America. For them, our
identity finds its roots and its soul in pre-Hispanic cultures and civilizations, whose development and modernization were brutally stunted by violence and subjected to censure, repression, and marginalization not only
during the three colonial centuries but also later, after the advent of re-
publicanism. According to indigenist thinkers, the authentic "American
expression" (to use the title of a book by José Lezama Lima) resides in all
the cultural manifestations—from the native languages to the beliefs, rites,
arts, and popular mores—that resisted Western cultural oppression and en-
dured to our days. A distinguished historian of this vein, the Peruvian Luis
E. Valcárcel, even affirmed that the churches, convents, and other monuments of colonial architecture should be burned since they represented the
"Anti-Peru." They were impostors, a negation of the pristine American
identity that could only be of exclusively indigenous roots. And one of
Latin America's most original novelists, José María Arguedas, narrated, in
stories of great delicacy and vibrant moral protest, the epic of the survival
of the Quechua culture in the Andean world, despite the suffocating and
distortionary presence of the West.

Hispanicism and indigenism produced excellent historical essays and   13
highly creative works of fiction, but, judged from our current perspective,
both doctrines seem equally sectarian, reductionist, and false. Neither is capable of fitting the expansive diversity of Latin America into its ideological straitjacket, and both smack of racism. Who would dare claim in our
day that only what is "Hispanic" or "Indian" legitimately represents Latin
America?

Nevertheless, efforts to forge and isolate our distinct "cultural identity"   14
continue today with a political and intellectual zeal deserving of worthier
causes. Seeking to impose a cultural identity on a people is equivalent to
locking them in a prison and denying them the most precious of liberties—
that of choosing what, how, and who they want to be. Latin America has
not one but many cultural identities; no one of them can claim more legitimacy or purity than the others. Of course, Latin America embodies the
pre-Hispanic world and its cultures, which, in Mexico, Guatemala, and the
Andean countries, still exert so much social force. But Latin America is also
a vast swarm of Spanish and Portuguese speakers with a tradition of five
centuries behind them whose presence and actions have been decisive in
giving the continent its current features. And is not Latin America also
something of Africa, which arrived on our shores together with Europe?
Has not the African presence indelibly marked our skin, our music, our
idiosyncrasies, our society? The cultural, ethnic, and social ingredients that

make up Latin America link us to almost all the regions and cultures of the world. We have so many cultural identities that it is like not having one at all. This reality is, contrary to what nationalists believe, our greatest treasure. It is also an excellent credential that enables us to feel like full-fledged citizens in our globalized world.

Local Voices, Global Reach

The fear of Americanization of the planet is more ideological paranoia than 15 reality. There is no doubt, of course, that with globalization, English has become the general language of our time, as was Latin in the Middle Ages. And it will continue its ascent, since it is an indispensable instrument for international transactions and communication. But does this mean that English necessarily develops at the expense of the other great languages? Absolutely not. In fact, the opposite is true. The vanishing of borders and an increasingly interdependent world have created incentives for new generations to learn and assimilate to other cultures, not merely as a hobby but also out of necessity, since the ability to speak several languages and navigate comfortably in different cultures has become crucial for professional success. Consider the case of Spanish. Half a century ago, Spanish speakers were an inward-looking community; we projected ourselves in only very limited ways beyond our traditional linguistic confines. Today, Spanish is dynamic and thriving, gaining beachheads or even vast landholdings on all five continents. The fact that there are some 25 to 30 million Spanish speakers in the United States today explains why the two recent U.S. presidential candidates, Texas Governor George W. Bush and Vice President Al Gore, campaigned not only in English but also in Spanish.

How many millions of young men and women around the globe have 16 responded to the challenges of globalization by learning Japanese, German, Mandarin, Cantonese, Russian, or French? Fortunately, this tendency will only increase in the coming years. That is why the best defense of our own cultures and languages is to promote them vigorously throughout this new world, not to persist in the naive pretense of vaccinating them against the menace of English. Those who propose such remedies speak much about culture, but they tend to be ignorant people who mask their true vocation: nationalism. And if there is anything at odds with the universalist propensities of culture, it is the parochial, exclusionary, and confused vision that nationalist perspectives try to impose on cultural life. The most admirable lesson that cultures teach us is that they need not be protected by bureaucrats or commissars, or confined behind iron bars, or isolated by customs services in order to remain alive and exuberant; to the contrary, such efforts would only wither or even trivialize *culture*. Cultures must live freely, constantly jousting with different cultures. This renovates and renews them, allowing them to evolve and adapt to the continuous flow of life. In antiquity, Latin did not kill Greek; to the contrary, the artistic originality and intellectual depth of Hellenic culture permeated Roman civilization and, through it, the poems of Homer and the philosophies of Plato and Aristotle reached the entire world. Globalization will not make local cultures disappear; in a framework of worldwide openness, all that is valuable and worthy of survival in local cultures will find fertile ground in which to bloom.

This is happening in Europe, everywhere. Especially noteworthy is   17
Spain, where regional cultures are reemerging with special vigor. During the dictatorship of General Francisco Franco, regional cultures were repressed and condemned to a clandestine existence. But with the return of democracy, Spain's rich cultural diversity was unleashed and allowed to develop freely. In the country's regime of autonomies, local cultures have had an extraordinary boom, particularly in Catalonia, Galicia, and the Basque country, but also in the rest of Spain. Of course, we must not confuse this regional cultural rebirth, which is positive and enriching, with the phenomenon of nationalism, which poses serious threats to the culture of liberty.

In his celebrated 1948 essay "Notes Towards the Definition of Cul-   18
ture," T. S. Eliot predicted that in the future, humanity would experience a renaissance of local and regional cultures. At the time, his prophecy seemed quite daring. However, globalization will likely make it a reality in the 21st century, and we must be happy about this. A rebirth of small, local cultures will give back to humanity that rich multiplicity of behavior and expressions that the nation-state annihilated in order to create so-called national cultural identities toward the end of the 18th, and particularly in the 19th, century. (This fact is easily forgotten, or we attempt to forget it because of its grave moral connotations.) National cultures were often forged in blood and fire, prohibiting the teaching or publication of vernacular languages or the practice of religions and customs that dissented from those the nation-state considered ideal. In this way, in many countries of the world, the nation-state forcibly imposed a dominant culture upon local ones that were repressed and abolished from official life. But, contrary to the warnings of those who fear globalization, it is not easy to completely erase cultures—however small they may be—if behind them is a rich tradition and people who practice them, even if in secret. And today, thanks to the weakening of the nation-state, we are seeing forgotten, marginalized, and silenced local cultures reemerging and displaying dynamic signs of life in the great concept of this globalized planet.

Thinking About the Essay

1. Is this essay about *culture* or *globalization*—or both? How do you know? Does the title provide a hint, or is it incomplete or misleading? What is Vargas Llosa's thesis, and how does this thesis provide an answer to the first question?

2. Vargas Llosa divides his essay into three sections. What is the focus of each section? How do the parts interrelate?

3. What types of illustration does he use to structure his definition and analysis of culture? Identify some of these.

4. This essay involves considerable causal analysis and comparison and contrast. What causal and comparative patterns of development can you detect? What assumptions does the writer make about the reader's ability to follow these patterns of thought and organization? In terms of audience analysis, how does his overall style of writing presuppose a highly literate readership?

5. Select three paragraphs that capture Vargas Llosa's optimistic tone. Does he deal adequately with the pessimistic side of his subject? Why or why not?

Responding in Writing

6. Vargas Llosa writes: "Cultures must live freely, constantly jousting with different cultures" (paragraph 16). Write a paper responding to Vargas Llosa's statement. Provide sufficient reasons and illustrations to support your position.

7. Define what you mean by *culture* and how this relates to your own family's cultural origins and attitudes.

8. Write an essay in which you tackle the problem of the relationship between culture and globalization. Feel free to consult the essays in the previous chapter for ideas.

Networking

9. In small groups, develop a formal outline of Vargas Llosa's relatively complex essay. Put your collective product on the chalkboard or on a transparency so that you can evaluate your outline against the results of the other class groups.

10. Search the Internet for reviews of Vargas Llosa's recent novel, *The Feast of the Goat*. After reading these reviews, decide whether you would like to read the novel, and explain your response to other members of the class.

On Seeing England for the First Time

JAMAICA KINCAID

Jamaica Kincaid was born Elaine Potter Richardson in 1949 in St. John's, Antigua, in the West Indies. After emigrating to the United States, she became a staff writer for *The New Yorker,* with her short stories also appearing in *Rolling Stone,* the *Paris Review,* and elsewhere. She has taught at Harvard University and other colleges while compiling a distinguished body of fiction and nonfiction, notably *Annie John* (1958), *A Small Place* (1988), *Lucy* (1991), *The Autobiography of My Mother* (1996), and *Among Flowers: A Walk in the Himalaya* (2005). The stories collected in *At the Bottom of the River* (1984) won the Morton Dauwen Zabel Award from the American Academy and Institute of Arts and Letters. Although Kincaid has turned recently in her writing to the relatively peaceful world of gardening, the typical tone of her fiction and essays is severely critical of the social, cultural, and political consequences of colonialism and immigration. In "On Seeing England for the First Time," published in *Transition* in 1991, Kincaid thinks about the time when Great Britain was associated with the forces of globalization throughout the world.

Before Reading

It was once said that the sun never sets on the British Empire. What does this statement mean? Could the same be said of the United States today?

When I saw England for the first time, I was a child in school sitting at   1
a desk. The England I was looking at was laid out on a map gently, beautifully, delicately, a very special jewel; it lay on a bed of sky blue—the background of the map—its yellow form mysterious, because though it looked like a leg of mutton, it could not really look like anything so familiar as a leg of mutton because it was England—with shadings of pink and green, unlike any shadings of pink and green I had seen before, squiggly veins of red running in every direction. England was a special jewel all right, and only special people got to wear it. The people who got to wear England were English people. They wore it well and they wore it everywhere: in jungles, in deserts, on plains, on top of the highest mountains, on

all the oceans, on all the seas, in places where they were not welcome, in places they should not have been. When my teacher had pinned this map up on the blackboard, she said, "This is England"—and she said it with authority, seriousness, and adoration, and we all sat up. It was as if she had said, "This is Jerusalem, the place you will go to when you die but only if you have been good." We understood then—we were meant to understand then—that England was to be our source of myth and the source from which we got our sense of reality, our sense of what was meaningful, our sense of what was meaningless—and much about our own lives and much about the very idea of us headed that last list.

At the time I was a child sitting at my desk seeing England for the first time, I was already very familiar with the greatness of it. Each morning before I left for school, I ate a breakfast of half a grapefruit, an egg, bread and butter and a slice of cheese, and a cup of cocoa; or half a grapefruit, a bowl of oat porridge, bread and butter and a slice of cheese, and a cup of cocoa. The can of cocoa was often left on the table in front of me. It had written on it the name of the company, the year the company was established, and the words "Made in England." Those words, "Made in England," were written on the box the oats came in too. They would also have been written on the box the shoes I was wearing came in; a bolt of gray linen cloth lying on the shelf of a store from which my mother had bought three yards to make the uniform that I was wearing had written along its edge those three words. The shoes I wore were made in England; so were my socks and cotton undergarments and the satin ribbons I wore tied at the end of two plaits of my hair. My father, who might have sat next to me at breakfast, was a carpenter and cabinet maker. The shoes he wore to work would have been made in England, as were his khaki shirt and trousers, his underpants and undershirt, his socks and brown felt hat. Felt was not the proper material from which a hat that was expected to provide shade from the hot sun should be made, but my father must have seen and admired a picture of an Englishman wearing such a hat in England, and this picture that he saw must have been so compelling that it caused him to wear the wrong hat for a hot climate most of his long life. And this hat—a brown felt hat—became so central to his character that it was the first thing he put on in the morning as he stepped out of bed and the last thing he took off before he stepped back into bed at night. As we sat at breakfast a car might go by. The car, a Hillman or a Zephyr, was made in England. The very idea of the meal itself, breakfast, and its substantial quality and quantity was an idea from England; we somehow knew that in England they began the day with this meal called breakfast and a proper breakfast was a big breakfast. No one I knew liked eating so much food so early in the day; it made us

2

feel sleepy, tired. But this breakfast business was Made in England like almost everything else that surrounded us, the exceptions being the sea, the sky, and the air we breathed.

At the time I saw this map—seeing England for the first time—I did not 3 say to myself, "Ah, so that's what it looks like," because there was no longing in me to put a shape to those three words that ran through every part of my life, no matter how small; for me to have had such a longing would have meant that I lived in a certain atmosphere, an atmosphere in which those three words were felt as a burden. But I did not live in such an atmosphere. My father's brown felt hat would develop a hole in its crown, the lining would separate from the hat itself, and six weeks before he thought that he could not be seen wearing it—he was a very vain man—he would order another hat from England. And my mother taught me to eat my food in the English way: the knife in the right hand, the fork in the left, my elbows held still close to my side, the food carefully balanced on my fork and then brought up to my mouth. When I had finally mastered it, I overheard her saying to a friend, "Did you see how nicely she can eat?" But I knew then that I enjoyed my food more when I ate it with my bare hands, and I continued to do so when she wasn't looking. And when my teacher showed us the map, she asked us to study it carefully, because no test we would ever take would be complete without this statement: "Draw a map of England."

I did not know then that the statement "Draw a map of England" was 4 something far worse than a declaration of war, for in fact a flat-out declaration of war would have put me on alert, and again in fact, there was no need for war—I had long ago been conquered. I did not know then that this statement was part of a process that would result in my erasure, not my physical erasure, but my erasure all the same. I did not know then that this statement was meant to make me feel in awe and small whenever I heard the word "England": awe at its existence, small because I was not from it. I did not know very much of anything then—certainly not what a blessing it was that I was unable to draw a map of England correctly.

After that there were many times of seeing England for the first time. I 5 saw England in history. I knew the names of all the kings of England. I knew the names of their children, their wives, their disappointments, their triumphs, the names of people who betrayed them; I knew the dates on which they were born and the dates they died. I knew their conquests and was made to feel glad if I figured in them; I knew their defeats. I knew the details of the year 1066 (the Battle of Hastings, the end of the reign of the Anglo-Saxon kings) before I knew the details of the year 1832 (the year slavery was abolished). It wasn't as bad as I make it sound now; it was worse. I did like so much hearing again and again how Alfred the Great, traveling in disguise, had been left to watch cakes, and because he wasn't used to this the cakes got burned, and Alfred burned his hands pulling them out of the fire, and the woman who had left him to watch the cakes screamed at him. I loved King Alfred. My grandfather was named after him; his son, my uncle, was named after King Alfred; my brother is named after King Alfred. And so there are three people in my family named after a man they have never met, a man who died over ten centuries ago. The first view I got of England then was not unlike the first view received by the person who named my grandfather.

This view, though—the naming of the kings, their deeds, their disap-   6
pointments—was the vivid view, the forceful view. There were other views, subtler ones, softer, almost not there—but these were the ones that made the most lasting impression on me, these were the ones that made me really feel like nothing. "When morning touched the sky" was one phrase, for no morning touched the sky where I lived. The mornings where I lived came on abruptly, with a shock of heat and loud noises. "Evening approaches" was another, but the evenings where I lived did not approach; in fact, I had no evening—I had night and I had day and they came and went in a mechanical way: on, off; on, off. And then there were gentle mountains and low blue skies and moors over which people took walks for nothing but pleasure, when where I lived a walk was an act of labor, a burden, something only death or the automobile could relieve. And there were things that a small turn of a head could convey—entire worlds, whole lives would depend on this thing, a certain turn of a head. Everyday life could be quite tiring, more tiring than anything I was told not to do. I was told not to gossip, but they did that all the time. And they ate so much food, violating another of those rules they taught me: do not indulge in gluttony. And the foods they ate actually: if only sometime I could eat cold cuts after theater, cold cuts of lamb and mint sauce, and Yorkshire pudding and scones, and clotted cream, and sausages that came from up-country (imagine, "up-country"). And having troubling thoughts at twilight, a good time to have troubling thoughts, apparently; and servants who stole and left in the middle of a crisis, who were born with a limp or some other kind of deformity, not nourished properly in their mother's womb (that last part I figured out for myself; the point was, oh to have an untrustworthy servant); and wonderful cobbled streets onto which solid front doors opened; and people whose eyes were blue and who had fair skins and who smelled only of lavender, or sometimes sweet pea or primrose. And those flowers with those names: delphiniums, foxgloves, tulips, daffodils, floribunda, peonies; in bloom, a striking display, being cut and placed in large glass bowls, crystal, decorating rooms so large twenty

families the size of mine could fit in comfortably but used only for passing through. And the weather was so remarkable because the rain fell gently always, only occasionally in deep gusts, and it colored the air various shades of gray, each an appealing shade for a dress to be worn when a portrait was being painted; and when it rained at twilight, wonderful things happened: people bumped into each other unexpectedly and that would lead to all sorts of turns of events—a plot, the mere weather caused plots. I saw that people rushed: they rushed to catch trains, they rushed toward each other and away from each other; they rushed and rushed and rushed. That word: rushed! I did not know what it was to do that. It was too hot to do that, and so I came to envy people who would rush, even though it had no meaning to me to do such a thing. But there they are again. They loved their children; their children were sent to their own rooms as a punishment, rooms larger than my entire house. They were special, everything about them said so, even their clothes; their clothes rustled, swished, soothed. The world was theirs, not mine; everything told me so.

If now as I speak of all this I give the impression of someone on the out-   7
side looking in, nose pressed up against a glass window, that is wrong. My nose was pressed up against a glass window all right, but there was an iron vise at the back of my neck forcing my head to stay in place. To avert my gaze was to fall back into something from which I had been rescued, a hole filled with nothing, and that was the word for everything about me, nothing. The reality of my life was conquests, subjugation, humiliation, enforced amnesia. I was forced to forget. Just for instance, this: I lived in a part of St. John's, Antigua, called Ovals. Ovals was made up of five streets, each of them named after a famous English seaman—to be quite frank, an officially sanctioned criminal: Rodney Street (after George Rodney), Nelson Street (after Horatio Nelson), Drake Street (after Francis Drake), Hood Street, and Hawkins Street (after John Hawkins). But John Hawkins was knighted after a trip he made to Africa, opening up a new trade, the slave trade. He was then entitled to wear as his crest a Negro bound with a cord. Every single person living on Hawkins Street was descended from a slave. John Hawkins's ship, the one in which he transported the people he had bought and kidnapped, was called *The Jesus*. He later became the treasurer of the Royal Navy and rear admiral.

Again, the reality of my life, the life I led at the time I was being shown   8
these views of England for the first time, for the second time, for the one-hundred-millionth time, was this: the sun shone with what sometimes seemed to be a deliberate cruelty; we must have done something to deserve that. My dresses did not rustle in the evening air as I strolled to the theater (I had no evening, I had no theater; my dresses were made of a cheap cot-

ton, the weave of which would give way after not too many washings). I got up in the morning, I did my chores (fetched water from the public pipe for my mother, swept the yard), I washed myself, I went to a woman to have my hair combed freshly every day (because before we were allowed into our classroom our teachers would inspect us, and children who had not bathed that day, or had dirt under their fingernails, or whose hair had not been combed anew that day, might not be allowed to attend class). I ate that breakfast. I walked to school. At school we gathered in an auditorium and sang a hymn, "All Things Bright and Beautiful," and looking down on us as we sang were portraits of the Queen of England and her husband; they wore jewels and medals and they smiled. I was a Brownie. At each meeting we would form a little group around a flagpole, and after raising the Union Jack, we would say, "I promise to do my best, to do my duty to God and the Queen, to help other people every day and obey the scouts' law."

Who were these people and why had I never seen them, I mean really 9 seen them, in the place where they lived? I had never been to England. No one I knew had ever been to England, or I should say, no one I knew had ever been and returned to tell me about it. All the people I knew who had gone to England had stayed there. Sometimes they left behind them their small children, never to see them again. England! I had seen England's representatives. I had seen the governor general at the public grounds at a ceremony celebrating the Queen's birthday. I had seen an old princess and I had seen a young princess. They had both been extremely not beautiful, but who of us would have told them that? I had never seen England, really seen it, I had only met a representative, seen a picture, read books, memorized its history. I had never set foot, my own foot, in it.

The space between the idea of something and its reality is always wide 10 and deep and dark. The longer they are kept apart—idea of thing, reality of thing—the wider the width, the deeper the depth, the thicker and darker the darkness. This space starts out empty, there is nothing in it, but it rapidly becomes filled up with obsession or desire or hatred or love—sometimes all of these things, sometimes some of these things, sometimes only one of these things. The existence of the world as I came to know it was a result of this: idea of thing over here, reality of thing way, way over there. There was Christopher Columbus, an unlikable man, an unpleasant man, a liar (and so, of course, a thief) surrounded by maps and schemes and plans, and there was the reality on the other side of that width, that depth, that darkness. He became obsessed, he became filled with desire, the hatred came later, love was never a part of it. Eventually, his idea met the longed-for reality. That the idea of something and its reality are often two completely different things is something no one ever remembers; and so when they meet and find that they are not compatible, the weaker of the two, idea or reality, dies. That idea Christopher Columbus had was more powerful than the reality he met, and so the reality he met died.

And so finally, when I was a grown-up woman, the mother of two children, the wife of someone, a person who resides in a powerful country that takes up more than its fair share of a continent, the owner of a house with many rooms in it and of two automobiles, with the desire and will (which I very much act upon) to take from the world more than I give back to it, more than I deserve, more than I need, finally then, I saw England, the real England, not a picture, not a painting, not through a story in a book, but England, for the first time. In me, the space between the idea of it and its reality had become filled with hatred, and so when at last I saw it I wanted to take it into my hands and tear it into little pieces and then crumble it up as if it were clay, child's clay. That was impossible, and so I could only indulge in not-favorable opinions.

There were monuments everywhere; they commemorated victories, battles fought between them and the people who lived across the sea from them, all vile people, fought over which of them would have dominion over the people who looked like me. The monuments were useless to them now, people sat on them and ate their lunch. They were like markers on an old useless trail, like a piece of old string tied to a finger to jog the memory, like old decoration in an old house, dirty, useless, in the way. Their skins were so pale, it made them look so fragile, so weak, so ugly. What if I had the power to simply banish them from their land, send boat after boatload of them on a voyage that in fact had no destination, force them to live in a place where the sun's presence was a constant? This would rid them of their pale complexion and make them look more like me, make them look more like the people I love and treasure and hold dear, and more like the people who occupy the near and far reaches of my imagination, my history, my geography, and reduce them and everything they have ever known to figurines as evidence that I was in divine favor, what if all this was in my power? Could I resist it? No one ever has.

And they were rude, they were rude to each other. They didn't like each other very much. They didn't like each other in the way they didn't like me, and it occurred to me that their dislike for me was one of the few things they agreed on.

I was on a train in England with a friend, an English woman. Before we were in England she liked me very much. In England she didn't like me at all. She didn't like the claim I said I had on England, she didn't like the views I had of England. I didn't like England, she didn't like England, but she didn't like me not liking it too. She said, "I want to show you my England, I want to show you the England that I know and love." I had told her many times before that I knew England and I didn't want to love it anyway. She no longer lived in England; it was her own country, but it had not been kind to her, so she left. On the train, the conductor was rude to her; she asked something, and he responded in a rude way. She became ashamed. She was ashamed at the way he treated her; she was ashamed at the way he behaved. "This is the new England," she said. But I liked the conductor being rude; his behavior seemed quite appropriate. Earlier this had happened: we had gone to a store to buy a shirt for my husband; it was meant to be a special present, a special shirt to wear on special occasions. This was a store where the Prince of Wales has his shirts made, but the shirts sold in this store are beautiful all the same. I found a shirt I thought my husband would like and I wanted to buy him a tie to go with it. When I couldn't decide which one to choose, the salesman showed me a new set. He was very pleased with these, he said, because they bore the crest of the Prince of Wales, and the Prince of Wales had never allowed his crest to decorate an article of clothing before. There was something in the way he said it; his tone was slavish, reverential, awed. It made me feel angry; I wanted to hit him. I didn't do that. I said, my husband and I hate princes, my husband would never wear anything that had a prince's anything on it. My friend stiffened. The salesman stiffened. They both drew themselves in, away from me. My friend told me that the prince was a symbol of her Englishness, and I could see that I had caused offense. I looked at her. She was an English person, the sort of English person I used to know at home, the sort who was nobody in England but somebody when they came to live among the people like me. There were many people I could have seen England with; that I was seeing it with this particular person, a person who reminded me of the people who showed me England long ago as I sat in church or at my desk, made me feel silent and afraid, for I wondered if, all these years of our friendship, I had had a friend or had been in the thrall of a racial memory.

I went to Bath—we, my friend and I, did this, but though we were together, I was no longer with her. The landscape was almost as familiar as my own hand, but I had never been in this place before, so how could that be again? And the streets of Bath were familiar, too, but I had never walked on them before. It was all those years of reading, starting with Roman Britain. Why did I have to know about Roman Britain? It was of no real use to me, a person living on a hot, drought-ridden island, and it is of no use to me now, and yet my head is filled with this nonsense, Roman Britain.

In Bath, I drank tea in a room I had read about in a novel written in the eighteenth century. In this very same room, young women wearing those dresses that rustled and so on danced and flirted and sometimes disgraced themselves with young men, soldiers, sailors, who were on their way to Bristol or someplace like that, so many places like that where so many adventures, the outcome of which was not good for me, began. Bristol, England. A sentence that began "That night the ship sailed from Bristol, England" would end not so good for me. And then I was driving through the countryside in an English motorcar, on narrow winding roads, and they were so familiar, though I had never been on them before; and through little villages the names of which I somehow knew so well though I had never been there before. And the countryside did have all those hedges and hedges, fields hedged in. I was marveling at all the toil of it, the planting of the hedges to begin with and then the care of it, all that clipping, year after year of clipping, and I wondered at the lives of the people who would have to do this, because wherever I see and feel the hands that hold up the world, I see and feel myself and all the people who look like me. And I said, "Those hedges" and my friend said that someone, a woman named Mrs. Rothchild, worried that the hedges weren't being taken care of properly; the farmers couldn't afford or find the help to keep up the hedges, and often they replaced them with wire fencing. I might have said to that, well if Mrs. Rothchild doesn't like the wire fencing, why doesn't she take care of the hedges herself, but I didn't. And then in those fields that were now hemmed in by wire fencing that a privileged woman didn't like was planted a vile yellow flowering bush that produced an oil, and my friend said that Mrs. Rothchild didn't like this either; it ruined the English countryside, it ruined the traditional look of the English countryside.

It was not at that moment that I wished every sentence, everything I 16
knew, that began with England would end with "and then it all died; we don't know how, it just all died." At that moment, I was thinking, who are these people who forced me to think of them all the time, who forced me to think that the world I knew was incomplete, or without substance, or did not measure up because it was not England; that I was incomplete, or without substance, and did not measure up because I was not English. Who were these people? The person sitting next to me couldn't give me a clue; no one person could. In any case, if I had said to her, I find England ugly, I hate England; the weather is like a jail sentence, the English are a very ugly people, the food in England is like a jail sentence, the hair of English people is so straight, so dead looking, the English have an unbearable smell so different from the smell of people I know, real people of course, she would have said that I was a person full of prejudice. Apart from the fact that it

is I—that is, the people who look like me—who made her aware of the unpleasantness of such a thing, the idea of such a thing, prejudice, she would have been only partly right, sort of right: I may be capable of prejudice, but my prejudices have no weight to them, my prejudices have no force behind them, my prejudices remain opinions, my prejudices remain my personal opinion. And a great feeling of rage and disappointment came over me as I looked at England, my head full of personal opinions that could not have public, my public, approval. The people I come from are powerless to do evil on grand scale.

The moment I wished every sentence, everything I knew, that began 17 with England would end with "and then it all died, we don't know how, it just all died" was when I saw the white cliffs of Dover. I had sung hymns and recited poems that were about a longing to see the white cliffs of Dover again. At the time I sang the hymns and recited the poems, I could really long to see them again because I had never seen them at all, nor had anyone around me at the time. But there we were, groups of people longing for something we had never seen. And so there they were, the white cliffs, but they were not that pearly majestic thing I used to sing about, that thing that created such a feeling in these people that when they died in the place where I lived they had themselves buried facing a direction that would allow them to see the white cliffs of Dover when they were resurrected, as surely they would be. The white cliffs of Dover, when finally I saw them, were cliffs, but they were not white; you would only call them that if the word "white" meant something special to you; they were dirty and they were steep; they were so steep, the correct height from which all my views of England, starting with the map before me in my classroom and ending with the trip I had just taken, should jump and die and disappear forever.

Thinking About the Essay

1. Based on your careful reading of this essay, summarize Kincaid's understanding of cultural imperialism. Does the fact that she writes about England and not the United States diminish the importance of her argument? Explain.

2. Kincaid divides her essay into two major parts. What is her intention? What is the effect?

3. Kincaid establishes several contrasts between England and Antigua. What are they? How does this comparative method serve to organize the essay?

4. The writer's paragraphs tend to be quite long. Analyze the way she develops her introductory and concluding paragraphs. Also examine the longest paragraph in the essay (paragraph 6) and explain how she achieves coherence in the presentation of her ideas.

5. How does Kincaid's use of the personal voice—the "I" point of view—affect the tone and purpose of her essay? By adopting this personal perspective, what does Kincaid want the audience to infer about her and her experience of cultural imperialism?

Responding in Writing

6. Write an account of your early education. What did you learn about the country where you were born and its relationship to the rest of the world? How did your early education influence or mold your global understanding today?

7. Write an essay analyzing Kincaid's various views on England and what they ultimately mean to her. Has she convinced you about her perspective on the subject? Why or why not? Be certain to deal with her concluding paragraph and her reference to the "white cliffs of Dover."

8. Imagine that you live in a country that has a history of colonization. (Perhaps you or your family has actually experienced this condition.) What would your attitude toward the colonizing or globalizing power be? Write a paper exploring this real or imaginary situation.

Networking

9. With three other class members, draw up a complete list of the contrasts that Kincaid establishes between Antigua and England. Arrive at a consensus about why she is so preoccupied with England—not just as a child but also as an adult writing about the experience. Select one member of your group as a representative in a class panel discussion that talks about these contrasts.

10. Go online and find information about Antigua. Evaluate Kincaid's impressions of her native island with what you have learned about it.

The Clash of Civilizations: Is Conflict Avoidable?

CHAPTER 8

The spread of Coca-Cola, McDonald's, and Levi's jeans around the world—all the trappings of American popular culture—combined with the broader economic and political forces generated by America's superpower status, has resulted in what some call a "clash of civilizations." The phrase, coined by the American political scientist Samuel Huntington, who has an essay in this chapter, suggests that we are in a new era in which the forces of globalization have brought entire civilizations, rather than mere nations, into conflict with each other. The nature of this conflict goes to the heart of what we mean by cultural identity—who am I, and where do I belong?—and how we see ourselves in relation to our civilization and others we come into contact with.

According to Huntington, whose long article appeared in the summer 1993 issue of *Foreign Affairs* and subsequently in an expanded book, *The Clash of Civilizations and the Remaking of World Order* (1996), the world can be divided into seven or perhaps eight contemporary civilizations: Western, Latin American, Islamic, Sinic or Chinese (which includes China, Taiwan, Korea, and Vietnam), Japanese, Hindu, Orthodox (Russia, Serbia, Greece), and African. "Human history," writes Huntington, "is the history of civilizations. It is impossible to think of the development of humanity in any other terms." Historically there have been numerous conflicts between and among these civilizations. However, Huntington's thesis is that with the rise of the West since 1500, other civilizations—notably the Islamic and Chinese—have resented this "rise" and reacted against it. Furthermore, in the inevitable cycles of history, other civilizations will rise in reaction to the dominance of the Western world and become dominant themselves, thus leading to a new clash with global consequences.

 *Online Study Center* This icon will direct you to web links, audio and visual content, and additional resources on the website college.hmco.com/pic/muller.NWR2e

Palestinian schoolgirls walk past Israeli soldiers in Hebron, one of the most contested and violent cities of the West Bank—a region jointly controlled by Israel and the Palestinian Authority. The tomb of Abraham, considered the patriarch of both Judaism and Islam, is located in Hebron; rivalries here extend for millennia.

Thinking About the Image

1. What elements make this photograph especially compelling? Consider the expressions on the faces of the schoolgirls, the size and positioning of the soldiers, and the details of the setting.
2. Do you think that the photographer reinforces conventional depictions of the Arab-Israeli conflict in the American media, or is the photographer trying to present a different perspective? Explain your response.
3. Do you believe that the photographer advances an argument concerning Israel's occupation of the West Bank? Why or why not?

Huntington's broad thesis has come under scrutiny and attack on all sides, and some of his critics appear in this chapter. Yet it could be argued that what we see most clearly in the world today—the conflict between the Western and Islamic worlds, or the gradual ascendancy of China as the next major world power—confirms Huntington's basic claim. Conversely, if you think that reality actually contradicts Huntington's thesis, then you could argue that Western forms of culture, democracy, and modernization actually are cutting across all civilizations and triumphing over them. Benjamin Barber (whose essay appears in Chapter 6) maintains that there will be raging conflicts among civilizations in the future, but that "McWorld," as he terms the West, will triumph over "Jihad." Thus Western civilization will not decline but will defeat the forces of fundamentalism and totalitarianism.

The essays in this chapter deal with the clash of civilizations from a variety of perspectives. We can't deny that conflicts among civilizations exist; some are religious, others ethnic, still others cultural. The writers invite us to consider our own loyalties, and whether we associate with one culture, nation, or civilization or with many. Are there commonalities among civilizations, or must we be forever in conflict? Must we always deal with threats to our gods, our ancestors, our civilization? Or, in a world of 6 billion people, are there tangible signs that we needn't think of "inferior" and "superior" civilizations but rather of a world showing signs of heightened tolerance, integration, and harmony? The way we answer these questions will determine the fabric of future civilizations.

American Dream Boat

K. OANH HA

K. Oanh Ha was born in Vietnam in 1973. As she relates in the following essay, she left Vietnam with her family in July 1979, journeying with other "boat people" to the United States. Raised in California, she is a staff writer for the *San Jose Mercury News*. She is working on a novel that is based loosely on her family's escape from Vietnam. In this personal narrative that she published in *Modern Maturity* in 2002, Ha provides a gentle affirmation of how—when it comes to love— civilizations need not clash.

Before Reading

Have you dated someone whose background represents a civilization entirely different from yours? If not, do you know of a couple who signify this coming together of civilizations? How do you—or they—work out any "clashes"?

The wedding day was only two weeks away when my parents called   1
with yet another request. In accordance with Vietnamese custom, they
fully expected Scott Harris, my fiancé, and his family to visit our family on
the morning of the wedding, bearing dowry gifts of fruit, candies, jewelry,
and a pig, in an elaborate procession.

"But it's not going to mean anything to Scott or his family. They're not   2
Vietnamese!" I protested. My parents were adamant: "Scott is marrying a
Vietnamese. If he wants to marry you, he'll honor our traditions."

Maybe there's no such thing as a stress-free wedding. Small or large,   3
there's bound to be pressure. But our February 12 wedding was a large do-
it-yourselfer that required a fusion of Vietnamese and American traditions—
a wedding that forced me and my parents to wrestle with questions about
our identities, culture, and place in America. After nearly 20 years here, my
family, and my parents in particular, were determined to have a traditional
Vietnamese wedding of sorts, even if their son-in-law and Vietnam-born,
California-raised daughter are as American as they can be.

And so I grudgingly called Scott that night to describe the wedding pro-   4
cession and explain the significance of the ritual. It's a good thing that he
is a patient, easygoing man. "I'll bring the pig," he said, "but I'm worried
it'll make a mess in the car."

"Oh! It's a *roasted* pig," I told him, laughing.   5

I was six years old when my family fled Vietnam in July 1979, just one   6
family among the thousands who collectively became known as the "boat
people," families who decided it was better to risk the very real possibility
of death at sea than to live under Communist rule. But, of course, I never
understood the politics then. I was just a child following my parents.

My memories are sketchy. There was the time that Thai pirates wield-   7
ing saber-like machetes raided our boat. Two years ago, I told my mother,
Kim Hanh Nguyen, how I remembered a woman dropping a handful of
jewelry into my rice porridge during the raid with the instructions to keep
eating. "That was no woman," my mother said. "That was me!" When we
reached the refugee camp in Kuala Lumpur, my mother used the wedding
ring and necklace to buy our shelter.

In September 1980, we arrived in Santa Ana, California, in Orange   8
County, now home to the largest Vietnamese community outside of Vietnam. Those who had left in 1975, right after the end of the war and the
American withdrawal, had been well-educated, wealthy, and connected
with the military. My family was part of the wave of boat people—mostly
middle-class and with little education—who sought refuge in America.

For nearly a year after we arrived, we crowded into the same three-   9
bedroom apartment, all 13 of us: brothers, sisters, cousins, uncles, aunts,
sisters-in-law, and my father's mother. There were only four of us children

in my immediate family then, three born in Vietnam and one born shortly after our resettlement in the U.S.

We started school and watched Mr. Rogers on PBS in the afternoons, 10 grew to love hamburgers and ketchup and longed to lose our accents. We older kids did lose our accents—and those who came later never had accents to begin with because they were born here. When we first came, I was the oldest of three children, all born in Vietnam. Now I have seven siblings, 22 years separating me from my youngest brother, who will start kindergarten in the fall.

In some ways, I was the stereotypical Asian nerd. I took honors classes, 11 received good grades, played the violin and cello. But there was a part of me that also yearned to be as American as my blond-haired neighbors across the street. I joined the school's swim and tennis teams, participated in speech competitions (which were attended by mostly white students) and worshipped Esprit and Guess. My first serious boyfriend was white but most of my friends were Asians who were either born in the U.S. or immigrated when they were very young. None of us had accents and we rarely spoke our native languages around one another. The last thing we wanted to be mistaken for was FOBs—fresh off the boat. I even changed my name to Kyrstin, unaware of its Nordic roots.

I wanted so badly to be a full-fledged American, whatever that meant. 12 At home though, my parents pushed traditional Vietnamese values. I spent most of my teenage years baby-sitting and had to plead with my then overly strict parents to let me out of the house. "Please, please. I just want to be like any other American kid."

My parents didn't understand. "You'll always be Vietnamese. No one's 13 going to look at you and say you're an American," was my mother's often-heard refrain.

I saw college as my escape, the beginning of the trip I would undertake 14 on my own. We had come to America as a family but it was time I navigated alone. College was my flight from the house that always smelled of fish sauce and jasmine tea.

At UCLA, I dated the man who would become my husband. Though 15 he's 17 years older than I am, my parents seemed to be more concerned with the cultural barriers than our age difference. "White Americans are fickle. They don't understand commitment and family responsibility like we Asians do," I was told.

Soon after I announced my engagement, my father, Minh Phu Ha, and 16 I had a rare and intimate conversation. "I'm just worried for you," he said. "All the Vietnamese women I know who have married whites are divorced from them. Our cultures are too far apart."

My father, I think, is worried that none of his kids will marry Viet- 17
namese. My sisters are dating non-Vietnamese Asians while my brother is
dating a white American. "It's just that with a Vietnamese son-in-law, I can
talk to him," my father explained to me one day. "A Vietnamese son-in-
law would call me 'Ba' and not by my first name."

Although my parents have come to terms with having Scott as their son- 18
in-law and to the prospect of grandchildren who will be racially mixed,
there are still times when Scott comes to visit that there are awkward si-
lences. There are still many cultural barriers.

I still think of what it all means to marry a white American. I worry that 19
my children won't be able to speak Vietnamese and won't appreciate that
part of their heritage. I also wonder if somehow this is the ultimate fulfillment of a latent desire to be "American."

Vietnamese-Americans, like Chinese-Americans, Indian-Americans, 20
and other assimilated immigrants, often speak of leading hyphenated lives,
of feet that straddle both cultures. I've always been proud of being Vietnamese. As my family and I discussed and heatedly debated what the wedding event was going to look like, I began to realize just how "American"
I had become.

And yet there was no denying the pull of my Vietnamese roots. Four 21
months before the wedding, I traveled back to Vietnam for the second time
since our family's escape. It was a trip I had planned for more than a year.
I was in Saigon, the city of my birth, to research and write a novel that
loosely mirrors the story of my own family and our journey from Vietnam.
The novel is my tribute to my family and our past. I'm writing it for myself as much as for my younger siblings, so they'll know what our family's
been through.

I returned to Vietnam to connect with something I can't really name but 22
know I lost when we left 20 years ago. I was about to start a new journey
with the marriage ahead, but I needed to come back to the place where my
family's journey began.

Scott came along for the first two weeks and met my extended family. 23
They all seemed to approve, especially when he showed he could eat pungent fish and shrimp sauce like any other Vietnamese.

During my time there I visited often with family members and talked 24
about the past. I saw the hospital where I was born, took a walk through
our old house, chatted with my father's old friends. The gaps in the circle
of my hyphenated life came closer together with every new Vietnamese
word that I learned, with every Vietnamese friend that I made.

I also chose the fabric for the tailoring of the *ao dai,* the traditional Viet- 25
namese dress of a long tunic over flowing pants, which I would change into

at the reception. I had my sisters' bridesmaid gowns made. And I had a velvet ao dai made for my 88-year-old maternal grandmother, *Bā Ngoai,* to wear to the wedding of her oldest grandchild. "My dream is to see you on your wedding day and eat at your wedding feast," she had told me several times.

Bā Ngoai came to the U.S. in 1983, three years after my family landed 26 in Orange County as war refugees. As soon as we got to the United States, my mother filed immigration papers for her. Bā Ngoai made that journey at age 73, leaving the only home she had known to be with my mother, her only child. Bā Ngoai nurtured and helped raise us grandchildren.

I had extended my stay in Vietnam. Several days after my original de- 27 parture date, I received a phone call. Bā Ngoai had died. I flew home carrying her ao dai. We buried her in it.

In Vietnamese tradition, one is in mourning for three years after the loss 28 of a parent or grandparent. Out of respect and love for the deceased, or *hieu,* decorum dictates that close family members can't get married until after the mourning period is over. But my wedding was only a month and a half away.

On the day we buried my grandmother, my family advised me to burn 29 the white cloth headband that symbolized my grief. By burning it, I ended my official mourning.

Through my tears I watched the white cloth become wispy ashes. My 30 family was supportive. "It's your duty to remember and honor her," my father told me. "But you also need to move forward with your life."

On the morning of our wedding, Scott's family stood outside our house 31 in a line bearing dowry gifts. Inside the house, Scott and I lighted incense in front of the family altar. Holding the incense between our palms, we bowed to my ancestors and asked for their blessings. I looked at the photo of Bā Ngoai and knew she had to be smiling.

Thinking About the Essay

1. How do you interpret the title? What aspects of the essay does it capture?

2. There are several characters in this essay. Who are they? How are they described? What sort of persona does Ha create for herself as the "I" narrator?

3. Why does Ha begin the essay in the present and then shift to the past? Trace the narrative pattern throughout her essay.

4. Often when you write a personal essay, it is valuable to create a central conflict. What is the conflict (or conflicts) in this selection? How does Ha develop and resolve it? Does this conflict lead to a thesis? Why or why not?

5. Explain the various moods and tones that Ha imbues her narrative with. Do they "clash" or not? Are they finally reconciled? Justify your response.

Responding in Writing

6. In a 500–750-word paper, explain why Ha's essay tells us about the clash of civilizations and how we might resolve it.

7. Write a narrative essay in which you tell of a relationship in which the people come from different civilizations. You can base this essay on personal experience, the experience of family or friends, or a situation drawn from television or film.

8. Do you think that the narrator and her husband will have a happy marriage? Why or why not? Cite what you have learned about them in the essay as support for your response.

Networking

9. In a group of four, discuss the relationship between Scott and "Kyrstin" Oanh. Do you think it is healthy and viable, or do you sense potential problems? Summarize your decision for the rest of the class.

10. Search the Internet for more information on the Vietnamese boat people. Where have they settled in the United States? How do they preserve their culture and civilization? How often do they intermarry with Americans outside their background? Discuss your findings with the class.

When Afghanistan Was at Peace

MARGARET ATWOOD

Margaret Atwood, born in 1939, is a Canadian novelist, poet, short story writer, and literary critic whose work explores the troubled contours of the modern world. Atwood's second collection of poetry, *The Circle Game* (1966), was published to critical acclaim. Equally impressive is a distinguished series of novels, including *Life Before Man* (1979), *The Handmaid's Tale* (1986), *Cat's Eye* (1988), *The Blind Assassin* (2000), and *The Penelopiad* (2005). Atwood's writing often blends the intensely personal experience with global realities. In "When Afghanistan Was at Peace," published in October 2001 in *The New York Times Magazine*, Atwood describes a world ruined by clashing civilizations.

Before Reading

Reflect on what you know about Afghanistan. How many "civilizations" have attempted to conquer and control it? What problems do you foresee for Afghanistan's future?

In February 1978, almost 23 years ago, I visited Afghanistan with my 1
spouse, Graeme Gibson, and our 18-month-old daughter. We went there
almost by chance: we were on our way to the Adelaide literary festival in
Australia. Pausing at intervals, we felt, would surely be easier on a child's
time clock. (Wrong, as it turned out.) We thought Afghanistan would make
a fascinating two-week stopover. Its military history impressed us—neither
Alexander the Great nor the British in the 19th century had stayed in the
country long because of the ferocity of its warriors.

"Don't go to Afghanistan," my father said when told of our plans. 2
"There's going to be a war there." He was fond of reading history books.
"As Alexander the Great said, Afghanistan is easy to march into but hard to
march out of." But we hadn't heard any other rumors of war, so off we went.

We were among the last to see Afghanistan in its days of relative 3
peace—relative, because even then there were tribal disputes and superpowers in play. The three biggest buildings in Kabul were the Chinese Embassy, the Soviet Embassy and the American Embassy, and the head of the
country was reportedly playing the three against one another.

The houses of Kabul were carved wood, and the streets were like a liv- 4
ing "Book of Hours": people in flowing robes, camels, donkeys, carts with
huge wooden wheels being pushed and pulled by men at either end. There
were few motorized vehicles. Among them were buses covered with ornate
Arabic script, with eyes painted on the front so the buses could see where
they were going.

We managed to hire a car in order to see the terrain of the famous and 5
disastrous British retreat from Kabul to Jalalabad. The scenery was
breathtaking: jagged mountains and the "Arabian Nights" dwellings in
the valleys—part houses, part fortresses—reflected in the enchanted blue-
green of the rivers. Our driver took the switchback road at breakneck
speed since we had to be back before sundown because of bandits.

The men we encountered were friendly and fond of children: our curly- 6
headed, fair-haired child got a lot of attention. The winter coat I wore had
a large hood so that I was sufficiently covered and did not attract undue
notice. Many wanted to talk; some knew English, while others spoke
through our driver. But they all addressed Graeme exclusively. To have
spoken to me would have been impolite. And yet when out interpreter negotiated our entry into an all-male teahouse, I received nothing worse than
uneasy glances. The law of hospitality toward visitors ranked higher than
the no-women-in-the-teahouse custom. In the hotel, those who served
meals and cleaned rooms were men, tall men with scars either from duel-
ing or from the national sport, played on horseback, in which gaining possession of a headless calf is the aim.

Girls and women we glimpsed on the street wore the chador, the long, 7
pleated garment with a crocheted grill for the eyes that is more comprehensive than any other Muslim coverup. At that time, you often saw chic
boots and shoes peeking out from the hem. The chador wasn't obligatory
back then; Hindu women didn't wear it. It was a cultural custom, and since
I had grown up hearing that you weren't decently dressed without a girdle
and white gloves, I thought I could understand such a thing. I also knew
that clothing is a symbol, that all symbols are ambiguous and that this one
might signify a fear of women or a desire to protect them from the gaze of
strangers. But it could also mean more negative things, just as the color red
can mean love, blood, life, royalty, good luck—or sin.

I bought a chador in the market. A jovial crowd of men gathered 8
around, amused by the spectacle of a Western woman picking out such a
non-Western item. They offered advice about color and quality. Purple was
better than light green or the blue, they said. (I bought the purple.) Every
writer wants the Cloak of Invisibility—the power to see without being
seen—or so I was thinking as I donned the chador. But once I had put it on,
I had an odd sense of having been turned into negative space, a blank in
the visual field, a sort of antimatter—both there and not there. Such a space
has power of a sort, but it is a passive power, the power of taboo.

Several weeks after we left Afghanistan, the war broke out. My father 9
was right, after all. Over the next years, we often remembered the people
we met and their courtesy and curiosity. How many of them are now dead,
through no fault of their own?

Six years after our trip, I wrote "The Handmaid's Tale," a speculative 10
fiction about an American theocracy. The women in that book wear out-
fits derived in part from nuns' costumes, partly from girls' schools' hem-
lines and partly—I must admit—from the faceless woman on the Old
Dutch Cleanser box, but also partly from the chador I acquired in
Afghanistan and its conflicting associations. As one character says, there is
freedom to and freedom from. But how much of the first should you have
to give up in order to assure the second? All cultures have had to grapple
with that, and our own—as we are now seeing—is no exception. Would I
have written the book if I never had visited Afghanistan? Possibly. Would
it have been the same? Unlikely.

Thinking About the Essay

1. Does Atwood provide a thesis sentence in this essay? Why or why not? How does her title imply a thesis? If you were writing a thesis sentence of your own for this essay, what would it be?

2. What is Atwood's purpose in writing this narrative essay? Consider that this essay was published shortly after the events of 9/11. Is narration an appropriate strategy for her purpose? Why or why not?

3. Narrative essays typically use description to flesh out the story. Find descriptive details that Atwood provides, and explain what these details contribute to the overall effect.

4. Analyze the point of view in this essay. Is Atwood an observer, a participant, or both? Is she neutral or involved? Support your opinion.

5. Consider the relationship of the introductory paragraphs to the conclusion. Why does Atwood use the introduction and conclusion to expand the time frame of her main narrative?

Responding in Writing

6. Write an editorial for your college newspaper supporting or attacking the role of Western powers in Afghanistan today.

7. Imagine that you are traveling to Afghanistan on assignment for a newspaper. Report back, telling readers about what you see and where you go. Feel free to research the subject prior to writing the essay.

8. What does Atwood say about the clash of civilizations in this essay? Answer this question by analyzing the strategies she uses to convey her thesis.

Networking

9. In groups of two or three, pool your knowledge of Afghanistan. Prepare a brief report to be presented to the class.

10. In her essay, Atwood alludes to some of the nations and civilizations that have tried to conquer Afghanistan over the centuries. For research, conduct a library or Internet search on the history of Afghanistan, and how it has been a crossroads in the clash of civilizations. Prepare a brief report on your findings.

The World in 1500—or the West as Backwater

DINESH D'SOUZA

> Dinesh D'Souza was born in 1961 in Bombay, India, and came to the United States in 1978 as an exchange student. After completing high school, he attended Dartmouth College, where he served as editor of the conservative magazine *Dartmouth Review* before graduation in 1983. Subsequently D'Souza contributed articles to several magazines, notably the *National Review,* before becoming a policy analyst for the Reagan administration. His longer work appears in *Illiberal Education: The Politics of Race and Sex on Campus* (1991), *The End of Racism: Principles for a Multi-Cultural Society* (1995), and *The Virtue of Prosperity: Finding Values in an Age of Techno-Affluence* (2001). D'Souza is a visiting scholar at the Hoover Institution. The following selection appears in his most recent book *What's So Great About America* (2002); here D'Souza offers an interesting perspective on the history of civilizations.

Before Reading

Think about all the great civilizations of the past and present. What causes them to rise and fall? Is it possible that Western civilization will suffer the same fate as other civilizations have? Why or why not?

For most of human history, other civilizations have proven far more advanced than the West. They were more advanced in learning, in wealth, in exploration, in inventions—and in cultural sophistication and works of the mind. We can see this clearly by taking an imaginative leap back in time to the year 1500, when "the West" as we know it now was just starting to emerge. 1

In 1500, there were several civilizations dotting the globe. However, two of them stood out in resplendence: the civilization of China—and the civilization of the Arab-Islamic world. During the Ming dynasty, the wealth, knowledge and power of China astonished all those who came into contact with it. Chinese astronomers knew more about eclipses and heavenly orbits than anyone else at the time. The Chinese were responsible for inventions of surpassing importance—printing, gunpowder and the compass. In the 15th century, the Chinese sent a fleet of ships—the largest and most sophisticated of their kind—to explore the shores of Africa, India and 2 other countries. At home, the Chinese ruling class presided over an empire distinguished by its size and cohesion. Confucian philosophy gave a kind of moral and intellectual unity to Chinese civilization. The Chinese had a merit system of government appointments. This was all the more impressive as most of the world operated on traditional systems of nepotism and patronage. Chinese society showed a refinement in porcelain work, in silk embroidery—and in social refinement—that no other society could match. No wonder the Chinese emperors regarded themselves as the "sons of Heaven"—and their part of the world as the center of the universe.

Equally impressive in the year 1500 were the achievements of Islamic 3 civilization. Starting in the 7th century, the Islamic empire spread rapidly until it sprawled across three continents: Europe, Asia—and Africa. The Muslims unified their enormous empire around a single faith, Islam—and a single language, Arabic. The Islamic world enjoyed a flourishing economy, enriched by trade with India and the Far East, and a largely uniform system of laws. The Muslims built spectacular cities—Baghdad, Damascus, Cairo, Istanbul, Seville, Granada—distinguished by architectural and literary splendor. Islamic literature and thought exhibited a richness, variety— and complexity—that far surpassed that of Europe at the time. Islam produced great men of learning, such as Ibn Sinha (Avicenna), Ihn Rushd (Averroes), Ibn Khaldun, al-Ghazali, al-Farabi and al-Kindi. Indeed, much of Greco-Roman knowledge—including the works of Aristotle—that had been lost in Europe during the Dark Ages was preserved in the Islamic world. It is no exaggeration to write, in the words of historian David Landes, that during this period "Islam was Europe's teacher."

Nothing could compare to China and the Islamic empire, but there were 4 other civilizations in the world in the year 1500. There was the civilization of India, renowned for its spiritual depth as the original home of two of the world's great religions: Hinduism and Buddhism. India was also famous for its wealth and mathematical learning. In Africa, there were the kingdoms of Ghana, Mali and Songhay—which were large, orderly and rich in gold. Finally, in the Americas, there were the Aztec and Inca civilizations. Despite their reputation for brutality and human sacrifice, these were impressive for their architecture, social organization—and city planning.

Meanwhile, Western civilization—then called Christendom—was a 5 relative backwater. Mired in the Dark Ages, Christendom was characterized by widespread ignorance, poverty and incessant clashes between warring tribes—and between kings and the Church. Indeed, Islamic writers who encountered the West in the late Middle Ages described it as remote, uninteresting—and primitive. A Muslim traveler described Europeans as "more like beasts than like men. They lack keenness of understanding and clarity of intelligence—and are overcome by ignorance and apathy, lack of

discernment and stupidity." Another Muslim writer gives an account of
the state of European medicine. He tells of a knight who came to a European physician complaining of an abscess on his leg. The physician seized
an ax and chopped off the leg with one blow—"and the man died at
once." Bernard Lewis, the Princeton historian, finds in such Muslim writings "the same note of amused disdain as we sometimes find among European travelers in Africa and Asia many centuries later."

How then did this relatively impoverished, backward civilization accu-   6
mulate so much economic, political and military power that it was able to
conquer and subdue all the other cultures of the world put together? The
truth is that, throughout history, Western civilization has gained immensely
from its absorption of the ideas and inventions of other cultures. From the
Muslims, the West recovered parts of its own Greco-Roman heritage. From
Hindus, the West learned its numeral system.

Civilizational development does not always go to the group that invents   7
things. It frequently goes to the people who are able to take the inventions—
and run with them.

Thinking About the Essay

1. What do you expect from D'Souza's title? Does he satisfy your expectations? Why or why not?

2. D'Souza is known as a conservative. Does he offer a conservative's view
   of the history of civilizations or not? Is his tone, for example, biased or objective? Explain your answer by referring to specific aspects of the essay.

3. Explain D'Souza's typical approach to paragraph development. What types
   of examples does he provide in these paragraphs? How does he achieve
   coherence?

4. How does D'Souza use classification as a main technique of organization
   in this essay?

5. Examine D'Souza's conclusion. What is significant about it?

Responding in Writing

6. Write an essay in which you maintain that the West *today* is or is not a
   "backwater."

7. In an argumentative paper, argue for or against the idea that the civilizations that D'Souza mentions in his essay are still vibrant and capable of coexisting.

8. Imagine that you represent a civilization *other* than the one you actually belong to. In an explanatory essay, tell why this civilization is noteworthy. You
   may want to conduct research for this paper.

Networking

9. In groups of four or five, review the drafts you have written. Focus on how well each writer has constructed a compelling presentation of the idea of civilization that has to be central to the essay assignment selected.

10. Search the Internet for information on D'Souza. Then join a class discussion in which you share your information and explore the reasons he is such a controversial figure.

Fundamentalism Is Here to Stay

KAREN ARMSTRONG

Karen Armstrong is one of the most highly regarded commentators on religion in North America and Europe. She currently teaches Christianity at the Leo Baeck College Centre for Jewish Education in London. Armstrong joined a Catholic convent at the age of seventeen but left her order after seven years. Her experience as a nun, and her departure from the Catholic Church, are recounted in the autobiographical *Through the Narrow Gates* (1982). Armstrong now describes herself as a "freelance monotheist" and compares religion to a raft: "Once you get across the river, moor the raft and go on. Don't lug it with you if you don't need it anymore." Armstrong's recent books include *The Battle for God: A History of Fundamentalism* (2001) and *Islam: A Short History* (2001). In the following essay, which appeared in globalagendamagazine.com in 2005, Armstrong defines religious fundamentalism as a reaction to—and a clash with—the perceived values of a secular modernity.

Before Reading

How do you define *fundamentalism*? Do you see the fundamentalist impulse as a feature common to all religions? Are there differences in degree or kind?

In the middle of the 20th century, it was generally assumed that secularism was the coming ideology and that religion would never again play a major role in world events. Today, religion dominates the headlines, and this is due in no small part to the militant piety that has developed in every single major world faith over the past century.

We usually call it "fundamentalism." Fundamentalist groups have staged revolutions, assassinated presidents, carried out terrorist atrocities and become an influential political force in strongly secularist nations.

There has, for example, been much discussion about the role of Protestant fundamentalism in the recent American elections. It is no longer possible to dismiss fundamentalism as a passing phase.

Fundamentalism Is Not . . .

We should begin by defining what fundamentalism is not. First, it should not be equated with religious conservatism. Leading American religious revivalist Billy Graham, for example, is not a fundamentalist. 3

Second, fundamentalism should not be linked automatically with violence. Only a tiny proportion of fundamentalists worldwide take part in acts of terror. The rest are simply struggling to live what they regard as a good religious life in a world that seems increasingly inimical to faith. 4

Third, fundamentalism is not an exclusively Islamic phenomenon. There are fundamentalist Jews, Christians, Hindus, Buddhists, Sikhs and Confucians, who all challenge the secular hegemony of the modern world. In fact, Islam developed a fundamentalist strain long after it had erupted in Judaism and Christianity. 5

Fundamentalism Is . . .

So what is fundamentalism? It is essentially a revolt against modern secular society. Wherever a western polity has been established that separates religion and politics, fundamentalist movements have sprung up in protest. Whatever the politicians or the pundits claim, people worldwide are demonstrating that they want to see religion reflected more prominently in public life. As part of their campaign, fundamentalists tend to withdraw from mainstream society to create enclaves of pure faith. 6

Typical examples are the Ultra-orthodox Jewish communities in New York or the fundamentalist Christianity of Bob Jones University in South Carolina. Here fundamentalists build a counterculture, in conscious defiance of the godless world that surrounds them, and from these communities some undertake a counteroffensive designed to drag God or religion back to centre stage from the wings to which they have been relegated in modern secular culture. 7

This campaign is rarely violent. It usually consists of a propaganda or welfare effort. In the United States, for example, the fundamentalist riposte attempts to reform school textbooks or to get Christian candidates elected to government posts. But if warfare is endemic in a region and has become chronic—as in the Middle East or Afghanistan—fundamentalists can get sucked into the violence that pervades the whole of society. In this way, originally secular disputes such as the Arab-Israeli conflict have been sacralized, on both sides. 8

The Road to Modernity

The ubiquity of the fundamentalist revolt shows that there is widespread 9
disappointment with modernity. But what is it about the modern world
that has provoked such rage and distress? In the 16th century, the peoples
of the west began to develop a new type of civilization unprecedented in
world history. Instead of basing their economy on a surplus of agricultural
produce, as did all premodern cultures, they relied increasingly on technology and the constant reinvestment of capital, which freed them from the
inherent limitations of agrarian society. This demanded radical change at
all levels of society—intellectual, political, social and religious. A wholly
new way of thinking became essential, and new forms of government had
to evolve to meet these altered conditions. It was found by trial and error
that the best way of creating a productive society was to create a secular,
tolerant, democratic polity.

It took Europe some 300 years to modernize, and the process was 10
wrenching and traumatic, involving bloody revolutions, often succeeded
by reigns of terror, brutal holy wars, dictatorships, cruel exploitation of the
workforce, the despoliation of the countryside, and widespread alienation
and anomie.

We are now witnessing the same kind of upheaval in developing coun- 11
tries presently undergoing modernization. But some of these countries have
had to attempt this difficult process far too rapidly and are forced to follow a western programme, rather than their own.

This accelerated modernization has created deep divisions in develop- 12
ing nations. Only an elite has a western education that enables them to understand the new modern institutions. The vast majority remains trapped
in the premodern ethos. They experience the incomprehensible change as
profoundly disturbing, and cling to traditional religion for support. But as
modernization progresses, people find that they cannot be religious in the
old way and try to find new means of expressing their piety. Fundamentalism is just one of these attempts, and it therefore develops only after a degree of modernization has been achieved.

The modern spirit that developed in the west had two essential charac- 13
teristics: independence and innovation. Modernization in Europe and America proceeded by declarations of independence on all fronts—religious,
political and intellectual—as scientists and inventors demanded the freedom to develop their ideas without interference from religious or political
authorities. Further, despite the trauma of modernization, it was exciting,
because the western countries were continually meeting new challenges
and creating something fresh. But in some developing countries, modernization came not with independence, but with colonial dependence and

subjugation, and the west was so far ahead that these could not innovate but only imitate. So they find it difficult to develop a truly modern spirit. A nation such as Japan, which was not colonized, was able to make its own distinctive contribution to the modern economy in a way that some Middle Eastern countries have not been able to do.

A Fight for Survival

Culture is always contested, and fundamentalists are primarily concerned 14 with saving their own society. Protestant fundamentalists in the United States want America to be a truly Christian nation, not a secular, pluralist republic. In Palestine, Hamas began by attacking the Palestine Liberation Organization, because it wanted the Palestinian resistance to be inspired by an Islamic rather than a secular polity. Osama bin Laden started by targeting the Saudi royal family and such secularist rulers as Saddam Hussein. Only at a secondary stage—if at all—do fundamentalists begin to attack a foreign foe. Thus fundamentalism does not represent a clash between civilizations, but a clash within civilizations.

Perhaps the most important factor to understand about this widespread 15 religious militancy is its rootedness in a deep fear of annihilation. Every fundamentalist movement I have studied in Judaism, Christianity and Islam is convinced that modern secular society wants to wipe out religion— even in America. Fundamentalists, therefore, believe they are fighting for survival, and when people feel that their backs are to the wall, some can strike out violently. This profound terror of annihilation is not as paranoid as it may at first appear. Jewish fundamentalism, for example, gained fresh momentum after World War II, when Hitler had tried to exterminate European Jewry, and after the 1973 October War, when Israelis felt vulnerable and isolated in the Middle East.

In some Muslim countries, modernization has usually been so acceler- 16 ated that secularism has been experienced as an assault. When Mustafa Kemal Ataturk created modern secular Turkey, he closed down all the madrasahs (traditional institutes for higher education in Islamic studies) and abolished the Sufi orders. He also forced all men and women to wear Western dress. Reformers such as Ataturk wanted their countries to look modern. In Iran, the shahs used to make their soldiers walk through the streets with their bayonets out, tearing off women's veils and ripping them to pieces. In 1935, shah Reza Pahlavi gave his soldiers orders to shoot at unarmed demonstrators in Mashhad (one of the holiest shrines in Iran), who were peacefully protesting against obligatory Western clothes. Hundreds of Iranians died that day. In such circumstances, secularism was not experienced as liberating and civilized, but as wicked, lethal and murderously hostile to faith.

The main fundamentalist ideology of Sunni Islam developed in the con- 17
centration camps in Egypt in which president Jamal Abd al-Nasser had in-
carcerated thousands of members of the Muslim Brotherhood in the late
1950s, without trial and often for doing nothing more incriminating than
attending a meeting or handing out leaflets. One of these prisoners was
Sayyid Qutb, who was executed by Nasser in 1966. Qutb went into the
camp as a moderate and a liberal. But in these vile prisons, watching the
Brothers being executed and subjected to mental and physical torture, and
hearing Nasser vowing to relegate Islam to a marginal role in Egypt, he
came to regard secularism as a great evil. He developed an ideology of committed armed struggle against this threat to the faith. His chief disciple today is Osama bin Laden.

Thus fundamentalism usually develops in a symbiotic relationship with 18
a secularism that is experienced as hostile and invasive. Every fundamentalist movement I have studied in each of the three monotheistic traditions
has developed in direct response to what is perceived as a secularist attack.
The more vicious the assault, the more extreme the fundamentalist riposte
is likely to be. Because fundamentalists fear that secularists want to destroy
them, aggressive and military action will only serve to confirm this conviction and exacerbate their fear, which can spill over into ungovernable rage.

Thus membership of al-Qaeda has increased since the recent Gulf War. 19
The offensive has convinced many Muslims that the West has really inau-
gurated a new crusade against the Islamic world. In the United States,
Protestant fundamentalists in the smaller towns and rural areas often feel
"colonized" by the alien ethos of Harvard, Yale and Washington DC. They
feel that the liberal establishment despises them, and this has resulted in a
fundamentalism that has gone way beyond Jerry Falwell and the Moral
Majority of the 1970s. (Falwell is an American fundamentalist Baptist pas-
tor, televangelist and founder of the Moral Majority—a group dedicated to
promoting its conservative and religious Christian-centric beliefs via support of political candidates.) Some groups, such as the Christian Recon-
structionists, look forward to the imminent destruction of the federal
government; the blazing towers of the World Trade Center would not be
alien to their ideology. When liberals deplore the development and persistence of fundamentalism in their own societies and worldwide, they should
be aware that the excesses of secularists have all too often been responsible for this radical alienation.

Here to Stay

Fundamentalism is not going to disappear, as secularists once imagined 20
that religion would modestly retreat to the sidelines and confine itself to

private life. Fundamentalism is here to stay, and in Judaism, Christianity and Islam, at least, it is becoming more extreme. Fundamentalism is not confined to the "other" civilizations. A dangerous gulf has appeared, dividing many societies against themselves. In the Middle East, India, Pakistan, Israel and the United States, for example, fundamentalists and secular liberals form two distinct camps, neither of which can understand the other.

In the past, these movements were often dismissed with patrician disdain. This has proved to be short-sighted. We have to take fundamentalism very seriously. Had the US made a greater effort to understand Shiite Islam, for example, it might have avoided unnecessary errors in the lead-up to the Iranian Revolution of 1978 to 79. The first step must be to look beneath the bizarre and often repulsive ideology of these movements to discern the disquiet and anger that lie at their roots. We must no longer deride these theologies as the fantasies of a lunatic fringe, but learn to decode their ideas and imagery. Only then can we deal creatively with fears and anxieties that, as we have seen to our cost, no society can safely ignore.   21

Thinking About the Essay

1. Why does Armstrong define fundamentalism first by stating what it is *not*? How do you respond to this tactic as a reader?

2. Where does Armstrong shift in the essay from definition to process analysis? How does Armstrong link the historical and economic factors that gave rise to modernity with the secular values that came to be associated with modernity? How is fundamentalism a response to modernity as both a process and a set of values?

3. Why does Armstrong make a point, throughout the essay, of dissociating the concept of fundamentalism from violence?

4. What examples does Armstrong give to acknowledge the militancy of twentieth-century attempts at rapid modernization? Do these examples strengthen or weaken her definition of fundamentalism? How has Armstrong prepared for this acknowledgment earlier in the essay?

5. Describe the symbiotic relationship between fundamentalist terrorism and secular modernity.

Responding in Writing

6. Respond to the term *militant piety,* which some would read as an oxymoron. How can piety take this form? In a brief essay, consider some ex-

amples of militant piety and explain why the term would, in your opinion, apply in each case.

7. Fundamentalism, according to Armstrong, "does not represent a clash between civilizations, but a clash within civilizations." How does Armstrong's concept of fundamentalism refute or qualify Samuel P. Huntington's "clash of cultures" theory? In an evaluative essay, point to some limitations that you see in both theories.

8. In a brief essay, offer some advice to American foreign policy makers on how to promote modernization in a Middle Eastern nation (like Iraq) so that it would not be experienced or perceived as an "assault."

Networking

9. In groups of three or four, make a list of three religious leaders or public figures in the United States whose views everyone in the group agrees would qualify as "fundamentalist" (according to Armstrong's definition). Share the list with the class, and justify the application of the label to each person on the list.

10. Go online and read at least three reviews of Armstrong's *The Battle for God: A History of Fundamentalism.* Do any of the reviewers take exception to her definition of *fundamentalism?*

The West and the Rest: Intercivilizational Issues

SAMUEL P. HUNTINGTON

Samuel Phillips Huntington was born in New York City in 1927. He received his education at Yale University (B.A., 1946), the University of Chicago (M.A., 1948), and Harvard University (Ph.D., 1951). A leading authority on international affairs, Huntington has worked and consulted for numerous government and private organizations, including the National Security Council, the National War College, and the Office of the Secretary of Defense. He is professor of government at Harvard University and director of its Center for Strategic Studies. Among his many books are *The Soldier and the State* (1957), *Political Order in Changing Societies* (1968), *American Military Strategy* (1986), and *The Clash of Civilizations and the Remaking of World Order* (1996), from which this essay is taken.

Before Reading

Do you think that Western civilization is under assault from Islamic, Chinese, or other civilizations? Why or why not?

Western Universalism

In the emerging world, the relations between states and groups from different civilizations will not be close and will often be antagonistic. Yet some intercivilization relations are more conflict-prone than others. At the micro level, the most violent fault lines are between Islam and its Orthodox, Hindu, African, and Western Christian neighbors. At the macro level, the dominant division is between "the West and the rest," with the most intense conflicts occurring between Muslim and Asian societies on the one hand, and the West on the other. The dangerous clashes of the future are likely to arise from the interaction of Western arrogance, Islamic intolerance, and Sinic assertiveness.

Alone among civilizations the West has had a major and at times devastating impact on every other civilization. The relation between the power and culture of the West and the power and cultures of other civilizations is, as a result, the most pervasive characteristic of the world of civilizations. As the relative power of other civilizations increases, the appeal of Western culture fades and non-Western peoples have increasing confidence in and commitment to their indigenous cultures. The central problem in the relations between the West and the rest is, consequently, the discordance between the West's—particularly America's—efforts to promote a universal Western culture and its declining ability to do so.

The collapse of communism exacerbated this discordance by reinforcing in the West the view that its ideology of democratic liberalism had triumphed globally and hence was universally valid. The West, and especially the United States, which has always been a missionary nation, believe that the non-Western peoples should commit themselves to the Western values of democracy, free markets, limited government, human rights, individualism, the rule of law, and should embody these values in their institutions. Minorities in other civilizations embrace and promote these values, but the dominant attitudes toward them in non-Western cultures range from widespread skepticism to intense opposition. What is universalism to the West is imperialism to the rest.

The West is attempting and will continue to attempt to sustain its preeminent position and defend its interests by defining those interests as the interests of the "world community." That phrase has become the euphemistic collective noun (replacing "the Free World") to give global legitimacy to actions reflecting the interests of the United States and other

Western powers. The West is, for instance, attempting to integrate the economies of non-Western societies into a global economic system which it dominates. Through the IMF and other international economic institutions, the West promotes its economic interests and imposes on other nations the economic policies it thinks appropriate. In any poll of non-Western peoples, however, the IMF undoubtedly would win the support of finance ministers and a few others but get an overwhelmingly unfavorable rating from almost everyone else, who would agree with Georgi Arbatov's description of IMF officials as "neo-Bolsheviks who love expropriating other people's money, imposing undemocratic and alien rules of economic and political conduct and stifling economic freedom."[1]

Non-Westerners also do not hesitate to point to the gaps between Western principle and Western action. Hypocrisy, double standards, and "but nots" are the price of universalist pretensions. Democracy is promoted but not if it brings Islamic fundamentalists to power; nonproliferation is preached for Iran and Iraq but not for Israel; free trade is the elixir of economic growth but not for agriculture; human rights are an issue with China but not with Saudi Arabia; aggression against oil-owning Kuwaitis is massively repulsed but not against non-oil-owning Bosnians. Double standards in practice are the unavoidable price of universal standards of principle.

Having achieved political independence, non-Western societies wish to free themselves from Western economic, military, and cultural domination. East Asian societies are well on their way to equalling the West economically. Asian and Islamic countries are looking for shortcuts to balance the West militarily. The universal aspirations of Western civilization, the declining relative power of the West, and the increasing cultural assertiveness of other civilizations ensure generally difficult relations between the West and the rest. The nature of those relations and the extent to which they are antagonistic, however, vary considerably and fall into three categories. With the challenger civilizations, Islam and China, the West is likely to have consistently strained and often highly antagonistic relations. Its relations with Latin America and Africa, weaker civilizations which have in some measure been dependent on the West, will involve much lower levels of conflict, particularly with Latin America. The relations of Russia, Japan, and India to the West are likely to fall between those of the other two groups, involving elements of cooperation and conflict, as these three core states at times line up with the challenger civilizations and at times side with the West. They are the "swing" civilizations between the West, on the one hand, and Islamic and Sinic civilizations, on the other.

1. Georgi Arbatov, "Neo-Bolsheviks of the I.M.F.," *New York Times*, 7 May 1992, p. A27.

Islam and China embody great cultural traditions very different from   7
and in their eyes infinitely superior to that of the West. The power and assertiveness of both in relation to the West are increasing, and the conflicts
between their values and interests and those of the West are multiplying
and becoming more intense. Because Islam lacks a core state, its relations
with the West vary greatly from country to country. Since the 1970s, however, a fairly consistent anti-Western trend has existed, marked by the rise
of fundamentalism, shifts in power within Muslim countries from more
pro-Western to more anti-Western governments, the emergence of a quasi
war between some Islamic groups and the West, and the weakening of the
Cold War security ties that existed between some Muslim states and the
United States. Underlying the differences on specific issues is the fundamental question of the role these civilizations will play relative to the West
in shaping the future of the world. Will the global institutions, the distribution of power, and the politics and economies of nations in the twenty-
first century primarily reflect Western values and interests or will they be
shaped primarily by those of Islam and China? . . .

The issues that divide the West and these other societies are increasingly   8
important on the international agenda. Three such issues involve the efforts of the West: (1) to maintain its military superiority through policies
of nonproliferation and counterproliferation with respect to nuclear, biological, and chemical weapons and the means to deliver them; (2) to promote Western political values and institutions by pressing other societies to
respect human rights as conceived in the West and to adopt democracy on
Western lines; and (3) to protect the cultural, social, and ethnic integrity of
Western societies by restricting the number of non-Westerners admitted as
immigrants or refugees. In all three areas the West has had and is likely to
continue to have difficulties defending its interests against those of non-
Western societies. . . .

The changing balance of power among civilizations makes it more and   9
more difficult for the West to achieve its goals with respect to weapons proliferation, human rights, immigration, and other issues. To minimize its
losses in this situation requires the West to wield skillfully its economic resources as carrots and sticks in dealing with other societies, to bolster its
unity and coordinate its policies so as to make it more difficult for other
societies to play one Western country off against another, and to promote
and exploit differences among non-Western nations. The West's ability to
pursue these strategies will be shaped by the nature and intensity of its conflicts with the challenger civilizations, on the one hand, and the extent to
which it can identify and develop common interests with the swing civilizations, on the other.

Thinking About the Essay

1. How would you characterize the tone of this essay? Does Huntington present himself as argumentative, opinioned, objective, fair-minded, liberal, conservative, or what? Identify words, sentences, and passages that support your assessment of the writer's voice.

2. Summarize Huntington's argument. What is his thesis or claim? What types of support does he provide?

3. What aspects of Huntington's language tell you that he writes for an audience that can follow his rapid sweep of the civilizations and institutions of the world? To what extent does he employ "loaded" language to advance his argument? Explain.

4. Huntington employs numerous rhetorical strategies to develop his argument, among them comparison and contrast, classification, and illustration. Locate examples of these strategies in the essay.

5. What, in Huntington's view, is the answer to the clash of civilizations? How does he prepare the reader for his answer? Trace the "logic" of his answer through the essay.

Responding in Writing

6. Compare and contrast the essays by D'Souza and Huntington. Establish a clear thesis concerning their views about the conflict of civilizations, and the different ways they approach the subject. Develop at least three key topics.

7. Do you agree or disagree with Huntington's analysis and argument? Explain your response in an argumentative paper of your own.

8. Respond in an analytical essay to Huntington's statement, "Alone among civilizations the West has had a major and at times devastating impact on every other civilization."

Networking

9. Discuss Huntington's essay in groups of three or four. Draw up a list of all the key elements in his argument. Then join a general class discussion on why his argument has caused so much controversy.

10. Go online and conduct a Boolean search on "Samuel Huntington" and "Clash of Civilizations." How has the debate developed since the time Huntington first published his ideas? Summarize the controversy in a brief paper.

It's the Women, Stupid

PIPPA NORRIS AND RONALD INGLEHART

> Pippa Norris is the McGuire Lecturer in Comparative
> Politics at the John F. Kennedy School of Government
> at Harvard University. A political scientist and public
> speaker, her research compares election and public
> opinion, political communications, and gender politics.
> Her most recent book is *Radical Right: Voters and Par-
> ties in the Electoral Marketplace* (2005). *Sacred and
> Secular: Religion and Politics Worldwide* (2004) was
> written with long-time collaborator Ronald Inglehart.
> Ronald Inglehart has been Professor of Political Science
> at the University of Michigan since 1978 and serves as
> Program Director for the Center of Political Studies at
> the Institute for Social Research. He is director of the
> World Values Surveys, the group whose most recent
> findings are discussed in the essay that follows. In the
> essay, which first appeared in *Ms.* magazine in April
> 2004, Norris and Inglehart look at recent survey results
> that complicate one key premise of Samuel P. Hunting-
> ton's "clash of cultures" hypothesis.

Before Reading

Do you distinguish between democracy as a form of government and what you
consider to be democratic ideals? Is it possible to endorse one without endors-
ing the other? Explain.

In the aftermath of 9/11 and American military intervention in Afghan- 1
istan and Iraq, many have characterized the current state of world affairs
as a "clash of civilizations." Simplistically, on one side stands the Western
world of democratic ideals; on the other, Muslim fundamentalist beliefs.

It is a flawed analysis. In fact, it is the matter of gender equality— 2
women's rights—that stands at the fulcrum of this divide.

In making the "clash of civilizations" analysis, popular commentators 3
commonly cite the thesis of Harvard University professor Samuel Huntington, who wrote in his 1996 book, The Clash of Civilizations and the
Remaking of World Order: "In the new world . . . the most pervasive, important and dangerous conflicts will not be between social classes . . . but
between people belonging to different cultural entities. Tribal wars and ethnic conflicts will occur within civilizations. . . . And the most dangerous
cultural conflicts are those along the fault lines between civilizations."

For 45 years, Huntington pointed out, the central fault line in Europe   4
had been the Iron Curtain created by the Soviet Union; now, he suggested, that line had moved east: "[It] is now the line separating peoples of Western Christianity . . . from Muslim and Orthodox peoples."

Huntington's "clash" thesis has been used to interpret the terrorist at-   5
tack on the World Trade Center as a reaction by Muslim fundamentalists against Western culture itself. Moreover, his prediction of cultural rifts has been used to explain violent ethnic conflicts in Bosnia-Herzegovina, the Caucasus, Israel/Palestine and Kashmir. But even if Huntington weren't literally predictive, many fear that the Bush administration has made his forecast self-fulfilling after 9/11 by invading two Muslim countries.

But is Huntington's thesis correct?   6

According to our analysis of research, no—at least not in the ways he   7
defined the clash of cultures.

For Huntington, the gap between the West and the Muslim East is   8
caused by a lack of shared political values, which, combined, create democracy. They include separation of church and state, respect for the rule of law, social pluralism, parliamentary institutions and the protection of individual rights and civil liberties. "Individually almost none of these factors was unique to the West," Huntington argued, but "the combination of them was, however, and this is what gave the West its distinctive quality."

We believe he's mistaken: New evidence reveals a surprising consensus   9
that both Muslim and Western societies find democracy to be the best form of government. The cultural fault line that does divide the world—and deeply—is the one labeled "gender equality." Muslim nations remain the most traditional societies in the world when it comes to determining the role of women or tolerating divorce and homosexuality. And the gap is widening, because as younger generations in the West become far more liberal on these issues, the Muslim world stands firm against any such change.

Democracy? Yes!

It's easy to see what inspired Huntington's thesis about democracy, given   10
the failure of electoral democracy to take root in most states of the Middle East and North Africa. In 2002 about two-thirds of the 192 countries around the globe were electoral democracies, yet only one-quarter of the 47 countries with Muslim majority populations were. And none of the core Arabic-speaking societies fell into this category. Although Saudi Arabia has announced that it will hold local elections, the Middle East remains decades behind electoral developments in Latin America, Asia and much of sub-Saharan Africa.

It's often assumed that Muslim countries are lacking in electoral democ- 11
racies because their citizens have little desire for democracy. Huntington
developed his provocative argument without any systematic evidence of
such public opinion, probably, in part, because few representative surveys
were available that examined social and political attitudes in both Western
and Muslim states.

In recent years, however, surveys have been conducted in several Mus- 12
lim nations by Gallup and by Pew. Also, the World Values Survey (WVS),
which has collected evidence from more than 65 countries since 1981, has
added research in the past four years from 13 majority Muslim states (Al-
bania, Algeria, Azerbaijan, Bangladesh, Bosnia-Herzegovina, Egypt, Indonesia, Iran, Jordan, Morocco, Nigeria, Pakistan and Turkey). Culture
does matter, as Huntington claimed, in that predominant religious traditions leave an enduring imprint on contemporary values. People living in
traditionally Christian nations, as well as in Muslim and Buddhist societies, continue to display distinct values from these religious systems even
if they've never set foot in a church, temple or mosque. But that doesn't
mean they're anti-democratic.

In fact, the World Values Survey shows that people in Muslim states 13
highly support the statement that having a democratic political system
would be "very good" for their country. Indeed, support for that notion in
countries such as Morocco, Algeria and Egypt is far greater than in many
established democracies, while attitudes in Jordan and Iran are very similar to those in the United States. The countries most critical of the notion
are not Muslim ones but the ex-Soviet states of Eastern Europe, which have
experienced radical economic dislocation and a flawed and incomplete
transition to electoral democracy.

Support for democracy involves many complex elements, however, and 14
any single survey question may prove unreliable. So we also examined a
broader range of social and political topics, including evaluations of democratic performance, since people may believe democracy is the best form
of government but remain dissatisfied with the way it works in practice.
Still, there is virtually no difference between Muslim and Western publics
on these measurements. The country least enthusiastic toward democratic
ideals turns out to be Russia, not a Muslim state. Even though it remains
unclear exactly what people, given their varied cultural experience, mean
when they express approval (or disapproval) for democratic ideals, the
loosely defined notion of democracy nonetheless maintains an overwhelmingly positive image throughout the world.

The WVS also includes two items monitoring respondents' attitudes to- 15
ward the religious leaders in government, and only here are Muslim states

in variance with the West: The less-secular Muslim publics prove far more favorable toward active public engagement by religious figures. It would be an exaggeration, though, to claim that this represents a clash only of Western-Muslim values; in fact, the survey shows widespread agreement with the idea of religious leadership in many other parts of the world, including sub-Saharan Africa and Latin America.

Gender Equity? No!

When survey questions turn to gender and sexuality issues, the gap be-   16
tween Western and Muslim publics widens into a gulf.

Support for gender equality was determined by weighing people's atti-   17
tudes toward women and men in the workforce, education, politics, and the family. The WVS also includes a 10-point scale, ranked from "never justifiable" to "always justifiable," that measures people's approval of homosexuality, abortion and divorce. It asks respondents to agree or disagree with five statements:

- On the whole, men make better political leaders than women do.   18
- When jobs are scarce, men should have more right to a job than   19
  women.
- A university education is more important for a boy than a girl.   20
- Do you think that a woman has to have children in order to be fulfilled   21
  or is this not necessary?
- If a woman wants to have a child as a single parent but she doesn't   22
  want to have a stable relationship with a man, do you approve or
  disapprove?

The survey results show two striking and significant patterns: First, there   23
is a persistent gap in support for gender equality and sexual liberalization between Western (most liberal), Muslim (most traditional) and all other societies (in the middle). More important, the gap between Western and Muslim publics steadily widens as we move from older to younger birth cohorts. Younger generations in Western societies become progressively more egalitarian than their elders, while younger generations in Muslim societies remain almost as traditional as their parents and grandparents. Moreover, breaking down survey results by gender, younger women prove just as traditional in their attitudes toward sex roles as do younger men.

The differences revealed in the survey results remain significant even af-   24
ter controlling for factors that could potentially affect them, including levels of human and political development, age, gender, education, income and degree of religiosity.

Policy Implications

The events of 9/11 caused immense interest in the root causes of conflict   25
between the Muslim world and the United States, and Huntington's "clash
of civilizations" thesis was but one way of understanding them. Any interpretation, by Huntington or others, carries important policy implications,
especially in deciding whether the failure of democracy to take root in
many Middle Eastern states reflects the hegemonic grip of governing
regimes or deeper currents of public opinion.

But what does it mean when research shows that issues involving gen-   26
der and sexual liberalization create more Muslim-Western divisiveness
than do beliefs about democratic ideals?

For one thing, although vitally important for the process of social   27
change, as well as for progress in human rights, the gender attitude gap is
unlikely to prompt international conflict of the sort predicted by the
"clash" thesis.

No matter how misguided the U.S. military intervention, analysis of po-   28
litical attitudes in a wide range of comparable Middle Eastern societies suggests that support for democratic ideals does exist in the region. Whether
these ideals can ever be translated into stable democratic institutions, however, remains a core challenge.

Thinking About the Essay

1. Where and how explicitly do the authors state their thesis or claim? What
   would have been the effect of stating the thesis less explicitly, or in a different place in the essay?

2. Why do the authors make a point of first addressing the "clash of civilizations" thesis as it has been adopted by various analysts, rather than addressing the author of the thesis (Samuel Huntington) or the theory in its
   original form?

3. What concessions do the authors make to Samuel Huntington in their critique of his argument? Why are these concessions made in the essay?

4. According to surveys quoted in the essay, what countries are least enthusiastic about democratic ideals? Do the authors devote adequate space to
   speculating about the reasons for this lack of enthusiasm? Why or why not?

5. Does the essay end on an optimistic, pessimistic, or an ambivalent note?
   How would you compare the attitude of the conclusion with the attitude expressed in the opening paragraphs?

Responding in Writing

6. How can a predictive theory become a self-fulfilling prophecy? What are some ways of constructing (or phrasing) theories like Samuel P. Huntington's that would protect against this danger?

7. In a brief essay, consider some examples of "progressive" thought in the United States that nevertheless contain what you see as regressive or dogmatic elements. Try to explain the compatibility of these attitudes.

8. In an essay of analysis, attempt to explain (or speculate about) the causes of the gender gap described in paragraphs 17–22.

Networking

9. In groups of three or four, come up with a list of five statements (similar to those that appear in the World Values Survey) that you consider to be "litmus tests" for democratic or progressive beliefs. Share your lists with the class.

10. Review some of the other results of the World Values Survey that are available for review online. Do you see any statistics that you feel ought to have been addressed in this essay? How would this information have qualified the argument of the essay?

A World Not Neatly Divided

Amartya Sen   Amartya K. Sen, the 1998 Nobel Prize winner in economics, was born in 1933 in Santiniketan, India. After studying at Presidency College in Calcutta, Sen emigrated to England, where he received B.A. (1955), M.A., and Ph.D. (1959) degrees from Trinity College, Cambridge. Master of Trinity College since 1998, Sen also has taught at Oxford University, the London School of Economics, Harvard University, and Cornell University. Sen is credited with bringing ethical considerations into the study of economics. He has done groundbreaking work in establishing techniques for assessing world poverty and the relative wealth of nations, the causes of famine, and the economic impact of health and education on developing societies. His study, *Collective Choice and Social Welfare* (1970), in which he uses the tools of economics to study such concepts as fairness, liberty, and justice, brings to economic theory a dimension of moral philosophy that has made Sen an influential figure in contemporary thought. Other notable works include *Poverty and Famines: An Essay on Entitlement and Deprivation* (1981), *On Ethics and Economics* (1987), *Development as Freedom* (1999), and *The Argumentative Indian: Writings on Indian History, Culture and Identity* (2005). As this essay from *The New York Times*, November 23, 2001, demonstrates, Sen commands a lucid prose style that enables him to make complex issues accessible to general readers. Here, he argues for a more nuanced approach to the idea of civilization than the one posed by Samuel Huntington.

Before Reading

Is it necessary to divide the world into various types of civilizations? What is the purpose of such classification, and what are the possible results?

When people talk about clashing civilizations, as so many politicians   1
and academics do now, they can sometimes miss the central issue. The inadequacy of this thesis begins well before we get to the question of whether civilizations must clash. The basic weakness of the theory lies in its program of categorizing people of the world according to a unique, allegedly commanding system of classification. This is problematic because civilizational categories are crude and inconsistent and also because there are other ways of seeing people (linked to politics, language, literature, class, occupation or other affiliations).

The befuddling influence of a singular classification also traps those   2
who dispute the thesis of a clash: To talk about "the Islamic world" or "the Western world" is already to adopt an impoverished vision of humanity as unalterably divided. In fact, civilizations are hard to partition in this way, given the diversities within each society as well as the linkages among different countries and cultures. For example, describing India as a "Hindu civilization" misses the fact that India has more Muslims than any other country except Indonesia and possibly Pakistan. It is futile to try to understand Indian art, literature, music, food or politics without seeing the extensive interactions across barriers of religious communities. These include Hindus and Muslims, Buddhists, Jains, Sikhs, Parsees, Christians (who have been in India since at least the fourth century, well before England's conversion to Christianity), Jews (present since the fall of Jerusalem), and even atheists and agnostics. Sanskrit has a larger atheistic literature than exists in any other classical language. Speaking of India as a Hindu civilization may be comforting to the Hindu fundamentalist, but it is an odd reading of India.

A similar coarseness can be seen in the other categories invoked, like 3
"the Islamic world." Consider Akbar and Aurangzeb, two Muslim emperors of the Mogul dynasty in India. Aurangzeb tried hard to convert
Hindus into Muslims and instituted various policies in that direction, of
which taxing the non-Muslims was only one example. In contrast, Akbar
reveled in his multiethnic court and pluralist laws, and issued official
proclamations insisting that no one "should be interfered with on account
of religion" and that "anyone is to be allowed to go over to a religion that
pleases him."

If a homogeneous view of Islam were to be taken, then only one of these 4
emperors could count as a true Muslim. The Islamic fundamentalist would
have no time for Akbar; Prime Minister Tony Blair, given his insistence that
tolerance is a defining characteristic of Islam, would have to consider ex-
communicating Aurangzeb. I expect both Akbar and Aurangzeb would
protest, and so would I. A similar crudity is present in the characterization
of what is called "Western civilization." Tolerance and individual freedom
have certainly been present in European history. But there is no dearth of
diversity here, either. When Akbar was making his pronouncements on religious tolerance in Agra, in the 1590's, the Inquisitions were still going on;
in 1600, Giordano Bruno was burned at the stake, for heresy, in Campo
dei Fiori in Rome.

Dividing the world into discrete civilizations is not just crude. It propels 5
us into the absurd belief that this partitioning is natural and necessary and
must overwhelm all other ways of identifying people. That imperious view
goes not only against the sentiment that "we human beings are all much
the same," but also against the more plausible understanding that we are
diversely different. For example, Bangladesh's split from Pakistan was not
connected with religion, but with language and politics.

Each of us has many features in our self-conception. Our religion, im- 6
portant as it may be, cannot be an all-engulfing identity. Even a shared
poverty can be a source of solidarity across the borders. The kind of division highlighted by, say, the so-called "anti-globalization" protesters—
whose movement is, incidentally, one of the most globalized in the
world—tries to unite the underdogs of the world economy and goes firmly
against religious, national or "civilizational" lines of division.

The main hope of harmony lies not in any imagined uniformity, but in 7
the plurality of our identities, which cut across each other and work against
sharp divisions into impenetrable civilizational camps. Political leaders
who think and act in terms of sectioning off humanity into various
"worlds" stand to make the world more flammable—even when their intentions are very different. They also end up, in the case of civilizations

defined by religion, lending authority to religious leaders seen as spokesmen for their "worlds." In the process, other voices are muffled and other concerns silenced. The robbing of our plural identities not only reduces us; it impoverishes the world.

Thinking About the Essay

1. How does Sen begin his essay? What is his argument and how does he present it in the opening paragraph?

2. Sen uses several illustrations to support his argument about "singular classification." Locate three of these examples and explain how they advance his claim.

3. Any discussion of types—whether types of civilizations or types of teachers—lends itself to classification. How does Sen use classification and division to organize his argument and his essay?

4. What transitional devices serve to unify this essay?

5. Does Sen's concluding paragraph serve to confirm his thesis or claim? Explain your answer.

Responding in Writing

6. What is so wrong about "singular classification," especially when considering nations, cultures, and civilizations? Write a response to this question, referring to Sen's essay in the process.

7. Write a complete analysis of the ways in which Sen composes his argument in "A World Not Neatly Divided."

8. Write a comparative paper analyzing the essays by Sen and Samuel Huntington.

Networking

9. In small groups, select a city, region, country, or civilization, and then draw up a list of traits or attributes—a singular classification—illuminating your subject. Present the list to class members, and as a group discuss the advantages and disadvantages of singular classification.

10. Conduct online research on an international city. Then write a travel blurb stressing both the singular nature of this city and also its diversity.

Andalusia's Journey

EDWARD SAID

> Edward W. Said was born in 1935 in Jerusalem, Palestine, and grew up in Egypt. His family moved to the United States in 1951. Educated at Princeton University (B.A., 1957) and Harvard University (Ph.D., 1964), Said was an influential literary and cultural critic and a noted supporter of the Palestinian cause. University Professor of English and comparative literature at Columbia, he was best known to the general public as a commentator on radio and television on Middle Eastern affairs. Perceived as a public intellectual, Said for decades advocated Palestinian rights even as he criticized Palestinian policies and leadership. His books *The Question of Palestine* (1979), *Covering Islam* (1981), and *The Politics of Dispossession: The Struggle for Palestinian Self-Determination* (1994) offer penetrating analyses of this troubled region. Said was also a distinguished literary critic, the author of the groundbreaking study *Orientalism* (1978), *Culture and Imperialism* (1993), and other books and collections of essays. In the early 1990s Said was diagnosed with leukemia; his illness prompted him to write an autobiography, *Out of Place: A Memoir* (1999), tracing his life and journeys as an exile. Said died in 2003. In the following essay, published in *Travel and Leisure* in 2002, Said offers a personal impression of one region in Spain that has been a crossroads in the convergence of civilizations.

Before Reading

Said speaks of Andalusia—the region in southern Spain where Arab, Latin, and Jewish civilizations came together for seven hundred years—as representing a dialogue rather than clash of civilizations. What is necessary for such a dialogue to occur in the world today?

> Poverty turns our country into a foreign land, and riches our place of exile into our home. For the whole world, in all its diversity, is one. And all its inhabitants our brothers and neighbors.
>
> —Abu Muhammad al-Zubaydi, Seville, A.D. 926–989

For an Arab, such as myself, to enter Granada's 13th-century Alhambra palace is to leave behind a modern world of disillusionment, strife, and uncertainty. In this, the calmest, most harmonious structure ever built by

1

A 16th-century plate from Valencia (once part of the Caliphate of Cordova), on which Arabic and Spanish designs merge.

Arab Muslims, the walls are covered with dizzying arabesques and geometric patterns, interspersed with Arabic script extolling God and his regents on earth. The repetition of a basically abstract series of motifs suggests infinity, and serves to pull one through the palace's many rooms. The palace's Generalife gardens, punctuated by cooling streams, are a miracle of balance and repose. The Alhambra, like the great ninth-century mosque-cum-cathedral of Cordova, La Mezquita, invites believer and nonbeliever alike with opulence and rigorous discipline of ornament, and almost imperceptible changes in perspective from one space to the next. The whole composition is always in evidence—always changing yet always somehow the same—a unity in multiplicity.

I have been traveling for four decades to southern Spain, Andalucía as 2 it is called by Spaniards, al-Andalus by Arabs, drawn there by its magnificent architecture, and the amazingly mixed Arab, Jewish, and Latin cultural centers of Cordova, Granada, and Seville. The turmoil of Andalusia's extraordinary past seems to hover just beneath the surface of its pleasant landscapes and generally small-scaled urban life. In its medieval heyday, Andalusia, established by the Arab general Tariq bin Ziyad and continuously fought over by numerous Muslim sects (among them Almoravids, Nasrids, and Almohads) and by Catholics as far north as Galicia, was a particularly lively instance of the dialogue, much more than the clash, of cultures. Muslims, Jews, and Christians co-existed with astonishing harmony. Today its periods of fruitful cultural diversity may provide a model for the co-existence of peoples, a model quite different from the ideological battles, local chauvinism, and ethnic conflict that finally brought it

The Alhambra's repeating arches.

down—and which ironically enough threaten to engulf our own 21st-century world.

When I first visited, in the summer of 1966, Franco-era Andalusia 3 seemed like a forgotten, if wonderfully picturesque, province of Catholic Spain. Its fierce sun accentuated the area's rigors: the scarcity of good accommodations, the difficulty of travel, the heaviness of the cuisine, the unyielding spirit of a people living in relative poverty and obdurate pride, the political and religious repression under which the country suffocated. The splendor of its great buildings was evident but seemed part of a distant backdrop to more urgent and more recent times: the Civil War of 1936–39 and Hemingway's sentimentalized view of it; the burgeoning and quite sleazy mass tourist trade that had put down roots in Málaga (not to mention the ghastly neighboring village of Torremolinos) and that was creeping slowly westward toward Portugal's Algarve (from the Arabic *al-gharb min al-Andalus,* "west of Andalusia").

Even in the summer of 1979, when I spent a few weeks in the area with 4 my wife and two young children, the Alhambra was all but deserted. You could stroll into it as you would into a public park. (Today, visiting the place is more like going to Disneyland. There are five gigantic parking lots and you must reserve well in advance.) For its part, Seville was a pleasant, somewhat subdued city of modest restaurants and family-style hotels.

The palace's Generalife gardens.

Swearing allegiance at the Alhambra, as imagined by Filippo Baratti, one of many 19th-century European artists captivated by Andalusia's history.

Franco had disappeared in 1975, of course, but the prosperous Spain of solidly based, open democracy had not yet arrived. You could still feel the Church's cold impress and the vestiges of the fascist dictatorship. Europe was a long distance away, beyond the Pyrenees, to the north.

In the 1980's and 90's Spain awakened into modernity and globalization. NATO's Spain, the EU's Spain, took over the peninsula's identity. There is now no shortage of excellent hotels or good restaurants, although 5 it must again be admitted, as the Michelin Guide put it in the 1960's, that for the most part "Spanish cuisine is more complicated than it is refined." But for me, and indeed for many Arabs, Andalusia still represents the finest flowering of our culture. That is particularly true now, when the Arab Middle East seems mired in defeat and violence, its societies unable to arrest their declining fortunes, its secular culture so full of almost surreal crisis, shock, and nihilism.

A spate of recent Arabic and Muslim writing has redirected attention 6 to Andalusia as a mournful, tantalizing emblem of what a glorious civilization was lost when Islamic rule ended. This literature serves only to accentuate the conditions of decline and loss that have so diminished modern Arab life—and the conquests that have dominated it. Thus, for instance, the 1992 appearance of Palestinian poet Mahmud Darwish's great *qasida,* or ode, *Ahd Ashr Kawkaban Ala Akhir Almashad Al-Andalusi* (Eleven Stars over the Last Moments of Andalusia). The poem was written about— and served to clarify—what the Palestinians felt they had lost not just once but time after time. The Palestinian national poet seems to be asking, What do we do after the last time, after the new conquerors have entered our palaces and consumed our still hot tea and heard our mellifluous music? Does it mean that as Arabs we exist only as a footnote to someone else's history?

> Our tea is green and hot: drink it. Our pistachios are fresh; eat them.
> The beds are of green cedar, fall on them,
> following this long siege, lie down on the feathers of our dream.
> The sheets are crisp, perfumes are ready by the door, and there are plenty of mirrors:
> Enter them so we may exist completely. Soon we will search
> In the margins of your history, in distant countries,
> For what was once our history. And in the end we will ask ourselves:
> Was Andalusia here or there? On the land . . . or in the poem?

It is difficult to overestimate the searing poignancy of these lines. They 7 recall not only the self-destructive demise of the Andalusian kings and their *tawai'f* but also present-day Arab disunity and consequent weakness. (*Tawai'f* is the plural of the Arabic *ta'ifa,* used to refer both to the independent Muslim kingdoms that began in 1023, and also to modern-day confessional sects, of the sort common in Lebanon during its recent civil war. The references are lost on no one whose language is Arabic.) For a visitor from either North Africa or the Arab countries east of Suez, including Egypt, Andalusia is idealized as a kind of lost paradise, which fell from the brilliance of its medieval apex into terrible squabbles and petty jealousies. This perhaps makes a rather too facile moral lesson of the place.

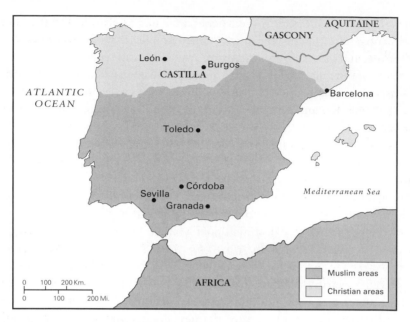

The Iberian Peninsula and North Africa
The map shows the extent of the Moorish conquest from the 9th through the 12th centuries C.E.

Andalusia's unthreatening landscape—tranquil hills, agreeable towns,   8
and rich green fields—survived a turbulent and deeply unsavory history.
Running through its convoluted past was a steady current of unrest, of trust
betrayed. It seems to have been made up of composite or converted souls,
Mozarabs (Arabized Christians) and *muwallads* (Christian converts to
Islam). Nothing and no one is simple. Several of its city-states (there were no
fewer than 12 at the height of the internecine conflict) were occasionally ruled
by poets and patrons of the arts, such as Seville's 11th-century al-Mutamid,
but they were often jealous and even small-minded schemers. Andalusia mul-
tiplies in the mind with its contradictions and puzzles; its history is a history
of the masks and assumed identities it has worn.

Was Andalusia largely Arab and Muslim, as it certainly seems to have   9
been, and if so why was it so very different from, say, Syria, Egypt, and
Iraq, themselves great centers of civilization and power? And how did the
Jews, the Visigoth Catholics, and the Romans who colonized it before the
Arabs play their role in Andalusia's makeup and identity? However all
these components are sorted out, a composite Andalusian identity an-
chored in Arab culture can be discerned in its striking buildings, its tiles
and wooden ceilings, its ornate pottery and neatly constructed houses. And

what could be more Andalusian than the fiery flamenco dancer, accompanied by hoarse *cantaores,* martial hand-clapping, and hypnotically strummed guitars, all of which have precedents in Arabic music?

On this trip I wanted to discover what Andalusia was from my per- 10 spective as a Palestinian Arab, as someone whose diverse background might offer a way of seeing and understanding the place beyond illusion and romance. I was born in Jerusalem, Andalusia's great Eastern antipode, and raised as a Christian. Though the environment I grew up in was both colonial and Muslim, my university education and years of residence in the United States and Europe allow me to see my past as a Westerner might. Standing before the monumental portal of Seville's Alcázar (the Hispanicized word for *al-qasr,* "castle"), every inch of which is covered in raised florid swirls and interlocking squares. I was reminded of similar surfaces from my earlier years in Cairo, Damascus, and Jerusalem, strangely present before me now in southern Europe, where Arab Muslims once hoped to set up an Umayyad empire in the West to rival the one in Syria. The Arabs journeyed along the shores of the Mediterranean through Spain, France, and Italy, all of which now bear their traces, even if those traces are not always acknowledged.

Perhaps the most striking feature of Andalusia historically was the care 11 lavished on such aspects of urban life as running water, leafy gardens, viewing places *(miradores),* and graceful wall and ceiling designs. Medieval Europe, all rough skins, drafty rooms, and meaty cuisine, was barbaric by comparison. This is worth noting, since the interiors of Andalusia's palaces today are presented as out of time, stripped of their luxurious silks and divans, their heady perfumes and spices, their counterpoint of din and lyrical poetry.

Except for Cordova's immense Mezquita, the choice spaces of what has 12 been known historically as Muslim Spain are generally not very large. Even Seville's Alcázar, big enough as a castle or palace, doesn't dominate at all. The Arabs who gave Andalusia its characteristic features generally used architecture to refashion and enhance nature, to create symmetrical patterns that echo Arabic calligraphy. Streets are pleasant to saunter in, rather than utilitarian thoroughfares. Curved ornaments—such as highly patterned vases and metal utensils—abound, all part of a wonderfully relaxed worldliness.

That worldliness, which reached its apex between the 9th and 12th cen- 13 turies, testifies to the extraordinary diversity of Islam itself, so often thought of today as a monolithic block of wild-eyed terrorists, bent on destruction and driven by fanaticism. Yes, there were feuding factions, but rarely before or after did the Islamic kings and princes produce a civilization of such refinement with so many potentially warring components. Consider that in

Seville's Alcázar palace, one of the best surviving examples of Mudejar architecture, a late Andalusian style.

Cordova's heyday the Jewish sage Maimonides and Islam's greatest thinker, Ibn Rushd (Averroës), lived in Cordova at the same time, each with his own disciples and doctrines, both writing and speaking in Arabic. Part of the Damascus-based Umayyad empire that had fallen to the Baghdad-based Abbasids in 750, the Spanish territories always retained an eagerness to be recognized by, and an ambition to surpass the achievements of, their Eastern cousin.

Quite soon, Andalusia became a magnet for talent in many arenas: music, philosophy, mysticism, literature, architecture, virtually all of the sciences, jurisprudence, religion. The monarchs Abd ar-Rahman I (731–788) and Abd ar-Rahman III (891–961) gave Cordova its almost mythic status. Three times the size of Paris (Europe's second-largest city in the 10th century), with 70 libraries, Cordova also had, according to the historian Salma Kahdra Jayyusi, "1,600 mosques, 900 baths, 213,077 homes for ordinary people, 60,300 mansions for notables, officials, and military commanders, and 80,455 shops." The mystics and poets Ibn Hazm and Ibn Arabi, Jewish writers Judah ha-Levi and Ibn Gabirol, the colloquial but lyrical *zajals* and wonderful strophic songs, or *muwashshah,* that seemed to emerge as if from nowhere and later influenced the troubadors, provided al-Andalus with verse, music, and atmosphere such as Europe had never had before.

The Arab general Tariq bin Ziyad and his desert army streamed across the Gibraltar straits in 711; on later forays he brought with him many North African Berbers, Yemenis, Egyptians, and Syrians. In Spain they encountered Visigoths and Jews, plus the remnants of a once thriving Roman community, all of whom at times co-existed, and at times fought with one another. No harmony was stable for very long—too many conflicting elements were always in play. Andalusia's reign of relative tolerance (three monotheistic faiths in complex accord with one another) abruptly ended when King Ferdinand and Queen Isabella seized the region and imposed a reign of terror on non-Christians. Significantly, one of the towering figures of the Andalusian cultural synthesis, Ibn Khaldun, a founder of sociology and historiography, came from a prominent Seville family, and was perhaps the greatest analyst of how nations rise and fall.

The last king of Granada, the luckless Boabdil (Abu Abd Allah Muhammad), was expelled along with the Jews in 1492, weeping or sighing—choose your version. The unhappy Moor quickly became the emblem of what the Arabs had lost. Yet most people who are gripped by the pathos of the king's departure may not know that Boabdil negotiated very profitable surrender terms—some money, and land outside Granada—before he left the city to the Castilian monarchs.

Despite the richness of Andalusia's Islamic past and its indelible presence in Spain's subsequent history after the Reconquista, for years the Church and royalist ideologues stressed the purgation of Spain's Islamic and Jewish heritage, insisting that Christian Spain was restored in 1492 as if little had happened to disturb its ascendancy in the seven preceding centuries. Not for nothing has the cult of Santiago (Saint James) been highlighted in Catholic Spain: St. James was, among other things, the patron saint of the Spanish in their battles against the Moors, hence his nickname Matamoros, "Killer of Moors." Yet, classical Mudejar art, with its typically florid arabesques and geometrical architecture, was produced after the Muslims were defeated. As far away as Catalonia, Gaudí's obsession with botanical motifs shows the Arab influence at its most profound. Why did it linger so if Arabs had represented only a negligible phase in Spanish history?

The Jews and Muslims who weren't thrown out or destroyed by the Inquisition remained as conversos and Moriscos, men and women who had converted to Catholicism to preserve their lives. No one will ever know whether the identity they abandoned was really given up or whether it continued underground. Miguel de Cervantes's magnificent novel *Don Quixote* draws attention to its supposed author, the fictional Arab Sidi Hamete Benengeli, which—it is plausibly alleged—was a way of masking Cervantes's own secret identity as an unrepentant converso. The wars between Muslims and Catholics turn up again and again in literature, including of course the *Chanson de Roland* (in which Charlemagne's Frankish army is defeated in 778 by Abd ar-Rahman's men) and Spain's national epic, *El Poema del Cid*. About 60 percent of the Spanish language is made up of Arabic words and phrases: *alcalde* (mayor), *barrios* (quarters of a city), *aceite* (oil), *aceitunas* (olives). Their persistence indicates that Spain's identity is truly, if perhaps also uneasily, bicultural.

It took the great Spanish historian and philologist Américo Castro, who taught for many years at Princeton, to establish the enduring pervasiveness of the country's repressed past in his monumental work *The Structure of Spanish History* (1954). One of Spain's finest contemporary novelists, Juan Goytisolo, has also inspired interest in Andalusia's Arab and Muslim origins, and done much to reassert Spain's non-European past. His *Count Julian*, which centers on the treacherous Catholic whom Spaniards hold responsible for bringing in the Moors, challenges the myth that Visigoth Spain's rapid fall in 711 can be explained by nothing other than the nobleman's betrayal.

Andalusia's identity was always in the process of being dissolved and lost, even when its cultural life was at its pinnacle. Every one of its several strands—Arabic, Muslim, Berber, Catholic, Jewish, Visigothic, Roman—calls up another. Cordova was a particularly wonderful case in point. A much smaller city today than under Abd ar-Rahman I, it is still dominated by the mosque that he began in 785. Erected on the site of a Christian church, it was an attempt to assert his identity as a Umayyad prince fleeing Damascus, to make a cultural statement as a Muslim exiled to a place literally across the world from where he had come.

The result is, in my experience, the greatest and most impressive reli- 21 gious structure on earth. The mosque-cathedral, La Mezquita, stretches effortlessly for acres in a series of unending double arches, whose climax is an incredibly ornate mihrab, the place where the muezzin or prayer leader stands. Its contours echo those of the great mosque in Damascus (from which Abd ar-Rahman I barely managed to escape when his Umayyad dynasty fell), while its arches are conscious quotations of Roman aqueducts. So assiduous was its architect in copying Damascus that the Cordovan mihrab actually faces south, rather than east—toward Mecca—as it should.

The great mosque was later barbarically seized by a Christian monarch 22 who turned it into a church. He did this by inserting an entire cathedral into the Muslim structure's center, in an aggressive erasure of history and statement of faith. He may also have had in mind the legend that Muslims had stolen the bells of the Cathedral of Santiago de Compostela, melted them down, and used them in the mosque, which also housed the Prophet Muhammad's hand. Today, though the Muslim idea of prayer remains dominant, the building exudes a spirit of inclusive sanctity and magnanimity of purpose.

Beyond the mosque's imposing walls, Cordova retains its memorial 23 splendor and inviting shelter. To this day, the houses communicate a sense of welcome: inner courtyards are often furnished with a fountain, and the rooms are dispersed around it, very much as they are in houses in Aleppo thousands of miles to the east. Streets are narrow and winding because, as in medieval Cairo, the idea is to cajole the pedestrian with promises of arrival. Thus one walks along without having to face the psychologically intimidating distance of the long, straight avenue. Moreover, Cordova is one of the few cities in the Mediterranean where the intermingling of Arab and Jewish quarters doesn't immediately suggest conflict. Just seeing streets and squares named after Averroës and Maimonides in 21st-century Cordova, one gets an immediate idea of what a universal culture was like a thousand years ago.

Only five miles outside Cordova stand the partially restored ruins of 24 what must have been the most lavish, and certainly the most impressive, royal city in Europe, Madinat al-Zahra (City of the Flower). Begun by Abd ar-Rahman III in 936, it, too, was a vast echo of palace-cities in the Arab East, which it almost certainly overshadowed for a time. It is as if Andalusia's rulers and great figures were unable ever to rid their minds of the East. They relived its prior greatness on their terms, nowhere with more striving for effect than in Madinat al-Zahra.

Now an enormous excavation, Madinat al-Zahra is slowly being re- 25
stored. You can stand looking down on the symmetrical array of stables,
military barracks, reception rooms, courtyards—all pointing at the great
central hall in which the king received his guests and subjects. According
to some scholars. Abd ar-Rahman wanted not only to assume the mantle
of the caliphate, thereby wresting it from the Abbasid king in Baghdad
(who couldn't have paid much attention to Abd ar-Rahman's posturings),
but also to establish political authority as something that belonged in the
West but had meaning only if snatched from the East. For an Arab visitor,
it is hard not to be struck by the rather competitive Andalusian reference
to the better-known Eastern Muslim empires, mainly those of the Abbasids
and Fatimids, who to this day form the core of what is taught and propa-
gated as Arab culture.

A special poignancy hangs over Andalusia's impressively animated 26
spaces. It derives not only from a pervasive sense of former grandeur but
also from what, because so many people hoped to possess it, Andalusia
tried to be—and what it might have been. Certainly Granada's Alhambra
is a monument to regret and the passage of time. Next to the wonderful
13th- to 14th-century Nasrid palace and superb Generalife gardens looms
the ponderous 16th-century castle of the Spanish king and Holy Roman
Emperor Charles V, who obviously wanted his rather ostentatious abode
to acquire some of the luster of the Arab complex. Yet, despite the Alhambra's opulence and its apparently hedonistic celebration of the good life
(for rulers, mainly), its arabesque patterns can seem like a defense against
mortality or the ravages of human life. One can easily imagine the belea-
guered and insecure Boabdil using it as a place of perfumed forgetfulness—
perhaps even at times reexperiencing the studied oblivion cultivated by Sufi
masters such as Ibn Arab.

The schizophrenia inherent in Spain's identity is more apparent in 27
Granada than anywhere else in Andalusia. Because the Alhambra sits on
one of several hills high above the city, Granada proper has paid the price
in clogged streets and overbuilt residential and commercial quarters
through which the Arab palace must be approached. Granada as a whole
embodies this tension between high and low. A mazelike system of one-way
streets connects the Alhambra to Albaicín, the old Muslim quarter. Despite
the wonders of the Alhambra, being in Albaicín is like feeling the fantasy
of summer and the realities of a grim winter very close to each other. The
resemblances between Albaicín and Cordova's barrios are striking, except
that, as the name suggests, Albaicín—Arabic for "the downtrodden and
hopeless"—was indeed an area for the poor and, one can't help feeling,
where the last Arabs and Jews huddled together before their eviction in

1492. Nothing evokes Granada's riven history more superbly than the "Albaicín" movement in Isaac Albéniz's greatest musical work, the redoubtably difficult-to-perform piano collection *Iberia.*

By contrast, Seville's spirit is very much of this world—part feline, part 28 macho, part dashing sparkle, part somber colonialism. Seville contains Spain's finest *plaza de toros* and also its largest cathedral. And it is here that all the archives of Spain's imperial conquests are housed. But before 1492, Seville was the administrative capital of the Arab monarchy that held sway over Andalusia. Where the Catholic empire-builders set their sights on the New World, the Arabs were taken up with the Old: Morocco, which before the final Reconquista was considered to be part of Andalusia. Similarities in metal, leather, and glazed pottery design between Spain and North Africa reinforce a prevailing unity of vision and religious discourse.

If Seville is a city where Catholic and Muslim cultures interact, it is to 29 the decided advantage of the former—though given Seville's special status in the Western romantic imagination as an extension of the Orient, it's probably truer to say that Seville is the triumph of Andalusian style. This, after all, is the city of Mérimée's and Bizet's *Carmen,* the heart of Hemingway's bullfighting obsession, and a favorite port of call for northern European poets and writers for whom citrus blossoms represent the salutary opposite of their dreary climates. Stendhal's *espagnolisme* derives from Sevillian themes, and the city's Holy Week parades and observances have gripped many peregrinating artists.

Not that the Arabs haven't made their own indelible mark on the city. 30 Standing watch over the landscape is the four-sided Giralda, a minaret built by an Almohad (basically an austere fundamentalist sort of Islam) king in the late 12th century. Its upper third was added to, for purposes of "improvement," by zealous Christians 400 years later. Despite some unnecessary flourishes, the tower was so magnetic that a contemporary chronicler observed, "From a distance it would appear that all the stars of the Zodiac had stopped in the heart of Seville." Incorporated into the cathedral, whose awesome bulk testifies to Catholic ambition and consolidation of power (Christopher Columbus's tomb is inside), the Giralda leads an independent existence as an ornate symbol of how even the harshest of ideologies can be filled with grace.

In the long run, and almost in spite of its kings and magistrates, the An- 31 dalusian style seems to have fostered movement and discovery rather than monumentality and stability. It enacted an earlier version of our own hybrid world, one whose borders were also thresholds, and whose multiple identities formed an enriched diversity.

Thinking About the Essay

1. Said wrote this article for *Travel and Leisure.* What does he assume about the readership of this specific magazine? How does he make the essay both an introduction to a tourist destination and a serious explanation of the importance of the region? Do you think he succeeds in his dual purpose? Why or why not?

2. Where does Said state his thesis? Why is his thesis personally important?

3. Trace the historical process that Said presents in this essay, moving section by section through the article. What are some of the main topics and points he draws from his historical analysis?

4. What mood or sense of place does Said create in this essay? Identify aspects of style and language that convey mood and atmosphere.

5. What *definition* of culture and civilization does Said present in this essay? Locate examples of various strategies he employs to create this definition.

Responding in Writing

6. Explain why, after reading Said's essay, you might want to visit Andalusia on your own or on a group tour. Where would you visit? What would you look for? What would you hope to learn from this trip?

7. Said raises the prospect that civilizations don't necessarily have to clash. Reread his essay, and then write a paper in which you outline the necessary conditions required for a dialogue of civilizations.

8. How can travel alert us to the history and contours of civilizations? Answer this question in a reflective essay. If you have traveled to the various centers of civilization or have read about them, incorporate this knowledge into the paper.

Networking

9. In small groups, work through Said's essay section by section. Then devise a sketch outline of the entire essay. Put your outline on the chalkboard or blackboard for the class to view.

10. Go to the library or online to find additional information on Andalusia. Then prepare a report in which you determine whether Said's presentation of the region is accurate or biased.

The Age of Terror: What Is the Just Response?

Just as changes in United States demographics, patterns of cultural change, the forces of globalization, and the "clash" of civilizations have brought us into expanding contact with the peoples of the world, recent events remind us of how dangerous this new world can be. Indeed, in the years since the September 11, 2001, attack, we have had to reorient our thinking about numerous critical issues: the war on terrorism; the erosion of our sense of individual and collective security; the need to achieve a balance between individual rights and common security. Above all, Americans now face the ethical, political, and historical challenge of being the world's single superpower. There are people and nations who hate America's standing in the world. And hatred and cruelty, as Isaac Bashevis Singer, a winner of the Nobel Prize for Literature, once observed, only produce more of the same.

The 9/11 terrorist attack was so profoundly unnerving that virtually all of us can remember where we were when the planes hijacked by terrorists crashed into New York's World Trade Center and the Pentagon in Washington, D.C. This was a primal national event, similar in impact to the raid on Pearl Harbor in 1941 or the assassinations of President John Kennedy and Martin Luther King Jr. in the 1960s. These prior events, whether taking the lives of thousands or just one, serve to define entire American generations. Today, America faces a new defining event—the war on terrorism. We seemingly live in an age of terror, and we have to find ways in which national and global communities can deal with this unnerving reality.

In a sense, the September 11 attack and subsequent assaults—from Bali to Spain and England to the Persian Gulf—have forced America to look inward and outward for intelligent responses. Looking inward, we

 **Online Study Center** This icon will direct you to web links, audio and visual content, and additional resources on the website college.hmco.com/pic/mullerNWR2e

Two women hold each other as they watch the World Trade Center burn following a terrorist attack on the twin skyscrapers in New York on Tuesday, Sept. 11, 2001.   (AP Photo/Ernesto Mora)

Thinking About the Image

1. On September 11, 2001, New York City was the center of the world's media attention. Cameras seemed to document every single moment of the disaster, from the first plane's impact through the seemingly endless search for remains. Why do you think the author of this textbook chose this particular image—rather than, say, an image of one of the buildings in flames—to illustrate this chapter?
2. Compare this photograph with others throughout this text. What is most strikingly different about this image?
3. Is the photographer violating the privacy of these women in a moment of obviously tremendous grief and distress? How do you think news photographers might cope with the responsibility of documenting such tragic or frightening events?
4. Which of the essays in this chapter do you think this photograph best illustrates? Why?

often have to deal with our own anger, insecurity, and hatred of other peoples who commit these crimes against unsuspecting humanity. These are primal emotions that affect our sense of personal identity. At the same time, we must understand how others around the world view our country and must gain knowledge of peoples and cultures we once knew little or nothing about. For example, are the terrorists who planned and launched the 9/11 attack a mere aberration—some delusional distortion of the great culture and civilization of Islam? Or do they reflect the consensus of the Arab street? Where do college students—who should be committed to liberal learning— go to find answers to such large and complex questions? What courses exist on your campus? What organizations foster transnational or global under- standing?

Ultimately—as writers in this chapter and throughout the text suggest—we have to read across cultures and nations to understand the consequences of 9/11. We have to reflect on our own backgrounds. We have to be candid about how our individual experience molds our attitudes toward "others"—most of whom are like us but some of whom want to do us harm. Liberal education, as the American philosopher William James stated at the beginning of the last century, makes us less fanatical. Against the backdrop of contemporary terrorism, we have to search for wisdom and for sustaining values.

To Any Would-Be Terrorists

Naomi Shihab Nye

Naomi Shihab Nye was born in 1952 in St. Louis, Mis- souri. Her family background is Palestinian American. She graduated from Trinity University (B.A., 1974) and subsequently started a career as a freelance writer and editor. Today Nye is known for her award-winning po- etry, fiction for children, novels, and essays. She has been a visiting writer at the University of Texas, the University of Hawaii, the University of California at Berkeley, and elsewhere. Among Nye's books are the prize-winning poetry collection *Different Ways to Pray* (1980); several other poetry volumes, including *Yellow Glove* (1986), incorporating poems dealing with Pales- tinian life; a book of essays, *Never in a Hurry* (1996); and a young adult novel, *Habibi* (1997), which draws on Nye's own childhood experience of living in Jerusalem in the 1970s, which at that time was part of Jordan. Among her many awards are the Peter I. B. Lavin Younger Poets Award from the Academy of American Poets and a Guggenheim Fellowship. Starting with the provocative title of the following essay, Nye speaks as a Palestinian American to an extremist audi- ence that needs "to find another way to live."

Before Reading

If you had an opportunity to address a terrorist, what would you say and how would you say it?

I am sorry I have to call you that, but I don't know how else to get your   1
attention. I hate that word. Do you know how hard some of us have worked to get rid of that word, to deny its instant connection to the Middle East? And now look. Look what extra work we have.

Not only did your colleagues kill thousands of innocent, international   2
people in those buildings and scar their families forever; they wounded a huge community of people in the Middle East, in the United States and all over the world. If that's what they wanted to do, please know the mission was a terrible success, and you can stop now.

Because I feel a little closer to you than many Americans could possibly   3
feel, or ever want to feel, I insist that you listen to me. Sit down and listen. I know what kinds of foods you like. I would feed them to you if you were right here, because it is very important that you listen.

I am humble in my country's pain and I am furious.   4

My Palestinian father became a refugee in 1948. He came to the United   5
States as a college student. He is 74 years old now and still homesick. He has planted fig trees. He has invited all the Ethiopians in his neighborhood to fill their little paper sacks with his figs. He has written columns and stories saying the Arabs are not terrorists; he has worked all his life to defy that word. Arabs are businessmen and students and kind neighbors. There is no one like him and there are thousands like him—gentle Arab daddies who make everyone laugh around the dinner table, who have a hard time with headlines, who stand outside in the evenings with their hands in their pockets staring toward the far horizon.

I am sorry if you did not have a father like that.   6

I wish everyone could have a father like that.   7

My hard-working American mother has spent 50 years trying to con-   8
vince her fellow teachers and choirmates not to believe stereotypes about the Middle East. She always told them, there is a much larger story. If you knew the story, you would not jump to conclusions from what you see in the news. But now look at the news. What a mess has been made.

Sometimes I wish everyone could have parents from different countries   9
or ethnic groups so they would be forced to cross boundaries, to believe in mixtures, every day of their lives. Because this is what the world calls us to do. WAKE UP!

The Palestinian grocer in my Mexican-American neighborhood paints   10
pictures of the Palestinian flag on his empty cartons. He paints trees and

rivers. He gives his paintings away. He says, "Don't insult me" when I try to pay him for a lemonade. Arabs have always been famous for their generosity. Remember?

My half-Arab brother with an Arabic name looks more like an Arab 11 than many full-blooded Arabs do and he has to fly every week.

My Palestinian cousins in Texas have beautiful brown little boys. Many 12 of them haven't gone to school yet. And now they have this heavy word to carry in their backpacks along with the weight of their papers and books. I repeat, the mission was a terrible success. But it was also a complete, total tragedy, and I want you to think about a few things.

1.

Many people, thousands of people, perhaps even millions of people, in the 13 United States are very aware of the long unfairness of our country's policies regarding Israel and Palestine. We talk about this all the time. It exhausts us and we keep talking. We write letters to newspapers, to politicians, to each other. We speak out in public even when it is uncomfortable to do so, because that is our responsibility. Many of these people aren't even Arabs. Many happen to be Jews who are equally troubled by the inequity. I promise you this is true. Because I am Arab-American, people always express these views to me, and I am amazed how many understand the intricate situation and have strong, caring feelings for Arabs and Palestinians even when they don't have to. Think of them, please: All those people who have been standing up for Arabs when they didn't have to.

But as ordinary citizens we don't run the government and don't get to 14 make all our government's policies, which makes us sad sometimes. We believe in the power of the word and we keep using it, even when it seems no one large enough is listening. That is one of the best things about this country: the free power of free words. Maybe we take it for granted too much. Many of the people killed in the World Trade Center probably believed in a free Palestine and were probably talking about it all the time.

But this tragedy could never help the Palestinians. Somehow, miracu- 15 lously, if other people won't help them more, they are going to have to help themselves. And it will be peace, not violence, that fixes things. You could ask any one of the kids in the Seeds of Peace organization and they would tell you that. Do you ever talk to kids? Please, please, talk to more kids.

2.

Have you noticed how many roads there are? Sure you have. You must 16 check out maps and highways and small alternate routes just like anyone else. There is no way everyone on earth could travel on the same road, or believe in exactly the same religion. It would be too crowded: it would be dumb. I don't believe you want us all to be Muslims. My Palestinian grandmother lived to be 106 years old and did not read or write, but even she was much smarter than that. The only place she ever went beyond Palestine and Jordan was to Mecca, by bus, and she was very proud to be called a Hajji and to wear white clothes afterwards. She worked very hard to get stains out of everyone's dresses—scrubbing them with a stone. I think she would consider the recent tragedies a terrible stain on her religion and her whole part of the world. She would weep. She was scared of airplanes anyway. She wanted people to worship God in whatever ways they felt comfortable. Just worship. Just remember God in every single day and doing. It didn't matter what they called it. When people asked her how she felt about the peace talks that were happening right before she died, she puffed up like a proud little bird and said, in Arabic, "I never lost my peace inside." To her, Islam was a welcoming religion. After her home in Jerusalem was stolen from her, she lived in a small village that contained a Christian shrine. She felt very tender toward the people who would visit it. A Jewish professor tracked me down a few years ago in Jerusalem to tell me she changed his life after he went to her village to do an oral history project on Arabs. "Don't think she only mattered to you!" he said. "She gave me a whole different reality to imagine—yet it was amazing how close we became. Arabs could never be just a 'project' after that."

Did you have a grandmother? Mine never wanted people to be pushed around. What did yours want? 17

Reading about Islam since my grandmother died, I note the "tolerance" that was "typical of Islam" even in the old days. The Muslim leader Khalid ibn al-Walid signed a Jerusalem treaty which declared, "in the name of God . . . you have complete security for your churches which shall not be occupied by the Muslims or destroyed." 18

It is the new millennium in which we should be even smarter than we used to be, right? But I think we have fallen behind. 19

3.

Many Americans do not want to kill any more innocent people anywhere in the world. We are extremely worried about military actions killing innocent people. We didn't like this in Iraq, we never liked it anywhere. We would like no more violence, from us as well as from you. We would like to stop the terrifying wheel of violence, just stop it, right on the road, and find something more creative to do to fix these huge problems we have. Violence is not creative, it is stupid and scary, and many of us hate all those 20 terrible movies and TV shows made in our own country that try to pretend otherwise. Don't watch them. Everyone should stop watching them. An appetite for explosive sounds and toppling buildings is not a healthy thing for anyone in any country. The USA should apologize to the whole world for sending this trash out into the air and for paying people to make it.

But here's something good you may not know—one of the best-selling 21 books of poetry in the United States in recent years is the Coleman Barks translation of Rumi, a mystical Sufi poet of the 13th century, and Sufism is Islam and doesn't that make you glad?

Everyone is talking about the suffering that ethnic Americans are going 22 through. Many will no doubt go through more of it, but I would like to thank everyone who has sent me a condolence card. Americans are usually very kind people. Didn't your colleagues find that out during their time living here? It is hard to imagine they missed it. How could they do what they did, knowing that?

4.

We will all die soon enough. Why not take the short time we have on this 23 delicate planet and figure out some really interesting things we might do together? I promise you, God would be happier. So many people are always trying to speak for God—I know it is a very dangerous thing to do. I tried my whole life not to do it. But this one time is an exception. Because there are so many people crying and scared and confused and complicated and exhausted right now—it is as if we have all had a giant simultaneous breakdown.

I beg you, as your distant Arab cousin, as your American neighbor, lis- 24 ten to me.

Our hearts are broken: as yours may also feel broken in some ways, we 25 can't understand, unless you tell us in words. Killing people won't tell us. We can't read that message.

Find another way to live. Don't expect others to be like you. Read 26 Rumi. Read Arabic poetry. Poetry humanizes us in a way that news, or even religion, has a harder time doing. A great Arab scholar, Dr. Salma Jayyusi, said, "If we read one another, we won't kill one another." Read American poetry. Plant mint. Find a friend who is so different from you, you can't believe how much you have in common. Love them. Let them love you. Surprise people in gentle ways, as friends do. The rest of us will try harder too. Make our family proud.

Thinking About the Essay

1. How does Nye address her primary audience—"would-be terrorists"? What tone or voice does she employ? What are some of the words and phrases she uses to get their attention? Of course, Nye also writes for a broader audience of readers—us. How does she make her message appealing to this larger audience?

2. Nye presents an elaborate argument in this essay. What is her central claim? What reasons or minor propositions does she give in support of her claim? How do the events of September 11 condition the nature of her argument? What types of appeal does she make to convince her audience to think, feel, and act differently?

3. Examine the introductory paragraphs—paragraphs 1–12. Why does Nye use a first-person ("I") point of view? What is her purpose? What is the effect?

4. Analyze sections 1–4 of Nye's essay (paragraphs 13–26). What is the subject matter of each? How does the sequence of sections serve to advance the writer's argument? What transitional techniques permit essay coherence and unity?

5. Why is Nye's last paragraph a fitting conclusion to the essay? What elements from the body of the essay does this concluding paragraph reinforce and illuminate?

Responding in Writing

6. Write your own letter to any would-be terrorists. Address this audience in a personal voice. Use a variety of appeals to make your case.

7. In an analytical essay, examine the ways in which Nye tries to make her case in "To Any Would-Be Terrorists."

8. Write a letter to Naomi Shihab Nye in which you agree or disagree with the content of her essay.

Networking

9. Exchange your paper with another class member and evaluate it for content, grammar and syntax, organization, and tone. Make revisions based on your discussion.

10. Either on the computer or in person, consult your college library's holdings for books by Rumi and works about this poet. Prepare a bibliography and also a brief biography of the poet, explaining why Naomi Shihab Nye would invite us to read Rumi.

Is Beauty Universal?
Global Body Images

Who Is Beautiful? Global Body Images

Not every society worships supermodels, but most societies do have notions about what constitutes beauty. Whereas a washboard stomach might set the standard for beauty for certain people in the United States, there are cultures and constituencies elsewhere that value ample stomachs and hips as the ideal body type. What one society values as beauty might not appeal—indeed might seem ridiculous—to another.

Of course, the age of globalization has spawned a fusion of styles, customs, and attitudes concerning beauty and ideal body images. Fashion magazines, advertisements, and television commercials—whether in the United States, Dubai, Japan, or anywhere on the planet—project transcultural (if not universal) standards of beauty. For example, the fashions of Africa and India adorn the bodies of Americans, and a fondness for tattoos (as one image in this portfolio reveals), appropriated from traditional societies by American teens, now seems to be spreading across continents like an unstoppable cultural virus.

The forces molding global definitions of beauty cannot escape the impact of American popular culture. Icons of American pop culture—whether Queen Latifah or Britney Spears—have an exaggerated impact on the attitudes, body styles, and beauty images of people around the world. Of course, cultural differences concerning beauty and body image persist, but the impact of American culture on how others perceive beauty can be irresistible and (as Susan Bordo observes in this book) insidious.

This portfolio presents images of the body and beauty from several cultural and transnational perspectives. These images reveal societies in transition and traditional values affected by (and at times resisting) the forces of globalization.

Tattoo Man. A participant displays his hand and head tattoos and face piercing at the Saint Petersburg International Tattoo Festival held in Russia in 2005.

Considering the Image

1. It is no longer unusual—at least in the United States—to see people with tattoos and body piercing. Do you think that global culture reflects these practices, or are they more specifically American or "Western" in orientation? Explain.

2. Do you think that the photographer makes an argument for or against tattoos and body piercing? Why or why not?

3. Why did the photographer choose to fill the frame with a close-up of the subject? What is the effect or dominant impression?

Kindergarten Kids. Children pose during a model contest held for kindergarten kids in Xiamen, east China's Fujian province.

Considering the Image

1. Identify the elements in this photograph that contribute to the overall effect. What aspects of the image do you find most effective?

2. What is your response to viewing these Chinese children dressed in Western clothing and posing as if they are models on a runway in New York or Paris? Do you find the scene amusing, charming, appalling, or what? Explain your reaction.

Dubai Britney. Two Arab women in traditional black burkas walk past a picture of pop singer Britney Spears in a posh shopping center in Dubai.

Considering the Image

1. What is your reaction to this photograph? Why do you believe you respond in this manner? How might the two women in burkas and Britney Spears serve as competing cultural symbols that condition your response? If you or a family member actually wears a burka, chador, or head covering, how might your reaction differ from others in the class?

2. What "message" or argument, if any, does the photographer convey in this shot? Does the photographer advance positive or negative connotations of the women in burkas and/or Britney Spears? Might there be an element of satire in the scene? Explain your responses to these questions.

Persian Beauty. An Iranian girl, surrounded by women in chadors, awaits admission to the Jamaran mosque in Tehran. The late Ayatollah Khomeini frequently conducted Friday prayers and made important speeches at this mosque.

Considering the Image

1. How does the photographer compose this image? Why does he bathe the girl in light while the people surrounding her are cast in shadows? What appeals to logos, ethos, and pathos do you detect?

2. Compare the representation of women in this image with that appearing in the Britney Spears photo. What similar and dissimilar cultural points do the two photographers want to make?

International Contestants.   Women at the June 2003 Miss Universe pageant pose for the photographer.

Considering the Image

1. What is your response to beauty contests in general and this photograph in particular? What media, cultural, and economic assumptions underlie such contests? Do such pageants exploit or celebrate women? Can you think of similar events involving men?

2. How does this photograph suggest or convey a "universal" definition of beauty? Where, for example, does each contestant come from? What other elements contribute to this definition?

Gay Pride.   Men and women celebrate Gay Pride Day in London in 2002.

Considering the Image

1. Analyze the composition of this photograph. What mood or dominant impression emerges from the scene? What representations of gender and sexual orientation does the photographer attempt to capture?

2. Do you think that the photographer has a point or argument to make about the globalization of gay lifestyles? Explain. What other issues concerning beauty, body image, gender, and sexual orientation are raised by this image?

Obese Girl Band.   Singers in a band named "Qianjin" (which in Chinese can mean both "girl" and "one ton") dance in celebration of the 2006 opening of a club for obese people in Beijing.

Considering the Image

1. Compare representations of women in this photograph with others in this folder, as well as with Susan Bordo's analysis in the essay that appears on pages 18–21.

2. An official at the Ministry of Health in China indicates that more than 200 million Chinese people are overweight. What cultural and economic values might serve to explain this phenomenon? How does the photograph articulate these values?

Blood Diamonds

GREG CAMPBELL | Greg Campbell, author of the book *Blood Diamonds: Tracing the Deadly Path of the World's Most Precious Stones* (2002), is a freelance journalist who reported on the war in Bosnia before traveling to Africa to write about the war in Sierra Leone. His reporting on the war in Africa led him to investigate the economy of the international diamond trade that financed the war and, as Campbell would discover, also played an important role in the financing of international terrorism. In the following article, which appeared in 2003 in the online publication *Amnesty Now*, Campbell traces the connections among the diamond trade, civil war, and terrorism.

Before Reading

Do you ever think of your purchase of a product as a moral act? Are there any products, or any products manufactured in a specific place and under certain conditions, that you would refuse to purchase on moral grounds?

In April 2001, when Jusu Lahia was fifteen years old, he was wounded by 1 an exploding rocket-propelled grenade. A lieutenant in Sierra Leone's Revolutionary United Front (RUF), Lahia was picked off during a battle in one of the most remote corners of the planet. He was among thousands of victims of a war fought for control of one of the world's most precious commodities: a fortune in raw diamonds that have made their way from the deadly jungles of Sierra Leone onto the rings and necklaces of happy lovers the world over.

Arms merchants, feeding on the diamond trade, bankrolled local 2 armies and made fortunes for transnational corporations. The profits also filled the coffers of al Qaeda, and possibly Hezbollah—terrorist organizations notorious for committing human rights violations, including crimes against humanity.

When Lahia sprawled to the earth—shards of hot metal ripped his body 3 from face to groin, destroying his left eye—few who eventually wore the gems he fought over could even locate Sierra Leone. And fewer still could find the Parrot's Beak, a small wedge of land that juts between the borders of neighboring Liberia and Guinea, directly into the line of fire between warring rebel factions in those countries. Rebel forces of all three nations were shooting it out with one another, as well as with the legitimate governments of all three countries and with an unknown number of local indigenous militias that were fighting for reasons of their own. The baffling and intense crossfire made the Parrot's Beak one of the deadliest 50-square-mile plots of land on the planet in 2001, and when Lahia went down in a hail of exploding shrapnel, he likely knew that he was far from the type of medical help that could save his life.

The RUF child soldier did not suffer alone. In the Parrot's Beak in mid-2001, some 50,000 refugees from Sierra Leone, Liberia, and Guinea were steadily dying from starvation, disease, and war wounds. The region was too hot for even the most daredevil humanitarian relief organizations.   4

Lahia was carried to a bare, fire-blackened hospital room in Kailahun,   5 the RUF's stronghold in the Parrot's Beak, and dumped on a pile of hay that served as a bed. When I first saw him there, surrounded by chaos, heat, and filth, I found it hard to remember that the cause of all this suffering—thousands of doomed refugees, well-armed but illiterate and drugged combatants, fallen wounded like Lahia, and injured civilian children—was brutally simple: The greed for diamonds. Certainly, there was nothing nearly as lustrous or awe-inspiring as a diamond in the bloodstained room where Lahia was dying of a tetanus infection, next to another felled fifteen-year-old. Powerless to treat him, the RUF field medics had simply taped his wounds shut and left him wracked with sweats and shivers.

Amputation Is Forever

Sadly, Kailahun wasn't the worst of it. The RUF began its jewelry heist in   6 1991, using the support of neighboring Liberia to capture Sierra Leone's vast wealth of diamond mines. Since then, the rebels have carried out one of the most brutal military campaigns in recent history, to enrich themselves as well as the genteel captains of the diamond industry living far removed from the killing fields. The RUF's signature tactic was amputation of civilians: Over the course of the decade-long war, the rebels have mutilated some 20,000 people, hacking off their arms, legs, lips, and ears with machetes and axes. This campaign was the RUF's grotesquely ironic response to Sierra Leone President Ahmad Tejan Kabbah's 1996 plea for citizens to "join hands for peace." Another 50,000 to 75,000 have been killed. The RUF's goal was to terrorize the population and enjoy uncontested dominion over the diamond fields.

While the RUF terrorized and looted the countryside, thousands of   7 prisoner–laborers worked to exhaustion, digging up the gems from muddy open-pit mines. Many ended up in shallow graves, executed for suspected theft, for lack of production, or simply for sport.

The international diamond industry's trading centers in Europe funded   8
this horror by buying up to $125 million worth of diamonds a year from
the RUF, according to UN estimates. Few cared where the gems originated,
or calculated the cost in lives lost rather than carats gained. The RUF used
its profits to open foreign bank accounts for rebel leaders and to finance a
complicated network of gunrunners who kept the rebels well-equipped
with the modern military hardware they used to control Sierra Leone's diamonds. The weapons—and the gems the rebels sold unimpeded to terrorist and corporate trader alike—allowed the RUF to fight off government
soldiers, hired mercenaries, peacekeepers from a regional West African reaction force, British paratroopers, and, until recently, the most expansive
and expensive peacekeeping mission the UN has ever deployed.

Throughout most of the war from 1991 to January 2002, this drama   9
played itself out in obscurity. During the RUF's worst assaults, international media pulled journalists out of the country in fear for their safety.
Local citizens were left to fend for themselves against bloodthirsty and
drugged child soldiers. Commanders often cut the children's arms and
packed the wounds with cocaine; marijuana was everywhere.

Until the deployment of the UN mission in 1999, the developed coun-   10
tries also washed their hands of the situation, doing little more than imposing sanctions on diamond exports and weapons sales to the small
country. These efforts did nothing to end the RUF's diamonds-for-guns
trade because most of the RUF's goods were smuggled out of Sierra Leone
and sold into the mainstream from neighboring countries.

Home to Roost

In a mistake that was to come home to roost, the West dismissed Sierra   11
Leone's war as little more than a baffling and tragic waste of life that had
little impact on their own economic interests—and even less on their national security.

Then on September 11, 2001, the world saw horrifying evidence of the   12
peril of ignoring such conflagrations and their related gross violations of
human rights.

For years, terrorists had been exploiting both the world's disdain for in-   13
tervening in Sierra Leone and the international diamond industry's tacit
funding of war. At least three African wars—in Sierra Leone, Angola, and
the Democratic Republic of Congo—had been good for business, ensuring
high and stable global prices for diamonds.

Beginning as early as 1998, the same year al Qaeda operatives report-   14
edly blew up U.S. embassies in Kenya and Sudan, Osama bin Laden's

terrorist network began buying diamonds from the RUF of Sierra Leone, according to FBI sources quoted in the *Washington Post*.

The paper also reported that two of the al Qaeda men implicated in those 15 attacks—Ahmed Khalfan Ghailani and Fazul Abdullah Mohammed—were in Sierra Leone in 2001, overseeing RUF diamond production.

As recently as mid-2001, a mere three months before the World Trade 16 Center and Pentagon attacks, al Qaeda had laundered millions of dollars by buying untraceable diamonds from the rebels. In the wake of 9/11, the United States and its allies in the "war on terrorism" froze more than $100 million worth of al Qaeda assets worldwide. But the terrorists likely have an ace in the hole in the form of diamonds from Sierra Leone, wealth that can be easily and quickly sold and is virtually untraceable.

Unspinnable Disaster

Even before 9/11, the diamond merchants were getting nervous. Media and 17 human rights groups began exposing the complicity of the romance industry in fueling wars. They also challenged the notion that Sierra Leone was simply another isolated post-cold war conflict that was troubling in its brutality but irrelevant to the national interests of developed countries.

Campaigns launched by Global Exchange and Amnesty International 18 against conflict diamonds threatened to replace the image of a diamond sparkling on the graceful hand of a lover with that of the truncated stump of a child amputee's arm. One diamond company executive is rumored to have had nightmares in which the tag line at the end of De Beers television commercials read, "Amputation is Forever."

The industry grew increasingly amenable to the idea of curtailing the 19 flow of blood diamonds. In 2000, Global Witness, a San Francisco-based non-governmental organization, joined with diamond industry representatives and officials from diamond exporting and importing countries to form the Kimberley Process. Amnesty International soon joined the negotiating effort, but according to Adotei Akwei, AIUSA's senior advocacy director for Africa, "the NGOs never had much power. We were allowed at the table but were seldom diners."

Despite many meetings, the panel failed to reach a consensus on how 20 to end the trade in blood diamonds. The U.S. Congress, too, faced intense lobbying. In 2000, Rep. Tony Hall (D-Ohio) introduced the Clean Diamond Act, a bill that sought to enact into law whatever import and export controls the Kimberley Process would adopt. The bill languished because of serious concerns over provisions added at the request of the Bush administration that—according to NGOs, the industry, and some senators—fatally compromised the bill.

The 9/11 terrorist attacks, along with a blistering *Washington Post* in- 21 vestigation by Doug Farrah into al Qaeda's large purchases of Sierra Leone diamonds, raised the stakes. While associating with bloodthirsty rebels was a formidable public relations challenge for the diamond industry, funding the terrorists who attacked the United States was simply unspinnable.

Last November, the Kimberley Process agreed to a set of regulations 22 that would require that all cross-border diamond transactions be accompanied by a non-forgeable paper trail, indicating when and where every imported stone was discovered. The Clean Diamond Act followed suit and was passed by the House of Representatives 408-6. It is currently awaiting a vote in the Senate.

Unfortunately, neither action is halting the lucrative trade: "Efforts to 23 end the trade in conflict diamonds ran into a major obstacle in the Bush administration, which has been reluctant to impede business in any way or have its hands tied by any international agreements, even when the U.S. diamond industry has called for it," says Akwei.

Nor is a better paper trail foolproof. Diamonds are sufficiently small 24 and portable to make it unlikely that any regime of certificates or guarantees will ensure that diamonds originate in conflict-free areas. Indeed, it seems that the only sure-fire way to eradicate conflict diamonds is to see an end to the conflicts where diamonds are found. As evidence, we can look again at Sierra Leone, where the war was officially declared over in January. With hostilities ended and the RUF disarmed and disbanded, diamond production is once again in the hands of the government and international exploration companies. The trick now is to see if the government can adeptly handle the complexities of mining and taxing so that the majority of revenue is reinvested, and to ensure that Sierra Leone finally benefits from diamonds rather than being torn apart by them.

The Shame of It All

Throughout the 1990s, children like Jusu Lahia armed themselves with 25 diamond-purchased AK-47s and, under the nose of the United Nations, helped the rebels sell the gems to terrorists. People had their hands chopped off by RUF units and were sent wandering hopelessly to spread the message of terror. West African "peacekeepers" were so inept in their defense of Sierra Leone's civilian population that charges of human rights violations are leveled at them as frequently as they are at the RUF. Nigerian soldiers serving a regional West African peacekeeping force killed civilians suspected of aiding RUF, tortured children suspected of being RUF, and slaughtered hospital patients in their efforts to rid Freetown of rebels. It is no stretch to say that Sierra Leone disintegrated during the 1990s into a murderous sinkhole of death and torture, all of it fueled by the sale of diamonds to respectable merchants throughout the world.

The shame of it all is that it took a catastrophic attack on American soil 26 for anyone to notice. Developed nations bought Sierra Leone's blood-soaked diamonds without question throughout the 1990s, apparently untroubled that the sales affected millions of Africans in a mostly forgotten and impoverished jungle.

Only after the effects of the RUF's diamond war were slammed home— 27 like a blade through the bones of a forearm—did anyone sit up and take notice.

If nothing else, the story of Sierra Leone's diamond war has proved un- 28 equivocally that the world ignores Africa and its problems at its peril. Events far from home often have very tangible impacts, and Sierra Leone has shown the world that there is no longer any such thing as an "isolated, regional conflict." Perhaps there never was.

Thinking About the Essay

1. How does Campbell weave narrative with exposition in the opening section of the essay? What is the effect of the rapid shifts from one rhetorical mode to another?

2. What is the significance of the titles given to sections, and how do they relate to the text that follows? Can you detect differences in tone among these titles? Explain the distinctions you make.

3. How does Campbell bridge geographical and psychological distance to make the issue seem urgent to readers in the West? Why does Campbell delay connecting the human tragedy of Sierra Leone with the national security interests of Western nations who had only recently regarded Sierra Leone as little more than a distant tragedy?

4. Why does Campbell characterize aspects of the issue of the blood diamond trade in terms of "spin"? How does spin reflect efforts in the West to rationalize and compartmentalize the problem?

5. How effective is the simile that appears in the penultimate paragraph of the essay's final section? Do you find it too dramatic or too contrived? Defend (or critique) the use of this simile as a rhetorical tactic.

Responding in Writing

6. Campbell claims that Sierra Leone proves that there is no longer any such thing as an "isolated, regional conflict." In an argumentative essay, attempt to refute Campbell's general statement (without necessarily disagreeing with Campbell's specific claim about the war in Sierra Leone).

7. Compose a letter to persuade your representative in Congress to vote "yes" or "no" on the Clean Diamond Act.

8. In an argumentative essay, respond to Campbell's account of the failures of the United Nations and other regional peace-keeping missions in Africa. Do you believe the United States, or some other Western power, can or should act unilaterally to stop wars in Africa? Justify your position on this policy issue.

Networking

9. In small groups, come up with advertising campaigns designed to inform consumers of the existence of the blood diamond trade and of the ways in which the "romance industry" is morally implicated. Conduct a focus group with the class to test the possible effect of the campaign.

10. Go online and visit the Amnesty International website. What actions do they encourage individual Americans to take in the cause of eliminating the blood diamond trade?

Letter from New York

PETER CAREY

Born in Victoria, Australia, in 1943, Peter Carey attended Monash University briefly before working part-time in advertising and starting a literary career, first as a short story writer and then as a novelist. His second collection of short fiction, *War Crimes* (1979), received numerous prizes, including Australia's National Book Council Award. In 1988, he won England's most prestigious literary award, the Booker Prize, for his novel *Oscar and Lucinda;* the novel was adapted as a film starring Cate Blanchett and Ralph Fiennes. Carey has written a number of other award-winning novels, including the acclaimed historical novel *True History of the Kelly Gang* (2000). In his fiction, Carey is a dazzling stylist and inventive formalist, often producing quirky and bizarre narratives in which eccentric characters cope with the mysteries of existence. Carey now lives in New York City with his wife, Alison Summers, who is mentioned in the following article. He wrote this piece in the form of an open letter to his friend Robert McCrum, the literary editor of the British *Observer,* only days after the 9/11 disaster.

Before Reading

Where were you on the day of the 9/11 attack on the World Trade Center? What do you remember? What were your immediate feelings and thoughts about the attack?

[September 23, 2001]
Dear Robert

The last week is a great blur with no divisions between night and day. 1
Time is broken. The events of the first day bleed into the next and all the powerful emotions and disturbing sights are now so hard to put in proper sequence.

I was sitting here in this office which you know so well, looking out 2 over that little garden. I heard a passenger jet fly over, very large, very low. I did feel momentarily alarmed. Air disaster crossed my mind, but only for a moment. It was probably 10 minutes before I went out to the street, and then only to buy a can of food for the starving cat. I wandered up to the corner deli. As I entered, a young Asian American woman smiled at me, as New Yorkers will when something weird is happening. I was puzzled. I wondered if she was a student I'd forgotten.

I got the cat food, and suddenly realised that the deli radio was playing 3 very loud. What is it? I asked the girl. She said: a plane has crashed into the World Trade Centre. Of course it was a terrorist attack. I never doubted it. Crowds were now gathering around the loudspeaker in the little doorway. They spilled into the street and looked down to the WTC. Smoke was already pouring from the upper floors.

In retrospect it seems an innocent and optimistic moment. We had no 4 idea how huge this disaster was. I knew my wife was in that building, not because she had told me, or told the kids where she was going, but because all three of us males knew that this was her favourite time to pick up discount clothes at Century 21, just across the street from the north tower. You go through the 1 & 9 subway in the Trade Centre concourse to get there. Of course you now know Century 21 from TV—that blackened broken jigsaw of disaster that has not yet fallen down.

I wanted to wait by the phone for Alison. But I wanted to be in the 5 street. I wanted to see my wife coming down from 6th Avenue, carrying those big plastic shopping bags filled with children's clothes. On the landing of our building I found my neighbour, Stu, crying. He had seen the plane crash into the building. So many friends were looking at the World Trade Centre at this moment. They now have this nightmare branded into the tissue of their cerebral cortex.

My friend Caz was jogging down the west side highway and witnessed 6
it. Pure evil. Rocky was working on a roof on 11th street. He ducked as the
757 flew over his head, then stood to see hell arrive just down the road.
Now he cannot sleep. Now none of us can sleep. Rocky thrashes and
moans all night long. Charley our 11-year-old cannot sleep. He didn't see
the plane but he was at school at Brooklyn Heights and his friends looked
out the window and saw what they should never have seen and then the
Manhattan kids all went through the difficulty, the uncertainty, of evacuation. Manhattan was burning. The bridges were closed. They did not know
where their parents were. Now Charley faces the mornings exhausted, tear-
ful, leaving a soggy bowl of half-eaten cereal on the table.

Our street drew us all outside. Our community was far more important 7
than the television. We huddled together, on our landings, in the laundromat, at the corner deli.

From my doorway I saw MaryAnn from across the street. She was 8
walking up and down with her baby in her arms. You could see, from the
way she kissed her baby's head, that she feared her husband dead. Feeling
her agony, we looked up towards 6th Avenue where the fire engines were
already appearing in huge numbers. They drove the wrong way down the
avenue, soon followed by black 4WDs with lights clamped on their roofs.

MaryAnn's husband entered the street. We were so happy to see him 9
alive. "Lloyd, Lloyd." We called to him but he did not even hear us. He
was a man who had seen something very bad. Now we started to hear
about the attack on the second building, then the Pentagon. I ran back and
forth between the silent phone and the street, like a madman on a leash. I
could not be anywhere. I could not miss the phone. Could not be away
from my neighbours.

Finally: a call. It was our friend Bea phoning from her apartment on 10
lower Broadway, just near City Hall. She had heard from my wife. Alison
had buzzed from the street just as the second plane hit the South Tower, almost next door. Bea was distraught. She had seen bodies falling past her
window. She was going to try to find my wife, but the street below was
chaos, billowing malignant smoke, stretching to engulf whoever fell or
stumbled. Bea said she would try to make her way to our house, a 15-
minute walk, just north of Houston.

So I now knew that Alison had escaped the first building, but was she 11
safe? How could I know? I paced like MaryAnn had paced but outside the
street was crowded. Pedestrians were fleeing from downtown. You could
recognise these people straight away, the stark, seared horror in their eyes,
the blankness, but also sometimes the frank appeals for human contact.
They now begin to stream along Bedford Street in ever increasing numbers.
These people have felt horror, they are like no other crowd I have ever seen.

Among them, finally, comes my wife, remarkable for the lack of trauma 12
her face reveals. It takes a little while for me to understand she was in the
building when it hit. Only when I read her own account do I appreciate the
extraordinary escape she has made, how lucky we are to have her alive.

We have two sons at different schools in Brooklyn and today we are 13
both very happy they are there. We discover our response is quite different
to many other Manhattan parents who immediately set out through the ruined city, fighting the problems of closed bridges and roads and subways,
to collect their children.

Bea's husband John is one of these. Why would you do that? I yell at 14
him. You're fucking nuts. Leave her there. She's safe. But his daughter
wants to come home and he is her father and he sets off into the chaos of
midtown traffic.

Although we believe that our kids are safe in Brooklyn, they are, just 15
the same, suffering their own traumas in their separate schools, knowing
their mother is probably in the building, seeing weeping friends whose parents had offices in the WTC. Some of these stories will have happy resolutions, but not all.

Our neighbourhood is now cordoned off from the city. You needed ID 16
to get beneath Houston, to get back from above 14th Street. John succeeded in his insane trip across the 59th Bridge and up the Brooklyn
Queens Expressway to Brooklyn Heights. He got his daughter, Leah, back
home on a train that the news said was not running. Bea and John and Leah
would not be able to return to her apartment for days. We cooked them
pasta and made them beds and in the evenings that would follow listened
to Bea as she arrived home after a traumatic day of grief counselling at
Bellevue—it was she who talked to all those people looking for husbands,
wives, children, lovers.

Late that night we discovered the F train was running. Charley came 17
back to Manhattan with his best friend Matthew. I walked him home. He
said the empty streets "creeped him out."

Our Brooklyn friend Betsy was caught in Manhattan with her beat-up 18
car and her cat and she too headed out on the 59th Street Bridge just as
John had, but now the expressway was closed down and so she started a
low meandering journey through the side streets of Queens and Brooklyn
until she found herself—ah, Bonfire of the Vanities—a white Jew alone in
the tough black area of East New York. "They were so sweet to me," she
said. "These young men guided me to safety, getting this little white girl
back to her own people."

Now our neighbourhood has become a command centre. That evening 19
we are standing on the corner of Houston and 6th Avenue watching the

huge earth-moving equipment and heavy trucks rolling, bumper to bumper, in a never-ending parade towards the devastation. Here is the endless might and wealth of America. Here are the drivers, like soldiers, heroes. These are not military vehicles but huge trucks from small companies in Connecticut and New Jersey, from Bergen and Hackensack. Seeing all these individuals rise to the crisis, with their American flags stuck out of windows and taped to radio aerials, I am reminded of Dunkirk. I am moved. We are all moved. The crowds come out to cheer them. I do too, without reserve.

This is the same corner where we will soon be lighting candles for the 20
dead and missing, where 11-year-old Charley and I will stand for 20 silent minutes watching those photographs, of lost firefighters, wives, mothers, fathers, sons. It's hard not to cry. We watch the tender way our neighbours lay flowers and arrange the candles. We do not know all these people in the pictures, but we do know our firefighters. We shop with them. We wait in line at the supermarket while they buy Italian sausage and pasta for their dinner.

Pleasant, hoarse-voiced Jerry from the laundromat is there on the cor- 21
ner. He is always on the street, but tonight he wears a stars and stripes bandanna and he cannot be still. He has three grown-up sons downtown right now, working in that perilous pile of deadly pick-up sticks. Jerry and I embrace, because what else is there to do? When one of his sons almost loses his hand, it is miraculously sewn on by microsurgery. I am praying, says Jerry, there is just a lot of praying to do.

Everywhere people are touched by death. Our friend David across the 22
road has lost his best friend, the father of a new baby. Silvano the restaurateur has lost a fireman friend, and Charley and I are dismayed to see the huge piles of flowers outside that tiny station on West 3rd Street. The station was always so small, it looked like a museum. But now we stand, Charley and I, and we close our eyes and say a prayer, although I don't know who I'm praying to. There is no God for me.

Alison needs to stay home. She nests, tidies, spends several hours on 23
small domestic tasks. Then, finally, she begins to write a powerful piece about her escape. She works all day, all night, she cannot stop. As for me, I have to be outside, among the people. It is all that gives me any peace. I want to stand in the deli by the radio. There I can be with my neighbours. We touch, embrace, cry, are half wild with anger. Emotions are close to the surface.

One night 15-year-old Sam says he wants to walk around the city. He 24
wants to see Union Square where there is the biggest massing of candles and memorials. We walk along Houston Street which is now a war zone.

Huge trucks from the New York Housing Authority stand in readiness to remove the rubble. We head east and then north. He is taller than me now, and likes to put his arm paternally around my shoulder. As we walk he says to me, apropos of nothing: "I love this city."

We walk to Union Square and I am proud of the complex, multifaceted 25 way Sam is talking about these events. He is concerned that local Muslims may be victimised because of our anger, cautious about retaliatory bombing, but mad too, like I am. We stand among the extraordinary shrine at Union Square where nuke-crazed groups stand next to pacifists, all united by their grief. The searing, murderous heat of that explosion has brought us all together.

We see so many people whom we know. The sweet-faced man from 26 our post office, whose continually lowered eyes have always given him a rather bemused and almost beatific expression, comes out of the dark to embrace me.

I am more vindictive than my son. I want to strike back, pulverise, kill, 27 obliterate anyone who has caused this harm to my city. I have become like the dangerous American the world has most reason to fear. This phase passes quickly enough. It has passed now. But on those first days and nights, I was overcome with murderous rage.

We are all changed by what has happened. Some of the changes have 28 been totally unexpected. Once, a year or so ago, I heard my son saying: "When we bombed Iraq."

"No," I said, "when they bombed Iraq." 29

"No," he said, "we." 30

It put a chill in me. I was very happy for him to be a New Yorker, but 31 I wasn't sure I wished him to be American.

But on the second day after the attack on the WTC, the day Sam turned 32 15, I bought him a large white T-shirt with an American flag printed on its front. Sam is a very hard guy to buy a T-shirt for, but he put this one on immediately, and then we went out together again, out among the people, giving ourselves some strange and rather beautiful comfort in the middle of all the horror that had fallen on our lives.

"I love this city, Dad. I love it more than ever." I did not disagree 33 with him.

Thinking About the Essay

1. Carey wrote this essay in the form of an open letter, probably with the expectation that it would be published. What aspects of the epistolary or letter style do you find in this piece? Cite specific examples. What are the benefits accruing to the epistolary style?

2. Who are Carey's primary and secondary audiences for this letter? Consider that Carey is an Australian, living in the United States, and writing to an English friend.

3. The writer is an acclaimed novelist. Point to examples of narrative and descriptive techniques that seem especially accomplished in this essay.

4. Does this essay contain a thesis, or is it simply a diffuse "letter from New York"? Justify your response by careful citation from the text.

5. What episode constitutes the writer's conclusion? Why is it so effective? What does Carey want to tell the reader at the end of his letter?

Responding in Writing

6. Write a letter to a close friend, reconstructing your response to the 9/11 disaster. Try to employ narration and description to re-create the experience in as vivid a manner as possible.

7. In an analytical and evaluative essay, explain why you think Carey's essay does or does not capture a sense of life in New York immediately after the World Trade Center bombings.

8. Carey writes that at first he wanted to kill all terrorists but that his ideas and emotions quickly changed. Are you able to trace a similar pattern to your own behavior? Why or why not? Answer these questions in a personal essay.

Networking

9. In small groups, explain to class members exactly where you were on 9/11 and how you responded to events during that first week. Then participate in a class discussion to create an inventory of responses.

10. Go to the Web and retrieve visual images of the World Trade Center disaster. Many are now famous. Which impress you, several years after they were taken? From a distance in time, how do you react to these images? Share one photograph with class members.

Generation Jihad

BILL POWELL   Bill Powell is the Asia editor for *Fortune* magazine and is currently based in Beijing. Powell joined the staff of *Fortune* in 2000. Prior to that, he reported for *Newsweek* as Moscow bureau chief (1996–2000), Berlin bureau chief and European economics editor (1994–95), and (simultaneously) Tokyo bureau chief and Asia economic editor (1989–94). Powell was also for many years a correspondent for *Business Week*. His many awards include an Overseas Press Club award for best economic reporting from abroad (1990, 1995) and the National Press Club Award for best reporting in a magazine (1987). In the following piece, which appeared in *Time* magazine in October of 2005, Powell profiles members of a new generation of disaffected Muslim youth in Europe and America who have become increasingly sympathetic to extremist causes.

Before Reading

How difficult is it for you to appreciate the grievances of disaffected youth who subscribe to an extremist politics that supports or defends terrorism? Do you make any moral distinction between "a suicide bomber and a B-52"?

The last time Myriam Cherif saw her son Peter, 23, was in May 2004, when the two of them stood at the elevator on the fifth floor of the gritty public-housing project where they lived, just north of Paris. Myriam, 48, was born in Tunisia, moved to France when she was 8 and became a French citizen. Peter's father, who died when the boy was 14, was a Catholic from the French Antilles in the Caribbean. But Peter took a different path. In 2003 he converted to Islam and became a devout Muslim. He took to wearing loose trousers and a long tunic instead of blue jeans and repeatedly told Myriam that she should wear the traditional Muslim head scarf. And then one day last spring, Peter told his mother he was heading off to Syria to study Arabic and the Koran.

At first, Peter e-mailed his mother every couple of days, sending her snapshots and news of his studies in Damascus. Last July he told her he was headed for a "spiritual retreat" and would be out of touch for a while. She heard nothing until December, when she received a brief phone call from a French government official who told her that Peter had been captured by U.S. soldiers in the Iraqi city of Fallujah.

Today Peter, one of five French citizens captured by U.S. forces in Iraq, 3
is being held at Abu Ghraib prison outside Baghdad, family members say.
More than a year since she last heard from her son, Myriam Cherif is still
trying to understand how, in the streets and cafes of Paris, Peter and other
young Muslims like him were lured into giving up their lives in the West
and pursuing jihad. "They saw aggressive, violent images on the Internet
and asked questions about why Muslims were suffering abroad while European countries were doing nothing," she says. "It's like they set off a
bomb in their heads."

Since 9/11, the Bush Administration has argued that the best way to 4
prevent further attacks by al-Qaeda and its sympathizers is to fight Islamic
extremists on their turf, in places like Afghanistan and Iraq, before they
make it to the West. But among Europeans, the suicide bombings in London on July 7 of this year, which were carried out by four British citizens,
shattered any lingering illusions that the threat can be kept from their
shores. In a videotaped message released last week on al-Jazeera, Osama
bin Laden's deputy, Ayman al-Zawahiri, claimed responsibility for the
London attacks—the first public acknowledgment that the bombers may
have received support and assistance from al-Qaeda operatives. In Europe
the message was a chilling reminder that the enemy is within. Jihadist networks are increasingly drawing on a pool of young Muslims living in cities
all over Europe—including many who were born and raised in the afflu-
ence and openness of the West, products of the very democracies they are
determined to attack.

Call it Generation Jihad—restive, rootless young Muslims who have 5
spent their lives in Europe but now find themselves alienated from their societies and the policies of their governments. While the precise number of
European jihadists is impossible to pinpoint, counterterrorism officials believe the pool of radicals is growing. Since 1990, the Muslim population in
Europe has expanded from an estimated 10 million to 14 million. (Estimates of the number of Muslims in the U.S. range from 2 million to 7 million.) A 2004 estimate by the intelligence unit of French police found that
about 150 of the country's indexed 1,600 mosques and prayer halls were
under the control of extremist elements. A study of 1,160 recent French
converts to Islam found that 23% identified themselves as Salafists, members of a sect sometimes associated with violent extremism. In the Netherlands, home to 1 million Muslims, a spokesman for the Dutch intelligence
service says it believes as many as 20 different hard-line Islamic groups may
be operating in the country—some simply prayer groups adhering to radical interpretations of the Koran, others perhaps organizing and recruiting
for violence. In London, authorities say, as many as 3,000 veterans of al-
Qaeda training camps over the years were born or based in Britain.

What explains the proliferation of Europe's homegrown radicals? And   6
what dangers do they pose? Interviews with dozens of Muslims across
Western Europe reveal a wide range of explanations for why so many are
responding to the call of radical Islam. A common sentiment among members of Generation Jihad is frustration with a perceived scarcity of opportunity and disappointment at public policies that they believe target
Muslims unfairly. Some lack a sense of belonging in European societies,
which have long struggled to assimilate immigrants from the Islamic world.
Many, in particular younger Muslims, suffer disproportionately from Europe's high-unemployment, slow-growth economies. Some are outraged
over the bloodshed in Iraq and the persistent notion—stoked by Osama bin
Laden but increasingly accepted among moderates—that the West is wag-
ing an assault on Islam.

The rage expressed by members of Generation Jihad has raised con-   7
cerns among European counterterrorism officials that policies pursued by
the U.S. and its allies in response to the Islamic terrorist threat may be further galvanizing radicals. Says a French investigator with a decade of an-
titerrorism experience: "There's a spreading atmosphere of indignation
among normal Muslims that's echoing among the younger generation."

The echoes can be heard in many neighborhoods of north and east Lon-   8
don, where Sajid Sharif, 37, a trained civil engineer who goes by the name
Abu Uzair, once handed out incendiary leaflets preaching his brand of extreme Islam. From the comfort of his home, he leads the Savior Sect, a
group that claims several hundred supporters and seeks to unite all Muslims worldwide under a strict conception of Islamic law. That might seem
fanciful—except that Uzair's mentor, Omar Bakri Muhammad, was one of
the first clerics to lose his right to live in Britain under the new antiterror-
ism laws. He was barred from returning after a holiday abroad. Uzair says
he isn't concerned about the threat of eviction because he is British born,
and his lawyer has reportedly told him he has little to worry about. "Anyway," says Uzair, "it is all in the hands of Allah."

Uzair is bearded, wears a long white gown and quotes nonstop from the   9
Koran and Hadith (a collection of the teachings of the Prophet Muhammad). His Pakistani parents are secular Muslims, he says, and speak very
little English. In his youth he smoked and went to night clubs. It was not
until he was a university student in Britain that he embraced Islam. "I
wanted some inner discipline," he says. "Since I have come to Islam, I have
a lot of tranquillity." Now he tries to steer people away from drugs, drink,
crime and smoking. Uzair's supporters refuse to vote in elections because
his sect recognizes only Shari'a, Islamic law. While he does not openly support terrorism, he declares that the July 7 attacks were retaliation for

Britain's support of the wars in Afghanistan and Iraq. "The majority of Muslims in the U.K. are frustrated, but they cannot speak," he says. "They will not condone the London bombings, but inside they believe that Britain had it coming."

The hostility Uzair feels toward the country of his birth is not atypical. 10 Many second-generation Muslims in Europe say they feel a part of neither their native countries nor their parents' heritage. Riad, 32, a French citizen who has been unemployed since 2002 and who asked to be identified by his first name, embodies the sense of estrangement. "They say we are French, and we would like to believe that as well," he says, sitting in a cafe in the Venissieux suburb of Lyons. "But do we look like normal French people to you?" His friend Karim, 27, says they are discriminated against because of their long beards. "Who will give us a job when we look like this? We have to fend for ourselves and find a way out."

That lack of connection to their native societies can often lead Muslims 11 in Europe to seek order in religion. Zaheer Khan, 30, who grew up in the county of Kent in southeast England, was drawn to radical Islam as a college student in the mid-1990s. The Wahhabi and Salafist recruiters, he says, "would tell you that things like taking out car insurance are against Islamic principles, or voting—this is haram, forbidden. Slowly the disengagement was there. You didn't say, 'Let's explore what it means to be living in Britain.' This didn't come up." The radical feelings that Khan had back then—although he is still devout, he has since moved away from radical Islam—are apparently widespread among second-generation Muslims. "The problem is that they have no real roots," says Dominique Many, a lawyer for one of the Muslim Frenchmen taken into custody by French officials on suspicion of volunteering to fight against U.S. forces in Iraq. "In Tunisia they are considered foreigners. In France they are considered foreigners. This is the new generation of Muslims."

Rootlessness is compounded by economic struggle. On the whole, Mus- 12 lims in Europe are far more likely to be unemployed than non-Muslims are. In Britain, almost two-thirds of children of Pakistani or Bangladeshi origin—ethnic groups that together account for three-fifths of Britain's Muslims—are categorized as poor; the national average is 28%. A French law-enforcement source says jobless Muslims are "the easy marks, the fodder of jihadist networks." Yassin el-Abdi, 24, a trained accountant in Mechelen, Belgium, who has been unemployed for three years, says extremists in Europe are making a bad situation for Muslims even worse. "These people who are planting the bombs are wrecking things for us," says el-Abdi. And the depressing reality, says his friend Said Bouazza, who runs a job-training center in Mechelen, is that unemployment is only adding to the jihadists' ranks. "It's like a ticking time bomb. There are people who fight back by opening their own store. Or they plant bombs."

The kinds of young people taking up the jihadist cause in Europe might 13 have been more inclined in the past to drift into a life of crime or drug use. The more committed would have had to journey to religious seminaries and training camps in places like Pakistan and Afghanistan to receive indoctrination in jihad. But now they don't need to leave home. The Internet has played a huge role in fostering a sense of community among both the fanatics and those who would join them. "They're becoming dedicated Islamists without ever leaving their home nations," a French counterterrorism official says.

What's more, TIME's reporting across Europe shows, the war in Iraq 14 has further radicalized some Muslims, convincing them that the U.S. and Britain are bent on war with Islam and that the only proper response is to fight back. Listen to Uzair, the Savior Sect leader in London: "Muslims are being killed all over the world through the foreign policy of the U.K. and U.S. Many feel they cannot sit around and do nothing about it. What is the difference between a suicide bomber and a B-52? I really feel that war has been declared on Islam." Iraq, says a senior French security official, "has acted as a formidable booster" for extremist groups.

In Belgium, a radical Muslim named Karim Hassoun who is head of the 15 Arab-European League, says flatly, "The more body bags of Americans we see coming back from Iraq, the happier we are." What's worrisome is how openly such rhetoric is received among ordinary Muslims, many of whom consider themselves moderates. In the Netherlands, where 1 of every 16 Dutch citizens is a Muslim, it's trendy for kids to hang on their bedroom walls half-burned American flags with Stars of David placed on them, says Mohammed Ridouan Jabri, founder of the eight-month-old Muslim Democratic Party.

What can be done to defuse the anger? European governments have 16 tried a range of approaches to contain radical Islam. In the wake of the July 7 bombings, British Prime Minister Tony Blair introduced a zero-tolerance policy toward hateful rhetoric, pledging, among other things, to deport clerics seen to be inciting violence. The crackdown represented a shift from Britain's tradition of tolerating militant speech. But some moderate Muslims fear that in his rush to get tough, Blair risks further estranging young European Muslims by heightening their sense that they are outsiders. "It reinforces bin Laden's arguments that citizenship is nothing, that nationality is a mirage blinding Muslims to their only real allegiance—to God, as jihadists define it," says Dounia Bouzar, a scholar and commentator on the lives of French-born Muslims like herself. Bouzar also laments France's 2004 law banning "conspicuous" religious symbols from public schools because its foremost target is the head scarves worn by certain devout Muslim females. Although enforcement of the law has not sparked the mass expulsion of hijab-wearing students that many feared, Bouzar says it has caused splits within the Muslim community.

The dilemma for Muslims across Europe is that in the wake of July 7, 17 public demand for tougher measures against terrorism is stifling open discussion of the grievances that are fueling extremism—which allows hardliners to crowd out moderate voices. "There is no middle ground now," says Naima Azough, 32, a Dutch parliamentarian from Morocco. "It's as if in the U.S. you heard only Noam Chomsky and Pat Buchanan."

Bolstering moderates will require change within Europe's Muslim 18 communities but also greater political sensitivity outside them—a willingness to acknowledge, for instance, the emotional impact that some policies enacted in the war on terrorism have had on Muslims. At a meeting of the radical Muslim group Hizb ut-Tahrir in Birmingham, England, the group's spokesman, Imran Waheed, 28, launched into a 40-minute lecture in front of about 80 people, insisting there's no need for the Muslim community to apologize for July 7. Many in the audience nodded in agreement. But some seemed ambivalent, caught between abhorrence for terrorism and a belief that their grievances are not taken seriously.

After praying with the other men in an adjacent room, a smiling twen- 19 tysomething, sporting pressed trousers and shirt and wearing neat, round glasses, began by pointing out that Islam forbids violence and the bombing of innocent people. "Our hearts are bleeding for the [July 7 victims]," he said, and in the next breath criticized the U.S. and Britain for ignoring the ways in which their policies may be adding to young Muslims' feelings of alienation. As a result, he says, the members of his generation "are frustrated. Their voices are not being heard." If the world hopes to understand—let alone overcome—the anger that roils Europe's young Muslims, it had better start to listen.

Thinking About the Essay

1. How effectively does Powell present the case of Myriam and Peter Cherif as symptomatic of a larger problem? Where is the transition made from this opening case study to a more general statement of the problem?

2. Why does Powell focus, in the second paragraph, on the chronology of diminishing contact between mother and son? What other details with larger thematic significance do you see in this opening narrative?

3. Where does Powell define the term *Generation Jihad*? How does the general definition relate to the case studies profiled in the essay? Could the term have been defined purely by way of illustration? Explain.

4. Trace the author's use of the word *rootless*. Find one other recurring motif in the essay and explain its function.

5. How does Powell address the war in Iraq as one factor that contributed to the rise of Generation Jihad? What importance does he attribute to the war as a factor?

Responding in Writing

6. Compose a profile of a group of people in the United States who are members of the same generation and who could be characterized as "restive, rootless, and alienated." What do these individuals feel alienated *from*? What term would you use to refer to this generation? Do you feel a member of this generation yourself?

7. Do you recall feeling alienated from your own mother or father when you were younger? In a brief essay, reflect on the nature of those feelings and some of their causes. In what way, if any, was your sense of alienation related to feelings of cultural or political alienation?

8. Write a letter to a politically moderate Muslim publication in which you attempt to relate (rather than equate) the problems facing a subsection of American youth today to the special problems facing American Muslim youths.

Networking

9. In groups of three or four, respond to the anti-American rhetoric described (in paragraph 15) as being prevalent among Muslim youth in Europe and America. Share your responses with the class. How would you have responded differently to the examples of this rhetoric if they had been reported in the opening paragraph of the essay, rather than later in the essay?

10. Go online and read at least three blog entries that represent the points of view of European or American Muslim youths on the international controversy over the 2006 publication, in a European newspaper, of a cartoon depicting the prophet Mohammed.

Bad Luck: Why Americans Exaggerate the Terrorist Threat

JEFFREY ROSEN | Jeffrey Rosen was born in 1964 in New York City and educated at Harvard University and Balliol College, Oxford University. He also has a J.D. degree from Yale Law School. Rosen currently teaches at George Washington Law School in Washington, D.C.; serves as legal affairs editor at *The New Republic,* where the following essay was published in November 2001; and also is a staff writer for *The New Yorker* magazine. In his recent book *The Unwanted Gaze: The Destruction of Privacy in America* (2000), Rosen explores the issue of privacy from the Middle Ages—when the Jewish ban on the "unwanted gaze" protected citizens from scrutiny—to such contemporary intrusions into the right of privacy as the Monica Lewinsky case. In this essay, Rosen (as we can infer from the title) offers a critical appraisal of our response to the terrorist threat.

Before Reading

What types of threats or fears have you experienced recently? Is the terrorist threat one of them? Why or why not?

The terrorist threat is all too real, but newspapers and TV stations around the globe are still managing to exaggerate it. As new cases of anthrax infection continue to emerge, the World Health Organization is begging people not to panic. But tabloid headlines like this one from *The Mirror* in London send a different message: "panic." A Time/CNN poll found that nearly half of all Americans say they are "very" or "somewhat" concerned that they or their families will be exposed to anthrax, even though only a handful of politicians and journalists have been targeted so far.

This isn't surprising. Terrorism is unfamiliar, it strikes largely at random, and it can't be easily avoided by individual precautions. Criminologists tell us that crimes with these features are the most likely to create hysteria. If America's ability to win the psychological war against terrorism depends upon our ability to remain calm in the face of random violence, our reaction to similar threats in the past is not entirely reassuring.

In the academic literature about crime, scholars have identified a para-   3
dox: "Most surveys discover that people apparently fear most being a victim of precisely those crimes they are least likely to be victims of," writes
Jason Ditton of the University of Sheffield. "Little old ladies apparently
worry excessively about being mugged, but they are the least likely to be
mugging victims." Women worry most about violent crime, though they
have the lowest risk of being victims, while young men worry the least,
though they have the highest risk. And because of their physical vulnerability, women tend to worry more about violence in general, even when the
risk of experiencing a particular attack is evenly distributed. In a Gallup
poll at the end of September, 62 percent of women said they were "very
worried" that their families might be victimized by terrorist attacks. Only
35 percent of the men were similarly concerned.

Why are people most afraid of the crimes they are least likely to expe-   4
rience? According to Wesley Skogan of Northwestern University, "it may
be the things we feel we can't control or influence, those uncontrollable
risks, are the ones that make people most fearful." It's why people fear flying more than they fear being hit by a car. We think we can protect ourselves against cars by looking before crossing the street—and therefore
underestimate the risk, even though it is actually higher than being killed
in a plane crash.

People also overestimate the risk of crimes they have never experienced.   5
The elderly are no more fearful than anyone else when asked how safe they
feel when they go out at night. That's because many senior citizens don't
go out at night, or they take precautions when they do. But when surveys
ask how safe they would feel if they did go out at night more often, old people say they would be very afraid, since they have less experience to give
them context. Instead they tend to assess risk based on media hype and rumors. "To be able to estimate the probability of an event occurring, you
first have to know the underlying distribution of those events, and second
the trend of those events—but when it comes to crime, people usually get
both hugely wrong," writes Ditton.

The media is partly to blame. A survey by George Gerbner, former dean   6
of the Annenberg School at the University of Pennsylvania, found that people who watch a lot of television are more likely than occasional viewers
to overestimate their chances of being a victim of violence, to believe their
neighborhood is unsafe, to say fear of crime is a very serious problem, to
assume that crime is rising, and to buy locks, watchdogs, and guns. And
this distortion isn't limited to television. Jason Ditton notes that 45 percent
of crimes reported in the newspaper involve sex or violence, even though
they only represent 3 percent of crimes overall. When interviewed about

how many crimes involve sex or violence, people tend to overestimate it by a factor of three or four. People believe they are more likely to be assaulted or raped than robbed, even though the robbery rate is much higher.

Will sensationalistic reports of worst-case terrorist scenarios exagger- 7 ate people's fear of being caught in an attack? There's every reason to believe that they will because of the media's tendency to exaggerate the scope and probability of remote risks. In a book called *Random Violence,* Joel Best, then of Southern Illinois University, examined the "moral panics" about a series of new crimes that seized public attention in the 1980s and '90s: freeway violence in 1987, wilding in 1989, stalking around 1990, kids and guns in 1991, and so forth. In each case, Best writes, television seized on two or three incidents of a dramatic crime, such as freeway shooting, and then claimed it was part of a broader trend. By taking the worst and most infrequent examples of criminal violence and melodramatically claiming they were typical, television created the false impression that everyone was equally at risk, thereby increasing its audience.

The risk of terrorism is more randomly distributed than the crimes the 8 media has hyped in the past. This makes it even more frightening because it is hard to avoid through precautions. (The anthrax envelopes were more narrowly targeted than the World Trade Center attack, of course, but they still infected postal workers.) Contemporary Americans, in particular, are not well equipped to deal with arbitrary threats because, in so many realms of life, we refuse to accept the role of chance. In his nineteenth-century novel *The Gilded Age,* Mark Twain described a steamship accident that killed 22 people. The investigator's verdict: "nobody to blame." This attitude was reflected in nineteenth-century legal doctrines such as assumption of risk, which refused to compensate victims who behaved carelessly. In the twentieth century, by contrast, the United States developed what the legal historian Lawrence Friedman has called an expectation of "total justice"— namely, "the general expectation that somebody will pay for any and all calamities that happen to a person, provided only that it is not the victim's 'fault,' or at least not solely his fault."

This effort to guarantee total justice is reflected throughout American 9 society—from the regulation of product safety to the elimination of legal doctrines like assumption of risk. Since September 11 the most egregious display of this total justice mentality has been the threat by various personal injury lawyers to sue the airlines, security officials, and the architects of the World Trade Center on behalf of the victims' families. One of their claims: Flaws in the design of the twin towers may have impeded escape.

Given America's difficulty in calculating and accepting unfamiliar risk, 10 what can be done, after September 11, to minimize panic? Rather than self-censoring only when it comes to the ravings of Osama bin Laden, the broadcast media might try to curb its usual focus on worst-case scenarios. Wesley Skogan found that when people were accurately informed about the real risk, they adjusted their fears accordingly. Politicians also need to be careful about passing on unspecified but terrifying threats of future attacks. In the middle of October the Justice Department warned that a terrorist attack might be imminent, but didn't say what the attack might be, or where it might strike. The vagueness of the warning only increased public fear and caused people to cancel travel plans. But it didn't make anyone more secure.

While Americans learn to take sensible precautions, we need to also   11
learn that there is no insurance against every calamity or compensation for every misfortune. There is something inegalitarian about risk: It singles out some people from the crowd for no good reason and treats them worse than everybody else. But even in the United States, there is no such thing as perfect equality or total justice. If the first foreign attack on U.S. soil helps teach Americans how to live with risk, then perhaps we can emerge from this ordeal a stronger society as well as a stronger nation.

Thinking About the Essay

1. In Rosen's opinion, who or what is to blame for Americans' preoccupation with threats of various kinds? How does a cause-and-effect pattern of development permit the writer to present a panorama of threats in this essay?

2. Rosen is trained in the law. How does his professional expertise influence the way he builds his "case" in this essay? What legal or "courtroom" techniques can you detect?

3. The writer constructs his argument through the use of numerous examples and forms of evidence. What types of evidence can you identify and where? What is the overall effect? Is his evidence convincing or not?

4. How does Rosen's level of language imply that he is writing for an audience that can follow logically the "rules of evidence" that he presents? Cite specific words and sentences to support your response.

5. To what extent, in your opinion, is Rosen's concluding paragraph an effective summation of his case? Is the tone of this last paragraph in keeping with the tone of the whole essay? Why or why not?

Responding in Writing

6. "The terrorist threat," says Rosen in the first sentence of paragraph 1, "is all too real, but newspapers and TV stations around the globe are still managing to exaggerate it." From your perspective, do you agree or disagree

with his assertion? Write an essay in which you provide sufficient evidence to support your response.

7. In a personal essay, explain how the terrorist threat has affected any other fears or apprehensions that you have had to deal with.

8. In an illustrative essay, address a question posed by Rosen in paragraph 10: "Given America's difficulty in calculating and accepting unfamiliar risk, what can be done, after September 11, to minimize panic?" Develop at least three ways to reduce our sense of panic.

Networking

9. In groups of four or five, discuss the ways in which each member has developed ways to cope with a range of fears and phobias—not just the terrorist threat. Then list all the strategies for coping and share them in class discussion.

10. Go online and locate at least four reviews of Rosen's book *The Unwanted Gaze: The Destruction of Privacy in America* (2000). Download and take notes on the reviewers' comments. (You will discover that some reviewers think that the book is brilliant, whereas others have negative opinions.) Write a comparative essay in which you explain these diverging appraisals of Rosen's book.

The Algebra of Infinite Justice

ARUNDHATI ROY | Arundhati Roy, born in Shillong, India, in 1961 and raised in Kerala, is the child of Syrian Christian and Hindu parents. Her first novel, *The God of Small Things* (1997), turned this former architecture student, actor, and screenwriter into an international celebrity. Steeped in the complex history of India, Roy's novel, which won the prestigious Booker Prize, is a dazzling portrayal of the lives of twin children as they move through the barriers of race, gender, and class on national and international levels of experience. To date, *The God of Small Things* has been published in twenty-seven languages. With her fame and royalties, Roy today is an activist, denouncing in extended essays the Indian government's destruction of the environment, criticizing nuclear proliferation, and subjecting other global issues to critical scrutiny. Her social and political criticism appears in *The Cost of Living* (1999) and *Power Politics* (2001). Roy received the $350,000

Lannam Foundation Prize for Cultural Freedom in 2002, announcing that she would donate the money to fifty educational institutions, publishing houses, and people's movements in India. In the following essay, published in *The Progressive* in December, 2001, Roy tries to explain why American foreign policy is so hated around the world.

Before Reading

Do you think that the United States government engages in policies around the world in order to promote "the American way of life"? Why or why not? What do you understand this term to mean? Why would peoples of other nations be skeptical of this effort?

It must be hard for ordinary Americans, so recently bereaved, to look up   1
at the world with their eyes full of tears and encounter what might appear to them to be indifference. It isn't indifference. It's just augury. An absence of surprise. The tired wisdom of knowing that what goes around eventually comes around. The American people ought to know that it is not them, but their government's policies, that are so hated.

Bush's almost god-like mission—called Operation Infinite Justice until   2
it was pointed out that this could be seen as an insult to Muslims, who believe that only Allah can mete out infinite justice, and was renamed Operation Enduring Freedom—requires some small clarifications. For example, Infinite Justice/Enduring Freedom for whom?

In 1996, Madeleine Albright, then the U.S. Ambassador to the United   3
Nations, was asked on national television what she felt about the fact that 500,000 Iraqi children had died as a result of economic sanctions the U.S. insisted upon. She replied that it was "a very hard choice," but that all things considered, "we think the price is worth it." Albright never lost her job for saying this. She continued to travel the world representing the views and aspirations of the U.S. government. More pertinently, the sanctions against Iraq remain in place. Children continue to die.

So here we have it. The equivocating distinction between civilization   4
and savagery, between the "massacre of innocent people" or, if you like, the "clash of civilizations" and "collateral damage." The sophistry and fastidious algebra of Infinite Justice. How many dead Iraqis will it take to make the world a better place? How many dead Afghans for every dead American? How many dead children for every dead man? How many dead mujahedeen for each dead investment banker?

The American people may be a little fuzzy about where exactly   5
Afghanistan is (we hear reports that there's a run on maps of the country),

Arundhati Roy *The Algebra of Infinite Justice* **397**

but the U.S. government and Afghanistan are old friends. In 1979, after the Soviet invasion of Afghanistan, the CIA and Pakistan's ISI (Inter-Services Intelligence) launched the CIA's largest covert operation since the Vietnam War. Their purpose was to harness the energy of Afghan resistance and expand it into a holy war, an Islamic jihad, which would turn Muslim countries within the Soviet Union against the communist regime and eventually destabilize it. When it began, it was meant to be the Soviet Union's Vietnam. It turned out to be much more than that. Over the years, through the ISI, the CIA funded and recruited tens of thousands of radical mujahedeen from forty Islamic countries as soldiers for America's proxy war. The rank and file of the mujahedeen were unaware that their jihad was actually being fought on behalf of Uncle Sam.

In 1989, after being bloodied by ten years of relentless conflict, the Russians withdrew, leaving behind a civilization reduced to rubble. Civil war in Afghanistan raged on. The jihad spread to Chechnya, Kosovo, and eventually to Kashmir. The CIA continued to pour in money and military equipment, but the overhead had become immense, and more money was needed.

The mujahedeen ordered farmers to plant opium as a "revolutionary tax." Under the protection of the ISI, hundreds of heroin processing laboratories were set up across Afghanistan. Within two years of the CIA's arrival, the Pakistan/Afghanistan borderland had become the biggest producer of heroin in the world, and the single biggest source on American streets. The annual profits, said to be between $100 and $200 billion, were ploughed back into training and arming militants.

In 1996, the Taliban—then a marginal sect of dangerous, hard-line fundamentalists—fought its way to power in Afghanistan. It was funded by the ISI, that old cohort of the CIA, and supported by many political parties in Pakistan. The Taliban unleashed a regime of terror. Its first victims were its own people, particularly women. It closed down girls' schools, dismissed women from government jobs, enforced Sharia law—under which women deemed to be "immoral" are stoned to death and widows guilty of being adulterous are buried alive.

After all that has happened, can there be anything more ironic than Russia and America joining hands to redestroy Afghanistan? The question is, can you destroy destruction? Dropping more bombs on Afghanistan will only shuffle the rubble, scramble some old graves, and disturb the dead. The desolate landscape of Afghanistan was the burial ground of Soviet communism and the springboard of a unipolar world dominated by America. It made the space for neocapitalism and corporate globalization, again dominated by America: And now Afghanistan is poised to become the graveyard for the unlikely soldiers who fought and won this war for America.

India, thanks in part to its geography and in part to the vision of its for- 10
mer leaders, has so far been fortunate enough to be left out of this Great
Game. Had it been drawn in, it's more than likely that our democracy, such
as it is, would not have survived. After September 11, as some of us
watched in horror, the Indian government furiously gyrated its hips, begging the U.S. to set up its base in India rather than Pakistan. Having had
this ringside view of Pakistan's sordid fate, it isn't just odd, it's unthinkable,
that India should want to do this. Any Third World country with a fragile
economy and a complex social base should know by now that to invite a
superpower such as America in (whether it says it's staying or just passing
through) would be like inviting a brick to drop through your windscreen.

Operation Enduring Freedom is being fought ostensibly to uphold the 11
American Way of Life. It'll probably end up undermining it completely. It
will spawn more anger and more terror across the world. For ordinary people in America, it will mean lives lived in a climate of sickening uncertainty:
Will my child be safe in school? Will there be nerve gas in the subway? A
bomb in the cinema hall? Will my love come home tonight? Being picked
off a few at a time—now with anthrax, later perhaps with smallpox or
bubonic plague—may end up being worse than being annihilated all at
once by a nuclear bomb.

The U.S. government and governments all over the world are using the 12
climate of war as an excuse to curtail civil liberties, deny free speech, lay
off workers, harass ethnic and religious minorities, cut back on public
spending, and divert huge amounts of money to the defense industry. To
what purpose? President Bush can no more "rid the world of evildoers"
than he can stock it with saints.

It's absurd for the U.S. government to even toy with the notion that it 13
can stamp out terrorism with more violence and oppression. Terrorism is
the symptom, not the disease.

Terrorism has no country. It's transnational, as global an enterprise as 14
Coke or Pepsi or Nike. At the first sign of trouble, terrorists can pull up
stakes and move their "factories" from country to country in search of a
better deal. Just like the multinationals.

Terrorism as a phenomenon may never go away. But if it is to be con- 15
tained, the first step is for America to at least acknowledge that it shares
the planet with other nations, with other human beings, who, even if they
are not on TV, have loves and griefs and stories and songs and sorrows and,
for heaven's sake, rights.

The September 11 attacks were a monstrous calling card from a world 16
gone horribly wrong. The message may have been written by Osama bin
Laden (who knows?) and delivered by his couriers, but it could well have

been signed by the ghosts of the victims of America's old wars: the millions killed in Korea, Vietnam, and Cambodia, the 17,500 killed when Israel—backed by the U.S.—invaded Lebanon in 1982, the tens of thousands of Iraqis killed in Operation Desert Storm, the thousands of Palestinians who have died fighting Israel's occupation of the West Bank.

And the millions who died, in Yugoslavia, Somalia, Haiti, Chile, 17 Nicaragua, El Salvador, the Dominican Republic, Panama, at the hands of all the terrorists, dictators, and genocidists whom the American government supported, trained, bankrolled, and supplied with arms. And this is far from being a comprehensive list.

For a country involved in so much warfare and conflict, the American 18 people have been extremely fortunate. The strikes on September 11 were only the second on American soil in over a century. The first was Pearl Harbor. The reprisal for this took a long route, but ended with Hiroshima and Nagasaki.

This time the world waits with bated breath for the horrors to come. 19

Someone recently said that if Osama bin Laden didn't exist, America 20 would have had to invent him. But in a way, America did invent him. He was among the jihadis who moved to Afghanistan in 1979 when the CIA commenced its operations there. Bin Laden has the distinction of being created by the CIA and wanted by the FBI. In the course of a fortnight, he was promoted from Suspect to Prime Suspect, and then, despite the lack of any real evidence, straight up the charts to "Wanted: Dead or Alive."

From what is known about bin Laden, it's entirely possible that he did 21 not personally plan and carry out the attacks—that he is the inspirational figure, "the CEO of the Holding Company." The Taliban's response to U.S. demands for the extradition of bin Laden was uncharacteristically reasonable: Produce the evidence, then we'll hand him over. President Bush's response was that the demand was "non-negotiable."

(While talks are on for the extradition of CEOs, can India put in a side- 22 request for the extradition of Warren Anderson of the USA? He was the chairman of Union Carbide, responsible for the 1984 Bhopal gas leak that killed 16,000 people. We have collated the necessary evidence. It's all in the files. Could we have him, please?)

But who is Osama bin Laden really? Let me rephrase that. What is 23 Osama bin Laden? He's America's family secret. He is the American President's dark doppelgänger. The savage twin of all that purports to be beautiful and civilized. He has been sculpted from the spare rib of a world laid to waste by America's foreign policy: its gunboat diplomacy, its nuclear arsenal, its vulgarly stated policy of "full spectrum dominance," its chilling disregard for non-American lives, its barbarous military interventions, its support for despotic and dictatorial regimes, its merciless economic agenda that has munched through the economies of poor countries like a cloud of locusts, its marauding multinationals that are taking over the air we breathe, the ground we stand on, the water we drink, the thoughts we think.

Now that the family secret has been spilled, the twins are blurring into 24 one another and gradually becoming interchangeable. Their guns, bombs, money, and drugs have been going around in the loop for a while. Now they've even begun to borrow each other's rhetoric. Each refers to the other as "the head of the snake." Both invoke God and use the loose millenarian currency of Good and Evil as their terms of reference. Both are engaged in unequivocal political crimes. Both are dangerously armed—one with the nuclear arsenal of the obscenely powerful, the other with the incandescent, destructive power of the utterly hopeless. The fireball and the ice pick. The bludgeon and the axe.

The important thing to keep in mind is that neither is an acceptable al- 25 ternative to the other.

President Bush's ultimatum to the people of the world—"Either you are 26 with us or you are with the terrorists"—is a piece of presumptuous arrogance.

It's not a choice that people want to, need to, or should have to make.   27

Thinking About the Essay

1. What are the writer's political views about the United States. What aspects of Roy's essay might prompt a counterargument? Do you disagree with Roy's assessment, or do you think that the writer actually has an important argument that we should treat seriously? Explain.

2. What does the title of the essay mean? Where does Roy expand on it? Why does she equate "justice" with "algebra"?

3. Point to paragraphs and sections of this essay where the writer uses process analysis, causal analysis, and comparison and contrast to advance her argument.

4. This essay seems to hop almost cinematically from point to point. Does Roy's technique damage the organization and coherence of her essay? Why or why not?

5. In the final analysis, does Roy make a compelling or logical argument in this essay? Explain your response.

Responding in Writing

6. Do you think that people around the world hate America's policies but not Americans—as Roy asserts? Write a paper responding to this question. Provide examples to support your position.

7. Write an argumentative essay in which you either support or rebut Roy's argument. Try to proceed point by point, moving completely through Roy's main reasons in defense of her claim.

8. What does the word justice mean to you? Did the American nation receive its due "justice" on September 11, 2001? Write an extended-definition essay responding to this notion.

Networking

9. In small groups, discuss each member's personal impression of Roy's essay. Try to explain the thoughts and emotions it prompts. Make a list of these responses, and share them with the rest of the class.

10. Enter an Internet forum dealing with American foreign policy and monitor what participants write about it. Prepare a summary of these responses, and post them—either on your own web page or as an e-mail attachment to friends.

10

CHAPTER

Global Aid: Can We Reduce Disease and Poverty?

The aftermath of Hurricane Katrina in 2005 was a reminder to many in the United States and around the world that major socioeconomic disparities exist even within a developed country. Poverty and a weak infrastructure made New Orleans and the surrounding region vulnerable to natural catastrophe, in much the same way that a compromised immune system invites disease. Observers compared the disaster in New Orleans to the humanitarian crises that result from floods and earthquakes in vulnerable, overpopulated Third World countries like Bangladesh. But the fact is that most of the world's population live under conditions like those found in Bangladesh and in the poorer parts of the United States.

We may like to think of such conditions as the provincial vestiges of a preindustrial world that, once exposed to the light of day, will naturally be assimilated into the modern world and corrected by the natural forces of progress. But globalization has also created new forms of poverty, isolation, and dependency. The new global economy has meant a return to what some would describe as an economics of colonial exploitation—although it is not clear who is exploiting whom, or even if "exploitation" is the correct label. Globalization has changed the relationship between "rich" and "poor" countries, but it is not clear whether the forces of a global free market will tend to bridge or widen the gap between rich and poor, whether global commerce will strengthen the socioeconomic infrastructures of poor countries or mask and preserve their deficiencies. Without infrastructures of their own in place, the poorest nations in the world may become even more dependent on international aid to address poverty-related health problems. And while some blame these negative

 *Online Study Center* This icon will direct you to web links, audio and visual content, and additional resources on the website college.hmco.com/pic/muller.NWR2e

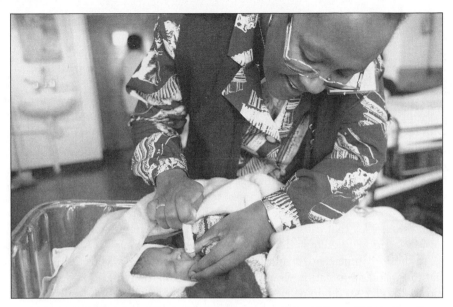

A health official administers a dose of Nevirapine to a newborn child at a clinic in Cape Town, South Africa. The drug substantially reduces the chance of HIV transmission from mother to child at birth.

Thinking About the Image

1. How would you describe your initial response to this image? For example, do you find the image to be optimistic or depressing? Explain your position.
2. How might your response be influenced by your attitudes toward gender, sexuality, race, geography, or cultural background?
3. The photographer shot this image at a time when the government of South Africa resisted the widespread dissemination of Nevirapine. What point or argument do you think the photographer was trying to make?
4. Conduct research on AIDS in South Africa, and then write a brief essay on one aspect of this problem. Insert at least three relevant images into the essay.

trends on the forces of an unregulated global free market, the philanthropic efforts of the Gates Foundation—which now spends nearly as much each year on global health projects as the World Health Organization—suggest that a corporate model of international aid may serve as a viable alternative to government-based infrastructures.

The essays in this chapter analyze global health and poverty issues in terms of a complex set of factors that have become even more complex in recent decades with the phenomenon of globalization. AIDS relief workers distribute condoms to miners in South Africa, but (as Alison Katz notes in her essay) the South African mines are run by unregulated transnational corporations, the miners are poor and underpaid migrant laborers, and their sex partners are often migrant workers who are forced into prostitution to feed and clothe their children. Often, the conditions that make people vulnerable to a disease are so closely connected with disease itself that cause and effect are nearly indistinguishable—hence, the term "Nutritionally Acquired Immune Deficiency Syndrome" (NAIDS).

In the early nineteenth century, British economist Robert Malthus predicted that the world's population would eventually outrun the world's food supply and that hunger and famine were the natural mechanisms for adjusting supply with demand. Malthus, as many have pointed out, failed to take into account future technological innovations that would radically improve the efficiency of world food production. Today, world food supply exceeds demand. The problem of world hunger is a failure of distribution, not a failure to produce enough food. And many of the diseases that result from poverty and hunger can be treated or prevented, depending on the approach taken. Globalization reminds us that certain disparities are the result of structural failure, and that the magnitude of a natural disaster is often a function of an unnatural vulnerability.

What I Did on My Summer Vacation

JEFFREY SACHS | Jeffrey Sachs is director of the Earth Institute, Quetelet Professor of Sustainable Development, and Professor of Health Policy and Management at Columbia University. Before his move to Columbia in 2002, Sachs was Director of the Center for International Development and Galen L. Stone Professor of International Trade at Harvard (where he was a faculty member for more than twenty years). Sachs serves as an economic adviser to governments in Latin America, Eastern Europe, the former Soviet Union, Asia, and Africa. He is Special Adviser to United Nations Secretary General Kofi Annan on the set of poverty alleviation initiatives known as the Millennium Project. In the following essay, which appeared in the December 2005 issue of *Esquire* magazine, Sachs describes his tour of places in Africa where, village by village, he witnesses evidence of the Millennium Project meeting its pragmatic goals.

Before Reading

Do you think of poverty and food shortage as a world problem that, like the poor, "will always be with us"? Can you imagine simple solutions to these problems that are also *long-term* solutions?

This summer, from June to August, my family and I took a trip. My daughter Hannah, who is ten, can now reel off the itinerary from memory: China, Tajikistan, Israel, United Arab Emirates, Yemen, Libya, England, Ghana, Mali, Nigeria, Kenya, Uganda, Ethiopia, Djibouti, Rwanda, Malawi, Indonesia, Cambodia. In these places, we spent most of our time in villages.

Throughout the world, the poor by and large live in villages. Thousands and thousands of villages: The fact of the matter is that these villages are communities of people who want out of poverty, who want their children to get out of poverty. They know they're poor. And they know the whole world is not poor and that they're stuck in a situation they don't want to be stuck in. That's the core concept of the Millennium Villages Project, which a few colleagues from the UN's Millennium Project and the Earth Institute at Columbia University and I started about a year ago.

Now, the basic ideas for how a poor village can be developed have been known for a long time among different groups of practitioners—those who grow food, and those who fight disease, and those who manage water supplies. What the Millennium Project does is bring these different groups together, because villages don't live only on farming or only on water or only on clinics. They live as whole communities that will get out of poverty wholly. If children are eating better because farmers are growing more food, it's going to improve the health of the children. Obviously, it will take the burden off the clinics. If the children are healthy, they are going to be in school. And they're going to be learning. If the children are in school, they're going to be the ones who will bring new ideas and new technologies to the community, so it's all mutually reinforcing.

My colleagues and I took a stand in our work several years ago that we would not look for the magic bullet, because there is none. These are just basic problems requiring basic work. Nothing magic about it. The strategy follows from that basic idea, but the idea of approaching this on a village-by-village basis came about accidentally.

Officialdom the world over is pretty slow moving, pretty impractical, and pretty darn frustrating many ways, so even when the proof of these concepts is clear, actually getting things done is not so easy. You need a little bit of money, and donors seem utterly capable of spending it on themselves, on salaries of consultants, on meetings and seminars and workshops, but not on actually helping people not starve to death in villages. Too much of

1

2

3

4

5

our aid money goes after an emergency comes, in shipping food aid instead of helping the farmers grow food, just as too much of it goes to razing and rebuilding a city rather than fortifying levees in advance of a disaster. Think of it as a smart investment: We can pay now or pay later. And it's a lot cheaper to pay now, and the return is incalculable. Yet this stuff doesn't actually get done, and that's why people are hungry, and that's why they're unable to access safe drinking water, and that's why they're dying by the millions.

It's not very satisfactory to see this and not act. And so in the last couple of years I've started to talk about these problems with business leaders and philanthropists, and over and over again I've heard the same response: Don't wait for the government. I'll help you. So what kind of accidentally dawned on us was that we could just go ahead and get these concepts proven on the ground. And that's what we are doing. And many philanthropists have come forward now and said, We'll give you some backing; show us what you can do.   6

The other day I was talking to the CEO of a major American corporation, a man who understands first and foremost the value of a good investment, and I was describing this effort to him, and he got it immediately. I hadn't even finished talking when he blurted out, "Sign me up for two villages!"   7

Our first village in Kenya, called Sauri, is actually a cluster of eight villages in what they call a sublocation in western Kenya, a very hungry, very disease-ridden, very isolated, extremely impoverished community. And it's a community that some of my colleagues knew because they had been analyzing the soils there and in nearby communities for many years. A colleague from Columbia University, Pedro Sanchez, who is a soils expert, felt strongly that there was an opportunity for quick development there. He told me that the soil simply lacked the nutrients to grow a proper crop. A little nitrogen, to be specific. He said to me, "You know, this situation could turn around quite quickly."   8

Now, when you have the experts saying that on one side and the philanthropists on the other side telling you, "Come on, let's do something," it gets pretty exciting. And that's how the Millennium Villages concept was born. The scientists said, Let's move. The philanthropists said, Let's move. A year ago we went and met with the community in Kenya and talked to people there about it. And they said, Let's move!   9

So we moved.   10

The trip this summer was timed to the harvest festival in Kenya, in which the community celebrated the biggest harvest that it had ever had. And it's stunning how easy it was. I had told Pedro that he'd better be right   11 about the nitrogen because a lot of people were watching, and lo and behold it was nitrogen! Putting in some basic fertilizer and helping the farmers use some improved seed varieties led to a doubling of their yields. Just like that, in one growing season. Very low cost, a few bucks per person in the village.

And we are not talking about just a few people being lifted out of poverty. We're talking about five thousand people. And that cluster of villages is already serving as the model for dozens of other villages for miles around. It's exponential. It's viral. This is how the world is changed. 12

On my trip this summer with my family, I got to visit with the leadership of ten African countries, from the village level to the heads of state. Each leader committed to working with us to establish ten Millennium Villages in the next year. That's a hundred altogether. 13

A year ago, we had two. 14

We first went to Sauri in the spring of 2004. Next, we decided to work in one of the toughest places on the planet, drought-ridden Ethiopia, where it's easy to just throw up your hands and say, It's impossible. But get on the ground, talk to the community, talk to the local experts, understand their distinctive problems, put it into bite-sized units, and what looks at first to be impossible becomes solvable. 15

We identified an area in northern Ethiopia, Tigray province. It is an hour from the regional capital, and then an hour off the road, and then an hour off the off-the-road. It's a beautiful, remote community of several thousand people in a valley that has tens of thousands of people. Again, we met with the community and found enormous enthusiasm and enormous organization—people who want to take their futures into their hands but need just a little bit of help to do it. They know about fertilizer, they know about improved seeds, they know about malaria bed nets, they know about cell phones, they know about trucks. They know they don't have any of these things. But they would like to have the chance. They're saying, Help us a bit and we can get out of this. In fact, that's what we find all over the developing world. The poor countries are saying to the rich countries: Look, we know you have an income a hundred times bigger than we have. We're starving, and you have more than enough to eat. You have everything you could ask for, and we have absolutely zero. We're not calling for revolution; we're not out to dismantle the world. We just want to have a chance to find a way over a long period of time to have some of the things that you have. 16

In Tigray province, their crop is a mix of teff, which is the staple grain of Ethiopia; sorghum, which is a dry-season grain; a little bit of finger millet, 17 which is another dry-season grain; and maize, which is pretty much grown all over Africa. Tree crops, papayas and mangoes, can grow in this kind of environment if there's a little bit of drip irrigation. And they provide both market opportunities and wonderful nutrition. So we started them with nurseries and improved seed. A local scientist, a wonderful young Ethiopian, was selected by the local government to head the project for us and get the community together. They built these remarkable check dams called gabions, which are just ways to preserve these mountainside villages from the short onslaught of floods and channel the water away from the crops so that the water running down the mountains doesn't create gulleys and destroy the land.

In other words, same point: simple steps, low-cost steps, all attuned to   18 the area's specific needs, led by the community, done by the community, but with a helping hand. That was early this year, and since then the local people have been out there doing the land reformation, doing reforestation, and getting ready for the planting season that was a couple months ago, and they'll be harvesting soon. In the meantime, the clinic is being built and the school is being expanded, all within a very modest budget of fifty dollars per villager per year for five years, which is our standard amount of intervention.

Then we've helped establish a local economy. And chances are, these   19 people aren't going to need us anymore. So the incessant talk in Washington about these corrupt people and their corrupt governments is just a galling excuse not to focus on practical things that we can do now to improve the world.

And for the hard-nosed among us, it bears repeating: Extreme poverty   20 is the best breeding ground on earth for disease, political instability, and terrorism.

Thirty-six years ago, the rich world began in earnest to figure out what it   21 would realistically take to help the poor world. A commission led by former Canadian prime minister Lester Pearson came up with the number 0.7. Here's how they arrived at that: They said that there should be a transfer of about 1 percent of GNP from the rich to the poor. That's one dollar out of every hundred. They said the public sector will do some and the private sector needs to do some, and that it should be about a seventy-thirty split. So that's where the seventy cents came from. And that was adopted by the General Assembly of the UN in 1970. The U.S. resisted for a long time. We didn't want to sign on even when the rest of the world did.

But in March 2002, the world's leaders met in Monterrey, Mexico, at a   22 conference that President Bush attended, and this conference adopted something called the Monterrey Consensus, which upheld the 0.7 target. This time, the United States signed on to it. The American signature came after a long, detailed negotiation. The U.S. finally said, Okay, it's only seventy cents. And the agreement it signed said this, in paragraph 42: "We urge developed countries that have not done so to make concrete efforts towards the target of 0.7 percent of GNP as official development assistance." Check it out, paragraph 42.

This fall at the United Nations, President Bush said that it is dangerous 23 to American security when countries are not achieving economic development. They become unstable; they become seedbeds for terror, for violence, for the major ills of the world. The whole U.S. national-security doctrine says that development is one of the pillars of national security. There's actually nothing wrong with what these tough, self-interested types in foreign policy have been saying, because what they have been saying is that it is completely within our national interest to be helping in these circumstances.

The problem is not in the words or the logic; the problem is in our lack 24 of action. We currently give about a quarter of our pledged assistance. We've pledged to give seventy cents out of every hundred dollars of U.S. income. Instead, we give about eighteen cents. For the safety of all Americans, we must insist that our government live up to its obligation.

When President Kennedy talked about helping the people in the huts 25 and villages around the world, he said we did it not to fight communism but because it was the right thing to do. Turns out that it was right on every level, not merely morally right. It was right for our national security, for our global health, for stopping violence. It was right from a hardheaded, bottom-line, conservative standpoint, and it was right for winning hearts and minds at a time when we needed allies. And we need allies again.

This is a tiny amount of our income that could save millions of people 26 and make a safer world, and it is really a measure of our times that we ask ourselves, Why should we give a few cents out of every hundred dollars to do something like this? And yet we do ask that question.

At the beginning of July, we flew to Libya for the African Union summit, 27 where I was honored to speak to the African heads of state for the second year running.

Then on to London for the G8 summit. I didn't actually go to the sum- 28 mit in Gleneagles but worked out of London and left the morning of the bombing.

And Tony Blair got it absolutely right that day, and President Bush 29 made a very good statement also, saying that it was all the more important to redouble our efforts in the fight against poverty and not let the terrorists take away from that agenda. And Gleneagles did produce important re- sults: The G8 leaders committed to doubling aid to Africa. It was a wel- come step in the right direction but a long way from what the world has promised.

After the G8, on to Ghana, where much interesting work is being done. 30 A lot of the agricultural concepts I am describing are drawn from Ghana's very vigorous scientific community of ecologists and agronomists, fruit growers and hydrologists. There's a tremendous amount of local research that's been done on African agriculture. And scientists there have solutions up and down the continent, and that's what they want to apply. We're not inventing any of this.

We went from Ghana to Nigeria. And Nigeria is quite another thing al- 31 together. It's the most populous country in Africa, one fifth of sub-Saharan Africa. The country has had an incredibly complex and difficult transition to democracy because it's a sprawling, multiethnic, unstable country with a long history of extreme corruption. Nigeria is led by President Obasanjo, who is fighting hard on every front to create a rule of law, decent systems, and a constitutional government.

I've been working with President Obasanjo for five years now on all 32 sorts of things. He has hosted an Africa-wide malaria conference and an Africa-wide AIDS conference that President Carter and I attended. He has hosted all sorts of other major initiatives because he's a real leader and he really understands the stakes right now. He's trying to get not only Nigeria on its feet but all of Africa.

So we will have many villages in Nigeria. In the north, we're going to 33 start one village project in Kaduna, working with the Islamic community there.

We also went south to the state of Ondo, which is led by a remarkable 34 reform-minded governor who I immediately took to. He was chairman of the geology department at Ibadan University for many years and got his Ph.D. in geology from the University of Texas. We decided together to launch a Millennium Villages project in his state. And that will be a site for two communities, Ibara and Ikaram, for about twenty thousand people, and we're getting that started right now. The governor is on e-mail with me, and he is very determined.

From Nigeria on to Mali, which is right next to Niger. People are hear- 35 ing about the hunger crisis in Niger, and the same basic crisis is also hap- pening in Mali. It had a massive locust crisis last year, which ate up the crops. Timbuktu is in northern Mali. We went from the capital, Bamako, to Timbuktu, both of which are on the Niger River. Timbuktu is just at the boundary of the desert and was the way station for caravans coming from the north through the Sahara on their way to Ghana and other parts of west Africa and back again. So it's a place of intersection, of nomads and farm people as well, and it's the northern extent of settled agriculture. The villages on the south side of Timbuktu are the worst of the worst.

I asked the village chief, What are you living on now? What are you go- 36 ing to do? It was obviously a very painful conversation. For him to be answering in front of everybody was not the easiest thing in the world, yet we needed to have the conversation. One option apparently was that they were going to borrow some seed, because they had lost everything—food, seed—to the locusts. And I asked what the terms would be. He had been looking down at the sand, and he raised his head and looked at me. The terms would be that they would have to pay it back twice, a 100 percent interest rate in one growing season, due in four months. Literally an impossible situation.

But we have an idea that we are testing. 37

A couple of months before I was in Mali, I had been to the Indian state 38 of Andhra Pradesh, which is along the Ganges River. The Ganges plain is home to hundreds of millions of people because you have intensive agriculture there. You go from farmhouse to farmhouse and everyone has a hand pump and many a treadle pump, which you use to pump water by foot. And the reason is that the water table is very close to the surface. You just dig down ten or fifteen feet and you hit water.

In Mali, you have the Niger River, but there are no pumps. And it 39 looked so familiar to me. I said, How far down is the water table? Three meters, they said.

Why don't you have a well down there? I asked, because everyone is 40 without water. And they said, Maybe we could do that. Maybe a large project could come in. I said, But you just need treadle pumps here. This is perfect for small-scale irrigation. Now a real expert will judge this. And we have great hydrologists and agronomists on our team. So we're going to start a village in Timbuktu, and we're going to prove that along the Niger you can have irrigation.

The south of Mali is a cotton-growing area where we're also going to 41 have a village. And it is here that you see the direct manifestation of how American cotton subsidies actually lead to the death of impoverished communities. There we had a community meeting sitting in the dirt. And I asked the people what had happened this season, and they told me something quite stunning.

At planting time, an agricultural collective provides some fertilizer and 42 seed. The farmers grow the crop. And then at the end of the growing season, this enterprise buys the cotton back from the farmers at the world market price. This year, the farmers were told, Well, you've just given us your crop and now you're deeper in debt because the value of your crop is less than the input we gave you four months ago.

So these people literally worked for months only to be deeper in debt   43 at the end of the season. The cotton prices are so low because we have heavily subsidized twenty-five thousand American cotton growers in a scheme that the World Trade Organization has declared illegal. Now, for cotton growers in Brazil it lowers their incomes and creates hardship, but in Mali it kills people. Because these people have no incomes, there's no nurse in the village, there's no school. And I turned to the chief. Have any children died recently? I asked. And I'll never forget his response. He waved his hand in violent disgust. "So many! *So many!*" he said before lowering his head and walking away. And then the village all piped in that they're losing children all the time because they get hungry, and then infection comes, and then the child's dead. We're not merely leaving these people to their fate but actually driving them into greater poverty without any sense of responsibility because we're not even compensating in other ways. Where's the other aid? Where's the "Oh, yes, we have to do it for our farmers, but here's what we can do for you"?

So that was Mali.   44

Then we flew to Kenya, and Kenya is where we started this discussion. 45 Not only is the village process working there, but the national government is very deeply engaged, so even though it's a village program, it's also a national program.

We had a good meeting with the Cabinet in Nairobi and then flew to 46 Sauri for the harvest festival.

And let me tell you, on that day in Kenya, the cornfields looked like Illi- 47 nois. And it was the most beautiful thing I ever saw in my life.

Thinking About the Essay

1. How is the essay structured as a "travelogue"? Why does Sachs open the essay with mention of his daughter?

2. How is the author's use of colloquial phrases and other language related, as a tonal gesture, to the argument of the essay?

3. Where does Sachs critique the shortcomings of the policy actions (or inaction) of nations in the developed world? What is the significance of the allusion to a recent domestic crisis in paragraph 5?

4. How does Sachs make the argument that alleviation of poverty in the developing world is in the national interest of developed nations? Where does he make this argument?

5. How does the concluding section of the essay connect with the opening paragraphs? What is the nature of the emotional appeal made in the final paragraphs of the essay?

Responding in Writing

6. In a brief essay, attempt to demystify the complexity of a current socioeconomic problem in the United States that could lead some observers to resign themselves to the problem's insolubility and to fall back upon the notion that "the poor are always with us."

7. In paragraph 25, Sachs states that John F. Kennedy's cold war rationale for world poverty relief was "right on every level, not merely morally right." In an expository essay, consider some *non*moral justifications for world poverty relief in the post–cold war era.

8. Compose a letter to a local philanthropist in which you attempt to persuade him or her to contribute to a poverty relief effort like the one Sachs describes.

Networking

9. In groups of three or four, plan a group vacation with an itinerary of places in the world that members of your group think are in most dire need of assistance. Share your itinerary with the class.

10. Go online and find out information about the most recent work of the Millennium Villages Project.

Cities Without Slums

NAMRITA TALWAR

Namrita Talwar is a science journalist based in New York City. She studied science and environmental reporting at New York University and currently works in the Department of Public Information at the United Nations headquarters in New York. In the following article, published in the *U.N. Chronicle* in 2004, Talwar reports on the alarming results of a study conducted by the United Nations Human Settlements Programme on the rapid expansion of urban slum populations throughout the world.

Before Reading

Why do urban slums exist in cities in the United States? Write down what you consider to be the features that define a slum, and return to this list after you have read the essay. Has the essay changed your definition of a slum? How?

Faeces fill up the deep ditches that pockmark the unpaved streets of nu-   1
merous slum cities in the industrializing world. Some 900 million slum
dwellers the world over inhale the foul air and walk through the narrow
lanes whose surface is splattered with fetid fluids and littered with plastic
bags. Matchbox tenements line the winding lanes, where inhabitants daily
battle buzzing flies and disease-injecting mosquitoes, and muddle through
ever-migrating rural populations that live under these festering conditions.

"*The Challenge of Slums: Global Report on Human Settlements*   2
2003"—the largest study ever done by the United Nations Human Settlements Programme (UN-HABITAT)—found that urban slums were growing faster than expected. With the locus of global poverty shifting rapidly
from rural areas to cities, almost one sixth of the world's population is already living in unhealthy areas, more often than not without water, sanitation or security. The report warns that if no concerted action is taken, the
number of slum dwellers worldwide will rise to 2 billion over the next
thirty years.

Despite all this, the number of people moving to cities, especially in   3
Africa, Latin America, Asia and in many parts of the Middle East, remains
high. The huge increase in the world's urban and urban slum populations
is a crisis of unprecedented magnitude.

"All of these people will need to be provided with shelter, employment   4
and with urban services," Naison Mutizwa-Mangiza, Chief of the Policy
Analysis, Synthesis and Dialogue Branch at the UN-HABITAT Monitoring
and Research Division, told the UN *Chronicle*. Many cities are caught in a
deep morass of haphazard growth and unplanned development of infrastructure, which analysts say is making some cities unable to cope with the
increasing burden of population. "The stretched capacity of most urban
economies in developing countries is unable to meet more than a fraction
of these needs," Mr. Mutizwa-Mangiza said.

Although at this stage there are no specific global estimates of urban   5
poverty, the report points out that the absolute numbers of poor and un-
dernourished in urban areas are increasing, as is the share of urban areas
in general poverty and malnutrition. Overall, half of the world's population—nearly 3 billion people—lives on less than $2 a day.

Similarly, globalization is another phenomenon, the report notes, bear-   6
ing down on the expanding slums. As the forces of globalization eddy
around the developing world, the opening up of economies may have offered opportunities for a few businesses and cities to grow. However, the
report says, the new insecurities that globalization has created surpass its
benefits, especially for the poor, who in the last decade have lost jobs, seen
their land seized, paid more for basic services and suffer from an absence
of a basic social infrastructure.

Despite growing globalization, little if any of the wealth amassed by the   7
rich has reached the poor, and this has only contributed to the increasing
gap between the haves and the have-nots. The task for now is to unbind
cities from slums. In its commitment to do so, world leaders in the United
Nations Millennium Declaration made a pledge to improve the lives of 100
million slum dwellers by the year 2020. The solution lies in improving
slums, as opposed to resettling slum dwellers. Relocating slums are known
to have created problems in the past, with people returning to the same
area in anticipation of better prospects for getting work. Upgrading of existing slums should be combined with policies that look at urban planning
and management, as well as at low-income housing development, according to the report.

"This should include supply of sufficient and affordable serviced land   8
for the gradual development of economically appropriate low-income
housing by the poor themselves, thus preventing the emergence of more
slums," Mr. Mutizwa-Mangiza said. At a broader national scale, decentralized urbanization strategies should be pursued, where possible, to ensure that rural-to-urban migration is spread more evenly, thus preventing
the congestion in cities that account, in part, for the mushrooming of
slums, he explained, adding that decentralized urbanization can only work
if pursued within the framework of suitable national economic development policies, inclusive of poverty reduction.

A major key to reducing slums lies in providing water, sanitation, storm   9
drainage, basic access to roads, and electricity at a satisfactory level. Although developing countries lack resources to build new infrastructure facilities, Mr. Mutizwa-Mangiza said that this should not be a problem, as
upgrading does not involve home construction since the residents can do
this themselves. They also offer optional loans for home improvements.

"With respect to the problem of limited resources, it has long been rec-   10
ognized that the poor play a key role in the improvement of their own living conditions and that their participation in decision-making is not only a
right, and thus an end in itself, but is also instrumental in achieving greater
effectiveness in the implementation of public policies," Mr. Mutizwa-
Mangiza explained. He also noted that the removal of environmental haz-
ards, providing incentives for community management and maintenance,
as well as the construction of clinics and schools, would be of great benefit to impoverished families. It costs ten times less to upgrade a slum for
clearance and relocation, which makes it an affordable alternative, the report says. The poor are often willing and able to invest their own labour
and finance resources in their housing. This has been demonstrated in
many slum upgrading and site and service projects for the poor, according
to the report.

The Orangi Pilot Project in Karachi, Pakistan, is one such example.   11
Residents in Orangi constructed sewers to 72,000 dwellings over twelve
years, from 1980 to 1992, contributing more than $2 million from their
own resources. The Project includes basic health, family planning, and education and empowerment components. The integrated programmes of social inclusion in Santo Andre municipality, Sao Paulo, Brazil, have
improved the living conditions of 16,000 favela inhabitants through part-
nerships with the poor, who are normally excluded from formal processes.

Slum upgrading in some countries also entails giving formal title deeds   12
or land ownership to poor dwellers. However, according to Mr. Mutizwa-
Mangiza, "combining tenure legalization and land titling programmes
with programmes to provide serviced land, upgrading and improvements
at settlement level has had limited success." When large-scale allocation of
property titles to households living in informal settlements has been made
possible, it has often resulted in increased housing prices within the settlements, or an increase in the cost of services. This often means that poor
households benefiting from such slum upgrading programmes sell their
houses to higher income households, thereby returning to their original status of shoddy housing.

The challenge for now is to ensure that the poor's contribution to slum   13
upgrading is made meaningful by investing in citywide infrastructure. The
going seems tough for developing countries, and the coming years will be
a test for nations seeking slum development. "Experience has shown the
need for significant investment in citywide trunk infrastructure by the public sector if housing in upgraded slums is to be affordable to the urban poor
and if efforts to support the informal enterprises run by poor slum dwellers
are to be successful," Mr. Mutizwa-Mangiza said.

Thinking About the Essay

1. How does the descriptive mode of the vivid opening paragraph contrast with
   the less vivid expository mode of the rest of the essay? Do any of images
   of the opening paragraph recur later in the essay as metaphors?

2. According to the UN-HABITAT report, what are the main factors that are contributing to the increase in the world's urban slum population?

3. Where in the essay does Talwar characterize the economic forces behind
   urban poverty as an unalterable "given"?

4. What are the unintended consequences of issuing of formal title deeds to
   poor slum dwellers and giving them ownership of property?

5. Do you detect a tone of optimism or pessimism in Talwar's reporting? Upon
   what evidence in the text would you base this attribution?

Responding in Writing

6. In a comparative essay, contrast Talwar's vision of urban poverty with the rural poverty of African villages as described by Jeffrey Sachs in the preceding essay in this chapter. Do the two forms of poverty have related causes?

7. In paragraph 10, Talwar reports that the poor in urban slums "are often willing and able to invest their own labour and finance resources in their housing." What does this fact tell you about the character of the average urban slum dweller? Respond in a brief essay.

8. How do you respond to the ironic "pricing out" phenomenon reported in paragraph 12 of the essay? Do you see an analogous phenomenon occurring in your own community? In an essay, analyze the nature of the economic mechanisms at work.

Networking

9. Divide the class into two groups and debate whether policies to relieve urban poverty should focus on the economic causes of expanding slums or on the more modest aim of improving conditions within urban slums.

10. Go online and read some of the other findings of the UN-HABITAT report that are not quoted or referred to in this essay.

A Threat Worse Than Terror

FAREED ZAKARIA | Foreign affairs analyst Fareed Zakaria was born and raised in Bombay, the son of politically progressive parents who were also practicing Muslims. (His father was a leading politician, and his mother edited the *Times of India*.) Zakaria moved to the United States to attend Yale and received a Ph.D. in political science at Harvard, where he studied under Samuel P. Huntington. At age twenty-eight, Zakaria accepted an offer to edit *Foreign Affairs* magazine. One of the first articles published in the magazine with Zakaria at the helm was Huntington's controversial essay on the clash of civilizations (later expanded into a book). Zakaria continues to make regular appearances as a foreign affairs analyst on television and in print, and he contributes a regular foreign affairs column in *Newsweek* (where the following essay appeared in October of 2005).

Before Reading

Do you distinguish between the threat of a "naturally" occurring disease and the manufactured threat of bio-terrorism? Which threat do you see as most pressing?

A flu pandemic is the most dangerous threat the United States faces to-   1
day, says Richard Falkenrath, who until recently served in the Bush administration as deputy Homeland Security adviser. "It's a bigger threat than terrorism. In fact it's bigger than anything I dealt with when I was in government." One makes a threat assessment on the basis of two factors: the probability of the event, and the loss of life if it happened. On both counts, a pandemic ranks higher than a major terror attack, even one involving weapons of mass destruction. A crude nuclear device would probably kill hundreds of thousands. A flu pandemic could easily kill millions.

Whether this particular virus makes the final, fatal mutation that allows   2
it to move from human to human, one day some virus will. The basic factor that is fueling this surge of viruses is China's growth. (China is the natural habitat of the influenza virus.) As China develops, it urbanizes, and its forests and wetlands shrink. That forces migratory birds to gather closer together—and closer to human habitation—which increases the chances of a virus spreading from one species to the next. Also, growth means a huge rise in chicken consumption. Across thousands of homes in China every day, chickens are slaughtered in highly unhygienic ways. "Every day the chances that this virus or another such virus will move from one species to another grow," says Laurie Garrett, author of "The Coming Plague," who has been writing brilliantly on this topic for years.

Nobody really disputes that we are badly unprepared for this threat. "If   3
some thing like this pandemic were to happen today," says Falkenrath, "the government would be mostly an observer, not a manager." The government can't even give intelligent advice to its citizens because it doesn't actually know what to say. We don't know whether people should stay put, leave cities, stay home or go to the nearest hospital. During the cold war, hundreds of people in government participated in dozens of crisis simulations of nuclear wars, accidents and incidents. These "tabletop exercises" were conducted so that if and when a real crisis hit, policy-makers would not be confronting critical decisions for the first time. No such expertise exists for today's deadliest threat.

Beyond short-term measures for this virus—mainly stocking up on   4
Tamiflu—the only credible response is the development of countermeasures. The best response would be a general vaccine that would work against all strains of the flu. That's a tall order, but it could be achieved.

The model of the Manhattan Project is often bandied about loosely, but *this* is a case in which it makes sense. We need a massive biomedical project aimed at tackling these kinds of diseases, whether they're natural or engineered by terrorists.

The total funding request for influenza-related research this year is 5 about $119 million. To put this in perspective, we are spending well over $10 billion to research and develop ballistic-missile defenses, which protect us against an unlikely threat (even if they worked). We are spending $4.5 billion a year on R&D—drawings!—for the Pentagon's new joint strike fighter. Do we have our priorities right?

The final sense in which we are unprepared is that we have weak global 6 organizations to deal with pandemics. The bird flu is a problem that began in Guangdong, China, and spread to Indonesia, Russia, Turkey, Romania and now possibly Iran. It may move next into Africa. Some of these governments are competent; others are not. Some hide information from everyone; others simply refuse to share it with the United States. We need a system that everyone will follow. The World Health Organization should become the global body that analyzes samples, monitors viruses, evaluates cures and keeps track of the best practices. Yet the WHO leads a hand-to-mouth existence, relying on the whims and grants of governments. A year ago its flu branch had five people. Now it has 12. It needs a much, much larger staff and its own set of laboratories around the world that would allow it to fulfill this clearinghouse function. Countries have finally agreed to a new set of conventions that give the U.N. and the WHO some of the authority they need. And Kofi Annan has appointed one person to coordinate the global efforts to fight pandemics.

Many people believed that globalization meant that government would 7 become less important. But as we see, today's world has actually made government more crucial. Only government can tackle a problem like this one, not by being big but by being smart and effective. And we need good governance not just at home but beyond. Without effective international coordination, we are doomed to failure. John Bolton once said that you could chop off 10 floors of the United Nations and we'd all be better off. Let's hope that the scientists fighting global diseases aren't on any of those floors.

Thinking About the Essay

1. How does Zakaria's economy of language, in the sentences of the opening paragraph and elsewhere in the essay, contribute to the force and urgency of his argument? Consider the effect of at least two examples. Why does he open the essay with a quoted statement, rather than with his own voice?

2. How does Zakaria compare the threat of a flu pandemic with various other threats in terms of the likelihood of their occurrence and the magnitude of their likely effects?

3. According to Zakaria, why is China the natural habitat of the influenza virus and the locus of concern about a future pandemic?

4. What historical analogies does Zakaria make in the essay? Why does he pause to reflect on one of these analogies once it has been made?

5. Why does Zakaria wait until his concluding paragraph to broach the topic of globalization? What is the purpose (and the more general implied target) of the polemical turn in the concluding paragraph? Who is John Bolton?

Responding in Writing

6. Respond to Zakaria's proposed criteria for a threat assessment. Are there other ways of assessing a global threat? How would these additional criteria apply to the threat of a flu pandemic?

7. Do you agree with Zakaria that only government can tackle the problem of a flu pandemic? Defend your position in an argumentative essay.

8. Compose a letter to your representative in Congress to persuade him or her to push for an increase in the United States contribution to the World Health Organization and for greater cooperation with the efforts of the United Nations.

Networking

9. In groups of three or four, decide on your immediate response to a flu pandemic in lieu of instructions from the government. Explain to the rest of the class why you would take this action; or, of you could not agree on a plan, explain the nature of your disagreement.

10. Go online to research the history of the flu pandemic that occurred in the aftermath of World War I and led to the deaths of more people worldwide than the number of soldiers and civilians killed in the war.

Technology Won't Feed the World's Hungry

ANURADHA MITTAL

> Anuradha Mittal, a native of India, is founder and di-
> rector of the Oakland Institute, a policy think tank that
> works to promote public participation and democratic
> debate on economic and social policy issues. Mittal is
> known internationally as an expert on trade, human
> rights, and agriculture issues. She has traveled widely as
> a public speaker and has appeared as guest and com-
> mentator on television and radio. Her articles on inter-
> national public policy issues have appeared in *The New
> York Times* and in other journals worldwide. In the fol-
> lowing article, which appeared in the July 12, 2001, is-
> sue of *Progressive Media Project,* Mittal argues that
> biotechnology cannot solve the problem of world
> hunger.

Before Reading

Do you see the debate over genetically engineered foods primarily in terms of
your choice as a consumer or in terms of the way such technology would
address world hunger?

Don't be misled. Genetically engineered food is not an answer to world 1
hunger.

The U.N. Development Program (UNDP) released a report last week 2
urging rich countries to put aside their fears of such food and help developing nations unlock the potential of biotechnology.

The report accuses opponents of ignoring the Third World's food needs. 3
It claims that Western consumers who do not face food shortages or nutritional deficiencies are more likely to focus on food safety and the loss of
biodiversity, while farming communities in developing countries emphasize
potentially higher yields and "greater nutritional value" of these crops.

But the UNDP has not done its homework. 4

In my country, India, for example, the debate pits mostly U.S.-trained 5
technocrats, seduced by technological fixes, against farmers and consumers
who overwhelmingly say no to these crops. The people who are to use the
modified seeds and eat the modified food often want nothing to do with
them.

The report rehashes the old myth of feeding the hungry through 6 miracle technology. As part of the 1960s Green Revolution, Western technology created pesticides and sent them to developing countries for agricultural use, which may have increased food production, but at the cost of poisoning our earth, air and water.

What's more, it failed to alleviate hunger. Of the 800 million hungry 7 people in the world today, more than 200 million live in India alone. It's not that India does not produce enough food to meet the needs of its hungry. It's that organizations like the International Monetary Fund (IMF) have slashed public services and social-safety nets so that the food can't get to the needy.

More than 60 million tons of excess, unsold food grain rotted in India 8 last year because the hungry were too poor to buy it. In desperation, some farmers burned the crops they could not market and resorted to selling their kidneys and other body parts, or committing suicide, to end the cycle of poverty.

A higher, genetically engineered crop yield would have done nothing for 9 them. And if the poor in India are not able to buy two meals a day, how will they purchase nutritionally rich crops such as rice that is engineered to contain vitamin A?

The report compares efforts to ban genetically modified foods with the 10 banning of the pesticide DDT, which was dangerous to humans but was effective in killing the mosquitoes that spread malaria. The Third World had to choose between death from DDT or malaria. It's appalling that even today the debate in developed countries offers the Third World the option of either dying from hunger or eating unsafe foods.

Malaria, like hunger, is a disease of poverty. When economic conditions 11 improve, it disappears, just as it did in the United States and Europe.

The focus ought to be on the root causes of the problem, not the symp- 12 tom. The hungry don't need a technological quick fix. They need basic social change.

In the Third World, the battle against genetically engineered food is a 13 battle against the corporate concentration of our food system. Corporations are gaining control of our biodiversity and even our seeds. This is a potential stranglehold on our food supply. In response, developing countries are imposing moratoriums on genetically engineered crops. Sri Lanka, Thailand, Brazil, Mexico and China, among others, have already done so.

The UNDP has been snookered about genetically engineered food. The 14 rest of us shouldn't be.

Thinking About the Essay

1. How does Mittal frame her paragraph-long paraphrase of the claims of the UNDP within the opening paragraphs of the essay?

2. Does Mittal's reference to India as "my country" have any effect on her argument? Would the argument be as strong without the personal element? Why or why not?

3. How does Mittal characterize the advocates of biotechnology who are the authors of the UNDP report?

4. According to Mittal, what is the role that corporations play in the promotion of biotechnology? How does this claim change her characterization of the motives for promoting such technology?

5. How effective is the colloquial language of the two-sentence concluding paragraph? Are there other examples of such language in the essay?

Responding in Writing

6. In a brief essay, connect Mittal's argument with other arguments presented in this chapter about economic infrastructure as the root cause of world health problems.

7. Argue for or against the use of biotechnology as a solution to world hunger by invoking an analogy of your own that you believe characterizes the reaction of opponents or supporters of such technology. Why is this analogy appropriate?

8. Do you think that adequate public services and social-safety nets exist in the United States that prevent the kind of failure of resource distribution Mittal describes in India? Why do people go hungry in the United States today? Is this hunger the result of a systemic failure? Answer these questions in an argumentative essay.

Networking

9. In small groups, discuss your reservations (or enthusiasms) about genetically engineered food. Do you feel that you are reacting according to your limited interests as a Western consumer? Why or why not?

10. Go online and engage in a discussion group debate over genetically engineered food from a global, hunger-relief point of view.

A Development Nightmare

KENNETH ROGOFF

Kenneth Rogoff was Charles and Marie Robertson Professor of International Affairs at Princeton University and is currently professor of economics and director of the Center for International Development at Harvard University. From 2001 to 2003, he served as chief economist and director of research at the International Monetary Fund. Rogoff has published extensively on government policy issues surrounding international finance, and he is also the co-author (with Maurice Obstfeld) of the widely used graduate textbook *Foundations of International Macroeconomics* (1996). In the following article, which appeared in *Foreign Policy* magazine in January/February 2004, Rogoff examines the foreign aid policies of "rich" nations whose efforts to promote the economic development of other nations are mixed with fears about the distribution (and dilution) of the world's wealth.

Before Reading

Do you measure your own economic prosperity in relative terms? What are those terms?

Indulge in a dream scenario for a moment: Suppose the world awoke to- 1 morrow and, miraculously, every country suddenly enjoyed the same per capita income as the United States, or roughly $40,000 per year. Global annual income would soar to $300 trillion, or some 10 times what it is now. And while we're at it, suppose also that international education levels, infant mortality rates, and life expectancies all converged to the levels in rich countries. In short, what if foreign aid worked and economic development happened overnight instead of over centuries?

A heretical thought, perhaps. But I wonder sometimes what voters in 2 rich nations must be thinking when they reward their politicians for cutting already pathetic foreign-aid budgets. Is it possible that, deep down, the world's wealthy fear what will happen if the developing countries really did catch up, and if the advantages their own children enjoy were shared by all? Would the dream become a nightmare?

Consider whether today's wealthy would materially suffer under such 3 a scenario. As things now stand, 290 million U.S. citizens already cause almost one-fourth of world carbon dioxide emissions. What if 1.3 billion Chinese and 1.1 billion Indians suddenly all had cars and began churning out automobile exhaust at prodigious U.S. rates? While the sun might not turn black and the ozone layer might not vaporize overnight, the environmental possibilities are frightening. And what of the price of oil, which is already notoriously sensitive to small imbalances in demand and supply? Absent huge new discoveries or brilliant new inventions, oil could easily reach $200 per barrel, as consumption and depletion rates accelerate. The mighty U.S. dollar would become a boutique currency and the euro experiment a sideshow. Investors would clamor for Chinese yuan and Indian rupees. The world's youth would grow up thinking that "Hollywood" must be a wordplay on "Bollywood," and McDonald's hamburgers would be viewed a minor ethnic cuisine. And a country such as Canada would suddenly have the economic heft of Luxembourg, with much of its population reduced to serving once poor, now rich, international tourists.

Let's face it: The rich countries would no longer feel rich. Humans are 4
social creatures; once we clear the hurdle of basic subsistence, wealth becomes a relative state of being. Even an optimist such as myself must concede that a world of equality between rich and poor nations would be shockingly different—and that is even disregarding the impact on global power politics. Still, such rapid economic development offers a clear upside for today's rich countries. Greater diversity and knowledge spillovers can breed much faster productivity growth, the ultimate source of wealth for everyone. Once properly educated, fed, and plugged in, inventive geniuses from South Asia and Africa might speed the development of clean and safe hydrogen power by two generations. And whereas commercial medical researchers might start spending more energy combating tropical diseases, now privileged citizens in temperate climates would still enjoy countless technological spin-offs. Indeed, such gains of rapid economic development could fully offset the losses to the rich.

By highlighting latent insecurities in rich countries, I certainly do not 5
mean to endorse or stoke them. But these underlying fears must be addressed. If globalization really works, then what is the endgame? What kind of political institutions are necessary to prepare—socially as well as psychologically—for success? It is easy for everyone to endorse the United Nations Millennium Development Goals (MDG), which aim to satisfy basic human needs by 2015. (Unfortunately, the specific objectives are so limited that MDG ought to stand for the Minimum Development Goals.) But how far are rich nations willing to take development? How much are we prepared to give?

Of course, no one has developed a magic formula for how to make coun- 6
tries grow, though economic researchers have identified a number of poisons. Corruption, overweening government intervention, and mountains of

debt are contraindicated for countries attempting to develop (which is one reason most foreign aid should be recast as outright grants instead of loans). Though critics are correct to argue that foreign aid stymies growth by breeding corruption and stifling private enterprise, the empirical evidence suggests that aid can be productive when it supports good policies. Does trade help countries grow? Again, my read of the evidence says yes: If Europe and Japan gave up their outrageous farm protection and if the United States stopped competing with India for the title of anti-dumping champion of the world, poor countries would gain far more than if their aid inflows suddenly doubled. And, by the way, if poor countries gave up their own trade protectionism, their citizens would benefit by even more.

Even so, rich countries could easily afford to triple their aid budgets   7
without running the remotest risk of the "nightmare" scenario coming true. They could channel money into health in Africa, into education, and into infrastructure and other necessities with little danger of any rapid catch-up. (Though why the World Bank still lends to China, with more than $350 billion in hard currency reserves and a space program to boot, is difficult to explain.) Gallons of aid money, such as what Northern Italy has poured into Southern Italy for almost 60 years, help assuage development's growing pains, but progress rarely occurs quickly. Growth economics suggests that poor regions have a hard time closing the income gap on rich countries at a rate greater than 2 percent per year, even under the best of circumstances. Catch-up—when it happens at all—takes generations.

Rich countries need not be ambivalent or stingy. Certainly, if sudden   8
and rapid economic development were possible and actually materialized, many citizens in wealthy nations would feel jarred, even threatened. And some day, world income distribution will be radically different than it is today, but not anytime soon. Nightmare scenarios and fear of success need never stand in the way of sensible—and generous—development policies.

Thinking About the Essay

1. How does Rogoff undercut the utopian vision presented in the opening paragraph of the essay?

2. What motives does Rogoff attribute to members of "rich" nations? What evidence does he offer to support this attribution? Does Rogoff express any sympathy with these motives?

3. How would you characterize Rogoff's brand of irony in this essay? Highlight at least three different ironic passages and note some similarities and differences in tone between them.

4. What negative effects of economic progress does Rogoff acknowledge in the essay? Why does he wait to acknowledge these effects?

5. What policies does Rogoff endorse that would promote international economic development? What past and current policies does he attack? Why does he attack them? How are these inadequate policies connected with the interests and perceptions of "rich" nations?

Responding in Writing

6. In a brief essay, construct a "dream scenario" similar to Rogoff's, in which you envision the solution to a world health problem, and consider some additional negative side effects of the solution if this scenario were to be realized.

7. Do you fear the loss or erosion of your privileges as a member of a "rich" nation? Reflect on these fears in an essay blending narrative and expository elements.

8. Define what you see as the "endgame" of globalization. Is this a world you would like to live in? How do you see your children or grandchildren adapting to this world?

Networking

9. In groups of three or four, list some other cultural transformations that might occur under Rogoff's scenario. Do you fear the possibility of becoming culturally (or economically) marginalized? Why? Discuss those feelings within your group, and share the results of the discussion with the class.

10. Go online and research foreign aid statistics in the most recent United States federal budget. Do these numbers surprise you? Why or why not?

Follow the Money

VIVIENNE WALT AND AMANDA BOWER

Vivienne Walt is a staff writer for *Time* magazine who currently lives in Paris. She has worked as a foreign correspondent for twenty-five years and has reported on wars in various parts of the world (including, most recently, the 2003 war in Iraq). Walt is also known for her extensive reporting on politics and health issues in Africa. Amanda Bower is a San Francisco–based writer for *Time*. A native of Australia, Bower won the 1995 Fulbright Post-Graduate Student Award in Journalism and moved to the United States to study journalism at

Columbia University. Her work as a freelance journalist has taken her to many parts of the world, including Cambodia, Vietnam, Guatemala, and Costa Rica. In the following article, which appeared in the Europe Edition of *Time International* in December of 2005, Walt and Bower investigate the newly documented transnational economy created by migrant workers who send the money they earn in foreign countries back home to their communities of origin.

Before Reading

What personal sacrifices would you make in order to support your family? Would you describe your motives as a "work ethic"? Why or why not?

Waly Diabira pats the cover on his bed in the cramped fifth-floor room   1
he shares with two men in a red-brick dormitory building for immigrants near Paris' Left Bank. "My father slept on this same bed, in this same room, for many years," he says. In 1950, his father, Mamadou Diabira, left their tiny village in Mali and caught a steamboat to Europe, where he worked as a street cleaner in Paris for about 25 years, receiving a certificate of thanks signed by then mayor Jacques Chirac. Waly, a 32-year-old building cleaner, only got to know his father when he sneaked into France at 18 on a boat from Morocco; he now works legally in France. A large photograph hangs above Waly's narrow bed, of his 2-year-old daughter, whom he has never met. The migrant tradition has continued into the next generation, fueled by the same force that kept his father rooted in France for decades—the need to send money home. Similar stories swell the immigrant population in Paris and other cities across France, and are multiplied millions of times across the world.

Such tales are nothing new. The color TV in a remote Turkish farmstead   2
and the concrete-walled house amid shacks of corrugated iron have often been paid for by absent family members. Plenty of church halls in Ireland have been funded by passing the plate around congregations in Boston and New York. But the scale of money flows is new. Mass migration has produced a giant worldwide economy all its own, which has accelerated so fast during the past few years that the figures have astounded the experts. This year, remittances—the cash that migrants send home—is set to exceed $232 billion, nearly 60% higher than the number just four years ago, according to the World Bank, which tracks the figures. Of that, about $166.9 billion goes to poor countries, nearly double the amount in 2000. In many of those countries, the money from migrants has now overshot exports, and exceeds direct foreign aid from other governments. "The way these

numbers have increased is mind-boggling," says Dilip Ratha, a senior economist for the World Bank and co-author of a new Bank report on remittances. Ratha says he was so struck by the figures that he rechecked his research several times, wondering if he might have miscalculated. Indeed, he believes the true figure for remittances this year is probably closer to $350 billion, since migrants are estimated to send one-third of their money using unofficial methods, including taking it home by hand. That money is never reported to tax officials, and appears on no records.

One reason for the growth in recorded remittances has its origins in the 3 global war on terrorism. To stop terrorist networks using informal transfer systems like hawala in Africa, the Middle East and South Asia (where it's referred to as hundi), European and U.S. officials have cracked down on them. That has shifted payments to easier-to-track official channels. Some migrants, however, still use methods that elude the bean counters. In Hong Kong, Endang Muna Saroh, 35, works as a nanny to two children in a comfortable residential neighborhood, and sends $200 home every month to her mother and 10-year-old son in Surabaya, Indonesia, wiring the money to her brother-in-law's bank account. The country receives recorded remittances such as this worth a total of $1.8 billion a year. Yet like many migrants, Endang also saved hundreds of dollars to carry by hand to her family in August, when she flew home for her first visit in four years.

In Paris, Waly keeps a notebook on his bedside table, in which he writes 4 lists of the cash amounts he gives each month to couriers. They fly to Mali—where remittances account for 3.2% of the country's national income—with wads of euros stuffed in their pockets and luggage. With about 300 people from his village of Ambadedi working in Paris—an estimated one-quarter of Ambadedi's entire population—the community has a well-organized network to transfer money, much of which is aimed at avoiding the hefty commissions from banks. "I write careful notes," Waly says. "'Here's a20 for my mother, a30 to my sister, and so on.'" Of the a1,000 he earns each month cleaning office buildings in Paris, he sends about a500 home, and then pays a240 for his share of the monthly rental. That experience is repeated across the world. The life of squirreling away money is grueling: it involves years-long separation from families, miserable living conditions, and the threat of deportation for the many who are working illegally. All the same, remittances play a vital role in recycling money from the rich world to the poor one. "Migration is going up," says Ratha. "We had better not wish it away, because it's very much there to stay."

On three continents, migrants and their families described how the trans- 5 fers worked. Nine years ago, Cornelio Zamora left his home in Zacapoaxtla,

Mexico, paying a smuggler $2,500 to take him across the Rio Grande into the U.S. He had been unable to support his wife and four children on the $7 a day he earned as a bus driver. Working as a house painter in San Jose, California, Zamora, 48, now sends about $700 a month home. His wife says she has based all family decisions—where to send the children to school, what house to live in—on Zamora's monthly earnings "on the other side."

In migrants' countries of origin, escalating desires—for things like bet-   6
ter education and bigger homes—help drive the remittances. Ironically, economists calculate that the poorer the migrants are, the more money they dispatch. "There is enormous social pressure to send money home," says Khalid Koser, a geography professor at University College London, who in October co-authored a report for the Global Commission on International Migration in Geneva, which researches governments' immigration policies. Koser found that many migrants scrape by in first-world cities, depriving themselves of basic comforts in order to "keep people alive" back home. "There are many people sending 40% of their income in remittances," he says, adding that many families save to pay the passage of a migrant to richer parts of Asia, or to Europe or the U.S. Ruhel Daked, a 26-year-old Bangladeshi, earns a1,300 a month working as a chef in Paris. Yet despite his modestly comfortable salary, he bunks with two other Bangladeshis in a dormitory building for immigrants, with one toilet shared among many men, because he says he has one goal: "To save! Save as much as I can. That is why I am here."

In visits to migrants' hometowns, the impact on their families and com-   7
munities is clear. Waly's village of Ambadedi has sent thousands of mi-grants to Paris since his father Mamadou first headed there. Set atop the steep northern bank of the Senegal River, the village at first glance looks like countless others in West Africa. Goats and donkeys meander down the dirt lanes, and women scrub clothes in the river. But Ambadedi has cher-ished luxuries that are absent from other remote parts of Mali. There is a generator that lights up most of the houses every night. A water tower feeds water to several collection points. And television antennas bristle from the rooftops of two-story concrete houses—a far cry from the mud hut in which old Mamadou was raised. Villagers have even started dreaming about building a bridge across the river to connect Ambadedi to the near-est highway, says Sekou Drame, Mamadou's brother-in-law, as he escorts a *Time* reporter back to the wooden pirogue that will ferry him across the river's muddy flow. "It depends on God," he says. "And our families in France."

In Mexico, the Zamora family home is another tangible indicator of the   8
impact of remittances. Zamora's work in California has paid for a new

three-bedroom house, the first his family has ever owned. The changes his cash have brought to his family within one generation are dizzying; one daughter has trained as a nurse, another as a teacher, and his son as a radio technician. "The first time I wore shoes, I was 14 years old," Zamora says. "I don't want my family to go through that." It's a similar story in Indonesia where Endang's monthly money transfers from four years' work as a nanny in Hong Kong finally paid off last July, when her 10-year-old son, her mother and several relatives moved into a renovated two-story concrete house in Surabaya, bought with Endang's savings for about $9,700. In Paris, Daked, the Bangladeshi chef, says his parents recently bought a family home with the funds he has sent home since sneaking into Europe in 1997; he estimated his total remittances at about a38,000 in eight years.

Vital though the flow of remittances may be, it cannot, on its own, lift 9 entire nations out of poverty. Those who study the impact of remittances argue that the money allows poor countries to put off basic decisions of economic management, like reforming their tax-collection systems and building decent schools. "Everyone loves money that flows in with no fiscal implications," says Devesh Kapur, a specialist on migration and professor of government at the University of Texas in Austin. "They see it as a silver bullet." But bullets wound; and skilled workers often understandably put the interests of their families before those of their countries, choosing to work abroad so they can send remittances back home. About eight out of 10 college graduates from Haiti and Jamaica live outside their countries, and about half the college graduates of Sierra Leone and Ghana have also emigrated, according to the Paris-based Organization for Economic Co-operation and Development.

Remittances to poor countries can also mask the fact that they don't 10 produce much at home. In the western Mali district of Kayes—where Waly's village of Ambadedi is located and where most migrants hail from— the region has done so well that farmers use remittances as a crutch. Studies have shown that they spend less time on their land than farmers in other parts of Mali: there is more money to be made by migrating to Europe. "You see poverty other places, but here, you see money," says Abdel Kader Coulibaly, a bank manager in Kayes. He says migrants' families spend all they get, rather than investing it to generate income locally. "All the money ends up with shopkeepers and traders from Bamako [the capital]," he says.

The trick now is to find programs that maximize the benefits of remit- 11 ted cash while avoiding some of its downside. Some migrants are now using their economic clout to perform work usually done by big aid organizations. Ambadedi's workers' association in Paris, for example, funds some village projects with its members' own earnings. But the association also solicits help from the French government and the European Union. "We have a project under way to purify the village water supply," says Ibrahim Diabira, 55, a relative of Waly, who works in Paris as a building cleaner and helps run the village association in the French capital. Elsewhere, host nations have created temporary legal work programs, in which migrants earn legal wages with benefits, before returning home. That way, migrants retain close links to their countries while developing skills abroad. "When they go back, they will take augmented skills, savings and networks," says Kapur. (He himself left his native India 22 years ago and settled in the U.S.)

In Paris, Waly is planning to return home in January to see his 2-year-   12
old daughter for the first time, and to spend time with his wife. But he won't stay long. "Frankly, people would die there if we didn't work here," he says. Come spring, he will be back in Paris, cleaning offices, and changing the way the world spreads its wealth around.

Thinking About the Essay

1. How is the migrant tradition described, in the opening paragraph, as a cyclical phenomenon?

2. How do the authors distinguish the current migration-based economies from transactions between immigrants to their communities of origin that occurred in the past?

3. What aspects of Waly Diabira's story are presented as being typical of the motives and experiences of migrant workers worldwide? What do the other case studies in the essay contribute to the authors' analysis of remittance economies?

4. Why is there generally an inverse relation between migrant workers' level of poverty and the amount of money they send back home? What other statistical correlations are noted in the essay?

5. Why do the authors return to the story of Waly Diabira in the final paragraph of the essay? What does this conclusion indicate about the authors' attitude toward the "changing way the world spreads its wealth around"?

Responding in Writing

6. What does it mean to put the interests of an immediate circle of family or friends above the interests of a native or adopted country? In a brief essay, reflect on how your feelings of national or community identity would change if you were forced (for economic reasons) to relocate to another country.

7. What are your concerns about the size and nature of the migrant work force in the United States? Do you feel that workers are being exploited? Or do you see the work force as parasitic upon the economy and tax-based infrastructure of communities where they work? List your concerns in an essay, and consider—point by point—an alternate perspective that would cast your concern in a different (more positive) light.

8. Respond to the statement (in paragraph 4) that remittances "play a vital role in recycling money from the rich world to the poor one." Are "recycling" and "redistribution" appropriate metaphors, given what you have read in this essay about the economy of remittances?

Networking

9. In groups of three or four, share the experiences you have had with the immigrant work force in your community. Have you engaged in one-on-one conversations with them? What did you learn about their backgrounds, current lifestyles, and long-term plans?

10. Go online and look up the nations listed as the top ten recipients of foreign-earned remittances in 2005, according to the World Bank. Do these rankings surprise you?

AIDS in Africa

ALISON KATZ

Alison Katz is a member of the People's Health Movement, an international organization of social activists, health professionals, academics, and researchers who are dedicated to reviving the principles and aims of the so-called Alma Ata Declaration of 1978 (issued by the International Conference on Primary Health Care). In the following essay, which appeared in *Z Magazine Online* in September of 2003, Katz argues that international efforts to battle the spread of AIDS in Africa have ignored the Alma Ata Declaration's findings about the connection between disease and poverty and the economic systems that create poverty in places like Africa.

Before Reading

To what extent are public health problems the result of individual behavioral choices? Do efforts to educate people about public health issues depend on the assumption that individuals have the freedom to choose their behavior and to change their environment?

Thirteen million AIDS deaths already in the worst affected countries. 1
Without care and treatment, there will be 68 million more between
now and 2020. The global figures on AIDS are terrifying, but the first reaction of a number of world experts (of other diseases) to the above an-
nouncement at the International AIDS Conference in Barcelona, July 2002,
was indignation. They protested that Peter Piot, executive director of
UNAIDS, must be stealing some of his figures from "their diseases." Such
is politics in the international health community.

Politics on a grander scale has prevented a rational and effective re- 2
sponse to the AIDS pandemic, which is killing up to a quarter of many
southern African countries' populations. The real scandal is not the un-
seemly scrambling after donor funds, but the imperceptible impact of international and national responses to AIDS over two decades of intense
and costly activity. In its sobering 2002 report, UNAIDS states that prevalence is climbing higher than ever previously believed possible. It is spreading rapidly into new populations in Africa, Asia, the Caribbean, and
Eastern Europe.

One-third of Zimbabwe's population is infected and the epidemic con- 3
tinues to expand even in countries that already had extremely high HIV
prevalence. In Botswana, for example, the country with the highest HIV infection rates in the world, almost 39 percent of all adults are now living
with HIV, up from less than 36 percent 2 years ago.

Are we doing something wrong? Is the approach ill-founded or even fa- 4
tally flawed? Neither UNAIDS nor any of its partners are even asking the
question let alone revising their strategies.

A Neo-Liberal Approach

For over 20 years now, the international AIDS community has persisted in 5
a reductionist obsession with individual behavior and an implicit acceptance of a deeply flawed and essentially racist theory.

In line with neo-liberal doctrine, it has explained the spread of AIDS— 6
and the extremely high prevalences in sub-Saharan Africa—in terms of individual sexual behavior. It has exaggerated the extent to which people
control their lives and circumstances and ignored larger macroeconomic
and political factors and poverty-induced population vulnerability in terms
of seriously weakened immune systems. The insistence on analyzing this
colossal public health catastrophe in terms of individual behavior has correspondingly restricted the response to action at the individual level, usually promotion of safer sex, condom use, and education for prevention.

Predictably, the impact of these peripheral efforts has been insignifi- 7
cant, although tired old success stories are still regularly wheeled out for

display. As long as the root causes of AIDS continue to be neglected, such efforts will remain cosmetic, unsustainable, and exceptions. Average HIV prevalences in the adult population of most sub-Saharan African countries are 25 percent. The figures for Europe and most of the industrialized world are still under 0.1 percent and, in many cases, under 0.01 percent. Individual behavior cannot possibly account for this enormous difference, which would imply that people in some African countries have at least 250 and even 2,500 times more unprotected/unsafe sex than people in Europe, the U.S., or Australia.

8 The absurdity of this proposition, which has its origins in racist mythology, is not confronted because assumptions about sexual behavior are usually implicit. Myths thrive precisely because they are unstated and therefore rarely subjected to scrutiny. Running parallel to this dubious proposition is the perverse refusal to confront the obvious, such as the almost perfect "coincidence" of high prevalence of HIV/AIDS (and all the diseases of poverty) with the poorest regions of the earth.

9 An epidemic of gigantic proportions is taking hold in Southeast Asia, home to an even larger number of powerless and poverty stricken people. It will be interesting to see if any notion of structural violence is at last invoked to advance our understanding of the dynamics of the pandemic or if we will discover that previously quite "well-behaved" Asians are as "promiscuous" as Africans.

10 The fundamental public health lessons of the past 150 years are known even to lay people. It is well understood that the overall health status of populations and their capacity to fight off infection is related primarily to food, water, sanitation, and housing. According to an article by E. Stillwaggon, "HIV/AIDS in Africa: Fertile Terrain," published in the *Journal of Development Studies* (August 2002): "A century of clinical practice demonstrates that people with nutritional deficiencies, parasitic diseases, generally poor health and little access to health services or who are otherwise economically disadvantaged have greater susceptibility to infectious diseases whether they are transmitted sexually, by food, water, air or other means."

11 Curiously, in the case of HIV/AIDS, seriously deficient immune systems have been ignored as a factor of vulnerability and determinant of the high levels of infection in desperately poor populations.

12 Pasteur's dictum, "the microbe is nothing, the terrain is everything," is still the best summary of century-old public health wisdom. The focus on individual behavior is almost as absurd in the response to AIDS as it would be if it were applied to the response to tuberculosis. A sound public health approach to TB does not exhort people in high prevalence areas not to

breathe too much on each other—not understanding that they are breathing more or less like every other human being on earth. It addresses the sanitary, nutritional, and housing arrangements, which determine their high vulnerability.

Breathing and having sex—though not quite in the same category—can   13
both reasonably be seen as everyday human behaviors. The peculiar focus on the exotic, the unusual, the immoral, and the illegal has obscured the simple fact that AIDS is overwhelmingly transmitted through heterosexual, penetrative, vaginal sex. Few people know that when AIDS hit the headlines as a "gay plague" in California it was already a well established heterosexual epidemic in Africa. The unimportance, in the eyes of the world, of African people in general, and of African women in particular, may partly explain this neglect. The common sense interpretation of the facts is that high risk physical and economic environments, coupled with dangerously weakened immune systems, leave people highly susceptible to all kinds of infections including HIV.

A Racist Theory?

The fight against AIDS in Africa has been dominated by long-standing   14
Western prejudices against African sexuality and cultural practices. A striking example was in the early 1980s, when speculation about the Haitian origin of AIDS and the role of bizarre voodoo practices led to a wave of anti-Haitian discrimination. As with Jamaica, the Dominican Republic, and Trinidad, it turned out that tourists (mainly U.S. homosexuals) were the most likely source of virus transmission. It has been pointed out that in the absence of penicillin, the war-ravaged Europe of the late 1940s would have been devastated by epidemics of syphilis and gonorrhea.

The international AIDS community has pursued a singularly unsuc-   15
cessful strategy with religious conviction, rather than with good science or even common sense. Evidence, in the rather odious academic area known euphemistically as "sexual networking," is flimsy. Rates of sexual activity do not appear to vary much between populations (though of course there are always groups within populations who either take more risks or have more risks imposed on them). What seems to emerge from the literature with consistency is that multiple, mostly serial, casual, and unprotected sex is common in Africa, Europe, the U.S., and parts of Asia, with most men everywhere having more partners than most women (WHO 1995).

Furthermore, rates/types of sexual activity do not appear to have a clear   16
relation with prevalence of HIV infection. A major multi-site study undertaken by UNAIDS in four sub-Saharan African cities showed that most parameters of risky sexual behavior were not consistently more common in the high HIV prevalence sites than in the relatively low prevalence sites.

Gender Diversions

The implicit assumption that African people have more or less "brought it   17
on themselves" through their "promiscuity" has evolved through a superficial, neo-liberal gender analysis into a much more explicit accusation of
African men. If such an apolitical gender debate has resulted in shifting the
blame from all African people to all African men, it has failed. No one disputes that women, particularly in developing countries, are not only biologically more vulnerable to sexually transmitted infections including HIV,
but they are also acutely vulnerable socially, culturally and economically.
Women have to exchange sex for material favors for their own and their
children's survival in many poor countries. For as long as they do not control when, where, with whom, with or without protection, they have sex—
they will be at risk.

However, women in Europe are clearly at far less risk than men in   18
Africa. If we take as a rough indicator of risk, the average prevalences of
less than 0.1 percent and 25 percent for Europe and Africa respectively, it
becomes clear that neither individual behavior nor gender inequality accounts for the spread and pattern of the pandemic. Sound feminist analysis, rooted in social justice, recognizes oppression of women in poor
countries within the context of the oppression of entire communities of
men, women, and children, none of whom have any meaningful control
over their lives.

Women in sub-Saharan Africa carry a risk of contracting HIV infection   19
at a rate 500–1,000-fold compared to women in the rest of the world. This
is quite a large difference to explain in terms of African and European male
sexual behavior.

A Disease of Poverty

In common with all sexually transmitted infections (STIs), HIV/AIDS has   20
a particular relationship to poverty. The poor are more vulnerable to HIV
infection than the rich—notwithstanding transient vulnerabilities of richer
men who can afford to use prostitutes—of which much has been made. The
fact remains that 95 percent of infections are in developing countries; and
more than 70 percent are in sub-Saharan Africa where over 80 percent of
the deaths have occurred. Women are more vulnerable than men; young
women are far more vulnerable (4 to 5 times) than young men. Oppressed
and marginalized "minorities"—blacks and Hispanics in the U.S., refugees
and street children everywhere—are more vulnerable than dominant
majorities.

There are plausible explanations, in terms of biological vulnerability,   21
for the very high rates of HIV transmission among poor populations. The

major biological factors of interest are malnutrition and chronic co-infection with other diseases of poverty, notably, parasitic infection, tuberculosis, malaria, and other tropical diseases. These factors are known to seriously impair and interfere with immune function, and to be responsible for the bulk of infectious disease—whether bacterial, viral, or parasitic.

The thesis that is proposed for the huge variation in prevalence between 22 countries is that HIV-negative people whose immune systems are weakened by poor nutrition and constantly challenged by co-infections are more vulnerable to HIV infection; and that HIV-positive people, in the same condition, are more infectious to others. The result is high population transmission rates.

There is no shortage of evidence on the adverse, even devastating effects 23 of malnutrition, under-nutrition, and specific nutritional deficiencies on immune function, susceptibility to infection and capacity to cope, once infected.

The term nutritionally acquired immune deficiency syndrome (NAIDS) 24 is applied to immunological dysfunction associated with malnutrition in infants and small children. Is it unreasonable to suppose that a similar mechanism may operate in adolescents and adults and may be worth investigating and even—as a precautionary principle—acting on? The average African household is caught in a poverty cycle of low food production, low income, poor health, malnutrition, poor environmental sanitation, and infectious disease. Food security, as primary prevention, should be a priority strategy in the fight against AIDS in Africa. With water and sanitation, it has the huge advantage of simultaneously reducing population vulnerability to all the other diseases of poverty.

This brings us to the second major factor, chronic co-infections, most 25 of which are also related to the failure to meet basic needs. There is ample evidence that co-infections not only interfere with immune function, but they also increase viremia—the level of HIV circulating in the body. High viremia, unsurprisingly, is associated with increased risk of transmission.

Parasitic infections, which affect over a quarter of the world's popula- 26 tion, overwhelmingly in developing countries, may play a particularly important role in high population transmission rates of HIV and TB. Some researchers have suggested that in order to control both these epidemics, parasitic infections must be controlled first. The only co-infection that has received due attention is sexually transmitted infection (syphilis, gonorrhea, chancroid, etc.), which is known to substantially increase vulnerability to HIV infection. Prevention and control of STI has been recognized as a key strategy in the fight against AIDS.

Interestingly, the fact that the modes of transmission are the same for 27 STIs as for HIV—both are blood borne diseases, which can be transmitted sexually—has meant that the focus on individual behavior and individual agency can go unchallenged. This would not be the case if the co-infection to be prevented or controlled as a factor of susceptibility to HIV infection were intestinal worms or enteritis.

With the exception of some brave and outspoken NGOs, the main- 28 stream international AIDS community steadfastly refuses to address poverty, powerlessness, and inequality. It is not that the AIDS community does not talk about poverty. On the contrary, it is the most fashionable subject at the moment. Poverty reduction (rather than eradication) is on everyone's lips in the alliance of WB/IMF/WTO/G8, the UN agencies dealing with AIDS, government aid agencies, and "charitable" foundations, such as Ford, Rockefeller, and Bill and Melinda Gates.

In sanctimonious tones, they lament the persistence of poverty, but in a 29 perverse reversal of logic, they advocate for massive attacks on a few killer diseases (malaria, TB, and AIDS) in order to "create prosperity." No amount of health delivered to Haitians or Tanzanians today is going to provide them with prosperity tomorrow or the next day. It will allow them to survive where others die in rather precarious conditions, perhaps until the next bout of illness.

Many will protest that the connections with poverty have been recog- 30 nized from the start. This is true, but it has invariably been in terms of the economic impact of AIDS on communities, in particular on their productivity rather than poverty as the root cause of extreme susceptibility to all infections including HIV.

Even when social and economic factors, such as labor migration, ex- 31 change of sex for survival, gender power imbalances and population movements, have been identified as contributing to vulnerability, the solutions proposed are still focused on the residual action possible at the level of individual behavior.

The most striking example of this is the provision of condoms at the pit- 32 head of mines in South Africa to tens of thousands of migrant laborers slaving to bring up gold for white-owned transnational corporations and to thousands of migrant women selling sex to feed and clothe their children. Migrant labor and sex slavery are unhealthy—even life threatening—socially constructed phenomena, which can therefore be socially deconstructed. Examination of poverty and powerlessness as root causes of AIDS would threaten these kinds of production arrangements. They would also imply a fundamental shift in the international economic order, massive redistribution of the earth's resources, and an end to the fantastically exploitative relations between North and South.

The overwhelming power of vested interests confines both the research 33 agenda and the strategies of the international AIDS community to the sphere of the individual in order that structural, economic, and political inequalities neither be brought to light nor questioned.

The Declaration of Alma Ata (International Conference on Primary   34
Health Care) in 1978 explicitly recognized structural inequalities and macroeconomic factors as determinants of poverty and therefore of population health status. As this approach threatened the status quo, it was politically sanitized and reduced to a few technological interventions. By the early 1980s, neoliberal dogma was already being imposed in international fora and primary health care had more or less been abandoned.

However, the only progress possible in public health today, and in the   35
fight against AIDS, is a return to the wisdom of Alma Ata—armed at the turn of the century with 20 years' more evidence of the negative health effects of savage, free market neoliberalism. The "triumph" of capitalism in the Russian Federation, for example, has been accompanied by the collapse of health services and spectacular increases in rates of illness and death.

Trillions Rather Than Millions?

The sums made available through international aid are pitiful compared to   36
the sums that would be released through debt cancellation, fair trade, and measures to end the continued pillage of developing country resources. These amount to trillions rather than millions. It is not hard to understand the preference for international aid. First, it brings about one and half times more back to the donor country than is received by the recipient country. Second, it is immediately used to service the debt to Northern banks—far larger sums than are available to the health and education sectors of debtor countries. Third, even though it may increase the size of the crumbs from the rich person's table, it does not threaten the international economic order. On the contrary, it deepens the dependency that is so profitable to the developed countries and so devastating to developing countries.

It is the responsibility of international health authorities to identify the   37
determinants of health (and disease) and to advocate for policy and action, which will contribute most effectively to the goal of health for all, even if this lies outside the health sector. If food, water, sanitation, basic health care, and housing are the quickest, cheapest, most effective ways of achieving health for all, then the international health community should be advocating this.

If these basic needs can only be met when countries' national capacities   38
are freed from the strangulation of debt and unfair terms of trade and from the destabilizing chaos of financial flows then they must recommend this. If national food security requires a degree of protectionism rather than unfettered free trade, it must be strongly advocated. There could be no clearer

public health imperative. If the obstacle to such advocacy is the hand that feeds the international AIDS community, then the time has come to bite it. That hand is the alliance of WB/IMF/WTO, the G8—even occasionally the UN—and the transnational corporations influencing their policies.

The beauty of a fair international economic order lies in the fact that 39 nations, communities, and families left to their own devices are quite capable of meeting their own basic needs. Removing the obstacles to self determination is the task to be accomplished.

The international AIDS community needs to ally with the tremendous 40 movement for social and economic justice today. As a start it might wish to make immediate debt cancellation and the introduction of a Tobin-type tax its funding source for the first few years, followed swiftly by the first steps towards fair trade, bringing trillions of dollars to public health efforts within the long promised new international economic order.

Thinking About the Essay

1. How does Katz shift from the local example of internecine politics related in the opening paragraph to political impediments on a larger scale?

2. According to Katz, why are women in the world, and particularly women in Africa, more vulnerable to the transmission of sexually transmitted infections?

3. What are the ideological tenets of neo-liberalism? According to Katz, how do these tenets translate into limited (and racist) appraisals of world health problems?

4. How does Katz argue for debt cancellation as an economic alternative to international aid?

5. How does the final section of the essay return to—and transform—the idea that public health issues may be understood in terms of individual behavioral choices?

Responding in Writing

6. Define some of the differences between a liberal (or neo-liberal) approach to reform and the kinds of reform movements proposed by Katz as an alternative for dealing with world health crises.

7. What is your vision of a "fair international economic order"? Do you believe this economic order could, in principle, be realized within your lifetime? Are you as confident as Katz is in economic reform is a realistically attainable solution to the AIDS crisis? Respond to these questions in a brief essay.

8. The Gates Foundation, whose efforts, along with those of other charitable organizations, is the object of Katz's direct and indirect criticism. Reflect on how your opinion of the Gates Foundation (and other philanthropic enterprises) has changed as a result of reading Katz's essay.

Networking

9. In groups of three or four, choose a public health issue (a communicable or non-communicable disease, the prevalence of smoking, etc.) and list some choices in individual behavior that would explain the magnitude of the problem. Exchange your list with another group and come up with a list of structural factors that could serve as an alternative explanation.

10. Go online and research the findings of the 1978 Declaration of Alma Ata (International Conference on Primary Health Care). How do the diagnoses in this report relate to the findings of the 1993 World Bank Development report that served as a blueprint for the efforts of the Gates Foundation?

The Fate of the Earth: Can We Preserve the Global Environment?

11

CHAPTER

I t is tempting to think that at one time—was it before 9/11, or before the explosion of the first atomic bomb, or before the Black Death?— the problems of the world were simpler and more manageable. But were they? After all, the Black Death of the thirteenth century liqui- dated more than a third of Europe's population. There have always been world conflicts, and challenges that Earth's inhabitants have had to confront. So far, we have survived; we have not destroyed the planet. However, as the writers in this chapter attest, the fate of the Earth is uncertain, for humanity continues to be a flawed enterprise.

What is certain is that for the last several decades we have been moving into a new era in global history. This new era, as the writers in earlier chapters have revealed, is both like and unlike previous historical epochs. We do not have to accept the thesis of Francis Fukuyama, whose writing appears in this chapter, that we have reached the "end" of history. At the same time, we do have to acknowledge that new chal- lenges—scientific, ecological, economic, political, and cultural—await us in the new millennium. Numerous local and global problems need our sustained attention. Over the past decade, in particular, we have come to recognize that we have relationships and obligations to the planet and its inhabitants. A dust storm originating in Africa can sweep across the Atlantic, affecting ecologies in other continents. A nuclear accident in Russia can affect the milk of cows in Nebraska. Even the cars that we purchase and drive—as one author in this chapter asserts— can have an impact on the world's climate.

Clearly, then, in this new millennial era, we are part of a global envi- ronment. We have mutual obligations not to waste natural resources, to respect the environment, to harness science and technology to human and

 *Online Study Center* This icon will direct you to web links, audio and visual content, and additional resources on the website college.hmco.com/pic/muller.NWR2e

Tourists on a camel safari in Egypt clearly affect the local ecosystem and indigenous community.

Thinking About the Image

1. This photograph originally accompanied an article about "ecotourism." What do you know about ecotourism? Why do you think people would plan an "ecotourism" vacation?
2. What kind of story does this photograph tell about the relationship between the tourists and the "natives"?
3. Are you amused or surprised by what the camels are carrying?
4. What do you think is the point of view, or opinion, of the photographer who took this picture toward the people on the camels? How can you tell? Is there anything else that is amusing, sarcastic, or ironic about this photograph?

nonhuman benefit, and so much more. This new era is not necessarily more corrosive than previous epochs, but the stakes do seem to be higher. We now have to comprehend our reciprocal relationships at the numerous crossroads of nature and civilization. The *process* of civilization wherein we harness our physical, creative, scientific, political, intellectual, and spiritual resources is well advanced. However, the current condition of the global environment, as the writers in this last chapter testify, demands our attention.

By and large, the writers in this chapter, all of whom deal with subjects of consequence—global warming, biotechnology, environmental degradation, population growth, weapons of mass destruction—are not doomsday prophets. In fact, while offering cautionary statements about our shortsightedness and wastefulness, they tend to find hope for the world's environment. Whether finding once again a small spot in Eden in a remote Amazon jungle or contemplating the consequences of driving an SUV, these writers try to establish a moral basis for the continuation of the species—not just our human species but all varieties of life on Earth. We are not caught in an endless spiral that will end in mass extinction. But we do have to harness what Albert Schweitzer called "the devils of our own creation." Ultimately, we must find ways to coexist on Earth with nature and all living things.

The Obligation to Endure

RACHEL CARSON | Born in Pennsylvania in 1907, Rachel Carson became a leading figure in the world's emerging environmental movement. Abandoning an early interest in English literature, she concentrated instead on zoology, ultimately obtaining an advanced degree from the Graduate School of Johns Hopkins University. She was a marine biologist on the staff of the United States Fish and Wildlife Service for fifteen years, serving as editor in chief. Her first book was *Under the Sea Wind* (1941). With *The Sea Around Us* (1951), which sold millions of copies, was translated into dozens of languages, and won the National Book Award, Carson emerged as the best-known spokesperson for the preservation of the world's resources. In 1952, Carson resigned her government position to devote her time to writing. Her last book, *Silent Spring* (1964), from which the following essay is taken, aroused immediate controversy for its indictment of the use of pesticides. Carson died in 1964.

Before Reading

In the decades since *Silent Spring* was published, numerous pesticides have been banned—especially in the United States. Do you think that the problem no longer exists? Why or why not?

The history of life on earth has been a history of interaction between living   1
things and their surroundings. To a large extent, the physical form and
the habits of the earth's vegetation and its animal life have been molded by the
environment. Considering the whole span of earthly time, the opposite effect,
in which life actually modifies its surroundings, has been relatively slight. Only
within the moment of time represented by the present century has one
species—man—acquired significant power to alter the nature of his world.

During the past quarter century this power has not only increased to   2
one of disturbing magnitude but it has changed in character. The most
alarming of all man's assaults upon the environment is the contamination
of air, earth, rivers, and sea with dangerous and even lethal materials. This
pollution is for the most part irrecoverable; the chain of evil it initiates not
only in the world that must support life but in living tissues is for the most
part irreversible. In this now universal contamination of the environment,
chemicals are the sinister and little-recognized partners of radiation in
changing the very nature of the world—the very nature of its life. Stron-
tium 90, released through nuclear explosions into the air, comes to earth in
rain or drifts down as fallout, lodges in soil, enters into the grass or corn
or wheat grown there, and in time takes up its abode in the bones of a human being, there to remain until his death. Similarly, chemicals sprayed on
croplands or forests or gardens lie long in soil, entering into living organisms, passing from one to another in a chain of poisoning and death. Or
they pass mysteriously by underground streams until they emerge and,
through the alchemy of air and sunlight, combine into new forms that kill
vegetation, sicken cattle, and work unknown harm on those who drink
from once pure wells. As Albert Schweitzer has said, "Man can hardly even
recognize the devils of his own creation."

It took hundreds of millions of years to produce the life that now in-   3
habits the earth—eons of time in which that developing and evolving and
diversifying life reached a state of adjustment and balance with its surroundings. The environment, rigorously shaping and directing the life it
supported, contained elements that were hostile as well as supporting. Certain rocks gave out dangerous radiation; even within the light of the sun,
from which all life draws its energy, there were shortwave radiations with
power to injure. Given time—time not in years but in millennia—life ad-
justs, and a balance has been reached. For time is the essential ingredient;
but in the modern world there is no time.

The rapidity of change and the speed with which new situations are cre-   4
ated follow the impetuous and heedless pace of man rather than the deliberate pace of nature. Radiation is no longer merely the background radiation
of rocks, the bombardment of cosmic rays, the ultraviolet of the sun that
have existed before there was any life on earth; radiation is now the unnat-

ural creation of man's tampering with the atom. The chemicals to which life is asked to make its adjustment are no longer merely the calcium and silica and copper and all the rest of the minerals washed out of the rocks and carried in rivers to the sea; they are the synthetic creations of man's inventive mind, brewed in his laboratories, and having no counterparts in nature.

To adjust to these chemicals would require time on the scale that is nature's; it would require not merely the years of a man's life but the life of generations. And even this, were it by some miracle possible, would be futile, for the new chemicals come from our laboratories in an endless stream; almost five hundred annually find their way into actual use in the United States alone. The figure is staggering and its implications are not easily grasped—500 new chemicals to which the bodies of men and animals are required somehow to adapt each year, chemicals totally outside the limits of biologic experience.   5

Among them are many that are used in man's war against nature. Since the mid-1940's over 200 basic chemicals have been created for use in killing insects, weeds, rodents, and other organisms described in the modern vernacular as "pests"; and they are sold under several thousand different brand names.   6

These sprays, dusts, and aerosols are now applied almost universally to farms, gardens, forests, and homes—nonselective chemicals that have the power to kill every insect, the "good" and the "bad," to still the song of birds and the leaping of fish in the streams, to coat the leaves with a deadly film, and to linger on in soil—all this though the intended target may be only a few weeds or insects. Can anyone believe it is possible to lay down such a barrage of poisons on the surface of the earth without making it unfit for all life? They should not be called "insecticides," but "biocides."   7

The whole process of spraying seems caught up in an endless spiral. Since DDT was released for civilian use, a process of escalation has been going on in which ever more toxic materials must be found. This has happened because insects, in a triumphant vindication of Darwin's principle of the survival of the fittest, have evolved super races immune to the particular insecticide used, hence a deadlier one has always to be developed—and then a deadlier one than that. It has happened also because, for reasons to be described later, destructive insects often undergo a "flareback," or resurgence, after spraying in numbers greater than before. Thus the chemical war is never won, and all life is caught in its violent crossfire.   8

Along with the possibility of the extinction of mankind by nuclear war, the central problem of our age has therefore become the contamination of man's total environment with such substances of incredible potential for harm—substances that accumulate in the tissues of plants and animals and even penetrate the germ cells to shatter or alter the very material of heredity upon which the shape of the future depends.   9

Some would-be architects of our future look toward a time when it will 10 be possible to alter the human germ plasm by design. But we may easily be doing so now by inadvertence, for many chemicals, like radiation, bring about gene mutations. It is ironic to think that man might determine his own future by something so seemingly trivial as the choice of an insect spray.

All this has been risked—for what? Future historians may well be 11 amazed by our distorted sense of proportion. How could intelligent beings seek to control a few unwanted species by a method that contaminated the entire environment and brought the threat of disease and death even to their own kind? Yet this is precisely what we have done. We have done it, moreover, for reasons that collapse the moment we examine them. We are told that the enormous and expanding use of pesticides is necessary to maintain farm production. Yet is our real problem not one of *overproduction*? Our farms, despite measures to remove acreages from production and to pay farmers not to produce, have yielded such a staggering excess of crops that the American taxpayer in 1962 is paying out more than one billion dollars a year as the total carrying cost of the surplus-food storage program. And is the situation helped when one branch of the Agriculture Department tries to reduce production while another states, as it did in 1958, "It is believed generally that reduction of crop acreages under provisions of the Soil Bank will stimulate interest in use of chemicals to obtain maximum production on the land retained in crops."

All this is not to say there is no insect problem and no need of control. 12 I am saying, rather, that control must be geared to realities, not to mythical situations, and that the methods employed must be such that they do not destroy us along with the insects.

The problem whose attempted solution has brought such a train of disas- 13 ter in its wake is an accompaniment of our modern way of life. Long before the age of man, insects inhabited the earth—a group of extraordinarily varied and adaptable beings. Over the course of time since man's advent, a small percentage of the more than half a million species of insects have come into conflict with human welfare in two principal ways: as competitors for the food supply and as carriers of human disease.

Disease-carrying insects become important where human beings are 14 crowded together, especially under conditions where sanitation is poor, as in times of natural disaster or war or in situations of extreme poverty and deprivation. Then control of some sort becomes necessary. It is a sobering fact, however, as we shall presently see, that the method of massive chemical control has had only limited success, and also threatens to worsen the very conditions it is intended to curb.

Under primitive agricultural conditions the farmer had few insect prob- 15
lems. These arose with the intensification of agriculture—the devotion of
immense acreages to a single crop. Such a system set the stage for explosive
increases in specific insect populations. Single-crop farming does not take
advantage of the principles by which nature works; it is agriculture as an
engineer might conceive it to be. Nature has introduced great variety into
the landscape, but man has displayed a passion for simplifying it. Thus he
undoes the built-in checks and balances by which nature holds the species
within bounds. One important natural check is a limit on the amount of
suitable habitat for each species. Obviously then, an insect that lives on
wheat can build up its population to much higher levels on a farm devoted
to wheat than on one in which wheat is intermingled with other crops to
which the insect is not adapted.

The same thing happens in other situations. A generation or more ago, 16
the towns of large areas of the United States lined their streets with the no-
ble elm tree. Now the beauty they hopefully created is threatened with
complete destruction as disease sweeps through the elms, carried by a bee-
tle that would have only limited chance to build up large populations and
to spread from tree to tree if the elms were only occasional trees in a richly
diversified planting.

Another factor in the modern insect problem is one that must be viewed 17
against a background of geologic and human history: the spreading of
thousands of different kinds of organisms from their native homes to invade new territories. This worldwide migration has been studied and
graphically described by the British ecologist Charles Elton in his recent
book *The Ecology of Invasions*. During the Cretaceous Period, some hundred million years ago, flooding seas cut many land bridges between continents and living things found themselves confined in what Elton calls
"colossal separate nature reserves." There, isolated from others of their
kind, they developed many new species. When some of the land masses
were joined again, about 15 million years ago, these species began to move
out into new territories—a movement that is not only still in progress but
is now receiving considerable assistance from man.

The importation of plants is the primary agent in the modern spread of 18
species, for animals have almost invariably gone along with the plants,
quarantine being a comparatively recent and not completely effective innovation. The United States Office of Plant Introduction alone has introduced almost 200,000 species and varieties of plants from all over the
world. Nearly half of the 180 or so major insect enemies of plants in the
United States are accidental imports from abroad, and most of them have
come as hitchhikers on plants.

In new territory, out of reach of the restraining hand of the natural en- 19
emies that kept down its numbers in its native land, an invading plant or
animal is able to become enormously abundant. Thus it is no accident that
our most troublesome insects are introduced species.

These invasions, both the naturally occurring and those dependent on 20
human assistance, are likely to continue indefinitely. Quarantine and massive chemical campaigns are only extremely expensive ways of buying time.
We are faced, according to Dr. Elton, "with a life-and-death need not just
to find new technological means of suppressing this plant or that animal";
instead we need the basic knowledge of animal populations and their relations to their surroundings that will "promote an even balance and damp
down the explosive power of outbreaks and new invasions."

Much of the necessary knowledge is now available but we do not use 21
it. We train ecologists in our universities and even employ them in our governmental agencies but we seldom take their advice. We allow the chemical death rain to fall as though there were no alternative, whereas in fact
there are many, and our ingenuity could soon discover many more if given
opportunity.

Have we fallen into a mesmerized state that makes us accept as in- 22
evitable that which is inferior or detrimental, as though having lost the will
or the vision to demand that which is good? Such thinking, in the words of
the ecologist Paul Shepard, "idealizes life with only its head out of water,
inches above the limits of toleration of the corruption of its own environment. . . . Why should we tolerate a diet of weak poisons, a home in insipid
surroundings, a circle of acquaintances who are not quite our enemies, the
noise of motors with just enough relief to prevent insanity? Who would
want to live in a world which is just not quite fatal?"

Yet such a world is pressed upon us. The crusade to create a chemically 23
sterile, insect-free world seems to have engendered a fanatic zeal on the
part of many specialists and most of the so-called control agencies. On
every hand there is evidence that those engaged in spraying operations exercise a ruthless power. "The regulatory entomologists . . . function as pros-
ecutor, judge and jury, tax assessor and collector and sheriff to enforce their
own orders," said Connecticut entomologist Neely Turner. The most fla-
grant abuses go unchecked in both state and federal agencies.

It is not my contention that chemical insecticides must never be used. I 24
do contend that we have put poisonous and biologically potent chemicals
indiscriminately into the hands of persons largely or wholly ignorant of
their potentials for harm. We have subjected enormous numbers of people
to contact with these poisons, without their consent and often without their
knowledge. If the Bill of Rights contains no guarantee that a citizen shall be

secure against lethal poisons distributed either by private individuals or by public officials, it is surely only because our forefathers, despite their considerable wisdom and foresight, could conceive of no such problem.

I contend, furthermore, that we have allowed these chemicals to be used 25 with little or no advance investigation of their effect on soil, water, wildlife, and man himself. Future generations are unlikely to condone our lack of prudent concern for the integrity of the natural world that supports all life.

There is still very limited awareness of the nature of the threat. This is 26 an era of specialists, each of whom sees his own problem and is unaware of or intolerant of the larger frame into which it fits. It is also an era dominated by industry, in which the right to make a dollar at whatever cost is seldom challenged. When the public protests, confronted with some obvious evidence of damaging results of pesticide applications, it is fed little tranquilizing pills of half truth. We urgently need an end to these false assurances, to the sugar coating of unpalatable facts. It is the public that is being asked to assume the risks that the insect controllers calculate. The public must decide whether it wishes to continue on the present road, and it can do so only when in full possession of the facts. In the words of Jean Rostand, "The obligation to endure gives us the right to know."

Thinking About the Essay

1. What is Carson's thesis or claim? Where does it appear, or is it implied? Justify your response.

2. Explain the tone of Carson's essay. How do such words as *dangerous, evil,* and *sinister* reinforce this tone?

3. Evaluate Carson's essay as a model of argumentation. What reasons does she provide to demonstrate the overpopulation of insects? How does she convince us of "the obligation to endure"? What remedies does she propose? What appeals does she make?

4. Identify all instances where Carson uses expert testimony. How effective is this testimony in reinforcing the writer's argument?

5. What is Carson's purpose in her final paragraph? How effective is it? Explain.

Responding in Writing

6. Write your own essay entitled "The Obligation to Endure." You may focus on pesticides or any other topic—for example, genetically altered foods or global warming—to organize your paper.

7. In an essay, argue for or against the proposition that we spend too much time and money worrying about the state of the world environment.

8. Write a paper in which you present solutions to some of the problems that Carson raises in her essay.

Networking

9. Working in small groups, find out more about Rachel Carson and her involvement with environmental issues. In class discussion, evaluate her relevance to the environmental situation today.

10. Go online and find out more about pesticides commonly used today. Share your findings with the class. How safe are they? Would you use them as a homeowner, landscaper, farmer, or forestry official?

Talking Trash

ANDY ROONEY

Andrew A. Rooney, better known as "Andy" from his regular appearances on 60 Minutes and his syndicated columns in more than two hundred newspapers, is one of the nation's best-known curmudgeons, a writer and commentator who is frequently at odds with conventional wisdom on various issues. Born in Albany, New York, in 1919, he attended Colgate University before serving in the U.S. Army from 1942 to 1945 as a reporter for *Stars and Stripes*. Rooney has written, produced, and narrated programs for some of the major shows in television history: he wrote material for Arthur Godfrey from 1949 to 1955, and for Sam Levenson, Herb Shriner, Victor Borge, Gary Moore, and other celebrities who define many of the high points of early television comedy. Over the decades, Rooney has also produced television essays, documentaries, and specials for ABC, CBS, and public television. A prolific writer, he is the author of more than a dozen books—most recently *My War* (1995), *Sincerely, Andy Rooney* (1999), *Common Nonsense* (2002), and *Years of Minutes* (2003). Known for his dry, unassuming, but acerbic wit (which from time to time has gotten him in trouble with viewers and television studios), Rooney is at his best when convincing readers about simple truths. In this essay, which appeared in 2002 in *Diversion*, he tells us the simple truth about our inability to moderate our wasteful ways.

Before Reading

Americans are perceived as being terribly wasteful. They discard food, appliances, clothing, and so much more that other peoples and societies would find useful. Do you agree or disagree with this profile of the wasteful American? And how do you fit into this picture?

Last Saturday I filled the trunk of my car and the passenger seats behind 1
me with junk and headed for the dump. There were newspapers, empty cardboard boxes, bags of junk mail, advertising flyers, empty bottles, cans, and garbage. I enjoy the trip. Next to buying something new, throwing away something that is old is the most satisfying experience I know.

The garbage men come to my house twice a week, but they're very 2
fussy. If the garbage is not packaged the way they like it, they won't take it. That's why I make a trip to the dump every Saturday. It's two miles from our house, and I often think big thoughts about throwing things away while I'm driving there.

How much, I got to wondering last week, does the whole Earth weigh? 3
New York City alone throws away 24 million pounds of garbage a day. A day! How long will it take us to turn the whole planet Earth into garbage, throw it away, and leave us standing on nothing?

Oil, coal, and metal ore are the most obvious extractions, but any place 4
there's a valuable mineral, we dig beneath the surface, take it out, and make it into something else. We never put anything back. We disfigure one part of our land by digging something out and then move on to another spot after we've used up all its resources.

After my visit to the dump, I headed for the supermarket, where I 5
bought $34 worth of groceries. Everything was packed in something–a can, a box, a bottle, a carton, or a bag. When I got to the checkout counter, the cashier separated my cans, boxes, cartons, bottles, and bags and put three or four at a time into other bags, boxes, or cartons. Sometimes she put my paper bags into plastic bags. One bag never seemed to do. If something was in plastic, she put that into paper.

On the way home, I stopped at the dry cleaner. Five of my shirts, which 6
had been laundered, were in a cardboard box. There was a piece of cardboard in the front of each shirt and another cardboard cutout to fit the collar to keep it from getting wrinkled. The suit I had cleaned was on a throwaway hanger, in a plastic bag with a form-fitting piece of paper inside over the shoulders of my suit.

When I got home, I put the groceries where they belonged in various 7
places in the kitchen. With the wastebasket at hand, I threw out all the outer bags and wrappers. By the time I'd unwrapped and stored everything, I'd filled the kitchen wastebasket a second time.

It would be interesting to conduct a serious test to determine what per-   8
centage of everything we discard. It must be more than 25%. I drank the
contents of a bottle of Coke and threw the bottle away. The Coca-Cola
Company must pay more for the bottle than for what they put in it. Dozens
of things we eat come in containers that weigh more and cost the manufacturer more than what they put in them.

We've gone overboard on packaging, and part of the reason is that a   9
bag, a can, or a carton provides a place for the producer to display advertising. The average cereal box looks like a roadside billboard.

The Earth could end up as one huge, uninhabitable dump.   10

Thinking About the Essay

1. What is Rooney's thesis? Where does he state it? What evidence does he provide to support his thesis?

2. Does Rooney, writing about a serious problem, maintain a serious tone in this essay? What evidence in the essay leads you to your view?

3. How does Rooney structure his argument? Does he provide enough supporting points to back up his major claim or proposition? Why or why not?

4. Is Rooney merely making value judgments about himself, or does he have a broader purpose? How do you know?

5. Explain the style of this essay. Are Rooney's language and sentence structure accessible or difficult? How does his style facilitate your reading and appreciation of the essay?

Responding in Writing

6. Argue for or against the proposition that we are a wasteful society. As Rooney does, organize your essay around your own personal experience or your knowledge of family and friends.

7. Write an imaginative essay about the year 2050. Center the essay on Rooney's last sentence: "The Earth could end up as one huge, uninhabitable dump."

8. Write a letter to your local congressman or congresswoman outlining the need for your community to do more about controlling its waste flow. Offer specific remedies for improvement.

Networking

9. Divide into groups of three or four, and jot down some of the instances of waste you have encountered on your campus. Compare your list with other group members' lists. Which problems seem to be most common? Which are singular? Share and discuss your results with the rest of the class.

10. Utilizing one or more web search engines, download information on waste management. What is the current status of this movement in the United States? Which cities or regions are doing the best job of managing their waste problems? Present your findings in class discussion.

Lessons from Lost Worlds

JARED DIAMOND | Jared Diamond is Professor of Geography at UCLA and formerly Professor of Physiology at the UCLA School of Medicine. His widely acclaimed *Guns, Germs, and Steel: The Fates of Human Societies* was awarded the Pulitzer Prize in 1998. Diamond is also known for his work as a conservationist and as director of the World Wildlife Fund. His field experience includes seventeen expeditions to New Guinea and neighboring islands, where he helped to establish Indonesian New Guinea's national park system. In the following essay, which appeared in the August 26, 2002, issue of *Time* magazine, Diamond derives some lessons from the historical precedent of past societies that failed to respond to environmental crises similar to those that currently face our global community.

Before Reading

What is your chief concern about the world your grandchildren will inherit? Why does this one concern take precedence over the others? How are your concerns logically related to one another?

Children have a wonderful ability to focus their parents' attention on the essentials. Before our twin sons were born in 1987, I had often heard about all the environmental problems projected to come to a head toward the middle of this century. But I was born in 1937, so I would surely be dead before 2050. Hence I couldn't think of 2050 as a real date, and I couldn't grasp that the environmental risks were real.

After the birth of our kids, my wife and I proceeded to obsess about the things most parents obsess about—schools, our wills, life insurance. Then I realized with a jolt: my kids will reach my present age of 65 in 2052. That's a real date, not an unimaginable one! My kids' lives will depend on the state of the world in 2052, not just on our decisions about life insurance and schools.

I should have known that. Having lived in Europe for years, I saw that the lives of my friends also born in 1937 had been affected greatly by the state of the world around them. For many of those overseas contemporaries growing up during World War II, that state of the world left them orphaned or homeless. Their parents may have thought wisely about life insurance, but their parents' generation had not thought wisely about world conditions. Over the heads of our own children now hang other threats from world conditions, different from the threats of 1939–45.

While the risk of nuclear war between major powers still exists, it's less   4
acute now than 15 years ago, thank God. Many people worry about terrorists, and so do I, but then I reflect that terrorists could at worst kill "only" a few tens of millions of us. The even graver environmental problems that could do in all our children are environmental ones, such as global warming and land and water degradation.

These threats interact with terrorism by breeding the desperation that   5
drives some individuals to become terrorists and others to support terrorists. Sept. 11 made us realize that we are not immune from the environmental problems of any country, no matter how remote—not even those of Somalia and Afghanistan. Of course, in reality, that was true before Sept. 11, but we didn't think much about it then. We and the Somalis breathe and pollute the same atmosphere, are bathed by the same oceans and compete for the same global pie of shrinking resources. Before Sept. 11, though, we thought of globalization as mainly meaning "us" sending "them" good things, like the Internet and Coca-Cola. Now we understand that globalization also means "them" being in a position to send "us" bad things, like terrorist attacks, emerging diseases, illegal immigrants and situations requiring the dispatch of U.S. troops.

A historical perspective can help us, because ours is not the first society   6
to face environmental challenges. Many past societies collapsed partly from their failure to solve problems similar to those we face today—especially problems of deforestation, water management, topsoil loss and climate change. The long list of victims includes the Anasazi in the U.S. Southwest, the Maya, Easter Islanders, the Greenland Norse, Mycenaean Greeks and inhabitants of the Fertile Crescent, the Indus Valley, Great Zimbabwe and Angkor Wat. The outcomes ranged from "just" a collapse of society, to the deaths of most people, to (in some cases) everyone's ending up dead. What can we learn from these events? I see four main sets of lessons.

First, environmental problems can indeed cause societies to collapse,   7
even societies assaulting their environments with stone tools and far lower population densities than we have today.

Second, some environments are more fragile than others, making some   8
societies more prone to collapse than others. Fragility varies even within

the same country: for instance, some parts of the U.S., including Southern California, where I live, are especially at risk from low rainfall and salinization of soil from agriculture that is dependent on irrigation—the same problems that overwhelmed the Anasazi. Some nations occupy more fragile environments than do others. It's no accident that a list of the world's most environmentally devastated and/or overpopulated countries resembles a list of the world's current political tinderboxes. Both lists include Afghanistan, Haiti, Iraq, Nepal, Rwanda and Somalia.

Third, otherwise robust societies can be dragged down by the environ- 9
mental problems of their trade partners. About 500 years ago, two Polynesian societies, on Henderson Island and Pitcairn Island, vanished because they depended for vital imports on the Polynesian society of Mangareva Island, which collapsed from deforestation. We Americans can well understand that outcome, having seen how vulnerable we are to instability in oil-exporting countries of the Middle East.

Fourth, we wonder, Why didn't those peoples see the problems devel- 10
oping around them and do something to avoid disaster? (Future generations may ask that question about us.) One explanation is the conflicts between the short-term interests of those in power and the long-term interests of everybody: chiefs were becoming rich from processes that ultimately undermined society. That too is an acute issue today, as wealthy Americans do things that enrich themselves in the short run and harm everyone in the long run. As the Anasazi chiefs found, they could get away with those policies for a while, but ultimately they bought themselves the privilege of being merely the last to starve.

Of course, there are differences between our situation and those of past 11
societies. Our problems are more dangerous than those of the Anasazi. Today there are far more humans alive, packing far greater destructive power, than ever before. Unlike the Anasazi, a society today cant collapse without affecting societies far away. Because of globalization, the risk we face today is of a worldwide collapse, not just a local tragedy.

People often ask if I am an optimist or a pessimist about our future. I 12
answer that I'm cautiously optimistic. We face big problems that will do us in if we don't solve them. But we are capable of solving them. The risk we face isn't that of an asteroid collision beyond our ability to avoid. Instead our problems are of our own making, and so we can stop making them. The only thing lacking is the necessary political will.

The other reason for my optimism is the big advantage we enjoy over 13
the Anasazi and other past societies: the power of the media. When the Anasazi were collapsing in the U.S. Southwest, they had no idea that Easter

Island was also on a downward spiral thousands of miles away, or that Mycenaean Greece had collapsed 2,400 years earlier. But we know from the media what is happening all around the world, and we know from archaeologists what happened in the past. We can learn from that understanding of remote places and times; the Anasazi didn't have that option. Knowing history, we are not doomed to repeat it.

Thinking About the Essay

1. How are the opening paragraphs of the essay structured around multiple, counterpointed analogies? Does the author modulate convincingly from one to another?

2. Highlight instances of the author's use of scare quotes and explain their function in the essay.

3. Where does Diamond introduce the issue of globalization? What connections are made in the essay between globalization, terrorism, and environmental problems?

4. What significance do you see in the order in which Diamond presents his four sets of lessons? Are any of the sets of lessons different in kind from the others?

5. How does globalization recur as a theme in the final paragraphs to distinguish the histories of past cultures from our own situation?

Responding in Writing

6. Write a letter addressed to your future grandchildren in which you relate your current concerns about the world they will inhabit. Is the future state of the environment near the top of your list of concerns? Why or why not?

7. Rwanda appears on Diamond's list of "political tinderboxes" with environmental problems related to resource exploitation or overpopulation (paragraph 8). In an essay, attempt to explain how overpopulation and limited resources (in a country like Rwanda) could lead to political unrest and (in the case of Rwanda) mass genocide.

8. In paragraph 3, Diamond observes of children who grew up during the Second World War that "their parents may have thought wisely about life insurance, but their parents' generation had not thought wisely about world conditions." In a brief essay, respond to this distinction between individual parents and a generation of individuals. How can someone belong to both categories at the same moment in history?

Networking

9. Do you share Diamond's optimism about the power of the media to inform and educate? Do you agree that "knowing history, we are not doomed to repeat it"? Divide the class into two groups ("optimists" and "pessimists") and debate Diamond's specific assertion about the media and the familiar and more general statement that ends the essay.

10. Go online and research the history of the collapse of a past culture alluded to in the essay. What are some other differences, not considered in the essay, between the environmental crisis faced by this past culture and the global problems that we face today?

Driving Global Warming

BILL MCKIBBEN | Bill McKibben was born in Palo Alto, California, in 1960 and studied at Harvard University (B.A., 1982). His writing focuses on the global ecosystem and the human impact on it. Frequently he brings moral and religious ideas to bear on the ways in which our behavior—from consumerism to industrial shortsightedness—degrades the natural world. McKibben says that with respect to nature and Earth's ecosystem, he tries "to counter despair." In books like *The End of Nature* (1989), *Hope, Human and Wild: True Stories of Living Lightly on the Earth* (1995), *Long Distance: A Year of Living Strenuously* (2000), and *Enough: Staying Human in an Engineered Age* (2003), McKibben balances a sense of alarm about our profligate waste of natural resources with a tempered optimism that we can revere and preserve our fragile planet. "What I have learned so far," McKibben observes, "is that what is sound and elegant and civilized and respectful of community is also environmentally benign." This essay by McKibben, which appeared in *The Christian Century* in 2001, poses a challenge: Why do we drive SUVs when clearly they degrade the environment?

Before Reading

What car or cars does your family own? Do you or other family members consider the impact on environment when purchasing vehicles? Why or why not? Is too much being made of the American propensity to drive large, gas-consuming cars? Justify your response.

Up until some point in the 1960s, people of a certain class routinely be-   1
longed to segregated country clubs without giving it much thought—
it was "normal." And then, in the space of a few years, those memberships
became immoral. As a society, we'd crossed some threshold where the benefits—a good place to play golf, a nice pool for the kids, business contacts,
a sense of status and belonging—had to be weighed against the recognition
that racial discrimination was evil. Belonging to Farflung Acres CC wasn't
the same as bombing black churches (perfectly sweet and decent people did
it) and quitting wasn't going to change the economic or social patterns of
the whole society, but it had become an inescapable symbol. Either you
cared enough about the issue of race to make a stand and or you didn't. If
you thought we were all made in God's image, and that Jesus had died to
save us all, it was the least you could do.

For the past decade, buying a sport utility vehicle—an Explorer, a Nav-   2
igator, a CRV, a Suburban, a Rover, and so on down the list—has seemed
perfectly normal. Most people of a certain station did it. If you went to a
grocery store in suburban Boston, you would think that reaching it required
crossing flooded rivers and climbing untracked canyons. In any given parking lot, every other vehicle has four-wheel drive, 18 inches of clearance,
step-up bumpers. They come with a lot of other features: leather seats, sur-
round sound, comfort, status. Maybe even some sense of connection with
nature, for they've been advertised as a way to commune with creation.

But now we've come to another of those threshold moments. In Janu-   3
ary, after five years of exhaustive scientific study, the International Panel
on Climate Change announced the consensus of the world's leading experts: if we keep burning fossil fuels at anything like our present rate, the
planet will warm four or five degrees, and perhaps as much as 11 degrees,
before the century is out. Those temperatures would top anything we've
seen for hundreds of millions of years. Already we can guess the effects.
The decade we've just come through was the warmest on record in human
history: it saw record incidence of floods and drought (both of which you'd
expect with higher temperatures). Arctic ice, we now know, has thinned 40
percent in the last 40 years. Sea level is rising steadily.

And what has the SUV to do with all of this? Well, it is mostly a ma-   4
chine for burning gasoline. Say you switched from a normal car to a big
sport "ute" and drove it for one year. The extra energy you use would be
the equivalent of leaving the door to the fridge open for six years, or your
bathroom light on for three decades. Twenty percent of America's carbon
dioxide emissions come from automobiles. Even as we've begun to improve
efficiency in factories and power plants, our cars and trucks have grown
bigger and more wasteful: average fuel efficiency actually declined in the

1990s, even as engineers came up with one technology after another that could have saved gas. That's a big reason why Americans now produce 12 percent more CO_2, the main global warming gas, than they did when Bill Clinton took office.

If you drive an SUV, then you're "driving" global warming, even more than the rest of us.

In Bangladesh people spent three months of 1998 living in the thigh-deep water that covered two-thirds of the nation. The inundation came because the Bay of Bengal was some inches higher than normal (as climate changes, sea level rises because warm water takes up more space). That high water blocked the drainage of the normal summer floods, turning the nation into a vast lake. No one can say exactly how much higher that water was because of our recent fondness for semi-military transport in the suburbs. Maybe an inch, who knows?

But the connection is clear. If you care about the people in this world living closest to the margins, then you need to do everything in your power to slow the rate at which the planet warms, for they are the most vulnerable. I was naked and you did not clothe me. I was hungry and you drowned me with your Ford Explorer.

Here's more: Coral reefs the world over are dying as warmer sea water bleaches them to death—by some estimates, this whole amazing ecosystem, this whole lovely corner of God's brain, may be extinct by mid-century. In the far north, scientists recently found that polar bears were 20 percent scrawnier than they'd been just a few years before. As pack ice disappears, they can't hunt the seals that form the basis of their diet. And on and on—according to many experts, the extinction spasm caused by climate change and other environmental degradation in this century will equal or surpass those caused by crashing asteroids in geological times. But this time it's us doing the crashing.

If we care about creation, if we understand the blooming earth as an exhibit of what pleases God, then we've got to do what we can to slow these massive changes. "Where were you when I set the boundaries of the oceans, and told the proud waves here you shall come and no further?" God asks Job. We can either spit in the old geezer's face and tell him we're in charge of sea level from here on out, or we can throttle back, learn to live a little differently.

Not so differently. Giving up SUVs is not exactly a return to the Stone Age. After all, we didn't have them a decade ago, when people with large families transported themselves in considerably more fuel-efficient minivans or station wagons. The only reason we have them now is that the car companies make immense profits from them. Ford's lucky to clear a grand selling you an Escort, but there's $10,000 clear profit in an Explorer. Save for a very few special circumstances, we don't need them—nine in ten SUVs never even leave the pavement. Where I live, in the Adirondack mountains of New York, we have snow and ice six months of the year, bad roads and steep mountains. But we don't have many SUVs because no one has the money to buy one. Somehow we still get around.

Sometimes people cite safety as their cause for buying a behemoth. They reason that they need them because everyone else has them or because in an accident the other car will suffer more (a position that would proba- bly not pass the test with many Christian ethicists). But even that's a flawed argument. It's true, says the *New York Times*, that in a collision an SUV is twice as likely as a car to kill the other driver. But because the things roll over so easily, overall "their occupants have roughly the same chance as car occupants of dying in a crash."

The big car companies are starting to sense that their franchise for may- hem is running out. Last fall, after fuel prices soared and exploding tires killed dozens, the big car companies said that half a decade from now they would try to increase their fuel efficiency by 25 percent. Which is actually a nice start, but also sort of like the country club board of directors saying, "Wait five years and we'll find a few token blacks." Twenty-five percent better than 13 miles per hour is still a sick joke. Already Toyota and Honda have hybrid vehicles on the lot that can get 50, 60, 70 miles to the gallon. And we don't have five or ten or 15 years to wait.

No, the time has come to make the case in the strongest terms. Not to harass those who already own SUVs—in a way, they're the biggest victims, since they get to live in the same warmer world as the rest of us, but have each sent 40 grand to Detroit to boot. But it's time to urge everyone we know to stop buying them. Time to join the SUV protest in Boston on June 2. Time to pass petitions around church pews collecting pledges not to buy the things in the future. Time to organize your friends and neighbors to picket outside the auto dealerships, reminding buyers to ask about gas mileage, steering them away from the monster trucks.

Time, in short, to say that this is a moral issue every bit as compelling as the civil rights movement of a generation ago, and every bit as demand- ing of our commitment and our sacrifice. It's not a technical question—it's about desire, status, power, willingness to change, openness to the rest of creation. It can't be left to the experts—the experts have had it for a decade now, and we're pouring ever more carbon into the atmosphere. It's time for all of us to take it on, as uncomfortable as that may be.

Calling it a moral issue does not mean we need to moralize. Every American is implicated in the environmental crisis—there are plenty of

direction

other indulgences we could point at in our own lives, from living in over-sized houses to boarding jets on a whim. But there's no symbol much clearer in our time than SUVs. Stop driving global warming. If we can't do even that, we're unlikely ever to do much.

Neg. Tone

Thinking About the Essay

1. McKibben published this essay in *The Christian Century*. What evidence do you find in the essay that suggests he writes for an audience interested in religious matters? What assumptions does he make about his intended audience? To what extent do you feel you are a member of that readership? Explain.

2. What exactly does the SUV symbolize? How does McKibben develop this symbol?

3. Why does McKibben create an introduction that seemingly is not directly relevant to the subject he develops? How is the content of this first paragraph relevant?

4. What is the author's argument? Where does he state his claim, and how effective is its placement? How does he employ personal experience, observation, and data to support his claim? Cite specific examples.

5. Explain the author's tone and how he achieves it. Is he optimistic or pessimistic about his subject? How do you know?

Responding in Writing

6. Write an essay explaining why you would or would not purchase an SUV. Be certain to provide reasons and evidence supporting your decision.

7. Argue for or against the proposition that moral and religious considerations should override personal preferences when we make decisions that might affect our environment adversely.

8. Write an essay that tries to present fairly both sides of the argument concerning SUVs. Create a thesis that reflects this attempt at objectivity.

Networking

9. Divide into groups of three or four and discuss your views on global warming. Do you think it is a serious problem or one that has been exaggerated? Share your answers with the rest of the class. Also, mention whether your views were modified or changed during group discussion.

10. Go online and read messages of some of the professional newsgroups whose members are in the environmental movement. Select several messages regarding global warming, and write a report on your findings.

In the Jungle

ANNIE DILLARD | Essayist, poet, autobiographer, novelist, and literary critic, Annie Dillard is best known for her keen descriptions and musings on nature. She was born in Pittsburgh, Pennsylvania, in 1945 and attended Hollins College in Virginia, where she received her B.A. (1967) and M.A. (1968) degrees. Her book *Pilgrim at Tinker Creek* (1974), a series of lyrical essays capturing the seasonal rhythms of her quiet life in Virginia's Roanoke Valley, received the Pulitzer Prize for general nonfiction. Among her other books are *Teaching a Stone to Talk* (1982), a collection of essays on nature and religion; *An American Childhood* (1987), an autobiography; *The Writing Life* (1989), a personal exploration of the creative process; and *Mornings Like This: Found Poems* (1995). She has been writer-in-residence at Wesleyan University in Connecticut since 1987. This essay, from *Teaching a Stone to Talk*, precise and poetic in style and meditative in its depiction of nature, reveals Dillard's unique ability to capture essential truths about our presence on Earth.

Before Reading

What do you expect to find in an essay with the title "In the Jungle"? What preconceptions do you have about jungles? What might you be able to learn about yourself and the human condition in a jungle?

Like any out-of-the-way place, the Napo River in the Ecuadorian jungle 1 seems real enough when you are there, even central. Out of the way of *what*? I was sitting on a stump at the edge of a bankside palm-thatch village, in the middle of the night, on the headwaters of the Amazon. Out of the way of human life, tenderness, or the glance of heaven?

A nightjar in a deep-leaved shadow called three long notes, and hushed. 2 The men with me talked softly in clumps: three North Americans, four Ecuadorians who were showing us the jungle. We were holding cool drinks and idly watching a hand-sized tarantula seize moths that came to the lone bulb on the generator shed beside us.

It was February, the middle of summer. Green fireflies spattered lights 3 across the air and illumined for seconds, now here, now there, the pale trunks of enormous, solitary trees. Beneath us the brown Napo River was rising, in all silence; it coiled up the sandy bank and tangled its foam in vines that trailed from the forest and roots that looped the shore.

Each breath of night smelled sweet, more moistened and sweet than any   4 kitchen, or garden, or cradle. Each star in Orion seemed to tremble and stir with my breath. All at once, in the thatch house across the clearing behind us, one of the village's Jesuit priests began playing an alto recorder, playing a wordless song, lyric, in a minor key, that twined over the village clearing, that caught in the big trees' canopies, muted our talk on the bankside, and wandered over the river, dissolving downstream.

This will do, I thought. This will do, for a weekend, or a season, or a   5 home.

Later that night I loosed my hair from its braids and combed it   6 smooth—not for myself, but so the village girls could play with it in the morning.

We had disembarked at the village that afternoon, and I had slumped   7 on some shaded steps, wishing I knew some Spanish or some Quechua so I could speak with the ring of little girls who were alternately staring at me and smiling at their toes. I spoke anyway, and fooled with my hair, which they were obviously dying to get their hands on, and laughed, and soon they were all braiding my hair, all five of them, all fifty fingers, all my hair, even my bangs. And then they took it apart and did it again, laughing, and teaching me Spanish nouns, and meeting my eyes and each other's with open delight, while their small brothers in blue jeans climbed down from the trees and began kicking a volleyball around with one of the North American men.

Now, as I combed my hair in the little tent, another of the men, a free-   8 lance writer from Manhattan, was talking quietly. He was telling us the tale of his life, describing his work in Hollywood, his apartment in Manhattan, his house in Paris. . . . "It makes me wonder," he said, "what I'm doing in a tent under a tree in the village of Pompeya, on the Napo River, in the jun-gle of Ecuador." After a pause he added, "It makes me wonder why I'm go-ing *back*."

The point of going somewhere like the Napo River in Ecuador is not to   9 see the most spectacular anything. It is simply to see what is there. We are here on the planet only once, and might as well get a feel for the place. We might as well get a feel for the fringes and hollows in which life is lived, for the Amazon basin, which covers half a continent, and for the life that— there, like anywhere else—is always and necessarily lived in detail: on the tributaries, in the riverside villages, sucking this particular white-fleshed guava in this particular pattern of shade.

What is there is interesting. The Napo River itself is wide (I mean wider   10
than the Mississippi at Davenport) and brown, opaque, and smeared with
floating foam and logs and branches from the jungle. White egrets hunch
on shoreline deadfalls and parrots in flocks dart in and out of the light. Under the water in the river, unseen, are anacondas—which are reputed to
take a few village toddlers every year—and water boas, stingrays, croco-
diles, manatees, and sweet-meated fish.

Low water bares gray strips of sandbar on which the natives build tiny   11
palm-thatch shelters, arched, the size of pup tents, for overnight fishing
trips. You see these extraordinarily clean people (who bathe twice a day in
the river, and whose straight black hair is always freshly washed) paddling
down the river in dugout canoes, hugging the banks.

Some of the Indians of this region, earlier in the century, used to sleep   12
naked in hammocks. The nights are cold. Gordon MacCreach, an American explorer in these Amazon tributaries, reported that he was startled to
hear the Indians get up at three in the morning. He was even more startled,
night after night, to hear them walk down to the river slowly, half asleep,
and bathe in the water. Only later did he learn what they were doing: they
were getting warm. The cold woke them; they warmed their skins in the
river, which was always ninety degrees; then they returned to their hammocks and slept through the rest of the night.

The riverbanks are low, and from the river you see an unbroken wall of   13
dark forest in every direction, from the Andes to the Atlantic. You get a
taste for looking at trees: trees hung with the swinging nests of yellow trou-
pials, trees from which ant nests the size of grain sacks hang like black goi-
ters, trees from which seven-colored tanagers flutter, coral trees, teak, balsa
and breadfruit, enormous emergent silk-cotton trees, and the pale-barked
samona palms.

When you are inside the jungle, away from the river, the trees vault out   14
of sight. It is hard to remember to look up the long trunks and see the fans,
strips, fronds, and sprays of glossy leaves. Inside the jungle you are more
likely to notice the snarl of climbers and creepers round the trees' boles, the
flowering bromeliads and epiphytes in every bough's crook, and the fan-
tastic silk-cotton tree trunks thirty or forty feet across, trunks buttressed in
flanges of wood whose curves can make three high walls of a room—a
shady, loamy-aired room where you would gladly live, or die. Butterflies,
iridescent blue, striped, or clear-winged, thread the jungle paths at eye
level. And at your feet is a swath of ants bearing triangular bits of green
leaf. The ants with their leaves look like a wide fleet of sailing dinghies—
but they don't quit. In either direction they wobble over the jungle floor as

far as the eye can see. I followed them off the path as far as I dared, and never saw an end to ants or to those luffing chips of green they bore.

Unseen in the jungle, but present, are tapirs, jaguars, many species of 15 snake and lizard, ocelots, armadillos, marmosets, howler monkeys, toucans and macaws and a hundred other birds, deer, bats, peccaries, capybaras, agoutis, and sloths. Also present in this jungle, but variously distant, are Texaco derricks and pipelines, and some of the wildest Indians in the world, blowgun-using Indians, who killed missionaries in 1956 and ate them.

Long lakes shine in the jungle. We traveled one of these in dugout ca- 16 noes, canoes with two inches of freeboard, canoes paddled with machete-hewn oars chopped from buttresses of silk-cotton trees, or poled in the shallows with peeled cane or bamboo. Our part-Indian guide had cleared the path to the lake the day before; when we walked the path we saw where he had impaled the lopped head of a boa, open-mouthed, on a pointed stick by the canoes, for decoration.

The lake was wonderful. Herons, egrets, and ibises plodded the saw- 17 grass shores, kingfishers and cuckoos clattered from sunlight to shade, great turkeylike birds fussed in dead branches, and hawks lolled overhead. There was all the time in the world. A turtle slid into the water. The boy in the bow of my canoe slapped stones at birds with a simple sling, a rubber throng and leather pad. He aimed brilliantly at moving targets, always, and always missed; the birds were out of range. He stuffed his sling back in his shirt. I looked around.

The lake and river waters are as opaque as rain-forest leaves; they are 18 veils, blinds, painted screens. You see things only by their effects. I saw the shoreline water roil and the sawgrass heave above a thrashing *paichi*, an enormous black fish of these waters; one had been caught the previous week weighing 430 pounds. Piranha fish live in the lakes, and electric eels. I dangled my fingers in the water, figuring it would be worth it.

We would eat chicken that night in the village, and rice, yucca, onions, 19 beets, and heaps of fruit. The sun would ring down, pulling darkness after it like a curtain. Twilight is short, and the unseen birds of twilight wistful, uncanny, catching the heart. The two nuns in their dazzling white habits—the beautiful-boned young nun and the warm-faced old—would glide to the open cane-and-thatch schoolroom in darkness, and start the children singing. The children would sing in piping Spanish, high-pitched and pure; they would sing "Nearer My God to Thee" in Quechua, very fast. (To reciprocate, we sang for them "Old MacDonald Had a Farm"; I thought they might recognize the animal sounds. Of course they thought we were out of our minds.) As the children became excited by their own singing, they left their log benches and swarmed around the nuns, hopping, smiling at us, everyone smiling, the nuns' faces bursting in their cowls, and the clear-voiced children still singing, and the palm-leafed roofing stirred.

The Napo River: it is not out of the way. It is *in* the way, catching sun- 20 light the way a cup catches poured water; it is a bowl of sweet air, a basin of greenness, and of grace, and, it would seem, of peace.

Thinking About the Essay

1. What is Dillard's purpose in writing this essay? Does she simply want to provide vivid description of a place that we might find romantic or exotic, or does she want to argue a point or persuade us to see something? Explain. How might description be used in the service of a larger purpose? Justify your answer with specific reference to the text.

2. Examine the first five paragraphs of this essay, which constitute the introduction. What is the effect of the first paragraph? How do paragraphs 1 to 5 set the stage for the ideas Dillard wants to develop in the rest of the essay?

3. Explain in your own words Dillard's thesis. How does she use comparison and contrast to advance this thesis?

4. What is Dillard's attitude toward the natives she encounters? How does her selection of detail and incident convey this tone? Would you say that her attitude is overly romantic? Why or why not?

5. Which paragraphs constitute the essay's conclusion? What evidence does the writer provide to support her conclusion?

Responding in Writing

6. Write a personal essay about the most unusual place your have encountered. What made it unusual? Try to capture the uniqueness of this place with vivid description.

7. Write a careful analysis of Dillard's style in this essay, especially her diction and descriptive talents. How does she harness the "poetry" of language to convey both an impression of a faraway location and a meditation on our place in the world?

8. Dillard asserts that since we "are on the planet only once," we should "get a feel for the place" (paragraph 9). Is it necessary to go to some out-of-the-way place to obtain this uncorrupted feel for our planet? Answer this question in a meditative essay.

Networking

9. In small groups, discuss the value of retreating to unspoiled nature to learn something about our life on this planet. Share with group members any experience of nature that you have had that is similar to Dillard's.

10. On the basis of outside reading and library or online research, write an essay in which you compare Dillard's experience in this essay to Henry David Thoreau's experience in *Walden*.

Digging Up the Roots

JANE GOODALL

British naturalist Jane Goodall, born in London in 1934, has spent much of her adult life in the jungles of Tanzania engaged in the study of chimpanzees. Fascinated by animals since childhood, Goodall, after graduating from school, traveled to Kenya to work with the famed paleontologist Louis Leakey, serving as his assistant on fossil-gathering trips to the Olduvai Gorge region. In 1960, at Leakey's urging, Goodall started a new project studying wild chimpanzees in the Gombe Stream Chimpanzee Reserve in Tanzania. In 1965, Cambridge University awarded Goodall a Ph.D. degree based on her thesis growing out of five years of research in the Gombe Reserve; she was only the eighth person in the university's history to earn a doctorate without having earned an undergraduate degree. Goodall has received dozens of major international awards from conservation societies and environmental groups, including the Albert Schweitzer Award, two Franklin Burr awards from the National Geographic Society, and numerous honorary doctorates from universities around the world. Among her many books are the widely read *In the Shadow of Man* (1971), *The Chimpanzees of Gombe: Patterns of Behavior* (1986), and a two-volume autobiography in letters, *Africa in My Blood* (2000) and *Beyond Innocence* (2001). She also has written books for children and participated in media productions based on her work. This essay from the winter 1994 issue of *Orion* reflects one of Goodall's core beliefs—that animals "have their own needs, emotions, and feelings—they matter."

Before Reading

Goodall says that "animals are like us." Do you agree or disagree, and why?

When we lose something that was very precious to us, whatever its na- 1 ture, we grieve. Our grief may be short-lived sorrow or lead to a lengthy period of mourning. The depth of our grief depends on the nature of the relationship that we had with what we have lost, not on who or what that person or thing actually was. We might grieve more for the loss of a dog or a cat than a person—it simply depends on the relative contributions made by each to our physical and spiritual well-being.

I have deeply loved several dogs and grieved correspondingly deeply 2 when they died. Just a few weeks ago at our family home in the U.K. we lost Cider, the dog who has shared our lives for the past thirteen years. I hate the thought of walking where she and I walked together. When I sit on "her" couch I feel a lump in my throat, and when the doorbell rings, and there are no fierce barks, it is not easy to go and let the caller in. I miss her snoring beside my bed at night. I am not ashamed to weep for her, as I wept for the other dogs who gave me so much.

The nature of my relationship with the Gombe chimpanzees is very dif- 3 ferent from that with my dogs. For one thing, dogs are utterly dependent on humans; for another, they become part of the household. From them I receive comfort when sad, and I can give comfort in return. With them I can share joy and excitement. With the chimpanzees it is different. They are free and independent. It is true that I have impinged on their lives, but only as an observer. (I speak here of the wild chimpanzees—relations can be very different with captive individuals.) The wild apes tolerate my presence. But they show no pleasure when they see me after an absence—they accept my goings and comings without comment. And this is as it should be since we are trying to study their natural lives. Moreover, the chimpanzees, unlike my dogs, do not depend on me for food or comfort. My relationship with them can best be described as one of mutual trust.

Nevertheless there have been Gombe chimpanzees whom I have most 4 truly loved—even though they did not reciprocate that love. One of these was old Flo. I shall never forget seeing her body as it lay at the edge of the fast-flowing Kakombe stream. I stayed close by for the better part of three days, to record the reactions of the other chimps. As I sat there I thought back over the hours we had spent together, that old female and I. I thought of all I had learned from her about maternal behavior, and family rela- tionships. I thought of her fearless, indomitable character. And I mourned her passing. Just as I grieved for old McGregor whom we had to shoot af- ter polio paralyzed both legs and he dislocated one arm as he dragged his body up a tree. And I was devastated when little Getty died. He had been everyone's favorite, loved by humans and even, I would swear, by the chimpanzees themselves. It was a long time before I could watch other infants without resentment, without asking the meaningless question: Why did it have to be him?

Of course, I was also very close to David Greybeard, the first chim- 5
panzee who ever let me approach. And I missed him very much when we finally realized he must have died. But we never knew exactly when this was, for we never found his body. Thus there was no sudden realization of his passing, no moment in time when grieving could begin.

Of all the Gombe chimpanzees I have known over the years, it was 6
Melissa whose death affected me the most, for I was there at the very end. I wrote about it in my last book, *Through a Window*.

> By evening, Melissa was alone. One foot hung down from her nest and every so often her toes moved. I stayed there, sitting on the forest floor. . . . Occasionally I spoke. I don't know if she knew I was there or, if she did, whether it made any difference. But I wanted to be with her as night fell: I didn't want her to be completely alone. . . . There was a distant pant-hoot far across the valley, but Melissa was silent. Never again would I hear her distinctive hoarse call. Never again would I wander with her from one patch of food to the next, waiting, at one with life of the forest, as she rested or groomed with one of her offspring. The stars were suddenly blurred and I wept for the passing of an old friend. Even now, seven years later, when I pass the tree where she died, I pause for a moment to remember her.

The nature of the grief I feel when a loved dog dies has one component 7
that is lacking from the sorrow caused by the death of one of my wild chimpanzee friends. Because dogs depend on us for food and comfort and help in sickness, there has always been an element of guilt in my grief for their passing. In their dog-minds, did I not let them down—however hard I tried to help? And could I, perhaps, have done more than I did? This nagging guilt, which we usually feel when a loved human companion passes away, has no place in my grieving for chimpanzee friends who have died. For they had no expectations of help.

The emotions triggered by the death of a chimpanzee I have loved are 8
different again from those that overwhelm me whenever I think of the vanishing wildlife of the world, of animals shot by hunters, snared by poachers, starved by the encroachment of farmers into their feeding grounds. I am angered, as well as saddened, when I think of their suffering, depressed when I think how hard it is to help them. The sight of a rhino killed for his horn is horribly distressing. It brings tears to my eyes, but the tears are part rage because we seem unable to stop the slaughter. True mourning, I

believe, can only follow the death of an individual we have known and loved, whose life for a while has been linked with ours.

I have always had a great passion for trees, for woods and forests. Of- 9 ten I lay my hand on the trunk of a tree, feeling the texture of its bark and imagining the sap coursing up the trunk, taking life to the leaves far above. Some trees seem to have characters of their own: the slim and elegant individual, rustling soft songs in the breeze; the helpful one, with wide branches and dense foliage, providing shade; and the strong and comforting tree with a friendly overhanging trunk to protect one from the rain. When I was a child I used sometimes to lie looking up at the blue sky through the leaves of a birch tree in the garden. I specially loved that tree in the moonlight, when the white trunk was bright and ghostly and the leaves were black with glinting silver where the soft light caught them. And when it died, like so many other birch trees in the drought of 1977, when no leaves burst out in the spring, I felt great sadness, and also a sense of nostalgia. In sorrowing for the tree, was I also grieving for my lost youth?

A little while ago I drove along a road in Tanzania that once ran 10 through miles of forest. Twenty years ago there were lions and elephants, leopards and wild dogs, and a myriad of birds. But now the trees are gone and the road guided us relentlessly, mile after mile, through hot, dusty country, where crops were withered under the glare of the sun and there was no shade. I felt a great melancholy, and also anger. This anger was not directed against the poor farmers who were trying to eke out a livelihood from the now inhospitable land, but against mankind in general. We multiply and we destroy, chopping and killing. Now, in this desecrated area, the women searching for firewood must dig up the roots of the trees they have long since cut down to make space for crops.

Gombe National Park is, today, like an island of forest and wildlife set 11 in a desert of human habitation. During a recent visit I climbed to the top of the rift escarpment and looked to the east, the north, the south. In 1980 I could look out from the same place, and there was chimpanzee habitat stretched as far as I could see. Now the steep slopes are bare of trees and have become increasingly barren and rocky, more and more of the precious top soil washed away with every heavy rain. And the chimpanzees, along with most of the other wild animals, have gone. But at least the little oasis of the park is safe, and in its ancient forests I can for a while take refuge from the problems of the world outside. If Gombe was destroyed I should know inconsolable grief. For Gombe, with all its vivid and unique chimpanzee characters, with all its tumbling memories, has been an integral part of my life for more than thirty years. It is, I have always said, paradise on earth. And who would not mourn expulsion from paradise?

Thinking About the Essay

1. How do you interpret the author's title in light of your reading of this essay? What "roots," in particular, does she seek to dig up?

2. Explain the tone of this essay. Do you find Goodall to be sentimental, overly romantic, or nostalgic for some vanished world? Why or why not? How does she create a certain mood, and how would you define it? How does her decision to insert the "I" point of view serve to strengthen tone and mood?

3. What comparisons does the author draw between human beings, dogs, and chimpanzees? How does she organize her essay around these subjects?

4. What, exactly, is this essay about, and what is Goodall's thesis? Does she state it in one sentence or a series of sentences, or does she imply it?

5. The last section of the essay focuses on trees. How does this last section capture and reinforce what the author wants to tell us about ourselves and the natural world?

Responding in Writing

6. Argue for or against the proposition that Goodall in this essay succeeds in getting to the "roots" of the human and nonhuman condition.

7. Write a personal essay in which you narrate and describe what you have learned from a family pet or from the natural world.

8. Goodall speaks of both the joy and grief that the natural world presents to us. Reread the essay, and explain in a brief paper which of these two emotions tends to dominate the other for the author.

Networking

9. Divide into groups of three and four and list examples of the destruction of natural habitats in the United States and around the world. Present your list to the class along with other groups.

10. Go online with another classmate and find out about the Gombe Stream Research Center and/or the Jane Goodall Institute. Share your findings in class discussion.

In Defense of Nature, Human and Non-human

Francis Fukuyama

Francis Fukuyama was born in 1952 in Chicago, Illinois; he studied at Cornell University (B.A., 1974), Yale University, and Harvard University (Ph.D., 1981). Fukuyama gained worldwide attention in 1989 with the publication in *National Interest* of his essay "The End of History?" In that sixteen-page inquiry, Fukuyama contends that history has reached its logical conclusion, which is liberal democracy. He expanded his thesis into the book *The End of History and the Last Man* (1992), which has been translated into more than a dozen languages. A clear, engaging prose stylist who makes political and economic ideas comprehensible to ordinary readers, Fukuyama is willing to present provocative and debatable theses for consideration both by specialists and by the public. Long associated with the RAND Corporation, Fukuyama today is Bernard Schwartz Professor of International Political Economy at the Johns Hopkins University School of Advanced International Studies. Among his books are *Trust: The Social Virtues and the Creation of Prosperity* (1995), *The Great Disruption: Human Nature and the Reconstitution of the Social Order* (1999), *Our Posthuman Future: Consequences of the Biotechnology Revolution* (2002), and *State-Building: Governance and World Order in the 21st Century* (2004). Fukuyama also writes frequently for magazines and journals. In this essay, from the July/August 2002 issue of *Worldwatch*, he poses an important argument about the connection between the defense of human and non-human nature.

Before Reading

What connections do you see between the need to defend nature against technological exploitation and the drive to limit experimentation in human genetics?

People who have not been paying close attention to the debate on human   1
biotechnology might think that the chief issue in this debate is about abortion, since the most outspoken opponents of cloning to date have been right-to-lifers who oppose the destruction of embryos. But there are important reasons why cloning and the genetic technologies that will follow upon

it should be of concern to all people, religious or secular, and above all to those who are concerned with protecting the natural environment. For the attempt to master human nature through biotechnology will be even more dangerous and consequential than the efforts of industrial societies to master non-human nature through earlier generations of technology.

If there is one thing that the environmental movement has taught us in the past couple of generations, it is that nature is a complex whole. The different parts of an ecosystem are mutually interdependent in ways that we often fail to understand; human efforts to manipulate certain parts of it will produce a host of unintended consequences that will come back to haunt us. 2

Watching one of the movies made in the 1930s about the construction of Hoover Dam or the Tennessee Valley Authority is today a strange experience: the films are at the same time naive and vaguely Stalinist, celebrating the human conquest of nature and boasting of the replacement of natural spaces with steel, concrete, and electricity. This victory over nature was short-lived: in the past generation, no developed country has undertaken a new large hydroelectric project, precisely because we now understand the devastating ecological and social consequences that such undertakings produce. Indeed, the environmental movement has been active in trying to persuade China to desist from pursuing the enormously destructive Three Gorges Dam. 3

If the problem of unintended consequences is severe in the case of non-human ecosystems, it will be far worse in the realm of human genetics. The human genome has in fact been likened to an ecosystem in the complex way that genes interact and influence one another. It is now estimated that there are only about 30,000 genes in the human genome, far fewer than the 100,000 believed to exist until recently. This is not terribly many more than the 14,000 in a fruitfly or the 19,000 in a nematode, and indicates that many higher human capabilities and behaviors are controlled by the complex interworking of multiple genes. A single gene will have multiple effects, while in other cases several genes need to work together to produce a single effect, along causal pathways that will be extremely difficult to untangle. 4

The first targets of genetic therapy will be relatively simple single gene disorders like Huntington's disease or Tay Sachs disease. Many geneticists believe that the genetic causality of higher-order behaviors and characteristics like personality, intelligence, or even height is so complex that we will never be able to manipulate it. But this is precisely where the danger lies: we will be constantly tempted to think that we understand this causality better than we really do, and will face even nastier surprises than we did when we tried to conquer the non-human natural environment. In this case, the victim of a failed experiment will not be an ecosystem, but a 5 human child whose parents, seeking to give her greater intelligence, will saddle her with a greater propensity for cancer, or prolonged debility in old age, or some other completely unexpected side effect that may emerge only after the experimenters have passed from the scene.

Listening to people in the biotech industry talk about the opportunities   6 opening up with the completion of the sequencing of the human genome is eerily like watching those propaganda films about Hoover Dam: there is a hubristic confidence that biotechnology and scientific cleverness will correct the defects of human nature, abolish disease, and perhaps even allow human beings to achieve immortality some day. We will come out the other end a superior species because we understand how imperfect and limited our nature is.

I believe that human beings are, to an even greater degree than ecosys-   7 tems, complex, coherent natural wholes, whose evolutionary provenance we do not even begin to understand. More than that, we possess human rights because of that specifically human nature: as Thomas Jefferson said at the end of his life, Americans enjoy equal political rights because nature has not arranged for certain human beings to be born with saddles on their backs, ready to be ridden by their betters. A biotechnology that seeks to manipulate human nature not only risks unforeseen consequences, but can undermine the very basis of equal democratic rights as well.

So how do we defend human nature? The tools are essentially the same   8 as in the case of protecting non-human nature: we try to shape norms through discussion and dialogue, and we use the power of the state to regulate the way in which technology is developed and deployed by the private sector and the scientific research community. Biomedicine is, of course, heavily regulated today, but there are huge gaps in the jurisdiction of those federal agencies with authority over biotechnology. The U.S. Food and Drug Administration can only regulate food, drugs, and medical products on the basis of safety and efficacy. It is enjoined from making decisions on the basis of ethical considerations, and it has weak to nonexistent jurisdiction over medical procedures like cloning, preimplantation genetic diagnosis (where embryos are screened for genetic characteristics before being implanted in a womb), and germline engineering (where an embryo's genes are manipulated in ways that are inherited by future generations). The National Institutes of Health (NIH) make numerous rules covering human experimentation and other aspects of scientific research, but their authority extends only to federally funded research and leaves unregulated the private biotech industry. The latter, in U.S. biotech firms alone, spends over $10 billion annually on research, and employs some 150,000 people.

Other countries are striving to put legislation in place to regulate   9 human biotechnology. One of the oldest legislative arrangements is that

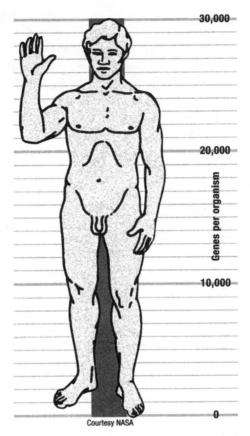

Courtesy NASA

A rendering of man from the plaque on *Pioneer 10,* the first manmade object to escape the so-lar system, and the number of genes in the human body. Although scientists initially expected the human genome to consist of 100,000 genes, it takes in fact only 30,000 genes to make up the human genetic code. The plaque on *Pioneer 10* was accompanied by a disk of music and languages from around the world; is there something greater than the genome that makes up what it means to be "human"?

of Britain, which established the Human Fertilisation and Embryology Agency more than ten years ago to regulate experimentation with embryos. Twenty-four countries have banned reproductive cloning, including Ger-many, France, India, Japan, Argentina, Brazil, South Africa, and the United Kingdom. In 1998, the Council of Europe approved an Additional Proto-col to its Convention on Human Rights and Dignity With Regard to Bio-medicine banning human reproductive cloning, a document that has been signed by 24 of the council's 43 member states. Germany and France have proposed that the United Nations draft a global convention to ban repro-ductive cloning.

One of the early efforts to police a specific genetic technology, recom- 10
binant DNA experiments, was the 1975 Asilomar Conference in California, which led to the establishment under the NIH of the Recombinant
DNA Advisory Committee (RAC). The RAC was supposed to approve all
recombinant experiments in which genes of different individuals and sometimes species were spliced together, initially in agricultural biotechnology
and later in areas like human gene therapy. A conference held in 2000 on
the 25th anniversary of Asilomar led to a general consensus that, whatever
the virtues of the RAC a generation ago, it had outlived its usefulness. The
RAC has no enforcement powers, does not oversee the private sector, and
does not have the institutional capability to even monitor effectively what
is happening in the U.S. biotech industry, much less globally. Clearly, new
regulatory institutions are needed to deal with the upcoming generation of
new biotechnologies.

Anyone who feels strongly about defending non-human nature from 11
technological manipulation should feel equally strongly about defending
human nature as well. In Europe, the environmental movement is more
firmly opposed to biotechnology than is its counterpart in the United
States, and has managed to stop the proliferation of genetically modified
foods there dead in its tracks. But genetically modified organisms are ultimately only an opening shot in a longer revolution, and far less consequential than the human biotechnologies now coming on line. Some people
believe that, given the depredations of humans on non-human nature, the
latter deserves more vigilant protection. But in the end, they are part of the
same whole. Altering the genes of plants affects only what we eat and grow;
altering our own genes affects who we are. Nature—both the natural environment around us, and our own—deserves an approach based on respect and stewardship, not domination and mastery.

Thinking About the Essay

1. What is the author's thesis or claim? Is it stated or implied? Explain.

2. How does Fukuyama structure his argument? What are his minor propositions? Where does he provide evidence to support his claims and
   assertions?

3. Does the author make any value judgments, or is he strictly logical and objective? Justify your answer by reference to the text.

4. Explain the comparative design of this essay. How does the author achieve
   both balance and unity in creating this comparative approach to his subject?

5. Describe the conclusion of this essay. How does it grow from the middle
   section? In what way does it reinforce the author's thesis? What is the final
   tone?

Responding in Writing

6. Argue for or against the proposition that a person who supports environmental causes should also oppose all forms of "a biotechnology that seeks to manipulate human nature" (paragraph 7).

7. Write an essay in which you explain whether or not you found Fukuyama's essay to be convincing.

8. Present your views on human cloning in a brief essay.

Networking

9. Form small groups and jot down all objections members have heard about biotechnological experimentation. Then develop a second list of positive outcomes to biotechnology research. Share your lists in class discussion.

10. Fukuyama refers to the Three Gorges Dam in China (paragraph 3). Conduct online research into this huge development project, and write a brief paper about its supporters and opponents.

A Hole in the World

JONATHAN SCHELL

Jonathan Schell was born in New York City in 1943. Following graduate study in Far Eastern history at Harvard University and additional study in Tokyo, Schell accompanied an American forces operation in South Vietnam in the winter and spring of 1967 that resulted in the evacuation of an entire village after "pacification" failed. He wrote a graphic description of the destruction of Vietnamese villages in *The Village of Ben Suc* (1967) and *The Military Half: An Account of Destruction in Quang Ngai and Quang Tin* (1968). Just as his first two books excoriated the American presence in Vietnam, Schell in his third book, *The Time of Illusion* (1976), offered a critique of the Nixon administration and the Watergate scandal. Schell's next book, *The Fate of the Earth* (1982), still one of the most persuasive treatments of the dangers of nuclear war, became a bestseller. Schell returned to the subject of nuclear proliferation in *The Gift of Time: The Case for Abolishing Nuclear Weapons* (1998). He currently is the peace and disarmament correspondent for *The Nation* and Harold Willens Peace Fellow at the Nation Institute. In the following essay, published in *The Nation* on October 1, 2001, Schell uses the events of 9/11 to raise the even more frightening specter of nuclear destruction.

Before Reading

How has 9/11 made you more aware of the dangers posed by weapons of mass destruction? Do you carry this awareness with you, or does the prospect of an attack with a weapon of mass destruction seem remote and unthreatening? Explain your response.

O n Tuesday morning, a piece was torn out of our world. A patch of blue   1
sky that should not have been there opened up in the New York skyline. In my neighborhood—I live eight blocks from the World Trade Center—the heavens were raining human beings. Our city was changed
forever. Our country was changed forever. Our world was changed forever.

It will take months merely to know what happened, far longer to feel   2
so much grief, longer still to understand its meaning. It's already clear, however, that one aspect of the catastrophe is of supreme importance for the
future: the danger of the use of weapons of mass destruction, and especially
the use of nuclear weapons. This danger includes their use by a terrorist
group but is by no means restricted to it. It is part of a larger danger that
has been for the most part ignored since the end of the cold war.

Among the small number who have been concerned with nuclear arms   3
in recent years—they have pretty much all known one another by their first
names—it was commonly heard that the world would not return its attention to this subject until a nuclear weapon was again set off somewhere in
the world. Then, the tiny club said to itself, the world would awaken to its
danger. Many of the ingredients of the catastrophe were obvious. The repeated suicide-homicides of the bombers in Israel made it obvious that
there were people so possessed by their cause that, in an exaltation of hatred, they would do anything in its name. Many reports—most recently an
article in the *New York Times* on the very morning of the attack—reminded the public that the world was awash in nuclear materials and the
wherewithal for other weapons of mass destruction. Russia is bursting at
the seams with these materials. The suicide bombers and the market in nuclear materials was that two-plus-two that points toward the proverbial
necessary four. But history is a trickster. The fates came up with a horror
that was unforeseen. No one had identified the civilian airliner as a weapon
of mass destruction, but it occurred to the diabolical imagination of those
who conceived Tuesday's attack that it could be one. The invention illumined the nature of terrorism in modern times. These terrorists carried no
bombs—only knives, if initial reports are to be believed. In short, they
turned the tremendous forces inherent in modern technical society—in this
case, Boeing 767s brimming with jet fuel—against itself.

So it is also with the more commonly recognized weapons of mass destruction. Their materials can be built the hard way, from scratch, as Iraq came within an ace of doing until stopped by the Gulf War and as Pakistan and India have done, or they can be diverted from Russian, or for that matter American or English or French or Chinese, stockpiles. In the one case, it is nuclear know-how that is turned against its inventors, in the other it is their hardware. Either way, it is "blowback"—the use of a technical capacity against its creator—and, as such, represents the pronounced suicidal tendencies of modern society. 4

This suicidal bent—nicely captured in the name of the still current nuclear policy "mutual assured destruction"—of course exists in forms even more devastating than possible terrorist attacks. India and Pakistan, which both possess nuclear weapons and have recently engaged in one of their many hot wars, are the likeliest candidates. Most important—and most forgotten—are the some 30,000 nuclear weapons that remain in the arsenals of Russia and the United States. The Bush Administration has announced its intention of breaking out of the antiballistic missile treaty of 1972, which bans antinuclear defenses, and the Russians have answered that if this treaty is abandoned the whole framework of nuclear arms control built up over thirty years may collapse. There is no quarrel between the United States and Russia that suggests a nuclear exchange between them, but accidents are another matter, and, as Tuesday's attack has shown, the mood and even the structure of the international order can change overnight. 5

What should be done? Should the terrorists who carried out Tuesday's attacks be brought to justice and punished, as the President wants to do? Of course. Who should be punished if not people who would hurl a cargo of innocent human beings against a fixed target of other innocent human beings? (When weighing the efficiency—as distinct from the satisfaction—of punishment, however, it is well to remember that the immediate attackers have administered the supposed supreme punishment of death to themselves.) Should further steps be taken to protect the country and the world from terrorism, including nuclear terrorism? They should. And yet even as we do these things, we must hold, as if to life itself, to a fundamental truth that has been known to all thoughtful people since the destruction of Hiroshima: There is no technical solution to the vulnerability of modern populations to weapons of mass destruction. After the attack, Secretary of Defense Rumsfeld placed US forces on the highest state of alert and ordered destroyers and aircraft carriers to take up positions up and down the coasts of the United States. But none of these measures can repeal the vulnerability of modern society to its own inventions, revealed by that heart-breaking gap in the New York skyline. This, obviously, holds 6 equally true for that other Maginot line, the proposed system of national missile defense. Thirty billion dollars is being spent on intelligence annually. We can assume that some portion of that was devoted to protecting the World Trade Center after it was first bombed in 1993. There may have been mistakes—maybe we'll find out—but the truth is that no one on earth can demonstrate that the expenditure of even ten times that amount can prevent a terrorist attack on the United States or any other country. The combination of the extraordinary power of modern technology, the universal and instantaneous spread of information in the information age and the mobility inherent in a globalized economy prevents it.

Man, however, is not merely a technical animal. Aristotle pointed out   7 that we are also a political animal, and it is to politics that we must return for the solutions that hold promise. That means returning to the treaties that the United States has recently been discarding like so much old newspaper—the one dealing, for example, with an International Criminal Court (useful for tracking down terrorists and bringing them to justice), with global warming and, above all, of course, with nuclear arms and the other weapons of mass destruction, biological and chemical. The United States and seven other countries now rely for their national security on the retaliatory execution of destruction a millionfold greater than the Tuesday attacks. The exit from this folly, by which we endanger ourselves as much as others, must be found. Rediscovering ourselves as political animals also means understanding the sources of the hatred that the United States has incurred in a decade of neglect and, worse, neglect of international affairs—a task that is highly unwelcome to many in current circumstances but nevertheless is indispensable to the future safety of the United States and the world.

It would be disrespectful of the dead to in any way minimize the catas-   8 trophe that has overtaken New York. Yet at the same time we must keep room in our minds for the fact that it could have been worse. To lose two huge buildings and the people in them is one thing; to lose all of Manhattan—or much, much more—is another. The emptiness in the sky can spread. We have been warned.

Thinking About the Essay

1. This essay appeared less than a month after the 9/11 disaster. Do you think that the writer exploited the catastrophe, or is his purpose valid? Explain your response.

2. Schell's credentials as a specialist on nuclear proliferation are impressive. Is this essay geared to a highly intelligent audience or a more general one? Cite internal evidence to support your response.

3. How is the essay organized? Where does the introduction begin and end? What paragraphs constitute the body? Where is the conclusion? What markers assisted you in establishing these stages of essay development?

4. Reduce the logical structure of Schell's argument to a set of major and minor propositions. Is his conclusion valid in light of the underlying reasons? Explain.

5. What assertion in the essay do you most agree with, and why? Which assertion do you find dubious or unsupported, and why?

Responding in Writing

6. Write an essay in which you agree or disagree with Schell's statement that the danger of the use of weapons of mass destruction is "of supreme importance for the future" (paragraph 2).

7. Schell asserts that the United States has neglected its role in international affairs, including its abandonment of international treaties, thereby endangering the nation's security. Argue for or against his claim.

8. Write an analysis of Schell's style in this essay. Begin with the title itself and how it resonates throughout the essay. Discuss the impact of such graphic uses of language as "the heavens were raining human beings" (paragraph 1). Identify those stylistic techniques the author uses to persuade us to accept the logic of his position.

Networking

9. Divide into groups of between three and five, and create a simulation game whereby a specific city is threatened by a weapon of mass destruction. Imagine the steps taken to thwart the attack, and determine if these steps would be successful or not. Present your scenario to the class.

10. Using an Internet search engine, locate information on nuclear disarmament. Using the information retrieved, write a report on what various groups, agencies, and governments are doing to reduce and prevent the spread of nuclear weapons.

Conducting Research
in the Global Era

Introduction

The *doing* of research is as important a process as the *writing* of a research paper. When scholars, professors, scientists, journalists, and students *do* research, they ask questions, solve problems, follow leads, and track down sources. The process of research as well as the writing of the research paper has changed radically over the last ten years, as the Internet now makes a whole world of resources instantly available to anyone. Skillfully navigating your way through this wealth of resources, evaluating and synthesizing information as you solve problems and answer questions, enhances your critical thinking and writing abilities and develops the tools you will need for professional success.

A research paper incorporates the ideas, discoveries, and observations of other writers. The information provided by these scholars, thinkers, and observers helps to support your own original thesis or claim about a topic. Learning how to evaluate, adapt, synthesize, and correctly acknowledge these sources in your research protects you from charges of plagiarism (discussed below). More importantly, it demonstrates to you how knowledge is expanded and created. Research, and research writing, are the cornerstone not only of the university but of our global information society.

The research paper is the final product of a process of inquiry and discovery. The topics and readings in this book bring together voices from all over the world, discussing and debating issues of universal importance. As you develop a topic, work toward a thesis, and discover sources and evidence, you will use the Internet to bring international perspectives to your writing. More immediately, your teacher will probably ask you to work in peer groups as you refine your topics, suggest resources to each other, and evaluate preliminary drafts of your final research paper. Although the primary—and ultimate—audience for your research paper is your teacher, thinking of your work as a process of discovery and a contribution to a larger global conversation will keep your perspective fresh and your interest engaged.

The Research Process

A research paper is the final result of a series of tasks, some small and others quite time consuming. Be sure to allow yourself plenty of time for each stage of the research process, working with your teacher or a peer group to develop a schedule that breaks down specific tasks.

The four broad stages of the research process are

1. Choosing a topic
2. Establishing a thesis
3. Finding, evaluating, and organizing evidence
4. Writing your paper

Stage One: Choosing a Topic

Reading and discussing the often urgent issues addressed in this book may have already given you an idea about a topic you would like to explore further. Your attention may also have been engaged by a television news report, an international website that presented an unexpected viewpoint, or a speaker who visited your campus. Even if your teacher assigns a specific topic area to you, finding—and nurturing—a genuine curiosity and concern about that topic will make the research process much more involving and satisfying. Some topics are too broad, too controversial (or not controversial enough), too current, or too obscure for an effective research paper.

Determining an Appropriate Research Topic

Ask yourself the following questions about possible topics for your research paper:

- Am I genuinely curious about this topic? Will I want to live with it for the next few weeks?
- What do I already know about this topic? What more do I want to find out?
- Does the topic fit the general guidelines my teacher has suggested?
- Can I readily locate the sources I will need for further research on this topic?

Exercise: Freewriting

Review your work for this class so far, taking note of any readings in the text that particularly appealed to you or any writing assignments that you especially enjoyed. Open a new folder on your computer, labeling it "Research Paper."

Open a new document, and title it "Freewriting." Then write, without stopping, everything that intrigued you originally about that reading or that assignment. Use the questions on page 486 to prompt your thinking.

Browsing

Having identified a general topic area of interest, begin exploring that area by *browsing*. When you browse, you take a broad and casual survey of the existing information and resources about your topic. There are many resources to consult as you begin to dig deeper into your topic, nearly all of which can be found at your campus library. Begin at the reference desk by asking for a guide to the library's reference collection.

- *General Reference Texts*. These include encyclopedias, almanacs, specialized dictionaries, and statistical information.
- *Periodical Index*. Both in-print and online versions of periodical indices now exist (the electronic versions are often subscription-only and available only through academic and some public libraries). A periodical index lists subjects, authors, and titles of articles in newspapers, journals, and magazines. Some electronic versions include both abstracts (brief summaries) and full-text versions of the articles.
- *Library Catalog*. Your library's catalog probably exists both online and as a "card catalog"—an alphabetized record organized by author, title, and subject—in which each book has its own paper card in a file. Begin your catalog browsing with a subject or keyword search. Identify the *call number* that appears most frequently for the books you are most likely to use—that number will point you to the library shelves where you'll find the most useful books for your topic.

Making a Global Connection

Unless you read another language, the information you find in books is not likely to be as international or immediate in perspective as that which you will find in periodicals and online. The information you find through the card catalog will direct you toward books that provide in-depth background information and context, but for the most up-to-date information as well as a perspective from the nation or countries involved in your topic, your online and periodical research will probably be most useful.

- *Search Engines*. For the most current and broadest overview of a research topic, a search engine such as Google, Altavista, or Yahoo can provide you with an ever-changing—and dauntingly vast—range of perspectives. Many search engines, including these three, have international sites (allowing you to search in specific regions or countries) as well as basic translation services. At the browsing stage, spending time online can both stimulate your interest and help you to focus your topic. Because websites change so quickly, however, be sure to print out a page from any site you think might be useful in the later stages of your research—that way, you'll have a hard copy of the site's URL (uniform resource locator, or web address). (If you're working on your own computer, create a new folder under "favorites" or "bookmarks" entitled "Research Project," and file bookmarks for interesting sites there.)

Stage Two: Establishing a Thesis

Moving from a general area of interest to a specific *thesis*—a claim you wish to make, an area of information you wish to explore, a question you intend to answer, or a solution to a problem you want to propose—requires thinking critically about your topic. You have already begun to focus on what *specifically* interests you about this topic in the freewriting exercise on page 486. The next step in refining your topic and establishing a thesis is to determine your audience and purpose for writing.

Determining Your Audience and Purpose

- Where have you found, through your browsing, the most interesting or compelling information about your topic? Who was the audience for that information? Do you consider yourself to be a part of that audience? Define the characteristics of that audience (e.g., concerned about the environment, interested in global economics, experienced at traveling abroad).
- *Why* are you most interested in this topic? Do you want to encourage someone (a friend, a politician) to take a specific course of action? Do you want to shed some light on an issue or event that not many people are familiar with?
- Try a little imaginative role playing. Imagine yourself researching this topic as a professional in a specific field. For example, if your topic is environmental preservation, imagine yourself as a pharmaceuticals researcher. What would your compelling interest in the topic be? What if you were an adventure traveler seeking new destinations—how would your approach to the topic of environmental preservation change?
- If you could have the undivided attention of anyone, other than your teacher, with whom you could share your knowledge about this topic, who would that person be and why?

Moving from a Topic to a Thesis Statement

Although choosing a topic is the beginning of the research *process*, it is not the beginning of your research *paper*. The course that your research will take, and the shape that your final paper will assume, are based on your *thesis statement.* A thesis statement is the answer to whatever question originally prompted your research. To narrow your topic and arrive at a thesis statement, ask yourself specific questions about the topic.

Using Questions to Create a Thesis Statement

General Topic	More Specific Topic	Question	Thesis Statement
Preserving the global environment	Preserving the rain forest	What is a creative way in which people could try to preserve the rain forest?	Ecotourism, when properly managed, can help the rain forest by creating economic incentives for the people who live there.
Economic security for women in the developing world	Creating economic opportunities for women in the developing world	What approaches could help women in the developing world establish economic security for themselves and their communities?	Microloans are a creative and empowering way of redistributing wealth that allows individual women to develop their own economic security.
AIDS in Africa	The incidence of AIDS in African women	How are international organizations working to stop the spread of AIDS among African women?	Improving literacy and educational opportunities for African girls and women will help to stem the spread of AIDS.
Dating and courtship between people of different religions	Dating behavior among second-generation American Hindu or Muslim teenagers	How are kids from conservative cultural or religious backgrounds negotiating between their family's beliefs and the pressures of American popular culture?	Encouraging multicultural events helps teenagers learn about each others' cultures and beliefs.

Stage Three: Finding, Evaluating, and Organizing Evidence

Developing a Working Bibliography

A working bibliography is a record of every source you consult as you conduct your research. Although not every source you use may end up cited in your paper, having a consolidated and organized record of *everything* you looked at will make drafting the paper as well as preparing the Works Cited page much easier. Some people use their computers for keeping a Works Cited list (especially if you do much of your research using online databases, which automatically create citations). But for most people—even if many of your sources are online—4 × 6 index cards are much more portable and efficient. Index cards allow you to easily rearrange the order of your sources (according to priority, for example, or sources that you need to double-check); they let you jot down notes or summaries; and they slip into your bookbag for a quick trip to the library.

Whether your working bibliography is on a computer or on index cards, always record the same information for each source you consult.

Checklists for Working Bibliographies

Information for a book:

❑ Author name(s), first and last
❑ Book title
❑ Place of publication
❑ Publisher's name
❑ Date of publication
❑ Library call number
❑ Page numbers (for specific information or quotes you'll want to consult later)

Information for an article in a journal or magazine:

❑ Author name(s), first and last
❑ Article title
❑ Magazine or journal title
❑ Volume and/or issue number
❑ Date of publication
❑ Page numbers
❑ Library call number

Information for online sources:

❑ Author (if there is one)
❑ Web page title, or title of an article or graphic on the web page
❑ URL (website address)
❑ Date of your online access

• *Some sites include information on how they prefer to be cited. You'll notice this information at the bottom of a main or "splash" page of a site, or you'll see a link to a "citation" page.*

Sample working bibliography note: Article

Honey, Martha. "Protecting the Environment: Setting Green Standards for the Tourism Industry." <u>Environment</u> July/August 2003:8–21.

Sample working bibliography note: Online source

World Tourism Association. "Global Code of Ethics for Tourism." <http:www.//world-tourism.org/projects/ethics/principles.html>.

Consulting Experts and Professionals

In the course of your research you may discover someone whose work is so timely, or opinions so relevant, that a personal interview would provide even more (and unique) information for your paper. Look beyond the university faculty for such experts—for example, if your topic is ecotourism, a local travel agent who specializes in ecotourism might be able to give you firsthand accounts of such locales and voyages. If your topic is second-generation teenagers balancing conservative backgrounds with American popular culture, hanging out with a group of such kids and talking with them about their lives will give you the kind of first-person anecdote that makes research writing genuinely fresh and original. Think of "expertise" as being about *experience*—not just a title or a degree.

Checklist for Arranging and Conducting Interviews

❑ Be certain that the person you wish to speak to will offer a completely unique, even undocumented, perspective on your topic. Interviewing someone who has already published widely on your topic is not the best use of your research time, as you can just as easily consult that person's published work.

❑ E-mail, telephone (at a business number, if possible), or write to your subject well in advance of your paper deadline. Explain clearly that you are a student writing a research paper, the topic of your paper, and the specific subject(s) you wish to discuss.

❑ An interview can be conducted via e-mail or over the telephone as well as in person. Instant messaging, because it can't be easily documented and doesn't lend itself to longer responses, is not a good choice.

❑ Write out your questions in advance!

Conducting Field Research

Field research involves traveling to a specific place to observe and document a specific occurrence or phenomenon. For example, if you were writing about the challenges and opportunities of a highly diverse immigrant community (such as Elmhurst, Queens), you might arrange to spend a day at a local school, park, or coffee shop. Bring a notebook, a digital camera, a tape recorder—anything that will help you capture and record observations. Although your task as a field researcher is to be *unbiased*—to objectively observe what is happening, keeping an open mind as well as open eyes— you'll want to always keep your working thesis in mind, too. For example, if your thesis is

> Allowing students in highly diverse American communities to create events that celebrate and respect their own cultural traditions within the general American popular culture helps to create understanding between teenagers and their immigrant parents

your field research might take you to a high school in an immigrant community to observe the interactions among teenagers. You'll want to record everything—both positive and negative, both expected and surprising—that you observe and overhear, but you won't want to get distracted by a teacher's mentioning the difficulties of coping with many different languages in the classroom. That's fascinating, but it's another topic altogether.

Checklist for Arranging and Conducting Field Research

❏ If your field research involves crossing a private boundary or property line—a school, church, hospital, restaurant, etc.—be sure to contact the institution first to confirm that it's appropriate for you to visit. As with the guidelines for conducting a personal interview, inform the person with whom you arrange the visit that you are a student conducting field research and that your research is for a classroom paper.

❏ Respect personal boundaries. Some people might not want to be photographed, and others might be uneasy if they think you are taking notes on their conversation or behavior. If you sense that your presence is making someone uncomfortable, apologize and explain what you are doing. If they are still uncomfortable, back off.

❏ When you use examples and observations from your field research in your research paper, do not use the first person as part of the citation. Simply describe what was observed, and under what circumstances.

Not recommended: When I visited the dog park to see how the personalities of dogs reflect those of their owners, I was especially attracted to the owner of a bulldog named Max. When I introduced myself to Max's owner, George T., and explained my project to him, George agreed with my thesis and pointed out that the owners of large, athletic dogs like Rottweilers tended to be young men, and the owners of more sedentary dogs (like Max) seemed to be a little mellower.

Recommended: A visit to a local dog park revealed the ways in which the personalities of dogs reflect those of their owners. George T., the owner of a bulldog named Max, pointed out that the younger men at the park were accompanied by large, athletic dogs like Rottweilers, while more sedentary people (like George) tended to have mellower breeds such as bulldogs.

Assessing the Credibility of Sources

After browsing, searching, observing, and conversing, you will by now have collected a mass of sources and data. The next step is to evaluate those sources critically, using your working bibliography as a road map back to all the sources you have consulted to date. This critical evaluation will help you to determine which sources have the relevance, credibility, and authority expected of academic research.

Checklist for Assessing Source Credibility

❏ Do the table of contents and index of a book include keywords and subjects relevant to your topic? Does the abstract of a journal article include keywords relevant to your topic and thesis? Does a website indicate through a menu (or from your using the "search" command) that it contains content relevant to your topic and thesis?

❏ How current is the source? Check the date of the magazine or journal and the copyright date of the book (the original copyright date, not the dates of reprints). Has the website been updated recently, and are its links current and functioning?

❏ How authoritative is the source? Is the author credentialed in his or her field? Do other authors refer to this writer (or website) in their work?

❏ Who sponsors a website? Is it the site of a major media group, a government agency, a political think tank, or a special-interest group? If you are unsure, print out the home page of the site and ask your teacher or a reference librarian.

Taking Notes

Now that you have determined which sources are most relevant and useful, you can begin to read them with greater attention to detail. This is *active reading*—annotating, responding to, and taking notes on what you are reading. Taking careful notes will help you to build the structure of your paper and will ensure accurate documentation later. As with the working bibliography, you can take notes either on your computer or on 4 × 6 index cards. For online sources, you can cut and paste blocks of text into a separate word processing document on your computer; just be certain to include the original URL and to indicate that what you have cut and pasted is a *direct quote* (which you might later paraphrase or summarize). Some researchers cut and paste material in a font or color that is completely different from their own writing, just to remind them of where specific words and concepts came from (and as protection against inadvertent plagiarism).

There are three kinds of notes you will take as you explore your resources:

- *Summaries* give you the broad overview of a source's perspective or information and serve as reminders of a source's content should you wish to re-visit later for more specific information or direct quotes.
- *Paraphrases* express a source's ideas and information in your own language.
- *Direct quotations* are best for when an author or subject expresses a thought or concept in language that is so striking, important, or original that to paraphrase it would be to lose some of its importance. Direct quotations are *exact* copies of an author's own words and are always enclosed in quotation marks.

Checklist for Taking Notes

❏ Take just one note (paraphrase, summary, or analysis) on each index card. Be sure to note the complete source information for the quote on the card (see the Checklists for Working Bibliographies on page 490 for what information is required).

❏ Cross-check your note-taking cards against your working bibliography. Be sure that every source on which you take notes has a corresponding entry in the working bibliography.

❏ Write a subtopic on top of each card, preferably in a brightly colored ink. Keep a running list of all of your subtopics. This will enable you to group together related pieces of information and determine the structure of your outline.

Sample note: Summary

Subtopic	Indigenous peoples and ecotourism
Author/title	Mastny, "Ecotourist trap"
Page numbers	94
Summary	The Kainamaro people of Guyana are actively involved with the development of ecotourism in their lands, ensuring that their cultural integrity takes precedence over financial gain.

Sample note: Paraphrase

Subtopic	Indigenous peoples and ecotourism
Author/title	Mastny, "Ecotourist trap"
Page numbers	94
Paraphrase	Actively involving indigenous peoples in ecotourism arrangements is important. A representative for the Kainamaro people of Guyana, Claudette Fleming, says that although this community first worried about maintaining their cultural integrity, they came to see that ecotourism would be a more beneficial way to increase their income and at the same time control their lands and culture than other industries such as logging.

Sample note: Direct quotation

Subtopic	Indigenous peoples and ecotourism
Author/title	Mastny, "Ecotourist trap"
Page numbers	94
Direct quotation	"The Kainamaro are content to share their culture and creativity with outsiders—as long as they remain in control of their futures and the pace of cultural change."

Understanding Plagiarism, Intellectual Property, and Academic Ethics

- *Plagiarism.* Plagiarism is the passing off of someone else's words, ideas, images, or concepts as your own. Plagiarism can be as subtle and accidental as forgetting to add an in-text citation or as blatant as "borrowing" a friend's paper or handing in something from a website with your own name on it. Most schools and colleges have explicit, detailed policies about what constitutes plagiarism, and the consequences of being caught are not pretty—you may risk anything from failure on a particular assignment to expulsion from the institution. There are two basic ways to avoid plagiarism: (1) don't wait until the last minute to write your paper (which will tempt you to take shortcuts); (2) give an in-text citation (see page 501) for absolutely everything you include in your research paper that didn't come out of your own head. It's better to be safe and over-cite than to be accused of plagiarism. For a straightforward discussion of plagiarism, go to http://www.georgetown.edu/honor/plagiarism.html.

- *Intellectual Property.* If you've ever considered wiping your hard disk clean of free downloaded music files out of the fear of being arrested, then you've wrestled with the issue of intellectual property. Intellectual property includes works of art, music, animation, and literature—as well as research concepts, computer programs, even fashion. Intellectual property rights for visual, musical, and verbal works are protected by *copyright law.* When you download, for free, a music track from the Internet, you are violating copyright law—the artist who created that work receives no credit or royalties for your enjoyment and use of his or her work. When you cut and paste blocks of a website into your own research paper without giving credit, you are also violating copyright law. To respect the intellectual property rights of anyone (or anything) you cite in your research paper, you carefully *cite* the source of the information. Using quotes from another writer, or images from another artist, in your own academic paper is legally defined as "fair use"— *if* you make it clear where the original material comes from.

- *Ethics and the Academic Researcher.* As you enter an academic conversation about your research topic, your audience—even if it's only your teacher—expects you to conduct yourself in an ethical fashion. Your *ethos,* literally, means "where you stand"—what you believe, how you express those beliefs, and how thoughtfully and considerately you relate to the "stances" of others in your academic community. In the professional academy, researchers in fields from medieval poetry through cell biology are expected to adhere to a code of ethics about their research. Working with the ideas and discoveries of others in their academic communities, they are careful to always acknowledge the work of their peers and the contributions that work has made to their own research. You should do the same. When you leave school, these basic ethical tenets remain the same. You wouldn't hand in another rep's marketing report as your own, you wouldn't claim credit for the successful recovery of another doctor's patient, and you wouldn't put your name on top of another reporter's story. To violate professional ethics is to break the trust that holds an academic or professional community together.

Stage Four: Organizing and Outlining Your Information

Now that you have gathered and evaluated a mass of information, the next step is to begin giving some shape and order to what you have discovered. Writing an outline helps you to think through and organize your evidence, determine the strengths and weaknesses of your argument, and visualize the shape of your final paper. Some instructors will require you to hand in an outline along with your research paper. Even if an outline isn't formally required, it is such a useful and valuable step toward moving from a pile of index cards to a logical, coherent draft that you should plan to create one.

Checklist for Organizing Your Information

❏ Gather up all of your note cards and print out any notes you have taken on your computer. Double-check all of your notes to make sure that they include accurate citation information.

❏ Using your list of subtopics, group your notes according to those subtopics. Are some piles of cards enormous, while other topics have only a card or two? See if subtopics can be combined—or if any subtopics could be further refined and made more specific.

❏ Set aside any note cards that don't seem to "fit" in any particular pile.

❏ Find your thesis statement and copy it out on a blank index card. Go through the cards in each subtopic. Can you immediately see a connection between each note card and your thesis statement? (If not, set that note card aside for now.)

❏ Do not throw away any of the note cards, even if they don't seem to "fit" into your current research plan. You probably won't use every single note card in your paper, but it's good to have a continuing record of your work.

Basic Outlining

Many word processing programs include an "outline" function, and your instructor may ask you to follow a specific format for your outline. An outline is a kind of road map for your thought processes, a list of the pieces of information you are going to discuss in your paper and how you are going to connect those pieces of information to each other as well as back to your original thesis. You can begin the outlining process by using the note cards you have divided into subtopics:

    I. Most compelling, important subtopic
        A. Supporting fact, quote, or illustration
        B. Another interesting piece of evidence that supports or illustrates the subtopic
           1. A direct quotation that further illustrates point B
           2. Another supporting point
             a. Minor, but still relevant, points

Another useful outlining strategy is to assign each subtopic a working "topic sentence" or "main idea." As you move into the drafting process, you can return to those topic sentences/main ideas to begin each paragraph.

The Writing Process

A research paper is more than a collection of strung-together facts. No matter how interesting and relevant each individual piece of information may be, your reader is not responsible for seeing how the parts make up a whole. Connecting the evidence, demonstrating the relationships between concepts and ideas, and proving how all of it supports your thesis is entirely up to you.

Drafting

The shape of your outline and your subdivided piles of index cards provide the framework for your rough draft. As you begin to write your essay, think about "connecting the dots" between each piece of evidence, gradually filling in the shape of your argument. Expect your arrangement of individual note cards or whole subtopics to change as you draft.

Remember that you are not drafting a final paper, and certainly not a perfect paper. The goal of drafting is to *organize* your evidence, to get a sense of your argument's strengths and weaknesses, to test the accuracy of your thesis and revise it if necessary. Drafting is as much a thinking process as it is a writing process.

If you get "stuck" as you draft, abandon whatever subtopic you are working on and begin with another. Working at the paragraph level first—using the evidence on a subtopic's note cards to support and illustrate the topic sentence or main idea of the subtopic—is a much less intimidating way to approach drafting a research paper.

Finally, as you draft, be sure that you include either an in-text citation (see page 501) or some other indication of *precisely* where each piece of information came from. This will save you time when you begin revising and preparing the final draft as well as the Works Cited list.

Incorporating Sources

As you draft, you will build connections between different pieces of evidence, different perspectives, and different authors. Learning how to smoothly integrate all those different sources into your own work, without breaking the flow of your own argument and voice, takes some practice. The most important thing to remember is to accurately indicate the source of every piece of information as soon as you cite it.

One way to smoothly integrate sources into your paper is through paraphrase. For example:

The educational benefits of ecotourism can help future generations to respect the environment. "Helping people learn to love the earth is a high calling and one that can be carried out through ecotourism. Ecotourism avoids much of the counterproductive baggage that often accompanies standard education" (Kimmel 41).

In revision, this writer used paraphrase to move more gracefully from her main point to the perspective provided by her source:

Teachers like James R. Kimmel have called the ecotourism experience a "nirvana" for educating their students. "Helping people learn to love the earth is a high calling and one that can be carried out through ecotourism," he observes, noting that the "counterproductive baggage" such as testing and grading are left behind (Kimmel 41).

This system of indicating where exactly an idea, quote, or paraphrase comes from is called *parenthetical citation.* In MLA and APA style, which are required by most academic disciplines (see pages 501–502), these in-text citations take the place of footnotes or endnotes.

Using Transition Verbs Between Your Writing and a Source

Using conversation verbs as transitions between your own writing and a direct quote can enliven the style of your paper. In the revised example above, the writer uses "observes" rather than just "states" or "writes." Other useful transitions include:

Arundhati Roy argues that . . .
Peter Carey mourns that . . .
Amy Tan remembers that . . .
Barbara Ehrenreich and Annette Fuentes compare the results of . . .
Ann Grace Mojtabai admits that . . .
Naomi Shihab Nye insists that . . .
Pico Iyer vividly describes . . .

Revising and Polishing

The drafting process clarified your ideas and gave structure to your argument. In the revision process, you rewrite and rethink your paper, strengthening the connections between your main points, your evidence, and your thesis. Sharing your essay draft with a classmate, with your instructor, or with a tutor at your campus writing center will give you an invaluable objective perspective on your paper's strengths and weaknesses.

Checklist for Your Final Draft

❑ Have I provided parenthetical citations for every source I used?

❑ Do all of those parenthetical citations correspond to an item on my Works Cited list?

❑ Does my essay's title clearly and specifically state my topic?

❑ Is my thesis statement identifiable, clear, and interesting?

❑ Does each body paragraph include a topic sentence that clearly connects to my thesis?

❑ Do I make graceful transitions between my own writing and the sources I incorporate?

❑ When I shared my paper with another reader, was I able to answer any questions about my evidence or my argument using sources already at hand? Or do I need to go back to the library or online to "fill in" any questionable areas in my research?

❑ Does my conclusion clearly echo and support my thesis statement and concisely sum up how all of my evidence supports that thesis?

❑ Have I proofread for clarity, grammar, accuracy, and style?

❑ Is my paper formatted according to my instructor's guidelines? Do I have a backup copy on disk, and more than one printed copy?

Documentation

From the beginning of your research, when you were browsing in the library and online, you have been documenting your sources. To document a source simply means to make a clear, accurate record of where exactly a piece of information, a quote, an idea, or a concept comes from, so that future readers of your paper can go back to that original source and learn more. As we have seen, careful attention to documentation is the best way to protect yourself against inadvertent plagiarism. There are two ways you document your sources in your paper: within the text itself (*in-text* or *parenthetical* citation) and in the Works Cited list at the end of your paper.

What Do I Need to Document?

- Anything I didn't know before I began my research
- Direct quotations
- Paraphrases
- Summaries
- Specific numerical data, such as charts and graphs
- Any image, text, or animation from a website
- Any audio or video
- Any information gathered during a personal interview

Parenthetical (in-text) Citation

The Modern Language Association (MLA) style for documentation is most commonly used in the humanities and is the format discussed here. Keep in mind that different academic disciplines have their own documentation guidelines and styles, as do some organizations (many newspapers, for example, have their own "style guides"). An in-text citation identifies the source of a piece of information as part of your own sentence or within parentheses. In MLA style, the parenthetical information includes the author's name and the page number (if appropriate) on which the information can be found in the original source. If your readers want to know more, they can then turn to your Works Cited page to find the author's name and the full bibliographic information for that source. Always place the in-text or parenthetical citation as close to the incorporated source material as possible—preferably within the same sentence.

Guidelines for Parenthetical (in-text) Citation

Page numbers for a book

The end of the Second World War began Samuel Beckett's greatest period of
   creativity, which he referred to as "the siege in the room" (Bair 346).

Bair describes the period immediately after the Second World War as a time of great
   creativity for Samuel Beckett (346).

In the first parenthetical citation, the author is not named within the student writer's text, so the parentheses include both the source author's name and the page number on which the information can be found. In the second example, the source author (Bair) is mentioned by name, so there is no need to repeat that name within the parentheses—only the page number is needed.

Page numbers for an article in a magazine or journal

Wheatley argues that "America has embraced values that cannot create a sustainable
   society and world" (25).

Page numbers for a newspaper article

Cite both the section letter (or description of the section) and the page.

Camera phones are leading to new questions about the invasion of privacy
(Harmon sec. 4:3).

A spokesperson for the National Institutes of Health has described obesity as the
greatest potential danger to the average American's health (Watts B3).

Website

Arts and Letters Daily includes links to opinions and essays on current events from
English-language media worldwide.

Article 2 of the proposed Global Code of Ethics for Tourism describes tourism "as a
vehicle for individual and collective fulfillment" (world-tourism).

When an online source does not give specific "page," screen, or
paragraph numbers, your parenthetical citation must include the name
of the site.

Works Cited List

Gather your working bibliography cards, and be sure that every source you
cite in your paper has a corresponding card. To construct the Works Cited
list, you simply arrange these cards in alphabetical order, by author. The
Works Cited page is a separate, double-spaced page at the end of your
paper.

Formatting Your Works Cited List

- Center the title, Works Cited, at the top of a new page. Do not underline it, italicize it, or place it in quotation marks.
- Alphabetize according to the author's name, or according to the title
  (for works, such as websites, that do not have an author). Ignore words
  such as *the, and,* and *a* when alphabetizing.
- Begin each entry at the left margin. After the first line, indent all other
  lines of the entry by five spaces (one stroke of the "tab" key).
- Double-space every line.
- Place a period after the author, the title, and the publishing
  information.
- Underline book and web page titles. Titles of articles, stories, poems, and parts of entire works in other media are placed in quotation marks.

Guidelines for Works Cited List

Book by One Author

Bair, Deirdre. <u>Samuel Beckett: A Biography</u>. New York: Simon, 1978.

Multiple Books by the Same Author

List the author's name for the first entry. For each entry that follows, replace the author's name with three hyphens.

Thomas, Lewis. <u>The Medusa and the Snail: More Notes of a Biology Watcher</u>. New York: Viking, 1979.

- - -. <u>Late Night Thoughts on Listening to Mahler's Ninth Symphony</u>. New York: Viking, 1983.

Book with Two or Three Authors/Editors

Moore-Gilbert, Bart, Gareth Stanton, and Willy Maley, eds. <u>Postcolonial Criticism</u>. London: Longman, 1997.

Book with More Than Three Authors/Editors

Nordhus, Inger, Gary R. VandenBos, Stig Berg, and Pia Fromholt, eds. <u>Clinical Geropsychology</u>. Washington: APA, 1998.

Book or Publication with Group or Organization as Author

National PTA. <u>National Standards for Parent/Family Involvement Programs</u>. Chicago: National PTA, 1997.

Book or Publication Without an Author

<u>The New York Public Library Desk Reference</u>. New York: Prentice, 1989.

Work in an Anthology of Pieces All by the Same Author

Thomas, Lewis. "The Youngest and Brightest Thing Around." <u>The Medusa and the Snail: More Notes of a Biology Watcher</u>. New York: Viking, 1979.

Work in an Anthology of Different Authors

Graver, Elizabeth. "The Body Shop." <u>The Best American Short Stories 1991</u>. Boston: Houghton, 1991.

Work Translated from Another Language

Cocteau, Jean. <u>The Difficulty of Being</u>. Trans. Elizabeth Sprigge. New York:
  Da Capo, 1995.

Entry from a Reference Volume

For dictionaries and encyclopedias, simply note the edition and its date. No
page numbers are necessary for references organized alphabetically, such as
encyclopedias (and, obviously, dictionaries).

"Turner, Nat." <u>Encyclopedia Americana: International Edition</u>. 1996 ed.

"Carriera, Rosalba." <u>The Oxford Companion to Western Art</u>. Ed. Hugh Brigstoke.
  Oxford: Oxford UP, 2001.

Article from a Journal with Pagination Continued Through Each Volume

Enoch, Jessica. "Resisting the Script of Indian Education: Zitkala-Sa and the Carlisle
  Indian School." <u>College English</u> 65 (2002): 117–41.

Do not include the issue number for journals paginated continuously.

Article from a Journal Paginated for Each Issue

Follow the same procedure for a journal with continued pagination, placing
a period and the issue number after the volume number.

Article from a Weekly or Biweekly Periodical

Baum, Dan. "Jake Leg." <u>New Yorker</u> 15 Sept. 2003: 50–57.

Article from a Monthly or Bimonthly Periodical

Perlin, John. "Solar Power: The Slow Revolution." <u>Invention and Technology</u> Summer
  2002: 20–25.

Article from a Daily Newspaper

Brody, Jane E. "A Pregame Ritual: Doctors Averting Disasters." <u>New York Times</u> 14
  Oct. 2003: F7.

If the newspaper article goes on for more than one page, add a + sign to the
first page number.

Newspaper or Periodical Article with No Author

"Groups Lose Sole Authority on Chaplains for Muslims." <u>New York Times</u> 14 Oct.
  2003: A15.

Unsigned Editorial in a Newspaper or Periodical

"The Iraqi Weapons Puzzle." Editorial. New York Times 12 Oct. 2003: sec. 4:10.

Letter to the Editor of a Newspaper or Periodical

Capasso, Chris. Letter. "Mountain Madness." Outside May 2003: 20.

Film, Video, DVD

If you are writing about a specific actor's performance or a specific director, use that person's name as the beginning of the citation. Otherwise, begin with the title of the work. Specify the media of the recording (film, video, DVD, etc.).

Princess Mononoke. Dir. Hayao Miyazaki. Prod. Studio Ghibli, 1999. Videocassette.
    Miramax, 2001.

Eames, Charles and Ray. The Films of Charles and Ray Eames, Volume 1: Powers of
    Ten. 1978. Videocassette. Pyramid Home Video, 1984.

Television or Radio Broadcast

"Alone on the Ice." The American Experience. PBS. KRMA, Denver. 8 Feb. 1999.

Arnold, Elizabeth. "The Birds of the Boreal." National Geographic Radio Expeditions.
    NPR. WNYC, New York. 14 Oct. 2003.

CD or Other Recording

Identify the format if the recording is not on a compact disc.

Bukkene Bruse. "Wedding March from Osterdalen." Nordic Roots 2. Northside, 2000.

Personal Interview

Give the name of the person you interviewed, how the interview was conducted (phone, e-mail, etc.), and the date of the interview.

Reed, Lou. Telephone interview. 12 Sept. 1998.

Dean, Howard. E-mail interview. 8 Aug. 2003.

Online Sources

Because websites are constantly changing, and "publication" information about a site varies so widely, think about documenting your site accurately enough so that a curious reader of your paper could find the website. When a URL is very long, give just enough information for readers to find their way to the site and then navigate to the specific page or image from there.

Web Page/Internet Site

Give the site title, the name of the site's editor (if there is one), electronic publication information, your own date of access, and the site's URL. (If some of this information is not available, just cite what you can.)

Arts & Letters Daily. Ed. Denis Dutton. 2003. 2 Sept. 2003 <http://www.aldaily.com/>.

Document or Article from an Internet Site

Include the author's name, document title, information about a print version (if applicable), information about the electronic version, access information, and URL.

Brooks, David. "The Organization Kid." The Atlantic Monthly April 2001: 40–54. 25
    Aug. 2003 <http://www.theatlantic.com/issues/2001/04/brooks-p1.htm>.

Book Available Online

The citation is similar to the format for a print book, but include as much information as you can about the website as well as the date of your access to it.

Einstein, Albert. Relativity: The Special and General Theory. Trans. Robert W.
    Lawson. New York: Henry Holt, 1920. Bartleby.com: Great Books Online. Ed.
    Steven van Leeuwen. 2003. 6 Sept. 2003 <http://www.bartelby.com/173/>.

Wheatley, Phillis. Poems on Various Subjects, Religious and Moral. Project Gutenberg.
    Ed. Michael S. Hart. 2003. 6 Sept. 2003 <http://www.ibiblio.org/pub/docs/books/
    gutenberg/etext96/whtly10.txt>.

Database Available Online

Bartleby Library. Ed. Steven van Leeuwen. 2003. 28 Sept. 2003 <http://www.bartleby.com>.

Source from a Library Subscription Database

Academic and most public libraries offer to their members access to subscription-only databases that provide electronic access to publications not otherwise available on free-access websites. When you cite a book, article, or other source that you have retrieved from such a database, add to your citation the name of the service and the institution that provided the access.

Mastny, Lisa. "Ecotourist Trap." Foreign Policy Nov.–Dec. 2002: 94+. Questia. 10
    Oct. 2003 <http://www.questia.com/>.

Rossant, John. "The Real War Is France vs. France." <u>Business Week</u> 6 Oct. 2003: 68.
   <u>MasterFile Premier</u>. EBSCO. Maplewood Mem. Lib., Maplewood, NJ.
   13 Oct. 2003 <http://0-web24.epnet.com.catalog.maplewoodlibrary.org/>.

Newspaper Article Online

Zernike, Kate. "Fight Against Fat Shifts to the Workplace." <u>New York Times</u> 12 Oct.
   2003. 12 Oct. 2003 <http://www.nytimes.com/2003/10/12/national/12OBES.html>.

Journal Article Online

Salkeld, Duncan. "Making Sense of Differences: Postmodern History, Philosophy
   and Shakespeare's Prostitutes." <u>Chronicon: An Electronic History Journal</u> 3 (1999).
   5 Apr. 2003 <http://www.ucc.ie/chronicon/salkfra.htm>.

E-mail

Give the writer's name, the subject line (if any) enclosed in quotation marks,
and the date of the message.

Stanford, Myles. "Johnson manuscripts online." E-mail to the author. 12 July 2003.

Electronic Posting to an Online Forum

Many online media sources conduct forums in which readers can respond to
breaking news or ongoing issues. Citing from such forums is difficult
because many people prefer to post anonymously; if the author's username is
too silly or inappropriate, use the title of the post or the title of the forum to
begin your citation and determine its place in the alphabetical order of your
Works Cited list.

Berman, Piotr. Online posting. 6 Oct. 2003. Is Middle East Peace Impossible? 13 Oct.
   2003 <http://tabletalk.salon.com/webx?13@@.596c5554>.

Glossary of Rhetorical Terms

allusion A reference to a familiar concept, person, or thing.

analytical essay An essay that defines and describes an issue by breaking it down into separate components and carefully considering each component.

annotation Marking up a text as you read by writing comments, questions, and ideas in the margins.

argument A *rhetorical strategy* that involves using *persuasion* to gain a reader's support for the writer's position.

assertion A statement that a writer claims is true without necessarily providing objective support for the *claim*.

audience The assumed readers of a text.

brainstorming An idea-generation strategy. Write your topic, a key word, or *thesis* at the top of a blank piece of paper or computer screen, and for ten or fifteen minutes just write down everything you associate with, think of, or know about that topic.

cause and effect/causal analysis A *rhetorical strategy* that examines the relationships between events or conditions and their consequences.

claim In *argument,* a statement that the author intends to support through the use of *reasons, evidence,* and appeals.

classification A *rhetorical strategy* that divides a subject into categories and then analyzes the characteristics of each category. See also *division.*

cognitive styles Different and individual approaches to thinking and understanding, especially in regard to how we process language and text.

coherence A characteristic of effective writing, achieved through careful organization of ideas and the skillful use of *transitions.*

colloquial language Informal language not usually found in an academic essay but appropriate in some cases for purposes of *illustration.*

comparison and **contrast** Two strategies that are often used to complement one another in the same essay. Comparison examines the similarities between two or more like subjects; contrast examines the differences between those subjects.

composing process The work of writing, moving from notes and ideas through multiple *drafts* to a "final" essay. All writers develop their own composing process as they become more comfortable with writing.

conflict A struggle between two opposing forces that creates suspense, tension, and interest in a *narrative.*

conventions The expectations general readers have of specific kinds of writing.

deduction An *argument* that begins with a clearly stated *claim,* and then uses selected evidence to support that claim. See also *induction.*

definition/extended definition A writing strategy that describes the nature of an abstract or concrete subject. Extended definition is a kind of essay based on that definition, expanding its scope by considering larger issues related to the subject (for example, the different ways in which different groups of people might define a term like *freedom*).

description A kind of writing based on sensory observations (sight, hearing, smell, touch) that allows readers to imaginatively re-create an experience.

diction The "style" of language, either written or spoken, from which inferences about the speaker's education, background, and origins can be made. Your choice of diction in a piece of writing depends on your intended *audience* and your *purpose.*

discourse Dialogue or conversation. In the study of rhetoric, *discourse* refers to the ways a specific group of people, organization, or institution speaks to and about itself.

division A *rhetorical strategy* that breaks a subject down into smaller parts and analyzes their relationship to the overall subject.

drafting Moving from notes and an outline to the general shape and form of a "final" essay. Writers often go through multiple "drafts" of an essay, moving ideas around, tinkering with the language, and double-checking facts.

editorialize An "editorial" in a newspaper offers the collective opinion of the newspaper's management on a *topical* issue. Writers "editorialize" when they offer opinions on a subject of topical interest. Unlike the approach of an *argument,* editorializing writers do not always consider the viewpoints of their opponents.

evidence In an *argument,* the facts and expert opinions used to support a *claim.*

exemplification See *illustration.*

expository essay An essay that seeks to explain something by combining different *rhetorical strategies,* such as *classification* and *description.*

extended definition See *definition.*

figurative language Imaginative language that compares one thing to another in ways that are not necessarily logical but that are nevertheless striking, original, and "true." Examples of figurative language are *metaphor, simile,* and *allusion.*

illustration Also called *exemplification.* The use of examples to support an essay's main idea. A successful illustrative essay uses several compelling examples to support its *thesis.*

imagery Descriptive writing that draws on vivid sensory descriptions and *figurative language* to re-create an experience for a reader.

induction In *argument,* a strategy that uses compelling evidence to lead an *audience* to an inevitable conclusion. See also *deduction.*

invective Angry or hostile language directed at a specific person (or persons).

irony A *rhetorical strategy* that uses language to suggest the opposite of what is actually being stated. Irony is used frequently in works of *satire* and works of humor.

major proposition See *claim.* In *argument,* the position a writer goes on to defend through *reasons* and *evidence.*

metaphor The comparison of two unlike things to one another for *figurative* effect.

minor proposition In *argument,* the position a writer goes on to defend through *reasons* and *evidence.* See also *claim.*

motif A simple theme (often a phrase or an image) that is repeated throughout a *narrative* to give it a deeper sense of *unity* and to underscore its basic idea.

narration/narrative A type of writing that tells a story. In an essay, narration is often used to describe what happened to a person or place over a certain period of time.

op-ed style Named for the "opinion and editorial" pages of newspapers, "op-ed style" describes brief *arguments* written for a general *audience* that are supported by *evidence* commonly accepted as "true" or "expert."

paraphrase Stating another author's opinions, ideas, or observations in your own words. When you paraphrase, you still give full credit (through in-text citation) to the original author.

persona The voice of the author of an essay or story, even if that voice never uses the first person or gives any further details about its "self." Your persona, in an academic essay, might be that of a concerned citizen, a sociological researcher, or a literary critic.

personal essay An essay written in the first person (the "I" point of view) that uses personal experience to illustrate a larger point.

persuasion A *rhetorical strategy,* often used in *argument,* that seeks to move readers to take a course of action or to change their minds about an issue.

point of view The perspective and attitude of a writer or narrator toward the subject.

précis A *summary* of the relevant facts, statements, and *evidence* offered by an essay, especially an *argument.*

prewriting Any idea-generation strategy that gets you "warmed up" for drafting an essay.

process analysis A kind of essay that describes, in chronological order, each step or stage of the performing of an action (a "how-to" essay).

prologue A brief statement or introduction to a longer work (originally, the introduction to a play spoken by one of the actors).

proposition A *thesis* statement, or *claim*, that suggests a specific action to take and seeks the support of readers to take that action. A proposition is supported by *evidence* demonstrating why this course of action is the best to take. See also *major proposition* and *minor proposition*.

purpose The reason a writer takes on a subject as well as the goal the writer hopes to achieve.

reader response theory Loosely defined, the idea that every reader brings an individual approach and background of knowledge to a text and responds to a text in a unique way.

reasons In *argument*, *evidence* you offer that your reader will accept as legitimate support for your *claim*. See also *minor proposition*.

rebuttal In *argument*, a considered response to an opposing point of view.

reflective essay An essay in which you examine and evaluate your own actions or beliefs, learning more about yourself in the process.

refutation In *argument*, proof that someone (usually the opposition) is incorrect.

revision The stage in the writing process in which you revisit your draft, reading and rewriting for clarity and *purpose*, adding or subtracting relevant *evidence*, and perhaps sharing your essay with additional readers for comment.

rhetoric The deliberate and formal use of language, usually in writing, to illustrate an idea or demonstrate a truth. The writer of rhetoric always has in mind an *audience* and a *purpose*.

rhetorical strategies Key patterns that writers employ to organize and clarify their ideas and opinions in an essay.

satire Writing that uses humor, often mocking, to call attention to stupidity or injustice and inspire social change. Satirists call attention to the foibles of groups, institutions, and bureaucracies rather than of individual people.

sensory detail Details based on the five senses (touch, sight, smell, taste, sound) that enhance descriptive writing.

simile A style of *figurative language* that compares two unlike things using *like* or *as*. See also *metaphor*.

stipulative definition Creating, based on your own experience and opinions, a definition of a term (generally an abstract term, such as *globalization*) for the purposes of your own *argument*.

style A writer's own unique sense for, and use of, language, *imagery,* and *rhetoric*. Some writers are immediately recognizable by their style; other times, a writer needs to consider *audience* and *purpose* when developing an appropriate style for a particular rhetorical task.

summary As a critical reading strategy, the brief restating (in your own words) of an essay's *thesis*, main points, and *evidence*. Summarizing can help you better understand the logic of a writer's argument and the way an essay is organized. See also *précis*.

symbol Something that stands for, or represents, something else. All numbers and letters are symbols, in that they stand for concepts and sounds.

thesis In an essay, a brief statement that concisely states the writer's subject and opinion on that subject.

tone The writer's "voice" in an essay that, through the use of *diction* and *figurative language,* as well as other *rhetorical strategies,* conveys the writer's feelings about the subject.

topical Relating to an issue or subject drawn from current events or that is of immediate interest to the *audience*.

topic sentence The sentence encapsulating the focus, or main idea, of each paragraph of an essay.

transition The language used to connect one idea to the next in an essay. Skillful use of transitions helps to give an essay *coherence,* allowing the reader to smoothly follow the writer's train of thoughts as well as to clearly see the connections between those thoughts and supporting *evidence.*

unity A quality of good writing that goes beyond *coherence* to an overall sense of completion. A writer achieves unity when the reader feels that not a word need be added to (or taken away from) the essay.

usage In rhetorical studies, the ways in which language is commonly used in speaking and writing.

visual texts Anything that conveys an idea without necessarily using language (photographs, advertisements, cartoons, graffiti, etc.).

voice See *tone*.

warrant In *argument,* a plausible *assertion* that a reader must agree with in order to accept the *claim.*

Glossary of Globalization Terms

acculturation The adoption by one *culture* of features from another, often as a result of conquest or colonialization—for example, the use of French as a primary language in many former French colonies in Africa.

anarchy The absence of any authority; total individual freedom.

assimilation The adoption of a society's *culture* and customs by immigrants to that society. At both an individual and a group level, the process is gradual and often reciprocal.

balkanization (From the breakup of the countries of the Balkan Peninsula, in Europe, into hostile and frequently warring nations after World War I.) To break apart into smaller, hostile nations or entities, as in the division of the former Yugoslavia and the breakup of the former Soviet Union.

bilingualism/multilingualism Functional literatcy in two or more languages; policies that promote the acquisition of more than one language.

biotechnology The application of science, especially genetic engineering, to living organisms in order to effect beneficial changes.

borderless economy Through alliances such as *NAFTA* and the European Union, the movement toward the *free trade* of goods and services across national borders.

capital The resources (money, land, raw material, labor, etc.) used to produce goods and services for the open market.

capitalism Economic system based on the ownership and exchange of goods and scrvices by private individuals, and through which individual accumulation of resources is relatively unchecked by governmental regulations.

caste An ancient Indian system of social hierarchy, now much in decline, that held that social status was inherited and could not be changed. The term is more broadly used to indicate a class of people who cannot move up the social hierarchy.

centrist Politically inclined toward moderation and compromise.

civil liberties Guarantees of certain rights, such as freedom of speech and right of assembly. In the United States, these rights are upheld by the Constitution (although they are also frequently challenged in society as well as in the courts).

cold war From 1945 to 1991, a period of tensions and hostilities between the Soviet Union and its Warsaw Pact allies and the United States and its *NATO* allies. The era was marked by massive arms proliferation and mutual paranoia and distrust.

collectivity The sharing of resources and responsibilities among a community or social group, rather than dividing and accumulating individually.

colonialism/postcolonial From the sixteenth through the mid-twentieth century, the conquest and ruling of peoples in Asia, Africa, and South America by European nations.

commercialization The transformation of a concept or idea into something that can be marketed, bought, and sold.

communism Political *ideology* based on the public ownership of resources and centralized planning of the economy. Based on the philosophy of Karl Marx (1818–1883), who sought alternatives to what he saw as the exploitation of the working classes by the rise of *industrialization*.

conservative In the United States, referring to a political *ideology* that supports individual liberties and minimal governmental involvement in the economy. Also, a social inclination toward traditional morals and values and a resistance to change.

consumerism Until recently, policies and practices meant to protect consumers from bad business practices. Has come to mean a lifestyle focused on the accumulation of material goods at the expense of other values.

Creole Refers to both languages and peoples, with different specific implications depending on the geographical region discussed. Generally, refers to a people or language that is the result of a mingling of *cultures, races,* and *ethnicities,* often due to colonization.

culture The shared customs, traditions, and beliefs of a group of people. These shared values are learned by members of the group from each other, and members of a specific culture share, create, contribute to, and preserve their culture for future generations.

democracy A political system through which *enfranchised* citizens (people who are acknowledged by the state as citizens and have been granted the right to vote) determine governmental courses of action through elections.

developing world Nations, especially those formerly colonized or under *imperialist* domination, now moving toward *industrialization* and economic and political stability.

diaspora Originally applied to Jewish people living outside of Israel; now applied to groups of people "dispersed" or widely scattered from their original homelands.

disarmament Originally a *cold war* term used to describe ongoing negotiations between the *superpowers* to limit and eventually dismantle weapons systems; now describes the diplomatic work of convincing nations to stop or reverse the production of weapons (especially nuclear).

disenfranchised See *enfranchisement.*

ecosystem The fragile web of relationships between living beings and their environment.

emigration Leaving one country for another. See also *immigration*.

enfranchisement The granting of the right to vote to an individual or a group. To be "disenfranchised" is to have no vote, and by extension no voice in determining your own or your community's governance.

ethnic/ethnicity Referring to a shared sense of common religion, *race,* national, and/or *cultural* identity.

ethnic cleansing An organized effort to force or coerce an *ethnic* group from a region. In recent history, efforts at ethnic cleansing in places like Rwanda and Serbia has led to *genocide.*

ethnocentrism The belief that one's own *culture* or *ethnic* identification is superior to that of others.

ethnology The anthropological study of *cultures.*

Eurocentric/Eurocentrism A worldview that believes European or Western values to be superior.

expatriate Someone who lives in a country where he or she is not a citizen.

fascism An extremely repressive political *ideology* that exercises complete control over individual and *civil liberties* through the use of force.

feminism The theory that women should have the same political, economic, and social rights as men.

free-market economy An economic system in which individuals, acting in their own self-interest, make decisions about their finances, employment, and consumption of goods and services. In a free-market economy, the government provides and regulates common services such as defense, education, and transportation.

free trade Unrestricted trade of goods and services between countries, free from tariffs (which artificially inflate the prices of imported goods) and quotas (which limit the importation of certain goods in order to protect a country's own industries).

fundamentalism Reactionary movement to establish traditional religious values and texts as the primary and/or governing *ideology* in a society.

genocide The organized destruction of a group of people because of their *race,* religion, or *ethnicity.*

global village Term coined in the 1960s by media critic Marshall McLuhan to describe the ability of new communications technologies to bring peoples together.

global warming A gradual increase in global temperature and resulting changes in global climate, caused by the accumulation of "greenhouse gases" from the burning of fossil fuels and the deterioration of the ozone layer (which shields the earth from ultraviolet rays).

globalization The consolidation of societies around the world due to international trade, economic interdependence, the reach of *information technologies,* and the possible resulting loss of local traditions, languages, values, and resources.

GMO (genetically modified organism) A living entity (plant, animal, or microbe) that has been altered in some way through the intervention of genetic engineering.

hegemony The domination of one state, entity, or social group over another.

homogenous Referring to a society or *culture* of very limited diversity whose citizens share very similar racial and/or *ethnic* backgrounds.

human rights The Universal Declaration of Human Rights ratified by the United Nations in 1948 seeks to guarantee that all human beings have a fundamental dignity and basic rights of self-determination.

ideology A belief system that determines and guides the structure of a government and its relation to its citizens.

immigration The movement of people from their homeland to a new nation. See also *emigration*.

imperialism/empire The economic and cultural influence, and occasionally domination, of nations or peoples by stronger nations. The motives of "imperialist" nations are usually economic (the seeking of raw resources, the opening of new markets for trade) and/or *ideological* (e.g., in the nineteenth century, the British imperialist idea that England had a "duty" to bring "civilization" to other parts of the globe).

indigenous Referring to peoples understood to be "natives" or original inhabitants of lands now threatened by *urbanization* or other factors. Opponents of *globalization* argue that the *cultures* of indigenous peoples are under particular threat from the forces of *globalization*.

industrialization The transformation of an economy from agricultural to industrial, often followed by *urbanization*.

information age Term coined by media scholar Marshall McLuhan in 1964 to discuss the rapidly expanding reach (at the time, through television, radio, and print) of technologies that spread information.

information technology Any electronic technology that enhances the production and dissemination of textual, visual, and auditory content, such as computers and cellular telephones.

liberal Implying a political and social tolerance of different views and lifestyles. In the United States, applies to a political preference for increased governmental involvement, especially in matters of social welfare.

Luddite From an early-nineteenth-century anti-*industrialization* movement in England; now describes a person who is opposed to technological progress because of its possible dehumanizing effects.

marginalization The effects of social and governmental policies that leave some members of a society *disenfranchised*, unable to seek or participate in common resources (such as education and health care) and/or unable to freely express themselves and their views.

Marxism A philosophy based on the work of political economist Karl Marx (1818–1883) and from which *socialism* and *communism* are derived. Marxist political thought focuses on the relationships between economic resources, power, and *ideology*, with the goal of redistributing resources equitably.

mestizo A Hispanic American of mixed European and *indigenous* ancestry.

monocultural Referring to a *culture* that is *homogenous* and resists diversification.

multiculturalism The belief that all *cultures* have intrinsic worth and that the diversity of *cultures* within a society is to be encouraged and celebrated.

multilateralism Cooperation between two or more nations on international issues.

NAFTA (North American Free Trade Agreement) An agreement between the United States, Canada, and Mexico that reduces governmental intervention in trade and investment between these countries.

nationalism Personal and communal feelings of loyalty to a nation; patriotism.

NATO (North Atlantic Treaty Organization) Defense alliance originally created in 1949 to counter the potential threat of the Soviet Union and its Warsaw Pact allies; now includes some of those former enemies in its membership.

naturalization The granting of citizenship, with its rights and privileges, to an immigrant.

NGO (nongovernmental organization) Organizations such as the International Red Cross, Doctors Without Borders, and the International Olympic Committee that provide aid or promote international cooperation without the specific involvement or oversight of governments.

patriarchy A society or worldview that subordinates women.

pluralism Encouragement by a society of competing and divergent political viewpoints.

political asylum Protection guaranteed by a government to refugees fleeing persecution in their own country because of their political beliefs or activism.

polygamy In some *cultures*, the practice of marrying more than one wife.

polyglot A person who speaks several languages, or referring to a community or *culture* in which several languages are spoken.

pop culture Values, traditions, and shared customs and references generated by the mass media, as opposed to values based on religion or *ideology*.

privatization The sale and transfer of formerly government-owned assets (such as utilities) to private corporations.

progressive Referring to a political inclination toward active reform, especially in *social justice*.

protectionism A government's efforts to protect its own agricultural and manufacturing industries from international competition. See also *free trade*.

race A group of people who have ancestry, physical characteristics, and *cultural* traditions in common. There is no genetic or "scientific" basis for the defining or classifying of an individual's "race."

rogue state A controversial term coined by the United States to describe states that act irrationally and that pose particular dangers to the United States and its allies. During the Clinton administration, the term was briefly replaced with "state of concern." Some opponents of *globalization* describe the United States itself as a "rogue state" for taking military, economic, and environmental actions without the participation or consideration of other states.

social justice A popular movement to redistribute wealth, resources, and political power more equitably among the members of a society.

socialism A political *ideology* based on considerable governmental involvement in the economy and other social institutions.

sovereignty The power of a state to govern itself and to defend its own interests.

Stalinism Referring to the methods of Joseph Stalin, general secretary of the Communist Party of the USSR and ruler of the Soviet Union from 1922 to 1953. A brutal dictator, his economic policies of forcing rapid *industrialization* and collectivization of agriculture resulted in massive suffering.

superpower During the *cold war,* term used to describe both the United States and the Soviet Union.

terrorism The use of random violence, especially against civilian targets, by ideologically motivated groups or individuals in an attempt to create social upheaval and to achieve recognition of their agenda.

Third World Term generally applied to nations moving toward *industrialization* and economic stabilization; the term *developing world* is now more commonly used.

totalitarianism An extremely repressive political system that attempts to completely control every aspect of a society through the use of force.

transnational A corporation or entity that conducts business and policy across national borders and has interests in several different nations.

urbanization The massive shift of a nation's peoples from rural, agrarian communities to large urban areas, usually as a result of *industrialization.*

utopia An idealized, speculative nation or system of government.

welfare state A nation that assumes primary governmental responsibility for the health, education, and social security of its citizens, often in exchange for heavy individual tax burdens.

Credits

Photo Credits

Chapter 1
P. 2: © AP/Kamran Jebreili

Chapter 2
P. 30: © Steve Kelley/The Times-Picayune

Chapter 3
P. 68: © AP/Chuck Stoody; P. 73: Michael S. Yamashita/Corbis

Chapter 4
P. 118: © AP/Robert Mecea

Chapter 5
P. 160: NY Times; P. 183: Metropolitan Museum of Art; P. 184: Darren Knight Gallery/Sydney; P. 207: SIPA Press

Chapter 6
P. 216: AP/D. Ross Cameron; P. 244: David Horsey/Tribune Media Services

Chapter 7
P. 273: AP/Christophe Ena

Chapter 8
P. 316: AP/Amit Shabi; P. 350: Christie's Images; P. 351: Thonig/Mauritius; P. 352: Thonig/Mauritius; P. 352: Christie's Images; P. 356: Brown Brothers, Inc.

Chapter 9
P. 364: AP/Ernesto Mora

Chapter 10
P. 403: Gideon Mendel/Corbis

Chapter 11
P. 444: Still Pictures/Peter Arnold; P. 477: NASA

Inserts

Culture or Conflict?: Images of Globalization
P. 2: AP/Enric Marti; P. 3: Joe McNally; P. 4: Bob Krist; P. 5: Joe McNally; P. 6: AP/Ramon Espinosa; P. 7: Michael Benanav; P. 8: Louise Gubb/Corbis/SABA

Is Beauty Universal? Global Body Images

P. 2: Igor Akimov/ITAR-TASS/Corbis; P. 3: China Newsphoto//Reuters/Corbis; P. 4: Steve Raymer/Corbis; P. 5: Morteza Nikoubazi/Reuters/Corbis; P. 6: Reuters/Corbis; P. 7: Patrick Ward/Corbis; P. 8: China Photos/Getty Images

Text Credits

Chapter 1

P. 11: From "Love and Race" by Nicholas B. Kristof, *New York Times,* December 6, 2002. Originally published in *The New York Times,* 2002. Reprinted by permission of The New York Times Co. P. 18: Reprinted by permission of the author. P. 26: From *Newsweek,* December 12, 2005, © 2005 Newsweek, Inc. All rights reserved.

Chapter 2

P. 31: Andrew Lam is an editor with New America Media and the author of "Perfume Dreams: Reflections on the Vietnamese Diaspora." P. 35: Introduction from *The Way to Rainy Mountain* by N. Scott Momaday. Copyright © 1969. Reprinted permission of The University of New Mexico Press. P. 42: Excerpted from the book, *Writin' Is Fightin'* by Ishmael Reed, Copyright © 2004 by Houghton Mifflin Company. Permission granted by Lowenstein-Yost Associates, Inc. P. 47: From *Newsweek,* March 22, 2004, © 2004 Newsweek, Inc. All rights reserved. P. 52: "American Dreamer" by Bharati Mukherjee. Originally published in *Mother Jones.* Copyright © 1997 by Bharati Mukherjee. Reprinted by permission of the author. P. 59: From "The Cult of Ethnicity" by Arthur M. Schlesinger, Jr., *Time,* July 8, 1991. © 1991 Time Inc. reprinted by permission. P. 63: Reprinted by permission.

Chapter 3

P. 70: "Stranger in the Arab-Muslim World" by Fouad Ajami, *The Wilson Quarterly,* Spring 2001, pp. 56+. P. 77: Reprinted with permission from YaleGlobal Online (www.yaleglobal.yale.edu), © 2006 Center for the Study of Globalization. P. 81: From "An Obsession the World Doesn't Share" by Roger Cohen. Published in *The New York Times Upfront,* March 28, 2005. Copyright © 2005 by The New York Times Company and Scholastic Inc. Reprinted by permission of Scholastic Inc. P. 86: Reprinted by permission of openDemocracy. P. 95: Reprinted by permission of The Hoover Institution. P. 101: Reprinted by permission. P. 109: Sasha Abramsky is a Senior Fellow at the Demos Institute and author of *Conned: How Millions Went to Prison, Lost the Vote, and Helped Send George W. Bush to the White House* (The New Press, 2006).

Chapter 4

P. 119: Copyright © 1990 by Amy Tan. First appeared in *The Threepenny Review.* Reprinted by permission of the author and the Sandra Kijkstra Literary Agency. P. 126: © 1996, The New York Times. Reprinted by permission. P. 130: Mary Blume, "If You Can't Master English, Try Globish." *International Herald Tribune* Apr. 22, 2005. Reprinted by permission of the author. P. 134: Reprinted by permission of the author. P. 138: Introduction, pp. 1–10, from *Spanglish* by Ilan Stavans. Copyright © 2003 by Ilan Stavans. Reprinted by permission of HarperCollins Publishers. P. 146: Reprinted with permission from the July/August 2002 issue of American Demographics. Copyright, Crain Communications, Inc. P. 154: Excerpt by Isabel Allende from *Speaking of Reading,* edited by Nadine Rosenthal. Copyright © 1995. Reprinted by permission of Nadine Rosenthal.

Chapter 9

Chapter 10

Chapter 11

Index

525